CONSTITUTION
OF
ANCIENT HINDU FAMILY

CONSTITUTION
OF
ANCIENT HINDU FAMILY

By

J.E. Padfield

BHARATIYA KALA PRAKASHAN
Delhi : : (India)

Published by :
BHARATIYA KALA PRAKASHAN
3421-A, IInd Floor, Narang Colony,
Tri Nagar, Delhi-110035.
Phone : 32967505 Telefax: 27393083
E-mail : bkp3421@yahoo.co.in

First Edition : 1918
Revised Edition : 2008

ISBN : 978-81-8090-168-3

Printed by :
BDH Printer at Salasar, Imaging Systems, Delhi.

Contents

Chapter 1

The Constitution of the Ancient Hindu Family and on the Import of the Expression "Joint Hindu Family"

The word 'family,' its primitive sense—Originally meant a slave-holding group—In that sense the word appropriate for units of early Hindu society—Slaves members of ancient Hindu families—Position of a slave similar to that of a son or wife—Hindu"slavery had few revolting features—Slave an article of property—Slaves classed with immoveable property-Slave concubines as members of the family— Heritable among barbarous people-Not so among the Hindus—Stealing a slave an offence similar to that of stealing a horse—Institution of slavery further developed in later years—Nārada's fifteen kinds of slaves—Slavery sanctioned and extended by Brahmanic law—Resemblance between ancient—Hindu and Roman families—Modern sense of the word family how evolved—Patria potestas the link between its ancient and modern sense—Patria potestas rudimentary amongst Hindus—Indications of Patria potestas in Sanskrit texts—Father's powers—The same in modern Hindu society—'Three ingredients in Patria potestas—No suit between father and son—Indication in Sanskrit texts—Father's absolute disposal of son's person—indicated by the law of adoption—Adoption a survival of a prepatriarchal state—Sale and gift of children common among barbarians—Brahmanic explanation of adoption misleading—'Family responsible for a member's torts—Family,

Guild, and 'Village courts—Popular machinery for administering justice—Family mulcted like a surety—no name in Sanskrit for Patria potestas—Kuṭumba and Kula the names in Sanskrit for 'family—Kuṭumba not necessarily a joint family–Notion conveyed by Kuṭumba—The word Kuṭumba of probable foreign origin-Kula and Sakulya—Family seldom joint beyond seven general. Lions-Sakulya meant a divided parcener—Kula probably a divided not a joint family. The word Hindu—Not Sanskrit-Naigma not equivalent, to Hindu—Personal law applied to Naigamas or sectaries—Hindu comes from Sindhu—No national name in Sanskrit for Hindu—Caste the chief characteristic of Hinduism—Hindu manners and customs a reason for applying Hindu law—Jains and Vaiṣṇavas Hindus in the eye of Law—The word 'joint' borrowed from English law—Joint tenancy compared with Hindu parceners—Ṛght of survivorship—Joint family not much treated of in Sanskrit texts—Further analogy between joint tenants and—Hindu joint' family—No express textual authority for right of survivorship—Survivorship deduced from joint family principles—Contrast between joint tenants and Hindu's family–Members rather than family spoken of as joint in Sanskrit tests.

The word 'family' its primitive sense, Originally mean a slave-holding group, In that sense the word appropriate for units of early Hindu society

The subject of the course of lectures which is about to commence being, the law relating to the Joint Hindu family, it may be not unimportant, at the outset, to direct our attention on to the ideas conveyed by each one of the component words of that well-known expression current in the literature of Hindu law. With that intention I shall first of all take up the leading word, namely the word 'family'.

This word is traceable to a certain noun signifying a 'slave' in of the many dialects of ancient Italy, the English lexicographers explaining the word 'family' as derived from the Latin *familia*, and adding by way of a note, that the word *famel*, meant, a 'slave' in the Oscan. From this it is clear that 'the word family' is calculated regard being had to its origin, to recall an age all in which slaves constituted, if not the most important, at least one of the important ingredients of what Sir Henry Maine has, in his treatise on Ancient Law, amply and lucidly demonstrated to have been the unit of society in very ancient days. But it is an exceedingly remarkable circumstance, that this term family, which from derivation, would be, a proper designation for a slave-holding group of individuals connected together by some tie of relationship, might be applied with equal propriety to the units of ancient Hindu society it was originally constituted. The word 'family' is foreign to the language of the Hindu, but it describes well the character of the Hindu family as it stood in early days. This will appear from a study of the primitive Hindu law. The primitive Hindu law, no less than the primitive law of the nation whom Sir Henry Maine had specially in view, while elucidating his generalizations upon the progress of ancient law, had to take cognizance of slaves as an intergal part of the elements of society in its earlier stages. Manu[1] enumerates seven descriptions of slaves, placing captives in war at the head of his list. "In seven ways" he says, "man becomes a slave : he may be brought home as a trophy in battle; he may give up his freedom, to obtain his daily food; or he may be born slave of the a house, or of the family; he may be bought or he may be made a, gift of; he may be a slave because his father was so; or he may have lost his liberty being unable 'to pay a fine." In the next succeeding śloka, he says:—"The wife, the son, and the slave; all these are known as incapable of owning wealthor property. Whatsoever they earn, belongs to him whom they themselves belong." 'In the śloka 299 of the same chapter he says;—"The wife, the son, the slave the pupil and the uterine brother, if found to be guilty of an offence, should be struck with a rope, or by means of bamboo split." In the śloka 167 of the same chapter he

1. Chapter 8, Sloka 415

says—Even a transaction. entered into by a slave; with a view to the maintenance of the family, whether in the native land or in a foreign land, should not be repudiated by the master." The above interpretation of the last śloka I have adopted by consulting the gloss of Kullūka, although the two words used in Manu's original text, namely *Adhyadhina* for slave," and *Jyāyān* for 'master', might be supposed as respectively implying, the first a 'dependent,' the second an 'elder brother.' This text of Manu, if Kullūka's explanation be right, will remind a student of Sir Henry Maine, of that passage in his treatise on Ancient Law, wherein he says[1]:—"That the government and representation of the family might under a particular state of circumstances devolve on the bondman." It also seems to me, that the question raised by Sir Henry Maine, as to whether slaves were members of the family or not, will have to be answered in the affirmative, if we are to suppose that in the days of Manu a slave was on occasions trusted with managing the affairs of a family. From the mention in the śloka, cited above, of the native land and the foreign land, the drift of the text appears to be, that the Hindu *pater familias* of those days used to leave a slave in charge of his family, when himself complled to quit his home by the exigencies of his worldly concerns; and that he used to depute a slave to manage such transactions of the family, as necessitated a journey away from home.

The position of a slave similar to that of a son or a wife

These extracts[2] from Manu are sufficient to indicate that in ealry Hindu society, as it is portrayed in the pages of that lawgiver who is generally supposed to be the most ancient of all, slaves were regarded in many respects much in the same light with a wife or a son. Even as regards the mode of domestic chastisement for trivial offences, the

1. Page 164.
2. See Appendix, Original Texts, No. 1.

treatment a slave received can scarcely be said to be at all hard or inhuman, since that chastisement did not involve any severity exceeding what is daily practised by way of school discipline in the most civilized parts of the world. This is certainly a redeeming feature in slavery as it existed under the Brahmanic regime, when we remember what Maine says connection with the lot *of a slave in* the ancient European world. According to his opinion, "it is more probable that the son was practically assimilated to the slave, than that the slave shared any of the tenderness which in later times was shown to the son." On the other hand, the state of things in the early Hindu society seems to have been, that the slave was regarded as a member of the family, that he, was occasionally employed to conduct important concerns in which the whole household was interested, that there was a public sentiment prevalent in society which prevented undue cruelty, even when it was thought necessary by way of correction to administer some punishment to him. Though the civil rights of a slave were neither Iarge nor varied, he yet enjoyed a certain consideration, and, a lot which in some respects at least he had hardly, reason to deem as more unbearable than that of a son.

Slave as an article of property

I shall next cite a few extracts from the early Hindu law, in order to point out the position of a slave as an article of property, liable to be bought and sold and inherited, like herds and cattle, and other subjects of ownership and proprietary right. Viewed in this light, he obtains the contemptuous name of a 'biped,'[1] in order to distinguish him from the domesticated quadrupeds, cows and buffaloes and goats and sheep, which in the ancient Brahmanic ďays, formed a large part of the wealth of a man.

1. See Dāyabhāga Chapter II, para. 14; Appendix, Original Text No. II.

Slaves classed with immoveable property

Vyāsa quoted in the Mitākṣarā, chapter I, section 1, para. 27[1] says:–Though immoveable property, and consisting in bipeds, be acquired by a man himself; there can be neither a grant nor a sale without convening all the sons." From this passage it is clear, that the early Hindu law classed slaves with, that more important kind or property which is-known by the name of immoveable. English text writers who have written on Hindu law generally set out with the observation that the Hindu law does not make any distinction between the immoveable and the moveable property. But strictly speaking, this is not altogether accurate.

Slave concubines as members of the family

In the above text of Vyāsa, there is an evident intention to exclude land from that unfettered power of disposition by the father of the household, which no doubt constituted one of his privileges with regard to the less stable descriptions of the subjects of proprietary right. There are passages also, here and there; to be noticed on a subsequent occasion, which have been construed by some schools of Hindu law as investing a Hindu widow with unrestricted right over the moveable property inherited by her from her deceased husband. Manu (9. 219)[2] says:— "Clothes, vehicles, ornaments, prepared food, women sacrifices and pious acts, as well as the common way, are declared not liable to distribution." Here slaves appear in the form of either female drudges employed in the menial household work, or concubines kept by a man in his house. In other places, these latter are known by the name of 'Avaruddhā,' the detained; and from the injunction of non-divisibility, it would seem that Manu in laying down this prohibition had in contemplation rather the female concubines, than

1. Appendix, Original Text No. III.
2. See Appendix, Original Text, No. IV.

bond-women in general. It will appear as the more probable view, when we remember how among various uncivilized races there is found a customs of dividing or appropriating by the heir of even the widows of a deceased relative.

Heritable among banborous nations

Herbert Spencer, in his work on Sociology,[1] cites instances of the widow of the deceased being transferred to his brother's harem; he mentions that among the Zulus the widow is transferred to the brother of her deceased husband on his death; that among the Damaras, when a chief dies, his surviving wives are transferred to his brother or to his nearest relation; that in Congo, if there be three brothers, and one of them die, the two survivors share his concubines between them; that in Samoa the brother of a deceased husband considered himself entitled to have his brother's wife; that in ancient Vera Paz,. the brother of the deceased at once took the widow as his wife even if he was married, and if he did not, another relation had a right to her; that among the New Zealanders, father's wives descended to their sons, and dead brother's wives to their surviving brothers ; that among the Mishmis, when a man dies or becomes old, it is the custom of these people for the wives to be distributed amongst his sons, who take them to wife; that in some provinces of Mexico the sons inherited those wives of their fathers who had not yet borne sons to the deceased; that among the Egbas the son inherits all the father's wives save his own mother; that on the Slave Coast, upon the father's death, the eldest son not only inherits all his goods and cattle, but his wives, except his own mother; and that in Dahomey, the king inherits the deceased's wives, and makes them his own, excepting of course the woman who bore him.

---

1. Ist Vol. page 680.

Not so among the Hindus

The same eminent authority has, in other parts of that very work, pointed out, that among the rudest societies of men, the distinction between a married wife and a concubine and a slave, is of an extremely inappreciable character. According to him, among such people, the marriage is so loose, that generally the act of capture by the male and cohabitation are sufficient to convert a couple into man and wife; he also says that women were the earliest of all slaves, and that the first differentiation in a social organism commences with the appropriation of the females by the males as slaves in order to perform all the necessary drudgery of the rude household life of those times. If we now remember these facts, which have been established by the observation of innumerable travellers, if we also recollect that one of the savage tribes to wit the Mishmis, named by Herbert Spencer as practising the custom of dividing the father's widows among his sons, is a tribe inhabiting a part of the north-eastern frontiers of India, the very land where Manu promulgated his Crode, we can hardly meet with a difficulty in understanding the text quoted above; we can easily see that the Brahmanic sense of refinement was shocked, by the contemplation of a custom of this kind observed by them as prevailing among neighbouring barbarians; and the adoption of a similar custom by the Āryan settlers is rigidly forbidden.

A like view no doubt is to be taken of the following text of Uṣanas, quoted in the Mitākṣarā (chapter I, section 4, pare. 26). "Sacrificial gains; land, written documents, prepared food, water and women, are indivisible among kinsmen even to the thousandth degree."[1] It is otherwise difficult to see why bond-women, if sufficiently numerous, should not be separately alloted among several co-parceners, when they are going to effect a partition of family

1. See Appendix, Original Text, No. V.

property. We can well understand when the Dāyabhāga says (Chapter I, section 10),[1] that as the division of a single slave woman among many co-parceners is impracticable, the proper mode of partition regarding such an article of property is to appropriate the services of the slave by turn for a specified number of days. But this indivisibility is confind to the case where only a single slave in this joint property of all. A nubmer of slaves, however, can be as easilydivided co-parcene as a number of cows, or horses, or sheep. The Mitākṣarā therefore; thinks it proper to add,[2] that women or female slaves, when unequal in number, must not be divided by their value, but should be employed in labour alternative, the word 'Viṣamah' or unequal, though not found in the text either of Manu or of Uṣanas, being supposed by that commentator to be understood. Be the interpretation what it may, whether. we consider the word 'women' as signifying 'concubines kept in the house,' or 'female' slaves , the two texts prove that at the time they were written, slaves, female at all events, formed a large part of the population of India, and that the lawyers often away had to take into their consideration the status and general position of these slaves.

Stealing a slave, an offence similar to that of stealing a horse

I shall next cite another text of Manu in order to illustrate the frequent recurrence of a slave as an article of property. Manu (chapter VIII, śloka 342)[3] says, that one who seizes and tethers animals belonging to another person which were roaming free, and one who unlooses such animals as are tied, and one who steals a slave, a horse or horse car, commits the same crime as is committed by a thief.

1. See Appendix, Text, No. VI.
2. Chapter I, Section 4, para. 22.
3. See Appendix, Original Text, No. VII.

The institution of slavery further development in later ages

Here the employment of the word 'stealing' as regards a slave is significant, and may be contrasted with the words kidnapping,' and 'abducting,' made use of in the Indian Penal Code, which along with the formal-legislative abolition of slavery had to create a new offence, unknown to the ancient criminal law of the Hindus, an offence which Indian Penal Code consistently with its principles of uni-versal freedom, could not class with theft.

Fifteen kinds of slaves according to Nārada

Although slaves were only of seven kinds in the days of Manu, as shown from a text quoted above, in the days of Nārada, who is evidently a subsequent writer, the number of classes into which slaves might be divided had swelled to fifteen. It is instructive to see how these classes were made up. As explained in the Mitākṣarā, being quoted in the midst of its comments on Yājñavalkya, third chapter, śloka 183,[1] the passage from Nārada relating to slaves says, that the first class of slaves consisted of those who were born in the house, being begotten on a female slave; the second class of those who were purchased; the third, of those obtained by gift; the fourth. class were the inherited slaves; the fifth were persons saved from starvation during a famine, on the condition of consenting to be slaves; the sixth were those pledged by their masters; the seventh, those who had become slaves on account of debt, whereby their debt was cleared; the eighth; were persons made captives in war; the ninth class were persons who got into slavery, being defeated in a lawsuit, upon a previous mutual understanding to that effect; the tenth class were persons who voluntarily gave themselves up to slavery; the eleventh were persons, who having in considerately relinquished the

1. See Appendix, Original Text, No. VIII.

householder's life, again came back to the same life; the twelfth temporarily made themselves slaves; the thirteenth were slaves for the sake of receiving food at all times; the fourteenth became slaves by marrying a female slave; the fifteenth sold themselves as slaves.

Brahmanic law sanctioned slavery and extened its range

From the above enumeration we see that there was hardly any legislative interference with an individual's giving up his personal freedom; the law seems to have stood quite aloof; it extended no protecting hand over the personal liberty of individuals, and had not as yet evolved even it rudimentary notion of the interest which the society has in such a matter. Not only did law give an indirect sanction to the institution of slavery by leaving persons to adjust their reciprocal status with' that regard just as they chose; but it extended the range of slavery by availing of it as a means of punishment for a religious offence; the law thus gave a direct and positive suppose to this hateful institution; for in no other light can we regard that part of the law of slavery set forth above, wherein it is enacted, that if a man gives up worldly life, and then being unable to conform to the austere and self-abnegating course of conduct enjoined upon a religious mendicant, resumes his position as an ordinary householder; law disallows him to do so ; he must become a slave, and thus expiate his vacillation; the dominant religion established by the sacerdotal caste thus avenged itself for trifling with its sacred rules.

Ancient Hindu Family in some respects similar to the ancient Roman family

The object for which I have dwelt upon the institution of slavery as it existed in ancient India at such a length, is to point out certain likenesses in the constitution of the family as it was conceived in our part of the world, with the elements of a family organization among the ancient Romans, the nation from whose language the word 'family' has been derived. How a word which originally meant only a number of slaves came gradually to stand for a legal and social conception, embracing in its range slaves and sons and daughters and wife,—in fact a household consisting of a man and all his dependents who looked up to him as either father or grandfather or husband or master, is not difficult to see. Such a man was head of the household; the slaves he held and sent about on his various errand's were entirely in his power; he was their master even up to inflicting the punishment of death. Now this absolute power he had not only over his slaves, but also over his wife and children and gradual children and great-grandchildren; if born during his lifetime.

Modern sense of the word family how evolved, Patria Potestas is the link between its ancient and modern sense

This power, as we learn from the treatise of Sir Henry Maine, gradually came to crystallize itself, if I may be allowed to use such an expression, under the name of *patria potestas*; which according to the same high authority, exerted so potent an influence in the development between its of Roman law, was a fact the centre round which much of the personal law of that nation turned.

Patria Potestas in a rudimentary form among ancient Hindus, Indications of Patria Potestas in the original Texts, Father's powers in primitive families.

Among the Hindus, the germ of a rudimentary form of *patria potestas* is not undiscernible; as even the extracts set forth above are sufficient to show. For, what is it but the manifestation of *patria potestas*, when it is said that neither the wife, nor the son, nor the slave can acquire wealth, and that all their earnings belong to him to whom they themselves belong ? We must remember that this rule is not to be interpreted as indicating the existence of the joint family system of the present day; it is not said that the earnings are to come into the common stock, to be used by each member as occasion requires; but it is emphatically declared to belong to him, to whom the wife, the son, the slave belongs ; that is to say, to the husband, the father, the master of the household, the sole chief ingested with a despotic power over everything, animate or inanimate, human or other than human, comprised within the area of that household. Everybody and everything, be it gold and silver, paddy and seeds, beasts of burden, cows and sheep and goats, be it his children or his slaves, all are at his disposal, all must conform to his wishes. The slave must till the ground, but the crop is not his, it is his master's; the wife may wear off her fingers in revolving the spinning-wheel, but the twist made belongs to the husband; the son may employ himself in any work he can perform, he may fish, may hunt, may trade; but what he gets must be brought to his father. This is what is implied by the text of Manu, setting forth the incapacity of the son, the slave and the wife to own the property earned by each. Even now after there has been developed an elaborate system of law regarding the peculiar property of women, after the inherent joint right of a son has been established over an area including almost nine-tenths of India, we may see the arrangement of a household described by Manu illustrated in many a poor family of the present day. The father takes everything that his wife or minor son may bring in, and often dissipates it in selfish and brutal enjoyment. Whoever is familiar with the facts of actual life in India, may bear witness to the persistency of the state of things, which has been portrayed by Manu in the text wherein he declares the son's incapacity to earn property for himself.

Traces is actual life of bygone patria potestas among HIndus.

Again, that a son and a wife are classed together, with

slaves, that the mode of administering domestic chastisement, upon each is identical what is this but an indication of something akin to *patria potestas*? It testifies to the existence of a general feeling, that the position of only one individual in the family is marked out as superior, namely, that of its head; the rest are all at the same level. Whether it be a slave, or a son or even a wife, the same degree of inferiority attaches to the ˘status of all. They are all equally incapable of owning wealth, all are associated with one another, being subject to nearly the same treatment as members of a joint household.

The Three ingredeints of Patria Potestas, No suit between father and son, The rule recognised in primitive Hindu law

Again, by referring to Maine's account of the rights and liabilities comprised under the institution of *patria potestas* among the Romans, I find that the *pater familias* was accountable for the torts of his sons under power that the parent and the child could not sue one another; and that the person of his were at the absolute disposal of the father; The two last features are directly trace to certain doctrines of ancient Hindu law, which we find noticed in the works of comparatively modem lawyers who have written on Hindu law. Thus, the Mitākṣarā,[1] in its comments on the śloka 32 of the second chapter of Yājñavalkya, cites a saying without naming the author, which runs as follows:—"There can be no lawsuit between a preceptor and his pupil, between a father and his son; between a husband and his wife; and between a master and his servant; although they may have mutually fallen out:" This text has been quoted by the author of Mitākṣarā, simply with a view to be qualified, and to be virtually dissented from. The author of the Mitākṣarā goes on to say, that the above declaration intends to lay down an absolute moral prohibition of such

1. See Appendix, Original Text, No. IX.

litigation, possibly because such litigation is calculated to scandalize society by a public exhibition, of the undutiful behaviour of a son, or the disrespectful attitude of a disciple, or the unpleasantnesses of the conjugal relation. But the Mitākṣarā forthwith adds, that there are duties enjoined. by law upon the preceptor or the father and the husband; and that if the preceptor or the father or the husband wilfully disregards any such duty, and infringes the correlative right, there could surely be no valid objection to the entertainment of a properly framed suit on the part of the disciple, or the son or the wife. Thus; the law as inculcated by Gautama says,, that a disciple is to be chastised either by a whip or by a split bamboo, so as to avoid causing death, and probably, any very serious hurt. The preceptor transgressing this rule, says the Mitākṣarā, must be punished by the king. So Manu lays down that in no care should a pupil be struck on the head. Now, if a; preceptor, says Mitākṣarā, highly incensed, were to strike the student on the head with a big staff, surely the student, having been subjected to a treatment condemned by law, may apply to the king for redress, and the king is bound, to listen to his complaint. So again, the law says that the immoveable property descended from a grandfather is owned by both the father and the son with an equal proprietary right; notwithstanding which declaration of law, if the father were to dissipate such property by selling it or giving it away, in that case the son can betake himself to a Court of Justice, and litigation between father and son must then necessarily ensue. So again, the law declares that during a famine, or for the sake of religious ceremonies or during an illness, or to ransom himself from the hands of a robber, if the separate property of the wife is appropriated by the husband, he need not pay it back, unless of his own free will. Therefore, if the husband without the justification of famine or any other lawful cause, were to spend his wife's property, and afterwards although solvent, were to withhold payment, when demand is made; in such a case, there is nothing to present litigation between a husband and his wife.

The rule indicates the past patriarchal stage of the Hindus

The above is the language of the Mitākṣarā, in connection with the text quoted by itself which negatives a law suit between a father and a son. But it seems to me, that we should not be guilty of drawing a far-fetched inference, were we to suppose that the text presents to our view the unmistakeable mark of a bygone state of the law, in other words a feature of primitive law, which had been dropped as the Brahmanic society had gradually advanced from its old patriarchal arrangement, under which, litigation between a father and his son, or a husband and wife, was out of the question. The treatise of the Mitākṣarā was no doubt written under inspirations, which would have precluded its Brahmanic author from admitting, that the Brahmanic society ever passed though that stage of social progress which is known as the patriarchal stage, and which has been almost demonstrated to have been the condition of all the different branches of the Indo-Germanic race; at a period anterior to the commencement of their respective written records, though these records fail not to afford ample evidence of the existence of such a condition.

The father's absolute disposal of the person of the son

The element in the aggregate powers vested in an ancient chief of the household; that, namely, which relates to the absolute control over the persons of the equally well evidenced by bits of indubitable primitive law cropping up in the Codes promulgated by the Brahmanic sages.

Evidence by the primitive law of adoption, The practice of adoption, a survival of a state ruder than the patriachal state. Sale or gifts of children common among barbarians.

Thus Vasiṣṭha, (chapter 15)[1] says;—"As the son owes

1. See Appendix, Original Text, No. X.

its origin to the seed and the blood, his father and his mother constitute the cause of his existence; the father and the mother are free to sell him, or forsake him or give him away. But one should not give away a single son; for, he is destined to continue the race of his forefathers. A woman should not make a gift of the son, unless there be permission, from her husband." This passage serves as an introduction to the very small chapter on the law of adoption to be found in the Institutes of Vasiṣṭha. Now, an orthodox expositor of Vasiṣṭha would indignantly scout the idea, that this power of giving away a son in adoption as declared by the holy sage Vasiṣṭha has anything to do with the power absolute disposal held by the chief of a patriarchal household over the persons of his sons. On the other hand, I should be disposed to see in the text of Vasiṣṭha, a mark, not simply of a patriarchal stage, but even of a state of society yet earlier and still more rude. In order to substantiate what I thus advance, I only need cite a few lines from the work on Sociology by Herbert Spencer. At p. 768, Vol. I it is said that though attached to their offspring, Australian mothers, when in danger, will sometimes desert them that. Fuegians sell their children for slaves; that the Patagonians often pawn and sell their wives and little ones to the Spaniard for brandy; that the *Sound* Indians sell, or gamble their children away; that the Pi-Edes barter their children to the Utes proper, for a few trinkets or bits of clothing; that the Macusi sell their childen for the same price as they ask for selling a dog. At P. 774, it is said, that the Japanese when pressed by distrers, sell their children to be waitresses, singers, or prostitutes and that parents in Japan have undoubtedly in some cases, if not in all, the power to sell their children, At p. 775, Mommsen is quoted to the effect, that the father of a Roman household might expose his children might exercise over them judicial powers, might punish them as he deemed fit, in life and limb; might also sell has child.

Similarty between adoption and such barbarian customs

When these facts are placed side by side with what Vasiṣṭha says as to the power of a father over his sons, can there remain and reasonable doubt, that there is a family likeness running through all these facts, exhibited, though some of these facts may be, in the most revolting practices of some of the most barbarous nations of the earth ? We may boast that our forefathers were at no previous stage in such an abject social conditon. But national pride ought, instead of ignoring facts too glaring to be overlooked, rather to rejoice that our ancestors had outgrown such conditions.

Though the modern law of adoption framed when civilization had advanced, Brahmanic explanation of the origin of adoption misleading

It is not intended here to maintain, that in the days of Vasiṣṭha, the sale or gift of sons as then practised among the Brahmanic people, had nothing to distinguish it from Constitution the custom of barbarians instanced above. On the other hand, I freely admit that motives, other than those which inspire a barbarian, had come into existence, and that the rude ancient practice, toned down and modified by advancing civilization and progressive ideas in religion, had then assumed a far more benign aspect than it originally had. But, it is impossible to resist the conclusion, that the origin of the practice; even among the Hindus, must have been the same, and that what Vasiṣṭha says with regard to the powers of a father, is nothing else than what is known to have been one of the characteristics of patriarchal groups among various other sections of the human race. It is curious to observe how the progress of metaphysical speculation led the leaders of Brahmanic thought in those days to discover, what they no doubt supposed to be a rational explanation of the custom of giving or selling sons, which they were dwelling upon. This custom of selling or giving away children had come down to them from the patriarchal period, and probably from a still under social stage. They saw it daily practised among the Brahman people whose law they were recording. They had no histories of their earlier days to guide their nescent speculations, nor any reliable accounts of the customs of contemporaneous savage societies. Therefore, the only explanation that could suggest itself to them was drawn from metaphysical ideas, coupled with such physiological notions as they possessed. What is the origin of a father's power of selling his son ? Because the father is the cause, the creator of the son; an artisan creates a saleable commodity, which therefore is at the absolute disposal of the artisan; the parents stood in a similar relation to their son; they had given him being, the son therefore should be at their absolute disposal. This is the explanation shadowed forth in Vasiṣṭha's text, but it is an explanation calculated to disguise the patriarchal origin of the custom of giving away a son; for, under the patriarchal system, the status of the mother is scarcely superior to that of the son, and yet the metaphysical explanation makes the mother a participator in whatever power the father had over the son. But the disguise is too transparent to cause a perplexity. For immediately after, it is said that a woman should not give away or accept a son, except with the permission of her husband. Had not the mother's power, deduced from metaphysical and physiological notions, been thus qualified, and in fact been cut short altogether, the law as laid down would have been at open variance with the practice of the period, which had no doubt then shaken off a good deal of the patriarchal characteristics, but nevertheless had not yet advanced sufficiently to sanction an entire independence of the wife. The advancement of society from the patriarchal stage is exactly measured by that vicarious power which Vasiṣṭha gives to the wife, and which no doubt was consonant to the current ideas of the day with regard to the status of the wife.

That the custom of giving away a son is a part of very primitive and very rude customs of uncivilized nations, is further confirmed by another indication, faint though it be, yet not to be mistaken, which can be drawn from a text of Manu.

In ch. 9, śloka 168,[1] Manu defines a given son to be one, whom either the mother or the father or both should give in distress. Now this word 'distress' has exercised much all his commentators, who betake themselves to strange shifts in order to give, an account of the word. Kulluka Bhatta, the great commentator on the Code of Manu, says[2] that the word 'distress' refers to the religious sentiment which is the origin of the doctrine of spiritual benefits. A dead man requires to be ministered to by his son, who must offer his deceased ancestors cake and water. Therefore, to have no son is to be in distress, when one is in next world. Therefore, Kulluka means to imply, that it is the absence of a son; which is equivalent to a prospective distressed condition in the next world, that authorizes a man to accept a son from a different family. This is how Kulluka explains the saying of Manu, that a son is given distress. But in order to arrive at the true meaning of Manu's text, we must remember what Herbert Spencer says. According to him, one of the many causes which induce savage people to part with their children, is the difficulty experienced in rearing them. It is the want of food both for themselves and for their children; that originated, along with certain other causes, the primitive germ of the custom, which gradually led to the elaborate law of affiliation and adoption. And Manu, who is said to be superior to all other promulgators of codified law, because he has incorporated the sense of the Veda,[3]

1. See Appendix, Original, Text, No. XI.
2. See Appendix, Original, Text, No. XII.
3. Vide Brihaspati, quoted by Kulluka in his comments on Manu, chapter 1, śloka 1, to this effect: "A law at variance with what Manu says is not acceptable, for Mann is superior; as he has incorporated the sense of the Veda." See Appendix, Original Text, No. XIII.

semingly remembers the origin of the law of adoption : probably in his days no given son was ever parted with by the natural father unless he was compelled by want to do so. Even in our days, we often witness that during times of general scarcity, children are given away by their parents, and sometimes are even abandoned.

This interpretation of the word 'distress,' so unaccountably found in Manu's text, had not become obsolete the days of the Mitākṣarā, since that treatise says[1] (chapter I, section 11, para 10); "By specifying distress, it is intimated that the son should not be given, unless there be distress. This prohibition regards the giver." We find it stated in Colebrooke's notes that both Balambhatta and Chandeswara adopt this interpretation. It was I believe, Apararka, cited by Nanda Pandita in his treatise on Adoption (section I, para. 7),[2] who was the first to propose the very unnatural and altogether forced construction, that 'distress' means the sonlessness of the adoptive father. But Nanda Pandita is evidently not satisfied with Apararka's interpretation, for he immediately after introduces the Mitākṣarā interpretation, and supports it by citing Kātyāyana, who says, " During a season of distress, the gift or even sale of a son may be otherwise the same must not be done; this is the injunction of the holy institutes."[3]

Here is an instructive instance of the manner in which the practice of a very rude state of society, transformely itself into a law which bears no resemblance to its primitive germ. People in distress part with their sons among uncivilized people; this practice is taken advantage of by persons of means, who, from various motives add to the number of their family by adopting male members from another family; the adopted member's acquire civil rights in the new family. At first none but persons in distress are

1. See Appendix, Original, Test, No. XIV.
2. Ibid, No. XV.
3. Ibid, No. XVI.

allowed to part with their sons; then this prohibition is converted into, a merely moral injunction; then the original practice is so far forgotten, that forced interpretations are fastened upon antique records of the custom.

Thus the modern law of adoption, having its origin in certain practices of our early ancestors, was developed under the patriarchal stage, through which we along with some other nations had to pass; and being helped by the progress of religious ideas, that law has gradually assumed the complex form in which we see it now. But our present concern with it is, that along with other facts in the history of our law, it testifies to the prevalence in early Hindu society, of that structure of social organization which is characterised by extensive powers vested in the father as the chief of a household-powers which extended to the gift or sale or even abandonment of a son.

Family responsible for a member's torts

The other feature of the Roman *patria potestas* which I have mentioned above, namely, the responsibility of the father for the wrongful acts of the son, cannot be so directly recognized in the remains of our ancient law, But I have lighted upon parts of that law which I cannot not understand in any other sense than that of joint responsibility attaching to the members of a household.

Thus Manu (chapter 8, śloka 169)[1] says, "Three suffer on account of others, namely, a witness, a surety, and the family." This text has been left in obscurity by Kulluka as regards the question; in what way does the family suffer on account of others ? We may well understand that a witness has to undergo a large amount of trouble in attending courts of justice, for the sake of parties to the suit; and this is suffering on account of others; that is to say, for persons other than the witness himself. Similarly, a surety, when he

1. See Appendix, Original, Text, No. XVI.—2.

is compelled to pay the sum for which he pledged his credit, no doubt suffers on account of the default committed, not by himself but by another, namely, his principal. But we are at a loss to understand how the family suffers for the fault of others. Kulluka says in explaining the text that a king should not compel the family to adjudicate matters of litigation.[1] The word employed in Manu is kula, the ordinary acceptation of which is, 'family' Adjudication of matters in litigation by a 'kula' or 'family' is adverted to in Yājñavalkya, (chapter II, śloka 30),[2] where it is said that the judicial functionaries employed by a king constitute the highest Court of justice; next to them are *pugas* or village communities and town communities, as explained by Vijñāneśvara; next to these communities, stand *Śreṇis or* guilds; lowest of all are the 'kulas' or 'families'. The Mitākṣarā explains the above text of Yājñavalkya in the following way, "*Pugas* are assemblages of persons who belong to different castes, live by different employments, but who all dwell in the same place, such as a village, or a town. *Śreṇis* are assemblages of persons who may be long to the same caste or different castes, but all of whom live by the same identical employment or calling; such as, horse-dealers, or sellers of betel, weavers, or workers in leather. Kulas or families are assemblages constituted by agnates, relatives and kinsmen.

'Family' Courts, guilds Courts and village Courts, Popular machinery for administering justice

What is intended to be said is, that if a certain matter of litigation has been decided by the royal. functionaries, the same matter is not cognizable again by the town communities, or the village communities, although the losing party be dissatisfied on the ground that the same has been wrongly decided. Similarly what has been decided by

1. See Appendix, Original, Text, No. XVII.
2. Ibid, Text, No. XVIII.

a town or village community cannot go for re-trial before guilds. Similarly a matter decided by a guild cannot be re-tried by a family. But what has been decided by the family may come up for re-trial before the guilds; the decisions of the guild can be revised by the tribunals of the village or town communities; and the juagments passed by these latter are open to revision by the royal functionaries." Smṛticandrikā[1] affords a further light on this subject, by explaining 'kulas' or 'families as persons of the same gotra with the plaintiff and the defendant, by which I suppose we are to understand that the members of the families to which the plaintiff and the defendant respectively belonged were invested with an original jurisdiction in administering justice, whether in civil or in criminal matters, from which tribunal, the appeal lay to the guild court; thence to the village or town Court, the decision of the royal functionaries being final. Whether these kula courts were. the ancient forms of the punchayets of the modern days, or of the caste meetings which are frequently convened in many parts of India in order to adjust matters relating to the caste, is a question difficult to solve. From what we find in Yājñavalkya and also in certain other old authorities quoted in the Smṛticandrikā, it is impossible to overlook the fact, that formerly there was an exceedingly well-organised system of administering' cheap and expeditious justice by machinery highly popular in its character. But, however that may be the question with which we are at present concerned is What on the interpretation to be given to the text of Manu, when, he says that families like sureties have to suffer on account of others ? Are we to understand in the sense which puts upon that familes are compelled to under go the trouble of administering justice when there are disagreements between either the members of the same family, or members belonging to different families, in which latter case both the families prabably united and formed a

1. See Appendix, Original, Text, No. XIX.

composite Court? Or are we to suppose that in this text of Manu we have found the indication of that customary law which a family jointly liable for the torts and wrongful acts of any of its members ? That such, a customary law prevailed extensively in early societies is borne out not only by what is known of the early law of the Romans, but also of the early custom of other societies. We have already seen what Sir Henry Maine says as to the responsibility of the *pater famileas* who was answerable for the delicts or torts his son under power. He was similarly liable for the torts of his slaves ; but in both cases he originally possessed the singular privilege of tendering the delinquent's person in full satisfaction of the damages. The same authority also explain that the *pater familias* was, it were, the representative of the family, and in fact was identifiable with it. Leveleye in his highly appreciated treatise on Primitive Property, says, that "Among the Germans, it was the family which received or paid the *wehrgeld*, or compensation for the crime; and there is exactly the same practice among the Albanians at the present day,, and among all Indian tribes" Herbert Spencer in his Sociology (Vol. 1, p. 734). says;–"Along with persistence of patriarchal structures under new conditions, naturally goes persistence of patriarchal principles. There is supremacy eldest male, sometimes continuing as in Roman law, to the extent of life and death power over wife and children. There long survives to the general idea, that the offences of the individual are the offences of the group which he belongs; and as a consequence, there survives the practice of holding the group responsible, and of inflicting punishment upon it" Manu when declaring that families suffer on of others, likens the liability of families with that sureties. Now what does he say with, the sureties ? In śloka 158 chapter 8,[1] it is laid down, that a man if a stands as surety for the purpose of producing another person, a debtor, when required by the creditor and if he fails to

1. See Appendix, Original, Text, No. XX.

produce the debts when rerquired by the creditor, he must pay the debt from own pocket. Yājñavalkya says upon the same subject - (chapter 2, śloka 54) to the following effect. Suretyship occurs for the purpose of producing the person of a debtor; or for guaranteeing his solvency,' or with a promise that the debt was to be paid by the surety in case the principal debtor fails. The first two kinds of sureties are compellable to make good the claim, if there is a failure to produce, or if the solvency of the debtor turns out not to be true.

Family multed like a surety

As regards the third kind of surety who undertakes expressly to pay, even his sons are liable to pay the debt which the father might be compelled to pay. Manu says that as a surety suffers for another, so a family suffers for another; we find that even the son of a surety suffers loss of money on account of the wrongful conduct of his father's principal; we may fairly conclude from the analogy between a surety and a family, that a family suffered for the wrongful conduct of one of its members, the family had to make, compensation to the injured party. In other words, one member of the family commits a wrong; 'but all the others suffer a loss, because they are liable to pay compensation; they suffer for something not done by themselves. This vicarious liability of a surety would perfectly resemble the liability of families, if we take the meaning to be in accordance with the above-named custom of other societies of the patriarchal type. Whereas what Kulluka suggests is hardly sufficient to render the parallel between the liabilities of sureties and that of families at all intelligible.

No name in Sanskrit for Patria Potestas

Thus we see that if we analyse portions of our ancient law by availing ourselves of the accounts of the customs of other primitive communities, especially communities which are ethnologically connected with the Hindoos, we may meet with many indications of the close relationships and likenesses which existed between our institutions and those of other communities; and particularly we find a striking analogy between the institution of ancient Brahmanic family and the institution of family in the early societies of a kindred origin. I shall in a future Lecture try to point out how the comparison can be carried still further; how in fact all the characterstics of the patriachal type enumerated by Herbert Spencer are plainly discernible in various parts of the law promulgated by our sages, although that law has undergone numberless modifications by the process of interpretation applied by our later jurists, who were under the necessity of reconciling the practices existing at their day with the written law handed down to them from early times. At the present moment, it will suffice to say that the germ of the family traceable in the early portions of the Hindu law did not greatly differ from the Roman family in its rudimentary condition. No doubt, we in Sanskrit have no name for the institution of *patria potestas*, but this is what was to be expected. The wide divergence in the political history of the two nations set in operation many causes, which checked the further development of *patria potestas* among the Hindus. At the same time, those causes must have been principally instrumental in giving a durability to the institution of family in India, which that institution did not obtain among the Romans, nor among those other nations which were at any time subjected to the Roman law. The name 'family' derived from the language of the Romans has been now applied by the British administrators of justice in India to groups of individuals belonging to the Hindu race, who being mutually related, live together and own property together. The name recalls the period when slaves constituted an integral parts of such groups. We have seen that in this respect the name would not have been inappropriate to the Hindu groups of kinsmen and relatives.

But somehow or others we never named our groups of kinsmen dwelling together as so many slave holding assemblages. Our name is different. The legal entity now understood by the expression family would be designated in the language of Hindu law either 'Kuṭumba' or a 'Kula.'

In Sanskrit 'Kuṭumba' and 'kula' are the names for a 'family'

In order that a clear idea may be obtained of the manner in which the word Kuṭumba used to be employed by our law givers, both ancient and modern,[1] I shall here cite a few passages in which that word has been used to family.' Manu (ch. 8, śloka 166.)[2] If the who contracted the debt has died, and if the expenditure was made for the propose of the 'Kuṭumba,' that debt should be paid by persons related to the deceased their own wealth, although the relatives may be devided:," Kulluka in his comments upon this śloka says:—When the expenditure of the loan was made by him for, the purpose of maintaining the 'Kuṭumba' of all the brothers, previously divided or undivided; then that debt should be paid by those who are divided, and by those who are undivided, from their own wealth." Manu (chapter 8, śloka 167).

"Even if a slave should enter into a transaction for purposes of the ' Kuṭumba, either in the native land or in a foreigned, the elder should not repudiate that transaction." Kulluka's comments on this śloka are: "Whether, the master be in that country, or in a different country; any loan and the like, that may be made by even a slave, on 'account of the expenses of the Kuṭumba of the master, that loan the master should adopt in its entirely. Here I have tired be as

1. By modern, I mean such authors as Vijñāneśvara, Jimūtavāhana, Aparāka, Medhātithi, and others whose works have no independent binding authority, but are professedly expositions of the law as propounded by the ancient sages.
2. See Appendix, Original Text, No. XXI.

literal as I possibly could. The meaning of 'Kulluka-evidenaly seems to be, that the word 'transaction', Vyavahara in the original, includes not only the making of a loan, but other dealings also, such as purchasing provisions for the consumption of the family, and therefore Kulluka says, 'and the like' means also to imply, that the transaction entered into by the slave should be allowed by the master without any modification; so, he says 'tatha,' just as it was,' in the original Yājñavalkya (chapter 2, śloka 45). 'When the head of a Kuṭumba is either dead or is sojourning away from home, then persons who have taken his property should pay the debt which may have been contracted by persons undivided, for the purposes of the Kuṭumba[1].'

The comments[2] of Vijñāneśvara on this śloka are,—"The debt which has been contracted by many, who are undivided, for the purposes of the Kuṭumba, or by one, that debt the head of the Kuṭumba should pay; he being dead, or gone away on a sojourn, all the participators of his wealth should pay."

Yājñavalkya (chapter 2, śloka 46 according to the

---

1. This śloka is numbered as the 46th of the second chapter of Yājñavalkya in the Edition of the Mitākṣara which was issued in 1829 by the Committee of Public Instruction in Calcutta (Kolkata). That Edition comprises only the Vyavahārādhyāya or the Chapter on Judicial Proceedings. I have cited the śloka from Viswanath Mandlik's edition of Yajnavalkya, Bombay, in this Edition the śloka stands as the 45th of the second chapter, My translation of the śloka varies slightly from that adopted by the abovenamed gentleman. He renders' proshita,' by 'gone to a remote country.' I should humbly think that the word has nothing to do with the distance from, or nearness to, home, of the country wherein a person may be sojourning. The word comes from the root ' Vas' preceded by the Upasarga 'pra,' which is in very ordinary use as signifying 'to go abroad or away from home,' 'to sojourn in another country *Vide* Wilson's Dictionary of the Sanskrit Language, the word ' proshita.'
2. See Appendix, Original, Text No. XXII.

Mandlik edition; 47 according to the edition issued by the Committee of public Instruction).[1]

A woman should not liquidate what was contracted by her husband, or by her son; a father, what was borrowed by the son; a husband, what was borrowed by the wife excepting the debt for the purposes of the Kuṭumba

The comments of Vijñāneśvara on this śloka are:

The sage in this is speaking of an exception to the rule of, who should pay. A woman, that is, a wife, should by no means pay the debt contracted by the husband; a woman, that is, a mother, should not pay what has been contracted by the son; similarly, the father' should not pay the same contracted by the son, similarly the husband should not pay the same contracted by the wife excepting that contracted for the purposes of the Kuṭumba this qualifies all. Therefore, the head of the Kuṭumba be should pay that contracted for the purposes of the Kuṭumba by any one soever. In his absence, it should be paid by the participators of his heritage; this has been already declared. 'Mitākṣarā, chapter I, section 1 para. 27[2] "Therefore ownership in the wealth of the father and of the grandfather is by birth alone. In spite of its being so, it is settled that the father is in making use of property other than immoveables on the occasions of religious acts indispensable to be performed; or of gifts of favour, support of the Kuṭumba, relief from distress and so forth, these being prescribed by, texts of law. But as regards immoveable property, whether acquired by himself, or received from *his* father and the rest, there is ' accountability to the son and the rest; since there is the following text of law:—

Although immoveable property, and that consisting in slaves be acquired by one's own self; there can be neither a gift nor a sale, without convening all the sons. Those that

1. See Appendix, Original, Text, No. XXIII.
2. Ibid, No. XXIV.

are born, and those that are unborn, and also those that are lying within the womb; they are in expectation of something to live—upon, there can be neither is a gift nor a sale.'[1]

"There is a limitation of the above. Even a single person may make a gift or a pledge or sale in respect of immoveable property at a time of distress, for the purposes Kuṭumba, and specially for religious purposes."

"The meaning hereof is, the sons, the son's sons, being minors and incapable of giving permission, or the brothers being in that condition, although undivided, on the occasion of a calamity affecting the whole Kuṭumba; and in support thereof, and on the occasion of the father's funeral rites etc. which are indispensable to be porformed, even a single capable person may effect a gift, or pledge or sale of immoveable property.

Nārada quoted in the Vivāda Cintāmaṇi of Vachaspati Misra.[2]

"That debt which has been contracted by an undivided paternal uncle, or a brother, or by a mother, for the purpose of old Kuṭumba–all the participators of the heritage should pay the same."

Vṛhaspati quoted by the same author at the same place. What has been taken by the paternal uncle, a brother, a son, a woman a slave, a disciple, and a dependent, for the purpose of the Kuṭumba—the owner of the house-hold is liable to pay the same.

Nārada quoted again by the same author at the same place.

---

1. The latter part of this text of Vyāsa has a different reading which as means: the destruction of that which is to be subsisted upon is condemned:
2. Page 18, Edition by Ramchandra Vidyavagishs, formerly Professor of Smriti in the Calcutta Government Sanscrit College. This Edition was issued under the patronage of the Committee of Public Instruction. See Appendix, Original, Text, No. XXV.

'Nor should a debt contracted by the wife devolve by any means upon the husband; excepting that contracted during a calamity; since, the exigencies of a Kuṭumba are paramount. The above does not apply to the wives of the washerman, the fowlers, the milkmen, and the liquor–sellers; and their calling is under the control of them; and the Kuṭumba is dependent upon them,' *i.e.*, it is the women of these castes who manage their house-hold affairs and also the duties of their calling.

The comments of Vachaspati Misra upon this text are— 'The above is intented for an illustration; since what is contracted by the wives of even a Brahmin and the rest, is to be paid by the owner of the Kuṭumba. Saṅkha and Likhita quoted by Jimutvahana and in his Dāyabhāga, (chapter I, para. 42). 'When the father is incapable, the eldest son should look after the affairs; or he who stands next, and understands business, being permitted by him; but there is no divsion of the heritage when the father is unwilling; in case of his being aged, unsettled in mind, or afficted with a prolonged illness, the eldest son should take care of the concerns of the rest, like to the father; for the support of the *Kuṭumba* is dependent on the heritage; those having a father are not free; similarly in case of the mother being alive.'

'Kutumba' does not necessarly mena a joint family.

In the above quotations, extraced for the purpose of illustrating the employment of the expression 'Kuṭumba' as it occurs in the original text-books, the context shows that it is a united 'family' composed of brothers and uncles and probably of other more distant relatives, which is intended by the word 'Kuṭumba' In fact all these passages view a 'Kuṭumba' as possessed of a heritage; and all those persons who may be unitedly interested in a haritage, or in any property descended to them from their forefathers, are taken to be included in the Kuṭumba. 'But from these instances of the use of the word 'Kuṭumba,' 'we are not at liberty to jump to the conclusion that the word is restricted to a family comprising many persons independent of one another, or of persons whose rights are co-ordinate. If that had been so, 'Kuṭumba' would have been a very proper rendering for the expression 'joint family,' as it is used in the English text-books on Hindu law. But the following śloka[1] from the Mitākṣarā, quoted there from the Institutes of Nārada, is an authority for saying, that the word 'Kuṭumba' is not confined in its meaning to only a 'united family' also means the wife and children of a single individual.

"He, who will support the 'Kuṭumba' of a brother, while the latter is engaged in pursuing his studies—is entitled althouth he be himself devoid of learning, to get a share of those, gains of knowledge."[2]

In this text, the word 'Kuṭumba' evidently stands for the aggregate of those individuals, who depend upon a single person for their support; in other words, his own wife and children. The other brother maintains them while he is

1. See Appendix; Original Teat, No. XXVI. Mitak. Ch. 1, S. 4, para 8.
2. I have here given a translation of the text which varies, but not essentially, from that of Colebrooke. It is my intention to follow a similar course when I have to cite, or refer to, a text of Hindu law; that is to say, I shall in most cases give my own translation, although there may be an extant English translation of the same text, previously public. This will not in every case imply that I either disapproved of, or disagreed with, each, previously published translation. My purpose in giving my own translation is as follows :-Those who have access to the original Sanskrit will require neither translation, in order to obtain the drift of the passage. Those who have no such access will certainly obtain clearer ideas of the purport of the passage, by having at their command two independent versions of the same text. It often happens in translating from one language into another, that a sufficient prominence cannot be given to all the important notions conveyed by the original. One transaction may possibly give prominence to one idea; the other to another. Hence a more correct notion as to what is contained in the original may be acquired by consulting two independent translations, than would be the case if sole recourse were had to either.

pursuing his studies, probably away from home in the house of his preceptor; thereby the other brother entitles himself to receive a share of whatever earnings will in future be made by the learned brother by means of his learning. We shall see on a future occasion that this rule has been greatly qualified by judge-made law.

Notion conveyed by 'kuṭumba'

Thus we arrive at the conclusion, that in the original text-books of Hindu law, the name of a family is, whether such family be the united assemblage of a number, of co-parceners having independent and co-ordinate rights, or it be composed of the wife and children of a single individual, is 'Kuṭumba.' It is a word of very extensive use in Sanskrit language and literature. It calls up the notion of a large group of persons, living within one enclosure, ordinarily taking their meals together, having a common fund and common means of support, owning extensive landed property, with herds and cattle; and probably slaves, before slavery was abolished by the British Government; having probably a common family idol whose worship is carried on out of the common funds, and performing the annual and the occasional religious ceremonies in honour of their departed ancestors. How this 'Kuṭumba' used to be conceived popularly may be seen from the following translation of a Sanskrit verse, which is often quoted as a proverb in ordinary parlance.[1]

"It is only persons of a small mind who are in the habit of reckoning, who is of their kin, and who not so; but to those who conduct themselves on generous principles, the whole world is of their own 'Kuṭumba'."

The word 'kuṭumba' of probable foreign origin.

Altough thus the notion of a 'kuṭumba' was and still is

1. अयं निजः परो वेति गणनां लघुचेतसां।
उदारचरितानां तु वसुधैव कुटुम्बकम्।।

very general among the Hindus, yet it is doubtful whether the word is of genuine Sanskrit origin. It has no derivation in that language, or whatever derivation it is said to have, is evidently a manufacture of the scholastic ingenuity of the Brahmanic Sanskritists. They can find or invent a roct for every word met with in Sanskrit Literature; but the canons of true philology are often against such ingenious derivation, which is wholly fruitless, and totally fails to throw any light on the true origin of the word. Thus, Wilson in his Dictionary of Sanskrit Language, wherein he has generally followed the guidance of the Pundit compilers of his justly valued work derives the word 'Kuṭumba' from a root of the same identical form, 'Kuṭumba,' which means 'to support family.' In other words, 'Kuṭumba,' 'a family,' comes from Kuṭumba, to support family.' This is specimen of Brahmanic etymological ingenuity. The suspicion that the word 'Kuṭumba' is not of genuine Sanskrit origin is further confirmed by the fact, that the word has get but a scanty number of derivatives in that language. The only two derivative words traceable to 'Kuṭumba' are 'kutumbin' and 'kutumbini.' The former literally means one who has a 'Kuṭumba,' a family man, and the head or chief of a family or household. The latter signifies the wife of the chief of a household, hence, the 'mistress of a household,' who regulates the zenana department and who in fact answers to the same idea which in Bengal is entertained of a 'Ginni,' a Bengali word derived from Grihini,' a matron, or the lady who stands as the female head of household on the other hand, the word 'Kuṭumba' bears a close resemblance to the Persian-Arabic word 'kaum,' signifying 'kinsfolk.' It is at this day difficult to determine which of the two nations, the Hindus or the Persians, were in debted to the other for the term, But if, as l am inclined to suspect, we are the borrowers, then it is a remarkable circumstance that the ordinary name of one of the most durable, institutions of the Hindu society should have been wanting in their own language, and should have been adopted by them from a neighbouring people.

Kula and Sakulya

The other national name for that institution, as I have already said, is 'Kula' This word occurs in the well-known legal term, of 'Sakulya,' which etymologically signifying persons born in the same family, is technically confined to a small specified number, out of the aggregate of all those who might be justly entitled to the appelleation. The three generations immediately above the paternal great-grandfather together with their descendants, and the three generations immediately below the great-grandson in the male line, are the kinsmen who have obtained the name of Sakulyas. This is the interpretation given to the word by Jimūtavāhana alone. The word is to be found in the Code of Manu; it also occurs certain extracts, severally attributed in the following law-givers, namely, Baudhāyana, Devala and Vrihaspati. In the extract from Baudhāyana, quoted by Jimūtavāhana in his Dāyabhāga, chapter 11, section 1, para. 37, the name occurs as follows. Baudhāyana says:—[1]

"Paternal great-grandfather, paternal grandfather, father, himself, brothers of the whole blood, a son born in a wife, of the same caste, son's son, and the son of a son's son, all these: participators of an undivided dāya or heritage, are spoken of as sapiṇḍas participators of a divided dāya or heritage,—are sopken of as sakulyas. Issue of the body existing, it is on them that, property devolves. In the absence of a sapiṇḍa, a sakulya, and in his absence the property, or the disciple, or the household priest, should take. In absence thereof, the king."

Then I came to the extract from Devala quoted in the Vivāda-Cintāmaṇi,[2] (Sanskrit, p. 154).

1. See Appendix, Original Text, No. XXVII.
2. Ibid, No. XXVIII.

Then the dāya or heritage of a sonless man should be divided by uterine brothers, or by daughters of equal caste, or by the father who is alive; by brothers of equal caste, by mother and by the wife, in due succession; in default of these, it should be taken by sakulyas dwelling together.'

The next extract is from Vṛhaspati, quoted in the Smṛti Candrikā (MS. Calcutta Sanskrit College, No. 2098, leaf 253, P. 2).

"Where there are many jñātis, sakulyas and bandhus—he who is nearer, out of them-should take the wealth of a childless man." To the above extracts I must add Manu, 9th Chapter, śloka 187.

"Every such person who would be the nearest, out of sapiṇḍas–the wealth should belong to him. Thereafter would come a sakulya, a preceptor or even a disciple.

Now, none of these extracts throws , any light as to what particular persons were designated by the term 'Sakulya'. Jimutavāhana attaches a special meaning to the text of Baudhāyana, the authority for his selecting certain specified kinsmen as entitled to that name, being a test from the Mārkaṇḍya Purāṇa, quoted in the Dāyabhāga (Chapter 11, Section 1, pares. 41.)[1]

"And the three others, from the paternal grandfather of the paternal grandfather, are the participators of the wipings of the piṇḍa, and he who offers the oblations is the seventh of them. In this way connection has been declared by the saints to be extending to seven generations."

To this text Jīmūtavāhana adds by way of explanation that this kindred relation regards the period of impurity to be observed by relatives. But Mārkaṇḍeya nowhere says that the three ancestors from the paternal grandfather of the paternal grandfather are styled 'Sakulyas.'

---

1. See Appendix, Original Text, No. XXIX.

Family formerly seldom joint beyond seven generations. Sakulya equivalent to 'divided parcener'.

The truth is, that Jīmūtavāhana, when departing in his, scheme of intestate succession from all the other schools, has given a forced and unnatural interpretation to the text of Baudhāyana, whose plain meaning is consonant to the doctrine of all the schools, excepting that of Bengal, that the sapiṇḍa relationship extends in every case to seven generations and that any kinsman beyond those degrees is 'a sakulya, that is a person born in the same family, that this 'sakulya' is often convertible to 'gotrajā' term used by Yājñavalkya, and to 'samaodaka'—another term used by other sages.

'Kula' probably meant a divided family, not a joint family.

An important fact which we may infer from a plain and natural construction of the text of Baudhāyana is that in his days joint-family relationship was supposed to be conterminous with the 'sapiṇḍa' relationship for he, after enumerating seven generations, calls them, as participators of undivided heritage. Here, the word in the original, dāya, which in every case means inherited property,' is construed by Jīmūtavāhana in the sense of a 'piṇḍa,' or oblation. Herein lies the forced character of his interpretation. If we disregard this interpretation, we may safely conclude, that in former days no family ever remained in union beyond seven generations–that being the utmost limit to which family union was even actually carried. Thus, we may get an idea of the constitution of an ancient joint family as it was contemplated by the old lawgivers of the Hindus. Although therefore the word 'kula' be a name for a family, it is seldom used in the sense of an undivided family had it been so, the word 'sakulya,' which literally means 'born in the same family,' would have never carried with it the notion of a divided participator of inherited property; for

Baudhāyana evidently defines a 'sakulya' to be a divided parcener.'

The word 'Hindu', Not a Sanskrit word.

I now come to the second component part of the expression "joint Hindu family," namely, the word ' Hindu.' At first sight no term appears to be capable of so easy a construction. The Hindus constitute the bulk of the population of India; it may be supposed therefore that we can without the least difficulty ascertain whether a particular individual or a particular family is Hindu or not. But if we consider the matter a little more closely, we shall find an accurate definition of the term 'Hindu' to be not so easy a task. In the first place, original Sanskrit law does not give us any help, because the term 'Hindu' nowhere occurs in the whole body of that law. Our ancient lawgivers were not under the necessity of regarding the population of India as classified according to different religious denominations. The idea of a territorial law for a society under a Brahmanic administration had not then dawned. A king no doubt was to be guided by a Brahman administrator of justice, but the law which was to be administered did not entirely depend upon the priesthood. Thus Yājñavalkya says:—

Chapter I, śloka 7.[1]

"The Veda the Smṛti, the practice of the righteous men, what is acceptable to one's own soul, and a desire produced by a virtuous resolve—all this is the root of law".

Manu, chapter VIII. śloka 41.

The king "should asscertain the laws of a state, and those prevailing in a particular inhabited country, the laws of the guilds, and the laws of families, and being versed in law, should establish every one in his proper law."

Śloka 46.

"What is practised by righteous men, and by learned

1. See Appendix, Original Text, No. XXX.

persons of the three regenerate castes–he should established the same,' in consistency with the law of the country, and families and castes."

Kulluka explains it thus:

"What is practised by persons of the regenerate castes, such as are learned and also virtuous—he having adopted the same, in consistency with the law of the country, and families and castes should establish it."

Yājñavalkya, chapter II, śloka 188.

"What may be customary, in consistency with his own law, and what has been enacted by a king–even that also should be kept up with care."

Upon this the comments of Vijñāneśvara are:—

"Without conflicting with the law promulgated in the Veda and the Smṛti, that law which arises from usagas for instance the law relating to the pasture of cows; the storing of the water, the keeping up of the templet of a divinity, and other like matters-that also should with care be observed. Similarly, the customary law by a king also, in consistency of course with his own Proper law—as for instance, the law to some such effect as this:– food should be given to all the travellers; horses etc. should not be sent to the dominions of our enemy' even this also should be maintained."

Yājñavalkya, chapter II, śloka 194.

"The same rule applies also to the laws of guilds, of 'naigamas' or those who acknowledge the authority of the Veda, of 'pāshandins' or those who deny that authority, and of societies; the king should maintain the distinction of the above; and should maintain the previous course of conduct."

Upon this text, the comments of Vijñāneśvara are:—

"The guilds are those who live by the same commodity or by the same mechanical art; the Naigamas are those who acknowledge the authority of the Veda as having been composed by persons of infallibility; such as the worshippers of Paśupati, (a particular religious sect); the pāṣandins are those who do not at all acknowledge the authority of the Veda, such as the followers of Buddha who go about naked; a society is a group of persons subsisting by the same calling, such as the fighting men; as regards all these four, the rule in the same—that is to say, the rule propounded in śloka 186. And the king should maintain the regulations of their law; and should maintain the course of conduct previously adopted."

'Naigama' not equivalent to 'Hindu', Personal law applied to 'Naigamas' or sectaries

In this text we nearly touch upon some class of people whom we may be inclined to take as Hindus; for if anything to acknowledge the authority of the Veda is certainly one of the undoubted characteristics of a Hindu in the ordinary acceptation of that term; and we might suppose that the Naigama, in other words, a follower of Nigama or the Veda must be the name of a Hindu. But a slight reflection will convince us that no special injunction was necessary in a Hindu territory for maintaining law of the Veda, for Yājña-valkya had already laid down in śloka 7 of the 1st chapter, that the Veda was one of the 'roots' of law. On the other hand, by seeing that Vijñāneśvara has instanced the worshippers of Paśupati as a sub-class included in the more general class of the Naigamas, we must conclude, that by the term 'Naigama' were intended all those Hindu sectaries, who did not altogether throw away the Veda, but whose departures from the Vedic religion as followed by the generality of the orthodox people were sufficiently striking to have made it desirable that they should be separately grouped. It is for this reason that an authoritative declaration was necessary, to induce the king to respect the particular observances followed by these Naigamas or sectaries, and to administer law in their case in accordance with those observances. Vijñāneśvara in fact mentions they very name, Pāśupata. It is a name, as every Hindu knows, still current, and still designates one of the most extensive sects by which at present the community professing the Hindu religion is mainly divided. In our days, the five sects, the worshippers respectively of Śakti, of the sun-god, of Śiva, of Gaṇeśa, and of Paśupati, are no longer regarded as so many sectaries or dissenters from the established Hindu religion. They are universally viewed as within the pale of Hinduism; but from what I have quoted above, it seems clear that in Vijñāneśvara's time their position was somewhat different, and that something like a personal law was applied to them by the rulers of the land. Thus we see that the classification of the inhabitants of India, as Hindus and non-Hindus, was hardly called for by the exigencies of the administration of law, at a time when Brahmanism was the dominant religion of the land.

There is hardly any likelihood, for the above reason, of our obtaining any help from the original Sanskrit text books, in ascertaining the real meaning of the term 'Hindu' or in defining the class or classes of persons who are entitled to that designation. The name itself is foreign; it is the Mahommedans who dubbed us with that designation. Themselves coming from the west of the river Sindhu, and from a country far away, it is probable that they began to call the people inhabiting the banks of that river as the 'Sindhus' and as the Persian language generally converts our dental sibilant into an aspirate, the name became changed into 'Hindu'. Gradually as the Mahommedans spread over the rest of India, they observed that there was general resemblance in the manners and customs and outward appearance of the people inhabiting the country to the east of the Indus; for this reason all the inhabitants of the new country obtained the appellation given to the borderers; and the land became the land of the ' Hindus', in other words , the 'Hindustan'. It is therefore a strange and a curious fact, that although the followers of the Brahmanic religion early attained to a high pitch of civilization, yet there is no national name for the Indian nation in the language of the people. This anomaly is accounted for by the fact, that the land of India was never under a really central government before the arrival of the Mahommedans. The tie which connected the different sections of the Indian community inhabiting its differernt parts was a religious one; and it is probable that this community of religion was indicated in Sanskrit by the two terms of the 'Ārya' and the 'Mleccha'. All within the pale of the religion were the Āryas; all beyond were the Mlecchas. Furthermore, if our ancestors wanted to say that a particular country was a Hindu country, they would probable have said that it was a 'Cāturvarṇiya', country, or a country in which the distinction of castes was observed. According to the popular idea, this was an essential distinction which separated the Brahmanic people from the rest of mankind. During the days when India was governed by the Hindu kings, it is probable that if a lawyer had been asked, who were amenable to the law of the Veda and the Smṛti, he would have answered, that the said law was binding upon those who observed the distinction of castes.

Caste the chief characteristic of Hinduism

Even at the present day, such a definition would not be wide of the mark. Although the religion of the Brahmans has from the earliest times been characterised by toleration, and has gradually obsorbed into his bosom many a faith which at first had no connection with it, yet it may be doubted whether a man who openly repudiated caste would at the present day be called a Hindu. This open repudiation will not consist in eating prohibited food, or in disregarding similar other regulations of daily life, or in holding particular doctrines as to the origin of the Vedas, or the sacredness of the idols, or even in the non-performance of the prescribed religious ceremonies. A man may be heterobox in all these respects, and yet remain a Hindu. But what will cut off one's connection with Hinduism is marriage into another caste. To marry into a different caste is a step from which there is no turning back. Constituted as Hindu society at present is, I do not see how any one who disregards caste regulations in this respect, can be at all admitted within the charmed circle of a Hindu community.

Of course, open renunciation of the Brahmanic faith, when evinced by the adoption of a different established form of religion, such as Christianity of Mahommedanism, would have a similar effect. But the rules of Hindu law may yet be applicable to such converts, at least so far as the native Christians are concerned. In a recent case decided by the Allahabad High Court (Raj Bahadur v. Bishen Dyal, I. L. R., 4 All. 347) the Judges observed:—

"Section 24, Act VI, 1871, makes Hindu law applicable in case of Hindus. The language expressaly limits the operation and application of the first para to those cases in which the parties are at the time of the litigation orthodox Hindus in religion. Their *status* before the law obsolutely depends upon their religious belief, and this in the strict sense of the term. For the very essense of the principles of Hindu law is drawn from, and may be traced to, religious sources, and it is only when the union of the two exists in its well-understood the rational sense that the rule of decision provided by the Act is to be followed. A Hindu who becomes a convert to some other faith, is not deprived *ipso fact* of his rights to property by inheritance or otherwise—*Prima facie* he loses the benefits of the law of the religion be has abandoned, and aquires a new legal *status* according to the creed he has embraced, if such creed involves legal responsibitlities and obligations. Thus a Hindu adopting the Mahommedan faith, from the moment of his conversion, by that act affects all the property he may subsequently acquire, so as to render it subject to the Mahommedan law of inheritance. His apostasy has an immediate and prospective effect and not a retrospective effect, and his subjection to the new law dates from the profession of the new faith. The mere fact that a man calls himself a Hindu, or is described by others by that term is not enough. His only claim to have a special kind of law applied to him is, that he follows and observes a particular religion that of itself creates his law for him. If he fails to establish his religion, his privilege to the application of its law, fails also.

"According to Abraham *v.* Abraham, (9 Moore, 199) a Hindu coverted to Christianity may renounce the Hindu law, or if he thinks fit, he may abide by the old law, notwithstanding that he has renounced the old religion. But Christianity is a religion which can scarecly be said to carry with it or invoice any legal rights or obligations. Therefore a Hindu, become a Chiristian, may still elect to be governed by Hindu law as regards succession and inheritance. But if he becomes an orthodox Mussulman, it is otherwise; for his new religion is concerned with, and directly provides for the devolution and distribution of estate, and he cannot adopt it in one respect, and refuse to be bound by it in the other. In Abraham *v.* Abraham, the Judicial Committee say—

'The convert may, by course of conduct after his conversion, have shown by what law he intended to be governed as to these matters. He may have done so, either by attaching himself to that class which had adopted and acted upon some particular law, or by himself having observed some family usage or custom; and nothing can surely be more just than that the rights and interests in his property, and his powers over it should be governed by the law which he has adopted, or the rules which he has adopted.'"

The case in which the above observations were made by the Allahabad High Court related to a certain wealthy family of the North-Western Provinces. This family, as appears from the facts disclosed in the judgement, exhibits in instance of a curious mixture of Hindu and Mahommedan practices in the life led by the members who composed the family. They seem to have observed the Mahommedan form of religious prayers, well-known by the name of Namaz and Kalma; they also observed the Mussulman fasts; gave alms in the Mussulman way during the festivals of Ramzan and Muhurrum; they venerated Pirs, or the Mahommedan saints. On the other hand, they went by the name of Srivastav Kayasthas and always selected their wives from that caste; they kept Hindu holidays and festivals, and distributed alms on those occasions; lived and fed like Hindus; did not bury their dead, nor practise circumcision.

The question which arose in the above case was, whether this family could be considered as joint undivided Hindu family, and whether partition a necessary incident to the property belonging to such a family, could be sued for by one of the members. Although under the circumstances detailed above, the Allahabad High Court felt a difficulty in deciding the question, yet ultimately they came to the conclusion that, as there were certain facts in the past history of the family from which the submission of the family to the Hindu law of inheritance and succession could be inferred, equity, justice and good conscience made it obligatory upon the Court to declare that the family were bound by the Hindu law.

This case illustrates instructively how nice it often becomes practically to discriminate between those whom the law ought to regard as Hindu from those who ought not be so regarded.

The case of Abraham *v.* Abraham, repeatedly referred to in the last case, was one of native Christians belonging to the Madras Presidency (Now Chennai). The family to which the parties to that suit belonged had been converted to Christianity many generations ago; yet the defendant in the suit contented that the law applicable to a Hindu joint family governed their case. The Judicial Committee expressly guard themselves from saying that such a contention was at once negatived by the fact of the family being Christian. Their decision was in the particular case against the contention; at the same time they say that if the family had all along conformed to a way of life followed by the Hindus, the law of the Hindu joint family might have been applied to them.

Another case in which a similar question arose was decided by the Judicial Committee in the following way. The facts of the case were, that an Englishman had lived with two Hindu concubines, one of whom belonged to some caste superior to the Śūdras. He had five sons by these two mistresses, and left all his property by a will to these five sons. Each one of the five illegitimate children had a right by the will in one-fifth share of the Englishman's property. The children were brought up as Hindus, and at first lived as an united family; but subsequently one of the five illegitimate sons brought a suit for partition, and obtained a decree. There was an appeal from this decree, and pending the appeal, a written compromise was executed by the five sons, the sum and substance of which compromise was, that the property was to remain undivided, and that one brother was to conduct the management of the same, paying over the profits to the others according to their respective shares, excepting Rampershad, who was to receive a particular sum as his share of the profits, whether the actual surplus profits did or did not entitle him to such a sum, he giving up his right to the share in any increase in the actual profits that might accrue in particular years. After the death of the first managing brother Taukoram, his uterine brother Rampershad both of whom were born of the Śūdra concubine, filed a suit for the recovery of the real and the account of being his brother of the whole blood. It was thus that the question arose, whether these five persons could be regarded in the light of an undivided family, and whether the law governing the reciprocal rights of the members of joint Hindu family could be applied to the case. The observations of theit Lordships are :

"Failing this arguments upon the construction of the razeenama, the respondents (the other brothers) contended that the title of the appellant (the representative of Rampershad) was nevertheless defeated by that instrument. They argued that all the illegitimate sons were to be considered to be Hindus; and that the sons, except Rampershad, having continued in common, Rampershad could not, by Hindu law, be entitled to any portion of Taukoram's estate. This argument renders it necessary to consider what sort of a partnership was constituted by the actual agreed union of the other sons. They were not an united Hindu family in the ordinary sense in which that term is used in the next writers on the Hindu law; a family of which the father was, in his lifetime the head, and the sons in a sense parceners in birth, by an inchoate, though alterable title: but they sons of a Christian father by different Hindu mothers, constituting themselves in the enjoyment of their property after the manner of a Hindu joint family; on the death of each, his lineal heirs, representing their parents, would by the effect of the agreement, enter into that partnership ; collaterals, however, could not so enter by succesion, unless the Hindu law gave, in the case under consideration a right of inheritance also to collaterals. The parties could not, by their agreement, give new rights of succession to themselves, or their heirs unknown to the law. The law of survivorship, which is the consequence of such a partnership among Hindus, would come in only on failure of the heirs." They further observe—"It is, however, impossible to treat these sons as the sons of a Śūdra father;

if the appellant and Taukoram be viewed as the sons of a Śūdra mother, still the property never was her's; and their heritable capacity even to property of her's has not been established."[1]

In the case their Lordships unhesitatingly consider the parties, the illegitimate sons of an Englishman by Hindu mothers, as Hindus; although, the Hindu society being constituted on the principle of division into castes, it is impossible to assign a particular caste to persons of the class to which the parties to the above suit belonged. But the reason for the decision of the Privy Council is plainly discernible. These persons led the life of Hindus; they evidently conformed to the manners and customs observed by people actually within the pale of the Hindu community; this was the criterion which guided their Lordships in declaring that the parties were to be considered as Hindus.

Hindu manners and customs a reason for applying Hindu law.

From the three cases cited above, the principles to be deduced would probably be, that in doubtful cases, conformity to the manners and observances of the Hindus is a safe guide for concluding that a particular family is to be governed by the Hindu law; that where a family conform to the manners and observances of two different religious communities such as the Hindus and the Mahommedans, the criterion will be, what law of inhertance and succession has been previously submitted to by the members of the family; that actual conversion to Christianity, if accompanied by Hindu observances and a Hindu mode of life, will render a family amenable to a Hindu law; but that conversion to Mahommedanism will have an opposite effect, as the profession of that religion carries with it the special law inculcated in the Koran with regard to the rights of property and inheritance. The above propositions will at

1. Myna Bayee v. Ottoram, 2 W.R.P.R. 4.

the present day have to be considered in connection with the provisions of the Indian Succession Act (Act X of 1865), which regulates the succession of all persons who are neither Hindus, Mahommedans, Buddhists, Sikhs, nor Parsis. How far this enactment affects the law of the joint family, it is difficult to say.

Jains and Vaiṣṇavas are Hindus in the eye of the law.

With regard to certian established religious communities of India, such as the Jains and Vaiṣṇavas, it may be safely affirmed that in those parts of India in which the Mitākṣarā law prevails, persons belonging to communities like that of the Jains and Vaiṣṇavas are to be considered as subject to the law relating to the joint Hindu family, notwithstanding that such communities have disowned for a long time the authority of the Vedas, and have varied in their tenets and observances from the generality of the Hindu population. It is indeed often difficult to say how far a particular religious community actually disowns the authority of the Hindu Shasters. Their isolated situation in the midst of surrounding Hinduism in many cases prevents an open profession of the real doctrines of their religion, while their condition in life is generally such that motives of convenience prompt them to live in conformity to Hindu manners, as was to be expected, seeing that whatever innovations in religion the may have adopted, they or their ancestors must have originally belonged to the Hindu race.

On the whole, therefore, religious persuasion within certain limits has not so much to do with the question of the applicability of the joint family law; the main consideration being the mode of life, Hindu of non-Hindu, followed by the family.

The last point which I have to consider is the notion conveyed by the term 'Joint' in the expression 'joint Hindu family.'

The word 'joint' borrowed from English property law.

This term has been borrowed from the language of English property law. In order to understand the import of this term, we shall have to refer therefore to that law.

Kent in his Commentaries (Vol. IV, p. 405) says:—

"Joint tenants are persons who own lands by a joint title, created expressly by one and the same deed or will. They hold uniformly by purchase. It is laid down in the text-books, as a general proposition, that the estate holden in joint tenancy must be of the same duration or nature, and quantity of interest, whether the estates of the several joint tenants be in fee or in tail, or for life or for years. But the proposition must be taken with some explanations. Two persons may have a joint estate for life, with remainder to one of them in fee, and if he who hath the fee first dies, the survivor takes the whole estate for his life.

"Joint tenants are seised *per my et per tout,* and each has the entire possession, as well of every parcel as of the whole. They have each (if there be two of them, for instance) an undivided moiety of the whole. A joint tenant, in respect of his companion, is seised of the whole, but for the purpose of alienation, and to forfeit, and to lose by default in a *proecipe,* he is the owner only of his undivided part or proportion.

"The doctrine of survivorship or *jus accrecendi,* is the distinguishing incident of title by joint tenancy; and therefore, the entire tenancy or estate, upon the death of any of the joint tenants, went to the survivors, and so on to the last survivor, who took an estate of inheritance. The whole estate or interest held in joint tenancy, whether it was an estate in fee, or for life, or for years, or was a personal chattel, passed to the last survivor, and vested in him absolutely. It passed to him free, and exempt from all charges made by the deceased co-tenant. The consequence of this doctrine is, that a joint tenant cannot devise his interest in the land; for the devise does not take effect until after the death of the devisor, and the claim of the surviving tenant arises in the same instant with that of the devisee, and is prefered. But the charges made by a joint tenant, and judgements against him, will bind his assignee, and him as undivided."

Joint tenants comparable to Hir du parceners, Ṛght of survivorship, Joint family not much treated of in Sanscrit texts.

Now, we shall see that the members of an undivided Hindu family stand very much in the same relation to one another as joint tenants under the English law do. Each members has possession over the whole of the joint family property, and if one member dies, his right devolves upon the rest under certain limitations. Thus we shall see that in a true joint family, that is, in a joint family governed by the Mitākṣarā law, the widow of a deceased member does not succeed her husband to his rights, but the whole joint property remains as before subject to the title and possession of his undivided co-parceners, in a case in which the deceased member had no lineal dèscendant to take his place. This is the feature of a joint family governed by the Mitākṣarā law which strikes every student of Hindu law of succession as the most distinctive. I have no doubt that it was this peculiar feature, which at once suggested to the minds of the early British administrators of Hindu law, the close resemblance between the joint tenants under the English law and the joint Hindu family under the Mitākṣarā law. This is called the right of survivorship—a term unknown to the original texts; nor do we know, nor can we pitch upon, any expression in Sanskrit which would convey the idea. This is not to be wondered at; for the original texts do not treat much of the law relating to undivided families; the sayings of the ancient sages, such as Manu and Yājñavalkya, directly making mention of undivided coparceners are few; nor have the later authors, such as Vijñāneśvara and Vācaspati Misra, dwelt at length upon the subject. We have at present a goodly mass of legal maxims which lay down the rights, the liabilities, the status, the obligation and the duties of the members of a joint Hindu family; but those maxims are to be gathered from the case-law as it has been developed by the British administrators of justice for the people of India. It consists of a number of deductions gradually made from the few principles to be obtained, generally in the Mitākṣarā, and sometimes also in another authorities. The number of such authorities is not very large. Bengal, by its peculiar doctrines on the question of ownership, as we shall subsequently see more at length, is cut off altogether from the law of true joint family. The authors of the Bengal school therefore are not of avail upon the matter. With regard to the authorities followed in the other schools, although there is a pretty large number of what are called the Nibandha treatises—original legal works as distinguished from commentaries on particular texts—yet these Nibandha treatises, many of which have been enumerated by Morley in his Introduction to his Digest of Cases, have generally gone on the model of the Mitākṣarā, and except on rare points of law, it would not be too much to say that these Nibandha treatises add but little to the stock of principles obtainable from the Mitākṣarā. Yet we ought not to depreciate them as helps in disentangling knotty questions connected with the law of the joint family. But be that as it may, the doctrine of survivorship, which was never put into a form of words by any writer of original texts of Hindu law, from the Mitākṣarā downward, has yet proved a powerful engine in the development of the case-law on the subject of Hindu joint families. As soon as it was observed that there was a very tangible analogy between Hindu co-parceners and English joint tenants, it was inevitable that incidents of English joint tenancy should have been extended to the legal position of the Hindu coparceners, at least in cases where such extension did not run counter to anything to be found in the original texts. We must remember that the judges who did this, had no other course left open to them; for they were familiar with the law of English joint tenancy; they saw nothing in the original texts, or in the translations, to guide them in the particular instances; certainly the most reasonable course for them was, avowedly or not, to take advantage of that other law they were familiar with, supported as this course was by the analogy already adverted do.

Further analogy between joint tenants and Hindu joint family.

This analogy may be carried somewhat further. It is said of the joint tenants that the estates held by them must be of the same nature. Now this must necessarily be the case as regards the Hindu co-parceners. Their right arises from relationship to some original single owner of the property, and the nature of this right must be identical as regards each co-parcener, although the share of each in the property, if a partition were made, might not be the same. Another principle of the law of joint tenancy is, that the beneficial acts of one of them respecting the joint estate will enure equally to the advantage of all. As regards Hindu co-parceners, this principle is not undiscernible in the following text of Manu, chapter 9, śloka 215.[1]

"If there be a joint enterprise of brothers who are not divided, the father by no means should give any unequal share to a son"

The comments of Kulluka are :

"If there be an enterprise for jointly acquiring wealth—of brothers, dwelling with the father, and undivided—then at the time of partition, the father should in no case give more to any one son."

---

1. See Appendix, Original Text, No. XXXI.

This would be an authority for holding, that supposing any one of the brothers had made greater exertions in the common enterprise, had probably, gone to a distant country to promote its interests, or had made a discovery whereby the profits of the enterprise had been enlarged, yet the division at the time of partition would be in equal shares. But the principle appears in a clearer from in the following passage from the Mitākṣarā. Chapter I, section 4, para 6[1]

"In this passage, the words, 'whatever has been self-acquired without detriment to paternal wealth.' qualify all. And for this reason—'what gains of friendship have been earned without detriment to the paternal wealth,—what has been a marriage gift, without detriment to the paternal wealth'—'what ancestral property has been recovered, without detriment to the paternal wealth'—'what has been gained by science, without detriment to the paternal wealth'—thus it is to be constructed in each case. And thus; what gains of friendship there may be, as benefits returned, by deteriment to the paternal wealth; what has been received in marriages of the asura and other forms; likewise, what ancestral property has been recovered by spending paternal wealth—likewise, what has been gained by science acquired by the expenditure of paternal wealth—all that must be shared by all the brothers and by the fathers."

The portion of the above extract which just now concerns us in wherein it is said that if ancestral property has been recovered by a single co-parcener with the aid of co-parcenary property, the recovery must enure to the benefit of all.

Again joint tenants are said to be seised *per my et per tout*, and each has the entire possession, as well of every parcel, as of the whole. Now this follows, as regards Hindu co-parceners, from the very definition of partition given in the Mitākṣarā. That definition runs as follows—[2]

1. See Appendix, Original Text, No. XXXII.
2. Ibid, No. XXXIII.

Chapter I, section 1, para. 4.

"Partition is the establishment of many ownerships regarding the whole of the property, upon several parts of the same."

Again para. 23.

Now the term ' partition' relates to wealth, of which the owners are many."

From the above it is evident that before partition, that is to say, when the property remains in the joint condition, every co-parcener is the owner of the whole property; being owner of the whole, each must necessarily be an owner of every parcel.

We have already seen that the principle resemblance consists in the right of survivorship; and this right depends for its authority upon but one single text of the Mitākṣarā, whatever other support it may have had from the custom of the countries governed by the Mitākṣarā law, and from the opinions of the Pundits who were the law officers in the Courts of the early British administrators of justice, and whose opinions in fact are the foundation of much of what is now accepted as Hindu law.[1]

That single text is as follows—

Chapter II, section 1, para. 30

"Therefore this interpretation (of Yājñavalkya's text) becomes established, that when a sonless person who is divided and not re-united, departs for heaven, the lawfully married wife first takes the wealth."[2]

---

1. Vide Collector of Madura *v.* Muttu Ramalinga Sathupathy, 10 W.R.P.R., p. 17 At p. 22, their Lordships say:—"Their Lordships cannot but think that the former (*i.e.*, the opinions of Pundits) have been too summaritly dealt the with by the Judge of the High Court. These opinions, at one time enjoined to be followed, and long directed to be taken by the Courts, were official, and could not be shaken without weakening the foundation of much that is now received as Hindu law in various parts of British India. Upon such materials, the earlier works of Europeon writers on the Hindu law, and the earlier decisions of our Courts were mainly founded."
2. See Appendix, Original Text, No. XXXIV.

With this we must piece together what is said at the end of para. 35.

"The saying of Sankha also applies to the re-united brothers." The saying of Sankha referred to here is found at the beginning of the para and is as follows—

Survivorship deduced from the principles governing a joint family.

"The wealth of one sonless, departed for heaven, goes to the brother; in default thereof the parents should appropriate; or the eldest wife." I apprehend that the doctrine of survivorship, as applied to the Hindu copar-ceners, has but a scanty texual authority. I apprehand that were we called upon to give an account of that doctrine from the original written texts, we should be at a loss how to do so, unless we argued in the following manner—

The Mitākṣarā says that before partition every coparcener has an ownership or right in the whole of the property; it also says that when any co-parcener dies leaving no male issue, his widow succeeds to the property of the husband, only in cases where he had been separated from his other co-parceners; hence it follows that when he had not been so separated, it is the unseparated co-parceners who take whatever interest the deceased co-parcener had in the whole of the property; his widow is simply entitled to food and raiment out of the family property.

Upon this point, Viramitrodaya, which has been declared by their Lordships of the Judicial Committee to be an acceptable authority in elucidating what has been left obscure by the Mitākṣarā,[1] says:—(Chapter III, Part I, section 10; p. 64 of the original Sanskrit.)

---

1. Vide Gridhari Lall Roy *v.* The Government of Bengal, 10 W.R.,P.R., 31; at p. 34, it is said that the Viramitrodaya, which by Mr. Calobrooke and others is stated to be a treatise of high authority at Benaras, is properly receivable as an exposition of what may have been left doubtful by the Mitākṣarā and declaratory of the law of the Benares School.

"Therefore the chaste wife of one sonless, who died unreunited and separated, is entitled to the whole wealth; but of one unseparated, and of one reunited, if sonless—even the chaste wife receives simply the maintenance, on account of the saying of Nārada etc. Here the first part of the saying is quoted. At the end of section 10 the same work mentions by name a number of authorities who maintain that the right of the widow to get the wealth of her deceased husband is confined to the cases where the husband had been separated and unreunited. These authorities are Vijñāneśvara, Lukshmidhara, the author of Smriti Chandrika, Viswarupa, Medhatithi and the author of the Madanaratna. Yet we see that nowhere in the Sanskrit treatises is it expressly laid down, that when a person dies in the state of being joint with his co-parceners , his share lapses of the other members of the undivided family. To find an authority for such a proposition, we must have recourse to the custom of those parts of India which have accepted the Mitākṣarā as the highest of all their guides in law. This custom must have been first made known to the British Judges by the written opinions of the Brahmanic law officers, and as I have already said, it must have been the British Judges who observed the similarity of ths custom with what obtained as law among joint tenants in England. They therefore very reasonably called this right at the Hindu co-parceners as right by survivorship—an application of language which has been fruitful in its results upon the Joint Family Law.

Contrast between joint tenants and Joint Hindu family.

Yet this similarly between the joint tenants of England and Hindu coparceners of India must not be supposed to be perfect or absolute. In the Full Bench case of Sadabart Poshad Sahoo *v.* Foolbash Kooer, 12 W. R. F. B. I. Sir Barnes Peacock makes a distinction between the two in the following way—

"According to the law of England, if there be two joint tenants, a severance is effected by one of them conveying his share to a stranger, as well as by partition; but joint tenants under the England law are in a very different position from members of a joint Hindu family under the Mitākṣarā law. For instance, if a Hindu family consist of a father and three sons, any one of the sons has right to compel a partition of the joint ancestral property; but upon the partition during the life of the father, his wives are entitled to shares, and if a partition is made after the death of the father, his widows are entitled to shares and daughters are entitled to participate." Other differences may also be pointed out. For instances:—The title of the joint tenants is said to be created expressly by one and the same deed or will. But the title of the Hindu coparceners is not created by a deed or will; nor does their title arise at the same time or by the same act. According to the principle applicable to them, their title is created by birth, as we shall see more at length; fresh coparceners come into existence at different dates; but as soon as born, the title of each such coparcener, whether a son or nephew, or a cousin, or even a more distant kinsman, fastens itself upon the aggregate of the joint property, however this accrual of a new right by the birth of a fresh coparcener may affect the previously existing interest of the rest. Again, on the death of a joint tenant under the English Law, his widow cannot claim any maintenance from the survivor; but the widow of a Hindu coparcener has an indefeasible right of receiving food and raiment from those to whom her husband's interest lapses on account of his death.

'Members' rather than 'family' spoken of as joint in Sanskrit Texts.

I have thus one by one considered the import of each one of the terms in the composite legal expression which has furnished a name to the subject of my Lectures. The observation with which I shall conclude this analysis of the name will be, that in the original texts, it is not the family which is ordinarily spoken of as joint or undivided, but it is the members composing the family who are said to be separated or unseparated.

Thus, Mitākṣarā, chapter I, section 1, para. 30.

"Whether separated or unseparated, the sapiṇḍas are equal as regards immoveable property."[1]

Yājñavalkya, chapter II, śloka 46.

"What debt may have been contracted by the unseparated" (in the plural; and therefore the word understood is 'members.')

Manu, chapter VIII, śloka 166.

"If the maker of the loan be dead, and if the expenditure have been made for the purpose of the family—that debt should be paid by kinsmen, although separated, from their own wealth."

---

1. See Appendix, Original Text, No. XXXV.

Chapter 2
The Probable Origin And Gradual Development of the Joint Hindu Family

How to distinguish archaic from modern Hindu Law—General truths in jurisprudence—Exclusion of females an archaic principle—Law not continuously progressive in every case—Individual proprietary right a modern notion —Daughter's heritable right under the Mitākṣarā—The same under the Dāyabhāga—The Dāyabhāga Law more modern than the Mitākṣarā Law—Evidenced by individual proprietary right—Extensive prevalence of the Institution of Joint Family—Their traits similar—Similarity no necessary indication of ethnic identity—Village communities—Indicated by Sanskrit texts properly interpreted—Interpretation helped by European investigations in other quarters—Essential features of a village community—Traceable in Sanskrit Texts—Land an impartible property—Dwelling-house a private property—Priestly influence opposed to community in land—Village fields inalienable except with village consent—Joint Families posterior to village communities—Village proprietorship indicated by law of village boundaries—Village lands in India included forests, as elsewhere—Included also pasture lands—Individual proprietary right indicated in Manu—Collective property preceded individual property—Justice administered by village communities and family groups—Pūgas or Indian village communities not groups of kinsmen—Joint family land not saleable—Mortgage of land preceded sale—Sale of land first introduced by Brahmanic influence—As evidenced by a text of the Mitākṣarā—Gifts to Brahmans the earliest alienations of lana—Sale of land to be permitted by jñātis and dāyādas—Jñātis probably the same as Samānodakas—Jñātis and cognationes—Dāyādas—The dāyāda group the root of joint family—Caste and village communities, how co-existed—Absence of intermarriage, the true characterisitc of caste properly so called—Probable origin of caste—Gotra—Eight founders of gotras—The gotra, the earliest type of a joint family—Modern Hindu community an expansion of eight patriarchal groups—characteristics of patriarchal groups—Traceable in recorded Hindu Law—Supremacy of the eldest—Female exclusion—Some females declared heirs by Manu—Daughter first inherited as putrika—Agnatic kinship—Agnatic kinship partially abandoned by later lawyers—A Sapiṇḍa according to Mitākṣarā—Ancestor worship—In the form of Śrāddhas—Summary.

How to Distinguish Archaic From Modern Hindu Law, General Truths in Jurisprudence, Exclusion of Females Anarchaic Principle, Law Not Continuously Progressive in Every Case

In this lecture I shall give a brief account of Institutions in the other parts of the world similar to our Joint Family, and shall then try to draw a comparison between the traits exhibited by them all. In doing so, constant references will have to be made to our own archaic law, by which I mean laws of the primitive stamp found in the writings of our ancient acknowledged promulgators of law. Yājñavalkya at the outset of the work which passes under his name enumerates some twenty Sanhitākārs or codifiers of Hindu law; but Viṣwanāth Māndlik of Bombay (Mumbai), in his very learned edition of the Vyavahāra-mayukha, furnishes us with the names of ninety-seven holy personages (see page xix of the Introduction) who may be styled as saints or sages, like Manu and Yājñavalkya, and whose *dicta* are binding on all orthodox Hindus as of the highest authority on all points of law. Now it may be asked, How am I to separate in the treatises of these authors what is primitive from what is modern? The difficulty of doing so is certainly not inconsiderable. But the researches of European authors among the laws of various nations have led to certain general results which are accepted on all hands; it is by the help of these inductions in the science of jurisprudence that we may approximately ascertain the earlier portions of our own law and distinguish them from those parts which evidently had a later origin. Thus : it is now generally known that the participation of women in the heritable property does not date from very early times. Now in the Hindu system, the traces of two antagonistic principles, one excluding them generally from inheritance, and the other giving them partial rights, but with jealousy and reluctance, are equally discernible. From this state of things, it would not be unreasonable, to my mind, to infer that the principle of exclusion is of the primitive type, while the principle admitting them to the enjoyment of partial rights, is modern. Sometimes, however, in the course of the development of law in the different parts of India, there has been occasionally a going back to the more ancient type. When such has been the case, the separation between the ancient and the modern parts of the law becomes a task of still greater nicety. But on the whole, the difficulties are not insuperable. A system of law of a later growth, even though reviving a primitive feature and incorporating the same with itself, can yet scarcely conceal its modern character so entirely as to frustate all attempts to find out the same. Thus; let us carry the illustration cited above relating to the rights of the females, a little further. Every body admits that the law of property promulgated in Dāyabhāga is of a later grown than the Mitākṣarā system. Yet the Mitākṣarā is certainly very much in advance of the Dāyabhāga as regards one department of female rights namely, the rights of the daughter in regard to the property of her father, where there are sons existing. Witness the following extract from that work. Yājñavalkya had said (chapter II, śloka 127)[1] that the daughters are to be given in marriage by their brothers after the death of the parents, on which occasion the brothers are to give their sisters a fourth from their own shares. After giving what appeared to him a rational explanation of this text, Vijñāneśvara notices a contrary doctrine, which embodies in it the principle of female exclusion. Chapter I, section 7, para. 11.

Daughter's Heritable Right Under the Mitākṣarā

"If it be said, that 'here also, the speaking of the fourth share is not intentional—that the real intention is to declare the payment of only as much wealth as is requisite for the sacrament of marriage,' this is not so. Because there is no authority for saying that both the Smritis (Manu and Yājñavalkya) have spoken of the fourth share to be given, without really meaning the same; and because we hear also of there being a sin in case of non-payment."

Again para. 14.

"Therefore after the death of the father, the unmarried daughter also is entitled to a share; before, however, (*i.e.,* before the father's death,) whatsoever the father gives, she gets—since there is no special text. Thus everything becomes unobjectionable."

Now compare the above with what is said on the same subject, in the Dāyabhāga of Jīmūtavāhana.

Chapter III, section 2, para. 36.

The Same Under the Dāyabhāga

"Where the property is small, the sons, taking out of each of their respective shares, should give the unmarried daughters one-fourth share. As says Manu, 'From their own shares should the brothers give severally to the unmarried

1. See Appendix, Original Text, No. XXXVI.

daughters, one-fourth share from each of their own respective shares; unwilling to give, they should become fallen (*i.e.*, degraded)."

Para. 37.

"As we are hearing here of a gift, in the expression 'should give,' and of degradation in case of not giving, the unmarried daughters should not take with the idea that they had a right; for to a brother who has a *right*, another brother does not *give*."

Para. 38.

"As says Yājñavalkya. 'Those not religiously initiated should be initiated by brothers previously initiated; and sisters also; giving, however, one-forth share from the self-appropriated share.' He is speaking of the indepensableness of initiating the unmarried daughters; (which in the case of women, means marrying); not of their right."

Para. 39.

"And thus, where there is much wealth, wealth requisite for the marriage should be given; there is no invariable rule of one fourth share. This is the conclusion."

Para. 40.

"And the above is to be understood in the case of there being an equality in the numbers of sons and unmarried daughters; in the case of the number being unequal, either there should a great deal of wealth come to belong to the daughter, or there should come about an impecuniosity of the son; and that is not right, for the superiority belongs to the son."

The Dāyabhāga Law More Modern Than the Mitākṣarā Law, As Evidenced by Individual Proprietary Ṛght

The above argument of Jīmūtavāhana is an extraordinary instance of special pleading. Because a word signifying 'a gift' has been employed in the Ṛṣi text, it is made a ground for holding that this is not language implying a 'right,' although the above texts of Yājnavalkya and of Manu are found in the same place with a large number of other texts, which discuss the *rights,* and nothing but the rights, of the various members of the family. This instance, of extending the inequality between males and females, as regards their civil rights, certainly bears a primitive stamp upon it. The course of legal development everywhere has been in an opposite direction—towards doing away with and lessening these inequalities, reducing the disabilities of women. Yet we should commit an error, were we to suppose, from this one instance, that the system of law advocated by Jīmūtavāhana is as a whole of an earlier date than that promulgated by Vijñāneśvara. We all know it as an indisputable fact that the Mitākṣarā preceeded the Dāyabhāga. The whole course of tradition points to it. But even were we left without the help of this universally accepted tradition, we should arrive at the same conclusion by internal evidence, by looking at the structure of each of these two bodies of law. Excepting the above mentioned solitary instance of the heritable right of an unmarried daughter, and possibly excepting two or more other similar instances, the Dāyabhāga is a great way in advance of the Mitākṣarā. The single fact of its having given greater prominence to individual property, as compared with the proprietorship of a joint family insisted upon in the Mitākṣarā, is quite sufficient to establish the relative ages of the two treatises and of the two systems of law severally advocated by each; comparative jurisprudence has made it clear that the principle of individual proprietary right is of later growth than the principle of joint proprietorship; consequently a system of law which is based upon the second of these two principles must necessarily be more ancient than the system which is founded on the opposite notion.

Extensive prevalence of the institution of joint family

I shall therefore examine the features of the Hindu joint family as they are exhibited in our ancient records of law; with a view to find similitudes in the joint family systems of countries in the other parts of the world. The investigation into the customs of the different nations, which has been carried on by the learned men of Europe with their accustomed vigour and success, has brought to light the existence of the institution of joint family in very many countries. A Hindu inhabitant of India, who must necessarily have daily opportunities of witnessing the actual working of the institution all over India, will have to marvel at the account given by European writers of similar groups of kinsmen in Russia, in Servia, in parts of France down to a very recent date, in England a few centuries ago, and even in parts of the New Continent. These accounts disclose such an amount of similarity with the mode of living followed by our Hindu coparcenary bodies, that the first idea entertained by one who contemplates this similarity, would be that of historical connection between these different assemblages. But such an idea, however plausible as regards those people who belong to the same identical Arian stock, must evidently be inadmissible in the case of American groups of joint kinsfolk. Our wonder at these resemblances is analogous to the wonder which must have struck the earlier savans of Europe, who for the first time compared the languages of the Greeks, the Romans, and the Brāhmans. When these savans found that not only the sounds of words, but even the grammatical changes and formations were wonderfully alike in the three languages, the conclusion was irresistible that these three people,—the Greeks, the Romans, and the Brahmanic nation, were kith and kin. No proof or demonstration or argument was necessary; to see the similarity was quite enough; and although if put in a syllogistic form, the reasoning on which such a conclusion is based may be open to cavil, yet to convince a person who dissents, all that is necessary is to put him to study the Greek, the Latin and the Sanskrit together; the constituion of his mind must be different from that of the ordinary human beings, if after studying the three languages, he does not rise with the same conviction which has now obtained universal acceptance with regard to the ethnic identity of the Greeks, the Romans, and the Brahmanic people.

Similarity no necessary indication of ethnic identity

A like observation may be made in connection with the similarity of traits in the joint family systems as prevailing among the peoples named above. The resemblance is of the same pervading and intimate character; and although opinion is not unanimous that this resemblance points to a kinship in race, we may yet safely conclude that wherever the kinship in race has been otherwise established, this further resemblance in manners and social structure is an additional confirmation of ethnic identity. However that may be, my concern here is to lay my finger on these points of likeness, to trace if possible the origin of the Hindu joint family, and to give an account of the probable course its history has taken.

In order to understand these likenesses in all their various aspects, we must widen our view, and must take into our consideration, another element of the social fabric, which is closely connected with the joint family, I mean the village community.

Village Communities

To a student who would confine his attention solely to the ancient Sanskrit documents of Hindu law and usage, the very existence of village communities in the ancient Hindu social structure would probably remain sealed. But if he has had some instruction from the European investigators as to how this institution was once almost universal—then to such a student many a scrap of old Sanskrit writing which he at first passed over as quite unimportant, assumes a new significance. He then learns to look at these scraps in the light of information received from his European instructors, and gradually a conviction gains upon him that not only village communities were very common in the Hindu societies described by Manu and Yājñavalkya, but that these village communities constituted an integral and most important element of the social and political organization of the day. Although in those Sanskrit writings, we hear a vast deal about how powerful a king was, how extensive and how all-pervading his functions were, yet the student learns to conclude that even much of the governmental work was left to these village communities. As an illustration of how light is thrown upon the study of Brahmanic antiquities by the general results obtainable from the works of European thinkers, I may cite a familiar topic. Every student of Sanskrit knows that in the early epic literature of that language, and even throughout that literature down to a very modern date, the usual way of designating a particular tract of land as inhabited by a particular nation, is to use the name of that nation, or rather of that tribe, in the plural number. Thus in the great epic of the Mahābhārata, we constantly hear of the Kurus, the Pāncālas, the Cedis, the Madras, the Aṅgas, the Baṅgas, and Kaliṅgas. These plural names on most occasions import nothing but the country inhabited by these people. Thus, in the Chāndogya Upaniṣad, it is said—

"The Kurus having been destroyed by hailstorms."[1] We are not to suppose that the race or tribe of Kurus was exterminated by hailstorms; the real meaning of the language is, that the country of the Kurus had its harvest

1. See Apendix, Original Text, No. XXXVII.

destroyed by hailstorms, as the subsequent part of the story in the Upaniṣad from which I have quoted the above phrase clearly shows. The story goes on to narrate how there was a wide-spread scarcity consequent upon these hailstorms, and so on. Were we to say, according to the true Sanscrit idiom, that the Bhagirathi flows through the country of Bengal, we must say what is tantamount to saying that the said river flows among the Baṅgas. Now, to a student of mere Sanskrit, this idiom must be perplexing— it must surprise him that a language, so rich as Sanskrit, should have had recourse to such a roundabout way of naming a country. But his perplexity at once disappears, when we remember the explanation given by Sir Henry Maine in his work on Ancient Law, wherein it has been shown that territorical aggregation is everywhere of later growth, and that in primitive periods people knew of no other way of grouping themselves except as belonging to the same family or race, and that the tribal name gradually came to designate the tribal habitat.This generalization at once removes all tinge of anomaly from the Mahābhārata method of naming a country, and the study of Sanskrit gains in accuracy of interpretation by having recourse to the notions propounded by European thinkers. It is hardly to be doubted that had Sir Henry Maine been conversant with the Sanskrit language, he would not have failed to illustrate his generalization by referring to the above circumstance. Nothing less than conversancy with the peculiar expressions in the original Sanskrit could have suggested to him this illustration, as otherwise the peculiarity of the plural number would have necessarily escaped him, however correct the translation consulted by him might have been.

Essential features of a village community traceable in sanskrit texts

With regard to the subject of village communities, by referring to Laveleye's work on Primitive Property, which has been eulogized by Cliffe Leslie as one of the most brilliant examples in literature of the application of the comparative method to historical investigation, I find that the general characteristics of these associations are, that the whole of the village land is owned in common by all the inhabitants, that these lands are periodically distributed to the several families for the purposes of cultivation, that there is left a portion of the land for pasturing cattle belonging to all the families, that this pasture land is seldom divided among them, but almost always remains in common, every number of the community having a right to send his cattle on to it. Speaking of the Russian *Mir*, which is the present name in Russia for a village association, Laveleye has said that all the adult male inhabitants of the village are entitled to a share of the land belonging to the association. In primitive times, there was no partition of the soil. I compare this statement with what is contained in the Mitākṣarā, (chapter I, section 4, para. 26).[1] In this para. Vijñāneśvara quotes a saying of Usanas, one of the reputed early promulgators of our law. I have already quoted this text for another purpose in my first Lecture. The said text runs as follows :

"Impartible among persons of the same gotra is—even as far as a thousand families—the gains of the priestly office, *the field*, the vehicles, the prepared food, the water and women." I find that Colebrooke has rendered this text thus :

Land an impartible property

"Sacrificial gains, lands, written documents, prepared food, water, and women, are indivisible among kinsmen even to the thousandth degree." The disagreements between the two translations are not of much importance, for what Colebrooke renders by "Documents," I render as "Vehicles"— the word in the original being 'pattra,' which

1. See Appendix, Original Text, No. XXXVIII.

is used in both the senses. I can cite Mitākṣarā, chapter I, section 4, para. 18,[1] for supporting my version. In this para the word 'pattra' is explained by Vijñāneśvara as "means of conveyance— horses, palanqueens, and so forth." But what Colebrooke translates 'even to the thousandth degree' is an important part of the text; and for my present purpose, I must direct particular attention to it. In the original, the word 'kula' is used; everybody knows that this word ordinarily signifies 'a family.' By looking into the Dictionary of Sanskrit language by Wilson, I do not find that he explains 'kula' as meaning 'a degree' or 'a generation'. If this portion of the original text be literally transformed into English equivalent words, it may be put into the form—'even, as far as, thousand, family.' Colebrooke may have been justified by the context in rendering the above, 'even to the thousandth degree.' It has been necessary for me to notice this discrepancy between the translation that I give here and the translation found in Colebrooke's rendering of the Mitākṣarā; since otherwise a reader who referred to the latter might have been taken by surprise. But the difference in the translations does not signify. It is clear that Usanas, in enumerating properties not to be divided even among persons of the same gotra, makes mention of the 'field.' The word in the original is 'Kṣetra.' Now, what is the meaning of the injunction against the partition of the field, even as far as a thousand families, or even to the thousandth degree, for both the ways of expression amount to the same thing? Vijñāneśvara is ready with an explanation. He says that (*vide* the last part of the para.[2]) this probhibition of the division of a field intends landed property acquired by a Brahman from the piers gift of religiously inclined individuals. Such landed property must descend to his sons of the Brahman caste, in exclusion of his sons by the wives of an inferior caste. There is

1. See Appendix, Original Text, No. XXXIX.
2. Ibid, No. XL.

overwhelming evidence in ancient texts that in those days intermarriage among the different castes was of very frequent occurrence. Vijñāneśvara apparently means to say that charitable gifts of immoveable property received by a Brahman are pre-eminently gifts made on account of his Brahmanic caste; and that although a Brahman has been led by the weakness of flesh to disregard the scriptural injunctions against marrying into inferior castes, yet it would be unreasonable to allow such property, as he acquired on the ground of his social pre-eminence, to be inherited by his issue of a mixed blood. And Vijñāneśvara quotes Manu to support his position; for in Manu's time the self-exaltation of the Brahmanic caste has already reached its utmost limits. This is one of the innumerable instances which bear out Sir Henry Manie's profound observation. "The religious oligarchies of Asia, either for their own guidance, or for the relief of their memory, or for the instruction of their disciples, seem in all cases to have embodied their legal learning in a Code, but the opportunity of increasing and consolidating their own influence was too great."

But are we bound to adopt the above interpretation of Vijñāneśvara as regards the injunction contained in the text of Usanas against the division of a field? In the practical administration of law, no doubt, it has been held to be inconvenient to go behind these Nibandha treatises, such as the Dāyabhāga and the Mitākṣarā, which have been accepted as repositories of prevalent Hindu customs for many generations. The Privy Council have certainly prescribed to a European Judge the duty of closely following the direction of these treatises in his daily task of administering justice. (*Vide* Collector of Madura *v.* Muttu Ramalinga, 10, W. R., P. R. 17.) But surely we are not debarred from questioning the accuracy of the Nibandha treatises, as to the interpretation they put upon ancient texts, especially the correctness of their explanation of fragments of usage discernible in those ancient texts. To construe the text of Usanas in the way of Vijñāneśvara is calculated to remind us of the well-known Bengali proverb—"Hymns to a divinity, while threshing the paddy." That construction may have been current and adopted in the days of the Mitākṣarā; but to my mind, Usana's text embodies a usage of the very early period when village communities flourished in all their pristine vigour—when all their peculiar features, comprising that of holding the land in common, were actual facts.

Again Laveleye writes with regard to the selfsame Russian village community that the dwelling-house, and the land on which it stands and the garden attached to it, form a private hereditary property. At p. 120, Laveleye says :—"Succession only applied to the dwelling house, with the appendant inclosure, and this passed to the eldest.' The meaning of this statement must be, that each inhabitant has a private and several right to his own dwelling-house, that it entirely belonged to him, and that on his death it descended to his son or other legal heir, free from the general rights of the community, whose proprietorship must have been confined to the cultivated lands and to the lands left fallow for pasturing purposes. Now I find in the second Maṇḍala of the Ṛg Veda, Sūkta 127, verse 5, the following curious comparison :—

आत् अस्य आयुः प्रभणवत् वीड्डु शर्मन सूनवे।

Dwelling house a private property

Following the commentary of Sāyaṇācāryya, I translate the above text thus:—"Therefore, food comes under his seizure—as a nice house comes under the seizure of a son." By "his" is meant the God of Fire; for the whole of this hymn has the God of Fire for its divinity, that is to say, the them or the topic of the hymn. The translation may be made clear thus :—As fire seizes food put into it on the occasion of a burnt-sacrifice; so a son seizes of possesses himself of a nice house belonging to his parents. The word "parents" is not found in the text of the hymn itself; but Sāyaṇa in his gloss supplies the word; and there is hardly any reason to dispute the correctness of the explanation given by him. At any rate, the word 'Sūnu,' which is a well-known word even in modern Sanskrit as implying 'a son,' is found in the Ṛg Veda text, and the correlative word, either 'the father' or 'the parents,' will have to be understood to imply the person or persons intended by the hymn to be owning the 'nice house' which the 'son' seizes.

This evidence no doubt is exceedingly scanty and indefinite; at the same time, it can hardly be passed over when we are trying to find traces of the institution of the village community in the early records of the Brahmanic race. It may fairly be asked, why among so many other articles of property, should this 'nice house' have been singled out to be mentioned as seizable by the son? I must not be supposed as implying, by my quotation of the above hymn of the Ṛg Veda, that even at so early a date as that of the Ṛg Veda hymns, the principle of collective proprietary right in land had not been displaced to a great extend. Were we so to suppose, proofs of an opposite tendency would meet us at every step. Somehow or other, the spirit of Brahmanic domination which established itself among the Hindu people even before the dawn of its history, was antagonistic to collective property. The Ṛg Veda times were evidently the age in which this ascendancy had nearly been complete. Although reasonable doubts have been thrown as to there having been at that date any organized or definite caste system, yet clearly there was a priestly class, and there were already keen contentions among different members within the bosom of this class, as to who should monopolize the gifts and charities proceeding from wealthy laymen of a religious turn of mind.

Priestly influence opposed to community of land

Among the solvents of the institution of collective

property, Laveleye mentions the practice of making gifts to the church. According to him the faithful in those times often left their house, and even their share in the collective domain, to the churchmen, who gradually withdrew from the community the portions come into their possession. Thus we see that in Europe the priestly class exercised a great influence in weakening the institution of collective property. We may therefore very reasonably suppose that in India also it was the early rise of the Brahmanic influence which operated most in obliterating the vestiges of the prevalence of a similar institution here. Such a supposition is corroborated by what the Brahmans themselves have said to be one of the reasons for effecting a partition among the members of a joint family. Manu (chapter 9, śloka 111)[1] says that religious rites are multiplied by there being several households in place of one, therefore he adds that partition is conducive to the growth of religion; the plain meaning of which text is that the Brahmans thrive best by the multiplication of religious ceremonies and that it is for the interest of the Brahmans to advise the separation of a joint family.

To continue our comparison.

Village fields inalienable except with village consent

By referring to the same authority, Laveleye, I find that village communities of all countries are averse to the alienation of land to strangers. "No one" he says "could sell his property to a stranger without the consent of his associates, who always has a right of pre-emption." At p. 120 he again says, "Originally at Rome, as well as in Germany, as in India, the pater familias could not dispose of the family property by testament." At p. 177—"Just as under the system of village communities, no one could dispose of his private property, his house and enclosure, without the consent of the other inhabitants of the mark;

1. See Appendix, Original Text, No. XLI.

so, in later times, he could not alienate land, except with the consent of the other members of the family." Every one of the above statements regarding the customs of village communities has its prototype in the records of our ancient-law. Thus the Mitākṣarā, chapter I, section 1, para. 31, quotes a text[1] without naming the authority. "Land passes by six (formalities)—by the consent of the same village, of the jñatis, of the dāyādas or the participators of the heritage, of persons living on its boundaries, and by the gift of gold and water." The meaning of the above text is :—There are six formalities necessary to be observed, in order that land may pass by sale from one person to another. One of these formalities is the consent of the village. Vijñāneśvara, living in times when all tradition as to the former prevalence of collective property had been lost, explains the necessity of taking the permission of the village by quoting another anonymous text which lays down that the acceptance of a gift should be publicly made, especially when the subject of donation is immoveable property. Vijñāneśvara says that the object of taking the permission of the village is to give publicity to the proceeding. But I have already said that in matters of the early history of our law, his authority is not likely to be a very safe guide. He had no access to the accounts of the law of any other people; the materials before him were the Brahmanic documents, and such oral instructions handed down from generation to generation, as generally go along with the study of Sanskrit learning in India. But oral traditions are peculiarly liable to be vitiated, and to be ultimately lost. It may even be doubted whether the author, whoever he may be, of the anonymous text inculcating the necessity of taking the permission of the village in alienations of land, knew anything about the past existence of village communities in India. His testimony is valuable as recording the fact, that in his time the sale of land was accompanied by six formalities, one of which was

1. See Appendix, Original Text, No. XLII.

the grant of permission by the village. It may also be doubted whether in the time of Vijñāneśvara, this fromality of taking the permission of the village was at all observed; for from all the evidence available to us, at that time joint family property had completely supplanted the older arrangement of property being vested in more numerous bodies of men. Vijñāneśvara says that the permission is taken solely for the purpose of giving a publicity to the transaction of alienation, not that the transaction would be invalidated by its absence. We may therefore conclude, that although at the age when the author of the anonymons text lived, the formality of the village consent was indispensable, the disintegration of village community had sufficiently advanced when Vijñāneśvara flourished, to have justified this last author in saying that the village consent was a mere unmeaning form which might or might not be observed in practice.

I have once intimated, that direct evidence of the past existence of village communities in India is not obtainable from the Brahmanic records, from in fact even the earliest of the records of Hindu Law; even in the Ṛg Veda period, it is only joint families, which are said by Laveleye to be later in their appearance, rather than the village communities, that meet our eye. Thus, supposing either the current Institutes of Manu or those of Gautama to be the earliest systematic record of Hindu law, we shall nowhere find either of those works recording as a fact that in India at any time, the 'gramas' or villages were the proprietors in common of the land with which the people of the village were connected. Nor do I intend to support any such proposition, as that the author of either of those two treatises actually witnessed in his days the occurrence of any collective proprietorship by the inhabitants of the village, at least so far as the Arian part of the Indian population was concerned. I am obliged thus to qualify my statement as to the improbability of either Manu or Gautama being an eye-witness of collective proprietorship, because I bethink myself of the fact, that we, even in this nineteenth century, can be eye-witnesses if we choose of such proprietorship; for in the Province of Madras (Chennai), the High Court of that Presidency has to adjudicate cases in which collective ownership in the village lands, and the custom of periodical re-distribution of the arable soil, are asserted by the parties to the suit. (*Vide* 2 Mad. H. C. Rep. p. 5, foot-note.) It was therefore not absolutely impossible for either Manu or Gautama to take note of the fact, that across the border of the land of four castes, there were rude barbarians who had no sense, how growth of religion might be promoted by partition of lands, and among whom all ownership in immoveable property was conceived as vested in the entire tribe. At all events, neither Manu nor Gautama has thought fit to put any such fact on record, intent as both were in giving an account of the customs of the people who followed the rule of the four castes. This people at the time had outgrown the stage of collective ownership; they had already become imbued with the principle of joint-families—a principle which is certainly an advance upon the other arrangement; there were already traces to show that even the joint family was on its way to gradual disintegration towards individual property. Such is the picture we are forced to draw of the society of Manu's or Gautama's time, now that we have the key in our hand as to the progress of primitive institutions, which key is furnished to us by the investigations and generalizations of European thinkers. Yet as we know from the instructions of those sure and safe guides, that the traces of no past social arrangement can be all effaced in the subsequent history of the society, although such arrangements must necessarily be modified and gradually displaced by the course of evolution which all societies are destined to run, it is expected that we should meet with the marks of the past arrangements in all accounts of the subsequent social stages, if such accounts are at all faithful, and if they are sufficiently comprehensive. And this expectation is not falsified, so far as the history of the Brahmanic society is concerned. But the evidence of the past stages is of an indirect nature. It is something like a side-light thrown by facts which have been recorded for other purposes. We must piece together the facts recorded at different places; and must gather the whole into an evidence of the lost social arrangement which the science of comparative jurisprudence leads us to expect.

I have thought it as well to make the above observations, lest I should appear in my manipulation of old Sanskrit texts, to be drawing from them unjustifiable inferences, and to be twisting them into a sense in which none of our Brahmanic authorities understood them. I have tried to shew how these Brahmanic authorities cannot be accepted as infallible guides on such a question, namely, the question of the course the development of Hindu law must have taken. If we accept what Sir Henry Maine, and Laveleye, and Herbert Spencer, have propounded as to the history and progress of social arrangements in general, we must not allow ourselves to be cramped by the narrow ideas of many a modern Brahmanic authority; we must attach plain meaning to plain words in what bits of statement we meet with in written Brahmanic records of the past customs of the Hindu race; and if by doing so, we can assimilate those customs with what eminent. European authorities say revailed elsewhere, we may rest sure that in putting a novel interpretation upon certain ancient Sanskrit texts, we need not give way to any misgiving as to the accuracy of our interpretation. It is thus I justify myself in my construction of the anonymous text quoted by the Mitākṣarā, the text, namely, which prescribes the taking of permission of the village as an indispensable accompaniment of all alienations of land.

Furthermore :—we must remember, of what nature these texts often are. Although a particular text is found imbedded in a particular treatise, it does not necessarily follow that the reputed author of the treatise was the first to put together the words composing the text. By the term 'text' here, I mean what is in Sanskrit called a 'vacana' or 'saying,' generally a verse of thiry-two syllables, embodying a particular custom or law or observance or rule of conduct. Were I to say that even at this day there are hundreds of Brahmans who have at their tongue's end a thousand such stray verses, you at least will be hardly inclined to suppose that I am exaggerating. Now what I gather from this practice among our educated Brahmins is, that the practice is immemorial, that at all times in our past history, rules of law put into the form of a verse were stored in the memory of literary men. I have no doubt that at all periods there was a vast number of such verses, considered as the general property of the whole nation. They were regarded somewhat in the light of proverbs. When an author had occasion to insert any of these proverbial texts in his work, he hardly thought it necessary to indicate that they were not his own composition; for no reader would have thought that they were. This is the only possible explanation of the fact that some of these texts of a very wide application are found in the treatises of more than one ancient sage. Viśvanāth Māndlik, whose edition of the Institutes of Yājñāvalkya exhibits great research, has noticed this identity of texts in different Institutes, and has suggested a similar explanation. According to him, some of these verses were traditional; they can furnish no clue as to the relative age of the authors in whose works they are found. Adopting this view, the conclusion I arrive at is, that their value as records of fragmentary ancient law and primitive custom cannot be over-estimated. They may not be congruous with the general spirit of the law propounded by the particular sage in whose work they are found, because in the time of that author, law had advanced, and progressive principles had modified the ancient custom. Thus, the anonymous text inculcating the necessity of taking the persmission of the village in alienating land may be found inserted in the work of an author, who lived at a time, when joint family system had fully established itself, and yet when the old formality of permission by the village had not entirely died out

Another indication of the fact that village communities prevailed extensively in Hindu society if furnished by the law of boundary disputes as promulgated by Manu. It will be remembered that Manu divided litigation into eighteen classes, (Manu, chapter VIII, ślokas 3-7), by which I understand that in his days there were eighteen forms of action prescribed by law. Just as under the English common law, an action is said to be 'on assumpsit,' or 'on tort,' it is probable that when justice was administered under the Brahmanic system, actions were regarded as falling either under the head of Debt, or Deposit or Unauthorized Sale, or Partition, and so forth. Now, one of these heads was called the Sīmāvivāda or Boundary Disputes. Manu therefore prescribes the mode of dealing with these actions on Boundary Disputes, and also with the general law on the subject of Boundaries, in the Ślokas 245-266 of his 8th chapter. This section on boundaries is well worth bodily citation; but I shall confine myself to such parts of it as furnish evidence upon the subject of village communities. The very first śloka of this portion runs thus :—

Law of village boundaries indicated village proprietorship

Manu, chapter VIII, śloka 245.

"Dispute having arisen between two villages in respect of boundary—in the month of Jait, when the raised earthworks are distinctly visible—one should trace the boundary."[1]

This verse speaks of a dispute between two villages on the question of boundary. On what other supposition can we explain it, unless we believe that collective proprietary right to the land was vested in each of the two villages?

1. See Appendix, Original Text, No. XLIII.

Within each village there may have been individual property established, or property owned by joint families; but at the same time we cannot but conclude that each village was regarded as a unit, holding its own land, and disputing with another similar unit as to whether a particular plot of land fell within the ambit of one or the other. By 'one should trace,' we are to understand 'the king' in his capacity of a Judicial functionary, and possibly also in his capacity of an executive functionary. It is the king to whom the law is being prescribed, and he is directed to ascertain the limits of the two villages in the month of Jyeṣṭha, when excessive heat has parched up the soil, and all vegetation has withered, and there is no impediment caused by shrubs and weeds to tracing the exact boundary line. The raised earthworks are the 'Setus' in the original,—a word which is now generally supposed to stand for a bridge, yet which is known to all students of Sanskrit to signify a line of earthwork extending over a large area of land, slightly raised from the ground. It also signifies that kind of a bridge which consists in a dam or a dyke constructed with earth and stones, and thrown across a water-course, by which men and cattle pass and repass from one side of the channel to the other. The earth-work 'Setu' it seems, anciently ran along the boundary-line between the lands respectively belonging to two villages. It is probable that as individual property advanced within the village, the practice of demarcating fields extended from the village boundaries to the fields, within, it,—a practice exemplified in our own days in the network of slightly raised earthen boundary lines met with all over the country in the fields surrounding a village. That each village was regarded as an individual unit in possession of landed property is further borne out by śloka, 248, which says:—"Reservoirs, drinking-places, elongated tanks, water-courses, and temples of gods, should be constructed at the spots where boundaries meet." Surely extensive works like the above, especially temples and reservoirs, could not be intended for boundary marks placed between small properties in land as belonging to particular individuals. When the area is extensive, it is then that large boundary marks like a temple or a reservoir can be useful; otherwise the boundary marks would take up a good part of the space, and would leave but little for the ordinary purposes of agriculture. On the contrary, if we suppose that it is the lands belonging to a whole village which age intended to be marked off, temples and reservoirs become reasonable as boundary marks.

The above view is further confirmed by what Manu says as proper to be done when the marks the difficult to trace. Śloka 258.

"In the absence of witnesses, four villages, situated on all sides round, should in the presence of the king, solemnly assist at the ascertainment of the limits."

Śloka 259.

"In the absence of such witnesses on the question of boundary, as dwell in villages on all sides round or as have inhabited the same village from father to son, the king should question the following persons also, such persons being frequenters of the wood."

Śloka 260.

"Namely, the hunters, the fowlers, the cow-herds, the fishermen, the diggers of roots, the snake-catchers, those who live by the gleanings of the field, and also other frequenters of the wood."

Śloka 261.

"As they, being questioned, should state the marks of the places where two boundaries meet—the king should so establish the same, in accordance with law, between two villages."

Village lands in india included forest, as elsewhere

The whole of these directions can become pertinent, only when one village claims as against another, particular plots to be belonging to itself. The testimony of persons frequenting the woods, as acceptable in determining the border of a village, points to another similarity between our old village communities and those of the other parts of the world. All over in the accounts given by Laveleye of these communities, whether in Russia, in ancient Germany, or in Switzerland, we see that the common domains were made up of three parts namely, the arable land, the pasture, and the forest, the last generally preserved for timber and fire-wood. Now Manu's text directs that testimonies of hunters and fowlers and similar other walkers of the forest tracts are of value in fixing the limits of the land of a village. Hence we infer that these lands usually included some forest tracts, and that the village marches at places ran into such tracts and mingled with similar lands claimed by a neighbouring village.

Included also pasture lands

As to the commons, or collectively owned pasturing grounds, our evidence drawn from the ancient lawgivers is direct, and beyond all doubt. Both Manu and Yājñavalkya are explicit on the subject, and their language is free from ambiguity in this respect at least.

Manu, chapter VIII, śloka 237[1].

"On all sides round a village should there be, a vacant space measuring one hundred bows, or measuring three casts of sami stick :—of a town, it should be thrice the same.

Kulluka's comments are :

"A bow is four cubits; śami means a stick of the śami wood, its cast is its throwing, In the vicinity of a village, in all directions, as far as four hundred cubits or three casts of a stick—for the purpose of pasturing the beasts, there

1. See Appendix, Original Text, No. XLIV. I am not quite certain whether the word 'sami' here means simply 'a stick,' or 'a stick of the sami wood.

should be kept a vacant space, free from the sowing of corn etc. But in the vicinity of a town, the same should be made thrice as wide."

Yājñavalkya, chapter II, śloka 169; first half.

"The pasturing place for cattle is to be, according to the desire of the village people; or as the soil may allow, or as the king may ordain."

Vijñāneśvara's comments.

"According to the desire of the village people—that is, according to the desire of the rustic men—or regard being had to the largeness or smallness of the area—or as the king may direct—a pasturing place for cattle should be made. For the purpose of pasturing the cattle, a certain portion of the land should be kept free from tilage."

In these two quotations, we may see how the custom of keeping common lands for the use of the village cattle was gradually modified. The Insititutes of Manu are admitted on all hands to be of a more ancient date than those of Yājñavalkya. In the first , the custom of keeping the common is definite; in the second are observable traces of its vitality having been weakened. The extent of the pastures is made dependent on the will of the villagers, or on the aggregate quantity of lands available, or lastly on the king's directions. This last evidently is a foreign element. As in Europe it is said that the feudal lords gradually encroached upon the village commons, and went on reducing their area; so here in India, the kings, whose number and extent of territory justify us in saying, that they occupied a position not dissimilar to that of the European feudal lords, encroached upon the village commons; and the villagers had in time to defer to his orders as regards the area of their cattle feeding grounds.

It must not be supposed, as I have more than once intimated, that communistic property was universal during Manu's period. Such a supposition would be inconsistent with a great part of the evidence furnished by him. Thus in śloka 254, chapter VIII, he says :

"In the presence of the families belonging to the village, and also of those two litigating persons, the witnesses on boundary should be questioned as to the marks of the boundary line."

Individual proprietary right indicated in manu

Here evidently, two private are intended; and such private litigation, other than a dispute between two villages, could only arise when individual proprietary right had been developed within the village. In Manu's Institutes, every distinction between the two kinds of boundary disputes, namely, that between two villages, and that between two individual inhabitants, does not appear to have been drawn. Even as regards the above śloka, Kullūka explains that the two litigating parties were the plaintiff and the defendent appointed by the inhabitants of the two villages, from which we might reasonably infer that even in this śloka, boundary disputed between two villages are in contemplation; that, possibly for the convenience of the judicial proceeding, each village was represented by some appointed agent, and that these agents are spoken of as the litigating parties. In śloka 252 also, Kullūka speaks of two litigating villages. But in śloka 262 we find unambiguous evidence of boundary disputes within the same village. That śloka is :—

"As regards fields, wells, and reservoirs, and as regards a garden and a house— the ascertainment of the boundary line is to be understood as depending on the testimony of persons living on all sides round." The comments of Kullūka are :—

"In the same village also, when there is a dispute as to the boundary line, with reference to fields, wells, reservoirs, gardens and houses, the ascertainment of the boundary limits is to be understood as depending on the evidence of witnesses who dwell in places on all sides round—not on the evidence of hunters and other." Kullūka no doubt means that neighbours are the witnesses in such boundary disputes as arise within the same village.

Collective property preceded individual property

Thus, we see that although individual proprietary right had fully established itself, yet some how or other villages were considered as owning their lands in common. The existence of such as notion can be explained only if we assume, that as elsewhere, so in India, individual property was preceded by collective property in land.

As to a part of the governmental functions having been discharged by these communities, I have already cited Yājñavalkya's śloka 30 of the 2nd chapter. In that śloka village communities and town communities are mentioned under the name of 'pūgas,' which word ordinarily signifies an assemblage, a group. The same signification also attaches to the word 'grāma,' the usual word in Sanskrit, and I believe in all the modern Indian dialects, for a village. That a word signifying a collection of men should in time be applied to their place of residence is another point of similarity between these communities here and in other countries. Laveleye says (p. 12),—The name of the Russian village, *derevnia,* has the same root as the German *dorf,* the Scandinavian *trup,* the Anglo-Sexon *throp,* and the French *troup, troup.* It signifies, as M. Julius Faucher remarks, union, aggregation, with a view to mutual protection. Men, in primitive ages, have to group together for common resistance against the attacks of enemies and beasts of prey, as well as to cultivate the soil by the association of hands and the co-operation of individual forces."

The word 'pūga,' used by Yājñavalkya, is evident by Vijñāneśvara, 'villages and towns etc. being assemblages of persons of different castes, different dwellings, dwelling in the same place. Here it must be there is a radical difference, between the Indian and the other village communities.

Everywhere else, the theory with regard to these communities is that all the inhabitants of the village are descended from a common ancestor. They consider each other as kith and kin, more or less remote. Sir Henry Maine goes even so far as to say, that in primitive times the grouping of men together on any other notion was impossible. But in India the institution of these 'pūgas' spoken of by Yājñavalkya must have been of a very early date; and the traditional meaning at least, attached to the word, as evidenced by the explanation of Vijñāneśvara, negatives the notion of common descent. The very fact of the members of the group belonging to different castes is inconsistent with that idea. At the same time, the other group, of 'Kulas', or 'families,' mentioned in that very śloka of Yājñavalkya, answers to the idea of a common descent. There cannot be the least doubt that these three institutions mentioned by Yājñavalkya, namely the village communities, the guilds, and the families—each being superior to the next that succeeds in the order of enumeration—must have lent a great assitance to the king in the administration of justice. This brings us face to face with a fresh likeness between the Indian and the Russian village communities, where, it is said, (Laveleye, p. 9), "The heads of families, assembled in council under the presidency of the *starosta* or mayor, whom they have elected, discuss and regulate all the affairs of the commune. The *starosta* is the chief of the police; he also has jurisdiction over the lesser offences. He can pronounce sentence to the amount of one rouble fine and two days' hard labour." Yājñavalkya as commented on by Vijñāneśvara, says something, which bears a close resemblance to the above. There might be a judicial proceeding, first of all, before the 'Kulas,' or 'families'. That decision might be appealed to the guilds; from their decision the appeal lay to the village communities; whence the ultimate appeal was preferred to the king, or to the functionaries appointed by him. We must suppose that both the civil and the criminal proceedings came under the above arrangement; for Vijñāneśvara employs the word 'Vyavahārā,' which is used in the sense of a judicial proceeding in general, and which, as explain by him in another part of the Mitākṣarā, is of two kinds—one relating to property, and the other having its origin in the evil propensities of men—the latter kind in fact being the class of proceedings governed by the criminal law. We are totally in the dark as to how the details of this popular mode of adminsitering justice were organized in Yājñavalkya's days. We cannot say, for instance, supposing it were a civil suit, the family of which party, whether the plaintiff's family or the defendant's family, or both together, presided at the trial; or whether the administration of justice by these family courts was confined to the cases where both the parties were members of it; or what was the constitution of these family courts, how many households were included in each family, what was the principle of union in each, whether simple, common ancestry, or some sort of joint proprietary right, or some communion in worship. To this latter surmise we may be led, by remembering that there is an expression very much in vogue in India, namely, the word 'Kula-devatā' or descended from a remote common ancestor, and who kept up the remembrance of this common ancestry by periodical joint worship of some common divinity were marginally grouped together as forming a 'Kula' such as is contemplated by the text of Yājñavalkya.

The above view is confirmed by what we read of the German communities, about whom it is said (Laveleye, p. 106);— "The mark, like the ancient gens, had its altars, and its sacrifices, and in later days, after the introduction of Christianity, its church and common patron saint. It has a tribunal which took cognizance of moral offences, and even, in the early times, of crimes committed within its territories."

Joint family land not saleable

The other likenesses, as disclosed in the Brahmanic records, between the Eastern and the Western communities, are referable to the institution of joint families, rather than to the larger groups constituted by villages and towns. I shall first enumerate these points of likeness. Of the Germans it is said (Laveleye, p. 118); "The ancient family group which constituted the social unit among nomadic nations, was preserved after the tribe has settled on the soil to devote itself to agriculture. As a result, the community exercised a right of eminent domain, even over what was private property. No one could sell his property to a stranger, without the consent of his associates, who always had a right of pre-emption." Compare the above with what is said in the Mitākṣarā, chapter I, section I, para. 30.[1]

"Whether unseparated or separated, sapiṇḍas, (persons of the same blood), are equal as regards immoveable property; for a single person is in all cases incompetent to make a gift, or a mortgage, or a sale."

Para. 27, Vyāsa quoted.

"Of immoveable property and slaves, although acquired by a man himself, there is no gift nor sale, without connecting all the sons. Those who have been born, and those who have not been born, and those who are lying in the womb—they are in expectation of means of subsistence. There is no gift nor sale."

Para. 32, anonymous text quoted.

"There is no sale as regards immoveable property— one should make a mortgage by permission."

Mortgage of land preceded sale of land first introduced by Brahmanic influence

---

1. See Apendix, Original Text, No. XLV.

From all these fragments of ancient law, we gather that in the Brahmanic society, as in other countries, the sale of lands was originally repugnant to the current notions of the communties; that the whole of the landed property, whether in the possession of families or of larger assemblages, was viewed as a common fund, on which the subsistence of all members, including the future generations, depended; that the principles of both law and religion were adverse to the dissipation of this fund; and that even when the growing requirements of a progressive society made it imperative in time that alienation of landed property should be allowed by law, the popular instincts were not violated all at once, but that the change in the property law was gradually established by first permitting mortgages, which acted as a transitional stage to an absolute transfer of immoveable property from one person to another. This revolution in the law of property was in India plainly brought about by the influence of religious principles. In the passage of the Mitākṣarā whence we have cited the above extracts, we may plainly observe how the crafty priesthood assisted at this revolution, one which is now admitted, by an eminent body of thinkers at least, to have been on the whole a salutary change. That Brahmanic influence was all important in preparing the popular mind for accepting the change, cannot be made clear unless we cite the whole of the passage from the Mitākṣarā,[1] demarcated as paras. 31 and 32 by Colebrooke in his translation.

"As to the text—

As evidenced by a text of the Mitākṣarā, gifts to Brāhmans the earliest alienations of land

'Land passes by six [formalities], permission of the same village, of *jñātis* or kinsmen, of participators of the inheritance, of the dwellers on all sides round, and by gift of gold, and of water,'—Here also, the village permission

1. See Appendix, Original Text No. XLVI.

in enjoined with a view to the publicity of the transaction; on account of the Smṛti text,— 'A gift should be public— specially of immoveable property;' not that there is an invalidity in the transaction, in the absence of the village permission. The permission of the dwellers on all sides round is, however, to do away with boundary disputes. The reason for the permission of the *jñātis* and co-heirs, however, has been already stated.—As to these words—'by gift of gold and water'— inasmuch as the sale of immoveable property is forbidden by the text,—'There is no sale of immoveable property—one should make a mortgage by permission,' and inasmuch as there is seen a eulogy on gift, in the text,— 'He who accepts a gift of land, and he who makes a gift of land—both of them thereby do a pious deed,— both destine themselves for a journey to heaven'— therefore even when a sale is to be made, one should effect a sale of immoveable property in the form of a gift, having given water with gold.—This is the meaning.' From this we gather that gifts were the earliest forms of alienation of land. Now gifts can be accepted only by a Brahman. Out of the eight modes of acquiring property enumerated by Gautama, whose text is quoted in the Mitākṣarā, chapter I, section 1, para. 8, acceptance of gift is said to be a mode exceptional for the Brahmans— it is peculiar to them; no other caste can accept gifts. This is the foundation of the well-known Bengali proverb, that a Brahman is a beggar, although he be master of untold wealth for to no other caste was it allowable to make his subsistence by the charity of others. Charity to Brahman therefore is constant theme of a goodly portion of our religious writings. That these injunctions have been followed in practice by laymen all over India from the earliest timed down to our own days, needs no special mention. However weakening an operation foreign ideas may have had on Hindu orthodoxy, charity to Brahmins still retains a powerful hold on popular ideas in religion. Much of what is now practised as part of Hindu religion, but furnishes occasions for making gifts to the priestly class. The Brahmans therefore had at an early date an instinct keen enough to perceive that the inalienability of immoveable property was in the way of their temporal prosperity. Thus the law, which was to a great extent in their hands, made a distinction between gift and sale, and created the notion in the popular mind, that though sales might be disallowed by the customary law, gifts of land were not barred by the divinely ordained law. This it seems to me is the origin of the observance of the so-called six formalities mentioned in the anonymous text. It was not for Vijñāneśvara, who was a Sanniyāsi, in other words a Brahman who had entered on the fourth stage of life, to point out such an origin for the aforesaid custom. But he has disclosed sufficient for us to make the proper inferences. If therefore the views which Sir Henry Maine and thinkers of his school hold with regard to the salutary character of the change from common property into individual property be well-founded, we are indebted to the Brahmans, whatever their motives might have been, for that salutary change in the law of property among the people of ancient India.

We have already seen, from a passage in Laveleye's work, that similar influences emanating from the Christian Church had a similar effect, in helping to diseslablished the community of landed property. That outhoe has noticed how one of the causes of a similar change in weastern Europe was the piety of laymen, no doubt incited by proper preachings from the Church, who transfered their shares in the common land to the religious Corporations. Here therefore we may see how two religions, so diverse in their forms and principles as Hinduism and Christianity are, have excercised a curiously similar influence on the progress of law.

Sale of land to be permitted by Jñātis and Dāyādas, Jñātis probably the same as Samānodakas

This prohibition of alienation, as regards landed property, seems to belong to a period, when common property was giving place to joint family property, although the tranformation was not yet complete, nor fully established. Along with what we hear as to there being no sale of immoveable property, we also hear that land might be mortgaged by permission. It is not said by the permission of whom this mortgage was to be effected. Vijñāneśvara is silent as to the name of the author, to whom either this text or the other text showing the necessity of village permission, is to be ascribed. Besides the permission of the village, this other text directs the necessity of consulting the *jñātis*, the dāyādas or co-heirs, and the neighbours. According to the explanations given by Vijñāneśvara as to the meaning of the formality mentioned last in the anonymous text, namely, the giving of gold and water, the text may be supposed to speak of either an act of gift or an act of sale. Under each supposition, we cannot overlook the circumstance that other elements, besides the original village community, have come into existence;—these are the jñātis, and the dāyādas. I have not met with any authority which gives a definite idea, as to how far this relationship, namely, that of being jñāti to one another, extends. It is a word still in use in the vernaculars. The root from which the word is derived is 'jñā', 'to know.' From this we may infer, that a kinsman whose relationship with ourselves we know or can ascertain, is a jñāti, We must couple this derivative sense with the other notion prevalent in all societies descended from a partiarchal root, that all relationship in the proper sense of the term is to be reckoned through males alone. Thus we arrive at the idea, that a jñāti is one whose relationship is ascertainable, and who has descended through males alone from a common male ancestor. The kinship of two persons who are *jñātis* to one another is to be counted from a common ancestor through males alone.

This accords well with the popular notion of a jñāti. We never apply that appellation to a maternal uncle's son, or to any one related through the mother. On the contrary, we understand by that term kinsmen like the paternal uncle, or his son, or his grandson in the male line. But how far does this relationship extend? To this, the only answer I can suggest is—that the same popular notion often vaguely indicates, that fourteen, generations are the utmost limit to which the kinship implied by the term jñāti can be carried. This I beleive is the idea entertained by the Brahman Paṇḍits, who, whether they can cite an authority or not for their view, would readily give the name of jñātis to two persons, descended from a common male ancestor through males alone, within fourteen generations in the ascending line. They would, at the same time, demur to do so, if a higher degree be taken as the root of relationship. Wilson, in his Dictionary of the Sanskrit language, explains jnāti as 'a distant kinsman, who does not participate in the oblations of food or water.' This is not accurate, for it does not exclude the relations on the mother's side, and at the same time it excludes many, whom ordinary usage is universally known to include; for instance, a paternal uncle. Tārānath Tarkavācaspati, in his Dictionary, includes in the name of jñāti, sapiṇḍas, sakulyas, samānodakas and sagotras, and illustrates by mentioning the paternal uncle. The explanation given by him is rather vaguely worded.[1] If it is intended to include all persons whatsoever who belong to the same gotra, then I am afraid it has given a go-by to the widespread popular idea noticed above; it also introduces the very novel notion, that any one belonging to the same gotra is to be viewed in the light of a jñāti. If, on the other hand, Tāranāth means to say that jñātis are such relations as are otherwise known by the name of sapiṇḍas, sakulyas or samanadokas, provided they are of the same gotra, then I believe he hits the correct signification of the term jñāti. The relationship of samānodaka extends as far as the

1. See Appendix, Original Text, No. XLVII

fourteenth generation. Mitākṣarā, ch. II, sec. 5, para 6[1] says, "In their absence, right to the wealth is of the samānodakas; and these are to be understood as the seven above the sapiṇḍas; or as far as there exists a knowledge of the birth and the name; as says Vrihanmanu : 'The relationship of being a sapiṇḍa ceases at the seventh male; but that of being a samānodaka should cease at the fourteenth; some [say], at the remembrance of the birth and the name;' thereafter it is called a gotra.'" By 'birth and name,' we are of course to understand and parentage, or the fact of a person's being descended from some common ancestor, whose name is known. This is said to be the opinion of some. Now, may we not put together all these indications, and may we not gather as the combined result, that 'jnāti' and 'samānodaka,' are synonymous? 'Jnāti' is derived from a root, which means 'to know,' or 'knowledge;' 'samānodaka,' according to some, is one whose descent from a common ancestor is 'known'; 'jñāti' is popularly confined to fourteen generations; 'samānodaka,' in its other acceptation, is also confined to fourteen generation; both are admittedly accepted as involving the additional fact that the person designated a 'jñāti' or 'samānodaka' must be of the same gotra; while the indefiniteness of the term 'jñāti' as to the number of generations it may be extended to has its correspondence in a similar indefiniteness disclosed in the text, as to the number of generations comprised in the samānodaka relationship. From this similarity between the two words, it seems to me, that ordianarily, when a text speaks of a jñāti, we may fairly suppose that it intends kinsmen characterised by a common male ancestry as far as the fourteenth degree in the ascending line.

Jñātis and cognationes

We cannot overlook here a difference between the Sanskrit word jñāti and the Latin word cognationes, though

1. See Appendix, Original Text, No. XLVIII.

both are derived from two similar roots, I mean similar in their sound, and most probably also identical in the eye of comparative grammar. The radical idea involved in the two words in not now the same; for the Brāhmanic root implies 'to know,' while the root of the Latin word mean 'to be born.' The Romans had a couple of words, 'agnates' and 'cognates,' for the purpose of designating a double set of relations. But the Brāhmanic jñāti answers to the agnates alone, the other set of relations, the cognates, included both the 'jñātis' and the 'bandhus.' Colebrooke translated 'bandhus' as 'cognates.' Yet the word 'cognate' as a term of the Roman Law is not equivalent to our 'bandhu', as appears from what I read in Laveleye. In his work it is said, that the German families, a number of which put together constituted a German village community, are called by Caesar 'cognationes' (Laveleye, p. 105). Surely we cannot suppose, that Caesar, while writing so elaborately about the manners and customs of the ancient Germans, was ignorant of the fact that their families were not made up of simply 'cognates' in the sense of 'bandhus,' for that word is confined to kinsmen of a different gotra, that is, kinsmen related through a female. Nor can we suppose, that these German families were really composed of only such kinsmen as stood in the relation of 'bandhus' to one another. Such an idea would be too preposterous to be entertained for a moment. That a nation belonging to the Aryan stock, which the ancient Germans are admitted on all hands to have been, should have excluded their relations through males from the constitution of their families, is repugnant to all the established notions relating to the usages of the Aryan race, wheresoever located. The idea is also in contradiction with what is known of all those nations, whose origin is traceable to what Sir Henry Maine has called a 'patriarchal cell.' We must therefore at once repudiate the supposition, that the ancient Germans, descendants of patriarchal groups, traced their relations through females, simply because their families have been called 'cognationes' by a Latin author, and because Colebrooke has assimilated 'cognates' with 'bandhus.' That being so, these German family groups, so described as a group of cognationes,' and separately occupying a portion of the common domain owned by the tribe, are analogous to the Hindu groups of jñātis, whose consent we are told was requisite for any transfer of immoveable estate.

Dayadas—what !

I now take up the element named last in the anonymous text, to wit, the 'dayādas,' who also seem to have that had a similar veto upon the transfer of immoveable property. Its derivation is plain, which furnishes us with this sense-that a dāyāda is one who takes the dāya. But what is this dāya ? According to Jīmūtavāhana, any property which a person obtains on account of his kinship to another, when that other's ownership has terminated, whether by death, or by retirement from the world, or by excommunication from the society to which he belonged is called dāya.' Any one therefore who takes, or is competent to take, the dāya, on account of such kinship is a dāyada. So that a son is a dāyāda to his father; the word in fact thus becomes synonymous with the English term heir.' But, in practice, the word is not so restricted in its sense. Those who take the same inheritance, whether by joint or by separate right, are frequently called dāyādas to one another. Often, persons simply of the same family are so called; and in general literature the word carried with it an idea of 'competition,' 'rivalry,' even 'enmity' in this respect it is not unlike the word 'jñāti,' which has given a name to a kind of bitter enmity arising among the same kith and kin. This hostility is denoted by two very current expressions, 'Jñāti sattru' and 'jñāti virodha,' the first signifying 'a kinsmen as an enemy, the second, 'mutual quarrels of kinsmen.' That the word dāyāda has a similar import would be borne out by a reference to the well-known Tales of the Pañcatantra, a work ascribed to an early period of later Sanskrit Literature. In that work, in the fable of the Frog Gangadatta, it is said that he was दायादैरुद्वेजित that is, harassed by his dāyādas. This idea of competition and rivalry involved in the meaning of the word dāyāda is explained by the definition of the word days given in the Vīramitrodaya, which quotes the following text. (Section 3, chapter I) " The paternal property which has to be divided, the leaıned call the dāya. The dāyādas therefore are those who inherit in combination the divisible paternal property, who in fact are co-heirs to one another. Hence, coupling the idea of rivalry popularly attributed to the word, with what is said in the above definition, I conclude that the word dāyāda stands rather for a co-heir than for an heir. I may also infer from the above definition, that the word would be more properly applied to a family of co-heirs living together in a joint condition, rather than to such as have separated. The definition says that the dāya is paternal property which has yet to be divided; it follows therefore that it has not actually been divided. Practice of writers, however, does not in every ease support such an inference. Baudhāyana cited in the Dāyabhāga and referred to in my first Lecture[1] evidently considers the dāyādas to be of two classes, unseparated and separated. The former he calls sapiṇḍas ; the latter he names sakulyas. But even this clean-cut division of sapiṇḍas and sakulyas as respectively standing for joint and separate groups of kinsmen is but little attended to by other writers. Thus, Manu in the Mitākṣarā, chapter I, section 1, para. 30,[2] says that sapiṇḍas, whether unseparated or separated are equal in respect of immoveable property. We must therefore reject the idea that any one of these words, jñāti, dāyāda, sapiṇḍa, sakulya and samānodaka, carries with it the incident of either separation or joint right. Each may be

1. See ante, p. 36.
2. See Appendix, Original Text, No. XLIX.

indiscriminately employed to denote either condition of a Hindu family, joint or divided.

The necessity of permission by village, jñāti and dāyāda, how explained.

Since it is now plain that division or non-division is not implied by the words jñāti and dāyāda, we must inquire why their permission was necessary in transferring land. The explanation given by the Mitākṣara is hardly satisfactory. The author of that work says, (*vide* chapter I, section 1, para. 30, *et seq*) that the permission of the village people is to make the transaction public; that the permission of jñātis and the dāyādas is of course indispensable when the land is joint property, all having a right in it; that if the property is not joint, yet the permission of the jñātis and the dāyādas is proper, in order that in future there may be no dispute as to the property being joint or otherwise; that such permission is enjoined by law for the purpose of facilitating judicial work in any future litigation relating to the property; and that the permission of the neighbours is with a view to avoid boundary disputes. The above explanation is so far correct, that in the time of Vijñāneśvara, usage prescribed the formality of taking the consent of all these different parties; that the usage was then generally followed, but sometimes disregarded, such departure being *not* visited with the penalty of the sale being invalid; that expounders of law explained the usage on the ground of expediency, but had no idea as to how the usage originally grew, or whether it had an intimate connection with any by-gone state of things. The notion of explaining national customs and usages by the past history of the nation is of modern origin. The Brahmanic mind, moreover, in the age of Vijñāneśvara was peculiarly unfitted to start an idea of that kind. Although the Brahmins may have had a dim perception of conditions of society other than that portrayed in Manu, they seldom turned their reflection towards the topic. We need not therefore be surprised, that in spite of indications which cannot be mistaken by one furnished with information from other sources, the Brahmanic authors could not draw proper inferences, nor could correctly account for much of what they saw around them. We being in a position to compare these usages with what has obtained in other parts of the world, may possibly arrive at conclusions which will explain better what is disclosed in our ancient texts.

To my mind, the whole of this part of the Mitākṣarā, to which I have repeatedly referred, I mean paras. 30 *et seq* of section 1, chapter I, together with the texts already quoted from Manu and Yājñavalkya, are sufficient to support the proposition, that landed property in ancient India passed through almost the same identical revolutions, which are pointed out by Laveleye as having had their day in successive ages among many of the communities described by him in his work on Primitive Property. We have first the absolute prohibition of the sale of immoveable property, and the generally prevalent notion that village people were collectively the proprietors of the soil which belonged to it as a single community, such soil including some forest land at least within its area. This is evidenced by Manu's provisions for regulating lawsuits regarding boundaries. We have then the gradual decay of this principle of inalienability. The decay is indicated by the introduction of mortgage by permission on the one hand, and by the practice charitable gifts to the priestly class on the other. We have then the formalities attendant on the act of donation extended to actual transfers. We have also indications of the gradual transformations undergone by the proprietary right, which was at first vested in the whole village, then in the smaller body of jñātis, then in the still smaller body of dāyādas till ultimately the individual became clothed with full dominion, inclusive of the right of using the subject of proprietary right absolutely at his own pleasure. The author of the Dāyabhāga emphatically declares that right on repeated occasions in discussing the topic of ownership in his renowned treatise. The several transformations are clearly evidenced by the usage which recognized the necessity of taking the consent of the above-mentioned different groups, even though such groups might be actually unconnected with the land to be sold. All these indications can be satisfactorily explained only on the supposition suggested above, namely, that land was originally held by men grouped together in single villages, then by a section of them known as jñātis, then by a still smaller section known as dāyādas—this the last group being the immediate root of the modern joint family so largely prevalent all over India.

The dāyāda group of the root of joint family

The only fact which seemingly clashes with the above supposition is the institution of caste, an institution that has inveterately fixed itself on the soil of India. How among so many nations, which originally started with similar ideas on several elements of the social structure, we alone have inextricably entangled ourselves in the meshes of a peculiar social arrangement, which has through all ages been in the way of our forming a real, genuine, and homogeneous nation; how notwithstanding innumerable political revolutions, this same obstinate arrangement, though at times rudely shaken by internal struggles, has yet, somehow or other, re-asserted its power, and has entered on a fresh career over an extending area; how from being originally four, the number of castes has now, I suppose, swelled into a thousand, or more than a thousand, dividing the Indian people into more and still more minute sections; is a topic, upon which much might be said, although it would be out of place here. I shall content myself by pointing out that the apparent incompatibility of caste with the existence of collective property as vested in groups of the form of village communities, will be removed if we consider certain facts, which I gather from the accounts of foreign village communities.

Caste and village community; how the two existed

Caste in its essence implies prohibition of intermarriage as its central feature; this is what gives caste its rigidity and its stability. When men divide themselves into separate groups which would not marry into one another, which would view with repugnance if any such marriage ties were actually formed, and which would in time pass a law making such marriages invalid and disinheriting the children, the fruits of such a marriage, it is then that the principle of caste can be said to have been introduced among those groups, who although descended from the same race, may thence-forward be regarded as so many separate tribes,-their local contiguity being but an unimportant accident. Caste did not in India take its rise all at once clothed with this essential characteristic of itself. Its origin is in the difference of occupations which men have to follow, when growth of society multiplies its necessities, and the advantages of a division of labour in promoting production are perceived.

Absense of intermarriage the true characteristic of caste properly to called

Now, the theory of village communities is inconsistent with caste only when caste has developed in itself its most essential feature, of allowing no intermarriage; not when caste displays itself simply in diversity of callings. All village communities, wherever developed, are imbued with the notion that the members are descended from a common ancestor; but this notion may co-exist with caste, when caste simply means that the son is to follow the trade of the father, and before the community has dictated to itself that there shall be no marriage between persons following one occupation and those following another. The organized difference in the occupations followed by the members, who compose a particular village group, is not irreconcileable with collective property; this I gather from two instances given by Laveleye. At p. 108, he cites the following passage from Caesar:— Those who remain in the country cultivate the soil for themselves and for the absent members, and in their turn take arms the next year, while the others remain at one. But none among them can possess the land in severalty as their own, and none may occupy for, more than a year the same land for cultivation. They consume little corn, but chiefly live on milk and the flesh of their herds, and devote themselves to the chase."

Probable origin of caste.

The above is said of the Suevi, one of the most power ful and warlike of the Teutonic tribes. The following from p. 143, Laveleye's work, relates to certain ancient colonists settled in Sicily. "They divided themselves into two separate classes : one was charged with the cultivation of the soil of the island, which was declared common property; to the other was entrusted the work of defence. Having thus put all their property into one lump, and eating together at public repasts, the inhabitants of the island lived in common for some years." The above division of the members of a society furnishes a picture of the process by which early Brāhmanic society branched off into separate castes. In that description we see the germ of the two of the four original castes, the Kṣatriyas and the Vaiśyas. When our Āryan ancestors first came into India from the steppes across the mountain border into the valley of the Indus, their position was similar to that of the Suevi in the German forests, and of the Sicilian colonists described above. In order to cope with the aboriginal hordes in their new land, it may be reasonably supposed that they adopted a similar contrivance of dividing the community into two groups who alternately fought and tilled the soil. In time they discovered that both the fighting and the tilling work were better done by men who had had some experience in either caste than if the fighting men and the tillers interchanged their places every year or at other short intervals. As yet the medicine-man of the savage period had not developed into a Brahmanic priest, offering the soma juice to ancestors near, and to ancestors more remote, promoted to the rank of gods.[1] The Brahmanic society had then been differentiated, to use the language of Herbert Spencer, into two classes, that of the Kṣatriyas, the fighting-men, and the class composed of the tillers of the soil, the Vaiśyas; possibly also, there was the slave class, composed of the captive Dasyus, the aborigines, who formed the root of the future Śūdra caste. But the priestly element could not have long remained undistinguished; with the extension of territory, the necessity for knitting together the elements of the social structure grew stronger; such a bond at that early age could be supplied only by religion in the form of ancestorworship; this ancestor-worship gradually transformed itself into the worship of the Ṛg Veda divinities, Indra, and Varuṇa, and the Aświns, and Vṛhaspati and Brahmanaspati. These deities evidently were at first but very renowned ancestors, having taken a powerful hold on the imagination of the people, by some extraordinary qualification—prowess or knowledge of the healing art, or the power of composing verses and songs, or skill in preparing stimulating drinks. The priestly class separated itself from the general community, devoting itself more particularly to the religious

1. See Herbert Spencer's Sociology. This eminent philosopher's theory regarding the origin of the notion of divinities has been established by such an array of indisputable facts, and furnishes a satisfactory explanation of so vast a number of the religious ideas of primitive ages, that it is impossible to withhold one's assent to that theory. In reading the Ṛg Veda, it seems to me, that this theory acts as a torch-light in the general obscurity pervading that venerable document of the Brāhmanic race.

department of the social needs; by composing the Ṛk verses, by offering and elaborating the soma sacrifices, and by developing the worship of ancestors and divinities. There was no prohibition then of intermarriage among these different classes. Even in Manu's time, such prohibition was but nominal; although the learned Brahmins had then taught themselves to regard with disfavour alliances between different classes. In the Ṛg Veda periods, the priests, who are often called Vipras, are simply persons following a particular calling, and Vipra meant nothing but a person of a retentive memory, in other words, one who could recite a number of verses at a sacrifice, and possibly could compose a verse, if need there were. Viśvāmitra, although a widespread tradition refers him to the Kṣatriya class, is the author of the Gāyatri, the most sacred of all the Vedic verses in the Brahmanic estimation; every orthodox Brahman believes that his salvation depends upon the daily recitation of this verse; that the holiest of the holy is concentrated in the few words of which the verse consists. Every day, if a Brahman is in the habit of repeating his three daily prayers, he must thrice commemorate the fact, that Viśvāmitra was the author of what he considers as his sole reliance and hope in the 'bhavasamudra,' or 'the ocean of existence.' What more convincing evidence could there of the exceedingly small importance attached to caste in the Ṛg Veda times, than that the holiest text in the whole body of the Veda should have been attributed to a member of the Kṣatriya tribe ?

Gotra.

Thus we see that caste as it was understood in the earliest period that our written records reach, did not carry with it the idea that a group, because composed of members belonging to different castes, could not have descended from the same ancestor. But there is another difficulty in connection with the subject under consideration. We do not see how to get over this difficulty with ease. This difficulty is raised by a well-known word having a patent bearing upon the joint family system, I allude to the word 'Gotra.' As Brahmanic society is at present constituted, theoretically at least, it may be divided into so many groups, each being named a gotra. By Brahmanic society I understand all persons who consider themselves governed by the Hindu Law, including all the Hindu castes, how large soever their number be. Every Brahman, or Kṣatriya, or Vaiśya or respectable Śūdra can say, to what particular gotra he belongs. The number of these gotras has been no where exhaustively enumerated; nor do the gotras named in one province of India exactly tally with those referred to in another, All over Bengal, the whole class of Brahmans who consider themselves descended from the five historic Brahmans brought over to this part of the country from the ancient city of Kanouj, refer themselves to five gotras. The five gotras are Śāṇḍilya, Kāsyapa, Bharadwāja, Vātsya, and Sāvarṇa. One of these gotras, at least, that of the Bharadwājas, I have ascertained by personal enquiry, is also found among the Maharastra Brahmans in the Western Presidency. The theory of gotra, as latterly developed by Brahmanic writers, denies that either a Kṣatriya, or a Vaiśyas, or a Śūdra, has a right, to say that he belongs to a special gotra in the proper sense of the term. Thus Nanda Pandita in his Dattaka Mīmāṁsā, section 2, para. 76,[1] says that the Kṣatriyas have no gotra of their own, that when a Kṣatriya refers himself to a particular gotra, we are to suppose the gotra of his spiritual preceptor is meant. I infer from this that the later theory of the institution of gotras negatives the idea that any one but a Brahman really has a gotra, since even those standing immediately below the Brahmans in the social ladder are excluded from the precincts of that institution. The theory of gotras also says, that a gotra is an association of persons who have descen-

1. See Appendix, Original Text, No. L.

ded from a common ancestor. In his erudite Bengali work on Widow Marriage, Pandit Iswar Chandra Vidyasagar says, quoting a text of Baudhāyana cited in Mādhavacārya's Gloss on the Institutes of Parāsara.

"Viśvāmitra, Jamadagni, Bharadwāja, Gotama, Attri, Vasiṣṭha, Kaśyapa—these are the seven Ṛṣis ; the issue of the seven Ṛṣis together with, Agastya as the eighth, this they call as the Gotra."[1]

Eight founders of gotras, Gotra the earliest type of a joint family.

The meaning of this text is, that a gotra is the aggregate of all such persons as trace their ancestry to any one of these eight Ṛṣis. According to the above enumeration, the whole Brahmanic community is divisible into eight sections; since every person comprised in that community, has for his own ancestor, or for the ancestor of his spiritual preceptor or rather of his family priest, one of the above-named eight Ṛṣis. But by personal enquiry, I have ascertained, that in the Madras Presidency (Chennai) there are Brahmans who name other Ṛṣis for their titular ancestors; in Bengal also, of the five gotras mentioned above, only two are identified with the Ṛṣis named in Baudhayāna's text as founders of the gotra communities. Madhāvācārya evidently had noticed this fact, or facts similar to this; for he, quoted at that very page of Vidyāsāgar's work, in the foot-note, says that[2] the sub-divisions of the eight primitive gotras number a thousand. It is therefore probable that the other gotras, which are often named, should be considered to be the subdivisions of the original eight. It is therefore exceedingly likely, that the priestly class of India has descended from eight ancestors, each of whom is said to be the head or founder of a gotra. Now, the question arises, why is each of these classes of Brahmans called a gotra? If we look to its modern derivation, it may mean a 'cow-pen—a place in

1. See Appendix, Original Text, No. LI.
2. Ibid, No. LII.

which cows are kept, or protected, it may be from the wild beasts, or from the plundering attacks of the Dāsyus who surrounded the early Brahmanic settlements formed in the upper part of the Indus valley. We might also say with some degree of plausibility, that this derivation of the word points to that pastoral condition, which originally characterised our remote ancestors ; that the number of patriarchal chiefs who directed their course to the land of India, in order to find suitable pastures for their cattle, was eight; and that the actual Brahmanic community, now spread over so large an area is but the expansion of those eight 'patriarchal cells,' as Sir Henry Maine has styled them. In this view of the gotra, it may be considered to be the earliest recorded type of the joint Hindu family. The innumerable modern groups of Hindu coparceners, wheresoever located, and howsoever diverse in form, may under that supposition be considered to be the direct lineal descendants of those eight 'gotra saints,' as they are often called. But the difficulty to which I have referred is—that our earliest record the Ṛg Veda, does not exactly sanction such an interpretation of the word 'gotra.' Had the word not been at all found in that book, then the difficulty would have been no doubt less. But in the earlier parts of the collected hymns supposing the actual modern arrangement of the text to be a chronological one, for which, however, there is little authority, the word gotra has been used only in the sense of a 'number' or 'collection of cows.' The Ṛg Veda is a work, which taken as a whole, speaks of a state of society that certainly had advanced beyond the pastoral stage. It speaks of cities and villages, and kings, gambling houses and courtezans, and various other features of a settled society, not likely to co-exist with the nomadic condition of man. If, therefore, it was in the form of pastoral groups that our ancestors first trod on the Indian soil, how is it that the name by which each of those groups was distinguished, I mean the name of gotra does not bear that sense in the Ṛg Veda ? Gotra may have first of all had the Ṛg Veda sense, namely, a collection of cows.' From this it came to mean each 'collection of cows' as belonging to a single patriarchal chief regarded as a social unit; the next transition of the meaning of the word 'gotra 'was that 'gotra' began to stand for a 'patriarchal family'. But in a work which was evidently composed at a time when the patriarchal condition had to a great extent been modified by the establishment of towns and villages, we should expect to find the wòrd gotra used in its secondary sense of a patriarchal family; whereas that work is found to employ the word 'gotra' only in its old and primitive meaning of 'a collection of cows.' Thus a doubt arises, whether gotra' in the sense of 'a patriarchal family' had really any connection with the 'gotra' in its modern sense of "all the descendants of each one of the eight gotra Ṛṣis", named a little while ago. This difficulty might be got over, if we could suppose, that a great part of the Ṛg Veda was probably composed before the arrival of our ancestors at the Indian soil ; but such a supposition would not, I am afraid, apply to every part of the Ṛg Veda, wherein the word gotra is used in the sense of cattle.

Modern Hindu community an expansion of eight patriarchal groups

Possibly we might set up a hypothesis to the following effect, in order to cover all the facts. Our ancestors came over to India in separate pastoral groups, whose principal wealth consisted in their collection of cows; it is not unlikely that eight such groups actually settled on the land of India. These groups remained in their pastoral condition for a very long period, even while settled on their new habitat; some portions of the Ṛg Veda they may have brought with them, as national songs and popular legends, from their original home; in the long interval which passed between their arrival here and their forming themselves into village communities living much more by tillage than by rearing of cattle, other portions of the Ṛg Veda were composed by their bards or Ṛṣis in India. The institution of gotras assumed a definite shape, the tradition of the eight primitive groups having never been lost; the Ṛg Veda was composed at different dates wide apart each from the other; and the indications found in one part of it have nothing to do with what we find in the other parts of it. By such a hypothesis, which is not tainted with any inherent improbability on the face of it, we may trace the modern undivided Hindu family to its earliest recorded root—its original type, the gotra. In so doing we need not be deterred by the later Brahmanic notion, that the Kṣatriyas and the Vaiśyas, are not lineal descendants of the eight founders of the gotras. It is our duty to disregard this notion; the notion was evidently generated by the immensely developed arrogance of the Indian priestly class–instances of this arrogance being met with at almost every page of the writings promulgated by them from the age of Manu. We must suppose that these gotras, or cattle tending pastoral groups, at whose head probably stood the renowned eight Ṛṣis, Vasiṣṭha and others, included not only the ancestors of modern Brahmans, but also the ancient progenitors of all the genuine Āryan Kṣatriya and Vaiśyas. The off-shoots of.these eight gotras gradually overspread the whole of India between the two northern and the central mountain chains; never letting slip the memory of their descent, and always organizing themselves on the parent type. Their numbers increased, and whatever the causes were, they overcame and drove from before them the aboriginal races; they outgrew in time the pastoral state; they established village communities, built themselves towns, founded kingdoms, divided into castes, adopted various manners and customs; but still the gotra organization was kept by them in remembrance and joint families were instituted on that early model. Thus we see, that the stock of ideas which governed their conduct when organized in the form of gotras or patriarchal groups, could never be altogether shaken off by them.

Characteristic of patriarchal groups.

Herbert Spencer has enumerated the chief characteristic of all patriarchal groups to be, the supremacy of the eldest male; the agnatic kinship and the resulting law of inheritance; and ancestor worship; to which we must add, as regards the Hindu patriarchal groups, the exclusion of females from inheritance; and the gradual development of the joint family system. The exclusion of the female from the rights of inheritance is a direct result of agnatic kinship, while joint family system is nothing but a modification of the patriarchal type.

Traceable in recorded Hindu law

The indications of all these characteristic principles are traceable in the recorded Hindu law; and as regards the last namely, the joint family system, the principle underlying the whole of Hindu law is, it is needless to add, the principle that governs the undivided family group.

The supremacy of the eldest is thus indicated by Manu, chapter IX, śloka 105.[1]

"The eldest alone should take in its entirety the paternal wealth ; the rest should live, depending upon him, in the same way as, upon the father."

Śloka 106.

"On the eldest. being born, a man becomes the pos sessor of a son, and free from his debt to his forefathers; therefore he is deserving of the whole."

Śloka 107.

"In whom one transfers the debt, and by whom one enjoys immortality; he alone is the son born in righteousness ; the others they deem to be born in lust."

1. See Appendix, Original Text, No. LIII.

Śloka 108.

"Like the father, should the eldest support the younger brothers ; and like to the sons should they comport towards the eldest brother, in accordance with law."

Śloka 109.

"The eldest exalts the family; or destroys it even; the eldest is most respected in the world; the eldest is above the censure of the Good."

Supremacy of the eldest.

Here, as elsewhere in Manu, the old custom current in the patriarchal state, by which the eldest took the place of the deceased father, is remembered; but the custom is put into the form of moral injunctions based on certain peculiar Brahmanic ideas. The tradition of a past age, when the eldest inherited all the paternal property, had not died out; but the practice of the day in Manu's time was in conformity to the later theory, that all brothers were equally entitled; possibly also there were frequent cases of all the brothers living together under the presidency of the eldest and thereby forming a joint family; Manu gives a recognition to the custom of the patriarchal period by dilating on the inherent merits of the eldest born; but the law which he propounds as proper to be really followed in practice is the law of equal partition, modified by some remnants of intermediate customs which gave something additional to the eldest in taken of honour. This additional something took at times the form of a double share; often it was only one-twentieth of the whole property. Jn these various usages, we but see the gradual modifications that the exclusive right of the eldest underwent, from the patriarchal days to the growth of equal right in all the brothers. A variety of these different usages is noticed by Āpastamba, quoted in the Mitākṣarā, chapter I, section 3, para. 6.[1] He there says, that according to some lawgivers, the eldest alone was entitled to the inheritance; that in some countries, gold and black cattle and soil of black loam are allotted to the eldest, and so forth ; and Āpastamba rounds off by declaring that all inequality in partition of ancestral wealth was against scriptural authority. When the Mitākṣarā was composed, the patriarchal practice of the whole property going to the eldest male, had lost its hold to such an extent, that the author demurs to allow the eldest even the smallest additional share, and anything in token of honour. In Chapter I, section 3, para. 4, he says, that although unequal partition has been mentioned in the scriptures, yet being repugnant to the feelings of mankind, it should never be followed in practice; but like many another usage of bygone days, such as the slaughter of an ox for hospitably receiving an honoured guest, or the procreation of a son by a brother on the widow of his deceased brother, should be repudiated by righteous men.

I shall not here enter upon the question, what was the connection between the institution of patriarchal family and the principle of inheritance by the eldest male. This connection has been vividly pointed out by Herbert Spencer in his work on Sociology[2]. I can add absolutely nothing to that explanation, from the Brahmanic source. The Hindu literature is totally silent on this topic; the indications the earliest specimens of that literature furnish as to any pastoral stage having been gone through by our ancestors, are scanty; we can only infer that such must have been the case, by reading the Ṛg Veda; in that work cows, and recovery of cows, and plunder of cows, and increase of cows, and gift of cows, are topics described in such permutations and combinations, that an impartial reader is forced to conclude that these descriptions bespeak a pastoral condition, either as actually present or as gone through within a period not long past. But as regards the principles

1. See Appendix, Original Text, No. LIV.
2. See Sociology, Vol. I, Part III, Ch. IX, on Family.

governing the ideas of men during the patriarchal stage, the Ṛg Veda does not help us in the slightest degree; in that matter we can gather but little from the dreary wilderness of those one thousand hymns, at but distant intervals redeemed by slight flashes of satire, or quaint flights of fancy.

Nor am I in a position to give a satisfactory account of the steps by which the exclusive right of the eldest son transformed itself into the equal rights of all. Upon that point, all that can be advanced must necessarily be but surmises and suppositions, based upon original texts recording usages of various kinds, such as obtained in different parts of the Brahmanic world. One inference may probably be ventured with some confidence, that it was through partition effected by the father that the other sons gradually came to share the estate along with their eldest brother. The principle by which the eldest monopolised the whole was founded on the reason, that he came to manhood earlier than the others, and that in times when security of life and property, had advanced but little, the regulation of the family affairs could not remain in abeyance, but it was imperatively necessary that some capable member should take the control of the family group. As times advanced, however, the influence of the older principle gradually waned; the younger members moreover, began to lend their help in materially furthering the family interests; and the father of the family began to perceive the inequitableness of excluding all his younger sons, he being attached to them all alike by the same tie of parental love. It was thus, I suppose, partly through the father's affection, and partly also through their own self-assertion, that the younger sons established their co-ordinate right to the paternal wealth.

Female exclusion.

The second principle originating in the patriarchal state, namely, the principle of female exclusion, is also exclusion testified to by our ancient texts. Upon this point, even the

Ṛg Veda happily furnishes us with a hint. In the 3rd Maṇḍala, the second verse of the 31st hymn[1] lays down the principle of female exclusion in unmistakeable terms. As explained by Sāyaṇa, the great commentator on a vast portion of our inspired writings, this verse may be rendered thus; " The son does not vacate the inherited wealth for his sister; he makes her the repository of the issue of him who takes her; although the parents procreate both the males and the females ; the one is a worker of good deeds; the other is graceful."

The meaning of this almost riddle-like verse is thus developed by Sāyaṇa—I simply reproduce the substance of what Sāyaṇa says.[2] The person who takes the sister is her husband; the son makes her a repository for that person's issue; that is to say, he gives his sister in marriage to a third person, who is generally a stranger, and the children of his sister begotten by that stranger belong to the stranger, they are his issue, and the brother simply converts his sister into an instrument as it were for bringing forth children to her husband. Then the author of this hymn, the Ṛṣi, I believe the renowned Viśvāmitra who occupies so distinguished a position in our sacred writings, remembers the iniquity and partiality of prefering the son; and therefore the Ṛṣi adds, that although both sons and daughters are no doubt the offspring of the same identical parents, yet the son is preferred in inheritance because he is the worker of good deeds, of religious oblations and sacrifices, says Sāyaṇa but the other offspring, a daughter, is but graceful, that is to say, she is decked and clothed, with fine dresses and ornaments, and thereby becomes but an ornamental member of the family,

---

1. न जामये तान्वो रिक्थमरैक्
   चकार गर्भं सनितु र्निधानम्।
   यदि मातरो जनयन्त वह्निम्
   अन्यः कर्त्ता सुकृतोरन्य बन्धन।।
2. See Appendix, Original Text, No. LV.

fit for no useful purposes. It is not therefore inequitable to exclude her from inheritance. Some portion of the above explanation might probably be taken exception to by those European scholars, who justly deny infallibility to Sāyaṇa in the matter of Vedic interpretation. But that the idea conveyed by this Ṛg Veda verse is one of excluding the female from inheritance, can I believe be scarcely disputed. In it we can also plainly catch hints of the very reasons for which the nations descended from patriarchal groups followed the principle of female exclusion. It was because the weaker sex was incapable of performing useful work, the most useful part of the work to be performed in early patriarchal stage being the fighting business. Herein we may overlook what Sāyaṇa says as to oblations and sacrifices. The fighting work necessarily fell upon the males; the very existence of the community depended upon an efficient performance of this indispensable work; the males therefore naturally came to be regarded as the only members of the community who could lay claim to the family, property. This most ancient declaration of the principle whereby males excluded the other sex, was followed by many of a more modern date. Thus Jīmūtavāhana in his Dāyabhāga, chapter XI, section 6, para. 11, quotes a text of Baudhāyana, which says:[1]—"A woman is not entitled to heritable wealth; for, according to the, authority of the Veda, women, and persons without a sense, are without heritable wealth." Mitra Misra in his Vīramitrodaya, chapter III, part I, conclusion of section 13, quotes a text, calling it a text of the Veda, and also a half-śloka from Manu. The text of the Veda is in the same identical words with the one ascribed to Baudhāyana. The half śloka from Manu, says:–"Persons without a sense, and women, have no heritable wealth; this is the law." The repeated reference to the Veda as an authority for, the principle of female exclusion, is a further confirmation, that the Ṛg Veda verse

1. See Appendix, Original Text, No. LVI.

I have quoted was generally understood substantially in the sense Sāyaṇa has put upon it. In fact, the consensus of all writers on Hindu law is, that a woman in general is not to be regarded as having a right to succeed to heritable property; and that in every case that she does inherit, she does so by virtue of special texts. We can therefore take it as a correct proposition, that from the earliest times reached by written Brāhmanic records, one of the fundamental principles of the Hindu law of inheritance has been the general exclusion of the female sex.

Some female declared heirs by Manu.

Yet we must not forget, that this principle was largely encroached upon even in Manu's days. He launches out into an encomium upon the daughter, in chapter IX, śloka 130,[1] which runs thus :—

"As one's self is, so is his son; the daughter is equal to the son ; she, the self, being alive, how can another take the wealth ?"

In the same chapter, śloka 217, Manu, says:—

"Of one deceased without issue, it is the mother who takes the inheritance ; the mother being dead, the father's mother should take the wealth."

Daughter first inherited as putrikā.

From this it is clear, that in Manu at least, the heritable right of three females we find expressly sanctioned. This introduction of the female right in place of the older law of the patriarchal period, seems to have been made step by step. The daughter was the first to come in for a share; her right was allowed only in cases where there were no sons at all. When society had arrived at a peaceful state, the parental love naturally yearned after making a provision for an unprotected daughter; even when she had by marriage

1. See Appendix, Original Text, No. LVII.

entered into another family, the father would much rather have seen his wealth participated in by his daughter, than that it should have gone to distant kinsmen, who were comparatively strangers to his affection. Yet, there is every reason to suppose, that the first introduction of the daughter into the regular list of heirs was brought about by what Sir Henry Maine would call a legal fiction. In that part of his Institutes where Manu makes a daughter the occupant of an equal rank with the son, it is not the ordinary daughter who is spoken of, it is a putrikā, that is, a daughter regarded in the light of a son. A putrikā could be made by a sonless man; the form of making a putrikā was, that a sonless man entered into an understanding with his son-in-law, whereby any male issue of the daughter given in marriage to him was to belong to him, the maternal grandfather; and he, the maternal grandfather, was to receive, after his death, the oblations to be given by his daughter's son. It was such a putrikā daughter, who evidently simulating the position of a son, first came in for a share in the inheritance. The principle of exclusive inheritance by the male sex had taken so deep a root in the national instinct, that the daughter had to be regarded as in the place of a son, before she could be admitted as an heir. This simulation of a son by the daughter had an assistance from some principles of the Brāhmanic faith. At the date when the daughter's right was first recognized, the Brahmanic religion had elaborated that complex system of ancestor-worship, which has come down to modern age with scarcely any appreciable change. It was the principle of ancestor-worship that gave a help to the daughter's right. She simulated a son, because *her* son was to perform those religious duties, that a son had to perform to his forefathers. It was the śrāddha to be performed by the daughter's son that constituted the consideration for the heirship of the daughter. Herein we see a noteworthy instance of a legal fiction, helped by religion, giving an impetus to the progress of law.

From the period when the son-simulating daughter first obtained a recognition of her right of inheritance, the advance in this direction has been steady. There was not much difficulty for the ordinary daughter to come in, when the putrikā had established her right. The position of the two was, in fact, undistinguishable. There is reason to believe that in Manu's days this advance had already been made; for he says in śloka 118, chapter IX, that the brothers must give one-fourth share to the unmarried daughters. We must not therefore suppose that in his time the law allowed succession to the putrikā daughter alone; all that we can gather from Manu's treatment of the daughter's right is, that originally the right must have been recognised only where there was no male issue born, when the daughter was viewed in the light of a son under a religious sanction.

Agnatic kinship.

With regard to the principle of agnatic kinship, we easily perceive that the same is closely connected with the principle of female exclusion, just now dwelt upon. The agnates are persons related to us through males alone; in other words, if two persons are related in such a way, that in tracing the descent of each from a common ancestor, we can do so without counting a single female, they are said to be standing in agnatic relationship to one another. We must remember that all relationship implies common ancestry, near or remote. Thus, two cousins on the father's side are kinsmen, because both are grandsons of the same common grandfather. In this way we may take any ancestor as the root, and may consider as relations, all persons who have descended from him, male or female. Relationship, as it is now understood in all civilized societies, is not confined to one sex alone, though there may be differences in the rights and privileges enjoyed by each sex. But within the four corners of this very India, there are communities, which count their relationship only in the female line. Thus, in

Malabar dwells a particular race of men, who call themselves Hindus, but among whom it is the sister's son who inherits the property of his mother's brother. In that country, one's own son is regarded as almost no relation at all. It has been found by those who have investigated the subject, that such a method of counting relationship through females alone has obtained in those societies, which have been characterized by the practice of polyandric marriage. The early Āryan society of India belonged quite to the opposite class of societies. It considered females as of no account in point of relation As the gotra was its cherished institution, it regarded the females as cut off from all connection with the stock from which she sprang, so soon as she was given in marriage. By marriage she became the member of a different gotra. A female is not mentioned as a sapiṇḍa in the text of Baudhāyana quoted by Jīmūta-vāhana in the Dāyabhāga, chapter XI, section 1, para. 37 which I have already cited once.[1] In that text it is the males alone who are spoken of as constituting a sapiṇḍa relationship; while another group of relations, known as the sakulyas, formed by those who were participators of a divided heritage, is also composed of males ; the next group, that of the samānodakas, is likewise understood to comprise males, as far as the fourteenth generation, or as far as kinship can be reckoned. The very word, in fact, ordinarily employed to define relationship I mean the word 'puruṣa,' a male,' in the sense of one generation, implies that males alone were counted in reckoning kinship. Manu says that the relationship of being a sapiṇḍa ceases at the seventh *male*; so also, elsewhere it is said that the sapiṇḍa relationship consists in being descended from seven males. The whole scheme of kinship, in fact, whether as regards mourning, impurity, performance of the Śraddha ceremonies, or participation of heritable property, is primarily based upon the notion of a male being the common root to trace one's descent from.

1. See *ante* p. 36.

Agnatic kinship partially abandoned by later lawyers.

From this original scheme of kinship, however, there have been in the later stages of the Brahmanic law, two lines of departure, under the auspices of those two celebrated modern lawyers, I mean Vijñāneśvara and Jīmūtavāhana who respectively stand at the head of the only two really antagonistic schools of Brahmanic law. Each of these two authors has, in elaborating the principles of their several doctrines, given a place in the group of sapiṇḍa kinsfolk, to persons who are not properly agnates. The older author, Vijñāneśvara, while discussing the question of the degree of consanguinity within which marriage is not allowable under the Hindu law, says: (leaf '7, page 1 of the old folio edition of the Mitākṣarā.[1]

" So that sapiṇḍas are the six, beginning with the father, and the six beginning with the son, and his own self the seventh. Even where there is a difference in the line of descent, one should count, beginning with and including the person from whom the difference in the line of descent occurs, till the seventh. This rule is applicable in every case."

Again he says-(leaf 6, page 1) :—

A sapiṇḍa according to Mitākṣarā

"The sapiṇḍa relationship arises on account of connection of the same body. Thus, the son is of the same piṇḍa or body with the father, because there is (in the son) the connection (*i. e.* the existence) of the parts of the father's body; similarly with the father's father etc., on account of the connection of the parts of his body, through the medium of the father; similarly with the mother, on account of the connection of the parts of his body; similarly with the mother's father etc. through the medium of the mother; similarly, with the mother's sister and the mother's brother, etc. on account of the connection of the parts of one identical

1. See Appendix, Original Text, No. LVIII.

body; similarly also, with the father's brother and father's sister, etc.; similarly the wife is of the same piṇḍa or body with the husband, on account of being the cause of one identical body; similarly also, mutually among the brothers' wives, on account of being the cause of one identical body with persons caused by one identical body. Thus, wherever there is this term 'sapiṇḍa,' there the connection of the parts of one identical body, either directly, or indirectly, is to be understood."[1]

Whatever physiological theory may underlie the above description of sapiṇḍa relationship, it is clear, that Vijñāneśvara considered the maternal uncle and the maternal aunt to be the sapiṇḍas of their nephew; so that in his scheme of kinship, the Roman rule that a female terminates relationship[2] has no place. Sapiṇḍa relationship of this more extended kind has now been adopted both by the Calcutta and the Bombay High Courts, as regards rights of inheritance.[3]

This description of sapiṇḍa relationship is a palpable deviation from the rule of agnatic kinship traceable in the earlier Hindu law. It simply follows out in its logical consequences the grammatical derivation of the word sapiṇḍa, having adopted one of the many acceptations in which the word piṇḍa is used in Sanskrit literature. That word signifies, among some thirteen or fourteen senses enumerated by both Professors Wilson and Tārānath in their respective dictionaries, the 'body' as well as 'a ball of food,'

1. This passage has been also translated in West and Buhler's Digest of the Hindu Law, 2nd Edition, page 1'74. I have kept close, as far as possible, to the original, leaving it to be interpreted as best it may be. The meaning of the original is not free from doubt. The process of reasoning by which Vijñāneśvara concludes that the wives of the brothers there are mutually sapiṇḍas to one another is rather obscure.
2. See Maine's Ancient Law, p. 148.
3. *Vide* Umed Bahadur c. Oodoi Chand ; I. L. R. 6 Cal. 119, and Lallubhai v. Mankuberbaio., I. L. R. 2 Bom. 388.

such as is offered in śrāddhas to the manes of a, departed ancestor. 'Sapiṇḍa' therefore is grammatically equivalent to 'one of the same body,' or 'one connected by the same funeral cake.' The two leaders of the two antagonistic schools of Hindu law, one prevailing in Bengal, and the other in the rest of India, have each accepted one of the above two senses in which the term piṇḍa is used in Sanskrit literature; and each has in that way worked out his special law of inheritance. Each differs widely from the other in the deductions he makes; and both have made a departure from the original sense of the word 'sapiṇḍa,' confined as it at first was to the relations of the strictly agnatic group. The Bengal lawyer excludes all females whatsoever from his list of sapiṇḍas, excepting only the wives of the male sapiṇḍas; but he confines his list within the first three ancestors in the father's line, and also within the same number of ancestors in the mother's line, beginning with the maternal grandfather. The author of the Mitākṣarā includes both male and female issue, provided they are descendants, in either the father or the mother's line, of a common ancestor, as far as the seventh degree. I am not here giving an exact account of sapiṇḍa relationship according to those two authors; but my purpose at present is simply to point attention to the fact, that in both, the systems the original agnatic principle has been entirely disregarded in preparing the list of persons known as sapiṇḍas. This is no doubt a progressive step in the development of the law of succession; but it is to be regretted that the step taken by each in this direction has not been of so decisive a character as to put an end to all uncertainity in that law.

Ancestor worship.

The last characteristic to be noticed as connecting the modern Hindu family with its ancient patriarchal prototype, the gotra, is the practice of ancestor-worship. It is somewhat surprising to find, that the great philopher of the day, Herbert Spencer, has had to labour, in order to make it clear that the Hindus have practised ancestor-worship. In section 150 of his Sociology, he quotes a statement, that no Indo-European race ever made a religion of worship of the dead. Herbert Spencer has controverted the statement by citing passages from Manu, and has discussed the point at some length. To a Hindu, the statement that ancestor-worship was not a part of his religion, must no doubt appear to be quite bewildering. To his mind, ancestor-worship, in some form or other, is the beginning, the middle.. and the end of what is known as Hindu religion. In order to support by illustrations drawn from the Hindu religion, his position that ancestor-worship is a necessary phasis through which most religions pass, Herbert Spencer had only the translation of Manu before him. But his truly philosophic instinct had sufficiently appreciated the bearing of many a Hindu custom which must have come to his knowledge. With a view to lay at rest all doubts on this subject, I shall translate an extract from the Mitākṣarā which I believe will be sufficient to convince every unprejudiced mind, that ancestor-worship, in the form of śrāddhas, was the be-all and the end-all of the religious life of a Hindu. The extract is taken from that part of the Acarādhyāya of the Mitākṣarā where he comments on śloka 217 *et seq* of the first chapter of Yājñavalkya. The passage is to be found in leaf 33, page 1, of the Calcutta Edition.[1]

In the form of Śrāddhas.

"Now the section upon śrāddhas is being commenced. A śrāddha is a gift, made with faith, having a deceased person for its object, of something to be eaten, or of something meant to be eaten. And it is of two kinds—the pārvaṇa and the ekoddiṣṭa ; of these (two), that which is made, having three male ancestors in view, is called the pārvaṇa that made, having one male ancestor in view, is the

1. See Appendix, Original Text, No. LIX.

ekoddiṣṭa. It is again of three kinds—constant or nitya; occasional, or naimittika; and voluntary, or kāmya. Of these three, that ordained for occaison fixed and invariable, is the nitya ; as every day, or at the new moon, or on the eighth days of the moon. That ordained for occasions which are not fixed and invariable are occasional, or the naimittika, as when a son is born, or on other similar occasions; that made, with a view to gain some object of desire is kāmya, as persons desirous of going to heaven make at the rising of the constellation of Kṛttikā. It is again of five kinds—the every day śrāddha, the pārvaṇa, the vṛddhi śrāddha, the ekoddiṣṭa, and the sapiṇḍīkaraṇa. Of these, the every day śrāddha is spoken of in (the following text) 'The śrāddha, the food, to the forefathers and the men,' etc. And so says Manu :—'One should give the every day śrāddha, with food, etc., or with water, or with milk and roots and fruits; to the forefathers, an exhaustless enjoyment ' The author [Yājnāvalkya] with a view to describe the pārvaṇa and the vṛddhi śrāddhas, is declaring the times thereof. ' The new moon ; the eighth days of the moon ; the dark fortnight ; the two solar journeys [North and South]; the presence of suitable articles ; and the presence of suitable priests ; the sun's transit to the Ram or to the Balance; the astrological conjunction called a vyatīpāta ; the astrological conjunction called gajacchāyā, the eclipse of the sun and of the moon; and the inclination of mind for performing a śrāddha; these are the times specified for a śrāddha. Upon this text of Yājñavalkya, Vijñāneśvara dilates at a great length; it would be wearisome to cite the passage here. In this passage we see, that the offer of food to be participated by the spirits of departed ancestors is a religious ceremony, which in the estimation of an orthodox Hindu is imperative at all times and on all occasions. His religion tells him that the chief value of a son consists in the son's capacity to perform these rites; it also enjoins upon him the duty of himself performing the same, so that he may not remain a debtor to his ancestors. If this is not practice of ancestor-worship,

I do not see what other name it ought to bear; nor what else can properly be so called.

Summary of Lecture II.

We have been thus able to lay our finger upon each and every one of the features which characterises a society of the patriarchal type as exhibited in the law of our own community. To recapitulate the substance of what has been attempted to be set forth in this Lecture. The modern Hindu community is mainly a continuation and expansion of the eight original gotras or patriarchal groups that came over to India from the regions which lie to the north-west of our country across the mountain chain which separates it therefrom. These gotras were absolutely homogeneous, excepting probably, the slave element, a portion of which element may have accompanied them from their old habitation, but by far the greater number were the aboriginal Dasyus made captive in war. The members of these gotras gradually supplanted the Dasyu race, and in the course of these struggles, themselves divided into a number of class divisions known as castes. When they had given up their nomadic life, they settled in agricultural communities characterised by all those attributes, which distinguish such groups in other parts of the world. These assemblages, known as the 'pūgas' or village communities, gradually disappeared, or at least lost all their essential traits, by operation partly of an inherent principle of decay, partly also by the disintegrating effect the Brahmanic religion had upon them. Throughout the whole career of those social groups so originated in the ancient gotras, the principal early traits were never altogether cast off, the supremacy of the eldest, the female exclusion the ancestor worship, having been either kept in remembrance, or partially followed in practice; while the most characteristic feature of a gotra group, the joint possession of all property, has retained its primitive vitality down to our own days; the result of this remarkable vitality being the undivided family of the modern Hindu Law.

Chapter 3

Joint Hindu Family Considered As a Whole

Family union seldom extending beyond seven generations—Sumanta's text an authority that property was never joint beyond seven generations—Married daughters of the family not members of it—Married women members of husband's family—Unmarried daughters members Unmarried daughter's rights under the various schools— Marriage portion of an unmarried daughter in Mithilā—An adopted son a member—In Mithilā, adopted son of the Kritrima kind—Shares of adopted and natural born members unequal—Radical difference between the Bengal and the Mitākṣāra joint families—Meaning of Jīmūtavāhana's dictum, 'a fact is not altered by a hundred texts—connection between father's absolute right and the supremacy of the Brahmins in Bengal—Ṛṣi texts relating to the rival rights of the father and the son—Gautama supports the son's right, Devala that of the father—Popular notion in the Mitākṣarā Provinces an authority for son's right by birth—Yājñavalkya, supports son's equality with father—Jīmūtavahana explains away Yājñavalkya text—Language of Jīmūtavāhana not explicit—Law settled in Bengal that father's right is absolute in all property—Jīmūtavāhana's work in developing the Bengal law—Special influence of Ṛṣi Devėla on Bengal law—Aggregate ownership and fractional owner ship—Unity of ownership as explained by Privy Council—In Bengal, no joint right between father and son—Area of aggregate ownership—Ṛght of survivorship a deduction from the principle of aggregate ownership—No right of survivorship in the school of fractional ownership— Inequitableness of the rule of survivorship—Large joint families are of a modern date-Large joint families probably date from the period of the Mahommedan rule—Butwarrah rarely resorted to—In a Mitākṣarā family, a female never a leading coparcener—In Bengal, a female's position often equal to that of a male—Double course of succession in schools of aggregate ownership—Yājñavalkya the only Ṛṣi who propounded a clear rule of succession—Questions of succession under Hindu Law were always unsettled—The expression 'joint in food, worship and estate'—Joint worship of the present day—Joint worship as formerly understood—Five great sacrifices Inequality in consumption of joint effects not taken account of—Expenses of daughter's marriage—Considered as family expenses Expenses of educating the youthful members of the family—Joint families not like Corporations in all respects—General propositions regarding joint family as a whole—Family expanded into village communities—Difference between modern and ancient village Communities—Joint condition occasionally recommended by Ṛṣis—Incapacities of undivided members—The principle of unity' not always applicable.

In this Lecture I shall first consider the Joint Hindu Family viewed as a whole, and I shall review in a general way the rights, privileges and obligations of the members, of whom the family is ordinarily composed.

Family union seldom extending beyond seven generation.

Before passing on to my observations on the family, viewed in the aggregate, it is proper to form a general conception of its composition. Upon this point I shall again refer to the text of Baudhāyana, cited in the Dāyabhāga for 'a different purpose, but which in its plain meaning gives us an insight into the constitution of a joint family as it was conceived in Baudhāyana's days. Jīmūtavāhana quotes this text in para. 37, section 1, chapter XI of his Dāyabhāga.[1] But we must not suppose that because it is quoted in the

1. See ante, p. 36.

Dāyabhāga, it has no authority in the Mitākṣarā system. The text belongs to a Ṛṣi, and provided it be authentic, has a binding force upon all the schools. That it is authentic, there can be no doubt, since Jīmūtavāhana founds his peculiar law of inheritance, confined solely to Bengal, upon this text; and it is reasonable to conclude, that when making so wide a departure from the law of all the schools led by the Mītākṣarā, Jīmūtavāhana could not have had recourse to any text, the authenticity of which was at all liable to be questioned. The text is also quoted by the Vīramitrodaya, chapter III, part I, section 11 ; and the Vīramitrodaya is admittedly a work of the Mitākṣarā school. In both these works that cite the above-named Baudhāyana's text, the Ṛṣi has been construed as inculcating the rules of śrāddha. Colebrooke also has translated it, as if the words used by Baudhāyana involve no ambiguity. The words used by Baudhāyana , are 'avibhakta dāyāda' and 'vibhakta dāyāda'. Colebrooke renders these words by those partaking of undivided oblations' and 'those who share divided oblations.' This is no doubt in accordance with the sense attached by Jīmūtavāhana to the word 'dāya' as used here. But I appeal to the experience of all Sanskrit scholars, whether the word dāya does not mean on all ordinary occasions, 'heritable property;' whether the use of the word 'dāya' in the sense of 'oblation' is not uncommon, in fact unique, solely I believe instanced in this text of Baudhāyana. Equally uncommon is the employment of the word 'dāyāda' in the sense of 'participator of oblation.' It means only 'participator of heritable property.' Jīmūtavāhana may have had a motive in twisting this text into an authority for the particular law of inheritance and succession obtaining in Bengal; and so far as that law is concerned, his interpretation must be accepted as final from a practical point of view. But it is impossible for ourselves to shut our eyes to the patent fact that Baudhāyana has used language, which if plainly read, furnishes an indication that in his day undivided family rarely held together beyond seven generations in the male line. For what does Baudhāyana do in the above passage ? He simply enumerates seven degrees of male descent, from the paternal great-grandfather down to the great-grandson in the male line; he also puts in the uterine brothers of the middle individual, namely, the person whose ancestors and male issue he is enumerating, and he calls them all put together as 'avibhakta dāyāda, in plain sense, 'undivided co-heirs.' He calls others 'sakulyas,' or 'vibhakta dāyāda,' or 'divided co-heirs.' Nor does it signify, that he makes the middle individual his starting point, instead of naming the series consecutively from either end. This method has been evidently adopted by him for the convenience of 'enumeration; for, after the fourth generation, either in the ascending or; in the descending line, the names become somewhat unwieldy ; inasmuch as for every degree to be named there must be an addition of 'vṛddha,' or of 'ati,' (which word serves the same purpose in Sanskrit, as the word 'great' does in naming the ascendants and descendants in the English language), in both the lines. Baudhāyana therefore has followed the convenient mode of naming three generations above and three generations below. His saying in fact is to be taken as evidence, that practically no joint Hindu family ever held together beyond those limits. Ordinarily division began long before those limits were actually reached. I doubt whether at this day there is a single undivided Hindu family throughout India, in which persons related to one another by a common ancestor beyond the seventh degree are to be found living together or holding property in common. There may be village communities of kinsmen, possibly holding the village lands in a joint condition, who are descended from a common ancestor still more remote. But such groups of kinsmen can hardly come under the appellation of an undivided Hindu family. Excepting the village lands held in different shares, these groups have hardly any other property in common; they cannot be joint in food; they cannot be living together around a single compound; nor can they be, in any sense of the expression, joint in worship. These large groups of remotely related kinsfolk, generally to be found in the North-Western Provinces and the Panjab, are rather examples of true and genuine village communities, than of undivided families, as these latter are understood in law. A joint family therefore may be taken to be composed of persons, whose common ancestor is not more remote than the seventh. There is, in fact, in the Hindu idea, something like a magical influence round this number 'seven' viewed in connection with the family organization. In questions of consanguinity as regards marriage, seven generations are primarily regarded; impurity and mourning, as national observances in honour of a departed kinsman, are confined within seven generations; sapiṇḍa relationship, the strongest and most important tie, whether from a legal or from a religious point of view is founded on the notion of seven generations ; the principal śrāddha ceremonies too, rarely extend beyond seven males, the first three being the recipients of the piṇḍa, the three above the recipients of the lepa *[vide* Dāyabhāga, chapter XI, section 1. pare. 41] . From all these circumstances taken together, from the indication furnished by Baudhāyana's text, and from the actual state of things obtaining at the present day, I conclude that in forming a definite notion of a joint family with regard to its constitution, we may view it as a group of individuals related to one another by their descent from a common ancestor within seven generations in the ascending line. Law does not declare that non-division is disallowed beyond these limits; but law has rarely to deal with an actual case in which non-division has not terminated, or separation in property has not taken place, within those limits. That some such notion must have been generally current all along in the history of Hindu law, I also gather from a particular Ṛṣi text, cited by Raghunandana in his work on Impurities. The text is there ascribed to the Ṛṣi Samantu—a name although seldom met with in the ordinary treatises on Hindu Civil law, yet not unfrequent in the works on ritual law. It is also a name found in the list of the Ṛṣi promulgators of law, which Viśvanāth Mandlik has inserted in his valuable edition of Yājñavalkya text.[1] The text itself may be thus translated— it is to be found in p. 221 of the Sudhitatwa of Raghunathnandana, Serampore Edition.[2]

"Of the Brahmans, having one identical proved as a Swadhā—the separation of religion takes is still the tenth; the separation of heritable proper father place from the seventh; and the separation of are takes place from the third." Here the word 'adobt as to original for' heritable property' is the well known member riktha.' When therefore the Rishi declares that a riktha' is separated at the seventh generation to furnish a direct and express authority for the proportion that 'riktha' or 'ancestral property' was ordinarily enjoyed in common by persons related within the seventh degree.

Married daughters of the family not members of it.

Such an assemblage of relations, when constituting a married joint family, must be understood as comprising individuals, every one of whom is a descendant of the common ancestor in an unbroken male line. Herein the fundamental rule regulating the Hindu family organization must be constantly kept in view. A Hindu female can seldom remain unmarried. A state of things partially oppose to this rule arose among some of the Kulin Brahmans of Bengal, whose regard for the purity of their caste led them to consign a good many females born in their family to a forced celibacy. But this state of things must be taken as

1. Vide p xix, Introduction, No. 96 in the list.
2. ब्राह्मणानामेकपिण्डस्वधानाम् आदशमात् धर्म्मविच्छित्तिर्भवति। आसप्तमात् रिक्थविछित्तिर्भवति। आतृतीयात् स्वधाविच्छित्तिर्भवति।

abnormal and unnatural. As a rule, no Hindu girl remains unmarried before the age of puberty is pasted. By marriage a girl passes into a different family; she becomes a member of the family of her husband; her connection with the family of her father ceasing from that date. This is an indication of the primitive gotra arrangement which distinguished our ancestors. The late marriage has all along laid down the strict rule which questions all connubial relation between persons of the generations ; it even goes so far as to declare the marriage resemble void if both the bride and the bridegroom to the same gotra. Thus Baudhāyana cited in Vdvāhalatra of Raghunandana (p. 62 Seramporetier text.)[1] "If one should unwittingly marry a girl of the same gotra, he should maintain her, like a mother." As palnary of this exogamous rule, there is the other rule a woman as soon as married, loses the gotra of her father and obtains the gotra of her father-in-law; in other words, after marriage, a girl is no longer referable to the family, of her father, but must be referred to the family of her husband. Every Hindu is familiar with this canon of social regulation. Raghunandana in his Udvāhatatwa (p. 72) has cited two Ṛṣi texts as authority for the above proposition. One he ascribes to Laghu Hārīta and the other to Vrihaspati. They are as follows:[2]

"A woman falls away from her own gotra, from the time of marriage, at the seventh step. Her oblations and libations must be made, naming the husband's gotra."

"The sacred verses recited at the time of taking the bride's hand take away the paternal gotra ; thereafter, offerings of food and water to women should be made, naming the gotra of her husband."

---

1. सगोत्रां चेत् अमत्या उपयच्छेत्। मातृवेदनां विभृयात्।
2. स्वगोत्राद् भ्रश्यते नारी विवाहात् सप्तमें पदे। पतिगोत्रेण कर्तव्या तस्याः पिण्डोदकक्रिया।।
पाणिग्रहणिका मन्त्राः पितृगोत्रापहारकाः। भर्त्तुर्गोत्रेण नारीणां देयं पिण्डोदकं ततः।

Married women members of husband's family.

This discontinuance of the father's gotra is to be considered as typical of the actual social fact, that ordinarily the married woman goes away from the house of her father and takes up her residence with the family of her husband. Thenceforward her rights and privileges are mostly associated with that family; she comes to be regarded as a member of the new family; and though there is still a possibility of her inheriting the property of her father under certain contingencies, yet these contingencies are remote and exceptional. There might be some doubt as to whether a married woman was to be regarded as a *member* of the family of her husband; but the doubt has been laid at rest by an authoritative decision of the late Hon'ble Justice Dwarkanath Mitter, who[1] has unequivocally laid down that "the wives and mothers of the members of a joint undivided Hindu family, so long as they continue to live in the family and are supported out of its income, are just as much members of that family as their sons, and husbands." Here, the words seem to imply a qualification namely, that of living in the family and being supported out of its income. From this we are not to suppose, that these persons cease to be members, if they are compelled by force of circumstances to live away from the family for a certain period, or if they do not actually receive maintenance from the income of the family property. Thus we may well suppose the case of a member of a joint family who is in Government employment, who may have to live with his wife and children far away from the family dwelling-house, and whose wife visits the common dwelling-house but on very rare occasions. It is not to be thought that the wife of such a member is no longer a member of the joint family. The qualification, however, is not without its value in certain other cases. Thus, female members of even

1. Chundernath Moitro v. Kristo Komal Singh, 15 W. R. 857.

respectable families sometimes go astray. Their connection with the family is thus cut off. These frail women generally betake themselves elsewhere. They thereby become dead to the family ; and are therefore no longer to be deemed members of the undivided family which they have disgraced by their misconduct.

Upon this point, modern custom and social feeling are certainly more strict than seems to have been the case in past times, when some of the authoritative treatises on Hindu law were composed. Thus the Vīramitrodaya, chapter III, part I, section 10, says:—Also let him act in the same manner even towards the fallen wives; food and raiment, however, should be allowed to them, if they reside in the vicinity of the dwelling-house." Mitra Misra, the author of that work, explains it as referring to the husband alone; but since he is not explicit, whether he intends thereby an unseparated or a divided husband, it is clear that in former times unchastity, if followed by submissive behaviour, was not visited so rigorously with banishment from society as is now the case in every instance.

Unmarried daughter to be supposed as members until marriage.

We have thus seen that the numerical strength of a joint family, as it is on the one hand reduced by the marriage of the daughters to other families, is on the other hand pretty nearly restored by the introduction of fresh members who are brought in as the wives of the males. To this we must add all the unmarried daughters, in order to realise a correct notion regarding the number of persons a joint family may be composed of. These unmarried daughters of the family are substantive, though subordinate, component parts of the household group. They have definite rights secured to them; and though the Bengal school, under the leading of Jīmūtavāhana, has cut down those rights to maintenance, and a mere pittance by way of marriage expenses; the

Benares School, at the head of which stands the Mitākṣarā, has emphatically laid down, that when a partition is made by brothers after the death of their father, the unmarried daughter gets one-fourth of the share alloted to a son. I have already cited a passage from the Mitākṣarā,[1] relating to this matter. I shall now cite passages propounding the law upon this subject from some other principal works of the different schools.

Unmarried daughter's rights under the Benares School.

Thus, Vīramitrodaya, chapter II, part I, section 21. "Hence in partition after the demise of the father, the maiden sisters are entitled to get shares out of the paternal property; and not that they are only to be disposed of in marriage. But if partition takes place previously to the School. father's decease, they get only whatever the father gives, for there is no particular text regarding the point."

Vyavahāra Mayūkha, p. 49, Mandlik Edition.

"The uninitiated sisters should have their ceremonies performed by those brothers who have been already initiated, giving them a quarter of one's own share. The sense is that a fourth part of such a share, as would be allotted to a son of the class to which the sister belongs, being given to each sister, they are to be initiated."

Vivādacintāmaṇi, Prosunno Kumar, p. 248.

The same in Mithila.

"Here the mention of a quarter is not essential. Property sufficient to defray the expenses of the nuptials should be given, for this is ordained by Viṣṇu."

Vivāda Candra.[2]

---

1. See *ante p.* 65.
2. MS. No. 2378, Calcutta Sanscrit College Library, leaf, 32, p. 1. भगिनीविवाहार्थमपि अविभक्तपितृधनादेयम। कन्याभ्यस्तु पिष्टद्रव्याद्देयं वैवाहिकं वसु। इति वचनात्। अविभक्तमृतकन्याविवाहार्थमपि पितृद्रव्यादेव दद्यात्। अपत्रस्य च या कन्या धर्म्मतः सापि पुत्रवत्। इति वचनात्। अविभक्तपितृद्रव्यं तस्यै देयमित्यर्थः। अविभक्तपितृद्रव्याभावे स्वांशदेव दद्युः।

"For the purpose of marrying the sisters also, (money) should be given out of the undivided paternal wealth; as the text is;—'To the daughters also, out of the father's wealth, should be given the nuptial money. Also for the marriage of the daughter of one who has died undivided, one should give (money) out of the father's wealth, as the text is,—'she who is the daughter of a sonless man, is life the son, in the eye of law.' The sense is that the undivided wealth of the father should be given to her. In the absence of undivided paternal wealth, they should give from their own share; since the argument that the initiatory ceremonies are indispensable applies equally; and since Viṣṇu says:—'Of the unmarried daughters, however, one should perform the initiatory ceremony in proportion to his own wealth.'

Madam Pārijāta.[1]

"The sense is that if there be brothers and sisters, uninitiated into the ceremonies ending with marriage, then having performod their ceremonies down to that of marriage, the partition should be made. The purport as regards the sisters, is, that having concluded the nuptials of the unmarried daughters, one should give them one-fourth share. Therefore the mode of division is as follows —A Brahmin has one wife, one son and one daughter. Then, having divided the father's wealth in two parts, and having

---

अवश्यकार्य्याः संस्काराः। इत्यतन्यायसाम्यात्। अनूढ़ानां तु कन्याना स्ववित्तानुरूपेण संस्कार कृर्य्यात्। इति वियूर्क्त।

1. MS. No. 1385, Calcutta Sanscrit Colledge library.
विवाहान्तसंस्कारैरसंस्कृतानां भ्रातृणां भगिनीनां च विवाहान्तसंस्कारं कृत्वा पश्च तु विभागः कर्त्तव्य इत्यर्थः। भगिन्यञ्च इत्य देरय तात्पर्य्यार्थः। भगिनानांमविवाहितीनां विवाहं दत्त्वां ताभ्य चतुर्थमंशं दद्यात्। तस्मादयञ्च विभागक्रमः। ब्राह्मणस्य एका पत्नी। तत्पचोऽप्येक एव एका च कन्या। तत्र पितृद्रव्यं द्वेध विभज्य तन्मध्ये एकमंशं चतुर्धा विभज्य चतुर्थमंशं कन्यायै दत्त्वा अवशिष्ट पुत्रो गृह्णीयात्। यदा पुत्रौ द्वौ कन्या चैका। तदा पित्र्यं द्रव्यं चेधा विभज्य तच एकमंश चतुर्था कृत्वा तुरौथाशं कन्याधै दत्त्वा अवशिष्टं द्वावपि पुत्रावर्धमर्धं गृह्णौयाती। एवं पुत्रहत्वे कन्यावहुत्वे चोहनीयं। यद्यकः पुत्रो द्वे च कन्ये। तदा पितृधनं त्रेधा विभज्य तत्रैकभागं चतुर्था कृत्वा तुरीयाशंमकर्मकं चतुर्थाशं द्वाभ्या कन्याभ्यां दत्त्वा अवशिष्टमखिलं धमं पुत्रो गृह्णाति। एवं पुत्रैकत्वे कन्यान्हत्वे चोहनीयम्।
leaf 135, p. 1.

divided one share out of the same into four parts, having given the fourth part to the daughter, the son should take the rest. Where there are two sons and one daughter, then having divided the paternal property into three parts, having made one part out of the same into four, having given the fourth part to the daughter, the two sons together should take the rest half and half. Thus it should be made out in case many sons and many daughters. If there be one son and two daughters, then having divided the father's wealth into three parts, having divided one share out of the same into four, having allotted to the two daughters one quarter share each, the son takes the whole of the remaining property. Thus it should be made out in the case of there being one son and many daughters."

The same under the Smṛticandrikā

What the Smṛti Candrikā, the Madras authority, intends to lay down upon this point, is not so clear. As understood by Mitra Misra, the author of the Vīramitrodaya the Smṛti Candrikā is to be supposed as siding with the Bengal and the Mithilā schools; for in the Vīramitrodaya it is said, (chapter II, part I, section 21)—"The author of the Smṛticandrikā has, however, (in accordance with the following text of Devala, namely, 'And to the maiden daughter, however, shall be given the father's wealth (and) nuptial property')—held, that property sufficient for marriage is to be allotted; his intention is that the qualifying term 'nuptial' in the phrase 'nuptial property' would be otherwise meaningless."

Both Manu and Yājñavalkya are explicit on the point. Manu chapter IX, Śloka 118.

"To the maiden sisters let their brothers give portions out of their allotments, respectively; to each the fourth part of the appropriate share; they who refuse to give shall be degraded."

Yājñavalkya, chapter II, Śloka 127, (Mandlik Edition, 124) .

"And sisters should be initiated into marriage, giving them the fourth part of one's own share."

Manu omits altogether to name marriage as the occasion for giving this one fourth share; and although Yājñavalkya seems to imply the doctrine that sisters at the time of a partition after the death of the father, have no independent and absolute right to a share of the paternal property; yet we have seen that three very high authorities, namely, Vijñāneśvara, Mitra Misra, and Viśveśvara Bhaṭṭa, the author of the Madana Pārijāta, already cited, are unanimous in regarding the texts of Manu and Yājñavalkya as declaring a substantive right of the unmarried daughters to obtain a share in the property of their deceased father. Nilakantha also, the Bombay authority, does not explain away this right by converting it into a marriage portion, as has been done by Jīmūtavāhana and probably by Devagaṇa Bhatta.[1]

The result therefore is, that the unmarried daughters as members of a joint Hindu family have a substantive right in the North-West and Bombay; while in Mithila, Bengal and the Madras Presidency (Chennai), their right is confined to receiving a portion requisite for being properly married.

Marriage portion of an unmarried daughter in Mithilā.

As regards the Mithilā territory, a recent decision by Mr. Justice Romes Chandra Mitter,[2] has given a definite shape

1. It is usually supposed, that the name of the author of the Smrti Candrikā is Devanda Bhatta. But in the MS. from the Government Sanskrit College of Calcutta, numbered 1492, which I have consulted, I find that the name given at the end of every section is Devagaṇa Bhatta ; the correctness of this latter form of the name is confirmed by the fact that it is referable to easily identified Sanskrit words. The names of the members of a Brahmin family are generally formed with Sanskrit words ; and although there are instances to the contrary, such as Kaiyata. Mammata, Appayya, etc., yet where an authentic MS. gives a name of the more usual form, I think that the same ought to be adopted as the real name of the anchor of the Smrti Candrikā.
2. Damuder Misser v. Seuabti, 10 C. L. R. 403.

to the right of the unmarried daughter. It has been laid down in that case, that this marriage portion must be regulated by the necessities of the particular case, and that the family is bound to spend a sufficient sum of money, such as may be necessary, in order to secure a suitable match for the daughter, regard being had to the practice of the family on previous similar occasions. Even a large sum, if allowed by the circumstances of the family, may be allotted for the purpose, if eligible bridegrooms are not otherwise to be induced to marry into the family. Thus defined by judicial decision, the unmarried daughter's right obtains a greater security than had been left to it by the unfortunate doctrines adopted by the Mithilā, the Bengal and the Madras authorities. Yet it is certainly a matter of regret that the step in the right direction, which was taken by such ancient writers as Manu and Yājñavalkya, should have been abandoned by the above three schools, and a retrograde movement, widening the distinction between male and female members of the family, should have been initiated afresh.

To the unmarried daughters as forming a part and parcel of a joint family, we must also add the adopted son, when any one of the leading members, being a sonless person, has thought proper to affiliate a son to himself ; for the right of adoption is not confined to separated Hindus alone. There is no law which prevents one who belongs to a family of undivided coparceners from making an adoption, if he thinks it fit. The only condition attached to the exercise of this right is that he must be without a son; neither youth, nor future probability of having issue begotten by himself, is at all considered an impediment. It is not intended here to enter into the details of the subject of adoption, which forms by itself a separate and extensive branch of Hindu Law. But in contemplating a joint family, we must not forget the fact that actual positive common parentage is not a necessary attribute of all the members.

Thus in the case of Ballabh Das *v.* Sundar Das, I. L. R., 1 All. 430, it is said:—"The joint Hindu family is constituted by the union of descendants, by heirship from some common ancestor, and there must be connexion among its members by blood relationship and marriage and adoption."

The rights of an adopted son, when introduced into a Hindu family, may be said to be generally of the same character with those of an ordinary member, a member, that is, claiming blood relationship. Thus in the case of Moharajah Juggurnath Sahai *v.* Muss. Mukhun Kunwar, (3 W. R. 24), it was held that "Under the Hindu Law the adopted son has the same rights as the son born." In this case the question was, whether a jaghir could descend to persons other than the direct heirs, and the Judges said, that if the jaghir in question in that case had been strictly hereditary, nothing could have prevented the succession of the adopted son. In a Bengal case, Tincowrie Chatterjee *v.* Denonath Banerji, (3 W. R. 49), the Judges said—"An adopted son has all the rights and privileges of a son born. He is the son of the father and of the mother, and succeeds to the paternal property, and also to the *stridhan* of his adoptive mother in the absence of daughters, as a son born would do." Then certain distinctions are pointed out between the status of an adapted son and that of a son born.

In a recent Bengal case,[1] the question of how far an adopted son can be said to occupy the position of a natural born son was discussed at great length by Mr. Justice Romes Chandra Mitten who reviewed in course of his decision all the authorities, ancient and modern, upon the point; the conclusion arrived at by him was expressed in the following words : "The position and status of an adopted son are precisely the same as those of a natural born son, except in a few instances which are expressly enumerated." He also

1. Joykisshore Chowdhry v. Panchoo Baboo, 1 C, L.R. 538.

says—"The rights of an adopted son unless curtailed by express texts, are in every respect, similar to those of a natural born son." He relies upon both the Dattaka Mīmāṁsā and the Dattaka Candrikā for the proposition of law laid down by him. As the Dattaka Mīmāṁsā is admitted on all hands to be an authority also in the Benares school, we must suppose the question of the status of an adopted son as settled, so far as the High Court of Bengal is concerned, in favour of the adopted son being regarded equal to a natural born son.

The High Court of the North-West also must be taken to have virtually decided the question in a similar way by having extended the heritable rights of an adopted son in the line of his adoptive mother.[1]

In Bombay (Mumbai),[2] it has been laid down that an adopted son takes from the date of his adoption a vested interest in the ancestral property of his adoptive father, as a natural born son does from the date of his birth.

In Madras (Chennai),[3] the adopted son is declared to be a member of the undivided family, who at his option may either continue a member, receiving his maintenance from the joint funds, or may demand a partition, and receive and enjoy his share separately from the rest. This is exactly the right universally admitted to be vested in the natural born son who belongs to a family governed by the Mitākṣarā Law.

Under the High Court of Bengal again, the case of Sudanand Mohapattar *v.* Soorjomonee Dabee, which was a case from the District of Cattack,[4] and was therefore governed by the Mitākṣarā Law, the language used by the judges implies that under that law, there is no distinction

1. Sham kuar *v.* Clyadin, I. L. R. 1 All. 255.
2. Rambhat *v.* Lakshman, I. L. R. 5 Bom. 635.
3. Ayyāvu Muppanar v. 'Niladatchi Ammal, 1 Mad. H. C. Rep. 48.
4. 6 W. R. 256; and 8 W. R. 455, in Review.

between the position of an adopted son and that of a natural born son in the matter of the co-ordinate rights which the law of the Mitākṣarā gives to both the father and the son, as belonging to one undivided family. The Judges say, (8 W. R. 458) : "The Mitākṣarā son is entitled equally with his father as well to the profits of the ancestral property as to the property itself from the moment (in this case) of, his adoption; and so, in this case, that is equally ancestral property which has been acquired out of the proceeds of such property, with that actually inherited from ancestors." As regards the soundness of the *dictum* pronounced in this case, that a son in a family governed by the Mitākṣarā has a right in the profits of the ancestral property, Mr. Justice R. Mitter has expressed his doubts.[1] But the grounds upon which his doubts are founded do not touch the position of an adopted son. Whether the profits or income accruing from the ancestral property in a joint family under the law of the Mitākṣarā, belong exclusively to the father, so as to be above all interference or interdiction on the part of the son, may be a question yet open to doubt; but howsoever this question may come ultimately to be decided, the adopted son will stand or with natural born son. There is nothing in the fact of adoption which can distinguish him so far as that point is concerned.

We may therefore consider it as settled that in Bengal, Madras, Bombay and the North-West, an adopted son has a secure position as one of the members of an undivided family.

In Mithila adopted son of the Kṛtrima kind.

In the Mithilā country, however, this proposition requires some qualification, inasmuch as there the ordinary mode of adoption has been obsolete for a few hundred years. In that part of the country, the form of adoption

1. Gunga Pershad *v.* Sheo Dyal, 9 C. L. R. 422.

which has been established from before the British administration is the Kṛtrima one. An adopted son of the Kṛtrima kind differs widely, from the Dattaka son. He does not lose his status in the natural family; he does not adopt the surname of the adoptive family; his relationship as a son is confined only to the person who affiliates him; the person affiliating may be either a male or a female; the husband and the wife are empowered to exercise the right of affiliation indepen dently of one another, and a son affiliated by either remains a stranger to the other. Such an adopted son therefore is not regarded as a member of the adoptive family. This no doubt is an anomalous position ; but the authorities are express.[1] It is not improbable that the anomaly is obviated in practice by the member of a joint Mithilā family rarely exercising his right of adoption. But as the law does not preclude of his so doing if he thought proper, it would be a nice question whether an adopted son in a joint Tirhoot family would be debarred from all rights of partition. In both the cases above referred to, the adoption was made by a woman, and it may well be that such an adoption, having no efficacy in affiliating the son to the husband, also fails in rendering the adopted son a member of the husband's family. It would also seem that in both the cases, the family of the husband was not an undivided one; for otherwise the property could not have come into the hands of the widow. The learned Judges at the same time say that a Kṛtrima adopted son does not become a member of the' family of the husband so far as collateral heirship is concerned. Such a decision leaves it still an open question, supposing a kurtaputtor (the local vernacular name for a Kṛtrima son) was adopted by the undivided member of a Hindu family domiciled in Tirhoot, and supposing the adoptive father died in the undivided condition, leaving the adopted son,—whether that son world be considered as

1. Collector of Tirhoot *v.* Huro Pershad Mohunt, 7 W. R. 500; Muss.. Shibo Kooeree *v.* Joognn Singly 8 W. R. 155.

having no rights in the family of his adoptive father; whether he would not be entitled to maintenance out of the family income; whether he would not receive a share, namely, that of his father, when a general partition of the family property took place; and whether he would not himself be entitled to demand a partition, if he chose. It would be difficult to support a negative answer to the above questions, when we remember that the Kṛtrima is one of the two forms of adoption authorized in this kali age; that, the affiliation produced by this form of adoption is complete so far as the adoptive parent is concerned ; and that he succeeds to all the rights and interests of such adoptive parent, when the latter dies. Probably it is the right of collateral succession which is intended to be denied to a Kṛtrima son; barring the same, probably the position of a Kṛtrima son in a Tirhoot undivided family, differs but little from that of an adopted son of the more ordinary kind in the joint families domiciled in the rest of India.

Shares of adopted and natural born members unequal.

Since the law of adoption is too vast to be adequately dealt with as a supplementary part of the course of Lectures to be delivered by me, I shall conclude the present topic by solely remarking, that it is when the partition of the undivided property comes about, that the distinction between an affiliated member and one actually related by blood becomes conspicuous. Thus, it has been held that if in an undivided Mitākṣarā family consisting of three brothers, one of the brothers dies leaving an adopted son, the share of that son, on partition of the property which descended to the three brothers, will be only half of that which his adoptive father could have claimed, had the latter been alive at the date of partition. In an undivided Hindu family governed by the Mitākṣarā law, an adopted son and the adopted son of a natural son stand exactly in the same position on partition.[1]

1. Kannngoe Raghavananda Das *v.* Sadhu Churn Das, 3 C. L. R. 534.

Under the Bengal school, some doubt may be entertained with regard to the applicability of the above rule of law, since in the case of Denonath Mukerji *v.* Gopalchurn Mukerji, 8 C. L. R. 57, the Judgment says that the passage in the Dattaka Candrikā declaring the share of an adopted son to be half of that of a natural born son is not to be construed as an express text limiting the share of an adopted son inheriting collaterally to half the share taken by the other collateral heirs. But it may well be that this restriction of the sense of the Dattaka Candrikā text applies solely to the case of collateral succession, and not to the partition of undivided property belonging to a joint Bengal family which comprises an adopted son as one of its members.

Redical difference between the Bengal and the Mitākṣarā joint families.

Having thus tried to sketch an outline of a joint family with reference to its constitution, in other words, the character of the different elements composing the same, I shall now enumerate its attributes considered as a whole. With that view, I must first of all premise that the conception of a joint family under the Bengal School differs radically from one obtaining in the rest of India. It is important to bear this radical difference always in mind. It is the source of the innumerably ramified peculiarities that characterise the property law governing three-fourths of the population of India. Joint family as it is understood in all parts of India other than Bengal, is founded on that feature of the property law of those provinces, which consists in the son and the father being coparceners in the ancestral estate. The idea under that law is, that, if there is any property, inherited by the father from his forefathers, his son obtains therein a vested right as soon as he is born. If there are two sons, then the father and each of the two sons are equally the proprietors of that property. If there be three or more sons, then the father becomes a co-proprietor with each one of his sons. This is the notion which has served as the germ of that complicated system of law, regulating under the name of the Mitākṣarā law the proprietor rights of all Hindus, who have their domicile beyond the region to which the Bengali language is confined. There are certain subordinate details in which the above named property law is not identical in all those parts of India just indicated; but the radical notion is the same throughout.

In Bengal, however, a stand was made in very early days against the co-ordinate rights of a son. The honour of inaugurating this departure from the prevailing law, which departure no doubt is regarded' as a progressive step by that school of modern thinkers, who consider the unrestricted transferability of landed property as a mark of advancing civilization, belongs to Jīmūtavāhana. Yet it may be questioned whether previous to the appearance of his treatise on the Law of Inheritance, Bengal had not been spontaneously tending towards the consummation of such a revolution. It would be unprecedented that a single author, however eminent, or a single-work however well-reasoned, should have been capable of at once producing so vast a change. The history of this subject, like that of everything connected with Hindu science, or religion, or law or literature, is not merely involved in obscurity, but may be said to be almost non-existent. The popular idea current in Bengal is, that Jīmūtavāhana was a judicial functionary under a renowned king of Bengal. As the Bengal property law differs so widely, from that of the rest of India, and as no other earlier authority is named in connection with the first introduction of this difference, it is not improbable that Jīmūtavāhana found an opportunity for propagating his peculiar doctrine from a judicial seat ; it is also probable that the germs of the doctrine were supplied to him by the legal usages of the province. Such a supposition is confirmed by a particular passage in the Dāyābhāga, wherein he establishes the unrestricted right of the father to do what he likes with the ancestral property. In ch. II, para 27, Jīmūtavāhana in effect says, that although there are ancient texts prohibiting the father from alienting the family property, yet those texts are to be construed as implying a moral injunction; they simply declare that if a father, being of dissipated habits, makes away with that which furnishes the means of subsistence to the family, he thereby incurs a sin; not that any sale or gift effected by him is inherently invalid. For, continues Jīmūtvāhana, the same texts which restrict the powers of the father also declare him to be an owner. How can ownership be separated from the right of unfettered disposition ? Does not the very word 'ownership' simply that power ? Is it not another name for that power ? Then he concludes by saying; (pats. 30) "Therefore, since it is the *propriety* of an act of gift or sale which is negatived, what happens by doing such an act is the infringement of a sacred ordination; not that there is and invalidity in the gift etc.; *for even a hundred texts cannot alter a fact."*

Meaning a Jīmūtavāhana's dictum a fact is not already by a hundred texts.

In this passage, the word in the original for 'fact' is *vastu*, which ordinarily signifies a ' thing.' Now, what does Jīmūtavāhana mean here by a thing' ? As a lawyer can he be reasonably supposed to be inculcating the astounding proposition, that all acts, howsoever contrary to the binding rules of conduct, must be valid, so soon as done by an unprincipled person ? Yet we cannot escape from the dilemma of attributing to him a proposition of that kind, if we are to construe him in the ordinary way. To my mind, the word 'vastu' here, as used by Jīmūtavāhana means 'a state of things.' He here seems to say, that a state of things is not to be altered by citing a hundred texts; that the state of things is, that sales of ancestral immoveable property by the father are of pretty frequent occurrence ; that this state of things has rooted itself too deeply to be subverted by the citation of passages from the old Ṛṣis ; and that all that we can do is to declare the moral delinquency of those persons who disregard the injunctions of those Ṛṣis.

By adopting such a construction of the above passage, we can give something like an intelligible shape to the striking difference between the property law of Bengal and that of the other parts of India. To harbour a notion, that all along the people of Bengal had been following the Mitākṣarā Law in all its integrity, and that as soon as Jīmūtavāhana brought forward his cogent arguments to show the unsoundness of all past interpretation of ancient law, Bengal threw aside Vijñāneśvara, and began to sanction the unrestricted sale of ancestral estate–to harbour some such notion involves an entire forgetfulness of the usual way in which similar changes in the laws and opinions of a people have been all over the world brought about.

Probable connection between fathers' absolute right and the supremacy of the Brahmins in Bengal.

We cannot therefore avoid the conclusion that Jīmutavāhana only gave a definite form to the tendency which usages in Bengal had already taken towards building up a paramount right in the father of the family with regard to all property, which by the nature of things, came under such a father's management. The origin of such a tendency is not traceable now. But as the tendency evidently was solely confined to Bengal, and as everywhere else the co-ordinate right of the father and the son remained intact, a conjecture may be offered to this effect; that the peculiarity of the Bengal law had some connection with the fact that the priestly class in Bengal obtained an influence unparalled in the other parts of India.

Tradition says that the ancestors of the modern superior class of Bengal Brahmins were invited over from the North-West by a renowned monarch, in order to assist him in the performance of his religious duties ; and that five Brahmins came from Kanouj and eventually settled in the country. We have seen that the influence of the sacer total class has in every part of the world had a good deal to do with the decay of joint rights, whether vested in large or small groups. It is the interest of such a class to promote one form of alienation, namely, donations of property to its own members. Such donations are more likely to be made where property is vested in a single in dividual, than where it is tied up in the hand of a group of persons, whether corporations, or joint families, or village communities. The Bengal Brahmins were, from the moment of their adopting the lower Provinces as their home, placed in the high position of religious advisers to the king of the land, and as a matter of course wielded a vast power, by becoming an agency for moulding the law. It is but natural to suppose that the administration of justice speedily fell into their hand. Their learning was superior, as the very reason of their advent in the country shows. It was because the indigenous Brahmins were utterly incompetent to perform the ordinary duties of the priestly class, that the Kanouj Brahmins were respectfully solicited to come by the sovereign of a benighted region. We must also remember that Bengal lay at the very border-land of Brahminism; the Brahmanic traditions therefore had a feebler hold here than in the central place where the Hindu religion had its birth. It is not improbable therefore that the Brahmin colonists of Bengal, placed at the head both of religion and of law by the ruler of the country, found an unoccupied field to plant the seeds of such doctrines as were most favourable to their self aggrandizement. The result therefore very probably was that from the days of Adisūra, the king whose name is connected with this religious regeneration of Bengal, an initial step was taken towards that individualization of property, which reached its utmost development when Jīmūtavāhana gave to the father an absolutely unfettered right, in all property, whether ancestral or self-acquired. A similar result was not arrived at in the rest of India, because the supremacy of the Brahmins had no such impetus given to it by royal favour.

That the peculiarity in the property law of Bengal had nothing to do with the cogency of the arguments brought forward by Jīmūtavāhana in order to refute the received interpretation of law, is plainly perceived, if we look at the texts upon which the rival schools rely in order to establish the peculiar doctrine espoused by each, These texts have been all brought together by Mitra Misra, in his Vīramitrodaya, he being the most recent text-writer who had to discuss the point with any seriousness. I shall therefore cite these Ṛṣis texts from this latest work, though almost all of them are noticed in the Mitākṣarā and the Dāyabhāga, these two works being taken as typical of the two contending doctrines, one inculcating an undivided right in the father and the son, and the other concentrating all the rights in the father alone.

Anonymous text cited in the Vīramitrodaya, chapter I, section 9.

Ṛṣi texts relating to the rival rights of the father and the son.

"Of gems and pearls and corals, in fact of all, the father is the lord; but of the whole of the immoveable property neither is the father, nor the grandfather, the rival (the lord). "From the favour of the father, might be enjoyed the garments and the ornaments ; but the immoveable property could not be enjoyed,-if there were a favour of the father."

Section 10, Gautama cited. " From the very moment of birth, one obtains the ownership of the wealth, thus say the authorities."

Nārada cited in that very Section.

"The father being dead the sons should divide the father's wealth."

Devala cited in that very Section.

"The father being dead, the sons should divide the father's wealth; since there cannot be ownership in them, while the father is living, being faultless."

Manu cited in that very Section.

"After the father and the mother, the brothers having assembled together should divide the paternal inheritance; since they are not the lords, while those two live."[1]

Śaṅkha and Likhita cited in Section 11.

"The father being alive,–the sons should not divide the inheritance; although ownership be obtained by them subsequently, the sons verily have no competency, on account of dependence in the matter of wealth and virtue."

Vyāsa cited in Section 30.

"Of the immoveable property, and the slaves, although acquired by one's own self, there is neither a gift, nor a sale, without assembling all the sons. Those who are born, those who are unborn, and those who are lying in the womb, they wish for subsistence. There is neither a gift, nor a sale."

Gautama supports the son's right, Devala that of the father.

These texts are the bones of contention between the respective followers of Vijñāneśvara and Jīmūtavāhana. The two most explicit are the sayings of Gautama and Devala. The former distinctly favours the Mitākṣarā doctrine, the latter as distincitly supports the Dāyabhāga law. The rest of the texts are capable of being interpreted either way, and have been so interpreted by each school in accordance with its peculiar proclivity. The Mitākṣarā school reads Devala as implying merely that the sons are not independent of their father respecting the use of the joint property; while Jīmūtavāhana says that Gautama's 'text declaring pro-

1. Manu, chapter IX, śloka 104.

prietary right to be contemporaneous with birth is not to be taken in its literal sense; that it simply intends to say that the origin of the heritable right of a son is his relationship to the father, and that birth is the initial point of this relationship; (Dāyabh. chapter I, para. 20) not that the son has .really any right in the ancestral property from the moment of his birth. His proprietary right dates from the moment of either the death or the degradation, or the retirement of the father.[1]

Popular notion in the Mitākṣarā Provinces an authority for son's right by birth.

There is one significant passage in the Mitākṣarā, regarding the question of this joint right between the father and the son, the drift of which has not, as far as I am aware, been sufficiently attended to. In para. 23, section 1, chapter I, it is said that as the subject of ownership is a temporal matter, in other words, is determinable by reference to the customs and usages observed by people at large, so the same popular usage sanctions the notion that the son has a right by birth. From this passage it is clear, that the chief authority relied upon by Vijñāneśvara for his position, that an equal right is vested in the father and the son, is popular usage. He, in effect, says, that everybody can perceive what people think about it ; that people understand right to be vested in the son from the moment of his birth; and that this universally recognized fact should not be captiously gainsaid. This sensible method of referring to the popular usage in order to establish right notions in law is forcibly pointed out by Mitres Misra, who says[2]:—"The Smṛti texts relating to litigation are but the repetitions of what prevails among the people; this has been so said by all the writers of treatises." We can therefore conclude that Vijñāneśvara laid down the law of equality between the father and the

---

1. Dayabh. chapter I, pares, 31.
2. Yiram, Chapter I, section 37.

son, because he found it established among the people for whom he wrote; on the other hand, Jīmūtavāhana also had no other course left open to. him than to advance in the direction indicated by the notions current in Bengal. Each gave prominence to that particular Ṛṣi-text which favoured his own special view; Jīmūtavāhana adopted Devala as his guide, and construed all other texts in conformity therewith; while Vijñāneśvara took as his authority the saying of Gautama, and subordinated the rest of the texts to that opinion.

Yājñavalkya supports son's equality with father.

There is one text, however, of Yājñavalkya, which while it furnished a tower of strength to the Mitākṣarā school, must have been felt by Jīmūtavāhana as a great stumbling-block in his way. I allude to the śloka, which I find numbered as 121 of the second chapter, in the Mandlik Edition, but as 124 in an Edition of the Mitākṣarā dated 1829, issued by the then Committee of Public Instruction in Calcutta (Kolkata). This śloka has been incorporated in the 3rd para, section 5, chapter I, of the Mitākṣarā by Colebrooke. Colebrooke again in a footnote numbers this śloka as the 122nd of the second chapter of Yājñavalkya. As the text is most important, and in fact, is by itself fit to be the foundation of the whole Mitākṣarā law, I shall first give the original Sanskrit and then the translation.

भूर्या पितामहोपात्ता निबन्धो द्रव्यमेव वा।
तत्र स्यात् सदृशं स्वाम्यं पितुः पुत्रस्य चाभयोः।।

Translation.

The land appropriated by the grandfather, or corrody or property-therein the ownership of both the father and the son, should be alike.

"The ownership of father and son is the same in land which was acquired by the grandfather, or in a corrody, or in chattels."-By *Colebrooke.*

"The ownership of both father and son is the same in land, a corrody, or wealth received from the grandfather." —*By Viswanath Mandlik.*[1]

On this text, the comments of the Mitākṣarā are as follows;-(chapter I, section 5, para. 4). "Land' means rice field etc.' A 'corrody,' 'out of one plantation of betel leaf, so many betel leaves, or out of one plantation of areca nut, so many areca nuts, thus described.' 'Property,' 'Gold, silver, etc.' What was obtained by the grandfather by acceptance of gift, or by conquest, etc. therein the ownership of the father and the son is wellknown among people; consequently, there is a partition. Since the same is 'alike; equal.' Therefore the partition is not solely by father's will, nor is there a double share for the father."

Jīmūtavāhana explains away Yājnavalkya's texts.

Jīmūtavāhana has quoted this text in chapter II, para.;— He there says;–(I am here giving the purport of the passage). As for the text of Yājñavalkya which declares that father and son have an equal ownership in property that belonged to the grandfather, the same applies to the case where two brothers and their father are living joint and then one brother dies leaving a son, and then the father dies. In such a case one might erroneously conclude in the first instance, that the living brother, being the nearest by relationship to the deceased father, should take the whole of the paternal, property. In order to obviate such a supposition, Yājña-valkya lays down, that under the above circumstances, the son of the previously deceased brother, standing as grandson by relationship should have a share, the same share, namely, that his father if alive would have got. In other words, the right of the father and his son is equal, the son should not be deprived of his share in his grandfather's property, be cause his father has predeceased the grandfather. In para. 15, Jīmūtavāhana gives an alternative

1. P. 215, Article 121.

interpretation of the same text, by taking the suggestion of a previous writer. He here says that the equality of ownership between the father and the son with regard to the grandfather's property simply implies, that the father has no right to make an unequal partition in respect of the grandfather's property. As regards his self-acquired property, a father can make any distribution he chooses, although his preferring one son to an inordinate extent would be morally culpable. But the grandfather's property a father cannot distribute at his pleasure. There the father and the son are equal. The father, can take a double share for himself, but he cannot make an unequal distribution among his sons.[1]

Language of Jīmūtavāhana not explient.

This portion of the Dāyabhāga dealing with the rival rights of the father and the son, seems to a certain extent involved in obscurity, if it even does not involve a direct contradiction. We have seen that in para. 30 of the 2nd chapter, Jīmūtavāhana in distinct terms declares the validity of all alienations actually made by the father. In para. 17 again he says that out of grandfather's property, the father can take a double share when making a partition with his sons. Now the question arises, of what property does he sanction an unfettered alienation in para 30 ? Is it of the self-acquired, or of that descended from the grandfather ? Para. 30 is the conclusion of a discussion which commences with para. 27. In para. 27 are cited two ślokas from Vyāsa, the purport of which is, that a single individual cannot alienate immoveable property which is common to the whole gotra, that whether divided or undivided, all sapiṇḍas are equal as regards immovable property, that a single person is in every case incompetent to make a gift, or mortgage or sale. In para. 29 is quoted another śloka from Vyāsa, as I gather from a foot-note' in Colebrooke's

1. Para. 17, 20, ch. II, Dāyabhāga.

translation of the Mitākṣarā, in which latter work the same śloka of Vyāsa appears in para. 27, section 1, chapter I. The purport of this second śloka is, that land and slaves, though acquired by one's own self, cannot be sold or made a gift of, without convening all the sons. From this it would seem that there was a doctrine abroad in Vyāsa's time, that even self-acquired property was not capable of being disposed of at one's own pleasure. Having quoted this doctrine in para. 29, Jīmūtavāhana, in the memorable para. 30 clinches his celebrated declaration of the Bengal property law, that alienations actually made by the father are not to be invalidated by a hundred texts. And in para. 31, he quotes Nārada, who says, that if one should give away or sell his own share, he has every power to do so, for he is the master of his own wealth. We may therefore very well suppose that the unrestricted power of alienation declared in the Dāyabhāga, chapter I, para. 30, is confined to one's self-acquired property, since there were ancient Ṛṣi texts whieh denied even such a right. This view is further confirmed by what is said in para. 17, that the father cannot make an unequal distribution of the grandfather's property among his sons. If he cannot do so, is it reasonable to think that he can alienate grandfather's property at his pleasure, thereby only incurring a moral culpability ? Yet it is now universally admitted in fact it is the settled law now, that in the Province of', Bengal a Hindu who has sons can sell, give or pledge, without their consent, immoveable ancestral property; without the consent of the sons, he can by will prevent, alter, or affect the succession to such property.[1] It is difficult to find an express authority for so sweeping a proposition in any original Sanskrit treatise on Hindu Law. Neither Raghunandana nor Srīkṛṣṇa, the two other Writers of the Bengal school who stand next to Jīmūtavāhana as authorities in Bengal, in so many terms countenances the notion that property inherited by the father, from the

1. Huro Lal Chowdhry v. Kripamoyee Dabee, 3 W. R.. 227.

grandfather can be disposed of by the father at his pleasure. The former in his Dāyatatva, and the latter in his Dāyakrama Saṁgraha, while discussing the subject of partition of grandfather's effects by the father, expressly limits the power of the father as, regards unequal distribution. Both of them quote the same text of Yājñavalkya declaring equal right of father and son, and both follow exactly the leading, of Jīmūtavāhana as regard its sense.

Jīmūtavāhana's work in developing the Bengal law.

The truth seems to be that the work done by Jīmūtavāhana in the development of the law of Bengal consisted in his denying the right of the son by birth, which right is the root, of all the peculiarities in the law of the other four schools. The actual Bengal law as enunciated in the decision quoted above from the 3rd volume of the Weekly Reporter, which in fact is one of an innumerable series of cases of a similar import, is a still later development, but foreshadowed in the treatise of Jīmūtavāhana. Probably in his time so unqualified an expression of opinion on the subject would have been of too startling a character. It is not unlikely therefore, that although he magnifies the father's rights as much as he safely can, Jīmūtavāhana has left the question of the father's disposing power over ancestral property in an intentional doubtfulness. In paras. 27-30 of the first chapter of the Dāyabhāga, although he appears to lay down the father's unfettered disposing power his self-acquired effects, he adduces a reason for it, which leaves but little to be desired by an unqualified advocate of the father's similar power over all property, whether ancestral or acquired. His argument is, that the father has a right, an ownership, that the very essence of ownership is absolute dominion—the right of doing with property what one pleases. The conclusion therefore is irresistable, that whenever there is proprietary right, the power of unrestricted disposition necessarily follows. The right of the son by birth having been negatived so elaborately in the preceding part of the work, Jīmūtavāhana left the consequences of his doctrine to take their own course. This course has been the extension of the father's power over all property in the Province of Bengal. The ultimate result has been consummated by Jīmūtavāhana giving prominence to the text of Devala,[1] wherein that Ṛṣi lay down in unmistakable terms, that so long the father is not tainted with any disqualification or degradation; the sons have no ownership at all.

Specise influence of Ṛṣi Devala on Bengal law

This Ṛṣi Devala seems to have had a very special and unique influence on the law of Bengal. It is his text which would seem to have had the effect of taking away the daughter's right to one-fourth share,[2] and it is his text Ṛṣi which is evoked here to establish the great distinction between the property-law of Bengal and that of other Provinces. I am not aware that any entire body of his Institutes is yet extant. Were it unearthed, it is not improbable that the source of many an other peculiarity in the Bengal law might be traced to the sayings of this very Ṛṣi.

Aggregate ownership and fractional ownership.

As a corollary of the doctrine set forth above, negativing the son's right by birth, is another peculiar doctrine of the Bengal school, that of what is called of the fractional ownership of the heirs, contracted with the doctrine of 'aggregati ownership expounded by all the other schools. The later text-writers of the Bengal school are careful in defining their own position to be that of the promulgators of the prādeśika svatva, 'calling their opponents as inculcating sāmudāy svatva, 'aggregate ownership.' This distinction is the outcome of the two definitions of partition opposed to one another, which are given by the two parties. In the Mitākṣarā, partition is defined thus—

1. For this text, see *ante* p. 160.
2. See *ante*, p. 145, last two lines. Although Jimutavāhana has not quoted this text, it is most explicit in cutting down an unmarried daughter's right to a mere marriage portion.

"Partition is the act of fixing diverse ownerships on particular parts of an aggregate of properties, which aggregate was previously subject to those diverse ownerships".[1]

This definition is repeated in the very same words in the Vīramitrodaya.[2] The leading authorities of the other three schools, namely, the Vivāda-cintāmaṇi of the Mithila, the Smṛti Candrikā of the Madras, the Vyavahāra of the Bombay schools are silent upon the point; all these treatises being of a later date than the Mitākṣarā, and usually following on the same lines, may be taken as having accepted the same definition. But in the Dāyabhāga we find a definition quits of a contrary import. There we find partition defined to be an act of particularizing an ownership, by casting of lots etc., which ownership had previously fastened upon an indefinite portion of an aggregate of properties, but which ownership was not previously ascertained.[3] If we ponder the meaning of these two definitions opposed to one another, the conclusion we come to is 'this:—In the opinion of the Mitākṣarā, before partition has taken place, every parcener has his ownership fastened upon the whole of the joint property, comprising lands and cattle, and gold and silver, and all other moveable effects, and even a trading business in which the family is concerned. There are as many ownerships, as there are parceners. These ownerships, each of them, has the whole property for its subject. No parcener can say that he singly is the owner of a particular share, one-third or one-fourth. As the Mitākṣarā makes the sons co-proprietors with the father, neither the father nor any one of the sons can at any given moment lay claim to a share numerically defined. A son can demand a partition; in that case, his share will be numerically defined. But while remaining joint, he at any

1. Chapter I, section I, para. 4.
2. Chapter I, section 4.
3. Chapter I, para. 8.

particular moment of time cannot positively assert that he is entitled to so much of the whole. If the family consists of a father and one son now, at a subsequent date another son may be born, and then another; and so on. So that by fresh additions to the joint family, the shares vary. Not only birth, but death also, affects the value of the shares. If partition be demanded when the family consists of one son and his father, the son gets half the property. But if two sons be born before partition, each son gets one-third. Thus it may seem advantageous for the son to divide the property as early as he can; but the son must come of age before he can demand partition; we shall subsequently see that during his minority, partition is not so easily granted. But before a son can come of age, which cannot be earlier than the sixteenth year according to the old Hindu law, or before the eighteenth or the twenty-first year according to Legislative enactmen other sons are generally born to the father. Again, the advantages of an early partition are not so obvious in every case. As fresh births diminish the pecuniary value of the shares to be allotted to the elder sons, so death among sons may swell again the shares of the survivors.

Unity of ownership as explained by Privy Council.

For the above reasons, before partition, a Mitākṣarā family may be likened to a corporation seized of property in its aggregate character. Admitting the rights of sons by birth, the author of the Mitākṣarā had no other course left open to him than to define partition in the way he has done. It is this that he means by saying that there are diverse ownerships regarding the whole before a partition has taken place; and when it does take place, these many aggregate ownership are made separate, each member comes to own an especial part of the whole, and has no more concern with other similar parts. This doctrine of the unity of ownership has been thus clearly set forth in the Privy Council case of Approvier *v.* Ramsubha Aiyan.[1] "According to the true

1. 11 Moore 75 ; S. C. 8. W. R. P. C. 1.

notion of an undivided family in Hindu law, no individual member of that family, whilst it remains undivided, can predicate of the joint and undivided property, that he, that particular member, has a certain definite share. No individual member of an undivided family could go to the place of the receipt of rent, and claim to take from the collector or bailiff of the rents, a certain definite share. The proceeds of undivided property must be brought according to the theory of an undivided family, to the common chest or purse, and then dealt with according to the modes of enjoyment of the members of an undivided family. But when the members of an undivided family agree among themselves with regard to particular property, that it shall thenceforth be the subject of ownership in certain defined shares; then the character of undivided property and joint enjoyment is taken away from the subject matter so agreed to be dealt with; and in the estate each member has henceforth a definite and certain share which he may claim a right to receive and enjoy in severalty, although the property itself has not been actually severed and divided." No doubt the Privy Council in the above case have made the observations with regard to an undivided Hindu family in general; yet these remarks would not be a correct description of a joint family under the Bengal law. Unless we lay it down as a proposition that under the Bengal law, there can be no joint family in the proper sense of the expression, we cannot say that undivided coparceners in Bengal have no defined shares in, the joint property. Herein lies the radical difference between the two descriptions of joint families.'

In Bengal, no joint right between father and son.

A Bengal joint family does not involve any joint rights as between a father and his sons. In it the joint rights are between brothers in general, or between those who claim under different brothers. A Mitākṣarā family, taking that expression in the sense of all joint families domiciled beyond the province of Bengal, involves joint rights as well between a father and his sons, as between different brothers or between those who claim under different brothers. Under the Bengal law, the members are not supposed to have their several rights fastened upon the whole of the joint property, but the right of each member is fastened upon one particular portion, which portion remains in an unidentifiable condition before partition, and becomes identifiable after partition. This is what Jīmūtavāhana intends by his definition of partition. The shares, according to that definition, can be numerically defined before partition. Nor does the value of these shares vary at different periods. There is no advantage or disadvantage to be gained or suffered by an early or a late partition. Even before partition, one member can go to the place of collection and can demand from the bailiff his particular share of the collected rent; at least the share which he will obtain is definite and not liable to be increased or decreased at any future date, unless by succession to some other member, which is quite a different matter altogether. It is possible that from the tenant himself the member of a Bengal joint family cannot demand his particular share of the rent; for there has been a current of decisions that a single co-sharer in tenanted landed property cannot insist upon the tenure of the tenant being split, by making the tenant liable to pay the rent in shares. But the force of these decisions must be supposed to have been greatly weakened by a Full Bench case which empowers every co-sharer to have his share defined in a particular fraction.[1] However that may be, there cannot be any doubt that the share of a member of a Bengal joint family is always definite. He can always say that he is proprietor to the extent of one-third, or one-fifth, and so forth. The Dāyabhāga expressly says that it is in particular portions of the whole property that the ownership of each coparcener attaches. Such a definition of partition was the obvious course for an advocate of the father's absolute ownership

1. Ishwar Chunder Dutt and others *v*. Ram Krishna Dass, I. L. R., 6 Cal. 902.

over all property. Under this view, the value of the shares remaining constant, it was not necessary to admit any joint right for each member over the whole property.

Area of aggregate ownership

From what has been said above, it is evident that there is no unity of ownership in a Bengal joint family, although there may be something like a unity of possession; while in a Mitākṣarā family on the other hand, there is both unity of ownership and of possession, as a natural consequence of its doctrine of 'aggregate ownership. Fractional ownership and 'aggregate ownership,' two expressions invented by the later writers of the Bengal school, convey well the two rival notions about the proprietary right as entertained by the two rival schools respectively; these two schools themselves, therefore, may be precisely designated, one as the school of 'aggregate ownership,' the other 'the school of fractional ownership.' The school of 'fractional ownership' is confined solely to Bengal, as is obvious from what has gone before; while the school of 'aggregate ownership' extends over the whole of the North-West from the Vindhya Hills to the banks of the Indus, includes the Provinces of Oude and Mithila, and includes also the whole of the Peninsula from the south of the Vindhya chain to the Cape Comorin. There are minor differences in the different localities of the extensive region indicated above;, but nowhere within the same is the general proposition at all denied, nor are its plain deductions disregarded or rejected.

Ṛght of survivorship, a deduction from the principle of aggregate ownership.

The most general of all the deductions from the theory of aggregate ownership is the rule of survivorship. I have already said that no single expression is to be found in the original Sanskrit texts which is of the same import with this term 'survivorship'. But there can be no doubt that the doctrine of aggregate ownership is the root from which the notion of survivorship has naturally sprung. In the Privy Council case of Kattama Natchiar *v.* Rajah of Sivagunga[1] their Lordships say[1]:—

'There are two principles on which the rule of succession according to Hindu law appears to depend: the first is that which determines the right to offer the funeral oblation, and the degree in which the person making the offering is supposed to minister to the spiritual benefit of the deceased; the other is an assumed right of survivorship. According to principles of Hindu law, there is coparcenaryship between the different members of a united family, and survivorship following upon it. There is community of interest and unity of possession between all the members of the family; and upon the death of any one of them, the others may well take by survivorship, that in which they had, in the deceased's lifetime a common interest and a common possession." Again in the Full Bench case of Sadaburt Pershad Sahool *v.* Muss. Foolbash Kooer[2] the Chief Justice Sir Barnes Peacock, said:—"According to the Mitākṣarā law, if a member of a joint undivided family dies without a son, leaving a brother, his widow does not take his share by descent. If he leaves a son, the son takes by descent, but if he leaves a widow, the survivors take by survivorship, and they hold the property which they take by survivorship, legally and equitably for themselves, and not in trust for the heirs of the deceased. The deceased's heirs have no interest either legally or equitably in the share which passes by survivorship to the surviving co-sharer. That will be made very clear if you suppose the case of a joint family consisting of a father and two sons and two uncles, the brothers of the father, taking property by descent from the father of the father and the two uncles. The father and the two sons take one-third, and the two uncles each take one-third, that is,

1. 9 Moore, 610; S. C. 2 W. R. F. C. 31.
2. 12 W. R. F. B. 1; S. C. 3 B. L. R. F. B. 31.

they take that which upon partition would be allotted. Then suppose that one of the sons dies without issue leaving a widow, his widow according to the Mitākṣarā law would not take his share in the estate." Then the Chief Justice continues and holds that the share of the deceased son passes by survivorship to the other members of the family; that the interest of the deceased son ceases with his death, and that the said interest is not seizable in execution for the debts of the deceased. We shall on a subsequent occasion see that this latter proposition has now become doubtful, since the series of decisions following on the lines of the celebrated Privy Council case of Girdhari Lal,[1] have been passed. But the doctrine of survivorship has remained untouched. Whatever interest the deceased son had in the family property must be vested in the other male members, although burdened, it may be, with the debts of the deceased son.

No right of survivorship in the school of fractional ownership, Inequitableness of the rule of survivrorship.

This doctrine of survivorship is totally inconsistent with the principle of fractional ownership. The school following that principle, in other words, the Bengal school, therefore, has developed a law of succession of a widely different kind. It gives the widow of a person dying without male issue the whole of his property, although he might have been joint, in the Bengal sense, with his brothers or other coparceners, at the time of his death. In this respect the law of Bengal contrasts most favourably with the school of aggregate ownership. The rule of survivorship, although not appearing to be inequitable to a very great extent, when the brothers are the survivors, assumes almost a repulsive form when it works the exclusion of the widow in favour of very remote sapiṇḍas, who may happen to have been united in interest with the deceased. Such union is not opposed to

1. 22 W. R. 56.

law. Modern joint families do often embrace within their precincts a large number of coparceners more or less distant in relationship; and the rigid rule of survivorship leaves the widow nearly unprovided where even a single survivor remains, however remote his connection with her husband may be. The widow no doubt has a right to maintenance from the joint property in the hand of a survivor. But this right often assumes so precarious a character, that one cannot but consider the rule of the Bengal school to be a referable provision of law, in favour of the widow. In whose helpless condition in Hindu society is too well known to require any comment. The mischievous character of the rule of survivorship becomes still more conspicuous when a large estate ultimately comes into the hand of the widow of the last survivor, although widows of the previously deceased members may be alive. Thus if there be five brothers in an undivided family, and each successively dies without male issue, leaving only a widow, then it is the widow of the brother who dies last that succeeds to the whole estate, the other four widows being entitled to receive only maintenance at her hand. The original texts have not, it is true, laid down in express terms the law to be so, but I do not see how a result of the above character, that is, the exclusion of many widows by the widow of the last member, can be avoided consistently with the rule of survivorship. The last member must be held as having died in non-union, and his estate must therefore, according to the law of succession applicable to separate property, devolve upon his widow, burdened with the payment of maintenance to the other widows.

Large Joint families are of a modern date.

It is remarkable that the writers of the Sanskrit digests seldom speak of such joint families as are found in modern days, I mean joint families of an unwieldy kind, including several branches, and comprising cousins even to the fourth remove, all living within the same inclosure, all concerned in the same landed property, or the same trading business, or sometimes even the joint profits of a popular idol-shrine, such as that of the goddess Kālī in the vicinity of Calcutta. The Haldar family, who are interested in the profits arising from the untold amounts of presents made by innumerable votaries belonging to every Hindu race, has now become so numerous that this single family might now occupy a whole village of a considerable extent. The family has had further facilities for growing in wealth and number, inasmuch as the income of the divinity has systematically increased under the prosperous condition of the country in general. This Haldar family may be taken as typical of a joint family in Bengal, not united in mess, it is true, but united in this one particular article of property, namely, the divinity. In the original texts I nowhere find traces of any family of so large a numerical strength. It is known to everybody, in fact it is a trite observation, that Hindu jurists view the law of inheritance in the light of the law of partition. All the questions of succession are discussed as parts of the law of partition; it is under that head that they deal with joint families, with the power of alienation, with the peculiar property of women, with disqualification, in fact generally with the whole law of property. The Brāhmanic religion at an early date inculcated the preferableness of separated ownership; and it would seem that the sermons of the priestly class had a durable effect on general practice; in other words, in those times when most of our Sanskrit treatises on Hindu law were written, separated families seem to have been the rule, and joint families the exception. I ground this inference upon the fact that nowhere in those treatises on partition, which constitute the majority of the literature of Hindu law, we find mention of large families. The division that those books speak of is generally a division either between the father and his sons, or between brothers, and on rare occasions, between uncles and nephews, and sometimes a grandfather and his grandsons and uncles. In re-union again, which as an incident of joint property is peculiar to India, we hear of a second coparcenaryship possible only between a father and his son, between two brothers, and between an uncle and his nephew.[1]

Large joint families probably date from the period of the Mahommedan rule,

From all this it is a legitimate inference that families in those days ordinarily divided in two generations, rarely remaining in union when the common ancestor of the male members was the third in the ascending line, counting from the members who were the eldest in age. Under such circumstances the exclusion of the widow by her husband's coparceneres did not work so great a hardship as when joint families began to assume a larger size, and when the widow had to give way to relations who could not entertain feelings of affection for her, who in fact were comparative strangers to her. The appearance of these large families, is attributable, probably to the establishment of Mahommedan rule in India. In spite of some highly creditable specimens of good sovereigns in the long list of the various Mussulman dynasties, the period of the Mahommedan rulers could never spread such a general security of life and property, as the Hindus had previously enjoyed under the mild despotism of their Kṣatriya monarchs, or as they are now enjoying under the sovereignty of Britain. An unsettled political condition amongst a people is conducive to such unions as are exemplified in these large joint families of later days; for the instinct of self-protection leads people having some mutual tie to come together and to be of assistance to one another. Another cause of the general prevalence of these large joint families may be found in the complicated system of land tenure, which appears to have been first introduced contemporaneously with the establishment of

1. Mitak chapter II, section 9, para. 8

the Mussullman supremacy. Under this complicated system—the parent of the zamindari method of the present day, landed property assumed new forms unknown to the ancient Hindu law. These new forms of immoveable property could not be so easily divided with satisfaction to all, by applying the principles deducible from the body of Hindu partition law. It may even be questioned, whether in that law a name can be found for rent. The thing that can be called as the nearest approach to rent is the 'Nibandha,' which Colebrooke and all the succeeding translators have rendered by the word 'Corrody'[1] The division of rent-paying lands therefore when joint property assumed the form of large estates paying revenue to the Mussulman rulers, came to be unusual, because it was difficult.

Butwarrah rarely resorted to.

Under even the butwarrah law of the present day, although it has been framed by jurists from England whose consummate skill equals their eminent practical knowledge, the partition of zamindari property is so cumbrous an affair, that coparcerers often prefer to remain joint, in spite of the manifold inconvenience of an undivided condition, rather than setting in motion the butwarrah machinery to unsettle everything for ten or fifteen years.

In a Mitāṣarā family, a female never a leading coparcener.

Another result of the rule of survivorship in a Mitākṣara family is that in no case can a female be a leading coparcener in such a family; she may be a member, entitled to certain rights and privileges; but she can never have a voice in the management of the undivided funds. Her position in the family is necessarily subordinate. The only instance in which she can lay claim to anything like an equality with the male members is, when she has minor male children, and when the joint interests of her sons are jeopardised by

1. Mitak. chapter 1, section 5, para 4.

the acts of the senior members of the family. Sometimes it may be her own husband, the father of her sons whose interests she is desirous to protect, whose acts become injurious to the sons. Thus[1] the High Court has held that under the Mitākṣarā law, the rights of the minor sons in the ancestral property may be protected by their mother who can bring a suit for declaration of right of partition as vested in her sons, when the father's acts are likely to imperil the minor's estate. In another case,[2] it has been held that although ordinarily it is the managing member of a joint Hindu family governed by the Mitākṣarā law who is entitled to a certificate under Act XXVII of 1860, yet when the members, appear to have fallen out, and do not agree with each other, it would not be the right course to pursue to grant the certificate to one of them as the managing member of the family. In the judgment in that case, it was also observed, that the certificate for a particular deceased member could not be withheld altogether, inasmuch as although the family was a joint Hindu family; still the debts that were due to the members of the joint family were the debts due to the deceased as well as to the other members of the family, and under section 2 of Act XXVII of 1860, so far as the deceased was concerned, no debtor could be compelled to pay the debts due to the joint family unless a person obtained a certificate under the Act to represent the deceased in the joint family. Therefore, there was a clear necessity that somebody should obtain a certificate to represent the deceased for the purpose of collecting debts. From these observations it is evident that if a member left minors under the guardianship of his widow, the widow, as representating the minors, would be entitled to the certificate on account of her deceased husband, where disagreements and quarrels have commenced to take place

1. Muss. Lekraj Kooor *v.* Sirdar Oval Singh 25 W. R. 497.
2. Chowdhry Kripa Sindhoo *v.* Radhacharun Das, 23 W. R. 234.

among the surviving members. Under such circumstances, even in a Mitākṣarā family, a female member would vicariously occupy a position of some authority generally denied by law to the female member on all other occasions.

In Bengal a female's position often equal to that of a male.

But in Bengal, joint families frequently exhibit instances of female members holding a position in all respects equal to that of the males. The reason is that the doctrine of fractional ownership does not make any difference in the course of succession, whether the family be joint or divided in interest. Whenever a member dies without leaving male issue down to the third generation, a female, either as the widow, or as a daughter, or as the mother, or even as the paternal grandmother, obtains a share in the joint estate; she in fact becomes a coparcener, having all the rights and privileges of the other male parceners ; she has a voice in the management of the property; she can even have a partition effected; and although her powers of alienation be of a qualified character, yet so long as she lives, hardly any distinction can be made between such a female member and her male coparceners.

Double course of succession in schools of aggregate ownership.

This leads us to that double course of succession laid down by the school of aggregate ownership, which is one of the many results of the above rule of survivorship, and which has added a fresh complication to the Mitākṣarā law. The line of succession in a separated family is entirely distinct from the persons in whom the property vests when an undivided member dies. In fact, it may in one sense be said that there is no succession or descent in a Mitākṣarā undivided family, or in a family of that school which has been formed by re-union after one separation. If the family is composed of different stocks, as for instance, if it consists of, say three brothers with the sons of each, then on partition the sons of each brother jointly take one-third of the estate, where all the brothers have died; or if any brother lives at the time of the partition, then he with his own sons takes one-third to be afterwards re-distributed in equal lots in case his sons demand a partition.[1] This may be said to be something similar to a succession or descent, inasmuch as where persons descended from different fathers constitute a joint family, then the shares to which the members are severally entitled must be calculated by considering the mutual position of their fathers in the family tree. Otherwise, whenever a person dies, what takes place is a lapse of his share or interest to the joint estate. When he leaves any male issue, such male issue quietly fills the place of the deceased member, but they cannot exactly be said to succeed the deceased to his interest in the family property, inasmuch as every male member as soon as born has his own substantive vested interest in the common property.

While therefore in a joint Mitākṣarā family, there is hardly anything like a succession to, or descent of, the interests of a deceased member, but only lapse of his share by virtue of survivorship; on the other hand, when the deceased was separate in interest, at the time of his death, such interest is succeeded to by a line of heirs, which is briefly indicated in the well-known text of Yājñavalkya which forms the para. 2, section 1, chapter II, of Colebrooke's Mitākṣarā and which is made up of the latter half of the 137th, the whole of the 138th, and the first half of the 139th ślokas of the second chapter of Yājñavalkya's Institutes.[2]

Yājñavalkya the only Ṛṣi who propounded a clear rule of succession, Questions of succession under Hindu Law were always unsettled.

Throughout the whole Hindu law, this text of

1. Mitak chapter I, section 5, para. 2.
2. Colebrooke in a footnote cites it as Yājñavalkya 2, 13r- 137; while Viśvanāth Mandlik in his Edltion of Yājñavalkya makes it as the 135th and 136th ślokas of the 2nd chapter.

Yājñavalkya is the only methodical and business-like statement of the course of succession; all the schools therefore have laid their hand upon it. All the schools have made of it what use was most subservient to their particular opinions. For in spite of its clear arrangement the text fails after a few steps, and is enveloped in the obscurity of such general terms as an 'agnate' and a 'cognate,' which are interpreted by different schools in numberless different ways, almost every original writer on this part of the law having his own particular views to support. As for the rest of the Ṛṣis, the law of succession has been laid down by them in a bewildering way; one may well despair of deriving any practical benefit from their texts in a disputed question of Hindu succession. It is not easy to understand how in Hindu days the practical administration of succession law was carried on with the help of such perplexing declarations of the line of heirs. The task of extracting from those texts anything like a general principle, so as to cover all the possible questions of inheritance has not yet been fulfilled, though the number of *nibandha* works commenting upon those texts is not small. In this most important branch of law, a branch having its application in the every day concerns of life, a systematic statement based upon clear principles that one can easily lay hold of, is still a want in the literature of Hindu law. The truth seems to be that after a certain number of heirs, I believe after the brother's sons the Hindu administrators of justice used to do just as their particular inclinations led them, and that there was no certainty whatever in this law. In those days, communications between different parts of the country were extremely difficult, and what was done in the practical working of the law of succession in one part of the country, never came to be known in another part; possibly as many schools of opinions grew up as there were tribunals. In the present course of Lectures, the law of success does not legitimately fall within them province of my subject, namely, a joint Hindu family; I shall therefore dismiss this matter simply by giving the general enumeration of heirs contained in Yājñavalkya's text, whose list is as follows;– the wife; (2) the daughters; (3) the parents; (4) the brothers; (5) the son thereof; (6) one born in the gotra ; (7) a bandhu; (8) the pupils; (9) the follow-students.

The expression 'joint in food, worship and estate.

Having thus briefly contrasted the joint families of the two descriptions, one prevailing in Bengal, and the other in the remaining parts of India, I shall now explain certain expressions, which are used with regard to both in the judge-made law. Thus in cases we often find a joint family described as joint in food, worship, and estate. What it is to be joint in estate, has to a certain extent already appeared, it is to have and hold in common the various kinds of property in which persons can be interested. This interest is one and the same for every member in a Mitākṣarā family; it is several and fractional for the different members in a Dāyabhāga family; yet so long as the properties themselves have not been severally allotted to those members, in a Dāyabhāga family also, the interest is in one sense joint or common at least, although there is no survivorship. To be joint in food implies only, that the arrangement for cooking the food of the family, is single and the same for the whole family. Generally speaking it is in the matter of this arrangement for cooking that the family separates first of all. Such separation in mess does not in every case necessitate a separation in estate or worship. Separation in mess is the easiest of all to be effected. It is necessitated usually when the male members begin to make earnings on their own account and are desirous to secure greater comforts for themselves and their own wives and children than can be afforded by the common family means. It, in most cases, co-exists with residence in a common dwelling house, only particular apartments being set apart for each married couple.

Joint worship of the present day, Joint worship as formerly understood.

As regards joint worship, the meaning of this expression, in Bengal at least, is in modern days somewhat different from what was formerly attached to it as used in our text writers. In Bengal it is tacitly supposed that every joint family has a common idol in the dwelling-house, and that all the members participate in the daily worship of that idol, either by themselves or vicariously with the help of a ministering priest. This supposition is so far accurate that in Bengal the well-to-do families generally have a household god, for the purposes of daily worship. These families also, in different seasons of the year, set up earthen idols for temporary worship on certain festival days, generally during the period from the beginning of' September till the end of March. On these occasions, large sums are spent from the common funds, the whole family being supposed to be participating in a common worship. The permanent idols kept in a family dwelling-house have their special festival days in different parts of the year, which also furnish occasions for extraordinary expenditure of the family funds. It may even be said without exaggeration, that our Brahmanic religious instructors have elaborated so minute a system of household devotion, that almost every day in the year may be made an occasion for spending goodly sums of money, if the members of the family were so piously inclined. These pious observances are generally practised by united families of large means, and so far they constitute what is known in law as joint worship. But our original text writers did not understand joint worship exactly in that sense. The custom of keeping permanent idols in private dwellings seems to have originated at a later period than when most of our original digests were written. It is remarkable that these digests nowhere mention Debutter property. Public opinion even now reprobates the profession of a *devala* Brahmin, that is, one whose calling it is to worship the idol of another person for wages received; household gods are seldom mentioned in the majority of the *nibandha* treatises; nor is it said in those works that the worship of these divinities is an indispensable liability attaching to the family property. On the contrary, the pious works alluded to by most original treatises are generally srads and other obsequial ceremonies. Thus Raghunandana[1] says:—"The father being dead, the rite should be performed by the son as ordained. When there are many sons of the father, dwelling at the same place, what is performed by the eldest, having taken the consent of all, and with undivided property, that is to be taken as performed by all. Ending with the sapiṇḍīkaraṇa, the sixteen srads that there are the sons should in no case perform them separately,though their property be separated." Mitra Misra says:[2]—"Partition with a view to the increase of pious deeds, however, is spoken of by Manu and Prajāpati. 'Thus they should either live together, or separately, with a view to pious deeds. Pious deeds increase by separation; therefore partition is conducive to piety.' And the piety consists in the worship of gods, etc., for that alone is spoken of as separate when there is no living together. Thus Vṛhaspati, 'of persons dwelling under one arrangement for cooking, the worship of the forefathers and gods and Brahmans is single, but among the separated, that same worship takes place in every house.' The author of the Saṅgraha, however, says that the expression 'increase of piety' means and includes also the increase of piety by means of the establishment of the sacred fires, etc.; thus he says, by

1. मृते पितरि पुत्रेण क्रिया कार्य्या विधानतः।
बहवः स्युर्यदा पुत्राः पितुरेकत्र वासिनः।।
सर्व्वेषां तु मतं कृत्वा ज्येष्ठनैव तु यत् कृतम्।
द्रव्येण चाविभक्तेन सर्व्वैरेव कृतं भवेत्।।
सपिण्डीकरणान्तानि यानि श्राद्धानि षोडश।
पृथक् नैव सुताः कुर्य्युः पृथक् द्रव्या अपि क्वचित्।।
Suddhitattwa, p. 212.
2. Viramitrodaya Ch. II Part I, see. 7.

partition the paternal property is rendered the property of the sons: when the right of property arises, they commence, hence separation is pious commence,' *i.e.*, accomplish the ceremony of establishing the sacred fires, etc. But this has already been refuted by us when establishing the right of sons to the performance of the ceremonies enjoined by the Śruti and the Smṛti, even before partition, by reason of the son's right to the paternal property accruing by birth alone. Therefore by the expression 'pious deeds' are to be understood such pious deeds as the five great sacrifices."

Five great sacrifices

These five great sacrifices are thus described by Manu, ch. 3, śloka 70. I am here giving the purport of the śloka, referring to the translation of Sir W. Jones for a more literal rendering of the original. The first is the sacrifices for the sacred writ, that is, the veda; this is performed by daily recital of its verses. The sacrifice for the forefathers is the libation of water to the manes ; the sacrifice for the gods is the making of burnt-offerings in the fire ; the sacrifice for the organized beings is the strewing of food, cooked or uncooked, on the surface of the earth; and the fifth and last is the sacrifice for mankind, which consists in hospitality to the strangers who unexpectedly visit the house and seek hospitable reception for the day. We must not therefore think that when our treatise-writers mention the worship of gods as a pious deed, they mean thereby the worship of such household idols as are permanently kept or periodically set up within Bengal families. The treatise-writers mean the making of burnt-offerings on the fire, mostly as an essential feature of the worship of such ancient Ṛg Veda divinities as Indra and Rudra and Varuṇa and others. Vācaspati Miśra[1] says:—"Or let them divide for the purpose of doing pious deeds. So says Manu, 'Either they should live together; or separately, with a view to pious deeds. Pious

1. Vivādacintāmaṇi, p. 227.

deeds multiply by separation, therefore separation, is a pious act.' How are religious duties multiplied by partition of property? Vṛhaspati speaks on this subject: 'A single performance of the ceremonies of forefathers and of the worship of the deities and Brahmans may answer for brothers, who reside together and eat food dressed in the same place. In a family the members of which live apart, these duties are separately performed in the house of each of them.' Divided estates being the exclusive property of every heir, each may perform the ceremonies, sacrifices, etc., according to his own choice, without reference to the others. Hence partition multiplies religious performances."

Smṛti-Candrikā (Krishna-Swami Iyer, p. 18, para. 41, &c.)

But where the co-heirs become divided, religious duties increase, as observed by Gautama in the passage, ' religious duties increase in case of partition.' If it be asked how they increase, Nārada:—"The religious duties of unseparated brethren are single. When partition, indeed, has been made, religious duties become separate for each of them. 'Religious duties,' duties relating to the worship of manes, deities and Brahmins Vṛhaspati too. 'Among co-heirs living in commensality, *i.e.*, with one dressing of food, the worship of manes, deities, and Brahmins takes place in one house only; but in a family of divided brethren, the above acts are performed in each house separately.'"

Vyavahāra, Mayūkha, (p. 73 Viśvanāth Mārdlik). "The religious duty of unseparated brethren is single. After partition even that becomes separate for each. * * In an unseparated family, whether it consist of father, grandfather, sons, grandsons, father's brothers, brother's sons, the religious duty is single." After this the author enumerates a number of religious observances, mostly consisting in the above-mentioned five great sacrifices, and a number of srad ceremonies, enjoined to be per formed at particular seasons of the year, and on certain special days, such as the new moon immediately before the Durgā pūjā. In this passage I find the only mention of something like our modern household deities, the worship whereof is directed to be single in an unseparated family. This is not to be wondered at; for Nīlkaṇṭha, the author of the Vyavahāra-mayūkha, is of a comparatively recent date ; he, must have flourished within two hundred years from the present time, as appears from a date given in a work of his paternal grandfather Nārāyan Bhaṭṭa.[1]

The result therefore is that when we meet with mention of joint worship in the original texts, we are to understand such religious ceremonies as the srad and the five great sacrifices enjoined by Manu; while in modern times, that expression stands also for the celebration of the worship of permanent household idols, and likewise the great periodical festivals, at the head of which stands the Durgā pūjā, so far as Bengal is concerned. This change in the worship performed by a joint family marks a silent change which has gradually supervened over the religion itself of the people. The five great sacrifices of the days of Manu are no more; hardly one in a hundred understands their nature. The worship of fire is altogether obsolete; while hospitality to guests arrived at the house by chance would be a religious duty too expensive to be performed by middle class families of the present day; for the facilities of intercourse between different parts of the country being great, the number of such unexpected guests would be a legion, were it understood that joint Hindu families were prepared to welcome them. The place of these old religious duties is now occupied by the periodical feeding of Brahmins on special days, and also in wealthy families by the daily worship of the permanent household gods.

Having thus explained the expression "joint in food,

1. Vide Maudlik Introduction, p. ixxv.

worship and estate," I shall here cite a number of propositions promulgated in the original texts and in the decisions of our Courts, in connection with that community of interest which obtains among the members of a joint family.

Inequality in consumption of joint effects not taken an account of.

On account of this common interest, so long as the joint character lasts, it is settled law that any inequality in the enjoyment of the common effects is not to be taken an account of. Where the value of the interests vested in the several members is the same, in other words, where the members on a partition would each be entitled to an equal share, it may be that one member has many children, and therefore the expenses of his special section of the family are much larger than those of any other member; one member may have more daughters to give away in marriage; and the marriage of a daughter in all high caste respectable Hindu families involves an amount of expenditure which is almost becoming oppressive day by day. As the marriages in all these families are invariably arranged by the parents or other guardians of the bride and the bridegroom, the consequence is, that when the bridegroom is a particularly suitable match, both on account of parentage and also on the ground of good worldly circumstances and of being an educated person, the sums or perquisites demanded by the guardian of such a bridegroom are so exorbitant, that the parent of the bride is often reduced to very great straits for paying the marriage same.

Expenses of daughter's marriage.

Instances are not rare of the father of a number of girls having had to sell his dwelling house to meet the expenses of their marriage. Sometimes these parent are absolutely ruined and are brought to penury and a state of starvation from a comparatively prosperous worldly condition. This state of things is becoming intensified day by day inasmuch as the spread of education under the beneficent British rule has made it easier for parents to train up their sons with greater perfection than was ever known amongst the Hindus in ancient days. As a result, eligible bridegrooms of high attainments are appreciated to a great extent; parents of girls are also alive to the fact that these high attainments lead to success in life, whether in the form of a lucrative professional career, or of highly paid Government situations. These bridegrooms therefore command their own price in the market of matrimony. Their parents, even though educated and of enlightened principles, in practical affairs do not abate a jot of their exorbitant demands, taking shelter under an excuse that they themselves have to give their own daughters similarly exorbitant marriage portions. This social abuse has become peculiarly deep-rooted in our country, inasmuch as its mischievousness cannot not correct itself by the influence of mutual love between the bride and the bridegroom; for all our marriages are marriages of convenience, in which anything like a reciprocal attraction or mutual choice has no place. From time immemorial we have been married by our parents to whomsoever chance leads our parents to select; we thus become encumbered with families before we know that we are ourselves inclined in that direction, and but literally fulfil the duty of perpetuating the race. Domestic happiness in the European sense of the term is beyond the reach Hindu living in the shell of Brahmanic social usages. Even now those amongst us who have had the blessing of an education under the guidance of principles from Western Europe, are willing slaves to this social despotism. So ineradicable is the conservative instinct of the race, that these men of education have now learnt to despise the idea of a marriage by reciprocal choice, and to cite the instance of Byron and Landor to show that even marriages by reciprocal choice often end in disastrous consequences. They argue therefrom that it is hardly worth our while to combat the usage that governs us in matrimonial concerns.

Considered as family expenses.

These large marriage expenses must be met from the family funds in an undivided group of Hindu coparceners; ono coparcener cannot complain because the expenses of another in this respect are unduly large. Nor will these inequalities be taller into account at the time of the future partition.

Expenses of educating the youthful members of the family.

Again the education of the children of one member may be unusually costly; his sons may possess peculiar aptitudes for learning; it may be thought proper to nurse and cherish such aptitudes, and to spend money that they may be adequately developed and may bear good fruit. In such a case, it is not open to another coparcener to say that a single coparcener's concerns ought not to engross so large a proportion of the family funds. If the means of the admit of incurring such legitimate expenses, "and if the managing member or the majority of the coparceners think it proper to go to these expenses for the education of the sons of a particular parcener, these expenses must be borne notwithstanding that it may excite the jealousy of another wrong-headed parcener. All that the latter can ask for is that his own concerns also should be looked after with the same assiduity. It is no doubt always open to him to demand a partition; but partition of large properties is so cumbrous a transaction, that coparceners seldom willingly resort to it, unless goaded by some insufferable inconvenience or by some instance of injustice specially injurious to the interests of a particular member. Although therefore the remedy of partition is lawfully open to any member dissatisfied with the way in which the joint effects are being dealt with, in practice this remedy is not commonly sought. On the other band, the law is clear that unequal consumption by different members is not a matter for which any special liability attaches to those members; the principle on which such unequal consumption is allowed being that all such concerns of a particular member, as are legitimate and reasonable, are the common concerns of the whole family. Thus the marriage of a daughter of the family is an obligation incumbent upon the whole family so long as it continues joint, and the expenses incurred on account of it must be necessarily borne by all without reference to the respective interests of the members. This is so because a joint Hindu family is not in all points subject to those principles which determine the reciprocal rights and obligations of a partnership.

Joint family not like corporations in all respects.

Joint families are often likened by English text writers to corporations; but it would be erroneous on that account to suppose that they are partnerships to all intents and purposes. In a partnership concern, every member is accountable to his co-partners for every pice that he has spent over and above his legitimate share in the business.[1] But in a joint Hindu family, whether the shares of the members be equal or unequal, the unequal consumption of the family property by the different members, is sanctioned by law, and the greater or smaller necessities for legitimate expenses under which the members may lie are the necessities of all. By way of textual authority for the above proposition, I may cite Vīramitrodaya.[2] "By reason of the right being common, the text of Kātyāyana, which says:—'A coparcener is not liable for the consumption of any article

1. *Vide* Reforring order of Mr. Justice Mitter in the F. B. case of Obhoy Chunder Roy Chowdry *v.* Peary Mohan Gooho, 13 W. R. F. B. 75.
2. English Translation, p. 41.

which belongs to all the undivided relatives,' becomes consistent in its literal sense; inasmuch as his own right extends over every article; accordingly there can be no theft in such a case, as will be shown hereafter. "

It has been said in another case[1] that the joint family is a single entity as regards the enjoyment of joint property. As long as the members choose to continue in a state of commensality and joint fruition and enjoyment of the profits of the property, they cannot be said to possess individually any several proprietary right, other than the right to call for a partition. For proprietary purposes, they exist as a whole, somewhat in the character of a corporation. I have already pointed out that although it may be convenient to liken a joint family to a corporation as conceived under European systems of Jurisprudence, yet all the incidents of a partnership concern are not attributable to a family.

"In another case[2] Mr. Justice Markby said:—"Each partner is entitled to consume on his own account no more of the partnership property than the share of the profits. Each partner is the agent of the others, bound by his contract to protect and further the interests of his copartners, unless relieved from that responsibility by special agreement. If a partner appropriates more than his due share of the profits, he becomes immediately a debtor to the concern. But in a Hindu family, it is wholly different. No obligation rests on any one member to stir his finger, if he does not feel so disposed, either for his own benefit, or for that of the family; if he does do so, he gains thereby no advantage; if he does not do so, he incurs no responsibility, nor is any member restricted to the amount of share, which prior to division, he is to enjoy. A member of a joint family has only a right to demand that a share of existing family property should be separated and given him, and so long as the family union remains unmodified, the enjoyment of the family property

1. Chuckun Let Sing *v.* Poran Chunder Sing, 9 W. R. 483.
2. Rungun Money Dassee *v.* Kassinath Dutt, 3 B. L. R, O. J. 1.

is in the strictest sense common as against each other." The conclusion arrived at in this decision by Mr. Justice Markby, namely, that a managing member is not responsible to the other parceners for an account of the family funds, was overruled in the Full Bench case of Abhoy Churn Roy Chowdry;[1] the Chief Justice Couch observing it to be an extra-judicial opinion not necessary for the determination of the particular case. But it does not seem to follow therefrom that the observations made by Mr. Justice Markby upon the character of a joint family have no longer any force. They may be accepted as a correct representation of the legal conception involved in such a family.

General propositions regarding joint family as a whole.

It has been held as a consequence of the community of interest that where the family consists of two brothers governed by the Mitākṣarā law, both must join in making a mortgage of the family property; and if both have joined, there is no other impediment to the mortgage being valid, if at the time the mortgage deed is executed, there be no other members interested in the undivided estate. If sons are born to one of the brothers subsequently to the date of mortgage, such sons cannot question its validity, inasmuch as their interest had no existence at its date. The mortgage made by the two brothers is also to be considered as a joint transaction; it is not a mortgage of one half share by one brother, and of the other half share by the other brother. The whole amount lent by tl e mortgagee is a charge as well upon one brother's share as upon the other brother's share. Where there is nothing to show that the joint family has been separated or the joint property partitioned, neither of the brothers can have any defined or certain share which he can call his own, or for which he can sue alone without making all the members parties.[2] It has been held that so

1. 13 W. R. F. B. 75.
2. Rajaram Tewaree *v.* Lachman Pershad, 12 W. R. 478.

long as a Hindu family under the Mitākṣarā law is living in the joint enjoyment of the family property, without having come to an actual partition among themselves of that property, or an ascertainment and partition of their rights in it, so long no member of the family has any such proprietary right as he can alien or encumber. The property, under such circumstances, belongs to all the members of the family jointly, as to a corporation; and no one of the individual members has any share in it which he can deal with as property.[1] A member of a joint family cannot be styled the owner of a khas share, that being a term expressly applicable to the members of families who have separated and are in possession of separate shares.[2]

Families expand into village communities.

Sir Henry Maine[3] says, "The possessions of a Hindu, however divisible theoretically, are so rarely distributed in fact, that many generations constantly succeed each other without a partition taking place, and thus the family in India has a, perpetual tendency to expand into a village community." He here evidently refers to that particular description of the village community, instances of which are found in the North-Western Provinces and the Punjab, where in many places the whole of the village lands is held by a single set of coparcener, whose descent from a common ancestor is yet remembered, and who jointly are known as the village zemindars, though the share of many a single individual has by division become almost infinitessimal.

Difference modern and ancient village communities.

These village communities must be of modern growth, to my mind after the introduction of the complicated system of land tenure under the Mahomeedan rule. Had it not been

1. Mohabeer Pershad *v.* Ramyad Sing, 20 W. R. 194.
2. Lalla Nukched Lal *v.* Futteh Bahadur Lal, 24 W. R. 39.
3. Ancient Law, p. 228.

so, Vijñāneśvara would not have defined a village community, as I have abundantly noticed[1] in a previous part of these ancient Lectures to be consisting of persons belonging to different castes; whereas the very description given by Sir Henry Maine precludes the idea that the village communities, which expanded from joint families as their root, can be composed of members belonging to different castes.

In his History of Early Institutions, p. 106, Sir Henry Maine has thus described a joint Hindu family—"If a Hindu has become the root of a joint undivided family, which is technically said to be joint in food, worship and estate, it is not necessarily separated by his death; his children continue united for legal purposes as a corporate brotherhood; and some definite act of one or more brethren is required to effect a dissolution of the plexus of mutual rights and a partition of the family property. The family thus founded by the continuance of several generations in union is identical in outline with a group very familiar to the students of the older Roman law, the Agnatic kindred. The Agnates were that assemblage of persons who would have been under the patriarchal authority of some one ancestor, if he had lived long enough to exercise it. The joint family of the Hindus is that assemblage of persons who would have joined in the sacrifices at the funeral of some common ancestor, if he had died in their lifetime."

Joint condition occasionally recommended Ṛṣis.

The Brāhmanic law-givers declare that the severance of the joint character described above is conducive to the multiplication of pious works. Yet we find some Ṛṣis pointing to the advantages of living together. Thus in the Vīramitrodaya, p. 52 "The common abode of the brethren, however, is preferable, as well while the parents are alive as likewise when they are dead. Thus Śaṅkha and Likhita declare;—'They may live together if they choose; since

1. *Ante*, pp. 23, 91.

united, they are likely to attain a flourishing state'; the meaning is–'united,' that is, 'dwelling together,' they may attain a flourishing condition through mutual assistance in the acquisition of wealth. So Nārada says:—'Let the eldest brother alone maintain all, just like a father; or, let a younger brother, if capable, do so; for the preservation of the family requires capacity."

Incapacities of undivided members.

In the original texts, speaking of the joint family as a whole, it is said that the undivided members labour under special incapacities. Thus there is a śloka of Nārada cited by each of the five leading authorities for the five schools of the Hindu Law; I mean by the Mitākṣarā as representing the Benares school, by the Dāyabhāga of Bengal, by the Vivādacintāmaṇi of Mithila, by the Smṛti-candrikā of Madras and by the Vyavahāra-mayūkha of Mahārāstra. The same text is also found in the Vīramitrodaya the supplementary authority for the first of the above five schools. The drift of the śloka is, that when the family is in an undivided condition, there cannot be any gift or sale between the coparceners, such transactions being only possible between coparceners when they are divided. The śloka also says that in an undivided state one member cannot be a witness for another, or a surety for another. The law as to witness promulgated in the original texts precludes the entertainment of the modern idea that any person could be sworn as a witness in his own cause. The Hindu jurists considered the parties in a suit and the witnesses as essentially distinct and separate; they had no conception that the same person could possibly bear two such inconsistent characters. The ślokas 72 and 73[1] of the second chapter of Yājñavalkya enumerates number of persons who were legally incompetent to give their

1. स्त्री बाल वृद्ध कितव मत्तोन्मत्ताभिशस्तका:।
रङ्गावतारि पाषण्डि कूटकृद्. विकलेन्द्रिय:।।
पतिताप्तार्थ सम्बन्धि सहाय रिपुस्तकरा:।
साहसी दृष्ट दोषश्च निर्धूताद्यास्त्वसाक्षिण:।।

testimony as witnesses in a cause; among these we find a friend of either party, and one interested in the disputed property. The Hindu Law of evidence in fact bears a close analogy to many other bodies of law upon the same subject which are framed upon the principle of excluding particular classes of evidence, not upon modern ideas which are for the admission of all kinds of evidence, leaving it to the Judge to determine what weight ought to be attached to such evidence. Under the Hindu law, one who had interest in the property in suit, was precluded from giving his own evidence as to the truth or falsehood of his claim. Practically, it is so even now; for few cases are decided solely on the evidence of parties alone; but the Hindu Law went a step further, and declared interest in the disputed property as a disqualification for being a witness. The śloka of Nārada, therefore, prohibiting one coparcener, from being a witness for another undivided coparcener, only embodies a deduction from the general rule; since such coparceners are interested in the same property. But supposing the disputed property were not common property belonging to all, but separate property exclusively owned by one, it is difficult to see why one member should not be a witness for another, unless we are to suppose that in such a case, he came under the category of a 'friend;' thus it may be, that 'friendship' being one of the disqualifications of a witness, a joint coparcener came, in the idea of the old jurists, within the general role. The Mitākṣarā simply cites the above-mentioned śloka of Nārada, to point out by what marks the joint or separate condition of a family may be determined.[1] It says:—"Similarly, other marks of previous separation are specified by the same author. 'Divided brothers may do the duty of a witness, of a surety, and may make a gift and an acceptance also; not the unseparated, by any means.[2]

1. Para. 4, section 12, chapter II.
2. I am at a loss to see, how this text has been translated by Colebrooke thus-"Separated and unseparated brothers may reciprocally bear testimony, become sureties, bestow gifts, and accept presents." Unless I suppose that the reading of the text

The Dāyabhāga quotes the same text of Nārada, in para. 7, chapter XIV. Here the translation made by Colebrooke is : "Separated, *not* unseparated brothers may reciprocally bear testimony, become sureties, bestow gifts and accept presents." In para. 9, Jīmūtavāhana explains the Ṛṣi text, namely, that of Nārada, by saying that where one brother gives and another accepts, or where one brother becomes a witness in a bond taken by another from a third party on lending money to him, or becomes surety for another brother, then the brothers are inferred to be separate ; since the law says that such transactions are illegal as between undivided brothers. In this instance also we see, as I have already noticed more than once, that the original texts seldom speak of joint families as constituted by distant relations, but generally confine their remarks to families composed of brothers, or of a father and his sons.

In the Vivādacintamaṇi the same text of Nārada has been thus rendered by Prasannakumar Tagore:—"Divided brothers can be witnesses to the concerns of each other ; can be sureties for each other; can make or receive presents; but undivided ones cannot do so" (p. 311).

Vyavahāra-mayūkha[1]:– "Separated brothers and not

which was used by Colebrooke was entirely different from what I find in the Edition of the Mitākṣarā, issued by the Committee of Public Instruction, the translation by Colebrooke is inaccurate. Even supposing the text to have been different we must pronounce that text to be incorrect since it makes the context meaningless. Vijñāneśvara wants to point out certain marks distinguishing separated coparceners, and he cites Nārada's text to show that certain transactions, if observed to be taking place mutually between the members of the same family, may legitimately lead to the conclusion that they are not joint. These mutual dealings are that one member is becoming witness for another, or his surety, or is accepting a gift from another. But if both the separated and the unseparated brothers can legally enter into such mutual dealings, how are these translations to be set down as marks of separation ?

1. Mandlik, p. 75.

unseparated brothers, may be witnesses or sureties; or may lend or borrow in respect of each other."

The same text is quoted in para. 8, chapter XVI, Smṛti Candrikā on which the author remarks that the acceptance of a present, and the fact of one becoming a witness for another, and so forth, are arguments for the inference that partition must have taken place.

In the Vīramitrodaya, the text is found in see. 2, chapter X, and has been thus rendered by Babu Gopal Chandra Sarkar. "Separated, and not unseparated kinsmen, may reciprocally bear testimony, bestow gifts, and accept presents."

Although thus we find in the original texts that these transactions are said to be invalid and inadmissible, when taking place as among unseparated members, the, law must be considered as practically obsolete now. We shall see in the next Lecture that the unseparated member is not precluded from holding property exclusively to his own use. That being so, there is nothing to prevent the transfer of such exclusive property from the ownership of one member to another, either by sale or by gift or by any other method of alienation. As regards the capacity for becoming a witness, Courts in British India are not bound to administer the Hindu Law of Evidence, and the Evidence Act has discarded almost all the disqualifications of a witness which prevailed in former times. No Court of Justice will now refuse to take the sworn testimony of any person in a suit simply because he happens to be undivided in estate with a party in the suit. Nor does the modern law declare that a deed or bond executed in favour of one member is inoperative because attested by his undivided coparcener; whatever weight the Courts may attach to it when a document so attested is proved in the trial of a suit by the sole evidence of such a member. He can also be accepted as a surely provided he has separate property from which, if any default be made by the principal, the proper compensation may be realized.

The members together constitute a single entity.

'This old law laid down by the original texts prohibiting the members from reciprocally bearing testimony, or becoming sureties or giving or accepting presents seems to be founded upon the principle that all the members together constitute a single entity in the eye of law. But the conception of this unity has no force when there is an infraction by the members of one another's undoubted rights.

This principle of unity not always applicable.

Thus where there was a Thakoorbaree belonging to all the members, and there was a certain pathway leading from the family dwelling-house to the said Thakoorbaree when the passage was bricked up by some of the members, it has been held that the members, whose access to the Thakoorbaree was thus obstructed, had a right to bring a suit to have the obstruction removed. Nor would the mere disuse of the pathway for four or five years constitute an abandonment of the plaintiff's right, inasmuch as such a claim was not a right of user but a right based on the status of a joint family.[1]

In another case one member wanted to build a nautchghur in an open space of the courtyard around which all the members had their dwelling-houses. On being stopped by another member from going on with the building, the first member brought a suit for a declaration of his right to carry on the building without obstruction on the part of the other members. The courtyard formed a portion of the dwelling-ground upon which the various members of the family resided. It was admitted to be joint

1. Chunder Kant Chowdhry *v.* Nandlal Chowdhry, 16 W. R. 277.

and undivided property belonging to the whole family. The plaintiff contended that it was a courtyard or compound attached to the particular house in which he lived, that he had exclusive possession of it for a long time, and that he could do with it what he liked. It was found as a fact that it had been held by the plaintiff for a long time. No family partition was alleged by the plaintiff. Upon these facts it was held that the plaintiff had no right to build on the spot. Pecar. J. observed, "In our judgement, as we understand joint possession under Hindu Law, that peculiar exclusive possession of a plot of a common dwelling house, or set of dwelling houses, which one member of a joint family obtains very commonly without an actual partition having been come to between the members of the family, is a possession which must be referred to the continuing consent of his co-sharers. So long as no actual partition is come to, either as a result of a suit, or formally between the parties themselves, or evidenced by long acknowledgement on the part of the members of the family, the possession is merely that which, for convenience sake, is conceded by all the members jointly to each one of them; and it may be put an end to, and a completely new arrangement come to at any time by the members of the family if they think fit to make the change. As long, however, as this peculiar state of exclusive possession is allowed to remain, it must be taken that the acquiescing members of the family concede to the person who has the exclusive possession, all reasonable rights of user of his separate plot, or separate portion of the dwelling house, as is necessary for the ordinary purposes of residence, having regard of course to the circumstances of Hindu life; but the concession on the part of the acquiescing members does not go to the extent of enabling the possessor of the dwelling house to alter the character of the property, or to do anything with it which is not consistent with such user of it as might be ordinarily expected to take place. If he desires to build a new and additional structure upon a portion of the house ground, he has no right to do so, and in that way materially to alter the condition of the property without obtaining the assent of his co-sharers."[1]

The exclusive possession by one member of a particular portion out of the joint immoveable property, such as has been described in the case cited above, seems to carry with it a right on the part of the member in exclusive possession to create a mokururee right in favour of a third party. In the case of Jotee Roy *v.* Bhuchuck Meah, 20 W. R. 288, it was held that when such a mokururee right had been created by one co-sharer during the undivided condition of the family without objection on the part of the other members, the said tenure could not be set aside by those to whom on a subsequent partition of the family property that particular portion of the joint immoveable property might be allotted. That a single member is not competent to deal at his pleasure with the joint property is further illustrated by the case of Nundun Lall *v.* Mr. Lloyd, 22 W. R., 74. In this case, Phear, J. in effect lays down that a joint proprietor is entitled to ask from his co-proprietors, to be allowed to enjoy his share of the property in any mode in which it can be enjoyed as an undivided share. And he has a right to insist drat neither his co-proprietor nor anybody claiming through him should without his consent take exclusive possession of any portion of the joint property to which he has not at the time a subsisting right of exclusive possession. He can complain that in the matter of sowing a crop of indigo, he has not been consulted; that he has good reasons as a joint cultivator to object to its being grown, and to ask for an injunction restraining another co-sharer from sowing indigo upon such joint land. This was not exactly the case of a joint family, inasmuch as the plaintiff alleged his share to be a particular fraction of the whole, whereas according to Appoovier's case, no member of a joint family can predicate

1. Sheo Pershad Sing *v.* Leelah Sing, 20 W. R, 160.

of himself that his share is such and such a fraction of the joint property. The above case seems much rather to be an instance of what Sir Henry Maine calls a joint family expanded into a village community. In the eye of law, such a village community, in which different co-proprietors, or groups of co-proprietors are registered as fractional shareholders, ought to be regarded as a group of so many separated families, whose patrimony, consisting of the village lands, has not been yet divided by metes and bounds. We shall subsequently see that the absence of such a division of the land by metes and bounds does not impress a joint character on the family. This case therefore is an authority that although a body of co-proprietors may be so far separated in interest from one another as to call themselves owners of particular fractional shares of the entire village lands, yet so long as the lands have not been divided by metes and bounds, the joint use of the lands must be made by all together in consultation with one another, and one cannot put the land to any use without a reference to the others. This is as regards the *use* of the lands; which in a manner, at least temporarily, alters the condition of the lands; as for instance, sowing indigo prevents the land from being used for sowing other ordinary crops, such as paddy and wheat, and the winter crops called the *rubby.* These crops are such as may come to the use of every co-proprietor, whereas indigo plant is a special kind of crop, which is not an article of ordinary consumption and which in fact is useless unless manufactured into an article of commerce by an elaborate process. A co-proprietor therefore may very reasonably raise objections if land in which he is interested should be grown with indigo plants without his consent.

If however, there are tenants upon the land, who have been inducted into their tenures, by the whole proprietary body, in that case it has been held that payment of rent to a single joint proprietor would discharge the tenant from his whole liability, provided the whole rent payable for his tenure has been paid by him.[1] But where no partition had been made of the joint landed property, and a tenant had been admitted into the tenure by some only of the coparceners, and where no such custom was proved as authorised them to admit a tenant without the consent of all, it was held that the tenant was liable to be ejected at the instance of those who did not take part in admitting him as a tenant.[2]

In one case the plaintiff sued for declaration of his right to occupy one half of a Chundee Mundub for *pooja* purposes, to a joint right in which he had been previously declared to be entitled. The Court said that the mode of enjoyment of ijmalee property was a matter for private arrangement, and not for judicial determination. The right having been once previously declared to be joint by the Court, the particular mode of its enjoyment must be left to the parties themselves, there being no rule of law by which that enjoyment might be regulated, save and except the general one that joint owners must occupy jointly.[3]

---

1. Baboo Oodit Narain Sing *v.* Mr. H. Hudson, 2 W. R. Act X Rulings, p 15.
2. Ghunshyam Sing *v.* Runjeet Sing, 4 W. R. Act X Rulings, p. 39.
3. Romes Chunder Bhattacharjee *v.* Soorjo Coomar Bhattacharjee, 5 W. R. 90.

Chapter 4

On The Managing Member of A Joint Hindu Family

A younger brother may be a manager—Son connot demand partition of father's self-acquisitions—'Father entitled to be the manager—Senior member of the family becomes the manager—The word 'karta' confined to Bengal—Whether in Bengal, father as 'karta' can be restrained by Sons–'Karta' accountable–Bengal father as 'karta' accountable–Manager's acts how, far binding upon the rest–Management of ancestral trade-Manager cannot enlarge period of limitations–Manager's power is confined to joint properly—Manager's powers terminated by partition—Bengal son cannot doomed partition.

A younger brother may be a manager

The united condition described in the last Lecture of a number of brethren, when the joint family is composed of the sons of the same parents, leads us to the consideration of the managing member, as in the text of Nārada quoted towards the end of the last Lecture, it is a managing member who is alluded to by saying that the family is kept up by capacity; although therefore ordinarily the eldest brother becomes the managing member, yet the text of Nārada clearly indicates that the same rule is not invariably followed, but that even a younger brother possessed of capacity, may undertake the family management and thus become its head or organ to the outside world. Instances of such headships vested in younger brothers are not rare in many an existing joint family of the day. I may mention a wealthy family of this very city, which was in a prosperous condition about forty years ago and lived in very great affluence. At present all traces of its former prosperity are nearly gone. I allude to the well-known family of Ram Doolal Sarkar, who left two sons Asutosh and Promothonath; of whom the younger brother, Prom-othonath was universally recognized as the manager of the vast estate left by their father Ram Doolal. When the family consists of a father and his sons, it is the father who ordinarily becomes the head, and even if it be a family governed by the Mitāsharā law, the sons are not competent to deal independently with the joint funds. Thus it is said in the Smṛticandrikā[1] that the sons have no right to independent while their father is alive. The author quotes a text from Sankha, which declares that although the sons obtain a ownership in all property immediately after their birth, yet they should not resort to a partition of the family effects so long as the father lives. They are not competent to do so; for whether in dealing with the property, or in religious works, they are not independent of the father, but should always abide by the father's advice and directions. The author of the Smṛticandrikā confirms the above *dictum* of Sankha by quoting Hārīta also. According to this latter authority, a son during the lifetime of the father, cannot make any acceptance of wealth, or any expenditure; he should not even reprimand the servants for misbehaviour on their part. In all these matters, the son must in every case take the permission of the father before he interferes with the affairs of the family. Hārīta says that the son is incompetent to accept wealth; this is explained by the author of the Smṛticandrikā as enjoyment of wealth. But considering that this acceptance of wealth is coupled with the expenditure of wealth; it seems to me that Hārīta intends to deny the competency of the son either to give an

1. Chapter 1, section 18.

acquittance or authorise an expenditure with out the permission of the father.

Son cannot demand partition of father's self-aquistitions.

Although in the above-quoted text of Sankha, it is declared that the sons are not independent of their father in making a partition, we must take the text to be confined to the father's self-acquisitions ; for in the Mitākṣarā[1] it is distinctly said that notwithstanding the mother's capacity to bear more children, and notwithstanding the father's unwillingness, the sons are competent to demand a partition of the grandfather's wealth. Similarly (para. 9) if an undivided father makes a gift of grandfather's property, or sells it, the son is not so far dependent as to be bound to abide by the same; for he is entitled to enter his protest against the same. As regards the self-acquisitions made by the father, the son, though a co-sharer, should not exercise his right of prohibition ; but should permit his father to make a sale or gift according to his pleasure. The reason for this distinction. between the father's own acquisitions and what has descended from the grandfather is stated rather in an unintelligible way by Vijñāneśvara. He says (para. 10) that although both in the paternal property and in the property left by the grandfather, the son has a vested right from the moment of his birth, yet the son is bound to obey the father so far as the paternal property is concerned; but in the property of the grandfather, the ownership of both is undistinguishable (such is the language); therefore the son has a right of prohibiting the disposition of the grandfather's property by the father at his pleasure. This mode of making a distinction can hardly commend itself as rational. It is declared that the son's ownership in the paternal property from the moment of his birth is complete; yet he should not control the disposition of it; but he should do so as regards

1. Chapter 1, section 5, para. 8.

grandfather's wealth. No reason, however, that we can understand is assigned for the difference. It would seem from another passage that upon this point the author of the Mitākṣarā had not himself a clear conception as to what law he intended to lay down. For in his Preliminary Discourse on the nature of ownership,[1] the author had in unmistakeable terms propounded the doctrine of the father's dependence upon the sons in dealing with all immoveable property, whether self-acquired or ancestral. But in para. 10, section 5 he generally says that the sons should permit their father to deal with his self-acquisitions just as he chooses. Here he does not confine this power of the father to moveable property alone. Probably the real opinion of the author was to declare the uncontrolled power of the father over only the moveable property acquired by himself ; while all immoveable property, whether acquired by himself or ancestral, was subject in its disposition to the control of the sons.

Mitra Misra, in his Vīramitrodaya, however, has come to a conclusion which involves the conception of a more enlarged power of disposition vested in the father. He says:– (p. 7.4) "'The substance of what is intended in the above texts is this : Although the ownership of the sons and the grandsons in the property of the father and the grand father arises by birth alone, still by reason of the texts previously cited, the sons being dependent on the father with respect to the father's self-acquired property, and the father being entitled to superiority on account of his being the acquirer, the sons must give their assent to the disposal by the father of his self-acquired property, excepting land and slaves, by reason of the previously cited text, namely, 'immoveables and bipeds, etc.' With respect to the grandfather's property, however, there is also the power of forbidding any disposal by the father; but with respect to property which was not recovered by the grandfather, but was recovered by the

1. *Vide* chapter I, section 1, para. 27.

father, the sons are certainly dependent on the father's will; although the property be the grandfather's; but as regards gems and pearls, etc., though inherited from the grandfather, the father alone has independence, by reason of the previously cited texts, namely, ' The father is master of all the gems, and pearls and corals, etc.' "

The two texts referred to in the above extract, are both found in the Mitākṣarā The, first is the text quoted in the Mitākṣarā chapter I, section 1, para. 27, and runs thus:—"Though immoveables and bipeds have been acquired by a man himself, a gift or sale of them should not be made without convening all the sons." The other text is found in para. 21, same chapter and same section, and runs thus-" The father is the master of the gems, pearls, and corals, and of all: but neither the father, nor the grandfather is the master of the whole immoveables estates." Mitra Misra thinks (p. 16, section 29, Eng.) that this latter text is an authority for saying that the moveable property of the grandfather is at the entire disposal of the father. But the Mitākṣarā does not make any distinction between the grandfather's moveable and immoveable property.[1] On the contrary, the Mitākṣarā restricts the father's power over even his self-acquired property of the immoveable class.[2] For chapter I, section 5, para. 10, says:—"Consequently the difference is this:–Although he has a right by birth in his father's and his grandfather's property; still, since he is dependent on his 'father in regard to the paternal estate and since the father has a predominant interest as it was acquired by himself, the son must acquiesce in the father's disposal of his own acquired property: but since both have indiscriminately a right in the grandfather's estate, the son has a power of interdiction." Chapter I, section 1, para. 27, says:—"Therefore it is a settled point, that property in the paternal or ancestral estate is by birth, although the father

1. *Vide* Mitak. chapter I, section 5, para. 10.
2. *Vide Id.* chapter I, section I, para. 27.

has independent power in the disposal of effects other than immoveables, for indispensable acts of duty, and for purposes prescribed by the texts of law, as gifts through affection, support of the family, relief from distress, and so forth: but he is subject to the control of his sons and the rest in regard to the immoveable estate whether acquired by himself or inherited from his father or other predecessor, since it is ordained;" and then follows the test of Vyāsa. (which has been repeatedly referred to in the course of my Lectures), (*ante*, p. 5) as an authority for the above proposition. Para. 29 says:—"While the sons and grandsons are minors, and incapable of giving their consent to a gift and the like; or while brothers are so and continue unseparated ; even one person who is capable may conclude a gift, hypothecation or sale of immoveable property, if a calamity affecting the whole family requires it, or the support of the family renders it necessary, or indispensable duties, such as the obsequies of the father or the like, make it unavoidable."

Now, what is the effect of all these passages, read together? Simply, this:—A son acquires a right by birth both in the paternal and in the ancestral property; that the father can dispose of moveable property, for the support of the family and certain other purposes; that if the other members are minors or otherwise incapacitated for giving consent to a transaction affecting the family funds, the father as well as any other single member, whereby seems to be intended a managing member, can deal with immoveable property for those purposes ; that he can dispose of his self-acquired moveable property absolutely at his pleasure; and that the immoveable property of all kinds is beyond his control, except in the case of what are called legal necessities. The Mitākṣarā explains the nature of these necessities by the mention of distress, family subsistence, and unavoidable religious duties. Even in the case of legal necessities, immoveable ancestral property can be dealt with by one when the other members are labouring under an incapacity by reason of minority, lunacy, imprisonment, and it may be absence in a far-off land. Vijñāneśvara nowhere says that the moveable property received from the grandfather is at the unfettered disposal of the father.

At this place I ought to notice the translation by Colebrooke of para. 24, chapter I, section 1 of the Mitākṣarā The conclusion of this para. has been rendered thus;–"So, according to our opinion, the father has power, to give away such effects, though acquired by *his* father," By' such effects' is intended 'moveable property.' Now the words in the original Sanskrit are :

एवमस्मन्मतेऽपि पित्रार्जितानामप्येतेषां पितुर्दानाधिकारी वचनात्।

As translated by Colebrooke, this passage of the Mitākṣarā would seem to sanction the proposition that the father's power over the moveable property inherited from the grandfather is unrestricted. But I am afraid that the translation here is not quite correct. The word '*his*,' in the midst of the words, 'though acquired by *his* father' is not in the original. The original text simply rendered would run:—'In this way, in our opinion also, the power to give on the part of the father as regards these, even though acquired by the father, follows from the text these" by 'their' are to be understood 'the gems, pearls and corals.' That is to say, moveable property, in general. What the author of the Mitākṣarā intends to say may be thus explained. We must remember that these passages form a part of that quaint discussion on the topic of ownership with which the author introduces the subject of partition. In the course of it he notices an adverse opinion which inculcates that ownership does not accrue by birth, but by the death of the previous owner. In fact this is the opinion of the Dāyabhāga school. He controverts that opinion on the strength of the text which declares that (para. 21) "of gems, pearls, and corals, of all in fact, the father is the master; but of the whole immoveable property, neither the father, nor the grand father is the master." Vijñāneśvara says to his opponent–you argue that although ownership arises by death, yet there being an express text giving ownership over moveable property to the father alone, the conclusion is clear that all moveable property is at the father's disposal. But I reply that even the grandfather himself being declared as not the lord of the immoveable property shows that the right of the son accrues by birth : otherwise, why should not the grandfather be the master of his own acquired immoveable property? And that being so, gems, pearls, and corals and such effects, although self-acquisitions of the father, are yet jointly owned by the father and the son. But there being an express text, the father can dispose of his self-acquired moveable property.

That this is the opinion of Vijñāneśvara as deducible from the above passages is confirmed by Visveśvara Bhatta the author of the well-known commentary on the Mitākṣarā, styled the Subodhinī, quotations from which are constantly to be met with in the footnotes of Colebrooke's Mitākṣarā. I cite the whole of that passage below.[1], "This is the purport:—Self-acquired property, either than immoveable, without even the permission of those entitled to permit (*i. e.*, entitled to be consulted)–can be given from affection. But (an objector says) if this be so, then there world result a conflict with the text of Viṣṇu, which speaks of an affectionate gift of even immoveable property. Therefore the author says:—[Viśveśvara Bhatta quotes a part of the Mitākṣarā test by way of reference]. This is the purport. As regards even self-acquired immoveable property-without

---

1. अयमभिप्रायः। स्थावरव्यतिरिक्तं स्वोपार्जित वस्तु अनुज्ञार्हानुमतिमन्तरेणापि पित्रा प्रीत्या दातुं शक्यते इति। ननु यद्येवं तर्हि स्थावरस्यापि प्रीतिदानप्रतिपादने (के?) न विष्णुवचनेन विरोध इत्यत आह। यत्रार्त्थं (यत्तु भर्त्रा?) प्रीतेनेत्यादि विष्णुवचनमिति। अयमाशयः। स्वोपार्जितेष्वपि स्थावरेषु अनुज्ञासमर्थासमर्थानुज्ञार्ह सर्व्वानुमतिमन्तरेण दानानधिकारः। इतरेषु तुन अनुमत्यपेक्षा इति। MS. Cal. Sans. College, No. 1342, leaf 61, p. 2.

the permission of all entitled to permit (entitled to be consulted), whether capable of permitting or incapable of permitting–there is no right to make a gift. As regards the other (kinds of property) there is no necessity for (taking) a permission."

By 'entitled to permit' is evidently meant 'a person whose permission is indispensable in making a transfer, he having a right in the property.' By 'capable of permitting' is evidently meant 'a person who has come of sage, or whose consent is valid in law.' The result of what Viśveśvara Bhatta writes is that he did not understand Vijñāneśvara to sanction the father's unfettered power of dealing with grandfather's moveable property.

The truth seems to be that in declaring the father as having an absolute right over the grandfather's moveable property, Mitra Misra has taken a hint from the Dāyabhāga school. Whether this declaration of law will ultimately receive judicial recognition or not, is a matter beyond my foresight, but I thought it my duty here to point out an inaccuracy in the current translation of the Mitākṣarā which might be supposed to countenance the view adopted by Mitra Misra.

In these passages just now discussed, we find repeated mention of grandfather's property as contrasted with the property of the father. Here, we must take the word 'grandfather' standing for any ancestor whatsoever. This appears from what Nīlakaṇṭha says at the very beginning of that section of his Vyavahāra-mayūkha which deals with the subject of Inheritance.[1] "Strictly speaking the wor' grandfather is indicative of a class, (not of the grandfather alone); otherwise, there would arise an absence of equal ownership of the great-grandson in the wealth received from the great-grandfather, etc."

---

1. P. 33, Mandlik.

Father's entitled to be the manager.

We have thus seen that so far as the right of partition is concerned, the dependence of the sons upon their father, is confined to the case of the father's self-acquisitions alone. In other matters, however, the sons are bound to be obedient to the father. Although it is now admitted as a proposition of law beyond all doubt that a son takes by birth a vested interest in immoveable ancestral property, although his interest in the father's lifetime and even before partition is a present interest of a proprietary or coparcenery nature; and although he has a right to enforce partition of the ancestral estate; yet until partition takes place, or until the death of the father, natural or civil, the father, by reason of his paternal relation, and his position as head and manager of the family, is entitled to make lawful disposition of the property in the interest of the family. In chapter I, section 5, paras 9 and 10 of the Mitākṣarā a, son is said to be dependent and bound to acquiesce, and has no right of interference, within certain limits ; the father is also said to have a predominant interest in his self-acquired property. Paras 9 and 10 have been held as an authority declaring how far the son's power of interdiction in the father's disposition of property extends, and showing that the power of disposition within certain limits is centred in the father. The son's enjoyment of the property is subject to the dispositions lawfully made by the father, and, if dissatisfied, the son's remedy will lie in any right that he may possess to enforce partition of the estate. Accordingly where a son did not like to live with his step-mother, and had taken forcible possession of an ancestral house after it had been vacated by a tenant, in spite of his father's opposition; it was held that the son was not competent to do so; that he could not insist upon occupying property which the father wanted to let to tenants on rent; that the father was entitled to make such arrangements with regard to ancestral property as he thought proper.[1] In this case the Chief Justice of the Allababad High Court, observed that the son's right to interfere in certain events to prevent waste, or to enforce partition in the father's lifetime even without the latter's consent, only implies a proprietary interest; it does not carry with it the incident of dominium. The sons have not independent dominion, although they have a proprietary right.

This dependence of the sons upon the father is termination by certain circumstances which are clearly set forth in, chapter I, para. 28, Smṛticandrikā, and in the following paragraphs. The main result of the explanations embodied in these paragraphs is connected with the question, what are the occasions which can justify sons in demanding partition, or even in making partition, without willingness on the part of the father. At the outset the author says in general terms that the dependent condition of the sons continues so long as the father conducts himself in an unexceptionable way, so long as he is blameless or faultless, as the language goes. Wherein consists this blameableness or faultlessness sufficiently clear from what follows. If he, the father; be addicted to vices proceeding from passion, the dependent condition of the sons immediately terminates. The word in the original is 'vyasana'; which term has a pecular meaning, thus explained by Wilson. A vyasana is a fault, vice, crime, or frailty, arising from desire or anger. This explanation is in accordance with what Manu says in verses 47 and 48 of chapter 7. In verse 47 he says:—"The group of vices taking their rise from desire are the following ten : hunting, gambling, sleeping in the day, calumny, whoring, drinking, the three amusements of dance and song and instrumental music, and purposelessly roaming hither and thither." In verse 48 he says:—"The group of vices taking their rise from anger or ill-feeling are the following eight: ill natured cavil, violence, malevolence, envy, hatred,

1. Bulldeo Das v. Sham Lal, 1. L. R. 1 All. 78.

misappropriation, abuse and assault." These eighteen descriptions misbehaviour are to be so called when a person is guilty of excess, some of these acts, such as instrumental music and hunting, being quite innocent when moderately indulged in. Probably Manu's meaning was, that people are naturally prone to run to excess in these propensities. He therefore proscribes them unqualifiedly. If modern Western society were judged by the standard thus set up, hardly a single gentleman would obtain a verdict in his favour as free from vice. Now Smṛti Candrikā lays down that this kind of vice disentitles a father to act as the head of the family, and emancipates the sons from their dependent position. The eldest son, under such circumstances, may assume the headship; may receive money or authorize expenditure or govern the household. Or even a younger may become the manager if the eldest give his assent to such an arrangement.' But the younger must have superior capacity for business , in order to lay claim to such a position. Capacity infact is the element which determines the qualification for being the head. Fitness and personal efficiency are the principles that guide the election of a managing member. The author of the Smṛti Candrikā, therefore says that a vicious life, imbecility and a prolonged invalid condition incapacitate the father from acting as the managing member. Even extreme old age, accompanied by dotage and weakened intellect, is a ground for taking from him the leading position in the family. In all these matters, Hindu Law, as developed by these later commentators, exhibits a just and rational regard for the welfare of the family, and subordinates to that end the claims of the father to respect and considerable. As I have said before, the original texts generally speak of a family as if it were composed wholly of the issue of a single stock; a father and his sons, or a number of brothers living together in a joint condition. But modern administrators have to deal with a large number of cases in which the family embraces cousins and uncles and grand-uncles. In such cases, the question, who ought to be the managing member, receives no assistance from the original texts; the judges therefore will have to apply principles of analogy drawn from the authorities, and from their own notions of equity. The procedure of applying the principle of analogy in cases not expressly provided for, is countenanced by the original texts. Thus in the Vīramitrodaya, Chapter II, Part I, Section 10,[1] it is said:—"Although this has beens ordained with reference to what the husband is to give, to a wife who is superseded by the marriage of another wife, still by parity of reason, it is to be applied in the present case where the question occurs (as to what should be allotted to a wife who has received woman's property). For Baudhāyana says:- 'What is affirmed of even one, among many that have a common attribute, same is to be extended to all, since they are declared to be similar." This therefore is an express authority for holding that analogy is a principle recognized from very early days, From the days of Baudhāyana, at least, in the working out of Hindu Law. If we apply this principle to the case of the managing member, we should probably lay down that where the family embraces cousins and uncles, seniority of age, and capacity for business, are the two qualifications constituting a title to the position of a managing member. I do not know the existence of any particular case where it has been so laid down. But Sir Henry Maine in his treatise on Early Institutions, (p. 199) Says:—"The family, according to the Hindu theory, is despotically governed by its head; but if he dies and the family separates at his death, the property is equally divided between the sons. If, however, the family does not separate, but allows itself to expand into a joint family we have the exact mixture of election and of doubtful succession which we find in the early examples of European primogeniture. The eldest son, and after him his eldest son is ordinarily the

1. P. 58, English.

manager of the affairs of the joint family, but his privileges theoretically depend upon election by the brotherhood, and he may be set aside by it, and when he is set aside, it is generally in favour of a brother of the deceased manager, who on the score of greater age is assumed to be better qualified than his nephew for administration and business."

Senior member of the family becomes the manager

The proposition that the eldest son of the eldest son assumes the managership is not borne out by actual practise. Nor is there, as far as we can see, anything like a formal election. What takes place is, that on the death of a managing member, the senior member in the fraternity, naturally and without any express sanction from the others, takes up the government of the joint concern. If the senior member be unfit or unwilling, then something like an informal consultation is held among the coparceners, and the member who in the estimation of all stands as a capable person, is nominated to the vacant headship. Sometimes in cases of families possessed of extensive properties, subordinate managership are constituted, these subordinate managers superintending different departments, one being placed at the head of the zamindary affairs, another supervising trading concerns, a third superintending the household expenditure, and so forth; while all may be subject again to the general control of a paramount head. In many cases, there is no paramount head, but the general control is vested in the whole of the parceners. No invariable rule, in fact, can be laid down with regard to the organization by which the management of joint family concerns is carried on; this organization being regulated by convenience and mutual arrangement among the members.

The word 'Kurta' confined to Bengal.

In Bengal, a manager is called a Karta. This term is not to be found in the original texts ; nor does the word bear any signification of that kind in Sanskrit, although. it is a Sanskrit word, and means simply' one who acts, who does something, an agent.' It also sometimes means 'the creator.' But in the Bengali language all other primitive significations of the term have been so absolutely merged in this sense of the manager of a joint family, that because the father in ordinary cases is the manager, the father is often called the karta. Thus sons arrived at manhood who live in the same house with their father generally refer to him by this name of the karta. Instead of saying that father did such and such a thing, they would in ordinary parlance say that the karta did such and such a thing. This is somewhat similar to the practice of fast young Englishmen refering to their father as the governor. In the Bengali, term karta when applied by the sons to their father does not imply the slightest disrespect, and is not indicative of any frivolous spirit on the part of the sons.

The position of the karta in a Bengal family has been thus described in a case:—"The coparceners manage the property together, and the karta is but the mouth-piece of the family, chosen and capable of being changed by themselves. The family may in this respect be likened to a committee with the karta as chairman. No doubt in practice, the members of the family often do leave pretty nearly everything in the hands of the karta and under his control, but this is in most cases the result of the respect which the seniority in age and generation is apt everywhere to engender, and most especially in the case of a Hindu joint family. When it takes place, it is a willing abdication of personal care and supervision. It is not a distinct agency or delegation of separate authority each member may still at all times interfere if he chooses. And he may always insist upon division, if he is dissatisfied with the management; even where the members of the family leave the most unrestricted power in the hands of the karta, it is, I believe, usual to hold a family conclave, at least once in the year to confirm and approve of what the karta has done, and to discuss jointly what should be done hereafter as to the family affairs. Unless, therefore, something is shown to the contrary, every adult member of an undivided family, living in commensality with the karta, must be taken as between himself and the karta, to be a participator in, and authorizer of, all that is from time to time done in the management of the joint property to this extent, namely, that he cannot, without further cause, call the karta to account for it. Of course, it may as a matter of fact be the case in a given family that the karta is the agent of, and stands in a fiduciary and accountable relation to, one or more of the members. It would be easy to imagine a state of things under which he had become the trustee of the property relative to his adult coparceners, or in which, by reason of his fraud or other behaviour, they or one of them had acquired an equity to call upon him for an account. But he does not wear the character of accountability, merely because he occupies the position of karta,"[1]

In Bengal, when the family is composed of a father and his sons, the position of the latter is entirely subordinate; the father must necessarily be the karta, and it would be wrong to suppose, as seemingly countenanced by the observations quoted above, that the sons are competent to set him aside from the position of the manager, or to interfere, or to take exceptions to the mode of his management. Supposing the joint property to consist of what has been inherited by the father from his ancestors, and of what has been acquired by himself, the power of the father in Bengal is absolute. He in fact is the sole owner; he can do just as he likes with the whole; and the sons occupy a position somewhat similar to that of the female members in a family governed by the Mitākṣarā law; or we may even go so far as to say that the position of the sons in a Bengal

1. Chuckun Lal Sing v. Poran Chunder Sing, 9 W. R. 483.

family is even lower than that of the female members in a Mitākṣarā family; for these female members at least possess a safe and secure right to maintenance; whereas it has been held that the father of a Bengal family is under no obligation to support a grown up son.[1] In the case so deciding Mr. Justice Mitter said that there was no authority either in the Hindu law, or in the Jain Śāstras, supporting the right of an adult son to demand maintenance from his father. The parties seem to have belonged to the Jain sect and were domiciled in Murshidabad, which is a part of the country governed by the Dāyabhāga law. It has been held that in the absence of proof of any special custom or usage, the Jains would be subject to the law obtaining in the part of the country where they reside.[2]

Wheter in Bengal, father as karta can be restrained by sons

It may be taken as settled therefore that so far as Bengal is concerned, the adult sons cannot even demand maintenance from their father. Any attempt therefore on the part of the sons of a Bengal family to depose the father from the post of managership is out of the question. A doubt may be entertained as to what the power of the sons will be, when the father of a Bengal family exhibits any such characteristic, as is declared in the passage of the Smṛticandrikā cited a little while ago, to incapacitate the father for management. For that passage is based upon the texts of Śaṅkha and Hārīta, two Ṛṣi authorities whose dicta, are binding upon the conscience of all Hindus wheresoever located, although the opinion of the Smṛticandrikā may not be so binding, Furthermore, those texts of Hārīta and Śaṅkha and Likhita have been, I find, cited in the Dāyabhāga, chap. I, Para 42. "Thus Harita says:—'While the father lives, the sons have no independent power with

1. Premchand Pepara *v.* Hoolas Chand Pepara, 12 W. R. 494.
2. Lalla Mohabeer Pershad v, Musst. Koondun Kooer, 8 W. R. 116.

regard to the receipt, expenditure and bailment of wealth. But if he be decayed, remotely absent, afflicted with disease, let the eldest son manage the affairs as he pleases.' So Śaṅkha and Likhita explicitly declare:—'If the father be incapable, let the eldest manage the affairs of the family; or with his consent, a younger brother, conversant with business. Partition of the wealth does not take place, if the father be not desirous of it. When he is old, or his mental faculties are impaired, or his body is afflicted with lasting disease, let the eldest protect, like the father, the goods of the rest ; for the support of the family is founded on wealth. They are not independent, while they have their father living, nor while their mother survives." On the strength of these Ṛsi authorities, it may well be contended that even in Bengal, a father is liable to be deposed from the managership, on the ground of weakened intellect or dotage. It may also be advanced with some force that if the father of a Bengal family gives himself up to a vicious course of conduct, the sons may hold a sort of family council, and may restrain the father from dissipating the property on which the welfare and subsistence of the family depend. In verse 51 of the 2nd chapter of Yājñavalkya, it is enjoined[1] that " if the father be sojourning away from home, or be dead, or be steeped in vice, the debt should be paid by sons and grandsons– when proved by witnesses if the debt be denied." In this verse, the same word 'vyasana'—which has been already explained as indulgence in a vicious course of conduct has been used by Ṛṣi Yājñavalkya. Being a Ṛṣi text, its operation is not confined to a Mitākṣarā family alone. Nor can it be said that the injunction directing the payment of the debt is a moral one; for it forms a part of that Ṛṣi's chapter on the law of litigation; there can therefore be no reason for doubting that in Hindu kingdom, whether the sons received any inheritance or not, they would be

---

1. पितरि प्रोषिते प्रेते व्यसनाभिप्लुतेऽथवा।
   पुत्र प्रौत्रेॠ णं देयं निह्ववे साक्षिभावितं।।

compellable in a Court of Justice to pay the debts of their father. If that be so, then a vicious course of life on the part of the father would be a reason for setting him aside from the headship of the family, and for placing the control of the joint concerns in the hands of the eldest son or some other qualified member. This rule might be enforced all over India without making any departure from the genuine spirit of the old Hindu law. Such a law might serve as an effective check on the reckless conduct of a misguided *paster familias* of the province of Bengal, where vast properties, built by generations of hard-working individuals, are not seldom dissipated, and highly respectable families are brought to ruin. The text of Yājñavalkya, therefore, in the hand of our judicial tribunals, might be worked to a salutary end. But the British administrators of justice are guided by far different principles. Interference with absolute rights of property is what they like the least; their training and education engender in them a deep-rooted sympathy for such jural notions as are favourable to absolute proprietary rights. The tendency of the development of Hindu Law in their hands has been towards the multiplication of these absolute rights. The Hindu widow's rights have now been greatly enlarged. The rights of the father of a Mitākṣarā family, as we shall see in a subsequent Lecture, have been now placed almost on a par with that of the Dāyabhāga father. Again, they have an instinctive repugnance to the idea of checking vice by the exercise, of judicial functions. It is for these reasons a forlorn hope that so far as the Bengal family is concerned, Yājñavalkya's text will be ever availed of in order to stop the ruin of families, or to check the reckless conduct of a vicious father. Nor is it certain that the enforcement of the law for deposing a father from the family headship on account of vicious life would be an unmixed good; in France, it is said that there is an institution of family councils, whereby a member who has over leapt all discipline is brought back to a more rational course of life ; but it is also said that these family councils are liable to abuse, and that sometimes by their means mere eccentricities of behaviour are made a ground for putting a person in a lunatic asylum. Who knows that in Bengal, were a similar law established, designing and evil-disposed sons might not take an undue advantage of it?

A karta therefore, so far as Bengal is concerned, may not be readily deposed from his post, when it is the father who occupies it. In any other case, probably the law as laid down in the decision quoted from the Ninth Volume of the Weekly Reporter is unexceptionable. Yet the ordinary remedy being a suit for partition, supposing the conduct of the karta were liable to censure, it might be doubted whether a suit would lie for deposing the karta and making some fitter person the managing member. The position of the karta depends upon the voluntary submission of the other parceners ; as soon as the relation between the karta and the rest becomes other than smooth, the inevitable result would be the disruption of the family. Under the Mitākṣarā also, I believe, it would be the same. The texts indeed declare the eldest son as entitled to succeed the father in the post of a manager under certain contingencies; but it is doubtful whether these texts are enforceable in a Court of Justice. If the manager that is, refuses to give up the headship, can the eldest son come to Court and ask to be placed in that position ? I believe not. The answer which the Court will make to him will probably be, Have a partition. But it is not so sure that a tribunal presided over by a Hindu Judge trained according to purely Hindu notions would not interpret these texts in their literal sense, and would not place an eldest son in the position of the head when the existing incumbent, whoever he may be, whether a father or any other relation, should bring himself within the purview of those texts; either by dotage, prolonged illness, imbecility, or a vicious' course of life.

'Karta' accountable.

With regard to the accountability of the karta, the case from the 9th Weekly Reporter gives an uncertain ring, and another case in which the judgment was given by Mr. Justice Markby, went very near saying that the karta was not accountable for the period during which he had managed the joint funds. In other words, it was held that the other co-parceners had no legal right to demand an account of the sums of money belonging to the whole family which came into the hands of the karta, as to what the karta had done with them, whether any surplus had been left, whether all the expenditure authorized by the karta had been proper and above objection; whether his management of funds had been conducted in good faith, and so forth. It was thought by Mr. Justice Markby that the demand for such an account from the karta would be repugnant to the true principle of a joint Hindu family; that such accountability of the karta would involve the very destruction of the joint family system.[1] At length, it was left for the late Mr. Justice Dwarkanath Mitter, whose honoured name is associated with the elucidation of many knotty questions of Hindu Law, to have it decided by a Full Bench, that the karta of a joint Hindu family could be sued by the other member for account, and that such suit' was maintainable even if the parties suing were minors during the period for which the accounts were asked.[2]

In this case the distinction between a joint family and a mercantile partnership was pointed out; it was also held that the managing member would obtain credit from his coparceners for all sums of money *bona fide* spent by him for the benefit of the family; as on the other hand he was liable to make good to them their shares of all sums which he had actually misappropriated, which he had spent for

1. Rungun Money Dasi *v.* Kasinath Daft, 3 B. L. R. O. J. I.
2. Obhoy Chunder Roy Chowdhry *v.* Peary Mohan Gooho, 73 W. R. F. B. 75.

purposes other than those in which the joint family was interested. The result of the referring order in this case, (in which Mar. justice Mitter, who was a member also of the Full Bench, set forth the reasons for his decision), and of the judgments delivered by the other Judges may be thus summed up:—The managing member of a joint family is not bound to repay, like the managing member of a partnership concern, such sums over and above his own particular share as he may have spent on his own special account, when these expenses are legitimate family expenses. Any other member can ask him what portion of the family income has been actually saved by him, whereupon the manager is bound to give an account of the receipts and disbursements. Chief justice Couch observed:–"The members of a joint Hindu family are entitled to the family property subject to such dispositions of it as the managing member is entitled to make, either by virtue of the power which is given to him by law as manager, or of the power that may be given to him by the consent of the other members of the family. Subject to the exercise of these powers, and to the disposition of any portion of the family property which may have been made by virtue of them, the other members of the family are clearly interested in that property. The principle upon which the right to call for an account rests, is not the existence of a direct agency or of a partnership where the manager may be considered as the agent of his copartners. It depends upon the right which the members of a joint Hindu family have to a share of the property, and where there is a joint right in the property, and one party receives all the profits, he is bound to account to the other parties who have an interest in it for the profits of their respective shares, after making such deductions as he may have the right to make." As the case in the 9th volume of the Weekly Reporter cited before had been decided by a judgment from Mr. Justice Phear, in the Full Bench case, Mr. Justice Phear thus explained his previous decision. Merely because one member happens to be the karta, it does not follow that he is bound to give an account, in a case where the other members were not only adult, but also had taken an actual part in the management of the family property. An adult member living in commensality with the others is to be presumed to take a part in the management of the joint property; this presumption can be rebutted by evidence that it was not actually so. The accountability of the karta rises from the principle of equity that every man who manages the property of another person, or property in which another person is beneficially interested, upon the foundation of a trust or confidence between the two, is on the principles of equity and good conscience accountable to the latter for the mode in which he does manage it, and for the profits which he has made out of it. The principle of equity is, that a person who has the control and management of another's property upon the footing of anything which amounts to a confidence or trust reposed in him by this other, shall not be allowed to abuse that confidence, and to make a profit out of his management without the owner's consent. Now this fact, whether a profit has been made or not by the manager from the property managed is ascertainable by compelling the manager to disclose the details of his management, in other words, by calling upon him to furnish an account; for these details must be within the knowledge of him alone who conducted the business of management. Equity therefore further lays down that accountability, is a necessary incident of the position of one who deals with another's property on the ground of trust or confidence.

Besides this principle of equity upon which the accountability of a managing member may be rested, an authority for the very same proposition is also found in a passage of the Digest of Jagannath Tarkapanchanan, quoted in the Reference Order of Mr. Justice Dwarakanath Mitter:—When some cause is shown for suspecting that effects are concealed, then only shall ordeal be performed. For example, the income is great, but expenditure small; but he who superintends the receipts and disbursements does not satisfactorily account for them."

The above decision by a Full Bench of the Calcutta High Court determines the point of accountability on the part of a manager in a Bengal family. But the principle upon which this liability is founded is equally applicable to the case of a Mitākṣarā family. In this latter there is the same community of interest, there is the same confidence or trust reposed by the others in the managing member, there is the same fact that profits of property belonging to many reach the hands of one among them. The result, therefore that the managing member will be bound to disclose at the instance of any one member what the history of the receipts and disbursements has been, necessarily follows. That it has been so understood appears from Muss. Nowalso Koeree *v.* Laljee Modi, 22 W. R. 202, in which case, although it was from a District governed by the Mitākṣarā Law, no question was made that the managing member was generally liable for an account; the point determined in this case being that he cannot be sued for an account with regard only to particular items of money. It was held that such a suit was liable to dismissal; that a suit for a general account of the joint property was the proper remedy open to an ordinary member, and that such a general account would of course embrace and include all those particular items of expense which might have appeared as specially objectionable to the other members.

Bengal father as 'karta' not accountable

In Bengal, the father as managing member, when the property is entirely ancestral, does not come within the principle of the Full Bench decision, that principle being that the profits of the property of one person, comes into the hands of another, must be accounted for, which is inapplicable when the other members, namely, the sons, are absolutely devoid of all proprietary interest. When it is open to the father to sell, mortgage, give or do anything he likes with inherited property, it would be inconsistent with so absolute a dominion that the father should have to disclose on the demand of the sons what he may have done with the profits. But the Mitākṣarā father's rights standing on a different footing, he as managing member is liable for an account at the requisition of the sons; though the law does not seem to deny him a very large discretion in the matter of expenditure, a discretion larger than that claimable for the managing member when he happens to be some other relation than the father. Thus if there are debts due for which the whole family is liable, the father of a Mitākṣarā family can borrow money at a less interest than the existing debts bear, and pay off the old debts by the new loans. In one case the father spent large sums in enlarging the family dwelling-house both on the ground-floor, and in building additions, and in adding an upper storey. It was found that the money laid out was not applied to ornamental or unproductive improvements, but to substantial and material additions.[1] In this case the Court observed that although necessary repairs only were a matter of family necessity, and not such improvements; yet the managing member had a discretion and could prudently and in good faith make additions and improvements in the family house. This discretion when exercised in good faith, and for the benefit of the family and of the estate should not be narrowly scrutinized. It should not be made a ground of objection that the money for the purpose of these improvements had been borrowed at a high rate of interest. The family had the benefit of such additions and improvements, which might enable them to take in additional lodgers. In this case therefore the other members, who were the sons, were held bound by the acts of the managing member, who was the father.

Manager's acts how far binding upon the rest.

The law as regards the question how far the acts of the

1. Ratnam *v.* Govindarajulu I. L. R, 2 Mad. 339.

managing member are binding upon the other members may be generally stated thus:—When the acts of the managing member proceed from an intention to provide for some family need, or to perform an indispensable religious duty, or to benefit the estate, they are binding upon the others.[1] The manager is the agent for the other members, and is supposed to have authority to do acts for their common necessity or benefit. A creditor dealing with such a manager has a reasonable ground to give credit to the acts of the manager in all matters, apparently and ordinarily within the scope of his authority.[2] In a Mitākṣarā family also, it is the father who has a right to be the manager of the family composed of himself and his sons.[3] This is a peculiarity in an undivided family composed of a father and his sons. Otherwise there is no distinction between such a joint family and one composed solely of brothers, as regards the powers of the managing member to deal with the joint property.[4] The foundation for the law relating to a managing member seems to be the passage in the Mitākṣarā which has been repeatedly cited in the course of these Lectures,[5] the purport of which is that even a single member who is labouring under no legal disability and who has capacity for conducting business may enter into transactions relating to the family property if a calamity affecting the entire household so requires, or if it be unavoidable for supplying the means of subsistence to the family, and of performing the religious ceremonies.

This passage seems to furnish an authority for the proportion that ordinary there is no difference between the

---

1. Saravana Tevar *v.* Muttyi Ambal, C Mad. H. C. Rep. 371; Honuman Prosad Pandey *v.* Musst. Babooe Munraj Koeree, 6 Moore, 393.
2. Kotta Ramswami Chetti *v.* Bangari Seshamma, see I. L. R. 3 Mad. 150.
3. Soorj Bunsi Kooer *v.* Sheo Prosad Sing, L. R. 6 I. A. 106.
4. Ponnappa Pillai *v*, Bappu Bhai Yangar, I. L. R. 4 Mad. 16.
5. Chapter I, suction 1, pats. 27 *et seq.*

position of a father and any other relative when placed at the head of the joint family as its managing member. Vijñāneśvara here does not impose any duty on the son, legal or religious, to pay the father's personal debt. Nor can this passage be cited as an authority for saying that the son ought to suffer for the extravagance of the father. If the father, as the managing member, incurs expense which are paybably unresonably it can hardly be said to benefit the estate, it can scarcely be contended that the payment of debts incurred for such expenses is a pious act. It is clear that such unreasonable expenses when authorized by a brother as the managing member would not be binding upon the rest; an elder brother often actually does occupy the position of the manager.

The indispensable duties alluted to in the Mitākṣarā are undoubtedly the annual śrādhs, the ceremony of investiture with sacred thread among the three superior castes, the marriage of the minor girls of the family, where such marrigae must be celebrated before the girls arrive at the age of puberty, and other religious ceremonies enjoined by the sacred writings, necessary to be performed at stated times, and the non-performance of which would be a cause of sin, or forfeiture of caste, or would lower the position of the family.[1] According to Giridharilal's case, 22 W.R. 56, the powers of a father as manager are superior to those of any other manager. His dealings with the joint property must stand unless they contravene law or morality. The High Court of Madras in the case just cited, say, that although in the Mitākṣarā, chapter I, section 5, para. 10, the son is declared to have a power of interdiction when the father dissipates the joint property, both the father and the son having equality a right in the ancestral estate; although therefore this passage may seem to negative the existence of any predominant interest in such property in the father's by virtue of his position as the head of the family; yet the text which lays the son under an obligation to pay the debts

1. Ponnapa pillai *v.* Bappa Bhai, I.L.R. 4 Mad. 16.

of his father may be said to be of superior authority as emanating from a Ṛṣi, while the author of the Mitākṣarā is only a commentator on the Ṛṣis texts; his *dictum* therefore cannot prevail against the express texts of Ṛṣis.

We shall see in a subsequent part of these Lectures that the author of the Mitākṣarā is not in conflict with the Ṛṣi authorities on the question of the son's obligation to pay his father's debts and that his *dictum* does not negative any such obligation.

Since the manager stands out to the rest of the world as the representative and organ of the family corporation, the law has invested him with powers and privileges enabling him to discharge effectively the functions of his position. Thus if any other member of the family dies, debts payable to the family might be evaded by the debtors on the plea that they were unable to pay, there being nobody competent to give them a discharge for the deceased member's share of the debts. The law therefore authorizes the managing member to apply for and obtain a certificate under Act XXVII of 1860 for the collection of the debts which may be wing to the deceased coparcener. The effect of such a certficate granted by the District Judge is, that the managing member when suing for the recovery of sums due to the joint family, cannot be met by any objection of the kind indicated above.[1] But this title to the certificate would be cut short by the fact of disagreements having arisen among the members, in which case it is the legal heir of the deceased member who would be entitled to obtain the certificate.[2]

Management of ancestral trade

The property of an undivided family often consists of an ancestral trade, which descends like other heritable property upon the members of the family in general. There

1. Chowdry Kripa Sindhoo Doss *v.* Radha Churn Doss, 23 W.R. 235.
2. Idem.

may be infant members comprised in a group of coparceners whose forefathers may have carried on a lucrative commercial business for many generations. The business may not only be the very foundation of the whole fortune of the family, but often is the only means of their subsistence. When therefore a member dies in such a family, it would be ruinous to apply the principle regulating ordinary partnerships, and to hold that the family partnership in the commercial business is dissolved by the death of a single member. Courts of Justice in consequence have held that a fresh family partnership immediately springs up between existing members, among whom are to be included even the infant heirs of the deceased. As a necessary incident of this fresh family partnership, the manager is immediately invested with all those powers and capacities which were his attributes' when no death had taken place in the family. A great many results will follow from the principle of this family partnership carried on from generation to generation. In carrying on a trade of this kind, the infant members will be bound by such acts of the managing member as must necessarily be done in order that the business may not suffer. He is legally authorized to pledge the property and the credit of the family for the ordinary purposes of the trade. Among these necessary acts must be included such as are indispensable for securing the material existence of the undivided coparceners and for the preservation of the joint property. In the case of Ramlal Thakursidas *v.* Lakhmichand Moniram, 1 Bom. H. C. Rep. Apply the law upon this subject was elaborately discussed. The following remarks made in the course of the judgment are most important. Third parties in the ordinary course of *bona fide* trade dealings should not be held bound to investigate the *status* of the family represented by the manager whilst dealing with him on the credit of the family property. Were such a power on the part of the managing member not implied by law, property in a family trade which is recognized by Hindu law to be a valuable inheritance would become practically valueless to the other members of the undivided family wherever an infant was concerned; for no one would deal with a manager if the minor were at liberty on coming of age to challenge as against third parties the trade transactions which took place during his minority. The general benefit of the undivided family is considered by Hindu Law to be paramount to any individual interest; and the recognition of a trade as inheritable property renders it necessary for the general benefit of the family that the protection which the Hindu Law generally extends to the interests of a minor should be so far trenched upon as to bind him by the acts of the family manager necessary for the carrying on, and the consequent preservation of that family property. But the infringement is not to be carried beyond the actual necessity of the case. It is not easy to draw a well-defined line between what is and what is not an act necessarily incident to the carrying on of a trade. But taking into account the intimate and fiduciary position of one partner towards a co-partner, and the anxious protection afforded by Hindu Law to the interests of a minor, I think it safer and more in accordance with its spirit, to hold in a case like the present (where the property so far as the minor's interest is concerned is of an ancestral character), that the compromise of partnership differences and accounts by a division and transfer of partnership property should not be treated as an act necessarily incident to the carrying on of a trade, but should be left to be governed by the law applicable to ordinary dealings with the manager of an undivided family when the interests of an infant member are concerned."

According to Sir Thomas Strange, the dealings of the manager with the joint property when minors have an interest in such property are liable to be scrutinized more strictly than when all the members are of age. Third persons who enter into transaction with such a manager are more strictly bound to see that the transactions are fair and *bona fide* so far as the minors' interests are concerned. The necessity of this precaution on the part of third persons is enhanced by the fact of minors being concerned, who in general will not be bound but by necessary acts or such as are evidently for their benefit.[1]

That a commercial or trading business is an inheritable property descendible from generation to generation in a joint family was laid down by Sir Lawrence Peel in Potum Doss *v.* Ramdhone Dass[2], wherein it was held that an ancestral trade, like other property, will descend upon the members of a Hindu undivided family, and that such a family can by its manager or adult members acting as managers enter into copartnership with a stranger.

In a Bengal case reported in the first volume of Shome's Reports, p. 1, Premchand Bauthra *v.* Radhika Lal Roy, the facts were that a silk-trade had been established by the father of two sons, one of whom appears to have been a minor when the father died, and for some years subsequent to that event. It was a trade which required at times a large outlay and was subject to considerable fluctuation; while the father was alive, trade had been in a flourishing condition. The trade had been carried on after the death of the father at his express desire, and it appears to have been carried on by the sons in much the same way as it had been previously. The father had been in the habit of borrowing money from time to time for the purpose of the business; and, although the dealings of the sons had been somewhat more extensive than those of the father, the business was carried on in the same manner. The elder of the two brothers had naturally acted as the manager, and had conducted the

1. Strange's Hindu Law, vol, I, p. 202.
2. Taylor's Rep. 279.

trading business. He had contracted loans on behalf of himself and of the minor brother in the course of managing the trade, and it was found that in doing so he had been actuated by perfect good faith. The result, however, of his operations, was unfortunate, owing to no mismanagement, but to a fall in the price of silk, which had affected others engaged in the trade in the same way as it did the two brothers. Chief Justice Garth observed, under the above circumstances:—"We cannot see any ground for relieving the minor from his liability. It was laid down by the Privy Council, in the 6th Moore's Indian Appeals, p. 383[1] that the power of a manager or guardian of an infant to charge his immoveable property by mortgage or otherwise, can only be exercised in case of necessity and for the minor's benefit, and that a lender under such circumstances is bound to enquire into the necessity for the loan and to ascertain as well as he can, that the manager is acting for the benefit of the estate. And the same principle has been laid down and acted upon in the cases cited at the bar (6 W . R. 16 : 20 W. R. 383 and 72 ; 23 W. R. 424) and in many others where it has been held that a guardian has no right to mortgage or sell the minor's property unless there is some necessity for it, and the transaction is for the minor's benefit. But a case like the present stands upon a different footing. The loan made by Premchand had nothing to do with immoveable property. They were made from time to time for the purpose of a trade which had been carried on by the minor's father, and which was in fact the patrimony of the two brothers; a trade of this kind is often the only property to which the family has to look for its livelihood, and having regard to the fact that here it was the father's express wish that it should be continued, and that there was no reason to suppose that it would cease to be profitable, the elder son would clearly not have been justified in excluding his brother from participation in it. Then if it was to be

1. Honooman Prosad's case.

continued, it could only be so by borrowing such sums as were reasonably necessary for the purpose; and it would be manifestly impossible for any one lending money to the brothers under such circumstances to enquire how far the state of the business from time to time required that such loans should be contracted. If it could have been shown that the sums borrowed from Premchand had been so unusually large as to excite suspicions in the mind of any prudent man, that the elder brother was exceeding his authority, that either from self-interest or other improper motive, the elder son had omitted to setup any defence upon that ground in Premchand's suit, this Court then very possibly might have interfered by injunction to restrain the execution." In the case of Johurra Bibee *v.* Sree Gopal Misser, I. L. R. I Cal. 470, the ancestral trade had been carried on by the members of a Mitākṣarā family, and when the last survivor of the family composed of a father and his son and an uncle, the brother of the father, failed in business, a house the joint property of the family came into the hands of the Official Assignee in the course of insolvency proceedings. The Official Assignee sold the house to Sree Gopal Misser. The widow of one of the members of the joint family sued this purchaser for a declaration of her right to maintenance from the rents and profits of the house. Pontifex, J. held that the widow was entitled to no such declaration, observing, "Persons carrying on a family business in the profits of which all the members of the family now participate have authority to pledge the joint family property and credit for the ordinary purposes of the business. And therefore debts honestly incurred in carrying on such business must override the rights of all members of the joint family in property acquired with funds derived from the joint business. In other words it seems to me that those who claim to participate in the benefits must also be subject to the liabilities of the joint business." In another case Joykisto Kower *v.* Nityanand Nundee, C. L. R. 443, the father of a family governed by the Dāyabhāga had carried on till the time of his death a trading business, which was continued after his death by his two widows, the family then being composed of these two widows and two sons, who appear to have been minors. The widows being *purda nashin* ladies, delegated their authority as managers to a son-in-law, who and the elder son, after he came of age, together conducted the management of the business. During the course of this management, debts were incurred, for the purpose of carrying on the business, and the question was whether the other son, the infant, was liable for these debts. Chief Justice Garth said:—" It seems to us, on the authority of decided cases, that the guardian of a Hindu minor is competent to carry on an ancestral trade on behalf of the minor. Consequently the contention raised that the infant is not liable to any extent for the debt is not welfounded. On the other hand, it seems to us only reasonable, as well as in accordance with legal principles, that a minor, on whose behalf an ancestral business is carried on, ought not to be held personally liable for the debts incurred in that business. There must be some defined limit to the minor's liability. The limit apparently laid down by Mr. Justice Macpherson is, that all the ancestral property will be liable. But there may be instances in which this limit would be found manifestly inadequate and unsuited to reach the justice of the case. For example, a petty trade in the time of the ancestor might expand after his death into a large flourishing business in the hands of a manager for the infants. Debts arising from this business would naturally become proportionately large, and it would seem unreasonable to hold that such debts should be recoverable only from ancestral property. On the other hand, the trade might not prosper; and in this case, the minor ought not to be accountable for trade looses, out of any property unconnected with the assets of the business, which he may have received from the ancestor." In another Bengal case,

Bemola Dossee *v.* Mohini Dossee, I. L. R. 5 Cal. 793, it has been held that in a joint family supported by the profits of a joint business, if a mortgage of the joint property be made by the managing member for the purpose of carrying on the said business, the same is binding upon all the members.

Manager cannot enlarge period of limitation.

On the other hand, it has been held that the managing member is not authorized as such to give an acknowledgement for a debt barred by limitation so as to bind the rest. In Kumara Saint Nadan *v.* Pala Nagappa Chetti I. L. R. 1 Mad. 386, the Judges said:–"The first and second defendants and the minor defendants were the members of an undivided Hindu family. The debt had been contracted for family purposes by the first defendant who was the managing member of the family, and the question is, whether an acknowledgment in writing, signed by him within the period, will bind his coparceners. The relation of the managing member of a Hindu family to his coparceners is a very peculiar one, and does not necessarily imply an authority on the part of the manager to keep alive, as against his coparceners, a liability, which would otherwise become barred. The words of section 20 of Act IX of 1871 must be construed strictly, and the managing member of a Hindu family is not under that section an agent generally or specially authorized by his coparceners for the purposes mentioned in that section."

This principle that it is not within the competency of a managing member to give a promise for the purpose of extending the period of limitation with reference to a joint debt does not seem to apply in the case of a family composed of a father and his son. In such a case, it is the father, who, unless labouring under a special disqualification, occupies the position of a managing member. In one case the father of an undivided family had been first sued for the recovery of a debt due from himself; the suit failed, the debt having been barred by limitation, when the father executed a promissory note undertaking to pay the bond. After the death of the father, his son was sued on the promissory note, and it was held that the son was liable to pay it; that this was not an immoral debt; that there was no illegality in the act of the father whereby he bound himself for the payment of a debt barred by limitation; and that limitation dose not affect the existence of a debt. The result therefore was that the son was declared bound to pay the amount of the promissory note from any assets of the father received by him.[1] In this case the principle regulating the power and privileges of a managing member was displaced by another for the first time brought into prominence by the Judicial Committee in the well-known case of Giridhari Lal *v.* Kanto Lal, 22 W. R, 56. This other principle is, that it is the pious duty of a son to pay such debts of the father as are neither illegal nor immoral. No court of justice or equity can countenance the notion, that if a man pays a debt which he may not be compellable by law to pay on account of lapse of time, or laches and negligence on the part of the creditor, he thereby commits an illegal or an immoral act. The suit on the part of the creditor for the recovery of a barred debt may in some sense be illegal, since limitation being a part of the law of procedure, such a suit contravenes the law of procedure. But no law declares that a man should not pay a stale or time-barred debt, in other words, a debt of a long standing ; all that the law says is that the creditor will not obtain the help of the tribunals in the recovery of a barred debt. Nor is the payment of a time-barred debt immoral. Hindu Law knows next to nothing as to rights being destroyed by lapse of time; in the Mitākṣarā in its comments upon verses 27, 28, and 29 of the 2nd chapter of Yājñavalkya, there is an elaborate discussion upon the point. This part of the treatise does not form a portion of Mr. Colebrooke's translation. But the result of the whole of that

1. Narayana Semi *v.* Sami Das, 1. L. R. 8 Mad. 293.

discussion may be stated to be that Vijñāneśvara in certain cases is against granting means profits when a suit for the recovery of immoveable property is brought after a long lapse of time. I believe there is no indication in any other part of the original texts which can be construed into even a remote resemblance of the conception involved in the modern law of limitation. Mr. Justice Mitter says in the case of Aparoop Tewaree *v.* Kandhjee Sahay, 8 C. L. R. 192, that it is a pious duty for a man to pay his own debts. Therefore, according to both the principles of Hindu Law and of morality, time-barred debts can be paid by the father as managing, member out of the joint property, and any arrangements made by him for such payment are binding upon the sons. This is an instance wherein the powers and privileges of a father as the head of an undivided family are superior to those of any other relative when occupying the position of the managing member.

Manager's power is confined to joint property.

Although we have thus seen that extensive powers are vested in the head of a joint family, and although he is the organ, mouth-piece and representative of the family corporation, we must not suppose that the legal individuality of all other members is merged in him so long as the family union lasts. A member of an undivided family continuing to be so, and enjoying in common with his co-heirs every advantage incident to the unseparated state may in the meantime acquire separate property to his own particular use in which, upon a division, the rest will have no right to share. This is so said by Sir Thomas Strange and recognized as correct law by Sir Richard Couch in the case of Buckshee Booniadi Lall *v.* Buckshee Dewkee Nundun, 19 W. R. 223. With regard to such property therefore, the managing member is not the representative of the coparcener who owns seperate property. The capacity of the member of a joint family to own property solely for his own use is recognized in the Sivagunga case (9 Moore, I. A. 610), where their Lordships observe:—"There being no positive text governing the case before us, we must look to the principles of the law to guide us in determining it. It is to be observed in the first place that the general course of descent of separate property, according to the Hindu Law, is not disputed. It is admitted that, accoding to that Law, such property descends to widows in default of male issue. It is upon the respondent therefore to make out that the property here in question, which was separately acquired, does not descend according to the course of the law. The way in which this is attempted to be done is by shewing a general state of coparcenership as to the family property; but assuming this to have been proved, or to be presumable from there being no disproof of the normal state of copercenaryship, this proof or absence of proof cannot alter the case, unless it be also the law that there cannot be property belonging to a united Hindu famil which descends in a course different from that of the descent of a share of the property held in union; but such a proposition is new, unsupported by authority, and at variance with principle." The whole judgment in fact in the Sivagunga case is based upon the idea that the member of an undivided family is competent to hold, at the same time that he is interested in the united funds, property which belongs exclusively to himself. This idea is sufficiently well-grounded on a large number of original texts. It forms the foundation of that chapter in the Hindu Law of Partition wherein is discussed what property is not liable to be divided at a general partition.[1]

Manager's powers terminated by partition.

Again the member of a joint family, though subject

1. *Vide* Mitāksharā ch. I, s. 4; Vīramitrodaya, ch. 7; Vivāda Cintāmaṇi p. 249; Smṛticandrikā ch. 7; Dāyabhāga. ch. 6; Mandlik's Vyavahāramayūkha, p. 66.

ordinarily to the control of the manager, has certainly an independent right to put on end to the joint condition by simply demanding a partition. This right is indefeasible and belongs to a son in a Mitākṣarā family. Innumerable cases have been decided on the basis of the existence of such a right. I shall cite only two. In the case of Mohabeer Prasad *v.* Ramyad Sing, 20 W. R. 195, the judgment of Mr. Justice Phear lays down that a partition of the joint property among the members of a Mitākṣarā family, amounting either to an ascertainment merely of the shares in which the joint property is to be thereafter held, or to an actual division by metes and and bounds, may be come to by the family at any time; and moreover every member of the family may, whenever he chooses, require that it shall be come to. The principle has been also established by a Full Bench Decision of the Allahabad High Court, Joogul Kishore *v.* Shib Sahai, I. L. R. 5 All. 431. "It is now settled law that the father and the son have equal vested rights in the joint ancestral immoveable property, and that the son can enforce a partition of his interest against his father's wish." The original texts upon which this right is founded are quite clear. Mitākṣarā ch. I, s. V, para. 8 "Thus while the mother is capable of bearing more sons, and the father retains his worldly affections and does not desire partition, a distribution, of the grandfather's estate does nevertheless take place by the will of the son." I have already said that the original texts generally contemplate the undivided family consisting of a father and his sons; it has also been seen that in such a family, the father must be the head and manager; moreover there are many reasons to suppose that the powers of the father as manager are more extensive than those of any other person occupying the same position. Consequently when the original texts declare even as against the manager whose powers are most extensive, namely, the father, the competency of the son to demand a partition; it follows necessarily that these texts must be in favour of similar competency on the part of the other members as against a manager invested with less extensive powers, such as an elder brother, or an uncle,' or a cousin senior in age. This is confirmed by what Vīramitrodaya says in ch. II, Part I, sec. 23. Here the author says that there is a partition during the lifetime of the son at the son's desire; and there is a partition after the death of the father, of course at the desire of the sons; both these kinds of partition, which have received special designation in Sanskrit at the hand of Mitra Misra and the author of the Smṛti-candrikā being respectively called living partition' and 'non-living partition'[1] can take place even at the desire of a single parcener. For this proposition Mitra Misra cites a text of Kātyāyana, the purport of which is, that if there be any coparceners who have not come of age, and if there be any who are absent, being sojourners away from home, then their portion of the wealth is to be deposited with their kinsmen and friends. This has been said by Kātyāyana in connection with the subject of partition: hence Mitra Misra argues, that in order to proceed to a partition of the joint effects, a unanimity of all the parceners is not indispensable; if the consent of all were indispensable, how could Kātyāyana speak of a partition when there were absent members or minor members? How could he speak of their share of the wealth being deposited with friends and kinsmen? For a minor is legally disqualified to give consent; and there can be no consent from a member who is absent in a remote region, by which no doubt was contemplated, the case of one who has gone so far away from his family domicile, as to have temporarily severed himself from all communication with his family. We must remember that in those days, in other words, before the establishment of postal communication between different parts of India, people gone abroad to travel could hardly keep up a regular correspondence with their home, though they may have never left the soil of the

1. Jīvadvibhāga and Ajīvadvibhāga.

Brāhminik fatherland. Nor were such distant journeys unfrequent ; for places of pilgrimage, to visit which a Hindu considers as meritorious from a religious point of view, are scattered over the land from Amarnath in the bosom of the Himālayas to Kanyākumārī opposite Ceylon (Shri Lanka); from Chandranāth on the borders of the Burmese territory to Dwārakānath on the shores of the western sea. When therefore Kātyāyana quoted by Mitra Misra in the passage above referred to, makes a provision for the divided shares of absent parceners, he lays down a rule which must have had extensive practical application. It is not unlikely that the universal practice of distant pilgrimages undertaken by our orthodox forefathers was the origin of this rule in the law of partition, that a single coparcener has a right to divide himself from the others, irrespective of what they wish. Were it not timely adopted, extreme hardship would have resulted in the matter of enjoying and improving property, in a peaceful and progressive community impatient of control in the free use of individual rights. The principle being once established in the case of absent members, was easily extended by analogy to the case of minors, whose incapacity for giving a legal consent ceased to be a bar to a partition among the rest. Accordingly Viṣṇu quoted by Mitra Misra in the very same passage says:—"So should be preserved the minor's wealth, until his attainment of majority."

On this question of an ordinary member's competency to demand partition irrespective of the father's or any other manager's desire, the Vyavahāra Mayūkha is not very explicit. It reads in a curious way the texts of Śaṅkha and Likhita, and Hārīta, which I have quoted as showing how the management of the joint property is to be carried on under particular contingencies.[1] Nīlakaṇṭha cites those texts, and on their authority bases the proposition that the father being incapable, partition takes place by the advice or

1. Mandlik, p. 40.

consent of the eldest son. He says what in effect amounts to this that any parcener who is capable of supporting a family, or probably the author's meaning is, that any parncener who has arrived at such an age of discretion as to be able to take charge of his family, may ask for partition. From this right, of case the minors would be excluded. Nor is it clear whether the father's incapacity for managing the family has anything to do with this right. At p. 38, the same author says:—"Even when there is a total absence of common property, a partition is effected by a mere declaration, 'I am separate from thee;'–for partition is but a particular condition of the mind; and this declaration is indicative of the same." This is an unqualified declaration of a single coparcener's right to divide himself, irrespective of the other members' wish. Nīlakaṇṭha therefore, who in general closely follows Vijñāneśvara, may be set down as one who not only admits the right of an ordinary member to demand partition irrespective of the manager's wish, but who extends that right to the son living under the managership of a father.

Bengal son cannot demand partition

The Dāyabhāga however, by its doctrine of the father's absolute right, allows no right of partition to the son while the father is alive. In para 44., chapter I, it says that if the father be degrated or retires from the world or dies, the sons can divide; or they can divide if the father wills it. Even as respects the grandfather's property, there may be a division when the mother is past child-bearing; even then it must be by the father's will, which will is controlled by the condition of the mother being incapable of bearing any more children. But when there is no father in tha case, the Dāyabhāga is explicit[1] that union depends upon the will of the parceners; and the author quotes Nārada who distinctly says that the eldest is to support them like the father, if they

1. Daya, para. 15, ch. III, sec. 1.

be so willing (icchath); and then Jīmūtavāhana says that 'partition may take place by the will of any one, as before intimated.' Here it is not said that there should be a desire on the part of the eldest as manager in order to brign about a partition. Then Jīmūtavāhana quotes the very same text of Kātyāyana which provides for the manner in which shares alloted to minors and absent members are to be dealt with.

As indicating the separate individuality of members other than the manager may be cited Babaji *v.* Shesha Giri, I. L. R. Bom. 593, wherein it has been held that a certificate of administration may be granted for the share of a minor who is a member of a joint Hindu family. It has also been held, where a joint family consisted of brothers, that one of these brothers could by a will appoint a guardian for his minor son. In this case the actual competition for guardianship was between the step-mother appointed as guardian by the father, and the natural mother, who claimed under the general priciples of Hindu Law, to set aside her husband's will in respect of the minor's guardianship. The Court observed that although the mother was the natural guardian of her child; although her right would under ordinary circumstances be supported, were any unauthorized person to deprive her of this right; yet the provisions of Hindu Law did not prohibit a father from appointing by writing prohibit or any other person than the mother to be the guard of her minor children. The will of the undivided member, though held to be inoperative as regards the disposition of the ancestral property, was not invalid as regards the appointment of a guardian. This is an authority for showing that an undivided member has a capacity for appointing a guardian for his minor sons; this capacity being declared to be inherent in such a member as the father of his sons; its exercise no doubt will be unobjectionable even though there were a manging member in the case.[1] Where an attempt was made to set up a plea

1. Soobah Doorga Lal *v.* Rajah Neelanand Sing, 7 W. R. 74.

in defence that a son in a Mitākṣarā family had no right to question fraudulent transfers of ancestral property made by the father, the Judges said that the son had an equal right with his father in the ancestral property; that he could compel his father tu divide the property during his lifetime, and that any alienation made by after the birth of the son, without the consent of the son, unless for a purpose justified by the Hindu Law as a legal necessity, would not bind the son. If therefore, the father during the minority of the son alienated the property in fraud of his creditors, such fraud would not bind the son, who was neither a party not a privy to the fraud ; for the son did not claim ancestral property through his father, his title from his birth being a title wholly independent of, and equal to that of the father. The acts of the father, therefore, if fraudulent, could not be binding upon the son. (Babu Beer Kishore *v.* Babu Hur Bullubh, 7 W. R. 502.)

Chapter 5
Limitation as Affecting The Rights of The Members of A Joint Family

Personal possession not necessary to bar limitation in joint property—widow presumed to be enjoying her share—Receipt by one member consistent with title of all—Act IX of 1871, Art. 127—Occasional visits to joint property do not bar limitation—Under Act XV of 1877, knowledge of being excluded the starting point—Limitation unknown to Hindu Law—Except as regards mesne profits in some cases—Rights of a member returned after a long absense–Procedure as affected by joint family law.

Personal possession not necessary to bar limitation in joint property, Widow presumed to be enjoying her share, Receipt by one member consistent with title of all.

We have previously seen that the members of a joint family are said to hold a united possession of the property common to all. It is said as between them that there is a unity of possession and of title. This principle of the unity of possession among the undivided member has given rise to a number of propositions in law which are solely applicable to the case of a joint family in connection with the question relating to the law of procedure. Thus as early as 1862 it was held that a suit for a share of inheritance by a single member would not be barred by limitation, if joint possession were shown within the period of limitation; the issue in such a case being, not whether the plaintiff was in possession up to date of suit, but whether' the joint possession continued up to any time within the period of limitation.[1] In this case the fact that the defendants had sent to the plaintiff within 12 years some portions rents of the estate was held sufficient to bar limitation. Receipt of Rs. 3 per month as a member of the family was held sufficient to show that the plaintiff had enjoyment of his share of the family property.[2] On the other hand, it was observed in a case which was one to the ground enforce to a share in immoveable property on that it was family property, that it was incumbent on the plaintiff to show that the estate within 12 years before the institution of the suit was in the possession claiming under his grandfather, namely his grandmother or mother, or that if not actually in their possession, that they received a portion of the profits from the defendant as the trustee in possession. This was evidently a case in which the plaintiff could not claim any relaxation of the law of limitation, on the ground of joint family, as his title was based upon inheritance from his maternal grandfather; and there cannot be any joint family as between a person and his mother's relation relatives.[3] If it had been paternal property, the Judges would not have said that the property would descend from the grandfather to the grandmother and then to the mother. Where two brothers domiciled in Assam had lived together it was held that the Dāyabhāga law applied; that the proper question with reference to a particular property was, whether it had been joint or not? If the property was joint, the fact of one brother having been in possession for 30 years did not affect the title of the other brother who claimed under him; for such possession, where the property was joint, was that of a trustee for the widow of his brother and could not be adverse to her.[4] On the other hand, if the family were not

1. Musst. Indur Money Debee *v.* Raj Naran, Sp. No. W. R. 52.
2. Umbikachuru *v.* Bhogobuttychurn, 3 W. R. 173.
3. Bydonath Ojha *v.* Gopalmat 6 W. R. 170.
4. Chundra Kanto Surmah *v.* Bungshee Deb Surmah, 6 W. R. 61.

joint, the possession by the brother's son of a deceased Hindu who had been separate would be adverse as against his widow and as against those who would be his heirs after the death of the widow. The Judges said that the acts of the brother's son, in getting a mutation of their names in the Collector's rent-roll, having taken place, more than 12 years before the death of the widow, were hostile to the widow, and the possession held by them of the estate of her husband was[1] held by them of the estate of her husband was adverse to the widow, inasmuch as the husband having been found by a decision of the Court to have been separate in estate from his brothers, and the case being governed by the Mitākṣarā Law, the widow ought to have succeeded to his estate, and not the nephews, the husband's brother's sons. These latter, however having obtained mutation of their names, and having held possession of the husband's estate for more than 12 years prior to the death of the widow, that act was hostile to the widow, and that possession adverse to her 2 Since under the Dāyabhāga law, even in a joint family, the widow succeeds her husband to his share of the joint property, and thereupon becomes a coparcener of the male members; in her case also therefore the principle of the unity of possession must apply; accordingly, if she continues living in the family house and in commensality with the family, the Court readily finds as a fact, that she must be receiving, in absence of evidence to the contrary payments of money or money's worth on account of her share. In such a case limitation does not apply because the widow did not receive payments in money on account of her husband's share and had been driven from the family house for four or five years.[2] Where the Lower Appellate Court had found in a case from Assam that the widow was actually residing upon a portion of the family lands and held a portion of it in her khas possession;

1. Gopal Sing *v.* Kanhya Lal, II W. R. 9.
2. Gobindo Chundor Bagchi v. Kripa Moyee Debia, 11 W. R. 338.

but that the defendant, who was a member of the joint family descended from a common ancestor with the deceasd husband of the widow, had been managing the property for the last 30 years since the death of the husband; it was held by the High Court that this was not possession adverse to the widow; that in Assam the Dāyabhāga prevailed; that under this law" the widow succeeded to her husband's share; that the very fact of her residing actually on the land and holding in her own sole possesion a portion of it, was sufficient to prevent limitation; that her name having been entered as a proprietress in the Collector's register conjointly with that of the defendant was enough to keep alive the widow's claim.[1] The Judicial Committee have made the following observations bearing on this unity of possession, in the case of Chand Hurree Maitee *v.* Rajah Norendro Naran Roy, 19 W. R. 231. It is perfectly well-known to all persons conversant with these matters in India that the receipt by one member of a family may be quite consistent with the title of the whole. One member of the family may be in receipt of one part of an estate, and another may be in receipt of another part of an estate, and they may have afterwards to account the one to the other in respect of the excess of receipts over their respective rights. "Their Lordships held that this would not amount to a proof of adverse possession on the part of either. In the cased of Amirto Lal Bose *v.* Rojonikanto Mitter, 23 W. R. 214, the Privy Council; said—"Their Lordships are induced by the evidence to a believe, that Ram Nursing's widow, Soorjomoney, continued to live with her deceased husband's brothers, and was supported by them, out of the income of the estate. Nothing could be more natural or consistent with the usage of Hindu families than that upon her husband's death, she should continue to reside at the family dwelling-house as a member of the joint family. Indeed the principal defendants state in their answer that

1. Deepo Debia *v.* Gobindo Deb, 10 W. R. 42.

'they retained their brother's 'wife, the said Soorjomoney and unmarried daughter under their own support and guidance, and they effected the marriage of the unmarried daughter into a suitable family and in a proper manner. If the widow and her daughter continued to live as the members of the joint family, the presumption would be that they were maintained out of the widow's share which she inherited from her husband unless it could be distinctly shown that she received only maintenance as distinguished from a participation in the profits of the estate, for even if she did not receive her full share of the profits, limitation would not run against her is the same manner as if she had been actually dispossessed of her husband's share of the estate." Where the family was admittedly a joint undivided one, the High Court held, that a single brother's possession would be the possession of all the brothers, and there would be no adverse holding.[1] On the other hand, Chief Justice Couch observed in the case of Gossain Dass Koondoo *v.* Seroo Coomaree Debia, 19 W. R. 192. "The question being whether a suit for the share of one of seven brothers in a tank was barred by the law of limitation the Judge has held that it was, sufficient for the plaintiff who claimed the share to show that Hullodhur whose share she claimed was one of seven brothers, being a joint family, and that the presumption that the possession of one was the possession of all, was sufficient to throw the burden of proof upon the defendant who set up the law of limitation. It appears that there have been conflicting dicta, if not decisions, in this Court upon the matter. The clause 13, s. 1, Act XIV of 1859 is clearly intended to apply to cases of joint family property, and it says distinctly that although it is a joint family property, the suit to enforce a right to a share in it must be brought within twelve years from the date of the last payment to the plaintiff on account of the share. If the law laid down by the Judge be correct, that in such a case it

1. Prithee Sing *v.* Court of Warda, 23 W. R. 272.

would be sufficient for the plaintiff to show that the property is joint family property, this provision in clause 13 would be practically inoperative, because all that the plaintiff need show is, that it is joint family property. But the clause says that the action must be brought within twelve years from the last payment on account of the share, plainly showing that the plaintiff, to be entitled to sue, there must be something more than the fact of the property being joint, and the possession of one being therefore the possession of all. We do not see how effect can be given to this provision of the law without holding that the suit must be brought within twelve years from the date of the last payment on account of the share, where one person is in possession of the property, or twelve years from the time of the plaintiff's' being in possession of his share, for we agree that it was not intended to bar plaintiff's right of action where he had been in possession of his share in any way within twelve years. If he is in possession of his share, there can be no payment by any person on account of his share. It is not enough for the plaintiff to prove his title to the property which is the subject of the suit, and leave it to the defendant to show that the suit is barred by the law of limitation by proving when the plaintiff was last in possession."

Act IX of 1871, Article 127.

Some members of a Hindu family had been absent from home for thirty years; it was not clear whether they were still joint with the remaining members who had all along remained at home; and had in the interval granted a mokurraree of a portion of the family property. The High Court held that this mokurreree could not be set aside by the members who had been absent, although their claim as against the other members for the family property might not have been barred under Article 127 of Act IX of 1871; for the mokurrereedar had got his lease from the members of the family who were in actual possession and managing the joint property, and had a perfectly good title as against the whole family, unless it could be shown that they had acted dishonestly.[1] If two brothers were joint in estate, on the death of one, the other would, according to the Hindu usages, be the manager and trustee for his brother's widow. His possession could not be adverse as against her.[2] The possession of one member of a joint family is to be regarded, as the possession of himself and his brothers; it is not adverse to the brothers.[3] In a suit by a widow to obtain her husband's half-share in property which had belonged to the paternal grandfather of her husband, it was held that if her husband had survived his grandfather, and thereby had inherited the property; then her husband and the defendant, another descendant of the grandfather, must have formed a joint family, and the fact that the widow lived in the same house, and in commensality with defendant was sufficient to prove her joint possession, so as to bar limitation.[4] Since the decision of the Chief Justice Couch construing clause 13, sec. 1, Act XIV of 1859, there have been two fresh enactments which govern the law of limitation relating to a suit for a share of joint family property. The first was Article 127 of Act IX of 1871, and the second the corresponding Article of Act XV of 1877. The three successive enactments may be as well cited here in order to see in one view the alterations made by the Legislature within the period of twenty years. Clause 13 is worded as follows:–"To suits to enforce the right to share in any property, moveable or immoveable on the ground that it is joint family property, the period of twelve years from the death of the person from whom the property alleged to be joint is said to have descended, or from the date of the last payment to the plaintiff, or any person through whom he claims, by the person in the possession or management of such property or estate on

1. Poshan Ram *v.* Bhowanee Deen, 24 W. R. 319.
2. Bheemram Chuckerbutty *v.* Huree Kishore R. Roy, 1 W. R. 359.
3. Deelah sing *v.* Toofanee Sing, 1 W. R. 307.
4. Bindoo Basinee Dassee *v.* Anundo Chunder Paul, 2 W. R. 179.

account of such alleged share." Under 'Act of 1871, the provision is, as laid down by Article 127 of the Second Schedule, that a suit by a Hindu excluded from joint family property to enforce a right to share therein must be brought within twelve years from the time when the plaintiff claims and is refused his share. Under Act XV of 1877, such a suit is to be brought within twelve years from the time when the exclusion becomes known to the plaintiff. It would seem that the principle of the unity of possession among the members of a joint family has been put upon a stronger footing by the last two Acts than it occupied before, inasmuch much as at first the plaintiff had to receive payment on account of his share, which payment might be supposed to consist even in receiving food in the family house, as some of the cases quoted above show.

Occasional Visits is joint property do not for limitation

Under the Act of 1871, there must have been a demand by the excluded member, and a refusal by the others, to set the period of limitation running; so that if a member did not make any demand, although he might not have been receiving anything on account of his share for very many years, his right would not have yet been barred. The latest law says that the period runs from the plaintiff's knowledge of his being excluded from the joint enjoyment; so that under it, if the other members anyhow act adversely to the plaintiff within his knowledge, (whereby as a reasonable man he must conclude that he has been excluded, as for instance, by the sale of the joint property, and by the purchaser taking possession of the same), possibly the period would run from the date of the purchaser's taking possession, unless the plaintiff was not aware of the fact by absence from home or for any other reason. In one case Mr. Justice Kemp held under clause 13 sec. 1, Act XIV of 1859, that occasional visits paid by a widow to the house of her husband's brothers' were not sufficient to bar limitation.[1]

1. Krishnadhone Chowdry *v.* Srimati Har Coomaree Chowdrain 25 W. R. 37.

In a recent case, the facts were that the Maharajah of Chota-Nagpore had made a grant of land to three brothers who constituted a joint family governed by the Mitākṣarā law. The grant was made for the performance of certain religious services in the temple of Juggurnath at Puri. The plaintiff was the adopted son of one of these brothers, and the defendant of another. During the minority of the plaintiff, the defendant had managed to get himself registered in the Court of Wards at Chota-Nagpore as the sole owner of the entire family property. The High Court in fact observed upon this point:—"We strongly suspect that after the death of Kumla, the defendant No. 1 took advantage of the tender age of the plaintiff, to deprive him of his rights both as regards the property in question and his turn of worship, and to obtain for that purpose an exclusive grant for himself. It is clear from the evidence on both sides, that the plaintiff has taken some part in the services of the idol, although an inferior part to that taken by the defendant No.1. The only other question is with regard to limitation. It seems to have been considered by the Court below, that the ordinary 12 years' rule of limitation was applicable to the suit; but we think that the appellant is right in his contention that the case comes under section 127[1] of the Limitation Act as being 'a suit brought by a person excluded from joint family property to enforce a right to a share therein'. It is true that under the Act of 1877, the time in such a case begins to run when the exclusion becomes known to the plaintiff; and it is probable that the plaintiff may have known that he was excluded from the property more than 12 years before the suit; but by section 2 of the Act, it is provided, that in any suit in which the period of limitation prescribed by that Act is shorter than the period prescribed by the Act of 1871, the suit may be brought within 2 years next after the 1st October 1877. Now under the Act of 1871, the 12 years under such circumstances would have run from the time when the

1. Meaning evidently Article 127 of the Second Schedule.

plaintiff claimed and was refused his share (see Art. 127). It does not appear that the plaintiff ever claimed or was refused his share, at any rate until 1875 ; and consequently he had 12 years from 1875 within which he brings his suit. That period was shortened by the Act of 1877; because the time under the latter Act would run from the time when the exclusion first became known to him. And therefore under section 2, the plaintiff was entitled to 2 years from the Ist October 1877 to bring his suit. He is therefore in ample time."[1] According to this decision, therefore, the enactment which was the most advantageous for the excluded member of a joint family was the provision under the Limitation Act of 1871.

In the case of Runjeet Sing *v.* Kooer Gujraj Sing, L. R. 1 I. A. 9, their Lordships held that under the aforesaid clause 13 of Section 1, Act XIV of 1859, there could not be any adverse possession by the managing member, although he held the bulk of the family property, and although the other members had received portions of the joint immoveable property for their maintenance. It was proved in this case that the members had continued to be joint and undivided in estate and that no actual partition had been come to. It was also found that important family expenses, such as the cost of marriages, had been defrayed by the manager, and entries had been made in the account books to that effect, and that the marriage of one of the members, all of whom had separate houses and were in the habit of taking their meals separately, had been celebrated at the house of the manager. Their Lordships observed:—"The question is whether there has been a payment", within the meaning of clause 13, section 1, Act XIV of 1859, "by the defendant to the plaintiffs in respect of their alleged share within twelve years before the commencement of the suit. Their Lordships entertaining the view they have expressed that there was no partition, but that the plaintiffs took the seer land as

1. Narain Khotia *v.* Lokenath Khotia, 9 C. L. R. 247.

equivalent to a payment in respect of their shares by the defendant, are of opinion that the proceeds of those seer lands have been substantially payments by the defendants within the meaning of that section, payments which have continued to the time of action brought, and that therefore the Statuts of Limitation does not apply."

Under Act XV of 1877, knowledge of being excluded, the starting point

In the case of Kallikishore Roy *v.* Dhununjoy Roy, I. L. R. 3. Cal. 228, Garth, C. J. observed, "The Article 127 of the Limitation Act of 1871 provides that the period of Limitation shall be 12 years, not from the time of the plaintiff's exclusion, but from the time when the plaintiff claims and is refused his share. Consequently if a plaintiff has been excluded for 50 years, and he then claims his share and is refused, he would have 12 years from the time of such refusal to bring his suit; or in other words, he would have 62 years from the time of his exclusion; and if he never claims or is refused, the period within which he may bring his suit appears to be indefinite. This apparent inadvertence has been rectified in the present Limitation Act." The last sentence refers to Act XV of 1877 wherein the provision upon the subject is, that the time will run from the plaintiff's knowledge on his being excluded.

Upon the question as to what would amount to such a knowledge on the part of the plaintiff, it has been held that an order of attachment directing the under-tenants upon the land which constituted the joint family property to cease to pay rent from a particular date, would be sufficient evidence in support of a finding that the plaintiff's became aware of their exclusion on the date of the attachment; Mitter, J. holding that in a suit to obtain a share of joint family property by partition, the proper Article applicable was No. 127 of Act XV of 1877.[1] Where however, the property in suit has been in exclusive possession of the defendants for

1. Issuridutt Sing *v.* Ibrahim, I. L. R. 8 Calc. 655.

upwards lof 12 years, and where it is an admitted fact that at the time of the institution of the suit, there was no joint family in existence consitituted by the plaintiff and the defendant, it has been held on the authority of Bamboo *v.* Kashiram, I. L. R. 3 Cal. 315, that it is not enough for the plainfiff merely to call the property in suit as joint family property, but it is necessary for him to actually prove that fact. Garth, C. J. observed, "The doctrine that because 30, 50 or 100 years ago the ancestors of the plaintiff and the defendant were joint, any property in the possession of the defendant is to be presumed as joint family property, appears to me a very dangerous one. If that doctrine were well-founded, it would seem to follow that, however long a Hindu may have been in exclusive possession of property, moveable or immoveable, he would always be subject to have his title to it questioned by any distant member of his family, who could prove that at some prior period, even 100 years ago, their common ancestore were members of a joint family, and not only so, but that in all such cases the *onus* of proving that the property was not joint would lie upon the defendant." (Abbhoychurn Ghose *v.* Govindchunder Dey, I. L. R. 9 Cal, 237) In the case of Herit Marut, I. L. R. 6 Bomb, 741 the High Court of Bombay held that a suit for possession of immoveable property was not barred, simply because the defendant, another member of the same joint family, had been in possession of the disputed property for more than 15 years if the plaintiff had not made any claim, the time would not run against him under Article 127 of Act XV of 1877 until his exclusion from the property had become known to him. In this case apparently no circumstance had been alleged on the part of the defendant to indicate any such exclusion of the plaintiff.

Limitation unknown to Hindu law

I have already said that the Hindu Law as propounded by the original texts had little to do with the question of actual possession by an undivided member. If an undivided member could prove his pedigree, his title to the joint property was at once established by the very law of inheritance, and it did not matter whether any such member was in receipt of the profits arising from the property or in actual possession of any part of it. There is a text in Yājñavalkya, śloka 24 of the Second Chapters[1] which might seem to countenance the notion that in Hindu days, there prevailed a doctrine very much resembling that of the lapse of legal rights by limitation. That śloka says, that if a person sees another enjoy his lands for twenty years, or sees another appropriate and use his moveable property for ten years without protest, he incurs a loss thereof. The very distinction made in this śloka between immoveable and moveable property in respect of the period during which the adverse enjoyment of each must respectively go on without protest would at once induce a modern jurist to conclude that this is a clear declaration of the law of limitation. Such a conclusion would not remain unconfirmed by many other texts cited in the Mitākṣarā in connection with its comments upon this śloka, and also in connection with its disscusion of the topic of title, and of the topic of possession as securing proprietary right. Those texts might be quoted as embodying a rudimentary law of limitation, and as evidencing a sufficiently advanced condition of the substantive law to necessitate recourse to that expedient of putting an end to litigation. But, however that may be, the commentators on the Ṛṣi texts distinctly deny that rights can cease to exist simply because they have not been asserted or enjoyed for a particular number of years. We must therefore suppose that although in the days of some of the Ṛṣis, such as Yājñavalkya and Hārīta, Hindu law had made a progress which is implied by the recognition of prescriptive rights, or rights created by long possession or enjoyment, the progress was checked in the

1. Mandlik's Ed. p. 203.

time of the commentators, at the head of whom stands, Vijñāneśvara. He, in his comments upon the above named śloka 24 of the Second Chapter of Yājñavalkya, dwells upon the question at great length. He sets out by raising the difficulty–How can rights cease to exist, because a person fails to make a protest ? Neither popular usage nor scriptural authority anywhere supports the notion that absence of protest, like an act of gift or of sale, operates in transferring proprietary right from one person to another. Nor can it be said that an enjoyment or possession for twenty years creates proprietary right. At best such an enjoyment can be but evidence of proprietary right; what is simply evidence cannot be the cause of the accrual of the right. He then quotes a text of Gautama, one of the Ṛṣi authorities, who has enumerated in a clear manner the circumstances under which proprietary right does arise ; or rather, as the Ṛṣi puts it, under which a person becomes the owner of some particular subject of proprietary right. This text is quoted by all the commentators, and forms a part of para. 8, sec. I, chap. I of Colebrooke's Mitākṣarā. In the foot-note the translator gives a reference to this text of Gautama from the Institutes of that Ṛṣi. The same text is again quoted in the Mitākṣarā under the above named śloka 24 of the Second Chapter of Yājñavalkya. This part of the Mitākṣarā full of interesting information, is not a part of Colebrooke's translation. I shall here give an abstract of it, so far as may be relevant to the question of the discontinuance of proprietary right by lapse of time. It will be found at p. 41 of the original Sanskrit. Now the purport of Gautama's text is, that a person can be the owner of property, either by means of inheritance, or by sale, or by partition, or appropriation of something that did not previously belong to anybody, or by the finding of hidden wealth. To these means of acquiring property must be added the act of acceptance on the part of a Brahman, that of conquest on the part of a soldier, and wages on the part of the two other castes.

Vijñāneśvara argues that in this enumeration there is no mention of long possession or prescription as an expedient for acquiring proprietary right. Nor, continues Vijñāneśvara, can we found the notion of long possession creating proprietary right on that very text of Yājñavalkya, construing him as declaring that twenty years, possession is a cause of ownership; for the causes of ownership must be ascertained from popular usage, not from the texts of the Ṛṣis. He then points out certain other texts which declare the liability to punishment suited to a thief, of who seizes and enjoys property without title, although his enjoyment may have continued for many hundred of years. Nor can it be contended, he adds, that although the right does not lapse, yet a suit for the recovery of such property after it had been adversely enjoyed for twenty and ten years respectively, would be ineffectual. For it would be inequitable to hold that where there is a right, there should not be a remedy A suit is nothing but an expedient for enforcing a right; and the cardinal principle which regulates the conduct of a suit is, that truth should be found out by all means in the power of the tribunal; and if an enquiry in that direction ends in establishing a particular state of things as true, the suit will have to be decided in accordance therewith. For these reasons, Vijñāneśvara concludes that the text of Yājñavalkya must be construed differently from its apparent sense. That construction is that the loss takes place not of the land or of the moveable property itself, but of its profits. This is the intention of the text.

Except of regards mesne profits in some cases

That is to say, after an adverse enjoyment for as twenty years without any protest on the part of the owner although the owner on principles of justice and equity in gets back the field, yet he does not get any' fruits' (that is the word used in the original) for the interval. The reason therefor being that he did not protest, whereby he committed a laches; and also because there is this authoritative text. If, however, the enjoyment has been without his knowledge, or in his absence, or in such a way that he could not be cognizant of the fact, then he must obtain the means profits also; since the texts[1] speaks of one who *sees* another enjoy. Again, if he sees an *protests*, then also he recovers the means profits; for, the text speaks of one who does not protest. Furthermore, within twenty years, although the adverse enjoyment may have been with one's knowledge and without protest, he should get back the profits; for the speaks of twenty years. It might no doubt be argued, says the author, that even these profits are the property of the rightful owner, and if the original property does not lapse, there is no reason why its profits should do so. To this argument the author answers that there would be force in such reasoning if the profits had been in existence after so long a period as twenty or ten years ; for instance, areca-nut trees or jack trees may have grown upon the land; and the land is recovered along with them, On the other hand, some fruits must be consumed during the wrongful possession; as regards these, they being no longer in existence, there cannot be any ownership in respect of a non-existent substance. Since, however, another Ṛṣi text cited before declares that a person enjoying for even many hundred years, but without title should be punished by the king with the same punishment which is meted out to a thief, it might be supposed that when land is recovered, what was consumed twenty years ago should be taken an account of, and the payment of a proper compensation for the same in the shape money should be enforced from the wrong-doer. In order to negative such a supposition, Yājñavalkya says

1. पश्यतोऽब्रुवतो हानिर्भूमे विंशतिवार्षिकी।
परेण भुज्यमानाया धनस्य दशवार्षिकी।।

Yājñ. ch. II, sl. 24.

"If one sees and does not protest, he loses in twenty yours land which has been enjoyed by another; moveable property he loses in ten years."

that the rightful owner has no right to obtain such compensation for what was consumed by the wrong-doer twenty years prior to the making of the claim by the rightful owner. This in fact is a special rule overriding the general principle that a thief or robber is to be compelled to give back what was stolen, either by restoring the article itself, or by paying a proper compensation in the shape of a money. The punishment by the king, however, adds the author, must in every case take place, even after twenty years; since enjoyment of another person's property without a title, is declared to be legally punishable in every case, and since there is no special rule limiting the rule. Therefore, as Vijñāneśvara winds it up, the true conclusion is that inasmuch as there has been a laches. on the part of the owner, and inasmuch as there is this express Ṛṣi text, fruits that have disappeared by consumption cannot be got back after twenty years. What the 'fruits' of a moveable property are is not clear from this passage; but I apprehend, from indications given in other parts of the work, that the meaning of the word 'fruits' in respect of moveable property may be explained by supposing the case of a milch cow; which may belong to one person, and may have been wrongfully seized by another. After ten years, the rightful owner could recover the cow from the misappropriator; but he could not, under this Hindu Limitation law, get back the price of milk produced by the cow beyond ten years before the making of the claim. He might, however; get back all the calves brought forth. Similar illustrations might be supposed with regard to some other descriptions of moveable property, as a boat for hire, and a bullock for bearing burdens, and so forth.

Rights of a member returned after a long absence.

A like spirit is manifested in a passage of the Smṛti Candrikā, the author devoting a special section upon the rights of the member of a joint family returned home after a long absence in a foreign country, when the partition of the joint family property has already been effected by the other members. I allude to paras. 21 to 26 of the 13th chapter of that work. The sum and substance of the law propounded in this passage is, that where a parcener has absented himself from home and been resident in a remote country, during which interval the family estate has been divided by the other parceners, he after his return is entitled only to half a share, which is to be made up out of the shares already allotted to the other parceners. This proposition is based upon the following texts of Bṛhaspati : " If a man leaves the common family and resides in another country, he will get on his return only half a share. There is no doubt this." This text is thus explained by the author of the Smṛti Candrikā." "Where one quits the place of residence of all his relations, and goes away to a very remote region, and the other parceners not knowing whether he is alive or not, make a partition among themselves of the whole estate,–If he should subsequently arrive, only, half a share is to be given to him out of the estate already divided. In such a case, as the division was made from ignorance of the existence of the absentee, and the absence were attributable to his fault, the alternative of giving him a full share in the estate has not been prescribed in his case. Hence it has been asserted at the conclusion of the passage that there is no doubt in this." A like share to be given also to one returning after a long absence, subsequent to partition. If the heir of an absentee, such as a grandson or the like, returns after partition, he will receive a share of only hereditary property. Where the lineal descendants of an absentee whom the neighbours and other inhabitants know by tradition to be the proprietor, appear, his kinsmen are to surrender to them his share of only the landed property, though there may be other hereditary wealth. An absentee appearing shall, subject to the above rules, receive a share of such wealth only as he proves, by tests divine or human, to be common property. The Ṛṣi texts upon which these propositions of law are founded, consist in five ślokas of Bṛhaspati. The first has been already set forth. The 2nd runs thus:—"Debts or documents or a house or a field, all this be property belonging to one's paternal grandfather, he although long absent and away from home, should, when come back, receive a share." The 3rd śloka is as follows:—"Whether it be the third or the fifth or even the seventh, on his name and parentage being ascertained–he should receive a share in what has come down in succession." The fourth śloka is as follows :—"He whom aged persons dwelling on all sides round know by tradition to be the proprietor, to his progeny when come back those born in the same family should allot the land." The fifth śloka is as follows:—"Whether a partition has made or has not been made, in every case where the heir asserts a claim—he should get a share in whatever may be common property."

That a co-sharer returning after a long absence receives only half a share is what I gather from Krishnasawmy Iyer's translation of the Smṛti Candrikā. On referring to the original Sanskrit of that work as edited by Pundit Bharatchandra Siromani, I find that the word, which in the text made use of by the translator must have been evidently *Ardhasah,* (half share) is printed as *Arthasah* which is rather obscure, but may mean, "from the wealth." In another part of the passage also there seems to be a similar discrepancy between the text before the translator and that before the Pundit editor, one text evidently containing a word which means half, and the other another word which means wealth. It is difficult to settle the real text of Brihaspati here. I would prefer the Pundit's text, inasmuch as the author of the Smṛti Candrikā does not give any reason, why a member come back after a long absence should receive half a share, and why his progeny should receive the full share of the landed property; as declared in the fourth śloka cited above. If the Pundit editor's text be co correct, then the law, according to the Smṛti Candrikā, would stand thus:—How long soever a parcener may have been absent from home, when he comes home after a general partition, he receives his proper share from the existing divided estate.

This passage of the Smriti Chandrikā is an authority for holding that there is no limitation as between undivided members of a joint Hindu family; if the law, as it was enacted by the Limitation Act of 1871, had not been altered by the later enactment of 1877, the Law of Limitation relating to this matter would have conformed almost exactly to the principles deducible from the original texts.

Procedure as affected by joint family law

As regards the question how far the procedure in a suit is affected by the circumstance of a party to the suit being a member of a joint family, it has been held, when the family consists of a father and his son governed by the Mitākṣarā law, that a single member has no right to sue alone for the recovery of property belonging to the whole family. It was observed, "The plaintiff is not the sole person entitled to the property which he seeks to recover, because his father who is not law a party to the suit is admittedly a member of the same joint family with the plaintiff. Of course if the plaintiff could not induce his father to join with him in bringing the suit, he might have made him a defendant, and so brought before the Court all the persons who were jointly interested in the property sought to be recovered." The reason assigned for this incapacity of a single member is said to be, that the other members interested in the disputed property would not be bound by the decree, which could not be made use of as a bar or otherwise by the defendant in any future proceedings which the other members might think proper to institute. (Gocool Persad *v.* Etwaree Mahto, 20 W. R. 138.) Something very similar seems to have been in the mind of Markby, J. who said on one occasion,–"As the properties claimed are all portion of the joint family property, the plaintiff's claim for a decree declaring his right to a four-anna share and for possession thereof cannot be granted, although his title to the said four-anna share is not disputed. It seems to me that the answer given by the Full Bench in the case of Sudaburt Persad Sahoo, 12 W. R. F. B. 1, to the 2nd of the two questions which we propounded precludes us from giving any such decree. As I have said, whether or no I concur in the principles laid down by these answers, I feel bound to apply them to the cases before us. And so doing it seems to me impossible to give the plaintiff a decree which he claims, which separate decree for possession for his fouranna share." (Sudaburt Persad Sahoo *v.* Lotf Ali Khan, 14 W, R. 9 sec page 344.) Upon a similar principle, it has been held that an eight anna shareholder in four mouzas out of six which constituted one revenue-paying estate was not entitled to sue alone under either section 10 or section 11 of Act XI of 1859, because he cannot bring himself under the words of section 10, and is not "a recorded sharer of a joint estate held in common tenancy " within that section. Neither is he "a recorded sharer of a joint estate, whose share consists of a specific portion of the land of the estate," for he has only an undivided moiety of four mouzas out of six. There are other sharers who, together with him constitute the entity which will be the sharer whose share consists of four mouzas out of six. If he had been joined with his co-sharers of the four mouzas, he might possibly have come before the Court with them as a party entitled to sue under section 11. (Nunhoo Sahai *v.* Rampershad Narain Sing, 21 W. R. 38.) In the case of Cheyt Narain Sing *v.* Bunwari Sing, 23 W. R. 395, Mitter, J. observed, "with respect to the first ground urged in Special Appeal, it seems to us that the plaintiff, if proved to be still a member of a joint Hindu family, would be precluded from maintaining a suit for his specific share which would devolve upon him an partition."

Chapter 6

Right To Maintenance

Male. member's right to food and raiment—Legal and moral obligations—Hardly known out of the Bengal School—In Bengal, doubtful if son can demand maintenance from father-Male members' wives entitled to maintenance- Wife co-owner with husband—But not to all intents and purposes—Wife entitled to separate maintenance for a just cause—Maintenance a charge upon husband's estate-Wife's maintenance in Bombay–Marrying a second wife no cause for separate maintenance—Superseded wife's rights under original texts—Widow's right to maintenance–As understood by the Allahabad High Court—Widow's maintenance in Madras—In Bombay—Widow's maintenance a charge on joint property—Purchases without notice relieved from widow's maintenance right—Modern case—law as to widows' maintenance not consonant with Ṛṣi texts—Fraudulent purchaser bound to pay widow's maintenance–Widow's right to residence—Not affected by the doctrine of factum valet—Widow may live elsewhere than in her husband's house—Separate maintenance from small joint property not allowed—Amount allowed in olden times—Amount once fixed may be altered—Female member occasionally entitled to maintenance in a double capacity—Limitation as to maintenance—Right of a daughter-in-law to maintenance—Texts relating to female member's-right Maintenance-right treated scantily in Nibandha treatises–Daughter-in-law's maintenance in Bengal–Jagannātha's influence on the development of Bengal law—Khetramoni Dasī v. Kasīnath Das—Position of Mitākṣarā daughter-in-law more secure—Other female members—How to make a maintenance right secure.

In this chapter I shall take up the subject of maintenance, so far as it bears upon the law of the Joint Family. In dealing with this part of the joint family law, I shall first consider the right to maintenance as vested in the male members, then the case of the wife, of the widow, of the, daughter-in-law, and lastly of the other female members.

Male member's right to food and raiment

Under the law of the four Schools other than the Bengal one, the male members are, as a rule, interested in the entire property belonging to the family. If the family consists of a father and his sons, and if the property is ancestral, the sons have a joint right in the property. The father may be the manager; in fact, he has a right to be the head of the family; the control over the undivided effects rests with him. But the sons certainly have a right to receive food and raiment at his hand, which being withheld, they, I apprehend, can compel him by a suit, to make arrangements for the family being provided with the means of subsistence. Any direct text laying down such a rule may not possibly be found; but there are texts which by necessary implication sanction such a rule. Thus the Mitākṣarā, which is an authority in all the four schools mentioned above, quotes twincle ślokas of Vyāsa in chapter I, section 1, para. 27, the last of which purports to say that all persons in existence within the family have a desire or necessity for subsistence; for this reason, the gift or sale of even self-acquired immoveable property would be improper. In the next section, Vijñāneśvara sanctions an alienation of immoveable property in order to procure subsistence for the family, when the co-owners, such as the sons and the grandsons are minors, and therefore incapable of consenting to the alienation. Here prominence is given to the necessity for procuring maintenance for the family ; and it would be unreasonable to suppose that persons having a substantive right in the property should not have the subordinate right of demanding maintenance. The same right, of the male members, to maintenance out of the joint property, is further inferrible from other parts of the four leading authorities of the above-named four schools, among whom there is hardly any difference upon this point, so far as the original texts are concerned. Thus is the Mitākṣarā chapter II, section 10, para. 5 says, after persons disqualified for taking a share in the inheritance have been enumerated, that these disqualified members of a family, though entitled to no allotment out of the joint property, are yet to be maintained by the others, who, unless they give them food and raiment, would be committing a sin that will entail upon them what is called a fallen state (*pātitya*) or degradation. For this proposition, Manu is quoted, who in śloka 202 of his 9th chapter, declares that to all these disqualified persons, it is proper to give, until the end of their lives, food and 'raiment, since if a person does not supply them with such subsistence, he becomes 'fallen' much is the language of Manu. Kullūka explains the same by saying that the person not giving the same becomes a 'sinner.' Here I may remark, by the way, that our modern administrators of justice are apt to suppose, when such language is used in the original texts, that the language implies, only a moral obligation, but does not impose any legal duty upon the person who is threatened with the risk of committing a sin. Thus I find in the judgment of Sir Barnes Peacock, in the well-known Full Bench case of Khettur Money Dossee *v.* Kasheenath Das, (see 10 W. R. F. B. p. 92), certain observations made by the eminent Chief Justice, which might lead one to suppose that no legal obligation can be inferred from the original texts unless they provide that the king should fine the person evading or neglecting to perform the duty promulgated by the text. Similarly in a recent Full Bench case decided by the High Court of Bombay, in which the Chief Justice Westropp delivered one of the most learned and elaborate decisions on the subject of maintenance,[1] I find that the Chief Justice remarked (see p, 602)—"Here no civil obligation is prescribed, but merely a moral duty."

The above rule laid down by modern tribunals for distinguishing legal and moral obligations would fail if applied to Manu's text declaring the right of disqualified members of a family to food and raiment. That this right is legally enforceable will I believe be admitted by all. Sir Barnes Peacock in the judgment already quoted from, elsewhere says that disqualified persons are members of the family in which they are born, and that though on the one hand they do not share in the joint estate, yet on the other, their maintenance is a charge on the estate, which but for the disqualification they would share with the qualified members.[2]

Hardly known out of the Bengal School

The truth is that the distinction between legal and moral obligations is hardly known out of the Bengal School. It was invented by this school, in order to make that wide departure from the general body of Hindu Law, the departure which consists in giving absolute power to the father over the joint ancestral property. The hint has been largely availed of by modern Courts, which under the bounden duty of administering Hindu law, have resorted to this expedient in order to avoid the manifest inconvenience of an unqualified application of ancient principles suited to a state of society widely different from what we see the present day. Ancient Hindu law, in fact, in many instances acts like the Procrustean bed upon the growing necessities of the present advanced stage. The old legal shell is too narrow to accommodate the grown-up modern social organism. Real conformity to Hindu law as it originally stood is not possible for the present Hindu

1. Savitri Bai *v.* Luxmi Bai, I. L. B. 2 Bom. 573.
2. *Vide* p. 91, col. 2, pare. 6, 10 W. R. Full Bench Rulings.

society; the judges, therefore, unable openly to repudiate its rules, have adopted principles which ensure a simulated and outward conformity to the ancient law. In this proceeding, the judges have trodden on the footsteps of Jīmūtavāhana, whose severance from the traditional system must have marked an era in the development of Hindu law.

With regard to the passage from the Mitākṣarā quoted above; relating to the disqualified persons, I have cited it to show that the male members in general have a right to maintenance out of the joint property, since even those debarred from claiming a substantive interest are declared to have that right. All the five schools are unanimous on this point.[1] Vivādacintāmaṇi quotes śloka 143 of the second chapter of Yajñavalkya, which has been thus translated (p. 243) "An outcast and his son, an impotent person, one lame, a madman, an idiot, one born blind, he who is afflicted with an incurable disease, and the like, must be maintained without any allotment of shares. "Vācaspati Miśra does not add any observation of his own to this declaration of a disqualified person's right to maintenance, but seems silently to endorse what is inculcated by the Ṛṣi text. Upon this point, the Smṛti Candrikā of the Madras School has dwelt a little more discursively.[2] The author first enumerates the disqualified persons and then adds that all these disqualified persons must be maintained; for an authority he quotes the same text of Yājñavalkya which we have found quoted in the Vivāda Cintāmaṇi. He then says, that this maintenance is to be supplied by those who take the inheritance. I believe that Smṛti Candrikā is the only original authority which is thus explicit as to the party liable to maintain excluded members; though the other original authorities pretty plainly leave the same to be inferred from the context. As to the party liable to maintain, the Smṛti Candrikā cites a text from Viṣṇu, the meaning of which is

1. Vīramitrodaya, ch. VIII, sec. 2.
2. Chapter V, para. 20 et *seq.*

that these persons should be given food and raiment by the participators of the inherited wealth. Then the author cites the same text of Manu which we find quoted in both the Mitākṣarā and the Vīramitrodaya, and which is an authority for saying that the excluded persons have a legal claim to a lifelong subsistence. Then the author quotes a text of Kātyāyana which being literally translated, would stand thus,—"Food and raiment, till the end of life, must be given by the *bandhus.* In default of even the *bandhus,* one should get the father's wealth. The kinsmen, who have received wealth other than paternal, should not be made to give." This text of Kātyāyana is explained by the author of the Smṛti Candrikā as meaning that the *bandhus,* or the kinsmen of the excluded person, the participators of his father's property, should give food and raiment, as laid down by Manu and others. The sense of the latter portion of Kātyāyana's text is that if the kinsmen have not participated in the excluded person's paternal wealth,, then the king, in other words, the Courts of Justice, should not compel the excluded person's kinsmen to maintain him. If a kinsman has not accepted or taken or received the excluded person's paternal wealth, then it is not necessary for him to maintain the excluded person. I may here remark that in modern decisions relating to the right of maintenance, we often find it propounded as a principle that a right to maintenance possessed by one Hindu against another is generally based upon the equity, casting that liability upon him who excludes another from participating in the wealth of a third person. This principle explains the rule which makes it incumbent upon a brother in a Mitākṣarā family to maintain the widow of his undivided brother. Why should such a brother maintain the said widow ? The answer is–he being undivided, prevents the widow from taking the property of her husband after his death; he takes that property; he in fact is in her way; therefore equity casts this liability upon him. Similarly in the case of disqualified members; for qualified members exclude them from sharing in the joint property; therefore equity makes it incumbent upon the qualified members to maintain the disqualified ones. I find the principle propounded by Norman, C. J. in Rajomoney Dossee *v.* Shibchunder Mullik, 2 Hyde 103, cited in p. 616, I. L. R. 2 Bom., the words of the Chief Justice were-'The present case is wholly distinguishable from those where an heir takes property, subject to the obligation of maintaining persons excluded from inheritance out of the estate of the deceased proprietor, or whom the deceased proprietor was morally bound to maintain, In such cases the Hindu Law seems to annex the duty as a burden on the inheritance in the hands of the heir, and the right of the party claiming maintenance appears to be a legal right analogous to the right of property.' Continuing the passage of the Smṛti Candrikā, I find it stated on the authority of Devala, that some of the excluded persons are not entitled even to maintenance; for Devala says that food and raiment are given to those other than the 'fallen person.' To which Smṛti Candrikā adds that the issue of a 'fallen person is also fallen; such issue therefore has no right to maintenance.' From a text of Vasiṣtha, the author makes out another disqualified person, namely, one who has become a religious mendicant, or one who having so become is unable to conform to the rules of that life, and re-assumes the condition of a householder. Both a religious mendicant and one re-assuming the householder's life are excluded not' only from a share, but even from an allowance for subsistence.

Referring to the Vyavahāra-mayūkha, I find it laid down (chapter IV, section 11, verse 9) that persons excluded must be maintained during life by those who take the inheritance. Then the same text of Manu, chapter IX, śloka 202, is quoted which has been cited in the Mitākṣarā and the Vīramitrodaya ; and also Yājñavalkya, chapter II, śloka 141, which has been quoted in the Vivādacintāmaṇi, and which declares the excluded person's right to maintenance.

In Bengal doubtful if son can demand maintenance from father

From all these authorities, the proposition that male members of a joint family possess an inherent right to have provision made for their subsistence by the person, whoever he may be, that stands out as the head of the family, is clearly deducible. As regards the Bengal school, however, the same proposition is not free from doubt, when the family is composed of a father and his sons, although there may be some ancestral property in the hands of the family. In favour of the sons' right to maintenance in such a case, it may be advanced that admitting the father's power to be absolute over the ancestral property, his absolute power contemplates only his right to alienate the same;–but where no alienations have been actually made, there is nothing to prevent the sons from asserting a right to subsistence out of the ancestral estate. The power of the father has been discussed by Jīmūtavāhana in paras. 20-31 of Chapter II of the Dāyabhāga. The purport of this passage may be thus set forth. "As regards ancestral property, when the partition is made by the father, he takes a double share; it is also the father with whom rests the choice of making a partition at all. Even though the property be ancestral, in Bengal the sons cannot demand that it shall be shared and allotments shall be given to them. Whether a division shall be made or not, the father alone will decide. If any ancestral property was lost to the family, and the father by exerting himself recovers the same, such property also must become the self-acquisition of the father. At the time of the particular the father may share it with his sons, or may not share it; but may wholly appropriate it to himself. The same power however, the father has not with regard to other ancestral property. If he thinks of making a partition, he must of force give shares to his sons; though he may reserve a double share out of it for himself; and he may postpone the actual partition to any date he chooses. Again, moveable ancestral property is entirely at his disposal, for Yājñavalkya has in one śloka said that the father is the lord of pearls, and gems and corals, of all forsooth; though of the whole immoveable property, neither is the father nor the grandfather the lord. From this text of Yājñavalkya, it follows that ancestral moveable property, even the whole of it, can be given away or sold or otherwise disposed of by the father; but not immoveable property, nor the *nibandha* or periodical receiptaccruing from land.[1] And since Yājñavalkya says that of the *whole* of the immoveable property, neither the father nor the grandfather the lord, we must give some force to this word *whole*. In other words, we must take the meaning of Yājñavalkya to be that the father cannot dispose of the *whole*, but he can dispose of a part of the ancestral property. The reason for prohibiting the disposal of the *whole* ancestral property is, that the subsistence of the family depends upon to. To provide subsistence for the family is an indispensable duty. Manu says that the approved means of attaining happiness in the next world is to provide maintenance for those who depend upon us. If they are left in misery, the hell would be in prospect for him who neglects them; for this reason dependents must be provided with subsistence. From this it is gathered that the father is not prohibited from alienating a small portion of the ancestral property, if such alienation does not interfere with the comfortable subsistence of the family. If, 'however, the family cannot be maintained without alienating the whole ancestral property, even the whole may be alienated for the purpose of subsistence, since the revealed law expressly declares that one must at all events be guided by the instinct of self-preservation. It is true that Vyāsa in a couple of verses seems to say that a single individual is not competent to make a sale or gift, in the absence of a consent on the part of the others, of the whole immoveable property—property

1. We shall subsequently consider the nature of *nibandha* more at length.

common to the family; whether separated or unseparated, the persons called sapiṇḍas have an equal right in the immoveable property; and a single person is incompetent to effect a gift or pledge or sale. But these two ślokas should not be cited as authority negativing the right of one to dispose of property belonging to himself; a man having a right to property must be supposed to have a power to do just as he likes with the same. The text of Vyāsa simply reprehends the conduct of a person of bad character, who unmindful of the claims of the family to receive subsistence out of the family funds, dissipates such funds and brings misery upon the family." I have already said that this passage is rather obscure. From it we cannot gather whether Jīmūtavāhana admits the father's power to alienate ancestral property, even though the father were thereby to bring on the starvation of the family. At the same time this passage is ordinarily appealed to as the textual authority of the Bengal school for the father's absolute power over ancestral property. However that may be, so far as the subject of maintenance is concerned, it may fairly be argued on the strength of this passage that even in Bengal, where there is ancestral property, and the sons live in commensality with the father, the sons can claim maintenance at his hand, and may even enforce that claim by a suit in a Court of Justice. Howsoever absolute the father may be with regard to such ancestral property in the matter of making an alienation, so long as the father retains it in his hands, the authorities seem to set a limit to his caprice. In making a partition, he is restricted to taking a double share. If his right be so very absolute, why should he not take three-fourths, or even the whole ? In Bengal therefore, ancestral property actually in the father's hands may probably be charged with the sons' maintenance. It cannot but be owned, however, that this right must be extremely precarious. If the father has quarrelled with his sons, and is seriously desirous to cut them off from all participation in the hereditary estate, all that he need do is to sell the estate. Then the sale is only a morally culpable act, not invalid in the eye of law. Considering the general consensus of opinion among the lawyers as to the Bengal father's absolute right over ancestral property, such a sale would hardly be regarded as subject to a charge for the maintenance of the sons, even though the purchaser took with notice. In spite of the circumstance that Jīmūtavāhana gives a great prominence to the duty of maintaining the family, his declaration that sons have no right during their father's life, so often repeated in his work and so laboriously established by general comparison of the early Ṛṣi texts, is a fatal stumbling block in the way of a Bengal son's right to maintenance. There is scarcely any case law upon the point. The dencision I have already once quoted from the 12th Vol. of Weekly Reporter, p. 494 (see *ante*, p. 226) does not mention whether there was any ancestral property in the hands of the father who was sued by his grown up son. It may be that if the father had been in possession of ancestral property, the judgment of the High Court would have been otherwise. This would seem to be so if we consider the very cautious expressions used by Sir Barnes Peacock in the Full Bench case of Khetter Money Dossee *v.* Kashinath Das, 9 W. R. 413. He there says, "There is no allegation 'in the plaint that the defendant has any ancestral property or any property upon which the planitiff's maintenance is a charge," (page 421). Again he says "There is no ancestral property upon which the daughter-in-law has a charge for maintenance. This is not a question of a charge upon an inheritance. The father-in-law is not stated to have inherited anything." (p. 423, Col. 1, para 2.)

On referring to Chapter V of the Dayābhāga, which deals with the subject of disqualified members, we find the same śloka of Yājñavalkya which we have seen cited in the Vivādacintāmaṇi and the Smṛti Candrikā. This śloka says that the excluded persons must be maintained; and in para.

11, ch. V, Jīmūtavāhana says, "Although they be excluded from participation, they ought to be maintained, excepting, however, the outcast and his son. "Again in para. 19, he says, "Their daughters also must be maintained until provided with husbands. Their childless wives, conducting themselves aright, must be supported: but such as are unchaste should be expelled; and so indeed should those who are perverse." It therefore appears that Jīmūtavāhana, in common with the authorities of the other four schools, endorsed the opinion that exclusion from inheritance on account of personal disqualification does not work the forfeiture of a person's right to maintenance. That being so, it is a fair deduction from the various passages of the Dāyabhāga quoted above that in Bengal where the family consists of a father and his sons, and where there is ancestral property in the hands of the father, the sons can demand from the father a provision for their subsistence, so long at least as the ancestral property has not been actually alienated by the father.

In Bengal, however, joint families often consist of brothers or other persons more distantly related to one another. In such a case, in whosesover management the joint property may be, every member is entitled to receive allowance out of the common funds for the purpose of maintaining himself and his branch of the family. The family may in course of time have grown to such large proportions that it may be inconvenient for the members to live in commensality and to dwell in separate apartments around a single compound. Members may choose to retain the common property in a joint condition, and at the same time to live in separate houses and separate mess. Quarrels and disagreements may have arisen among them, more especially among the female partion of the different branches of the family ; and yet cumbrous operation of having the whole joint property divided by metes and bounds may be deemed undesirable. Under these circumstances the members necessarily live apart from one another and receive an allowance by way of maintenance from the managing member, under whose care and supervision the undivided property is left. The property of many wealthy joint families in Bengal consists not only of lands and ordinary moveable property, but comprises profitable mercantile business; money lending business, putnees, durputnees and julkurs, and various other subjects of proprietory right. A fair and satisfactory partition of all these different kinds of property, when they have become large and extensive by accumulation during many generations is a task beset with difficulties. Practically therefore coparceners much rather like to leave them in a joint state even when disagreements have arisen among themselves, and content themselves by living and messing separately. If in such a case a manager withholds the maintenance allowance which may be reasonably claimed by one coparcener, notwithstanding that there are sufficient joint funds in his hands,—I believe the member to whom maintenance is denied may bring a suit to compel the manager to pay him a proper allowance. And I apprehend that the courts of justice will not meet such a suitor with the impracticable advice that his remedy lies in a suit for partition. Cases of this character rarely arise, and the reason is obvious. Wherever the affairs of a joint family are in the management of one coparcener occupying the position of its head, he generally knows how indisputable the rights of the other members are, and, therefore scarcely ever ventures to withhold an allowance for maintenance, when a particular member refuses to live in the family dwelling house. He knows that such a member can easily bring a suit for partition and thereby throw the family affairs into utter confusion for a number of years. He himself is interested in the joint property, and therefore knows how to avoid the inconvenience of such a partition suit.

Male member's wives entitled to maintenance

With regard to the right of the wives of the undivided members to receive maintenance from the joint property, this right also, like that of the male members, has been nowhere in the original texts declared in express terms, but is inferrible from various passages scattered among those texts. The nearest approach to any such declaration is seen in śloka 55, chap. III, Manu. That śloka,—"Married women must be honoured and adorned by their fathers and brethren, by their husbands, and by the brethren of their husbands, if they seek abundant prosperity. " But this can scarcely be taken as the declaration of a legal right. Here the father and the brother and the husband are all placed on the same footing. But modern Hindu Law as administered by our courts will hardly allow the contention that a woman has a legal right receive maintenance from her brother. On the other hand, there can be no doubt that a Hindu wife is entitled to receive maintenance at the hands of her husband. Such a right on the part of the wife seems to be taken for granted by the writers of the original texts. It is implied by various provisions of law which these texts contain. Thus in the Mitākṣarā ch. I, see. 2, paras 8, 9 and 10, it is said that when the father at his own desire distributes equal shares to all his sons, he should give a share equal to that of a son to every one of his lawfully married wives, unless any peculiar property had been given them by their father-in-law or their husband, in which latter case the wives are entitled to only a half share. Again in ch. II. sec. 11, para. 34, it is said that if another wife is married by the husband during the lifetime of his first married wife, the latter is called the superseded wife. Such a superseded wife is entitled to receive an amount of money from her husband equal to what has been spent by him on his second marriage. The right of the wife to a share on the division of an undivided estate or of the superseded wife to a certain amount, money on the occasion of her being superseded is generally considered to be in the nature of a maintenance. Again in ch. II, sec. 10, para. 15 it is said that the sonless wives of excluded persons must be maintained when their conduct is unexceptionable. In the Vīramitrodaya, ch. V, part 1, sec. 6, it is said, "But if the husband have a second wife and do not show honour to his first wife, he shall be compelled by force to restore her property, though amicably lent to him. If food, raiment and dwelling be withheld from the woman, she may exact her due supply, and take a share of the estate with the co-heirs." In the Vivādacintāmaṇi, page 265, it is said, "If suitable food, apparel and habitation cease to be provided for a wife, she may by force take her own property, and a just allotment for such a provision; or she may if he die take it from his heir." In page 244, it is said, "their childless wives (meaning the wives of disqualified persons) who preserve chastity must be supplied with food and apparel; but disloyal and traitorous wives shall be banished from the habitation." In the Smṛticandrikā, chapter V, para. 43 the author says "that the lawfully married wives of those who do not receive a share, if sonless and of unexceptionable behaviour, should be maintained by those very participators of the excluded person's paternal wealth upon whom it is incumbent to give subsistence to the excluded persons themselves."In the Vyavahāra Mayūkha, ch. IV, sec. 12, para. 12, the author says "the childless wives of the disqualified persons conducting themselves aright should also be supported; but if they are unchaste, they should be expelled; and similarly those who are perverse." In the Dāyabhāga also the śloka 145 of the 2nd chapter of Yājñavalkya has been quoted without any remarks (*vide* ch. V, para. 19, Dāyabhāga). This śloka is the authority referred to by the leading treatises of all the five schools to show that the chaste wives of excluded persons have a right to receive food and raiment.

This right is spoken of in connection with the partition property when effected by the qualified coparceners. As the disqualified parceners do not receive a share, the law of partition lays down that they have a right to receive food and raiment in lieu of a share; the same law also declares a similar right in favour of their wives. The irresistible conclusion from those provisions of law is, that while the family remains undivided, these persons and their wives as a matter of course continue to live is the a same mess and in the same dwelling-house with the other coparceners. That being so, we must conclude that the wife of every coparcener in a joint family has a right to maintenance from the common fund. It would be absurd if the law were otherwise. The disqualified persons and their wives are evidently placed on a more precarious footing. If even they have their right to maintenance provided for in unmistakeable terms, the other members and their wives, whose status is certainly superior, must necessarily possess the right given to the less favoured members.

Wife co-owner with husband, But not to all intents and purposes.

Under the Benares law as administered by the High Court of Allahabad, it is sometimes said that a wife is in a subordinate sense a co-owner with her husband; he cannot alienate his property or dispose of it by will in such wholesale manner as to deprive her of her maintenance. (Jamna *v.* Machul Sahu, I. L. R. 2 All., 317.) In this case the husband had made a gift of the whole of his property to his nephew, and the wife when she had become a widow, raised a contention before the High Court that the nephew was equitably bound to maintain her, inasmuch as no provision had been made for her maintenance by her husband. The High Court allowed the contention, Pearson, J. basing his opinion upon the Privy Council case of Sanatan Bysack *v.* Sreemutty Juggut Soondery Dossee, 8 Moore's I. A. 66. But the doctrine that a wife is a coowner with her husband in his properties cannot safely be made the foundation of the wife's right to receive maintenance from her husband. Original texts do not uphold the doctrine to its full extent. Vīramitrodaya, ch. 3, part 1, section 13, says, "Her (meaning the wife) right is only fictional, but not a real one: the wife's right to the husband's property, which to all appearance seems to be the same as the husband's right, like a mixture of milk and water, is suitable to the performance of acts which are to be jointly performed, but is not mutual like that of the brothers; hence it is that there may be separation of brothers, but not of the husband and wife ; on this reason is founded the text, namely,–'Partition cannot take place between the husband and wife; therefore it cannot but be admitted that on the extinction of the husband's right the extinction of wife's right is necessary." Accordingly it has been said by Oldfield, J. that too much stress should not be put on any of the texts which speak of wife's ownership in her husband's property. (Sham Lal *v.* Banna, I. .L. R. 4 All., 298.) The principle laid down in the above quoted case of Jumna *v.* Machul Sahu has been somewhat qualified by the more recent case of Gur Dyal v. Kausila, I L. R. 5 All., 368, where the wife sued for setting aside a deed of gift of two houses made by her husband, also for a declaration of her right to reside in both the houses, and also for a declaration of her right to maintenance personally against her husband, as well as against the two houses which had been alienated by him. The judgment was delivered by Straight, J.:—"Much stress is laid upon the ruling of this Court in Jumna *v.* Machul Sahu, I. L. R. 2 All., 315, in which it was held that where husband in his lifetime made a gift of his entire estate, leaving his widow without maintenance, the donee took and held such estate subject to her maintenance. But the circumstances of that and of the present case are somewhat different ; for here the donees of the alleged gift asserted that it was made to them by the husband in consideration of their discharging certain debts due from him, and it would seem that a mortgage the two houses was first made to raise money sufficient to pay such debts; and then house No. 2 was subsequently sold the appellant Guru Dayal in order to release the mortgage. Now it must be admitted that the payment of her husband's debts, whether he be alive or dead, must take precedence wife or widow's maintenance, and we are unable to find anything in the Hindu Law authorising the notion that such maintenance can stand in the way of sales or alienations being made by the husband during his lifetime or by his heirs after his death to satisfy his creditors."

The High Court of Bengal has held in one case where the wife was obliged to leave the house of her husband under the influence of her religious feelings, because her husband had kept a Mahomedan woman as his concubine, that such conduct was a sufficient justification to leave her husband's house, and that she was entitled to maintenance when she was living a chaste life with her mother. "(Lalla Govind Persad *v*: Dowlut Butee, 14 W. R. 451). But it is clear from both text-books and cases, that if a Hindu wife leaves her husband's house without sufficient cause, she cannot claim maintenance from him. It is also clear that adultery on the wife's part terminates all her right to receive subsistence at the hand of her husband, unless her guilt is condoned by him and she is taken back into the family. Therefore where her departure from her husband's house is accompanied by unchastity, the reason is the stronger that she should lose all right to maintenance. In this matter the Hindu Law seems to be in agreement with the English Law, under which latter, a wife's departure from her husband without sufficient reason exempts him from the duty of supporting her, and her elopement with adultery discharges him from all obligations to find her necessaries, and he will not be bound by her contracts for them, unless of course he pardons her and takes her back. (Ilata Shavatri *v.* Ilata Narayan Nambudiri, I Mad. H: C.Rep. 372.) The Vīramitrodaya seems to support the notion that even an unchaste wife receives an allowance of food and raiment. It quotes a text saying that fallen wives should have subsistence given them if they reside in the vicinity of the dwelling-house. The Vīramitrodaya says that this text applies only to the husband, it does not intend to favour any right on the part of such unchaste wives to receive food and raiment from the husband's family. (Ch. III, part 1, sec. 10, last para. page 153). This passage seems to make a distinction between the liability of the husband for the maintenance his wife, and that of the joint family for the maintenance of the wife of an individual member. In every other case there is no ground for making any such distinction. If when the husband is separate, the wife is entitled to receive maintenance from him, there is no reason to suppose that the said right on her part should be affected by the fact of her husband being joint in estate with others. The law therefore which regulates the maintenance right of the wife as against her husband must also govern her right as against the joint family of which her husband is a member.

In one case the question was, whether a wife who was living apart from her husband could bind him by her loans made for the purpose of supplying herself with necessaries, of prosecuting a suit for maintenance against her husband. It was held that upon this question, the Hindu law was governed by the same principles which have been adopted by the English law. 'A person dealing with and seeking to charge her husband, must show either the that wife is living with her husband and managing the household affairs, in which case an implied agency to buy necessaries is presumed or he must show the existence of such a state of things as would warrant her in living apart from her husband and claiming support and maintenance—when of course the law would give her implied authority to bind him for necessaries supplied to her during such separation, in the event of his not providing her with maintenance."

In this case it was held that because the husband married another wife, the first wife was not justified in separating herself and remaining apart from him of her own freewill. Any debts therefore that she contracted under the above circumstances were not binding upon her husband (Virasvami Chetti *v.* Appasvami Chetti, 1 Mad. H. C. Rep. 375).

Wife entitled to separate maintenance for a just cause, Maintenance a charge upon husband's estate.

Under certain circumstances, the property of the husband has a charge fastened upon it for the maintenance of his wife and sons. If such property is sold to a third person, he may be sued by the wife for a declaration that maintenance be awarded to her out of the profits of that property in the hands of the purchaser. But as it is one of the first principles of law that debts due from the family must be met from the family estate, if the purchaser can show that the sale was necessitated by the exigencies of the family, then neither the wife nor the sons, can demand any maintenance out of the profits of property come into the hands of a third party by sale. The head of the family is in every case responsible for such debts; his power extends to disposing of the joint bead estate in order to meet liabilities, and a claim to maintenance gives way to the rights of the purchaser who has advanced money to extricate the family from its liabilities[1].

Wife's maintenance in Bombay.

In Bombay (Mumbai), the wife's right to maintenance is not based upon the doctrine of her co-ownership with her husband. There the right is said to be latent and inoperative, unless she be deserted. The right comes into operation only when natural affection, which usually prompts the mutual

1. Natchiar Ammal *v.* Gopala Krishna I. L. R. 2 Mad. 127.

acts of members of families, fails of its proper effects; it is then that law steps in with its rigid rules and imperfect remedies. Such were the views expressed in a case in which the husband had made a gift of a house which was his self-acquisition in favour of his son, after having taken a release from his wife that she would not assert her right of maintenance against that house. The High Court of Bombay decided in this case that the release did not free the house from a liability for the widow's maintenance. In the course of the judgment delivered, the rights of the wife as against her husband were lengthily discussed, and many propositions of law were laid down which are not endorsed in any other quarter.[1] In order to establish the rule that right to maintenance as vested in a wife could not be transferred by her to another person, it was laid down that her right before the division of the family or before desertion or supersession by her husband were of a subordinate character. The other reason for holding, that a release given by a Hindu wife in favour of her husband of all her rights to maintenance is invalid, is stated to be the peculiar necessity for protecting the rights of a Hindu female who must ordinarily be presumed to be helpless liable to be taken advantage of by their male relation. Her independent contracts to which her husband is not a joint party require close scrutiny before a court of justice and equity. "Usage as well as the law of the Śāstras prescribes her submissive dependence; and a release to her husband, in return for a bare maintenance to which she was already entitled, of something going far beyond that maintenance fails to satisfy the essential conditions. Her position would thus remain after her release what it was before it."

In Bengal the law is not clear how far the circumstance of the husband being a member of a joint family will affect the wife's right to maintenance. But the very same reason which will disentitle her to assert this right when her

1. Narbada Bai *v*, Mahadeo Narayan I. L. R. 5 Bom, 99.

husband is separate will also apply when he is not so. Where a wife without her husband's sanction goes away from her husband's house to live with her own family, she has been held to have no right to ask subsistence from her husband. (Kullyanessuree Debee *v.* Dwarkanath Sarma Chatterjee. 6 W. R. 116). From the report of this case it does not appear whether the husband was joint or separate; but it is certain that his being joint would not enlarge the maintenance right of the wife. The only way in which the undivided condition of the husband will affect the question is, that when the husband is separate, the party whom the wife will have to sue for maintenance will be the husband himself, whereas in the case of a joint family, she probably has her choice in suing either the husband or the managing member where there is one; if there be no managing member, then she may probably sue all the coparceners, provided there be joint property in which her husband has an interest. Cases involving the wife's right to maintenance during the lifetime of her husband are rare; ordinarily a wife is bound to live under the protection of her husband, which means that she lives in the same house with her husband, said is as a matter of course provided with her necessaries, along with the other members of the family, male or female. It is when ill-usage or improper behaviour on the part of her husband drives her from the family dwelling house that her claim to separate maintenance comes into existence. What would amount to ill-usage or improper behaviour is a question on which no general rule can, laid down. In one case we have seen that a Hindu wife can properly quit her husband's house, if the latter so far forgets himself as to consort with a Mahomedan woman, and thereby hurts the religious feelings of the wife. In another case it happened that the wife had left her husband's house and had earned her own living by working as a day-labourer without any objection protest on her husband's part, or any offer to her to come back to his house. It was held that if the wife under such circumstances were subsequently desirous to return her right to claim maintenance would revive, and that her previous independent life during which she made her a own livelihood was not a bar to, or a waiver of, her claim against the husband. (Netye Laha *v.* Soondaree Dossee, 9 W. &. 475.)

Marrying a second wife no cause for separate maintenance, Superseded wife's rights under original texts.

Upon the question of the reasons justifying the wife to leave her husband's house, and then to claim a separate maintenance, the case of Sitanath Mookerjee *v.* S. M. Haimabutty Dabee (24 W. R. 377) is a recent authority which lays down that the fact, of the husband having married another wife does not amount to such a justification. The suit was brought by the wife of a Kooleen Brahmin, upon the allegation that she had been compelled by her husband's cruelty to leave her husband's house and seek a home among her own relations. The facts were, that she had been married at seven years of age, had been the first wife, and had lived very happily with her husband for several years. She had then gone to live her at father s house where she had been visited by her husband from time to time. After this the husband had married a second wife when the first wife came over to her husband's house, but was not treated by him with sufficient cordiality. A rupture took place between her and her husband chiefly because the two wives could not agree with each other, and then on one occasion the first wife was repulsed by her husband with some show of anger and impatience, and was pushed with his hands away from himself. A day or two after this she left the house, and did not any more attempt or was willing to return to it, but claimed a very large sum by way of separated maintenance. Garth, C. J. observed, " In this state of facts we have to consider whether the plaintiff has disclosed any sufficient grounds for absenting herself from her husband's house, and claiming at our hands a separate maintenance from her husband, either past or future. It is clear according to Hindu law, a wife's first duty to her husband is to submit herself obediently to his authority, and to remain under his roof and protection; and although it might be very difficult to deduce from the authorities at the present day any definite rule as to the causes which would justify a wife in leaving her husband's house, it may safely be affirmed that mere unkindeness or neglect short of cruelty would not be a sufficient justification." The Chief Justice then refers to the provisions in the Criminal Procedure Code, in order to point out the modern law, those provisions being that the husband will be ordered to maintain his wife who refuses to live with him, if there be satisfactory evidence that the husband is living in adultery or has habitually treated his wife with cruelty. Those provisions further say, that she is not entitled to any separate allowance if she refuses to live with her husband without any sufficient reason. Merely because the husband does not speak to, or consort with the wife, she is not justified in leaving him. This decision may at first sight seem to run counter to our original texts. Yājñavalkya says, in śloka 151 of the 2nd chapter (para. 34, see. 11, ch. II, Colebrooke's s Mitākṣarā)—"To a superseded wife one should give an equal sum of money on account of supersession, to her that is, to whom no peculiar property has been given; when it has been given, however, a half is declared as proper to be given. Upon this the comments of the Mitākṣarā are "*She* is superseded, over whom a marriage takes place. To such a superseded wife an equal sum of money by reason of the second marriage–equal to so much as has been spent on the second marriage–should be given, provided no woman's property has been given either by her husband or by her father-in-law. In case that has been given, a half of the sum spent on the occasion of the second marriage should be given. Here the word 'half' does not signify an equal moiety of the whole. As much as would make what has been previously given equal to the sum spent on the second marriage ought to be bestowed." This is an authority declaring;. the first wife's right to a sum of money for the sole and simple reason that her husband has married a second wife. Whether our ancient law-givers intended this liability on the part of the husband as taking the place of his liability for supplying subsistence, is not manifest. The obligation imposed on the husband with such refinement in its details cannot be explained away as a moral obligation. Nor can it be supposed to be confined solely to the Mitākṣarā School; for the Dāyabhāga recognises it in ch. IV, sec. 1, para. 14. "That wealth which is given to gratify a first wife by a man desirous of marrying a second, is a gift on a second marriage; for its object is to obtain another wife." The decision of Garth, C. J., however, is reconcilable with the original texts by supposing that these texts intend by what they call supersession something like a judicial separation under the English Law; for the husband's right so to supersede is hedged in by certain restrictions. (See Manu, ch. 9, sl. 80-82.) In the case decided by the Chief Justice, the husband apparently did not claim to exercise any such right of supersession according to the ancient law, nor did the wife advance her claim on that ground. It was simply an instance of the practice which has prevailed in Bengal few hundred years among the Kooleen Brahmins, practice equally repugnant to the law of the śāstras and to the dictates of universal morality.

Widow's right to maintenance.

I now come upon the widow's right to maintenance. This is the most important section of the Hindu Law of maintenance. It may be conveniently dealt with under five heads, first as to a widow's right to maintenance in general; 2nd, as to her right being a charge upon the joint property; 3rd, as to the necessity of her residing in the family house for the purpose of retaining her right; 4th as to the amount she can properly claim; 5th and last, as to how far the Law of Limitation affects this right. In the schools guiding themselves by the paramount authority of the Mitākṣarā this right of the widow stands on the same foundation; but the law in its developement in the course of its administration by the four High Courts has undergone certain separate modifications which may be more conveniently considered apart under the decisions of each High Court. I shall begin by noticing the decisions of the Allahabad High Court.

As understood by the Allahabad High court

The Allahabad High Court mainly guides itself in questions of Hindu Law by the provisions of the Mitākṣarā as explained and supplemented by the Vīramitrodaya which closely follows the older treatise and may be said to be a running commentary and gloss upon the work of Vijñaneśvara. The author of the Mitākṣarā has, after a lengthy discussion, established that a chaste and lawfully married wife of a sonless person who died; while he was divided and not re-united with any other coparcener, succeeds as an heir to all his wealth (ch. II, sec. 1, para. 39); but the author nowhere says what her rights are if the husband died undivided. Upon this point we are left by him in the dark. In other parts of his work he quotes a text or two, which might be construed into the widow's right to maintenance. Thus in ch. II, see. 1, paras. 7, 20, he quotes two ślokas from Nārada, which run as follows–"If among brothers any one dies without leaving issue, or retires from the world, the rest should divide his wealth among themselves, excepting, however, the property of the woman; and they should also provide subsistence to his women, until the termination of their lives, if they keep unsullied the bed of their husband; in case of their being otherwise, they should *snatch* the same." But these two ślokas have been put by the author into the mouth of the imaginary opponent whose position denying the widow's right to inherit her husband's property he is controverting so elaborately in this part of his work. Again in para. 20 of the same section and chapter, the author refers to those two ślokas of Nārada, and says that they are applicable to the case of re-united brothers. Therefore those two texts may be an authority for the right of the widow of a re-united brother to demand maintenance from the coparceners of her deceased husband. So far as the express text of the Mitākṣarā is concerned, we find no authority for the well understood proposition of law that the widow of an undivided Hindu receives maintenance from the family of which he was a member. We must therefore have recourse to the text of the Vīramitrodaya for such an authority. Ch. III, part 1, section 10, para. 3, (p. 153) of this latter work says:—"Hence the chaste wife of a sonless deceased person who was separated and not re-united, is entitled to take the entire estate ; but of a sonless person who was unseparated or re-united, even the chaste wife is entitled to mere subsistence, by reason of the texts of Nārada and others, such as,—'If any one among brothers die without issue, etc. An unchaste widow, however, is not entitled even to maintenance, for it is declared,–'But if she behave otherwise, they may resume the allowance." Here Mitra Misra cites the initiatory words of the very two ślokas of Nārada which we find quoted in the Mitākṣarā as authority for an undivided widow's right to maintenance. He does not notice that in the Mitākṣarā the two ślokas of Nārada are said to be applicable to the case of re-united brothers. The truth seems to be that writers of the original texts assimilate the undivided condition with re-union, and generally extend the incidents of the one to the other. There is another text in the Mitākṣarā which speaks of the widow's maintenance. It is found in ch.-II, sec. 1, para. 37, and is a quotation from Hārīta. "If a widowed woman, who is in the prime of youth, be self-willed, then subsistence should be given to her for the purpose of enabling her to live her life out." But this text the Mitākṣarā construes as implying a prohibition against a woman of suspected chastity taking the whole wealth. The Vīramitrodaya quotes a text of Kātyāyana which seems to be a clear authority on the point of widow's right to maintenance (see page 173, para, 2) "But when the husband dies unseparated, the wife is entitled to food and raiment—a portion of the however, she gets till her death." Mitra Misra explains this text by saying that here the word, 'however, 'is equivalent to an alternative particle, and means the same thing as the word 'or' would have meant, That is to say, the widow can get food and raiment in kind, or she may get as much money out of her husband's property as would be sufficient for her subsistence and for the performance of such religious ceremonies as it is competent to her to perform. This contemplates both the alternatives open to the widow of an undivided member; she may either choose to live in the same mess with the coparceners of her deceased husband, or she may receive a separate maintenance and live apart from them. A little further on, another text of Nārada is quoted, "All the chaste widows should be maintained with food and raiment by the eldest, or by the father-in-law or even by any other person born in the family." The author explains it by saying that in every instance it is to be understood that the person responsible for the widow's maintenance must be one who has appropriated the husband's property, for the liability to give maintenance is an incident to the participation of wealth. Here is an authority for the well-known rule of law which has been generally adopted in decisions involving the question of a Hindu's maintenance, the rule, namely, that if one person anyhow intercepts another's right of inheritance to the property of a third person, the first is liable for the maintenance of the second.

In the F. B. case of Gunga Bai *v.* Seetaram, I. L. R. I. All. 175, Pearson, J. observed, "In the case of Latlykuer *v.* Gunga Bishen, H. C. R. N. W. P., 1875, p. 261, to which allusion is made in the referring order, I assented, not without doubt and hesitation, to the doctrine that a Hindu widow was entitled to be maintained out of the joint ancestral estate of the family of which her husband was a member, although he had pre-deceased his father. That doctrine, although not expressly laid down in the Hindu Law, was supported by many considerations of reason and equity, and had been recognised by several decisions. But I am not prepared further that a widow is legally entitled to be maintained by her husband's relations after his death merely in consequence of such relationship. The texts which countenance such a view appear to be of the nature of moral or religious precepts." Oldfield, J. said, "The legal right of a widow to maintenance from her husband's family can, I apprehend, scarcely be supported with reference solely to those texts of Hindu Law which indicate the position a woman obtains by marriage in her husband's family, and those which generally inculcate the duty of maintenance of the female members of a family."

In an early case decided by the Privy Council, it was held that where there was joint ancestral property, the widow was entitled to maintenance out of it, although the rights of three of her sons had been confiscated by Government on account of absconding to evade a summons to appear and answer a charge of rebellion.[1] This was a case from Benares and therefore governed by the Mitākṣarā law.

Widow's maintenance in Madras

The High Court of Madras holds that woman divorced for adultery who has continued in adultery during her husband's life, and who has lived in unchastity after his death, is not entitled to maintenance out of the property of her deceased husband.[2] In this case, the Court in its judgment alludes to a rule of Hindu law which allows a bare subsistence to an adulterous wife, but draws a

1. Golab Koonwar *v.* Collector of Benares, 8 Moore I. A. 447; 8. C. 7 W. R. P. C. 47.
2. Muttammal *v.* Kamakshi Ammal, 2 Mad. H. C. Rep. 337.

distinction between the case of such a wife and that of a widow, who leads an unchaste life after her husband's death. This distinction is also made in the passage from the Vīramitrodaya I have already quoted, which imposes a duty upon the husband alone to give a bare subsistence to his unchaste wife.

The widow, though entitled to maintenance at the hand of the members of the family who have appropriated her husband's undivided share, cannot, however, bind them by her contracts for necessaries supplied to her. The heir no doubt is liable to pay the proper debts of the person from whom they inherit property; it is also a rule of law that debts contracted for necessary family expenses whilst the family are living together, must be paid from the family property. The power of contracting such debts is possessed even by a wife or a widow living in the family. But this rule cannot create a liability on the part of the heir to pay debts contracted by a widow to obtain her own necessaries.[1]

In Bombay

According to the Vyavahāra Mayūkha, if a coparcener dies without leaving issue, his widow is entitled to maintenance where he was unseparatcd or re-united with the rest.[2] It says:—"But says Nārada:—'Among brothers, if any one dies without issue, or enters a religious order, the rest should divide his wealth, except the wife's separate property. They should allow maintenance to his wives to the end of their lives, provided they preserve unsullied the bed of their lord. If they behave otherwise, the brothers may resume that allowance.' It relates according to Madana to the wives of one dying unseparated or re-united ; because the text occurs under that head. Kātyāyana says:—'If her husband have departed for heaven, *strī* (the wife) obtains food and raiment; if unseparated, she will receive a share

1. Ramasami Aiyan *v.* Minakshi Ammal, 2 Mad. H. C. Rep. 409.
2. Chapter IV, section 8, paras. 4–7.

of the wealth, so long as she lives.' The term ' unseparated' is illustrative of the class, such as the re-united. The word 'but' has here the sense of 'or.' There would thus result two propositions according to Madana, the latter referring to a wife lawfully married; the former to a concubine. The foundation of this exposition is questionable. The same author (Kātyāyana) thus makes a correct statement:–'She who is intent upon her service to the elders of the family, is fit to enjoy her legitimate share: should she not perform her proper duty, raiment and food [only] should be assigned to her. The meaning is, that at the elder or *guru's* pleasure, she may receive a share; otherwise merely food and raiment. The same:–'A wife who does malicious acts, who is immodest, destroys wealth, or is unchaste, is not fit to inherit wealth.' As for the text, 'this same course should be followed in the case of degraded females; food and raiment are to be given to them ; and they should reside near the house,—it, in the opinion of some authors refers to the husband while living."[1] In this passage, the same texts of Nārada and Kātyāyana are cited which are found in the Vīramitrodaya and are explained in the same manner. It assimilates non-separation with re-union in respect of the law of maintenance; it recognises the rule that an unchaste wife gets a bare subsistence at the hand of husband, but not a widow at the hand of the coparceners. It notices the alternative of the widow's getting a share of the wealth, even in case of non-separation; only it makes a dutiful conduct on her part a condition to that alternative.

The question that even an unchaste wife gets a bare subsistence, or what is otherwise called a starving maintenance, arose in the case of Honamma *v.* Timanna Bhat, I. L. R. 1 Bom. 560, where Westrop, C. J. held that a widow who has already obtained a decree for maintenance does not forfeit her right under it merely because she has since then been leading an incontinent life. The Chief Justice refers to

1. Mandlik, p. 78.

the Mayūkha, ch, IV, sec. 8, pl. 9, and the Mitākṣarā, ch. II, sec. 1, paras. 37, 38. The passage from the Mitākṣarā I have already noticed (see p. 306). The text of the Mayūkha referred to is as follows:—"To even a woman suspected of incontinence,, only maintenance should be given. Since Hārīta says:—'If a widowed woman in the prime of youth be self-willed, then subsistence should be given in order that she may live out her life. 'Self-willed' means 'suspected of incontinence. So says the Mitākṣarā." This is but an echo of the Mitākṣarā passage. I am afraid that this text of the Mayūkha does not support the rule that an incontinent widow gets starving allowance, as the Chief , Justice of Bombay has supposed. Were it so, the author of the Mayūkha. would not be consistent with himself. A few lines back the author has said that an unchaste woman can advance a claim of that kind solely against her husband, a view of the law adopted by the Vīramitrogaya (Vīram., p. 153). Therefore an incontinent widow is precluded from demanding a starving allowance from her deceased husband's family. The meaning of Hārīta as understood by the authors of the Mitākṣarā and Mayūkha seems to be this:—The widow of a separated Hindu ordinarily inherits his property; if, however she be very young and disobedient to those whom by usage and law she is bound to defer to, law gives her only a bare subsistence; this rule applies when there are good reasons to suspect her unchastity. It does not apply to the widow of an unseparated Hindu is Hārīta is interpreted as laying down a special rule limiting the ordinary rule of widow's succession to her husband. This succession does not occur unless her husband had been separate; the special rule must therefore regard the case of separation. At the same time it is impossible to question the soundness of the decision arrived at in the particular case quoted above. There a decree had already been obtained by the widow; and though Nārada says (see *ante, P. 306)* that in case of subsequent lapse, the widow's allowance may be *snatched* or resumed, yet modern courts have on considerations of equity turned a deaf ear to those harsh directions of the ancient Ṛṣis. Equity necessarily implies impartiality. Were the law, as laid down by the ancient Ṛṣis to be strictly enforced, many a Hindu youth who in the heyday of life has walked roughshod over the religious directions of our śāstars by eating forbidden food and drinking forbidden beverage, would be disinherited, if he may not have to give back inheritance already vested in him. If in his case, the rigorous ancient law is to be overlooked and disregarded, I do not see any reason why the weaker sex should be tied down to a more rigourous interpretation of those very texts. The above decision of the Chief Justice Westropp was dissented from in Valu *v.* Ganga, I. L. R. 7 Bom. 86, in which the judgment was delivered by Sargent, C. J. Referring to the above quoted text of Hārīta, the Chief Justice Says:–"It is plain therefore that the authors of the Mitākṣarā and Mayūkha regarded the text of Hārīta as exclusively intended to qualify the right of the widow on her not being a person of such conduct as to subject her to grave suspicion, or to make it likely that she will dishonour his name. The contract between actual chastity and the conduct which is described in the translations as headstrong or perverse is also drawn with marked distinctness in Mitākṣarā ch. II, sec. 10, para. 14 and Mayūkha, ch. IV, sec. IX, pl. 12, where the authors are discussing the rights of daughters and wives of disqualified persons. In the latter text, it is said:—'If she be unchaste, a woman must be turned out of doors and without a maintenance. A perverse woman should also be turned out of doors, but a maintenance must be provided for her, according to Madana and others. Regarding the question from the stand point of humanity, few people would probably care to justify the husband's relations who had succeeded to his property, in leaving his widow in a state of complete destitution, (provided she was then leading a respectable life), however much she might in the past have failed in her duty of maintaining inviolate the bed of her lord. But in the absence of any text distinctly imposing this obligation, or of any expression qualifying the right which is reserved by so many texts to those who take the husband's property of withdrawing maintenance from an unchaste widow, it cannot (except perhaps in the case of a son) be regarded as a legal liability to be enforced in a Civil Court."

In noticing above the case of Honamma, *v.* Timanna Bhat, I. L. R. 1 Bom. 559, I have said that Hārīta's text quoted in the Mitākṣarā, ch. II, sec. 1, para. 37 applies to the case of the widow of a separated parcener. I find that in Savitri Bai *v.* Lukshmi Bai, I. L. R. 2 Bom. p. 606 the same text has been explained by Westropp, C. J, himself as a denial of the right of a widow suspected of incontinency to take the whole estate, and therefore as implying that a widow not suspected of incontinency has a right to take the whole property of a husband separated from his family and dying without leaving issue male–"Vijñāneśvara is there regarding such maintenance of a headstrong woman as one of the liabilities of the inheritence, the descent of which was his main topic."

The case Savitri Bai *v.* Luximī Bai, I. L. R. 2 Bom. 573, in which the question of the Hindu widow's maintenance was considered by a Full Bench of the High Court of Bombay, and an exhaustive judgment, reviewing most of the prior decisions and discussing the original texts at a great length was delivered by Westropp, C. J. is a leading authority. This was not exactly the case of a joint family, for the widow's husband had separated himself before he died, and the claim was made against the uncle of the deceased husband. The points decided were that no claim to maintenance could be sustained in favour of a widow as against the relatives of her deceased husband, whether separated or not, unless there was ancestral property in their hands. This Full Bench Decision overruled some of the prior rulings which had gone far as to have laid down that mere destitution would entitled a widow to claim maintenance from her husband's relatives. One case was that the widow had obtained her deceased husband's share and had lived by money-lending for thirty years. (Bai Lakshmi *v.* Lakshmi Das Gopal Das, 1 Bom. H. C. Rep. 13.) Notwithstanding these facts, it had been held that the obligation of maintaining the widow would still attach to the husband's relatives, should she then be destitute of the means of living. In another case Chandrabhaga Bai *v.* Kashinath Vilpal Bom. H. C. Rep. 323, a widow whose husband had been separated in estate from his father, and who herself stopping with her own father sued her father-in-law for a money allowance by way of maintenance. The High Court of Bombay held that if the widow's present circumstances were such as to give her a claim to maintenance, the father-in-law would be bound to support her; and in determining what sum ought to be paid her as maintenance, any peculiar property in her hands should not be taken into account. In the case of Timmappa *v.* Parmeshriama, 5 Bom. H. C. Rep. 130 A. C. J., the High Court laid down that every Hindu widow, whether her husband was divided from the family or not, was entitled, when in needy circumstances, to claim maintenance from her husband's relatives, the whole policy of the Hindu Law being not to allow even a distantly related widow to starve. In Rama Bai *v.* Trimbak Ganesh, 9 Bom. H. C. Rep. 283, the High Court of Bombay said that although according to the authorities the relations of a deserted wife are not under a personal liability to maintain her, yet the proceeds of her husband's property to the extent of one-third might be claimed by her as maintenance. In the case of Udaram Sitaram *v.* Sonka Bai, 10 Bom. H. C. Rep. 483, the widow of an undivided son alleged that she had been maltreated by her father-in-law, who had expelled her from the family house. On these facts the Court awarded to her a residence in that house and a separate maintenance of rupees 10 per mensem. Soma of these older decisions were overruled and others welt distinguished, in the Full Bench case of Savitri Bai *v.* Lakshmi Bai, I. L. R. 2 Bom. 573.

Widow's maintenance a charge on joint property

I now come to the question of how far the maintenance of a Hindu widow is a charge on the joint property. When it is said that the widow's maintenance is a charge upon the estate, what is intended is that a claim on the part of a Hindu widow for maintenance is good, not only against the persons allied by relationship to the deceased husband, but also against any person into whose hands the husband's property may have come. Upon this point the original texts do not furnish us with any direct authority. We might possibly contend from some of these texts that so long as there are persons in the family having a just claim for subsistence out of the joint estate, any alienation of such estate would be absolutely and void in the eye of law.[1] But this ancient rule has been disregarded by the modern administrators of justice for a long time. In doing so, they have been mainly influenced by the principles governing the Bengal School, the authorities of which were the first to propound the doctrine that ownership means the power of dealing with property absolutely at one's pleasure. From this doctrine follows the corollary, that if a person is the lawful owner of property, a sale of it made by him must be legally valid notwithstanding that other persons may have a right to receive maintenance out of it. In a joint family when a coparcener dies, the rule of survivorship vests in the surviving members the interest the deceased member had. The survivors are the owners of the whole after a death of this kind, as they and the deceased were together owners of it before his death. Although therefore the widow may be entitled to subsistence, there is nothing to invalidate an actual sale by the owners of the property. The transaction

1. See Mitākṣarā, chap. I, see. 1, para. 27.

is legally good, though it may be morally reprehensible. Such is the view the tribunals of the present day have come to take of this matter, under the guidance of Jimūtavāhana and his followers. The work of Jimūtavāhana is nominally an authority for only the Bengal School; but his principles have imperceptibly overspread the law of the other four schools as actually administered. It should be borne in mind that the first considerable part of India which came under British dominion was the province of Bengal. The British administrators of Hindu Law therefore had become to a great extent familiar with the Bengal law before they addressed themselves to the task of mastering the law of the other four schools. What might be expected to happen did really take place. Analogies from Bengal law were largely availed of in deciding cases in the rest of India. The aggregate case-law as developed by the Courts of British India, exhibits a superabundance of Bengal rules, some of which are either in direct conflict with the recognised original authorities of the other four schools, or are entirely ignored by them. Another reason which has recommended the Bengal principles to the British administrators of justice is, that this law approaches more nearly to the ideas and opinions underlying the legal principles of Western Europe. In India the law of Bengal alone has given to individual proprietary right that absolute character which is in conformity to European notions. The effect of this tendency in the modern courts is visible on the law of maintenance as being a charge on joint property. Many an earlier case recognises the notion that a widow's maintenance follows the estate in whosesoever hands it may have come. In Mussamut Khukroo Misrain *v.* Jhoomucklall Dass, 15 W. R. 263, which was a case from the district of Tirhoot, and so governed by the Vivādacintāmaṇi, the Judges say:–"But with the finding that her husband died a member of the joint family, all her claim disappeared, and she has no interest whatever in the family estate. It has been contended that her claim for maintenance is a charge on the estate, and that therefore she has an interest in keeping that estate in the family; but as a matter of fact, change of ownership would not affect her lien, and if she failed in getting her maintenance from the members of her late husband's family, she could make the estate chargeable with it into whose hands soever it had fallen under the foreclosure". In Ramchunder Dikshit *v.* Savitiri Bai, 4 Bom. H. C. Rep. A. C. J. 73, the High Court of Bombay held that the maintenance of a widow was by Hindu Law a charge upon the whole estate and therefore on every part thereof. In this case the widow had sued for maintenance only one of the brothers of her deceased husband who raised a plea that as there were other persons interested in the property from which the widow's maintenance was to be received, the suit could not proceed unless they were made parties. The High Court said that it was not a good defence against the suit, inasmuch as the defendant might sue his brothers for contribution. In Gunga Bai *v.* Administrator General of Bengal, 2 I. J. N. S. 124, Phear, J. said that the widow's right to maintenance had by the death of her husband become an actual charge on the estate which devolved upon the four sons of the said husband in joint coparcenery. Three of these sons became afterwards concerned in a rebellion against the British Government, and having absconded, their rights were forfeited under Reg. XI of 1796. The Privy Council in Mussamut Golab Koonwar *v.* The Collector of Benares, 4 Moore's Ind. Ap. 246, held that the forfeiture of the sons' right did not interfere with the widow's right to maintenance out of the whole ancestral property. It was with reference to the facts of this case that Phear, J. said that the widow's claim was an existing burden on the share which her sons took in the estates at the time their shares were confiscated, and of course the Government took subject to her claim for maintenance. In Hiralal *v.* Muss. Kousillah, 2 Agra H. C. 42, the widow asserted her right to maintenance and objected to the conveyance of the property. The court held that this constituted a charge of which the purchaser had notice, and that the maintenance remained claimable out of the property notwithstanding its alienation by the heirs. In Baijun Doobey v. Brijbhooken Lal Awasti, L. R. 2 I. A. 279, Judicial Committee held that the maintenance of the widow was a charge upon the inheritance which had descended from her husband to her daughter-in-law; that the liability to maintain the widow passed to the son when he got the estate of his father, and when the estate passed from the son to the son's widow, the liability to maintain the father's widow still attached to the inheritance, the son's widow being bound to maintain the father's widow out of the inheritance. In Sreemutty Bhagabutty Dossee *v.* Kanailal Mitter, 8 B. L. R. 225, Phear, J. said:-" As against an heir who has taken the property, the widow has a right to have her maintenance treated as a charge on the property. She may doubtless follow the property in the hands of any one who takes it with notice of her having set up a claim for maintenance against the heir. I do not think that in Bengal she has a lien on the property in respect of her maintenance against all the world, irrespective of such notice. No such lien as far as I know has ever been established in these courts." In Babu Goluk Chunder Bose *v.* Rancee Ahilla Dai, 25 W. R. 100, Mitter, J. said:—"It has been settled by more than one decision of this court that where a purchaser purchases property from the heir with notice that a Hindu widow is entitled to be maintained out of it, the property in the hands of the purchaser continues to be charged with that maintenance. It is not a correct proposition of Hindu law to say that in all cases a Hindu widow is not entitled to follow properties from which she is entitled to obtain her maintenance in the hands of the purchaser, unless she at first attempts to recover her maintenance from the heir-at-law. It may be that in certain cases where the defence is that sufficient property is still in the hands of the heir-at-law from which the maintenance can be recovered, the person entitled to maintenance might not be allowed to recover it from the purchaser of a small portion of the family property without first attempting to recover it from the properties in the possession of the heir-at-law." In Subramania Mudaliar *v.* Kaliani Ammal, 7 Mad. H. C. R. 226, the court said:—"During the marriage and the life of the husband, the claim to maintenance against his estate was a mere possibility. If he had wrongfully put her away or refused to support her, the possibility would have become a present interest; the right is a charge on the husband's estate in some circumstances while he still lives, in all cases when he lives no longer. The husband's estate in the hands of the survivor is therefore that to which the charge attaches, and the husband's death is the period at which the statute begins to run against the claim."

Purchaser without notice relieved from widow's maintenance right

From a consideration of these different cases it would appear that originally the widow's claim to maintenance out of the joint property in which her deceased husband had an interest was supposed to override all other rights, including even those of a purchaser from the survivors to whom the husband's interest had lapsed. But latterly it has been held that a purchaser would not be affected if he had no notice of the widow's claim, and that even if he had notice the rights created by purchase from the hands of the survivors of the widow's deceased husband would remain intact if the alienation was caused by the necessity of paying such debts of the family as would be a just and valid burden upon the joint property. The necessity of notice has been strongly insisted upon in Adhirani Narain Kumari *v.* Shonamali Patmohadai, I.. L. R. 1 Cal. 365. In this case the widow sued the purchaser of the joint property for her maintenance, after having obtained a decree against a member of the joint family namely, the younger brother of her deceased husband. The property had been sold in execution of a decree against this person. It was found that the purchaser had no notice of any claim for maintenance on the part of the widow. The judgment was delivered by L. Jackson, J, who after reviewing many previous cases on the point held that the property in the hands of the purchaser was not liable for the maintenance claimed; that there was a distinction between the member of a family in whose hand the property had come either by right of inheritance or by survivorship, and a *bona fide* purchaser without notice; that it was exceedingly probable in this case that the debts which led to the sale of this property were partly ancestral; that the widow's right to maintenance was subject to the duty of paying these debts and was enforceable against only the residue after paying such debts; that her right to maintenance had been modified by her having previously obtained a personal decree against her deceased husband's younger brother; and that having omitted to give notice to the purchaser of her claim, the widow could have enforced her right only against the surplus proceeds of the property when sold.

The Full Bench case of Shamlal *v.* Banna, I. L. R. 4 All. 299, decided by the Allahabad High court, lays down that the maintenance of a Hindu widow is not such a charge on the joint estate in which her deceased had an interest, as can be enforced against a *bona fide* purchaser without notice, until the said maintenance has become fixed and charged by decree of court or contract on particular property. "The right to maintenance is of an indefinite character: the hier who succeeds to the estate may be said to take it with a trust for widow's support which will give her a right against him to have the allowance ascertained and fixed and made chargeable on particular property; but till this has been done, a charge cannot be said to exist in the sense of a title issuing out of the land itself, and binding every person who comes into the estate; and a *bona fide* purchaser for value without notice of the claim will therefore be protected. The principle of protecting a *bona fide* purchaser without notice cannot be objected to as being something peculiar to English Law, as it rests on grounds of public convenience which are of universal application."

Modern case law as to widow's maintenance not consonant to Ṛṣi texts

To a Hindu mind not penetrated with European notions, and still retaining the spirit of ancient Hindu law as propounded by the Ṛṣis and their earlier commentators, this exposition of the law relating to a widow's maintenance would appear harsh and unsympathetic. The life of a Hindu female is one of seclusion; outside the zenana, her knowledge is as limited as that of a tender child; culture, training, or education, she has absolutely none. If her rights are invaded by the male members the family, she is utterly helpless; or she falls under the influence of persons whose motive for lending her a help are the furthest from those of philanthropy disinterested goodwill. Females belonging to the respectable classes are incapable of earning their own livelihood; if the family property is transferred by the male relations, what can these females do to keep then rights of maintenance 'secure ? If the law holds that the purchaser of such property is not bound to give them maintenance, the law in fact forfeits an inherent right vested in them. To insist that the female member claiming maintenance must prove that her existence and claim were known to the purchaser is to impose upon her the performance of an impossibility. This is the light in which the modern exposition of the law of maintenance would be viewed by an orthodox Hindu. On the texts other hand, it is not easy to shut our eyes to the changes which Hindu society has undergone since the time when the Ṛṣi texts were written. Transfers of immoveable property have now obtained a frequency that the people of those days could not even dream of; the idea of property being tied up in the hand of a single individual or a single family would create an amount of inconvenience quite disproportioned to the advantage that might be gained if the law set its face against property changing hands. The ordinary arrangements of society would be unsettled if the law were so. Again, to declare invalid all transfer of joint property so long as maintenance of any person is to issue out of it, would be inconsistent with the undoubted proprietory right of the male members. To the outside world, they represent the joint property; all necessary expenses are incurred by them; third parties give them credit in proportion to the amount of property visibly in their possession; the female members are unknown to the public at large. Third parties become accustomed to advance loans to the male members, and to regard them as the sole proprietors, as the holders of an absolute and unfettered right over the property. If these third parties, so accustomed should buy it from them, their conduct cannot be blamed as unreasonable. On the contrary, it would be unresonable to hold them liable for unknown claims first brought to their notice after they have parted with their money. Unreasonable in this sense that the balance of convenience would be in favour of upholding the purchasers rights, regard being had to the present condition of Hindu society. The later decisions disclose principle upholding transfers of joint family property where the purchaser is not affected with fraud. Fraud may be imputed to him, if he knowingly and willingly buys from property from which a widow derives her maintenance. Lukshman Ramchandra Joshi *v.* Satyabhama Bai, I. L. R. 2 Bom. 494, is an authority for what has been said above.

Fraudulent purchaser bound to pay widow's maintenance

That was a suit for maintenance brought by a Hindu widow against her husband's brother (against whom she had previously obtained a decree), who was the sole surviving member of her husband's family, and purchaser against certain *bona fide* purchasers for value of certain immoveable ancestral property. It was contended that the widow's maintenance was not such a charge on the estate as to give her any kind of proprietary interest in it; that her right, although its value was dependent on the amount of her deceased husband's share in the property, was merely a personal one against her husband's brother; and that notice of what was not really a charge, in the sense of an interest in the property, could not convert the merely personal obligation into a real right by way of incumbrance on the property, accom-panying it into whosesoever hands it may pass. West, J. held that the sole surviving proprietary member was competent to sell the estate vested in him; that the right of the widow would not be affected thereby if by a decree of court it had become a charge adhering to the estate; that previous to its being made a precise and actual charge on the property, the proprietary member might deal with it at his discretion; that if the alienation were made with a view to defraud the widow, and if the purchaser were privy to the fraudulent transaction, the property in such purchaser's hand would still be liable for the widow's maintenance, and that mere knowledge on the purchaser's part of the existence of such a widow and of her claim would not be sufficient notice affecting the purchaser, who in good faith thought that the alienation would not work any wrong upon the widow. Where the sale of the family property is brought about by what is called a legal necessity, which among other matters includes the payment of a family debt, the claim to maintenance cannot take precedence of such debt, nor, will it be a charge on the husband's property as against a purchaser. (Natchiarammal *v.* Gopal Krishna, I. L. R., 2 Mad. 126.)

Widow's right to residence

Connected with the widow's right to maintenance is her

right to residence in the family dwelling house. The leading case on this subject is Mongola Dabee *v.* Dinonath Bose, 4 B. L. R. O. C. J. 73. In this case the judgment was delivered by Sir Barnes Peacock, the question being whether the purchaser of the family dwelling house from the adopted son of the widow's husband was entitled to dispossess her, she having lived in the house so long as her husband lived, and having continued to live in it after his death. Sir Barnes held that neither the adopted son nor the purchaser from him was entitled to turn the widow out of the house in which she was left by her husband at the time of his death; at any rate she could not be turned out unless some other suitable dwelling were provided for her. His words are:—"It seems quite contrary to every principle of Hindu Law, by which the property taken by an heir is for the spiritual benefit of the deceased, to suppose it would not have contained some provision to protect a Hindu widow from being turned out of the dwelling in which her husband had left her at the time of his death without notice or even after a week's notice." This decision is based upon two texts. The first is a text of Kātyāyana cited in 2 Colebrooke's Dig. p. 133, and is as follows:—"Except his whole estate and his dwelling house what remains after the food and clothing of his family, a man may give away, whatever it be, whether fixed or immoveable; otherwise it may not be given." The other text is verses 56 and 57, sec. 1, ch. 11 of the Dāyabhāga. Verse 56 is, "But the wife must enjoy her husband's estate after his demise. She is not entitled to make a gift, mortgage or sale of it. Thus Kātyāyana says 'Let the childless widow, preserving unsullied the bed of her lord, and abiding with her venerable protector, enjoy with moderation the property until her death. After her let the heirs take it'" The beginning of verse 57 is' "Abiding with her venerable protector, that is, with her father-in-law or others of her husband's family." I apprehend that these words have been construed by Sir Barnes as creating a right in the widow to dwell in her father-in-law's house. They clearly imply a duty on the part of the widow to adopt her residence in that house; the performance of this duty necessarily involves her right to reside therein, otherwise she would be unable to perform the duty. The considerations, however, which weighed most with the Chief Justice are disclosed in the following words of his judgment:—"I have very great doubt whether a son, either natural born or adopted, is entitled to turn his father's widow and the other females of the family who are entitled to maintenance out of the dwelling selected by the father for his own residence, and in which he left those females of his family at the time of his death. No one who is at all acquainted with the usages and customs of the Hindus can doubt, that it would be highly injurious to the reputation of the females of a family to be turned out of the residence, at least until some other proper place has been provided for them."

Not affected by the doctrine of factumvalet

With regard to the question whether the text of Kātyāyana might not be considered as a moral injunction the judgment says:–"If a man's right is not *factum valet.* restricted, *factum valet* applies; his act is valid if he has title, although he may be guilty of an immoral act in doing what he has a legal right to do; but if his right is restricted, the rule, *factum valet,* does not enable him to go beyond the restriction. The most difficult question is, whether this passage of Kātyāyana, which says a dwelling house may not be given, is a mere moral precept or a restriction on a man's right to convey. It seems to me at present that it is a restriction and not mere moral precept, and that the son and heir of the father has not such a right in the dwelling of the family that he can at once, of his own pleasure, turn out all females of his family, or sell it and give the purchaser leave to turn them out." This decision shows that even in Bengal the right over ancestral property is not unrestricted. In a former part of these Lectures I have attempted to show how such a conclusion could be arrived at by considering the drift of different parts of the Dāyabhāga especially where the author restricts the father's power as regards partition of inherited property. In Mongola Dabee *v.* Dinonath Bose, the Chief Justice comes to the same conclusion and says;— "That shows that, with regard to ancesteal property the father's inability to make an unequal partition of ancestral property among his sons depends on restricted ownership, and that he has not an unlimited discretion over his property. In those cases where a man has no title to convey, or where his right is restricted, the rule of *factum valet* not apply." Were these observations carried out to their legitimate consequences, the Bengal property law might be assimilated to the property law as sanctioned by the Mitākṣarā. But the local usage and numberless decisions have established the Bengal father's absolute power over inherited property too firmly to be shaken by remarks like the above, they being regarded as *obiter dicta.* The only restriction which the above case establishes over one's s power in respect of ancestral property in Bengal is, that the ancestor's widow and probably some other female members will not be driven out of the family dwelling house by persons claiming under alienations to which they are not parties. Mongola Dabee's case has been followed in cases decided by the other High Courts. Thus Gouri *v.* Chandermoni, I. L. R. 1 All. 262, the auction purchaser of the rights and interests of one member in a certain dwelling house endeavoured to obtain possession of the house, but was resisted by the childless widow of member, who was residing in the house, and claimed the right to reside in a moiety thereof as her husband's widow. The High Court said:—"It does appear to have been admitted that the property was held by Lachman Persad and Baney Madhub in equal shares, but assuming it was the joint property of the two brother, the widow of Baney Madhub is entitled to live in it, it being the house in which she resided with her husband. She cannot be ousted by a purchaser of her nephew's rights. The house is a small one, and it is not shown that one moiety is more than sufficient as a residence for the Mussamut." In Talemand Sing *v.* Rukmina I. L. R. 3 All. 358, one member of a joint family had been sued by a third party on a bond for money, upon which a decree had been obtained, and the family dwelling house had been sold in execution of the decree and purchased at the court sale by the decreeholder, when he tried to oust the widow of another member from the house. The High Court said that the widow of a member of a joint Hindu family could claim a right of residence in the family dwelling house, and could sert it against the auction purchaser. In Dalsukhram Mahasukhram *v.* Lallubhai Moteechand, I. L. R. 7 Bom. 282, two houses had been sold by the son of a joint family, one of which was occupied as residence by his mother. The purchaser sued both the vendor and his mother to recover possession of the houses. Upon these facts the district judge held that by Hindu Law and custom of the country a widow was entitled to residence in the house of her husband during her lifetime not with standing the sale of it by her son. The High Court that as no proper reasons were disclosed for the alienation by the son, and as the widow was in possession, and the purchaser had purchased with full knowledge of such possession, the sale by the son did not affect the widow's right to residence. On the authority of the passage from Kātyāyana already quoted, found in Colebrooke's Dig. b. 2, ch. IV, sec. 2, text 19, the High Court held that the requisites for the maintenance of the family were on the same footing as the family dwelling; and although the rule regarding maintenance that the ancestral property in the hands of a purchaser continues to be charged with it might be subject to certain conditions, yet it was undoubtedly a correct proposition of law, that a son could not evict his widowed mother or authorise a purchaser to do so without providing some other suitable dwelling for her. It has been held, however, in an Allahabad case that this right of residence would not prevent the auction sale of the family dwelling house merely because the judgment debtor's widow might be residing in it. In this case the suit was for certain moneys charged on, amongst other properties, the ancestral family dwelling house which was occupied by two widows, one the mother, the other the wife of the mortgagor, Their plea was that they had no other place to be in except that house, that they possessed a right residence therein, and that the mortgage was invalid. The decree of the first two courts refusing the sale of the house was upset by the High Court observing that the question of the right of residence was not involved in the case, that the hypothecated house could be sold in a execution of the mortgage decree, and that it was a matter for decision in a future case whether the widow could be ousted by the auction purchaser. (Bhikham Das *v.* Pura, I. L. R. 2 All. 141.)

Widow may live elsewhere than in her hunband's house.

Allied to the subject of a widow's right to reside in the family dwelling house is the question whether a widow affects her rights by refusing to live in the family of her husband. Such refusal may be dictated by either innocent or vicious motives. At one time there seems to have been a notion abroad that a widow was bound in duty after the death of her husband to live under the protection of her husband's family, and that should she, without any just cause, quit such protection, and go elsewhere she would, be guilty of a dereliction of duty, although there might be no vicious motive in her doing so. Nor would such a notion be devoid of all show of authority in its favour. Thus Kātyāyana quoted in the Dāyabhāga ch. 11, see. 1, verse 56, says that the sonless widow should preserve inviolate the bed of her husband, that she should stop with the 'venerable preceptor' or 'guru,' as the word in the original is Verse 57 explains what is meant by stopping with the guru. She must dwell near her 'father-in-law and such others, and must stop in her husband's house. This is the same text from which Sir Barnes Peacock has inferred that the husband's house is the proper dwelling place for the widow, and that she cannot be driven cut from it by her husband's heirs or third persons claiming through them. The word 'guru' in Sanskrit means 'one who is entitled to respect and veneration.' The father and the elder brother are often respectfully called 'gurus.' When therefore Kātyāyana says that the widow is to stop with the 'guru,' the reasonable construction is, that she is directed to live in the same house in which such persons live, as were entitled to respect and veneration from her husband ; it may be his father, or elder brother, or uncle, or senior cousin, or mother, somebody is fact belonging to the husband's family, to whom the husband used to pay deference when he was alive. After marriage, a woman's identity is to a great extent merged in that of her husband; she is according to Hindu notions, half his body; his house is her house; and his gurus would be her 'gurus.' The text of. Kātyāyana therefore, supplemented by Jīmūtavāhana's explanation, fairly indicates the prevalence of a pretty general notion among Hindus, that for a widow to be independent in her actions and to dwell elsewhere than in her deceased husband's house, would be improper conduct, Again Nārada quoted in verse 64, sec. I, ch. XI, Dāyabhāga, says that after the death of the husband, it is his family that has a claim to the obedience of the sonless widow. They have a right to be consulted when she makes any disposition of her property; they are the guardians of her wealth; they should supply her with all necessary things. When the family of her husband has become extinct to a man, when the family domicile even is gone to wreck, when there is not a soul of the same blood with her husband, it is then that she is allowed to place herself under the guardianship of her father's family. Modern usage also seems to be in conformity with the notion that it is proper for a widow to with her husband's family. The Hindus are superstitiously particular as to the honour of their females. The inevitable consequence of a single lapse of virtue on the part of a woman is absolute excommunication. Among the more respectable castes, actual unchastity is not unfrequent; but that the public excommunication of fallen women belonging to these castes is not so often seen is due to the fact that there is abundant concealment. There can be no condonation of an act of unchastity. Years of virtuous conduct cannot efface the stigma attaching to a woman to whom even a single guilty act has been brought home. Not only she herself, but even both her families, on the husband's and on the father's side, are involved in the infamy, according to the popular idea. No matter that all connection between the guilty woman and her family may have ceased; no matter that she may have gone elsewhere, dead to the community she belonged to. The memory of the guilt pursues her husband's and her father's family; and a certain social degradation is fastened upon all connected with her in the relationship of blood or affinity. It is for this reason, that the family of the widow's husband, when tolerably well-to-do, generally insist upon her residing with them. Except among the Kulin Brahmins, with whom the idea prevails that a man's proper home is his maternal grandfather's house, the residence of the widow with her husband's family is the rule; her residence in her father's house is exceptional. This usage of the Hindus furnishes an explanation of the circumstance that some of the earlier cases, where a widow sued either for succession to her husband's property or for maintenance out of the same, we meet with a plea in defence set up, that the widow did not reside in her husband's family. One of these very early cases was that of Gopinath Bysack *v.* Hurrosoondery Dossee.[1]

1. *Vide* the ones noticed at length at p. 22, of 20th vol, of the weekly Reporter.

Here the question seems to have been whether the widow did not forfeit her right to her husband's property by reason of refusal to live in the residence of her deceased husband, and with his family. Thin case was decided in 1826. In those days all questions of Hindu Law were referred to a Pundit attached to the court, who held an appointment from Government, and whose duty it was to enlighten the judges on Hindu law. The answer of the Pundit in the present case was; that unless the widow left her husband's residence for unchaste and improper purposes, her refusal to dwell with the family of her husband did not interfere with her right to inherit her husband's property. The case came ultimately before the Privy Council. Their lordships approved the Pundit's opinion, and observed with reference to the circumstances of that particular case that the widow was only fourteen years old at the time of her husband's death; that the husband's brothers were then young men, and the widow thought it more prudent and decorous to retire from their protection, and live with her mother and her family after the husband's death; that she did not forfeit the right of succession to her husband's estate on account of removing from the brothers of her late husband; and that the brothers had no right to insist upon her not with drawing from them in order to put herself under the protection of her mother. The observations with regard to the widow being of fourteen years of age, and the husband's brothers being young men, were not meant to the reasons upon which the decision of the Judicial Committee was founded. (*Vide* p. 22, 20 W. R. Raja Prithi Sing *v.* Ranee Rajkowar.) Those observations were made for the purpose of showing that the widow was not removing from her husband's house for unchaste or improper purposes. In the case of Shibu Soondery Dossee, cited in Shamacharan Surkar's Vyavasthā Darpaṇa, the widow after the death of her husband had left her father-in-law's house without any cause, and had sued the defendants who were the surviving brothers and representatives of the other brothers of her husband; the suit was for separate maintenance. The court said that the fact of her having left her father-in-law's house did not disentitle her from a separate maintenance. In Jadumonee Dossee *v.* Khetter Mohun Seal, published at p. 384, of the Vyavashthā Darpaṇa, the judgment was delivered by Sir Lawrence Peel, whose words are—"The question is whether a Hindu childless widow, who some time after the death of her husband, uncompelled by cruelty or ill usage, left the house of the family of her deceased husband, to dwell at first in the house of her own father, and subsequently with her aunt, living with her own relations, the residence being in all respects a proper one and her conduct unimpeached, forfeits her right of maintenance out of the property which was that of her deceased husband in his lifetime and which a had devolved on his heirs. * * * The Privy Council has, on the subject of the right of the Hindu widow to return to the home of her parents, laid down a broad rule, upon which it is not desirable to infringe." Then Sir Lawrence Peel cites the passage which I have already cited from the judgment of the Privy Council in Kashinath Bysack's case, and continues:-" In the Privy Council the question was whether the Hindu heiress forfeited her estate by selecting without impropriety her father's roof for her residence. But it is to be observed that the opinion of the, Pundits was generally expressed as to forfeiture of rights, and the court expressed in general terms that the widow had a right under the circumstances to select that residence, and could not be compelled to reside under the roof of her husband's family. This freedom of choice had respect to causes as applicable to a widow not an heiress, as to one who inherited. "The meaning of this last part of Sir Lawrence Peel's judgment is that even in Bengal the widow may not sometimes inherit her husband's estate, as for instance, when she is a disqualified person being affected by an incurable disease. But she is then entitled to maintenance out of her husband's property, and her right to select her own residence remains when she is entitled simply to maintenance. In Surnomoyee Dossee *v.* Gopal Lal Doss, Marshall 497, the widow sued for maintenance, and it was held that she was entitled to it notwithstanding that she had left the residence of her deceased husband:–The court said:—"In this case a widow sues for maintenance. The defendant, who is her stepson, objects that she resides in the house of her father, and alleges that she is therefore not entitled to maintenance. The widow alleges that she left the family house because she was tortured or rendered uncomfortable, but did not prove that allegation. We find, however, that it is laid down in the Vyavasthā Darpaṇa of Shama Charan Sarkar, the learned Interpreter of the late Supreme Court, Vol. I, p. 319, see. 160, that 'should a woman, without unchaste purposes, quit the family house and live with her parent or own relations, yet still she is entitled to maintenance;' and in sec. 161, ' The widow, however is not entitled to maintenance by residing elsewhere without a cause, if she was directed by her husband to be maintained in the family home.' We think, therefore, that the widow is entitled to retain the decree for maintenance which she has obtained."All these cases were considered by the Privy Council in Raja Prithi Sing *v.* Rani Rajkowar, (20 W. R. 21 S. C. 2 Suth. P. C. 846, S. C. 12 B. L. R. 238), where the widow sued the adopted son of her husband for maintenance, and was met by a plea of unchastity having been committed by her. This fact could not be proved by the defendant. The widow had left her husband's house, and the question considered by the Privy Council was whether a Hindu widow lost her right to maintenance by reason of her leaving her husband's house, provided she did not leave it for the purposes of unchastity or for any other improper purpose. The decision of the Privy Council was that a Hindu widow was not bound to reside with the relatives of her husband ; that the relations of her husband had no right to compel her to live with them ; that she did not forfeit her right to property or maintenance merely on account of her going and residing with her family, or leaving her husband's residence from any other cause than unchaste or improper purposes; that the law did not require her, for the purpose of maintaining her reputation, necessarily to live with her husband's relatives, and that she did not injure her reputation by living with her own father or own mother or with her relations on her father's side. Their Lordships also in this case point out a distinction between the position of a widow and that of a wife. "A wife cannot leave her husband's house when she chooses, and require him to provide maintenance for her elsewhere; but the case of a widow is different. All that is required of her is, that she is not to leave her husband's house for improper or unchaste purposes, and she is entitled to retain her maintenance unless she is guilty of unchastity or other disreputable practices after she leaves that residence." The distinction between a wife and a widow is founded upon the law relating to husband and wife. A husband has a right to his wife's society and she is bound to perform her conjugal duties towards him. The performance of these duties precludes the idea of her living at a distance from him. Unless therefore there are positive reasons for her quitting the protection of her husband, she is bound to live in the same house with him and to receive her maintenance there. In none of the earlier cases noticed by the Privy Council in Prithi Sing's case, the two texts, (see *ante*, pp. 331, 332) one of Kātyāyana and the other of Nārada, which I have already quoted, seem to have been placed before their Lordships. But even if brought to their notice, these texts would have hardly influenced the decision. No court of justice now would attribute an imperative character to the direction contained in such texts; nor would it be reasonable, in the present altered condition of Hindu society, to suppose that whenever a widow leaves her husband's house, she must be actuated by some improper motive. No other reason can be assigned for the direction given by Kātyāyana and Nārada to a Hindu widow to reside with the family of her husband, except this that such residence is the best safeguard of her virtue and reputation; modern tribunals have looked more to the reason of the law than the letter of its text, and have accordingly decided that improper behaviour is the only cause for which maintenance can be withheld from a widow.

In Ahallabhai Dabia *v.* Lukshimoney Debia, 6 W. R 37, the widow sued the heiress of the nephew of her husband for maintenance. The defendant did not impute unchastity or criminal conduct to her. Her plea was that the widow to receive maintenance ought to residence with the family or relatives of her late husband; two cases decided by the Sadder Dawany Adalut in 1850 and 1852 respectively seem to have been cited, which the judgement of the High Court says support the position that a widow, after a voluntary separation, not based any plea of ill-usage, has no right to a separate maintenance. The High Court, however, held, that "residence with the relations of the deceased husband is, after all, a moral and not a legal duty, and no forfeiture ought to be imposed on a widow who, for no immoral purposes, shows a preference for a residence elsewhere than with her husband's family, who are bound to give her support." Seton-Karr J. also observed that the Hindu Law as applicable to widows ought to be administered by the courts of this country with a liberal spirit. Macpherson, J. said that the widow's leaving the house of her husband's relatives did not entail forfeiture of her right to maintenance. This principle, that a liberal interpretation should be given to the old texts, does not seem to have been conformed to in Umacharan Chowdry *v.* Nitambini Dabia, 10 W. R. 359, where a Hindu widow sued to obtain a monthly allowance as maintenance from the brothers of her deceased husband, the family property having descended to them. They stated in their answer that they were willing to maintain her if she resided with them as a member of the family. The High Court held that the widow could get subsistence on condition that she returned to and resided with her brothers-in-law as a member of the family. The judges say that their opinion was based on the ruling of the Full Bench upon the subject. I believe the Full Bench ruling referred to here is the case of Khettermoney Dossee *v.* Kashinath Doss, to W. R. F. B. 89, which has decided that a daughter-in-law cannot claim a money allowance from her father-in-law who was not in possession of any ancestral property: The case of Umacharan Chowdry, does not disclose how in Bengal the widow came to be in the position of suing for maintenance, instead of inheriting the property. Supposing, however, that by some reason or other she was excluded from heirship, the decision of the High Court refusing a separate maintenance to her is not in accordance with the cases which went before, already noticed by me. In Srivirada Pratapa Raghunada Deo *v.* Sri Brojo Kishore Patta Deo, I. L. R. 1 Mad. 81, there are some observations made by the Judicial Committee which might support the idea that a widow was bound to reside in her husband's family. They are:—"The joint and undivided family is a normal condition of Hindu society. An undivided Hindu family is ordinarily joint not only in estate, but in food and worship; therefore not only the concerns of the joint property, but whatever relates to their commensality and their religious duties and observances, must be regulated by its members, or by the manager to whom they have expressly or by implication delegated the task of regulation. The Hindu wife upon her marriage passes into and becomes member of that family. It is upon that family that, as a widow, she has her claim for maintenance. It is in that family that, in strict contemplation of law, she ought to reside. It is in the members of that family that she must presumably find such councillors and protectors as the law makes requisite for her." But we must remember that this was said in a case in which the question was, who should be consulted by a widow desirous to adopt a son after the death of her husband. The above words of the Privy Council cannot be taken as overruling the clear expression of their views in their judgement in Raja Prithi Sing's case (20 W. R., 22).

In Rangovinayak Deo *v.* Yamuna Bai, I. L. R. 3 Bom. 47, the facts were similar to those of Umachurn Chowdry's case (10 W. R., 359). In this Bombay case, the widow had gone to reside with her parents after the death of her husband. For nine years she did not make any demand on her husband's family, but at the end of that period she sued her husband's brother and cousins for nine years' arrear of maintenance. The defence was, that the widow had voluntarily withdrawn from association with the joint family of which her husband had been a member, that she had not been harshly used, nor had been forced to incur any debts, but of her own free will had lived with her paternal family; and that she had no title to a money allowance. West, J. reviewed a number of cases most of which were from Bombay, and stated their effect in the following words:–"These cases make it plain that a separate maintenance may be awarded to the widow of a Hindu deceased as against the members of his family. Some of them seem to support the proposition that a separate maintenance may be claimed, although the husband's family may be willing to support the widow as a member of the household, and although there may be no particular reasons for withdrawing from it. The others would leave a discretion to the courts, which should be exercised so as not to throw on the deceased husband's family a needless or oppressive burden at the caprice of the widow or her family. None of them goes so far as to deprive the court of a discretion as to awarding or refusing arrears; while several of them support the exercise of such a discretion. It is we think probable that a close examination of the replies of the Pundits in the earlier cases would show that they did not intend, in denying that withdrawal from the husband's family involves forfeiture of proprietorship, to widen a dependent widow's liberty beyond the range defined by the Madras and Bombay Shastris, or to impose a heavier burden on her, husband's family. In a case like the present, where the widow has taken her residence permanently with her own family, and never even asked for anything on account of maintenance for many years, so as to create an impression that she abandoned any claim that she might have, where her own family seem to be in comfortable circumstances, and the defendant's people of rather straitened means, we think that it will be a right exercise of our discretion to reject the claim to a money annuity. There seems to be no necessity in the present case, and the defendants are petty traders on whom the burden of a fixed payment might bear oppressively. If the plaintiff chooses to take up her residence with her husband's family, they must support her in such comfort as their means allow; but in the absence of any special circumtances necessitating her withdrawal and separate residence, we do not think she can claim cash payments from them to enable her to add to her luxuries while living apart.

In this case, the reasons which weighed most with West, J., were that the widow was living more comfortably with her father's family, while the members of her deceased husband's family were weaking out a small inheritage by their own insignificant exertions for gaining livelihood; and absence of demand on the widow's part for nine years seems to have been regarded in the light of a waiver of her right. But the widow might have claimed a share of the property, whatever it was, had her husband died separate. She might then have sold it for her subsistence and deprived the family of even a reversionary right to it. For a sonless widow to live in the house of her deceased husband, in the same mess with her brothers-in-law and their wives, often becomes irksome and uncomfortable. Even in Bengal, where separation or its absence does not affect a widow's right, and where her position as a coparcener in respect of her deceased husband's share is secure, the family of her husband find means to render her condition unendurable. That she is a widow that no addition can be made by her to the family income, as her husband if alive might have made is a circumtance which renders her an object of contempt and dislike. If she consents to be the general drudge, patient to endure in silence all ill-treatment she may be subjected to, obedient to the slightest indications of a wish on the other members' part, it is then that her life in her deceased husband's family may become tolerable. Where there is good treatment, and consideration is shown to her, she seldom evinces a desire to quit her deceased husband's family. The petty jealousies, the mean annoyances, the nameless small vexations, which are the features of Hindu zenana life in too many cases, may be a sufficient cause for a widow's withdrawal from her husband's family, but are not capable of proof in a court of justice. Positive cruelty in the mutual treatment of the female members may not be so frequent; but the wear and tear caused by daily bickerings of an insignificant character is certainly a matter deserving consideration; it would therefore be a humane procedure to allow a widow a separate allowance when ever she is desirous for it. Her right to be maintained is beyond all doubt, and considerations of the hardship entailed upon the husband's family and their straitened means ought not to be imported to cut down this right. The judgement of Mr. Justice West in the above case therefore is open to criticism from this point of view. The truth seems to be, that in the decisions of our modern courts of justice, two opposites tendencies are dicernible. In some dicisions we percieve a tendency to revert to the spirit of the ancient Ṛṣi texts in all their primitive rigidity. These texts often display an utter disregard of the ordinary instincts of human nature; a literal and unqualified application of many of them now would cause much unhappiness and injustice. On the other hand, we find in other decisions a sedulous attempt to temper the severity of the ancient texts by introducing broader principles of justice, humanity and impartiality borrowed from the advanced civilization of Europe. Where these principles do not go against any express declaration of the Ṛṣis, or where they are not repugnant to any cherished notion of the Hindu community, no consummation is more devoutly to be wished for than the gradual incorporation of such liberal principles into the body of the current Hindu law. I am afraid that among our countrymen many suppose that the administration of Hindu law would be placed on a more satisfactory footing, were it left in the hand of our Pundits. The Pundits are more extensively acquainted with the original texts, no doubt. But the texts are of no help in new combinations of facts met with in actual cases. New principles must be had recourse to. It is remarkable that the original texts are rather poor in principles. What better storehouse is there to resort to, than the learning and experience and acumen of European judges whose education is infinitely superior that of the Pundits, and whose minds mirror the incomparably more progressive civilization of Western Europe? The effects of the administration of Hindu law by such superior intellects are seen in the gradual improvement of the position of widow. From the Vedic days of absolute exclusion to our own times when the widow has been placed on almost an equal footing with the male members, this gradual improvement can be traced step by step. Much was done towards it by Vijñāneśvara and some of his immediate predecessors; but it was left for the European judges, to give the right of the widow that definite from which has rendered it secure. I am afraid that the judgement of Mr. Justice West betrays an unconscious tendency of a retrograde character. It relegates the widow's right to maintenance to its primitive insecure condition, and puts an unnecessary fetter upon her freedom of action. It is therefore satisfactory to find that the rulling in the case of Rangovinayaka was dissented from by three judges of the High Court of Bombay including Westrop, C. J. in Kasturbi *v.* Shivaji Ram Devkurna, I. L. R., 3 Bom. 372. In this case the Chief Justice says, that in all the five schools, it was a settled point that a Hindu widow does not forfeit her right to maintenance, out of the property chargeable therewith, by reason of non-residence with the family of her husband, except when such non-residence is for unchaste or immoral purposes. The authorities for Bengal with regard to this point are Kashinath Bysack v. Harasoondery Dossee, 2 Morley's Digest (Easl's notes) 198, noticed by Peacock, C. J. in 12 B. L. R. 241 and 242, and Shibusundery Dossee *v.* Kristo Kishore Neogy, 2 Taylor and Bell, 190. For Madras it is settled by Visalatchi Ammal *v.* Annasami Shastri 5 Mad. H. C. Rep. 150; for the North-Western Prirovinces by Raja Prithi Sing *v.* Ranee Rajkowar, 12 B. L. R. O. C. 238; and for Bombay by the decision of the Privy Council in Narayan Rao Ramchander Pant *v.* Rama Bai, I. L. R. 3 Bom. 415. In the case before Westrop, C. J., the widow sued her husband's father and brother for separate maintenance on the allegations that having quarrelled with their wives, she was turned out, and had since lived in separate lodgings. The defendants answered that they neither turned out nor ill-treated the plaintiff; that she left their house of her own accord; that they were willing to maintain her if she lived with them; and that neither she nor her deceased husband was entitled to any ancestral property. Westrop, C. J. said:—"It has not been alleged that the late husband of the plaintiff was separate in estate from his father and brother, or that he held any estate separately from them, or that she lived apart from them for unchaste or immoral purposes." It was directed therefore to try the question whether there was any family property in the hands of the defendants, and if so, what amount was proper to be alloted to the widow for her maintenance? In the Privy Council case referred to in the judgement of the Chief

Justice, the widow sued the eldest son of her husband, to whom the father had left his self-acquired property by a will; this will recognised the claims of the younger brothers and the widow's to maintenance. The Privy Council interpreted the will as imposing an obligation on the eldest son to make allowances for the support of the widows, the obligation being held analogous to the rights vested in Hindu widow in ordinary cases where there is no will. It was objected by the defendant there that the widow had disentitled herself to maintenance by living apart from the family of the eldest son. Their Lordships held that no condition was to be found in the will imposing an obligation upon the widow to reside under the same roof and in joint family with the eldest son. The widow therefore, they held, was to be taken to have been left in this respect in the ordinary position of a Hindu widow, in which separation from the ancestral house did not disentitle her to maintenance suitable to her rank and condition.[1] In the Madras case of Visalatchi Ammal, also referred to in the decision of Westrop, C. J., the point decided was that a Hindu widow was entitled to charge on account of her maintenance a piece of land in the possession of her father-in-law, which originally formed a part of the ancestral property, and had been alloted on partition to the father-in-law; and that the widow's refusal to live in her father-in-law's house did not disentitle her to maintenance.

Separate maintenance from small joint propery not allowed.

In Ramchunder Bishnu Bapat *v.* Saguna Bai the widow had at first consented by a written agreement to receive rupees sixteen per annum as her maintenance from the brothers of her deceased husband. She subsequently sued for her maintenance being fixed at rupees four per mensem. Westrop, C. J. said[2]:—"A Hindu widow in not bound to

1. I. L. R. 3 Bomb. 421
2. I. L. R. 4 Bomb. 261

reside with her late husband's family, and if he were in union with that family at the time of his death, she is entitled to seperate maintenance where there is family property, and it is not so small as not reasonably to admit of allotment to her of separate maintenance. But though the family property may not be so small as to prevent any allotment of maintenance to her, yet it may be so small, or the family may be so numerous, as to admit only of a very moderate payment for a separate maintenance. Here the plaintiff was satisfied with the sum stipulated in the agree-ment for several years, and there is no proof that she was imposed upon. The family property is small and the family large; hence although the sum named in the agreement is itself small, yet we do not think that, under the circumstances of this case already noticed, the Court ought to increase that amount. The only variation which this court is disposed to make is to give to the widow the right to elect between taking the sum named it that agreement and living separately from her late husband's family, or of living with that family and being fed and clothed by them in the same manner as the members of that family." Upon the authority of this case, it would be a good defence in a suit for separate maintenance by a widow from the surviving members of the joint family to which her deceased husband belonged, that the family property is too small to admit of a separate payment being made to the widow for maintenance.

Amount of maintenance.

The next question is, what is the amount of maintenance claimable by a widow from the joint property in which her deceased husband was interested. Upon this point, the only general rule is, that in no case will it exceed the value of the share to which her deceased husband would have been entitled if a partition had been effected in his lifetime. In the Smṛticandrikā,[1] there is a passage indicating the state

1. P. 62, Sanskrit.

of society for which the author was providing the law. It will appear from this passage how unsuitable such provisions of law are to the present condition of the Hindu community.

Amount allowed in olden times.

The author quotes Nārada to answer the question what ought to be given to the widow for her subsistence where the property out of which the maintenance is to proceed is small. Nārada says that the claims of a chaste widow are limited to twenty four *arhakas* of paddy and forty *paṇas* in current money for every year. The author explains an *arhaka* to be one hundred and ninety two *prasthas,* and one *paṇa* as equal to one *kārshāpana.* He says that this *kārṣāpaṇa* is equivalent to an eightieth part of one *nishka* of current money in some parts of the country. The quantity of paddy implied by these different measures and the value of these descriptions of current money are not easily ascertainable now. Innumerable are the variations in the meaning attached in different parts of India to these different names for measure and currency. If we adopt what is understood by these terms in Bengal, the annual maintenance claimable by a Hindu widow according to Nārada would amount to 48 mauṇḍs of paddy and two rupees and a half in money.

Amount once fixed may be altered.

The High Court observed in one case that it was not necessary to maintain a Hindu widow in the same state as her husband would maintain her, that it was difficult to lay down a general rule, that where the net receipt amounted to ten thousand rupees, an allowance of rupees eight hundred a year was an ample and liberal provision for the widow.[1] In another case, the High Court of Bengal held rupees twenty-five per month as a reasonable and sufficient sum to allow to the widow where the income was proved

1. Kalipershad Sing *v.* Kupoor Kowari, 4 W. R. 65.

to be rupees 7,000 a year.[1] In this case Seton Karr. J. says that in determinig the amount of maintenance to be awarded to the widow, regard must be had not only to the annual value of tne property out of which the allowance was to proceed, but also to the circumstances of the family as well as to the requirements of the widow. In Bhogabanchunder Bose *v.* Bindoo Basini Dossee, Sumbhoonath Pandit, J. said that the amount of maintenance could be fixed only with reference to the amount of the income, and not solely on the necessities of the widow; it was also to be kept in mind that where the income was small, it might be more convenient for the party liable to supply the maintenance, to maintain the widow if she lived in his house, than if she were to live separate.[2] It was held in Sriram Bhattacharjee *v.* Puddomookhee Debia,[3] where the widow at first used to receive an allowance of three rupees per month, but subsequently left the house of her husband's family, removed to her own father's house, and since then being refused the payment of any further allowance, claimed rupees 4½ and half per mensem; that there was nothing in the law to prevent an increase of the amount, as there was nothing to prevent a decrease, should sufficient cause be shown. It was also held that the widow's right did not cease on her leaving her husband's house. The principle enunciated, that it is legally competent to a court of justice to direct the payment of an increased allowance or a reduced allowance where maintenance has once been already fixed, has been also propounded by L. Jackson, J. in Rajendronath Roy *v.* S. M. Rani Puttosoondry Dossee.[4] The court said:— "The previous decree based upon a compromise awarding a specific sum by way of maintenance, and the particular mode of realising that sum has neither more or less effect

1. Ahalla Bai Debia *v.* Lukshimonee Debia, 6 W. R. 37.
2. 6 W. R. 286
3. 9 W. R. 152
4. 5 C. L. R. 18.

than a decree would have, if it were founded on a judgment of Court, arrived at after hearing of evidence. Such decrees apportion maintenance always with reference to the circumtances of the parties, to the reasonable wants of the widow, and the extent of the property out of which the maintenance is to come. So long as the circumstances remain unaltered, the maintenance of course will be paid at the rate agreed upon, but if by circumtances not arising out of the default of the holder of the property the assets of it are greatly reduced, so that he can no longer be reasonably called upon to pay the amount of maintenance fixed, I think it is open to the court to reconsider the allowance and to adjust it to the altered circumtances." In this case the suit was by the widow against the adopted son of her husband upon the basis of a compromise whereby the adopted son had agreed to pay the sum of rupees 264 and three *bish* of paddy annually. At the time the suit was brought, the entire estates left by the widow's husband had been flooded by salt-water, and the income of the property had been so diminished that even the Government revenue could not be paid out of it. Upon these facts, the High Court held that rupees 15, the amount which she was then receiving, was sufficient. In Prithi Sing's case, (20 W. R., 22), the income of the property was two lacs a year, and there were four widows who had a right to receive an allowance out of it. Their Lordships held that the amount of maintenance must always be determined with reference to the income of the joint ancestral property; and that Rs. 200 per mensem for each of the four widows out of an income of two lacs a year was not an exorbitant or unreasonable provision.

According to Couch, C. J., if there has been a decree awarding maintenance to be paid by a particular person, if subsequent circumstances render it improper to continue the allowance originally made, the alteration in the amount connot be directed by the court at the time of the execution of the decree. Therefore where the property was ancestral, and had come into the hands of the minor successor of the party against whom the decree for maintenance had been made, the minor defendant was held precluded from raising the question in the execution of the decree, that there were circumstances under which the sum decreed was not a proper sum to be allowed. The only course left open to the judgment-debtor in such a case would be to apply to the court which made the decree for maintenance, for a review.[1] In Nobogopal Roy *v.* S. M. Amritomoyee Dossee, the question was whether the civil court had power to make an order that the husband should pay to the wife maintenance at a particular rate, in cases where the wife was residing apart from him for lawful cause, and whether such order could be operative in respect of payments to be made in future. The case was decided by a single judge, Markby, J. who held that such an order was subject to any modification which future circumstances might render necessary; that under some circumstances the allowance might be altogether stopped although there might not be any special direction to that effect contained in the order; that if the wife were shown to have been guilty of such misconduct as would forfeit her maintenance, or if it were shown that under changed condition of things, the wife could be called upon to return to her husband's house, or that the rate of allowance should be changed, the court would have power in all such cases either to set aside or to modify the order as circumstances might require; and that the safer course would be to insert special directions in the decree to that effect, the law upon the whole of this subject being not altogether settled.[2] In Hurry Mohun Roy *v.* S. M. Nayantara, 25 W. R. 474, a stepmother sued her stepson for separate maintenance upon the allegation that she had been obliged by ill-treatment on the part of her stepson to leave his house, and to seek accommodation elsewhere. The income from the

1. Ramkali Koer v. The Court of Wards, 18 W. R. 478.
2. 24 W. R. 428

ancestral property was not less than rupees 7,000 yearly. The court of first instance made a decree for maintenance at the rate of rupees 30 a month, together with an extra rupees 10 per month if no proper accommodation were provided for the stepmother; adding a proviso to the decree that if the stepmother insisted on living at her father's or at her son-in-law's house against the will of the defendant, she was to forfeit the larger portion of her allowance and to receive only rupees 12 per mensem. The High Court altered it into an absolute decree for rupees 25 per mensem, observing that the ill-feeling between the parties was so strong, that they could not be expected to live in comfort and peace in the same house; that the circumstances of the case necessied the award of a separate money allowance without reference to the possibility of the stepmother's getting accommodation any where on her stepson's premises; that rupees 30 per month together with rupees 10 for house-rent was not a reasonable amount of an income of rupees 7,000 a year, such a sum being too large a proportion to take away for the maintenance of one member of the family only; and that an unreserved allowance of rupees 25 per month was such as the reasonable and probable needs of a person in the plaintiff's position in life would warrant, regard being had to all the circumstances of the case. It was also said by the Judges in this case:—"It is in the highest degree improbable, considering the terms on which the parties to this suit are, that the stepson could ever agree to his stepmother's living either with her father or son-in-law, specially when her determination to live with either of those relatives contrary to the stepson's wishes could have the effect of saving him half the allowance he would be otherwise obliged to pay. To uphold the proviso in the decree of the Court of first instance would be practically to cut down the allowance to rupees 12 per mensem, for a widow woman would naturally desire to live with her relatives, and not amongst strangers. As to the objection, that by her living with her relatives the expenses of cook, etc., would be saved, and that the stepson is entitled to the benefit of such saving, we do not think that the circumstance ought to be taken into account in this case. What we have to do, is to give the plaintiff a reasonable allowance for maintenance, her position and that of her step son being considered, and we do not think rupees 25 a month is too largo a one, even if some small items of expense be cut off by the plaintiff's living in her father's or son-in-law's house. As to the life of semi-starvation and wretchedness in which it is argued that according to the Śāstras a Hindu widow ought to live, that is a matter of religious or ceremonial observance rather than of law. A Hindu widow in these days at all events is entitled to decent food and clothing if the head of the family is in a position to supply them, and rupees 25 a month does not seem too large a sum for the purpose."

If the allowance be payable out of the assets of a firm, such firm constituting, according to the well-known principle of Hindu law, the ancestral joint family property, a suit lies by the proprietor of the firm for the reduction of an allowance preciously fixed by a decree of the Court, upon the ground that the business of the firm has been gradually failing. In such a case, the business is considered as the estate charged with the payment of the maintenance; the diminution of its income is regarded as a sufficient cause for its reduction. If in time the estate yields no income at all, the maintenance will altogether cease; the rule being that in every case the amount of maintenance should bear a reasonable proportion to the amount of income.[1]

Female member occasionally entitled to maintenance in a double capacity.

Sometimes, the female member entitled to maintenance may claim it in a double capacity. Thus where there are three brothers constituting a family joint in estate, and one

1. Ruka Bai *v.* Ganda Bai, 1. L. R. 1 All. 594.

dies, leaving a widow and a minor son, and then the minor son dies, the family still continuing joint, the widow of the deceased brother may claim maintenance both as a widow of one of the coparceners joint family in its earlier stage, and as the mother of one of the coparceners of the family in its later stage. But I apprehend that this would not be a ground for the female member's receiving any increased allowance. Maintenance is allowed to a female member simply with a view to subsistence; and the amount necessary for the subsistence of a single individual not being subject to any variation on account of the party entitled to it being invested with a double right, the courts of justice I believe will allow that amount of maintenance which will be reasonable under the particular circumstances of each case. But if a woman being a member of a joint Hindu family, first loses her husband, and then her son, it cannot be reasonably advanced that as a mother she is entitled to a less amount of maintenance than what was at first thought necessary for her when she only lost her husband. The position of a Hindu mother of a child deceased since her husband's death is not inferior to that of a widow without a children, in respect to the amount of allowance claimable by her. In one case of this kind, Straight, J observed that there was no distinction between a widow and a mother. "It is impossible to avoid remarking that if matters of feeling can be admitted and we are not sure they should not in arriving at the amount of what is a reasonable allowance–the case of a widowed mother deprived of her only son and of the contingent advantages that might have accrued to her had he survived, seems the more deserving of sympathy and consideration. It is a fact not to be lost sight of in this case, that down to the death of the respondent's (the widow's) son, the appellants (the members of the joint family who were sued for maintenance) made due provision for her and her child according to their position and the family custom, but immediately after the letter's decease, they stopped the allowance not only for the one but as to both. Such a proceeding appears indefensible and altogether inconsistent with the position they now take up. They are actually in enjoyment of the profits of the share of the villages to which, had the respondent's husband lived, he would have been entitled, and it is relatively to the amount of these profits that the sum to be allowed here should be calculated. No precedent was quoted fixing any principle of computation to apply a case like the present, and it may well be that there are none, for the question that now arises involves equitable considerations that must of necessity be affected by the peculiar circumstances of each individual case."[1] In this case, another proposition laid down is, that the amount of maintenance is to be fixed, not only with reference to the income of the whole joint family but also with reference to the value of the particular share to which that member of the family was entitled, on account of relationship with whom the female member claims the maintenance. Thus, if she claims maintenance as the mother of a particular member, then the value her son's share should be looked to as a factor in determining the quantum; if as a widow, then the value of her husband's share is the matter to be considered. In the above case, the value of such share was rupees 3,000 odd per annum, and rupees 60 per mensem was allowed as maintenance, the court of first instance remarking that an estate incurred other expenses than the usual ones, and that the rents entered in the rent-roll of an estate were for different reasons never actually realised.

It is not a valid objection to fixing a money value of the maintenance to be paid, that the income varies according to the seasons, that a given sum should not be fixed, but should be determined as occasion may arise. Convenience requires that a reasonable definite sum conformable to all the circumstances of the case, should be ascertained and made payable by an order of the court, with a view to

1. Narharsing *v.* Dirghnath Koer, I. L. R. 2 All. 407.

prevent the recurrence of litigation between the parties.[1] In Sreemutty Nittokishoree Dossee *v.* Jogendro Nath Mullick,[2] the Judicial Committee declare that the elements to be considered in fixing the amount of maintenance are Firstly the value of the estate; Secondly the proper proportion which ought to be given to the widow out of it; and that the maintenance should include not only the ordinary expenses of living, but also what she might reasonably spend for religious and other duties incident to her station in life. In that case the contending parties were an adopted son and a widow of the adoptive father. The widow from the beginning repudiated the fact of adoption and contested for the whole estate. The *factum* of adoption was proved to the satisfaction of the court, but the conduct of the widow in having all along denied that fact, was regarded by the High Court as a circumstance which ought to lower the amount of maintenance awarded to the widow. The High Court said, that the fact of adoption was perfectly well-known to the widow and all the members of the family. The adoptive father had left a will by which he had bequeathed a lac of rupees absolutely to the widow, besides a right to live in the family dwelling house and to be maintained out of his general estate, as she had been in his lifetime. Upon these facts the High Court observed:—"If it had been left to the court to determine the sum which should be awarded to the defendant in future for her maintenance, we should only have given her the most moderate provision which, having regard to her husband's property and position, the law woulu allow." The Privy Council., however, said:—"One cannot read that passage without perceiving that the court reduced as low as they could, upon the principle upon which they proceeded, the maintenance which they allowed, as a kind of punishment to her for having defended a suit which they thought she must have known

1. I. L. R. 2 All. 777, Jhunna *v.* Rum Surup.
2. 3 Suth. P. C. 505.

was properly brought against her. That the court being under this influence, should have allowed its judgement to be affected by it, their Lordships think, was a departure from the strict principles which ought alone to have guided it." Their Lordships threw out an intimation that as a lac of rupees had been left her by her husband, the proper maintenance would be an annuity of rupees 6,000.

Limitation as to maintenance

Having thus considered the amount of maintenance claimable by a widow, I ought to say a few words upon the question, whether a claim to maintenance is ever barred by limitation. The law of limitation enacted in 1859, provides for suits for maintenance, and says that where the right to receive it is a charge on the inheritance of any estate, a suit for it will be barred, if instituted after twelve years from the death of the person on whose estate it is alleged to be a charge. In the Privy Council case of Narayan Rao Ram Chunder Pant, (I. L. R. 3 Bom. 415), the Judicial Committee has held, upon the terms of the will propounded in the case, that no charge was created upon any specific portion of the property, but that the adopted son, the general legatee under the will, was directed to allow maintenance to the widows. The terms of the will relating to maintenance were, "Nana the eldest son, shall provide for both the mothers; treating them with great respect." These terms were not sufficient, according to their Lordships' opinion, to create a right which was a specific charge upon the inheritance of any estate, within the meaning of the Limitation Act of 1859. So that upon the authority of this case, it would seem that a suit for the declaration of a right to receive maintenance personally against a member of a joint family would be barred by no lapse of time; for cl. 13, Sec. I, Act XIV of 1859, is silent as to a case where the maintenance is not sought to be made a charge upon the inheritance of any property. There have been two new enactments relating to limitation since the passing of Act XIV of 1859. The first is Act IX of 1871, and the second Act XV of 1877. Under the earlier of the two Acts, the provision relating to maintenance is general and simple; it simply says that[1] a suit by a Hindu for maintenance will be barred if instituted after twelve years from the date when the maintenance sued for is claimed and refused. The corresponding provision in the later of the two Acts, namely, Act XV of 1877, which is now in force, has been split up into two separate Articles 128 and 129. The first provides for arrears of maintenance; the second relates to a suit for the declaration of a right to maintenance. The suit for arrears will be barred in twelve years from the date when the arrears are payable; the suit for declaration will be barred twelve years from the date when the right is denied. As these provisions are general, and contemplate maintenance of the various kinds that one person may claim from another, it is not easy to find from a consideration of these provisions, an answer to the question, when does a widow's maintenance become payable, or when is the denial of her right to be supposed to take place? It is now settled that so far as the law of maintenance concerns a joint Hindu family, a widow need not live in that family to preserve her right. Supposing she withdrew from the family dwelling-house immediately after her husband's death, and supposing that for a number of years, she has not asked for any allowance, nor has any been paid to her; have any arrears become payable, under these circumstances? Has there been any denial of her right ? I apprehend that, unless there has been a positive assertion of right to maintenance on the widow's part, and a positive denial of it by the party sought to be made liable, limitation does not run against the widow. So again, with reference to the arrears, if no maintenance money has been expressly fixed to be paid by one party to the other, namely by a member of the joint family to the widow, there are no

1. Articles 128 of the Second Schedule.

arrears which can be said to be ' payable.' I am confirmed in this supposition by what I find in the judgment of the Privy Council in the case already referred to, namely, that of Narayan Ramchandra Pant; in that judgment it is said that the terms of the Act of 1859 are not quite clear; that under the principles of Common Law, the right to maintenance is one accruing from time to time, according to the wants and exigencies of the widow; and that the Statute of Limitation might do much harm if it should force widows to claim their strict rights, and to commence litigation, which, but for the purpose of keeping alive their claims' would not be necessary or desirable.

The above words may seem to rule that a claim to maintenance would be subject to no law of limitation. And some of our earlier cases might be supposed have been decided under an idea like that. In one case decided by the High Court of Bengal, Seton-Karr, J. said in a rather summary way that limitation could not apply to the suit so far as it was brought to fix the maintenance for the future. Macpherson, J. said that the case was not barred by limitation, because it was evident, that from the time of her husband's death, up to within twelve years from the institution of the suit, the widow had been maintained out of her husband's estate.[1] In this case the widow had sued both for large arrears and also for future maintenance at a particular rate. The case was under the Mitākṣarā law, and governed by the Limitation Act of 1859. The question of the widow's right to the large amount by way of arrears did not arise in the High Court; it had been disallowed in the court below, and there does not seem to have been an appeal upon that part of the claim by the widow, before the High Court. The appeal was by the party made liable for the maintenance, on various grounds, among others, that of limitation. The ruling by Macpherson J., that the suit was not barred, because the widow had been supported down

1. Aholla Bai Debia *v.* Luckimoney Debia, G W. R. 37.

to within twelve years before the institution of the suit, cannot refer to cl., sec. 1, Act XIV of 1859 ; for in that clause, 12 years from the death of the person on whose property the maintenance is a charge is mentioned as the period within which the suit is to be brought. It is not clear, therefore, what law of limitation is here referred to. The ruling seems to be that, if the widow has received her support from the joint family property within 12 years previous to the suit for a declaration of her right to future maintenance at a specified sum; her suit will be in time. But the words of Seton-Karr, J. warrant the supposition that under the Limitation Act of 1859, future maintenance may be claimed by the widow at any time during her life. To a like purport is a decision of the High Court of Bombay, the substance of which is stated to be that in a suit for maintenance the cause of action ordinarily arises at the time when the maintenance having become necessary is refused by the party from whom it is claimed; and that clause 13, sec. 1, Act XIV of 1859 does not apply to all suits for the recovery of maintenance brought by a Hindu widow against her husband's family, but only to suits in which the plaintiff seeks to have her maintenance made a charge on a particular estate[1]. In another case, the son's widow had sued her father-in-law, in a family governed by the Mitākṣarā. She had made no claim for twenty-two years after her husband's death, but alleged that she had been forced to sue, disputes having recently arisen between herself and her mother-in-law; that previously she had no cause of complaint against her father-in-law. The case was decided by a single judge; who said that such a claim was not governed by limitation, a claim for maintenance being a recurring cause of action[2]. The High Court of Madras has held that if there be two undivided brothers, and one of them dies leaving a widow then as the joint property in the

1. Timappa Bhat *v.* Paramesharïamma, 5 Bom. H. C. Rep. A. C. 130.
2. Muss. Heema Kooeree *v.* Ajudhya Pershad, 24 W. R. 474.

hands of the surviving brother is charged with the maintenance of the widow, limitation against her claim for maintenance runs from the date of her husband's death.[1] From this decision, it would seem that in every case of a claim by a Hindu widow for maintenance against the surviving members of the joint family to which her husband belonged, the limitation must run from the date of her husband's death. We have seen that the surviving members are not liable for such maintenance unless there is some joint property in their hands, property that is, in which the deceased husband of the widow had an interest. The High Court of Madras in the above case, in discussing the right of the widow, in effect says that in every such case the widow's maintenance is a charge on the joint property. Therefore wherever a widow can legally claim maintenance, she must do so by way of a charge upon an inherited estate; consequently every such claim would came within the words of cl. 13, sec. 1, Act of XIV of 1859; for there is no escaping from the necessary sequence of these propositions; all claims for maintenance by a widow depend upon the existence of joint property; all such maintenance is a charge on such property; therefore all such maintenance is barred in 12 years from the husband's death. But the Privy Council in Narayan Ramchandra Pant's case seem to be against such a rule. There is also another reason against the application of this cl. 13 to a maintenance right charged upon joint family property. The clause says that the maintenance must be a charge upon the *inheritance* of an estate. Now it is doubtful whether there is any 'inheritance' in the case when one undivided members dies, and his interest survives to those who remain. Sir Barnes Peacock has on one occasion said that the right of the surviving coparceners of a joint Hindu family governed by the Mitākṣarā law depends upon survivorship and not upon inheritance[2]. This opinion is

1. Subramania *v.* Kaliani Ammal, 7 Mad. II. C. Rep. 226.
2. Lalla Mohabeer Pershad *v.* Musa. Koondun Kooer, 8 W. R. 116; see p. 118, Col. 2, pare. 4.

based by the Chief Justice upon the authority the Sivaganga case.[1] If that be so, then calling in the principle that all law of limitation must receive a strict interpretation, it may be said that the maintenance of the widow of an undivided member is not a charge upon the inheritance of an estate in the case of a joint family governed by the Mitākṣarā law, and Clause 13 therefore would not apply; whether the inapplicability of that clause would be of any advantage to the widow may be doubted; for, if that clause does not apply, then clause 16 will, for clause 16 is a general provision applicable to all cases not otherwise provided for, and fixes six years as the period of limitation for all such cases. In one case, kemp, J. said that it is wrong to suppose that a right to maintenance is one to which limitation does not apply. Here, however, as the receipt by the widow of a separate money allowance was proved up to Kartik, 1275, within a short time after which date the suit seems to have been brought, the High Court held that the question of limitation did not arise. This decision has no reference to clause 13, since here limitation was taken to have run from the date of the last receipt of the money allowance; not from the date of the husband's death.[2] The case must have been under the Mitākṣarā law, since the appeal to the High Court was from the District of Patna, and the names of the parties indicate that they belonged to the up-country race, and were not from Bengal.

The effect of the change of law brought about by the enactment of Act IX of 1871 came to be considered by the High Court of Bombay in Jivi *v.* Ranji, I. L. R. 3 Bom. 207. There the widow sued for arrears of maintenance for four years from 13th June 1873 to 13th June 1877, alleging her cause of action to have assured on the last mentioned date, inasmuch as she on that date having claimed maintenance from her late husband's brother, the defendant, had been

1. 9 Moore's Ind. A. p. 539.
2. Choony Kooer *v.* Joonka Kooer, 12 W. R. 524.

refused by the latter. The Lower Appellate Court had held that no maintenance could be claimed for a period previous to a demand and refusal. The ground for so holding was that the provision relating to maintenance in Act IX of 1871, was a deliberate and decided change from the law of 1859, the earlier law giving a period of 12 years from the husband's death, and the later law the same period from the date of a demand and refusal. This finding of law on the part of the Lower Appellate Court, was upset by the High Court, Melvill, J. observing that it was not a sound proposition to lay down that a Hindu widow had no right to recover arrears of maintenance, excepting such as accured due after a demand and refusal; or that a demand and refusal created a prospective right to maintenance; or that there was no cause of action in respect of arrears claimed for a period prior to such demand being made. The result of this decision by Melvil, J. is that arreas of maintenance to the extent allowed by the law of limitation for the time being in force are legally claimable by a widow; that the new provision in the Limitation Act of 1871, enacting that the period of limitation is to run from the date when the maintenance sued for is claimed and refused, is not to be interpreted as creating the right to maintenance from that date; that a Limitation Act is not intended to define or create causes of action; that a widow has a legal right to maintenance, and may recover arrears for any period not excluded by the law of limitation applicable to the suit; that in a suit coming within the operation of Act IX of 1871 a widow may recover arrears for any period, unless it appear that there has been a demand and refusal, in which case she can recover arrears for 12 years only from the date of such demand and refusal. In this decision the effect of Art. 118, Second Schedule, of the Act of 1871, has not been considered. That Article provides six years as the period of limitation for a suit for which no period is provided elsewhere in the Schedule. Of course, Article 128 *does* provide a period for such arrears. But supposing that a widow were to live for fifty years after the death of her husband—a supposition borne out by actual facts in many instances—that she keeps silent for 25 years and makes no demand whatsoever, and then comes at once upon the members of the joint family with a claim for twenty-five years arrears, which may sometimes amount to an enormous sum. We have seen that in wealthy families, sometimes ever Rs. 300 per mensem has been allowed as widow's maintenance. In such a case 25 years' arrears would come up to a lac of rupees. It is difficult to believe that any court of justice will be inclined to award such a sum by way of arrears of maintenance. The law now in force, Act XV of 1877, makes the period run from the date of the arrears becoming payable. There is a difficulty in making out, when an arrears becomes payable, in a case where the two parties, the party claiming, that is, the widow, and the party liable, that is, the surviving member or members, have never come to any understanding upon the matter. Are we to suppose that such arrears become payable at the expiration of every month, or of every year subsequent to the husband's death? Unless we can answer that question, the observation of Melvil, J. in the Bombay case cited above, may apply, and arrears for any period may be legally sued for. Upon this point, the law is not quite clear.

Right of a daughter-in-law to maintenance, Texts relating to female members rights

I shall now deal with the maintenance of some other female members of the family. First and foremost among them is the daughter-in-law. With reference to the daughter-in-law the Bengal and other schools materially differ. In discussing her case, we must bear in mind that in Bengal the son is not regarded as a coparcener of his father in respect of the ancestral property. Whatever conclusion stray passages of Dāyabhāga might warrant as to the restrictions upon the father's power over ancestral property, current law and usage have rendered the father's right over ancestral property at once obsolute. Now the result of this doctrine of obsolute power on the father's part, a doctrine favoured by various parts of the Dāyạbhāga itself—is that the father can in Bengal do all he likes with ancestral property. It he sells it, the son cannot prevent him; he thereby commits what is only morally wrong; the sale is nevertheless valid in the eye of law. That being so, can a daughter-in-law, the wife of a son living in the same family with the father, prevent the sale, on the ground that her maintenance will be jeopardized thereby? It is clear, whatever the rights of a daughter-in-law may be with regard to maintenance to come out of ancestral property in the hands of the father-in-law, those rights cannot be affected by the circumstance of her husband being alive or dead. *Prima facie*, every member of a joint family, male or female, must have subsistence supplied to him or her by the karta or the managing member, provided there be family property, in other words ancestral property. Ṛṣi texts, if not directly inculating the necessity of supplying such subsistence, at least indirectly indicating the views and opinions of the authoritative law-givers in this regard, are too numerous to be overlooked. Thus Manu, ch. 8, śloka 389. "Neither the mother, nor the father, neither the wife, nor the son; can with propierty be abandoned. One abandoning them, when they are not *fallen*, (that is, not degraded by having committed a sin), should be fined by the king six hundred coins." The comments of Kullūka are that abandonment here means 'not maintaining them,' or 'not obeying them,' and so forth, as the case may be. The same author, ch. 3, ślokas 55-59. "These (that is, women of the family) should be respected by fathers, and brothers;—by husbands, and by husband's yonger brothers; and should be adorned with ornaments, if they desire to obtain abundant blessing. Where the women are respected, there the deities are pleased; where, however they are *not* respected, there no rites and ceremonies bear any fruit. Where the females grieve, that family quickly comes to an end; but where they do not grieve, that family is always in a flourishing state. Those houses which the females curse, on account of not being cherished and respected, dwindle away on all sides round as if smitten by a malevolent spirit. Therefore should these females be always respected and cherished with ornaments and clothing and food, by those men who are desirous of obtaining prosperity, on all occasions, on festival days and on days of auspicious rites." Colebrooke's Dig. B. 4, ch. I, sec. 2, text 41. "Women must be honoured and adorned by their own fathers and brethren, and by the fathers and brethern of the husband, if they (*i.e.* husband and father) seek abundant properity." Text 42. "Married women must be honoured by their fathers and brethern, by their husbands and by the brethern of their husbands, if they seek abundant prosperity." Text 43. "Females must be honoured by their husbands, brothers, fathers and paternal kinsmen; by the fathers, mothers and brethern of their husbands; and by all kinsmen; with gifts of ornaments, apparel, and food." Text 37. "These women, graced with the name of goddesses of abundance, should be treated with honour by him who desires wealth: a lovely woman kept from vice is the goddess of abundance." Text 38. "Where females are honoured, there the deities are pleased; but where they are unhonoured, there all religious acts become fruitless. When female relations are made miserable, even than is that family annihilated; for the houses on which they pronounce a curse perish, as if destroyed by a deadly sacrifice: those houses, which are not graced by the goddess of abundance, neither flourish nor increase." Upon this text the comments of Jagannātha are— "Female relation'means sisters, and women of a family. The meaning is, that houses on which female relations pronounce a curse, that is, on which they pronounce an imprecation in consequence of suffering from the want of a suitable maintenance and the like, are extirpated." Colebrooke's Dig., b. 2, ch. IV, sec. 2, Art. 18. "A man may give what remains after the food and clothing of his family: the giver of more, who leaves his family naked and unfed, may taste honey at first, but shall afterwards find it poison." Colebrooke's Dig., B. 2, ch. IV, sec. I, Text 11. "The ample support of those who are entitled to maintenance is rewarded with bliss in heaven; but hell is the portion of that man whose family is afflicated with pain by his neglect: therefore let him maintain his family with the utmost care." The comments of Jagannātha on this text are:—"This text forbidding the family to be left to pain and distress, the prohibition would be ill-observed by maintaining them for one day only; the prohibition is observed by maintaining them for life. 'Then, anyhow estimating the duration of life, and setting apart a sufficiency for their maintenance during that period, a man may give away the remainder of his immoveable property and the like?' This is not consistent with common sense; and Nārada declares it necessary to preserve wealth." Text 12. "Even they who are born, or yet unborn, and they who exist in the womb, require funds for subsistence; the deprivation of the means of subsistence is reprehended." Upon this text the comments of Jagannātha are:—"Funds for subsistence signifies means of living. This is supposed by Jimūtavāhana to be intended of wealth inherited from ancestors; and immoveables consititute the best property; therefore the term is used in its acceptation of wealth generally. Reserving a sufficiency for consumption until other immoveable property be obtained, a man may give away his moveable effects. This is the whole meaning."

I have quoted a sufficient number of texts to show in what direction the views and opinions of our Ṛṣis went with regard to the maintenance rights of the female members of the family. We must not suppose that because in some of these texts some relations are directed by name to pay honour and respect to the female members, and in other texts other relations are named, the interpretation is to be taken as literal and strict. If we consider the general spirit in which the directions have been given, we cannot overlook that all the male members are intended to be a menable to those directions, at all events such male members as are living in the same family. For instance, in one of the texts quoted above, the husband's younger brother is mentioned; but neither the husband's elder brother, nor the father-in-law. Are we to consider that the direction of law does not apply to them? In other texts again the father-in-law is expressly mentioned as bound to maintain the daughter-in-law and deck her with ornaments and clothes; but some other relations are not so mentioned. Surely the Ṛṣis who composed those texts did not intend to say that only the relatives specially named come under the direction. I believe that the drift of these texts taken together is that female members in a family are worthy of particular regard on the part of the females; that they usages of the Hindu society prevent the assumption of any independence on the part of the females; that they are unable themselves to make any arrangements for their food and clothing, even though they have property belonging to themselves; and that if possible, not only necessaries, but even moderate luxuries, within the means in the possession of the family may be reasonably supplied to them. It will be seen that the texts quoted above are Ṛṣi authorities, and therefore binding equally upon all the schools. Nor can we disregard them on the principle once enunciated by the privy Council that the duty of a European Judge is to consult the special treatises belonging to a particular school, rather than to have recourse to the texts of the ancient Ṛṣis.[1]

Maintenance right treated scantily in Nibandha treatises

For these special treatises, namely, the Mitākṣarā, the

1. See Collector of Madura *v.* Muttu Ramalinga, 10 W. R. P. C. 17.

Vīramitrodaya, the Vivādacintāmaṇi, the Dāyabhāga, the Smṛticandrikā, and the Mayūkha, have not handled the subject of maintenance at any length. Thus the Dāyabhāga gives up no help when we have to decide whether in Bengal the daughter-in-law is entitled to maintenance. The general rule as regards maintenance is started to be that when the deseased member of a family has left property, they who take it to the exclusion of his widow will be legally bound to maintain her out of the property. Now in Bengal, as regards a daughter-in-law, facts covered by such a rule can rarely arise. If the father and the son constitute a joint family, all the ancestral property belongs absolutely to the father. On the death of the son, the same property remains in the father's hands under the same title which the father had prior to the son's death. Unlike what takes place under the Mitākṣarā, the father's right is not enlarged in the slightest degree by the death of the son. It cannot therefore be said that in such a case the son has left any property from which his widow has been excluded by his father. If there is any proposition free from doubt under the Dāyabhāga law, it is this that during the lifetime of the father, the son is totally devoid of all ownership whatsoever in property which has descended to his father from any ancestor, either on the male or on the female side. Then suppose a case where the father and the son are living together, and earning money, and bringing their earnings into a common fund. They may be said to be constituting a joint family in one sense; but not in the Mitākṣarā sense, for there is no survivorship. If the father dies, then the son no doubt takes the whole property as his father's heir, and is bound to give maintenance and residence to his father's widow: but if the son dies, then the father does not take whatever share the son had in the joint estate, but the son's widow takes the same. Even in Bengal, if the son has been earning money, and paying it into his father's hands, and properties are purchased from the joint funds of the father and the son, there connot be any doubt that the son has a vested right in some share of the property. There may in such a case be a partition between the father and the son and thus the son's share may become tangible and definite. But after the son's death, the son's widow would be a co-heir of her father-in-law; and she does not stand upon the precarious right of receiving maintenance from her father-in-law. This therefore is not a case covered by the above rule of law; the widow is not excluded. The only combination of facts of which the above rule can be applied in Bengal is where a son's widow is a disqualified person; then she does not inherit the property of her husband; but the father does; in such a case the father-in-law in Bengal is bound to maintain his daughter-in-law, the reason being that the son's property, to which the son's widow would have succeeded but for her disqualification, has come into his hands.

Daughter-in-law's maintenance in Bengal.

I do not therefore see that in Bengal, as regards the right of the daughter-in-law to receive maintenance from her father-in-law, the existence of ancestral property can make any difference. Ancestral property or no ancestral property, if we literally follow the directions of the ancient Ṛṣis with regard to the treatment of females in the family, we must conclude that a father-in-law should maintain the widow of a deceased son. I believe that in the earlier days of the administration of Hindu law by European Judges, those directions of the ancient Ṛṣis were followed strictly to the letter. Thus in 1865 the High Court of Bengal said that a son's widow was according to Hindu law entitled to maintenance so long as she led a chaste life, whether she elected to live with her father-in-law, or with her own relations; that in any case, she was absolutely entitled to it, whenever she might choose to take it, so long as she should be leading a chaste life; and that the rate of maintenance was to be assessed with reference to the father-in-law's means. The Judges rely for this law upon Vyavasthā, No. 160 in the Vyavasthā-Darpaṇa of the late Babu Shamacharan Sarkar.[1] In the succeeding year the same question again arose in a case before the High Court of Bengal, in which the judge do not question the soundness of the previous ruling, but said that there must be means in the hands of the father-in-law in order that his obligation to maintain his daughter-in-law could be enforced in a court of justice; that the father-in-law should be exempted if he had absolutely no means; and that rate of allowance must be proportioned to the amount of such means.[2] Cases still earlier than these seem to recognize the right of the daughter-in-law to maintenance. Thus Case 2, Vol. 2, Macnaghten's Hindu Law, p. 104, holds that where the brother's sons succeeded to their uncle's estate, they were bound to support the widow of his son who had predeceased his father. Case 4 is one where two out of three sons succeeded to the father's property, the third having died before the father; the third son's widow was held to the have a lawful claim upon her husband's surviving brothers for maintenacne. Case 8. p. 116. says that the widow of the son predeceasing his father gets one share of the ancestral property, nor of the acquisitions made by her husband's brothers, but gets subsistence from the heirs and representatives of her father-in-law. Case 11 says that if a son dies before his father, and if his widow lives virtuously and is obedient to her husband's family, she gets maintenance from her father-in-law or other successor to his property; but not so, if the son, her husband, had once become separated to from his father, and had obtained his share of the family property. In p. 33, Select Reports, vol. 3, is a case of a widow whose husband died before his father, and whose right to food and raiment was sustained by the Court. In p. 223, is a case in which the amount of maintenance receivable by such a widow was considered,

1. Khoodee money Debea *v.* Tarachand Chuckerbutty, 2 W. R. 134.
2. Rutton Chand Shooree *v.* Srimati Hurro Money, 5 W.R. 225.

it being held that the calculation was to with reference to the circumstances of the family. Oojulmoney's case, p. 491, Sud. D. A. Decisions for 1848 makes the maintenance of a brother's widow, the brother having predeceased his father, dependent upon the widow's living in her husband's family. Then there is the case of Huro Soondary Goopta, p. 422, S. D. A. "Decis. 1850, where the right itself is not denied, but the amount alone is discussed. Another case, p. 796, S. D. for 1852, is one in which the claim was made against the Father-in-law by a son's widow who had been expelled from the family house. The court held that her departure from her husband's family having been a compulsory act, her right to maintenance had not been forfeited. In p. 1220, S. D. A. D. for 1858, a case is given in which the sons widow had been driven by ill-treatment on the part of her deceased husband's brother to dwell with her husband's nephew; and it was held that she had incurred no forfeiture of her right to maintenance. I believe the decision reported in 2 Hyde's Reports, p. 103 was the first in which the texts inculcating the duty of the father-in-law to support the widow of his deceased son were construed as imposing a moral and not a legal obligation. The words in this decision are,—"According to Hindu Law, probably the plaintiff should be maintained in the house of her father-in-law who ought to find her in food and raiment. But when the father and the son are not joint in estate, the maintenance of the son's widow appears to be a mere moral duty on her father-in-law, to performance of which he is not compellable by law. The absolute power of a father as master and head of the family over property acquired by himself, his right to distribute it at his pleasure, and to keep and reserve what he thinks fit for himself, is asserted in the most distinct manner in numerous texts; Colobrooke's Dig., B. 5 ch. I, sec. 2, pl. 23 to 26, and ch. II, p. 88. In p. 90 the commentator Jagannātha treats the maintenance of a family out of a man's own wealth as preceptive merely, and says, at p. 88, that a father slighting such precept, commits a moral offence, but incurs no civil penalty. A son's widow cannot have larger legal rights against her father-in-law, than her husband would have had if alive, and such husband could not have compelled his father to give him any share of his property."

I have already said that this distinction between a moral and a legal injunction is hardly countenanced by the Ṛṣi texts. By Ṛṣi texts I mean the sayings of the saints who were supposed to be inspired. Inferior; as authorities to these Ṛṣi texts are the writings of the commentators, including Jimūtavāhana and Raghunandana and Srikrishna who seems to be the latest; of the writers on Hindu Law in original Sanskrit whose opinions carry with them an independent authoritative character. The treatise of Jagannātha cannot be placed in the same rank with the works of those earlier authors named above. In spite of the high eulogium pronounced upon Jagannātha by Sir Thomas Strange; it is difficult to forget the origin of Jagannātha's bulky' Incubrations. The book was made to order; the British administrators were eager for a general resume of the law of the Hindus for the purpose of daily use in the administration of that law; Jagannātha at the time deservedly occupied the highest post in the world of Bengal Pandits. The days of the first establishment of British power in Bengal were the days when the study of Nyāya had won for the Bengali scholars a paramount position in the republic of Sanskrit Literature in northern India. Popular estimation had then placed the Nyāya philosophy above all the other branches of learning. Jagannātha stood at the top of the list of Pandits who then expounded the Nyāya philosophy. He no doubt used to receive what is called the highest Vidāy (presents made to Pandits on occasions of śrādhs, marriages etc.), in all assemblages of Sanskrit scholars invited by wealthy, persons on great family ceremonies. I believe it was for these reasons that the task of preparing a general

Digest of Hindu law was entrusted to him by the British authorities. The learned Pandit's knowledge to a certain extent was encyclopedic; but his specialty was the Nyāya; whatever information he for the occasion gathered on the subject of Hindu law in order to prepare his work was put together by him in the spirit befitting a student of his special branch of learning, the Nyāya or the Hindu Dialectics. Rules of logic or rather of what may be called the Indian scholastic philosophy, he has applied in his work on Hindu Law to a very great extent; and the easiest way to reconcile the mutual conflicts of the ancient texts, and to convert the aggregate of these texts into a logical and harmonious body of propositions, is to adopt the distinction between civil and moral obligation.

Jagannātha's influence on the development of Bengal law.

In this device he had been partially anticipated by Jimūtavāhana, the great founder of the school to which Jagannātha belonged. Yet the extent to which Jagannātha carries the application of this ingenious expedient might have startled his great master himself. Jagannātha's close reasoning and logical method of exposition seem to have recommended his work to the esteem of European Judges, who were trained in law, experienced lawyers themselves, I mean the Barristers from European Inns of Court, who were appointed to administer Hindu Law in the Presidency towns. They had a sympathy for symmetry in systems of law; they could appreciate wire-drawn distinctions in legal questions; and they found in Jagannātha's work a ready-made position of Hindu law on a logical basis. I believe in Jagannātha's method has influenced in an unacknowledged way the practical administration of Hindu law to a very great extent. Sir Thomas Strange was an admirer of Jagannātha, and Sir Thomas Strange was the father of most of the principles of Hindu law which actually guide the judicial sense of our European Judges.

With regard to the daughter-in-law's right to receive maintenance from her father-in-law, the keen logical perception of Jagannātha at once caught hold of the incongruity between the Bengal father's absolute right and such right to maintenance. The Dāyabhāga of Jīmūtavāhana must have been deeply pondered by him. What other conclusion can possibly result from a serious study of the Dāyabhāga, except this that the Bengal father can do as he likes with all property in his hands, both ancestral and self-acquired ? The dictum that sons are no owners during their father's lifetime has laid the axe at the root of a son's widow's right to maintenance. And the case quoted above from Hyde's Reports is nothing but a close syllogism founded upon that dictum as its major premiss. Yet a more humane lawyer than either Jagannātha or Jimūtavāhana was, might have drawn a distinction; might have said that although the father's power is absolute to sell the ancestral property inherited by him, yet so long as he does not sell, the helpless daughter-in-law can follow the property in his hands; or even the proceeds of sale, if they can be traced to be in his hands. I apprehend that in Hindu days, when sales of immoveable property were rather rare, the father-in-law was compelled to support his deceased son's widow, when he was able. I also believe that the public opinion had then sufficient strength to compel the father-in-law to follow a course of conduct which had been sanctioned by long-established usage, and from which few persons then cared to depart.

Khetramoni Dasi v. Kasīnath Das

The question of the son's widow's maintenance has received from the High Court of Bengal as much discussion and consideration as it is possible for a single question ever to receive from any tribunal. On 31st March 1868, it was once before a Bench composed of Sir Barnes Peacock, Chief Justice, and Loch, Kemp, A. G. Machpher son, Judges. On the 10th September, in the same year, it was again before another Bench composed of seven Judges, Bayley, Norman, L. S. Jackson, Phear, E. Jackson, Glover and Hobhouse. So that altogether eleven Judges have seriously considered the question.[1] The different decisions delivered on the two occasions illustrate what I have already once noticed—the fact that some European Judges are for restoring the Hindu Law to its original condition as disclosed in the ancient Ṛṣi texts, and others again are for tempering the literal interpretation of the texts by the introduction of European notions. The facts of this case were, that the father-in-law had no ancestral property in his hands, and the widow of the deceased son sued for a separate maintenance, unwilling to live in the family of her father-in-law. The ultimate result of the elaborate discussion by eleven Judges of the High Court of Bengal was that under the facts of the case, the son's widow was held to have no title to the maintenance she claimed. But I am Afraid that many minor questions relating to the matter remain still unsettled. For instance, where there is ancestral property in the father-in-law's hand, we do not know whether the son's widow can claim maintenance; we do not know if she can get it, in case she is willing to live in her father-in-law's family; and so forth. I believe it is generally supposed that the abovenamed case has settled the law in all cases against the right of the son's widow; and this generally prevalent idea has almost put an end to all assertions of claims to maintenance by a son's widow in Bengal. Maintenance suits are generally brought by persons in indigent circumstances; and it is not likely that the question of the son's widow's maintenance will soon be brought before the Courts of Justice in Bengal on a foundation of facts different from those of Kassee Nath Doss *v.* Khettur Money Ossee. A case may arise where the

1. *Vide* the case of Kashee Nath Doss *v.* Khettur Money Doseoo, 9 W. R. 413; and Khottur Money Dosseo *v.* Kasseo Nath Doss, 10 W. R. F. B. 89.

father-in-law has large ancestral property in his hands, and the widow of a deceased son of his has quarrelled with him, and has the prospect of powerful support from her paternal relations or maternal relations; it is difficult to say what the decision will be in such a case.

It will be seen that all the eleven Judges who delivered judgment in Khetramoni's case are cautious in confining their remarks to the facts of the particular case. They were unwilling to lay down broadly that the very relationship which subsists between a father-in-law and his son's widow is a sufficient reason for the latter's receiving a money allowance by way of maintenance. At the same time the strong array of texts inculcating the indispensableness of supporting the female members deterred the judges from pronouncing against the son's widow's right in all cases; for instance, where she is willing to live in the father-in-law's family; or where she has left it on account of harsh treatment. Chief Justice Peacock is for negativing her right even in this latter case.

It is not easy to apply adverse criticism to his opinion. It ought to be borne in mind, that Kulinism had not yet come into existence when the ancient texts were written. There is every reason to suppose that in those days plurality of wives was exceptional, and required the sanction of law to authorize it. But in a country where plurality of wives among the Kulin Brahmins is absolutely unrestricted either by law or public opinion, no European Judge can be expected to see the fitness of a legal principle which would lay on the father the burden of supporting fifty widows of a single deceased son. For the principle being once admitted, the number of widows a son may leave would not affect the liability of the father-in-law. At the same time, we must not forget, on the other hand, the very great share a father in Bengal has in bringing about the marriage of his son. He in most cases marries his son before the latter has arrived at years of discretion. That early marriage is so common is owing to the foolishness of the bridegroom's father. Equity and good conscience would be little outraged if the father-in-law were saddled with the liability of maintaining his son's widow, where the father gave his infant son in marriage, before the latter had acquired any sense as to what grave responsibilities he was incurring. Surely such a solemn act of life as marriage between two individuals ought to be accompanied by an adequate idea, that momentous changes in the personal status of the parties were taking place by the virtue of the act. As regards the infant son, he is but a puppet in the hands of his father. In all civilized countries, a married woman looks for her support to her husband; but where the husband is an infant at the time of marriage, who is to be supposed as making a promise that he will support the woman? Surely the father, who is the only free agent in the transaction. If therefore the law were that wherever the father was responsible for the marriage of his infant son, a promise should be fastened upon him, of supporting the son's widow, I believe the old texts inculcating the maintenance of a daughter-in-law might become something more than meaningless moral precepts.

Position of Mitākṣarā daughter-in-law more secure

Such is the position of the daughter-in-law in Bengal. In the other four schools, however, her rights are hardly distinguishable from those of the widow. There the son is a coparcener in the ancestral property; she has therefore, like the widow of every other coparcener, an indefeasible right to receive even a separate allowance out of the joint property in the father-in-law's hands. I do not see how it can be insisted in her case that she ought to dwell under the protection of her father-in-law any more than in the case of the widow of any other coparcener, such as a brother or an uncle. Some of the cases which I have already noticed in dealing with the question of the amount of maintenance place a daughter-in-law in a joint Mitākṣarā family exactly in the same rank with the father's widow. This superiority in the position of a daughter-in-law in a family governed by the Mitākṣarā law is recognized by our judges. In Muss. Hemu Kooeree *v.* Ajudhya Pershad, 24 W. R., 474, (although this case was decided by a single judge, and therefore the judgment, according to the opinion entertained in some quarters, may not carry with it the same weight as if the case had been decided by a Bench of two or more judges) Kemp, J. said that under the Bengal law, the widow of a son who left no property, could not compel her father-in-law to make her a pecuniary allowance in lieu of maintenance, if she refused to reside in his house as a member of his family; but that in a case governed by the Mitākṣarā law, the question would be whether the father and the son were joint in estate, and whether any joint estate was left which was burdened with the payment of a proper maintenance to the daughter-in-law. In this case the existence of ancestral property in the hands of the father-in-law is impliedly taken to be a condition precedent to the validity of the daughter-in-law's claim. The daughter-in-law in fact is in all respects like the widow of a coparcener; and the existence of such a widow's right to subsistence in a joint family is expressly declared in the Vīramitrodaya (p. 173). But in Bombay (Mumbai), as in the case of other widows in the family, there have been cases which sanction the claim of any destitute widow to maintenance from any male relation of the husband's family, whether there be any joint property in their hands or not, and whether the claim be made before separation or after separation; so in the case of a daughter-in-law also, a Bench of the High Court of Bombay, one of the members of which was a Hindu, has ruled that a Hindu father-in-law is legally bound to maintain his deceased son's widow, notwithstanding that no property belonging to his son may have come into his hands.[1] In this case the words

1. Udaram Sitaram *v.* Sonkar Bai, 10 Bom. H.C. Rep. 483.

used by West, J. were:-" The result is that the Hindu law, which still, notwithstanding separation, leaves to the other members of the family, an interest in the property of the separated member to be realized on his widow's death, conversely gives to him and to his widow a claim to maintenance if, through destitution, they should come to need it' Mr. Justice Nanabhai says:—"According to Hindu law, among the duties of the head of a family, that of maintenance by him of all the dependent members of that family is considered a primary duty. There can be no question but that the widow of a son is a dependent member of her father-in-law's family. She is therefore entitled to maintenance from the head of the family, her father-in-law. This right of hers would seem to be quite independent of any property acquired by her father-in-law from his deceased son as well as of any ancestral property in which such son had a joint interest with him. "The interest which West, J. says, a separated member has after the death of the widow is the interest of a reversionary heir which follows the property whenever it comes into the hands of a sonless widow after separation. This observation is intended to show that separation does not put an end to all mutual interest among the sometime members of a joint family that was, and the widow's maintenance, like the reversionary interest, may well follow separated property.

The High Court of Allahabad, however, has by a Full Bench decision settled the law of that part of India to be that the widow of a son who predeceased his father will get maintenance out of ancestral properties or funds in the possession of her father-in-law.[1] Another Full Bench of the same High Court has held the converse of the above proposition; that where there is no ancestral property in the hands of the father-in-law, the son's widow has no valid claim for maintenance against him.[2] In this case there was

1. Lalti Kuer *v.* Ganga Vishan, H.C.R.N.W.P. 1875, p. 261.
2. Ganga Bai *v.* Sita Ram, I.L.R. 1 All. 174.

ancestral property at first; but the father-in-law parted with them in order to pay off his debts. After his having done so, the son's widow sued him for maintenance out of a charitable allowance which he used to receive. The son's widow also claimed a right of residence in one moiety of the house which had been sold by the father-in-law. Upon these facts, Stuart, C. J. said that if the father-in-law had neither ancestral property nor any immoveable property in his hands, and if he had no such property in his possession with the disposal of which, his son, if alive, could have interfered, he was not legally bound to maintain his son's widow. The judgment further says that there may be some moral obligation to do so on the part of the father-in-law ; in the same way as it is morally obligatory on the part of the son's widow to dwell under the protection of her father-in-law. But the Privy Council in Pirthee Sing's case have decided that the necessity of residence in the family is not absolute; similarly the moral duty of supporting the son's widow, may be violated by him without his incurring any civil penalty, however discreditable his conduct may be in the estimation of the world. In this case the position of the son's widow was assimilated to that of her husband the son. Such a son cannot question a father's sale of ancestral property, if such sale has been necessitated by his debts; similarly the support of his widow cannot override the right of the purchaser where the purchase money went to pay off the father's debts. I believe the comparison may be extended by adding that as a Mitākṣarā son can question the validity of the illegal or immoral debts of his father, so his widow can seek maintenance upon the allegations that the debts contracted by the father-in-law are immoral, and that the purchase from him was affected with notice. There is also another noticeable part in the judgment of Stuart, C. J., who seems to throwout a hint that if there be self-acquired immoveable property in father-in-law's hand, the maintenance right of his son's widow attaches to it. This would be in accordance with an express passage of the Mitākṣarā. (Ch. I, See. 1, para 27). Immoveable property, even though acquired by the father himself, has been considered by Vijñāneśvara as part of the joint funds; and though he is not explicit upon the question of the father's power of disposal over his self-acquired property, it seems to me that the only way to reconcile all the different passages of his work relating to this matter would be by supposing that the Mitākṣarā father's absolute power of disposition is confined solely to his self-acquired moveable property. Chief Justice Stuart, I believe, was thinking of these passages of the Mitākṣarā when he says that the father-in-law's exemption from liability for his son's widow's maintenance depends also upon the absence of all self-acquired immoveable property in his hands. The part of his judgment I allude to runs thus—"We must assume for the purpose of this reference that the father-in-law is in possession neither of ancestral nor of immoveable property." These words seem to show that the possession of any kind of immoveable property, whether ancestral or acquired, would have raised a doubt as to the father-in-law's exemption from the liability which was in question in the Full Bench Reference.

The High Court of Bombay had to consider the question whether self-acquired property in the hands of the father-in-law could be legally claimed by a son's widow as a source of her maintenance.[1] There the son's widow claimed maintenance both for herself and her minor children. Sargent, C. J. overruled the claim. He relies upon Sabitri Bai *v.* Lakshmi Bai, I. L. R. 2 Bom., 574, and endorses the opinion expressed therein that when Hindu jurists speak of the right of the females of the family (other than a wife or mother) to maintenance without reference to the exis-

1. Kalu *v.* Kashi-bai, I.L.R. 7 Bom., 130.

tence of the family property, their tone is only precep-tive, and their injunction is of rather ethical than of legal obligation.

Other female Members

The other female members of the joint family whose maintenance has been touched upon in decided cases are a grandmother and a daughter. If there be a joint family composed of a father and his son; then the father dies leaving his widow and his son; then the son dies leaving a son; this latter son, the grandson of the first mentioned person, would be bound to maintain her, whether in Bengal or in the other provinces of India. But the grandson must have received ancestral property in order to be so liable. This right of the grandmother to receive maintenance is incidentally admitted in Sheodyal Tewaree *v.* Jadoonath Tewaree, 9 W. R., 62, in which Mitter, J. said;–"The mother or grandmother, as the case may be, is entitled to a share when sons or grandsons divide the family estate between themselves. But the mother or the grandmother can never be recognized as the owner of such a share, until the division has been actually made. She has no pre-existing vested right in the estate except a right of maintenance." This right of the grandmother also comes within the general rule relating to maintenance, that the heir is bound to provide out of the inherited, estate maintenance for persons whom the ancestor was legally or morally bound to maintain.[1] The grandmother's husband was both legally and morally bound to maintain his wife; the grandson is the heir of the grandfather; he is therefore liable to support his grandmother. The right also comes within another form of the same rule which says that when the deceased member of a family has left property, they who take it to the exclusion of his widow will be legally bound to maintain her out of the property.[2]

1. *Per* Sir Barnes Peacock in Khettromoney's case, 9 W.R. 422, Ist Column, beginning of the last para.
2. See per Oldfield, p. 176, I.L.R.I. All, last para.

The grandfather is the deceased member whose property is taken by the grandson to the exclusion of his widow, the grandmother; liability for her maintenance therefore attaches to him as the possessor of the joint estate. Puddum Mooknee Dossee *v.* Rayee Money Dossee is a Bengal case,[1] in which the judges on the authority of a passage from Macnaghten say that the Hindu law recognizes the right of the mother to maintenance on the part of one in the position of the grandmother in that particular case. The passage from Sir William Macnaghten is:—"She has a right to participate in all the comforts which are enjoyed by his family in its undivided state, and a legal as well as a natural claim to that protection which may be derived from a union of her descendants. If, therefore, she is deprived of such advantages, it is but just she should be enabled to take care of herself and not be obliged to go from door to door for her support."

The right of the grandmother also is subject to the rules applicable to that of a widow. Ordinarily, her maintenance is a charge on the estate in the hand of the heir. But if the heir alienates it, and the purchaser has no notice that there is such a charge upon the property, in other words, no notice that the grandmother of the vendor has a lawful claim to get her maintenance out of it, the purchaser's rights are not affected. She is competent to have her claim made a specific charge on a particular property; but so long as it has not been reduced to certainty by a legal transaction, she has a mere equity to a provision.[2] Therefore, where the joint property was first inherited by a widow's son, and then after the death of the son, by the grandson; and the son had mortgaged the whole property in order to pay off debts contracted by him to carry on his business transactions, the High Court of Madras held that the purchaser had purcha-

1. 12 W.R., 409
2. See Kalagathachi *v.* Ganapathi Pillai, I.L.R. 3 Mad. p, 191–2nd para.

sed it free from the widow's right, when there had been a decree on the mortgage followed by an auction sale. At the time of the auction sale the grandson had succeeded to the joint property. The widow after the auction sale asserted her right to maintenance out of the property in the auction purchaser's hand; she also claimed a right to have accommodation in one of the houses sold. The judges said that the mere right to maintenance did not create a lien on the family property. "To affect a *bona fide* purchaser the right must have been ascertained by contract, or by a decree of court, and charged on specific property. The widow (in the present case the grandmother of the party in whose hands the family property had come at the time of the court sale) took no steps to secure a charge on the property before the mortgage was created, and it is not shown that the mortgage was created in contemplation of any fraud on her rights; she cannot resist the sale on the mortgage decree." The judges also said that if the grandmother liked, she might enforce her right to maintenance on the surplus proceeds of the auction sale come into the hands of her grandson. Her right to residence in the house, however, which she had been all along occupying, was upheld, and it was directed that it should be sold subject to such right.[1] The daughter's right to maintenance is recognized in Kooloda Debia *v.* Ramjotee Debits, 12 W. R., 453, where the judges say that where the property is held jointly, it is a rule of the Mitākṣarā law, that the widow or the daughter does not succeed, but is only entitled to maintenance.

Some members in the family seem to be entitled to maintenance, independently of the existence of ancestral property. Thus Manu cited in Colebrooke's Dig. B. 5, ch. VI, sec. 2, Article 1, (p. 406, vol. 3, London Ed., of 1801) says:— "A mother and a father in their old age, a virtuous wife, and an infant son, must be maintained even though doing a

1. Venkantammal *v.* Andyappa, I.L.R. 6 Mad. 134.

hundred times that which ought not to be done." In Strange's Manual, sec. 209, it is said:—"Where there may be no property, but what has been self-acquired, the only person whose maintenance out of such property is imperative, are aged parents, wife and minor children." Sargent, C. J., in a case already noticed[1] says in connection with the above text of Manu:—"A man's aged parents, his wife, and his infant children, appeal to his protection in a special manner in which no other relations do, and the strength of the expression used in the injunction as to their protection points to children only being intended. To extend the legal obligations to descendants would impose in many cases a heavy burden." So that according to this opinion, one's infant sons are always entitled to get maintenance from him, but not his grandsons, nor any other descendants.

I have already noticed that in many instances the right of a female member to maintenance founds itself upon two or even three relationships. Thus, since a Mitākṣarā family may be composed of brothers, or cousins of the first degree, or those of the second and third degrees; as soon as any one of the members dies, his widow as such gets maintenance from all the surviving members together. If he left a son, and then that son dies, the widow then as the mother of a member is yet entitled to maintenance. If that son again dies leaving a son, who then dies, the original widow, then the mother of a deceased member, subsequently the grandmother of another deceased member, in every one of these capacities, she gets her maintenance. It does not, however, make any difference in what capacity she has a right; the root of her right being the same in every case, namely, her marriage with a member of an undivided family. So long as the undivided family lasts, and so long as any family property lasts, her maintenance attaches to that property in the hands of any surviving member, be it a son, or a

1. See I.L.R. 7 Bom. p. 130.

grandson, or a husband's uncle, or a husband's cousin, or a husband's nephew or grandnephew, or even a father-in-law. The rights of the different female members therefore hardly need a separate discussion, at least in the four schools submitting to the Mitākṣarā as their guide. The sole consideration is, whether the husband of the female member is or was an undivided coparcener, and whether there is any joint property.

How to make a maintenance right secure

When there is any such property in existence, the best advice for a female member is, that as soon as her husband dies, she should demand a specific portion of the joint property to be set apart for her maintenance. If she cannot have it done amicably, she ought to come to court; the decision of the Madras High Court quoted above, tacitly endorsed by all other High Courts,[1] will sustain the assertion of such a right. Once her maintenance being fixed as a charge upon the property, any disposition by the male members will leave it unaffected ; her maintenance will rest safe and secure. If she however, from disinclination to place herself in a position hostile to the male members, should hesitate in asserting her right, or should even defer it, she only will have herself to blame if the courts do not help her after the property has been dissipated either intentionally and fraudulently, by the male members; or after they have been compelled by force of circumstances to alienate the family funds. To fix the purchasers with either fraud or notice of the widow's claim, is not an easy task for any person; it is almost an impossibility for the retired inmate of a secluded Hindu Zenana. The tendency of the tribunals is, guided as they are, and must necessarily be, by notions derived from the latest culture of modern Europe, is to loosen the ties impeding the free circulation of property from hand to hand. When once property changes hands,

1. *Vide* I.L.R. 1 Cal. 365; I.L.R. 2 Bom 494; I.L.R. 4 All. 209.

intangible rights, like that of maintenance—rights which do not accompany the visible and bodily possession of property, do not obtain a proper consideration. Hindu society is fast drifting away from its former defined course; the old law gathered from the early Ṛṣi texts is becoming more and more unsuited to its present condition; the society itself, in spite of its strong conservative instincts, is being forced by uncontrollable circumstances to fashion itself on the European pattern. It is thus that among many rights and privileges formerly recognized, but which are now becoming obsolete, the widow's right to maintenance is one; and I am afraid, that unless attempts are made to protect it from the attack of notions of which the ancient Hindu Law knew next to nothing, the right are long will practically become a thing of the past.

Chapter 7
The Disqualified Members of A Joint Family

Exclusion for infirmity peculiar to Hindu law– Degradation as cause of exclusion added by Brahmins—Disqualification under the Benares school—Rule that estate once vested is not divestod—Disqualification under the Vīramitrodaya—Bearing religious mark a disqualification—Disqualification under the Mithilā law—In Bengal—In Bombay—In Madras—Disqualified list—Impotent—Absence of disqualification prosumed by law—The leper—The insane person—The rule that estates once vested are not divested has its exceptions—Insanity need not be congenital Idiot—Nirindriya or a person who has lost a sense— The fallen, the vicious and the heterodox—Sins classified—List of minor sine—Lex Loci Act, XXI of 1850.

There is another class of members of a joint Hindu family, who like the females, are devoid of any independent and substantive interest in the family property, but whose existence as members of a joint family can scarcely be kept out of sight. I allude to the class of persons known as the disqualified members of a family. I have once already had occasion to notice their case, when considering the right of the male members to receive subsistence from the undivided funds. I shall here have to point out who these disqualified persons are, of how many kinds.

Exclusion for infirmity peculiar to Hindu Law

This law of exclusion is peculiar to the Hindu system. Where there is a partition of the joint family property, that system says that persons affected with certain bodily or mental infirmities do not get a share, Yājñavalkya, ch. II, śloka 143, enumerates them, saying that an impotent person, a fallen person, the issue of a fallen person, a cripple, a lunatic, an idiot, a blind person, one afflicted with an incurable disease, and others, should be supported, being incompetent to get a share. In this enumeration may be perceived the remains of the influence of patriarchal traditions, as well as the effect of Brahmanic religious notions. In the patriarchal days, the very existence of the family group depended upon the vigour and capacity of its head. The cripple, and the blind, and similar other incapable persona were therefore summarily set aside, although they might be the eldest born; and the government of the household was entrusted to a younger, but more capable member. The tradition survived even when peaceable days supervened, and the practice remained whereby infirm persons were excluded from all share in the family property.

Degradation as cause of exclusion aded by Brāhmins

The effect of Brāhminic religion is plain in the superaddition of a *fallen* person, to the disqualified list. It is evident that to be *fallen* is to commit some act proscribed by religion; and before Brāhmanic religion had established its sway over the Hindu community in general, commission of acts proscribed by religion could not have had so serious a consequence as disinherison. It is also evident that the general establishment of Brāhmanic religion must have been subsequent to the days when the Hindu community still retained the marks of a patriarchal condition. I therefore infer that the inclusion of a fallen man in the iist of excluded persons is a later addition, made at a time when the Brāhmins thought that the interests of religion would be promoted by a rule of law which fastens disinherison upon persons who went against the commands of religion. The list of disqualified persons not exactly the same in all the Ṛiṣis. This we might expect from the manner in which Yājñavalkya concludes his enumeration, for he says that persons affected with incurable disease and similar others get no share, leaving it to be inferred that his enumeration is not exhaustive. The comments of Vijñāneśvara upon this śloka and the two following ślokas of Yājñavalkya have summed up the whole law of disqualification as understood in the Benares school.

Disqualification under the Benares school

According to him, by an impotent person we must understand what he calls the 'third sex,'-one who can be called neither a male nor a female, but is of a sex different from both. A 'fallen person' is one who has committed the sin of killing a Brāhmin, the most heinous that one can possibly be guilty of, under the Brāhmanic creed; or who has committed any other sinful act. To be fallen is to have committed a sinful act; and the commentator, to illustrate the fallen condition, mentions the most opprobrious of all sinful acts. A cripple is one who has no use of his legs. The derivative meaning of the word in the original (*Paṅgu*) is, one who does not walk upon his legs.' Therefore one who is only lame, and simply limps, would not be disqualified. A lunatic is explained as one who is subject to one of the many forms of insanity, which works on Hindu Medicine ascribe to an undue preponderance of any one of the celebrated physiological agents according to the Hindu medical theory, namely, the Wind, the Bile, and the Phlegm. Insanity is also said to be caused by the possession of a malevolent spirit called a *graha*. 'An idiot is one who has no internal sense and who is unable to ascertain what is for his good and what is not for his good. A blind person is one devoid of his visual organ. One afflicted with an incurable disease is a person subject to some illness which is beyond the power of medicine to heal, such as consumption and the like. And similar other excluded persons, are those who have retired from a householder's life, or who hate their fathers to the extent of doing an evil turn to them, or persons guilty of a minor sin, as specifically mentioned and described in Manu and in other Institutes.

Then Vijñāneśvara cites Vasiṣṭha to show that one retired from the householder's life is excluded; he cites Nārada law to show that the enemy of one's father and the perpetrator of a minor sin are excluded; and he cites Manu to add three other persons to the list.[1] These are a deaf person, a dumb person, and one who has lost a sense; according to Manu, blindness to be a cause of exclusion, must be congenital. If a person loses an organ of sense, by illness, he also is a disqualified member. Then Vijñāneśvara says that they do not get a share of the joint inheritance at partition, but should have food and raiment, and other necessary articles supplied to them; for Manu has said that a sensible man should furnish subsistence to them so long as they live; one who does not give, himself becomes a sinful man. They do not get a share if the disqualification has affected them before the partition takes place.

Rule that estate once vested is not divested

But if the disqualifying cause is of a date subsequent to the division, their shares are not taken back. This might be cited as an authority for the well-known proposition of Hindu law that an estate once vested is never divested. But its effect is neutralized by the sentence which follows in the Mitākṣarā immediately after; that sentence is, that if after partition the disqualifying cause is removed by medical treatment, then surely they should get a share. This rule necessarily involves the divesting of an already vested estate. Thus, suppose a congenitally blind man restored to eye-sight by medical skill, after the family has already divided, and the several members have taken their shares. The blind man that was, but who is no longer so, will get a share, if the rule laid down by Vijñāneśvara is to prevail. The other members must make up his share out of their own; which is nothing else than the divesting of an already vested interest. Vijñāneśvara then says that not only males, but females also, would be excluded, if affected by one of

1. Mitāk, ch. II, sec. 10.

the enumerated disqualifications; so that a blind or deaf widow, or daughter, or mother of a sonless divided Hindu would not inherit from him. If the disqualified persons have legitimate sons then these sons have a right to the proper share of the father; and their daughters get maintenance until given away in marriage; Vijñāneśvara adds that the duty of celebrating the nuptial ceremony of the daughters of the disqualified members falls upon the qualified ones.[1]

Disqualification under the Vīramitrodaya

In the Vīramitrodaya, the other treatise of the Benares school, we find the subject of disqualified members dealt with in ch. 8, which contains the following new rules upon the matter, not to be found in the Mitākṣarā. It says that impotency and sightlessness must both be congenital in order to work exclusion from inheritance; and that if at a subsequent period the infirmity is removed by medical treatment, then such persons' shares are to be made up from the remains of the divided property. The author then says that a person who has lost a sense is distinguishable from one afflicted with the infirmity of impotence, which is an attribute received at the hand of nature. According to some, he adds, one who has not got a hand or a leg comes under the category of having lost a sense. He further adds that a heinous sin and minor sins work exclusion if not expiated by proper atoning rites; for an atheistically inclined man, scoffing at religion and its commands from the pride of his heart, deserves to lose all rights in the family property. Yājnavalkya has said in general terms that all disqualified persons should receive subsistence from the qualified members; but the Vīramitrodaya quotes a passage of Devala, according to which an impotent person, a leper, a lunatic, an idiot, a sightless person, a fallen person and his issue, a person bearing marks on his body of a particular religious denomination, do not get a share of the

1. *Vide* Colebrooke's Mitāksharā, ch. II, sec. 10.

inheritance. " Out of these rice and clothing are given to all but the fallen person. Their sons, if free from defect, get the share of their father's inheritance." On this text the maintenance of fallen persons is cut off, also that of their issue, as laid down in the Vīramitrodaya.

Bearing religious marks, a disqualification

In the text of Devala we find another disqualified person added to the list, namely, one bearing the marks of a religious denomination on his body. This would be the natural and proper sense of the term need by Devala; but the Vīramitrodaya explains it as one who has become a hermit, etc. Then the author starts an objection, that since the impotent person and others cannot be invested with the sacred thread, they must be classed with the fallen. But the objection is answered by saying that this absence of investiture is caused by their incapacity to be invested with the thread; they on that account become like Śūdras, but are not fallen. Then Āpastamba is quoted, who says that an excommunicated person loses his share in the inheritance. An excommunicated person is one in whose company water is not drunk by his castemen. Then Vṛhaspati is quoted, according to whom a son destitute of virtue is unworthy of the paternal wealth, in whose stead the wealth goes to such kinsmen as are versed in the Vedas, and offer oblations to the last owner of the wealth. This is another addition to the disqualified list. A fresh addition is made from a passage of Manu, who says that one addicted to vice loses his title to inheritance.

Disqualification under the Mithilā law

According to the Vivāda-cintāmaṇi, the authority for the Mithilā School, one who is not virtuous is the first of the disqualified persons; then comes the excommunicated man. Then the author quotes those very texts of Manu and Yājñavalkya and Nārada and Devala and Vasiṣṭha, which we find either in the Mitākṣarā or the Vīramitrodaya; and has summarised the result by saying that a vicious person, one who is excommunicated from society for heinous crimes, an outcast, an impotent person, one who is incurably blind or deaf, a madman, an idiot, a person who is dumb or destitute of limbs, a leper, an enemy to his father, one afflicted with consumption, an impostor, and a person who has relinquished worldly concerns, are excluded from inheritance, and get only sustenance.[1]

In Bengal

In the Dayabhaga of Jīmūtavāhana the subject of disqualification has been treated in ch. 5, where he first of all cites Āpastamba, according to whom parceners are entitled to share, if they be endowed with virtue, and even if the eldest born exhibits a disposition for dissipating wealth in unrighteous purposes, he should go without a share. The vicious man therefore is, according to Jīmūta, the first of disqualified persons; then comes one who is called an *apapātrita*, the excommunicated person of the Vīramitrodaya, the outcast of the Vivādacintānaṇi, This term would literally mean 'one whose vessel or plate must be kept afar'—who would not be allowed to eat off the same plate that is used by his kinsmen.

Both Jīmūtavāhana and Mitra Misra, the author of the Vīramitrodaya, explain an *apapātrita* to be one with whom there is no drinking of water together by his kinsmen. But Vācaspati, the author of the Vivādacintāmaṇi, explains it as ' one in whose name, on account of an outrageous offence, a water-jar has been abandoned by his kinsmen, and who therefore has no right to offer oblations and libations to his father, and does not get the paternal property.' This practice of abandoning a water-jar is performed when kinsmen come home after cremating the corpse of a relative in the burning site. I therefore suppose that in some parts of the Hindu world, excommunication takes this form of assimilating the

1. See Vivāda-chintāmani, p. 242.

excommunicated person with one dead. It may be that this explanation was in the mind of Jīmūta and Mitra when they say that an *apapātrita* is a person who has been 'made one of separate water;' the expression used by these two authors being भिन्नोदकीकृत:. I have followed Colebrooke's translation in saying that the word signifies a person excluded from drinking water in company. But I find that Colebrooke quotes Achyuta who says that the expression used by Jīmūta means a person banished with the ceremony of kicking down a jar of water, as described by Yājñavalkya.[1] The ceremony is described in śloka 295, 3rd chapter of Yājñavalkya who says:—"The own kinsmen of a fallen man should carry a jar on the head of a female slave, outside the town, and should set him apart in all transactions."

Jīmūta says that the receipt of the inheritance is like the receipt of wages, for the recipient is bound to perform the duty of offering oblations and libations to the person whose property is inherited by him. Therefore one who is incompetent to perform that duty is equally incompetent to obtain the property. Then Jīmūta quotes the text of Manu saying that all addicted to evil deeds are not entitled to the wealth. He also gives a curious definition of an impotent person, from Kātyāyana, which furnishes an instance of strange physiological notions entertained by some of our Ṛiṣis.[2] A deaf man is not excluded, unless his infirmity dates from the moment of birth. A dumb person is defined as one who is unable to articulate vowel or consonant sounds. An idiot is one incapable of understanding the sense of the Veda. For the proposition that a fallen person and his issue do not get subsistence, he cites Baudhāyana, whose text no doubt is express on the point. Then Jīmūta cites certain other texts dealing with intermarriage between different castes; these are therefore obsolete in the present age.

---

1. See Colebrooke's Dāyabhāga, ch. V, para 3, footnote.
2. See Dāyabhāga, ch. V, para. 8.

In Bombay (Mumbai)

I now come upon the same subject in the Vyavahāra-mayūkha of Nīlakaṇṭha, whose views may be found in ch. IV, sec. 11 of the English translation. The list of disqualified persons given by Nīlakaṇṭha does not differ from that given by the others. But he explains *apapātrita* or 'excommunicated' in a special manner. He says that according to Madana that word intends one disloyal to his sovereign, and who has therefore been driven away by his kinsmen with the ceremony of breaking a water jar. To this Nīlakaṇṭha demurs and says that disloyalty to the sovereign does not cause excommunication. But he adds that if a man takes a sea voyage for the purposes of trade, he thereby violates an express scriptural prohibition, and should not be allowed to have any social intercourse with his blameless kinsmen; he here quotes an anonymous text, the purport of which is that if a regenerate man goes to sea in a vessel, there can be no social intercourse with him, though he may have undergone an expiatory rite. By a person retired from the householder's life Nīlakaṇṭha understands a life-long student, a hermit dwelling in the forest, and a mendicant having no fixed dwelling. All these are in the excluded list. For the proposition that the fallen man and his issue do not get maintenance, Nīlakaṇṭha cites Vasiṣṭha, Devala and Baudhāyana. Vasiṣṭha says that the impotent and the lunatic get support; hence Nīlakaṇṭha applies the principle that express mention of one implies the exclusion of others. He also quotes the obsolete texts relating to intermarriage. The rest of his law on the subject is conformable to that of the Mitākṣarā.

In Madras (Chenai)

The chapter on Exclusion (ch. V) in the Smṛti-candrikā is more lengthy and elaborate than in the other leading treatises. The author Devagana quotes the very same Ṛiṣi texts I have already noticed, and generally lays down the same law, adding, however, the following rules as peculiarly his own. We have seen that Devala mentions 'a mark-bearer,' (*liṅgin*) as disqualified. This word 'mark-bearer' has been explained in the Smṛti-Candrikā as intended for a life-long student, an anchorite retired into the forest, and so forth; it also signifies according to this treatise, a Bhudhist monk, a sectary of the *Śaiva* class, and so forth. The author also says that although in the text of Devala, the death of the father is mentioned as the occasion on which the impotent person and others are excluded from a share, yet that is not to be taken in its literal sense, but simply as illustrative of all the authorised periods for making a partition; therefore even during the lifetime of the father, when a partition is made, the impotent person and the rest do not get a share; for which lie cites a text of Āpastamba saying,—"While alive, he should equally divide the inheritance amongst his sons, excepting the impotent, the lunatic and the fallen." The author of the Smṛti-candrikā then quotes all the usual texts on the subject of disqualification from Manu, Nārada and Vasiṣtha. In the text of Nārada quoted, there is a reading different from that found in the Mitākṣarā. The reading according to Mitākṣarā fastens the disqualification upon a person guilty of a minor sin. But the reading in the Smṛticandrikā puts another word in that place, which the author explains as meaning' one who has been turned out by his kinsmen on account of a great offence.' Vasiṣtha says,–"Persons in another stage of life are shareless." According to the ancient arrangements of the Hindu society there were four stages of life, namely, that of the student, the householder, the dweller in the forest, and the mendicant. Students were of two kinds: some were called life-long students, because they made a vow for a celebate life; others were those who finishing the course of their studies in the preceptor's house, used to betake themselves to the householder's life. A literal reading of Vasiṣtha's text' would exclude even this latter class of students. Therefore the author of the Smṛti- candrikā says, that Vasiṣṭha's intention is to exclude such only as have taken a vow of life-long celebacy. Then he cites a text of Viṣṇu which runs thus:—"The fallen, the impotent, the incurably diseased, the defective, are not partakers of a share." The word 'defective' is to be understood as implying a person who is devoid of an organ of sense. It ought to be remembered that an organ of sense according to Hindu ideas includes the five organs of sense properly so called, and also the organ of speech or larynx, hand, foot, anus and the generative parts. The author says that the expression 'incurably diseased' indicates that if the impotence or the defect of sense be curable, then the persons affected therewith will get a share. It also indicates that the impotence and the deafness and the other defects need not be congenital to work exclusion; if at the time of the partition there is any disease beyond the power of medical skill to heal, the person affected with such a disease is disentitled.

This is the law of disqualification as expounded in the five leading treatises of the five schools of Hindu law. The connection of these rules with the law relating to joint Hindu families is this. The persons excluded from getting a share at the time of a general partition are all directed to be maintained by the heirs or the divided members. They have no vested right to get a portion of the joint property; but they have a vested interest in the joint effects, so as to entitle them to food and raiment and to all the necessary things, whether the property remains in a joint condition, or is separated into the different allotments taken by the several members. That during the joint condition of the family, these unfortunate members of the household group do get a subsistence out of the joint funds, there cannot be a question; although there may not be an original text exactly to that effect. The original texts are express that these persons get subsistence from the members dividing the property. I believe there was no necessity for any similar declaration touching the period of non-division. It is when property is severed, and its different parts come into the hands of the different individuals, that the necessity for the declaration of a right to maintenance arises. During non-division, all the members are regarded as a single whole, some members being endowed with larger rights and privileges and responsibilities than others; but the smallest and least of such rights and privileges must no doubt be that of getting subsistence.

Disqualified list— impotent

An exhaustive list of these disqualified persons is obtainable from the Smriti- chandrikā, which omits none mentioned in the other treatises, but is specially full and discursive on the subject. An enumeration should therefore be given here for a collective view of the whole number. This list comprises : (1) the impotent, (2) the leper, (3) the insane, (4) the idiot, (5) the blind, (6) the fallen, (7) the issue of the fallen, (8) the mark-bearer, (9) the deaf, (10) the dumb, (11) the defective in an organ of sense, (12) the enemy of his father, (13) the turned out by the kinsmen, (14) the life-long student, (15) the dweller in the forest, (16) the religious mendicant, (17) the incurably diseased, (18) the unworthy, (19) the vicious, (20) the negligent of the ancestral śrādhs.

Absence of disqualification presumed by law

With regard to the first in the above series, the impotent, it will be perceived that the most obvious and the least disputable instance of exclusion on this ground would be that of a hermaphrodite, who, according to the opinion of Vijñāneśvara, would be referable to neither the male nor the female sex, but to a third sex, different from both. Any other form of impotence, as for instance, the form characterised, in the definition given by Jīmūta in ch. 5, would be difficult to prove before a court of justice. In a decision of L. S. Jackson, J., it has been observed with reference to crippleness as a cause of exclusion, that the presumption of law would be against the existence of any disqualifying cause. A party whose right depends upon the existence of any such defect or infirmity in another person, must prove the fact of such infirmity.[1] Now the kind of impotence characterised in the Dāyabhāga is not open to any proof ; and I apprehend no court of justice will consider itself warranted in these days to give a verdict of exclusion on the ground of this form of impotence.

The leaper

With regard to the second in the series, the leper, it is not quite clear whether leprosy must be incurable in order to work disinherison. That most of the Ṛṣis have made out two separate causes of exclusion, by naming both a leprosy and an incurable disease, would lead to the supposition that simple leprosy, whether curable or not, is a disqualifying cause. At the same time the law of disqualification must in the name of humanity and also according to all legal principles receive a strict interpre-tation. Some of the Ṛṣis mention leprosy separately; but one of them Viṣṇu, as quoted in the Smṛti-candrikā, ch. 5, para. 8, mentions only the incurably diseased, and not the leper. Now there is a principle of interpretation often adopted by the commentators of Hindu Law, which consists in supposing the different Ṛṣis intending the same identical rule of law; this principle they call that of एकवाक्यता (identity of intention). Thus, if of two Ṛṣis, one says something explicitly, and another says something which is a near approach to the first, but not quite explicit, this principle of interpretation would make the opinion of the second Ṛṣi conformable to that of the first. Applying this principle to the case of a leper, it would not be a forced interpretation of the law on the

1. Futteck Chunder Chatterji *v.* Juggot Mohini Debi, 22 W.R. 348.

subject, if we hold that leprosy is no disqualification unless incurable. Then we may apply the other rule as to the burden of proof, that the party relying on the plea of disqualification must prove that fact. The law says that the disease must be incurable to be a cause of exclusion; in other words, it must be established beyond all possibility of doubt that the taint is absolutely incapable of being removed by medical art. No human testimony can establish such a fact. It is not the opinion of one medical man, or two, or ten that can be sufficient as proof; it is not even the opinion expressed, say in some of our own old medical treatises, such as that of Suśruta or Caraka, which can be regarded as sufficient. These are but the judgments of human beings, amongst whom none can lay claim to infallibility. Every day instances occur of diseases pronounced by the highest medical authority as beyond the power of the healing art, being cured by simple means suggested most probably by an ordinary or even an illiterate person. The law of leprosy causing disinherison therefore ought to be relegated to the category of obsolete rules. There is a case in the 2nd volume of the Weekly Reporter, p. 125, that of Issurchunder Sein *v.* Ranee Dossee, in which the contention was that a certain widow could not inherit, as she was a leper, and also as she was afflicted with another incurable disease. The observations of the judges were—"Persons, who, under ordinary circumstances, would undoubtedly inherit, are not to have their claim lightly set aside on the ground of disease; and in our opinion, no such person ought to be set aside or declared to be diseased, within the meaning of the Hindu law upon this subject, except upon the clearest and the most unquestionable evidence. In the present case, the evidence is of the weakest possible description. * * It is said that although the defendants have failed to prove leprosy, still, on the testimony of the native doctor, the plaintiff has atrophy of the bones, an incurable disease, which is a cause of disinherison. It is true that the native doctor says that the plaintiff has had some affection which he calls 'drying up of the bones,' for which he has treated her for six years or more; and he adds that inasmuch as this disease has not yielded to his treatment, be considers it to be incurable. But it would need far stronger evidence than the mere opinion of one native doctor to convince us that the plaintiff is labouring under some other disease of a different description, not leprosy—but incurable and rendering her incapable of inheriting. If, under ordinary circumstances, the strictest proof would be required of the disease causing disinheritance, still further proof, if possible, is requisite, when the disease, which it is attempted to prove, is different from the disease pleaded, and on which the defence was originally rested." In this case, as the leprosy was not proved, it is not clear what the decision of the judges would have been, if it had been really a case of leprosy; whether they would have held that leprosy, bare and simple, curable or not, was a disqualification.

The question arose in a Bombay case, Ananta *v.* Rama Bai, 1. L. R. 1 Bom. 554, in which Westropp, C. J. decided against a contention raised in that case that leprosy to disqualify must be congenital, but held also that leprosy must be of the sanious or ulcerous kind in order to cause exclusion from a share. That the incurability of leprosy is a necessary condition to its being, a disqualification is a view of the law which seems to have been first adopted by Sir Thomas Strange, and followed in Madras and Bombay; as the above decision of Westropp, C. J. refers to Muttuvelayuda Pillai *v.* Parasakti, Mad. S. D. A. Rep. 1859-62, p. 239, and Janardan Pandurang *v.* Gopal, 5 Bom. H. C. Rep. 145, A. C. J. Westropp, C. J. seems to lay down that if the leprosy be of the virulent or aggravated type which is generally regarded as incurable, then it will cause exclusion. But with deference to the learned Chief Justice, it may be said that this would be giving to popular opinion a degree of importance and weight which it hardly merits. If the law requires incurable leprosy, then the fact of incurability must be demonstrated before a person should be deprived of his birthright. Popular opinion is proverbially fallible, specially in such questions, the determination of which requires sound physiological knowledge of the highest type.

The insane person

The third kind of disqualified members is an insane person. Insanity need not be absolutely incurable to disqualify, for the texts speak of incurable disease in general; but madness is a separate head of disqualification, to which incurability is not attached. This has been held in a case in which the medical evidence went to show that the lucid intervals grew rarer in course of time, and there was no suspension of insanity for years. The doctor also expressed it as his opinion that it was not a case of insanity which had a chance of being cured. Upon these facts, Couch, C. J. said:— This evidence shows a state of madness for a long period of time, and certainly, if not without an absolute possibility of cure, without a probability of it. It is not necessary to show, by clear and positive evidence, the absolute impossibility of a cure. There is no authority for that either in the texts or in the decisions. When the succession fell in, he was certainly a madman, and not in a condition to offer funeral oblations, which is given as a reason why such a person, should be excluded from inheritance."[1] The criticism that suggests itself in respect of the above decision is that, if madness works exclusion, because a madman is incapable of offering funeral oblations; then there are actual instances in which no oblations are in point of fact offered. But the omission of this indispensable duty, though mentioned as a disqualification by most of the texts from Manu downwards, is not supposed to be a sufficient cause for exclusion. It seems to me that, as religious motives and reasons have been gradually done away with so far as they formerly affected questions of

1. Dwarakanath Bysack *v.* Dinobundhoo Mullick, 18 W. R. 305.

inheritance, the whole law of disqualification might well be confined to as narrow limits as possible. It is not necessary that insanity should be congenital to disqualify a person.[1] This conclusion is based upon the circumstance that Manu quoted in Mitākṣarā ch. 2, sec. 10, verse 3, says:—"Shareless are the impotent and the fallen; likewise the blind and the deaf from the moment of birth; and the insane, the idiot and the dumb; and all persons whatsoever who are devoid of an organ of sense." Here the only defects to which he attaches the condition of being congenital are blindness and deafness. Thereupon it follows from the maxim that express statement in one case excludes another case, that no other defects need be congenital to be a cause of exclusion. To a similar effect has been a decision of the Allahabad High Court, Deo Kishen *v.* Budh Prokash, 1. L. R. 5 All., 512. Here the insane person was a female; a Full Bench of the Court held that insanity at the time the succession opens, in other words in the case of a widow, when her husband dies, will debar her succession to the property of the husband. The court also held that her subsequent cure will not entitle her to demand the property back from the heir who has once already excluded her on account of her madness. This latter proposition has gone clearly against the opinions of the authors of the Mitākṣarā and the Vīramitrodaya. The former says[2]:—"If the defect be removed by medicament or other means, at a period subsequent to partition, the right of participation takes effect by analogy to the case of a son born after separation." The latter[3] says, after nothing the above opinion of Vijñāna, that this is nothing but proper, since the exclusion is a consequence of the defect, and the removal of the defect ought to be followed by the removal of the incapacity. I therefore fail to see how in the teeth of such express passages, the so-called doctrine of Hindu Law, that estates once vested are never divested, can be applied to the

1. Ram Sahye Bhagat *v.* Lalla Lalji Sahay, I. L. R. 8 Cal. 153.
2. Colebrooke's Mitāk., ch. 2 sec. 10, verse 7.
3. Ch. 8 sec. 4, para. 2.

case. In the joint judgment delivered by Straight, Oldfield, Brodhurst, Tyrrel, J J. in the above-mentioned Full Bench case of the High Court of Allahabad, the following passage occurs:—"But when property has once vested in the heir by succession, his subsequent insanity will not be a ground for its resumption. On this point, Vīramitrodaya, ch. 8,verse 4, is explicit. After stating that the exclusion takes place if the disqualification occurs previously to succession, the author proceeds,—'But not also, if subsequently to the partition (or succession) ; for there is no authority for the resumption of allotted shares.' And on the same principle that property once vested cannot be divested, although a person previously insane will become qualified to inherit property on the defect being removed, he cannot resume it from an heir who succeeded to it in consequence of his disqualification when the succession opened, and the property will thenceforward follow the line of succession under the Hindu Law." It is remarkable that the second paragraph of the very same verse 4, ch. 8, Vīramitrodaya, the first para. of which the judges, have quoted in the above passage, contains the provision that the subsequent removal of the defect will entitle the person to a share. It may be exceedingly inconvenient, no doubt, to re-open a partition already concluded. But the same is done when the pregnancy of a widow of one of the coparceners is not known at the time of the first partition; if the widow gives birth to a posthumous male child after partition has been made, it must be effected anew. In fact, both Vijñāna and Mitra refer to this very instance of re-opening a partition, and say that the parallel will apply when the insanity or any other disqualifying defect of a coparcener is removed after a partition.

The rule that estates once vested are not divested has its exception

The truth seems to be that the doctrine that under the Hindu law estates once vested cannot be divested, is like all general principles of law, subject to exceptions. It was applied to the case where a blind man did not succeed to his father's estate; but after the estate had been intermediately enjoyed by the two widows of the propositus, the surviving widow's death left the estate to his nephew. Subsequent to this event, the blind man had a son born to him, who claimed the estate back, no doubt on the authority of the following passage of the Dāyabhāga, ch. 5, para. 19. Therefore the sons of such persons (meaning all disqualified persons), being either their natural offspring or issue raised up by the wife, as the case may be, are entitled, provided they be free from similar defects, to take their allotments according to the pretensions of their fathers. Their daughters must be maintained until married, and their childless wives must be supported for life. It is so declared by Yājñavalkya:—'Their sons, whether legitimate or the offspring of the soil, are entitled to allotments, if free from similar defects. Their daughters also must be maintained until provided with husbands. Their childless wives conducting themselves aright, must be supported; but such as are unchaste should be expelled; and so indeed should those who are perverse." The court of first instance constituted by Norman, J., held that the grandson of the propositus, the son of his excluded blind son, was entitled to get back from the nephew the property from which his father the blind man had been excluded. The question before him was, whether it is necessary for the son of a disqualified person to be born in the lifetime of the propositus, or before the property has been taken by another heir, in order to take the place of his disqualified father. Norman, J. chiefly relied upon Manu, ch. 9, śloka 203, which says that if the eunuch (meaning an impotent person) and the rest should at any time desire to marry, and if the wife of a eunuch should raise up a son to him by a man legally appointed, that son and the issue of such as have children, shall be capable of inheriting. Norman, J. observed:—"There is no provision that the son who is to be capable of inheriting is to be born within the lifetime of the ancestor, as heir of whom he will take. Unless full force is given to the words 'at any time,'the result would follow that, although the wife and daughter of an excluded person would, under all the circumstances, be entitled to maintenance, yet the son of such person born after the death of the ancestor who could offer the funeral cakes, would be excluded from all participation in the ancestral property, and even from maintenance, because there is no provision, that such a son is to receive maintenance." But the decision of Norman, J. was upset in appeal by Sir Barnes Peacock, who said that when a male person succeeds to an estate as heir under the Hindu law, he obtains a full, absolute and indefeasible right thereto, and that the subsequent birth of the son of a disqualified person whom he excluded would not divest the heir's estate, and vest it in the son of the disqualified person.[1] This case was under the Dāyabhāga, which contains no provision similar to what is found in the two Benares treatises, namely, that the subsequent removal of the defect causing the disqualification entitles the formerly excluded person to a share. There is also an important difference between the cases of succession and partition. Partition is frequently re-opened, on the ground of the previous division having been imperfect, or fraudulent, or liable to exception for any other reason. Therefore, it would possibly be right to say that if a person's insanity be removed subsequent to the partition effected by his coparceners, he may get his own proper share, to be made up from the divided allotments.

Insantity need not be congenital

The real question before the Full Bench of the Allahabad High Court in the case cited above was whether the disqualifying insanity must be congenital; and that they decided in the negative. It was therefore an *obiter* that the

---

1. Callydoss Doss *v.* Kissen Chunder Doss, 11 W. R., Appeal from original jurisdiction, p. 11. S. C. 2 B. L. R. F. B. 190.

removal or the cure of lunacy would not cause the restoration of a right to the proper share.

Idiot

Allied to lunacy is the idiotcy of a coparcener. The difference between lunacy and idiotcy is, that the latter is a necessarily congenital defect, Vijñāna explaining an idiot as a person of imperfect or defective understanding, and Jīmūta defining him as a person incapable of understanding the Veda. I am afraid that the latter definition is too extensive, since a person may not be an idiot so as to be excluded from inheritance, and yet may be without an aptitude for the pursuit of letters. To have sufficient aptitude for literary culture, so as to be able to understand the Veda, by which no doubt must be intended the Veda in original Sanskrit, will signify an intellectual capacity, that cannot be properly laid down as an indispensable requisite for inheriting ancestral wealth. Since the study of the Veda as a bounden duty of every regenerate person, has become obsolete, and since Jīmūta names *incapacity* to understand the Veda to be the disqualification, and not simply actual ignorance of the Veda, I believe such incapacity cannot be predicated of a person unless he is put to the test, by being set to study the Veda. I believe only those persons will be excluded under this head, to whom possession of wealth is of little use, they being without sense or rationality. In Goureenath *v.* Collector of Monghyr, 7 W. R., 5, Markby, J. has said that under the Hindu Law the born idiots are excluded, and are absolutely without any right of inheritance.[1] At the same time he holds that a born idiot can hold property, and can have property duly conveyed to him. This has also been held with respect to the lunatics.[2] The original texts nowhere say that idiotcy to disqualify must be congenital. On the contrary, the Smṛti-candrikā, in

1. See p. 7, Column 1, para, 4.
2. See 17 W. R. 422; 18 W. R. O. J. 305; 19 W. R. 163.

para. 3, ch. 5, says:—" Since it is said that the disease must be incurable, it must be inferred that persons affected with such impotency and defect as are removable by medical treatment do get a share. Therefore, any person affected with incurable disease at the time of partition is debarred from a share; not simply such as are affected by congenital impotency and deafness. This ought to be understood." Here the Smṛti-candrikā lays down that a person deaf at the time of partition is excluded, although he may not have been deaf from the moment of birth. This is contrary to para. 9, ch. 5, Dāyabhāga. This para refers to the text of Manu enumerating disqualified persons, and says that the word 'birth' in that text is to be joined with both blindness and deafness. If we look to the text of Manu itself, we find an ambiguity. Sanskrit grammar would authorize either explanation. The text may be rendered "blind-born and deaf-born;" or 'blind-born and deaf.' The ambiguity may be made clear to those unacquainted with Sanskrit by asking them to imagine, as if the text were, 'born blind and deaf.' Such an expression may mean eithor 'born-blind and born deaf,' or it may mean 'a deaf man, and a man blind from birth.' Again, the term for 'birth' in the original text of Manu is Jāti, which may mean either 'birth,' or 'a class or species: If the latter meaning is adopted, then the text would be rendered thus:—'persons of the blind class and deaf persons.' This latter signification no doubt would be somewhat forced. But I am not sure that the author of the Smṛti-candrikā had not this kind of an explanation in his mind when he in sweeping terms says that the disease need not be congenital to disqualify, and he expressly mentions deafness as not necessary to be congenital.[1] Blindness he does not so expressly mention. But he has quoted the text of Manu specifying the 'born blind and deaf.'[2] If he thought that blindness must be congenital to exclude, it was to be

1. Ch. 5, para. 9.
2. Para. 4, ch. 5.

expected that he should have made some special remark with reference to blindness. In Bengal therefore deafness and blindness must be congenital to exclude; but in Madras, deafness according to its leading authority, need not be congenital; while it is doubtful whether blindness according to that authority, need be so.

With regard to idiotcy, excepting the above-quoted remark of Markby, J., there is nothing to guide us, whether it should be congenital or not. I apprehend that in the case of idiotcy which has supervened subsequent to the birth of a person, as in extreme old age it sometimes does, the disease will be classed with lunacy, and will so cause exclusion under a different head. We have seen that cases have settled that lunacy need not be congenital to exclude.[1] The High Court of Madras has said that the idiotcy to disqualify need not involve an utter mental darkness; if there is an unsoundness of mind since the time of birth, that will in point of law amount to idiotcy. The reason why idiots are excluded is that they are unfit for the ordinary intercourse of life.[2]

Nirindriya or a person who has lost a sense

In Bengal it is now settled law that blindness, unless congenital, is no cause of exclusion. If it has supervened two years before the succession opens, it cannot be contended that as a person who has least a sense, he is disentitled. Manu no doubt in his śloka on exclusion, winds up by mentioning निरिन्द्रिय, 'one who has lost a sense.' The word 'indriya' has a double meaning in Sanskrit; it means an organ of sense, such as the eye, etc.; it also means an organ of action, as the hand, the foot, the tongue as an organ of speech, etc. In the first part of this sloka Manu expressly mentions a born blind person. It would be plausible to argue

1. See *ante*, p. 414.
2. Tirrumanagal Animal *v.* Ramaswami Ayyangar, 1. Mad. H. C. Rep. A. C. 214.

that a person may not be born-blind, yet if he becomes blind at a subsequent period, he may come under the head of a *nirindriya,* or one who has lost a sense; but such an argument has been overruled. In Mohesehunder Roy *v.* Chundermohan Roy, 23 W. R. 78, S. C. 14 B. L. R. 273, L. S. Jackson, J., says:—"If it be contended that by the expression 'such as have lost the use of a sense or limb,' the exclusion is carried beyond what is implied in the former part of the śloka, it must be clear that the person to be excluded must be incurably blind, or such as has lost the sense of sight. Here the evidence does not show anything of that sort. The plaintiff has not lost his eyes, nor is there anything to show that he is incurably blind. Therefore if we are to go on that śloka, we do not think that he would be necessarily excluded. Speaking for myself, I should rather base my judgment on the two authorities on Hindu law current in Bengal, I mean the Dāyabhāga and the Dāyakrama Saṅgraha. A rule of Hindu law which is relied upon as preventing the natural course of inheritance ought to be clear and unmistakeable." The passage of the Dāyakrama Saṅgraha relied upon in this. decision is:—"Born blind and deaf, that is, by nature, not those who have become so from some adventitious cause."

In Murarji Gokuldas *v.* Parvati Bai, I. L. R. 1 Bom., 177, the question was discussed by Westropp, C. J. with his usual elaborateness; he comes to the same conclusion with the High Court of Bengal, and decides that blindness to cause exclusion must be congenital. In his lengthy judgment, the Chief Justice of Bombay was much exercised to find out whether the text of Yājñavalkya enumerating the excluded persons, which has been quoted by Jagannātha in his Digest, Book 5, ch. 4, PI. cccxxxi, and also by Vācaspati Miśra in his Vivādacintāmaṇi, contains the word 'born' preceding the word 'blind' in the original Sanskrit. Now this text of Yājñavalkya is the śloka 143 of his 2nd chapter, or 140 according to the edition of Viśvanāth, Mandlik. In the original of this text, the word 'born' does not precede the word 'blind:' In fact, Yājñavalkya does not expressly say that a person must be born blind to be excluded. It is Manu who says जात्यन्ध, Jātyandha, or 'blind by birth.' Colebrooke, in rendering Yājñavalkya-text, has no doubt put in the word 'born,' in order to effect a harmony between the two Ṛṣis, relying on the generally prevalent opinion, among the Pundits of Bengal at least, that congenital blindness alone is a 'disqualification. The text in the Vivāda-cintāmaṇi is no other than the above-named śloka of Yājñavalkya, and is in *ipsissima verba.* Upon the effect of the expression *'nirindriya,'* 'one who has lost a sense or limb' the Chief Justice says:— "But, even assuming that Manu meant by *'nirindriya'* to indicate deficiency in a sense, organ, or limb, or member, we think that, in including deficiency in a sense or organ, he must thereby have meant deficiency in a sense or organ not already provided for, and that we should give a forced or unnatural construction to his language if we were to hold that, after expressly providing that congenital blindness or deafness should disquaiify, he meant by *'nirindriya'* that blindness or deafness from any cause should have the same effect. The rule *expressio unius exclusio alterius,* might be properly applied, and would thus leave the phrase *'nirindriya'* in the text of Manu to' operate, not only where there is a deficiency in limb or member, but also a deficiency in any sense or organ not expressly provided for by Manu. We are not, however, to be understood as deciding that a deficiency in any sense or organ is in those passages implied in the word *'nirindriya* as employed by Manu in ch. 9, p1. 201, or anything more than that he is not by that term to be understood as referring to deficiency in any sense or organ already specially provided."

Although the original texts seem to confine congenitality to blindness and deafness, and I am not aware that dumbness has been declared by any Ṛṣi as a disqualification only when congenital, the High Court of Bombay has in one case said:-" Dumbness if from birth, is a cause of disinherison in females as well as in males. A Hindu widow born dumb is incapable of inheriting from her husband. Such widow is, however, entitled to her maintenance out of the property of her deceased husband."[1]

The principle which was expounded in the case of Kallydoss Doss,[2] has been extended to the case of a deaf and dumb person, and it has been held both in Bengal and in Bombay that the subsequently born son of a deaf and dumb man who was excluded on account of his disqualification cannot take back the estate from the member in whom it has vested.[3] The decision, however, of the High Court of Bombay seems to conflict with the spirit of the Mitākṣarā text, already quoted by me,[4] which expressly says that the removal of the disease would re-entitle the parcener to a share. It therefore *does* contemplate the divesting of an already vested estate. The facts in the Bombay case were that a Hindu lived in joint family with his nephew; that he had a deaf and dumb son, who did not possess any interest in the undivided property, and on the death of his father the whole joint property vested in the nephew; the deaf and dumb man then had a son free from all personal defects; who claimed a half share in the property. It was very forcibly argued on his behalf by Viswanath Mandlik, on the authority both of the Vyavahāra-mayūkha and the Mitākṣarā that the son being a co-owner in the schools other than that of Bengal, the son of the deaf and dumb as soon as born had an interest in the undivided property. But Kemball, J. relied upon the Bengal case of Kallydoss Doss

1. Vallabhram Sibnarayan *v.* Bai Hariganga, 4 Bom. H. C. Rep. A. C. J. 135.
2. 2 B. L. R. F. B. 103, S. C. 11 W. R. O. J. 11.
3. Poresh Money Dossee *v.* Dinonath Doss, 11 W. R. Appeals from original jurisdiction, p. 19, footnote; S. C. 1 B. L. R. 117; Bapuji Lakshman *v.* Pandu Rang, 1. L. R. 6 Bom. 616.
4. See *ante*, p. 411.

and decided against the claim advanced by the son of the deaf and dumb. In this case there had not been any division of the property; it must be admitted on all hands that in a Mitākṣarā family, interests in the joint property are frequently enlarged and diminished by births and deaths; it is clear upon the express texts of all the schools that blameless sons of the disqualified persons are entitled to a share; I therefore fail to see how the principle that estates once vested cannot be divested can have any application in a Mitākṣarā family. In Bengal, there is no survivorship, but it is always a descent or inheritance. In a Mitākṣarā family, it would be wrong to say that when one coparcener dies, the survivor inherits his estate; what takes place is that the interest of the survivor is enlarged; it is liable to be diminished by the birth of a son to himself or to some other coparcener; there must therefore be partial vesting and divesting from time to time. If this *does* happen on account of the birth of a son to an unexcluded coparcener, it is difficult to see what difference it makes when the son is born to an excluded person. That the son of an excluded person, if himself free from personal defect, *does* possess an interest in the family property, is borne out by the following passages which I quote from each of the leading treatises:

Colebrooke's Mitākṣarā, ch. 2, sec. 10, verse 9.

"The disinherison of the persons above described seeming to imply disinherison of their sons, the author adds: 'But their sons, whether legitimate, or the off-spring of the wife by a kinsman, are entitled to allotments, if free from similar defects:'

Golap Chandra Sarkar's Vīramitrodaya, ch. 8, sec. 6.

"Though the impotent and the rest are excluded from inheritance, still their sons are entitled to the shares, which would have been allotted to them. This is declared by Yogīśvara :— 'But of these, the *aurasa* or true son and the *kṣetraja* or the son of the wife, if free from defect, take the shares' 'Free from defect' means having no defect such as is mentioned above which causes exclusion from inheritance."

Vivāda-cintāmaṇi, p. 244.

"But their sons, whether begotten in lawful wedlock, or procreated by a kinsman on the wife duly authorised, may take shares, provided they have no disability."

Dāyabhāga of Jīmūta, ch. 5, para. 19.

"Therefore the sons of such persons, being either their natural offspring, or issues raised up by the wife, as the case may be, are entitled, provided they be free from similar defects, to take their allotments according to the pretensions of their fathers."

Smṛti-candrikā, ch. 5, para. 32.

"When the sons of the disqualified persons are not affected with impotency or any other defect, they might be supposed, simply as sons of disqualified persons to be disentitled from the grandfather's property;—therefore Devala has laid down a special rule—'Their sons should get their fathers' share, if free from defect:.' 'Their sons' that is, 'the sons of the shareless.' Devoid of defects, such as the impotency and the rest;— 'Fathers' share,' that is, 'a share of the grandfather's wealth' they should receive. This is the sense. Nor should it be supposed that this text, speaking generally of their sons, intends to declare a title in the sons of the fallen man to receive the grandfather's wealth. For the text says that the sons must be free from defects, 'which qualification excludes the fallen man's son; for the male issue of the fallen man is itself fallen. So says Vasiṣṭha. 'Begotten by the fallen becomes fallen; so they say; barring a woman; for she goes to the stranger.'

Vyavahāra-mayūkha, ch. 4, sec. 11, para. 11[1]

"But the blameless sons of those excluded from inheritance do inherit, according to the text of Viṣṇu. 'The legitimate sons of those alone out of the persons excluded from inheritance inherit, but not the song born to a degraded man.'

1. P. 101, Mandlik.

The only way to get rid of the effect of these clear declarations of law would be to say that these passages refer to the actual occasion of partition; that is to say, if when a partition is being effected, there be in existence blameless sons of disqualified persons, they shall receive that share which would have been received by their fathers but for the disqualifying cause. Even in that case, so long as the joint character lasts, or so long as there has not been any actual division, such as would be valid in the eye of law, the blameless son of the disqualified should have an interest in the property. In the Bombay case, there had not been any occasion for an actual division, since there had originally been only two coparceners of the joint family, the uncle and the nephew; and the whole property vented in the nephew after the uncle's death; but this ought not to have the effect of barring the rights of the subsequently born grandson.

The fallen, the vicious and the heterodox

I shall close this subject of disqualification by offering a few remarks on the fallen person, the vicious person, and the heterodox person who is negligent of the duty of performing the religious rites for the sake of his fore fathers.

Sins classified

You are no doubt aware that a fallen person is one who is called *patita* in Sanskrit. It is difficult to say what used to be considered in former days as an act rendering a person 'fallen.' *Patita* and *pātaka* come from the same root, the latter word meaning an act of sin, which causes a fall. Acts of sin have been classified by Manu as (1) great sins, (2) minor sins, (3) sins causing the loss of caste, (4) sins causing an intermixture, (5) sins causing unworthiness, (6) sins causing a stain.[1] The five great sins are : (1) killing a Brāhman, (2) drinking spirits, (3) theft, (4) cohabitation with the preceptor's wife, (5) intercourse with one guilty of any one of the above four sins.

1. Manu, ch. 11, slokas 55-70.

List of minor sins

The minor sins are: (1) killing a cow, or rather an animal of the bovine species, (2) acting as a priest to an inferior caste, (3) adultery, (4) selling one's self, (5) abandonment of the preceptor, of the parents, of a son, of the Vaidic study, and of the household fire, (0) to marry when an elder brother has not yet been married, (7) to be such an elder brother, (8) to marry one's daughter to either of the above, (9) to act as a priest to either of the above, (10) cohabitation with an unmarried girl, (11) usury, (12) sexual intercourse committed in the student stage of life, (13) selling a pond, a garden, or a wife, or a child, (14) to be uninvested with the sacred thread, (16) abandonment of a kinsman, (16) tuition on wages, (17) to be instructed by a hired tutor, (18) selling articles prohibited to be sold, (19) working mines, (20) erecting dykes to obstruct streams of water, (21) destroying medicinal plants, (22) living by the prostitution of one's wife, (23) attempt to kill persons by in cantation, (24) attempt to subjugate persons by incantation, (25) felling raw trees for the purpose of fuel, (26) cooking sumptuous food solely for one's own self, (27) eating prohibited food, (28) not keeping a household fire, (29) theft, (30) non-payment of debts, (31) studying bad books, (32) living as an actor, (33) theft of paddy, or base metal, or animals, (34) cohabitation with a drunken woman, (35) killing a woman, or a Śūdra, or a Vaiśya, or a Kṣatriya, (30) denying the next world.

Sins causing a loss of caste are: (1) causing hurt to a Brāhman, (2) smelling a thing prohibited to be smelt, or smelling spirits, (3) want of candour, (4) unnatural offence. Sins causing an intermixture are killing an ass, a horse, a camel, a stag, am elephant, a goat, a sheep, a fish, a serpent, or a buffalo.

Sins causing unworthiness are: (1) acceptance of wealth from base persons, (2) trade, (3) service of a Śūdra, (4) a telling a lie. Sins causing a stain are: (1) killing a worm, an insect, or a bird, (2) eating food in contact with spirits, (3) theft of fruit, or fuel, or flower.

I have thus given a detailed list of sins according to Manu, in order to show how impracticable this part of Hindu law is in the present state of society, or rather in any conceivable state of society. As far as the texts of Ṛṣis go, any one of these acts of sin would be sufficient to render a man fallen, and so entail upon him the consequence of either losing his birthright in the shape of ancestral property, or his right to maintenance if he be a member of a joint family. This list includes some heinous offences liable to severe punishments; and it may be that in Hindu days persons guilty of such offences were utterly excluded from all rights of property. The list also mentions many acts which must now be considered as entirely innocent. In former times, I believe, expiatory ceremonies were undergone by persons who had committed these conventionally sinful acts, which at once restored them to all their ordinary rights. Srikrishna Tarkalankara, in his comments on para. 31, ch. of Jīmūta's Dāyabhāga, throws some light on this point. That para. of the Dāyabhāga runs:-" Mere demise is not exclusively meant; for that intends also the state of the person degraded, gone into retirement, or the like; by reason of the analogy as occasioning extinction of property." This is how Colebrooke has translated. I would translate it thus:—"Nor is death alone intended to be spoken of ; but it refers as well to fallenness and so forth; since there is the similarity of extinguishing proprietary right." The purport is that when our texts say that proprietary right is extinguished by death, they also mean that it is extinguished equally if the proprietor becomes a fallen person by a sinful act, or retires into the forest, quitting the concerns of a householder's life, or becomes a religious mendicant, relinquishing all concerns. As regards 'fallenness,' Srikrishna explains:—अत्र पतितस्यापि सर्व्वस्वदानादि प्रायश्चित्तश्रवणात् प्रायश्चित्तपराङ्मुखेति विशेषणं देयं। तेन प्रायश्चित्तप्रागभावाभाव सहकृतं पातित्यं स्वत्वनाशहेतुरिति बोध्यं। that is,— "Since we hear that even a fallen man can perform an expiatory rite involving the gift of his whole property, we must add a qualification when we say that a fallen man loses all proprietary rights, that is to say, we must say that a fallen man so loses, if he be averse to perform an expiatory ceremony. Therefore it should be understood that only where there is an improbability of an expiatory ceremony being performed, that the fallen condition causes the extinction of proprietary right." In other words, the loss of proprietary rights on account of sinful acts had become all but obsolete in the days of Srīkrishna. The outcry therefore which was raised by our countrymen when Act XXI of 1850 was passed by the Government of British India, was ill-advised, and a result of ignorance. Previously to that enactment, by the *dictum* of the Hindu lawyers themselves, the commission of even the most heinous crimes, the most opprobrious sins, had ceased to be attended with any consequences affecting the civil rights of the guilty persons. It may be that where the Government is in the hands of a Hindu king, the king by a fitful exercise of his kingly authority, would in some cases visit certain sinful acts with deprivation of civil rights, and would overlook others. He would probably pass by such sins as he himself and his courtiers would be habitually guilty of, and select other very innocent acts for this kind of punishment, if he supposed that he would thereby be raised in popular estimation as the Defender of the Brāhmanic faith. But all this fitful exercise of kingly authority would be detrimental to the interests of society. In 1850, the British Government put an end to the uncertainty of the law by passing Act XXI of that year, the provisions whereof run thus:-" So much of any law or usage now in force within the territories subject to the Government of the East India Company, as inflicts on any person forfeiture of rights or property, or may be held in any way to impair or affect any right of inheritance, by reason of his or her renouncing, or having been excluded from the communion of any religion, or being deprived of caste, shall cease to be enforced as law in the courts of the East India Company, and in the courts established by Royal Charter within the said territories:; The passing of this law no doubt had the effect of taking off one of the hindrances to the spread of Christianity. That the Hindu community considered the Act as an attack on their religion was not to be wondered at. At the same time the hold of the ancient Hindu religion has been so far weakened, that an impartial consideration of the matter will lead every person to pronounce the enactment of Act XXI of 1850 as wise and proper, whatever its effects may have been.

That the so-called great sins according to the classification of Manu rendered a man 'fallen' or *patita.*, there cannot be the least doubt. Mitākṣarā quotes Nārada also in para. 3, see. 10, ch. 2, to show that even a person guilty of one of the so-called minor sins (upapātaka) is liable to lose his civil rights. Now in the list of minor sins I have given above, there are some, such as 'working mines,' and 'felling an unwithered tree for fuel,' which no form of modern ideas can regard as sinful. No modern court of justice would pronounce against a person's civil rights for such sinful acts. That being so, where is the authority for making a distinction between acts like these and the act of embracing the Christian religion? The weakness of Hindu religion lies in confounding acts which must be sinful for all ages and societies, with acts which were sinful under certain peculiar and inexplicable notions of the Brāhmanic lawyers.

Lex Loci Act, XXI of 1850

It may be remarked that Act XXI of 1850 is not happily worded. It abolishes all disabilities arising from conversion to a different religion, or from excommunication, or from loss of caste. Manu particularizes certain acts as causing loss of caste.[1] Now suppose a Brāhmin acts as a priest to a prohibited caste; he thereby commits a so-called minor sin. Would he lose his civil rights or not? It is doubtful if he has been excluded from the communion of any religion, or has been deprived of caste, in the language of the Act. In that

1. See *ante*, p. 425.

case, the Act will not apply, and the general Hindu law, laying down that a person guilty of a minor sin will lose his rights, will apply. In other words, such a member of a joint family will be deprived of all interest in the joint property. It is nearly certain that no court will ever pronounce deprivation of civil rights for any such cause. But the strict application of Hindu Law, in accordance with its most authoritative exposition, demands of a court of justice, that it should pronounce such a deprivation of rights. Similar questions may arise in actual administration of Hindu law in connection with many another minor sin. That they have not yet arisen in any appreciable number is owing to the circumstance that the world of lawyers is not so well acquainted with these obscure corners of Hindu law, where so many 'glorious' uncertainties are lurking unsuspected by the keen research of the practising lawyers of the day.

Similar remarks will apply to the two other diss-qualifying causes, consisting in a vicious course of life, and in the omission of rites for the forefathers. Manu is as express in excluding a vicious person, as in excluding a blind man or a leper. His verse has been quoted and adopted in all the leading treatises excepting the Mitākṣarā. Though opinions may differ as to what may constitute a vicious course of conduct with regard to certain acts, there are other acts which must be universally acknowledged as undoubtedly deserving to be so characterised. The śloka of Manu I allude to is No. 214 of the 9th chapter. The expression in the original is विकर्मस्थ, Vikarmasṭṭha, 'one staying in bad deeds,' literally; this phrase therefore seems to imply a person pursuing a vicious course of life, Manu says:—"All the brothers, pursuing a vicious course of life, lose their right to the wealth." Kullūka explains:–"Although not fallen, yet those brothers who are addicted to such bad deeds as gambling, whoring and so forth, do not deserve to got the inheritance." Vīramitrodaya says:—"All the brothers who are addicted to vice lose their title to inheritance. The purport is, that those who are incapable of performing the rites enjoined by the Śruti and the Smṛti, as well as those that are addicted to vice, are not entitled to get shares."[1] All these leading treatises, excepting the Mitākṣarā, exclude also a son who does not perform the srāddha of his forefathers. Thus Vīramitrodaya:—"Though born of a woman of equal class, a son destitute of virtue is unworthy of the paternal wealth; it is declared to belong to such kinsmen offering funeral oblation to him as are versed in the Vedas. A son redeems his father from debt to superior and inferior beings; hence there is no use for one who acts otherwise. What can be done with a cow which neither gives milk nor bears calves? For what purpose was that son born, who is neither learned nor virtuous? * * The meaning is this:–A son who performs the obsequies of his father or other ancestors, is of approved excellence, though he be uninitiated : not a son who acts otherwise, be he the eldest and conversant with the whole Veda.[2] Again a 'mark-bearer' is also excluded. The author of Smṛti-candrikā explains it as 'one who bears some mark to show that he belongs to a particular religious denom-ination.' Thus some of the Śaiva sectaries bear marks made with sandal-wood paste or with ashes on their foreheads; the Vaiṣṇavas bear what is called a 'tilaka' on the ridge of their nose ; most Buddhists wear red undergarments ; infact, there is I believe a special personal mark adopted by each one of the later religious sects; the special mark is recognized and known to the whole body of each sect. A strict interpretation of Devala's law—Devala being the only Ṛṣi who includes a 'mark-bearer' in the list of excluded persons[1] would exclude

1. Viram., chap. 8, sec. 11, last but one para.; Jīmūta's Dāyabhāga, chap. 5, para. 6, towards the end of it; Vivāda-cintamaṇi, p. 242, para. 2; Smṛti-candrika, chap. 5, para. 19; Vyavahāra-mayūkha, chap. 4, sec. 11, para. 8. p. 101, Mandlik.
2. Chap. 8, para. 11; sea also Jīmūta's Dāyabhāga, chap, 5, para. 6; Smṛti-candrikā, chap. 5, para. 15; Vyavahāra-mayūkha, chap. 4, Sec. 11 para. 8.

nearly three-fourths of the modern Hindu population. Hardly a single modern Hindu but secretly or openly belongs to a particular religious sect, and has his guru, who has taught him the *mantra,* or a formula consisting of two or three letters of the alphabet, to be recited by the disciple as many times as he can in the course of every day. Every Hindu who is ambitious of the reputation for orthodoxy, would bear some mark made either by sandal-wood paste, or vermilion, or red ochre, or yellow earth, or any other authorized dye-stuff. A stern Brāhmaṇa jurist of former time, who knew no other authorities on questions of law than the extant Smṛtis, would have rigidly excluded all these heretical sectaries, under the head of 'mark-bearer' in Devala's text. But nobody now even seems to be aware that these sectaries are under the ban of the genuine Hindu law, and that our courts of justice might be placed in an embarassing position if these provisions of Hindu Law were placed before them in a case involving the question of exclusion from inheritance. Nobody would dream of excluding them. I apprehend that the *dictum* of the Privy Council would be a help in such a case. For that highest of all tribunals has authoritatively declared that clear proof of usage would outweigh written texts of law.[2] The clear usage in connection with the subject under discussion has for a pretty long time been that neither sinful acts, nor a viciouscourse of life, nor omission to perform forefathers' obsequies, causes disinherison. Therefore the written texts of law declaring forfeiture of rights on those grounds may be disregarded. Nevertheless, it should not be forgotten that the *dictum* of the Judicial Committee is itself inconsistent with what Vasiṣtha says as to the authoritative character to be ascribed to usages when in conflict with written law. In the very commencement of his Institutes, Vasiṣtha has laid

1. See *ante*, p. 402.
2. See Collector of Madura, *v.* Muthu Ramalinga Sathupatty, 12 Moore, 397.

down; लोके प्रेत्य च विहितो धर्म्मः। तद्भावे सदाचारः प्रमाणं। "In this world, and with regard to the world to come, what has been *laid down* is to be the Law—In absence thereof the practice of the righteous men is the authority." So that it would be difficult to say that we should be administering Hindu Law according to its most approved principles, were we to give effect to every usage in conflict with, declared Law.

The truth is that the administration of Hindu Law, whether in the present matter of exclusion from inheritance, or in many other matters, that might be named, is hardly in a sastisfactory condition, or can be in a satisfactory condition, under the circumstances which actually exist. Hindu Law itself is in a hopeless state of uncertainty, on account of the vast body of the legal literature. In the second place Hindu society has long outgrown its original framework to which the laws embodied in the original texts, even the most recent of them, were suited. The law again is administered by tribunals that are in the main lacking in some of those qualifications which should be indispensable in an administrator of Hindu Law. I mean knowledge of the language in which that law is contained, and something approaching to an acquaintance with the inner working of the Hindu society. The absence of such qualifications is not sufficiently made up for by general ability and intelligence and conversancy with other systems of law. We cannot be sure that this unsatisfactory state of things is likely to be removed by returning to the days of law officers. One patent objection that system would be liable to is, that such law officers will not be adequately paid; and this want of adequate payment will inevitably lead to the abuses for which the arrangement for employing them as assessors of the courts was abolished. The only means of removing the difficulty appears to me to be the appointment of elective synods of Brāhman Pandits for each of the five different schools. Such an expedient would be on the lines indicated by Manu himself. I shall here give *in extenso* his observations upon the expedient of removing uncertainties in law. They begin at śloka 108 of the 12th chapter. "If it be asked, how are we to determine the rule in cases not provided for by the written texts, the answer is, what the well-trained Brāhmins should declare—that should be unhesitatingly adopted as law. By well-trained Brāhmins are meant such as in the proper form have acquainted themselves with the whole of the Veda, and with all the accessory branches of learning. They are the sources from which the Vedic authority is to be drawn. Or what a 'parishad,' (synod) consisting of not less than ten persons, should declare to be the law, or one consisting of not less than three persons of a righteous life, that law should not be disregarded. A person versed in the three Vedas, a logician, one versed in reasoning, argument and debate, a philologist, one versed in the Institutes of Manu, a householder, a student, and a forest-dweller-these together constitute a synod of not less than ten. One versed in the Ṛg-veda, one in the Yajur-veda, and one in the Sāma-veda, these three together constitute a synod of not less than three, for the ascertainment of the rule in cases of uncertain law. A single superior Brāhmin, versed in the Veda may declare what the law is to be, the same is to be considered as the authoritative law-not what has been propounded by ten thousand dunces."

It may be difficult exactly to follow in these days the directions of Manu for calling together a synod of learned men to fix the law. Yet I believe that if the Government took the matter in its hands, much might be effected in removing the present unsatisfactory state of things. In each of the five provinces professing a distinctive school, I mean in the North-West, Mithila, Bengal, Madras, and Bombay, every district might be invited to appoint a delegate by election to form a Provincial Synod of Hindu Law. A delegate might receive a salary of say Rs. 100 per mensem. The electors of the delegates should be all the professing Brāhmin Pandits of the District, who might receive a trifling remuneration for giving their votes in electing the District delegates. The Provincial Synods might be left to decide by majority of votes all disputed questions of Hindu Law. I believe under such a system, there would scarcely be any cause for dissatisfaction on the part of any person, or body of persons; nor would there be the least chance of the decisions of the synods being influenced by wholesale bribery. Even if there were, the Hindu community would hardly have reason to murmur at the result—the whole proceedings being as public as can possibly be, and a finality being given to all the disputed points. Considering the overwhelming preponderance of the Hindu element in the aggregate Indian community, it is not too much to expect from the Government that some outlay of money should be incurred by the ruling authorities in order to give satisfaction to that inherent love of their own ancient laws, which the Hindu races have always felt, notwithstanding innumerable radical chances their society has undergone since the days when these laws were framed for the guidance of their remote forefathers.

Chapter 8

The Property of A Joint Hindu Family

Property purchased with joint money is joint— A serf, called kīnāsa, considered as a kind of joint property—Nature of landed property among ancient Hindus—yogakṣema—yogakṣema the nearest approach to the modern endowed property—Prachīra, a kind of joint property—Yājya or poojah dalan—Joint trade—'Nibandha: what—Family idol a joint property—Family idol worshipped by turns, called a 'pala'—Family idol to be worshipped in its shrine-A 'pala' a periodically recurring right—Priestly earnings a loud of joint property—In Madras, divinity strictly importible—Dhammakatta—In Bombay, share of earnings from a temple alienable—Landed estate the usual joint property—Precautions in purchase or joint land—Name of a single member in title deeds of joint land—Registry in Collector's Books—Sale certificates in a single member's name–Purchase in the name of the family priest held as joint—Texts establishing the joint character of acquisitions—Purchases from ancestral funds joint, even though no coparcener exists—Property distributed by grandfather juice as between father and son.

Property purchased with joint money are joint

In this Lecture, it is my intention to enumerate and describe the several kinds of joint property which it is possible for an undivided family to be in possession of, and then to state certain ruled in answer to the question, under what circumstances a givan subject of proprietary right ought to be considered as joint. Strictly speaking, this latter question should more properly fall under a different head of my subject, which might be dealt with as the Law of Presumptions applicable to a joint Hindu family. Yet there are certain propositions of law, and certain principles established by the decisions of our courts, which cannot very well be included in that head. Thus it has been held that if the profits and income of joint property are laid out in the purchase of additional properties, the additional properties *ipso facto* become a part and parcel of the undivided family funds, no matter that only a single member had conducted the negotiations in connection with the purchase, or that only a single member's time and trouble had been mainly instrumental in increasing the original stock of joint property. This proposition has been repeatedly laid down and acted upon in decided cases, as I shall show further on; yet no obvious principle relating to the law of presumption has any application in it. It might be said that according to the law of presumption applicable to a joint family, courts are bound, in the first instance, to take it that all property in the possession of any member of a joint family is joint ; but this rule does not necessarily involve the other, that purchases made by the income of the joint funds are also joint. The latter rule is rather a deduction from the general principle of the joint family system, namely, the principle that all the members are jointly interested in every part of the joint property; that the income accruing from such property must necessarily be a subject of ownership belonging to all; hence it must follow that if the income be converted into land, or into a trading business, or into a house or a garden, the land, the business, the house, or the garden, itself becomes a joint property. It is in fact the old income in a new form ; the most elementary principles of law have established that the alteration in the form of property cannot interfere with its ownership. It therefore becomes convenient to consider rules similar to that set forth above apart from the Law of Presumptions applicable to a joint family.

A Serf, Called Kīrāsa, Considered As A Kind of Joint Property, Nature of Landed Property Among Ancient Hindus, Yogakshema, What?

Now, first as to the several descriptions of joint property a family may be in possession of. The kinds of property which appear to have been familiar to the writers of our original texts were extremely simple. Lands and houses, fields, cattle, sheep and goats, gold and silver and corals, clothing, vehicles—these are the ordinary subjects of proprietary right spoken of by ancient authors, such as Manu among the Ṛṣis, and Vijñāneśvara among the commentators. Thus Manu, ch. 9, śloka 119:— "Flocks of sheep and goats, together with animals of a single or uncloven hoof, if unequal in number, should not be divided; such property, when not evenly divisible, should be allotted to the eldest-born son." Here we find mention of horses as animals of an uncloven hoof. In śloka 123, Manu says:— "The son of a senior wife should appropriate as his special allotment the best of the bulls the family has got; the sons of junior wives will take bulls of an inferior kind." In the next śloka he says:—"If the son of the senior wife be the eldest born of the sons, then he has a right to fifteen cows and one bull; then the other sons shall divide the rest according to the seniority of their mothers." In śloka 150, it is said that a tiller, a bull for breeding purposes, vehicles, ornaments, and a dwelling house should form the special allotment to be received by the son of a Brāhman born of a wife of the same superior caste. Here we find mention of a peculiar kind of property, called 'kīnāsa' in the original, explained by Kullūka as a ' tiller of the called soil,' and meaning evidently a serf attached to the cultivated land, and probably' passing by transfer from owner to owner with the soil itself. I believe this kīnāsa is the bāhīka, mentioned in other parts of Sanskrit literature, who is sometimes compared to cattle in simplicity and harmlessness of character. Thus there is a proverb in Sanskrit,

गौर्वाहीक: quoted by writers of rhetorical treatises in Sanskrit, which means that an agriculturist is comparable to a cow. This kind of property, consisting in slaves attached to the soil, and cultivating it on account of the owner of the land, is probably the remote original, from whom the modern cultivating ryots have sprung—a supposition corroborated by the circumstance that there is no name for 'rent' in Sanskrit; nor is there any mention of any tenure in land, nor of any arrangement similar to the European metayer system, or the Indian 'adhiar' system, under which half the crops goes to the owner of the soil and the other half to the cultivator. Landed property seems to have been in remote Hindu days owned in the form of absolute feesimple, liable simply to a tax payable to Government, the rate of which ranged from one-sixth of the crops to one twelfth. Since the establishment of the British dominion, more specially since the abolition of slavery in all its form throughout British possessions, the 'kīnāsa' kind of joint property must be considered as obsolete. Then in śloka 219, ch. 9, Manu, we find mention of clothes, vehicles, prepared food, such as sweetmeats and flour, water as contained in a well or tank, women, some obscure kind of property called योगक्षेम, yogakṣema, and pasturing lands. The word 'yogakṣema' is very unsatisfactorily explained by Kullūka, according to whom the word means 'ministers and officiating priests, since by their means the welfare of the family is maintained'. The explanation throws no light upon the meaning of the word, or upon the kind of property intended to be spoken of by Manu when he makes use of that word. The primary object of this śloka of Manu is to point out, what properties should not be divided by the parceners at the time of a general partition. To say that ministers and priests should not be divided, in the same way as tanks and wells are incapable of a division, is to declare something which is specially unintelligible even in a writer of the Ṛṣi class—whose writings certainly are not always characterised by luminous statement. I apprehend what Kullūka means to say is this—Ministers, or Mantris, as Kullūka has it, should not be severally allotted to each one of the princes who divide among themselves a particular kingdom. A kingdom no doubt is said to be indivisible property; yet in our legendary history, there are instances recorded of a division of an empire having been come to by the several sons of a single emperor. Thus it is recorded in the Raghuvaṁśa that Rāma, the celebrated hero of Vālmiki's poem, divided his empire among his three other brothers; he also allotted seperate states to his two sons, Lava and Kuśa when he departed this life at the end of his reign. On the occasion of such a division, the different ministers, entrusted with the several departments of the administration, such as the army, the police, the taxes, etc., were not severally assigned to the different princes.[1] The officiating priest of the family also, whose ministrations are necessary on the occasions of all the religious rites and sacramental ceremonies to be performed by every Hindu family, comes under the same category of indivisibility. This seems to be the meaning of Kullūka.

The same śloka is cited in the Mitāksharā, ch. 1, sec. 4, para. 16 ; and Vijñāna has given a detailed explanation of it in a number of paragraphs that immediately follow. In para. 23 is found the explanation of the word 'Yogakṣema.' That para. has been thus translated by Colebrooke :— "The term *yogakṣema* is a conjunctive compound resolvable into *yoga* and *kṣema*. By the word *yoga* is signified a cause of obtaining something not already obtained; that is, a sacrificial act to be performed with fire consecrated according to the Veda and the law. By the term *kṣema* is denoted an auspicious act which becomes the means of conservation of what has been obtained; such as the making of a pool, or a garden, or the giving of alms elsewhere than

1. *Vide* the Drama of Mudrārākṣasa, where the, different ministers of State are enumerated in great detail; see also the Work on Hindu Polity, or Nītisāra, by Kāmandaki.

at the altar. Both these, though appertaining to the father, or though accomplished at the charge of the patrimony, are indivisible; as Laugakṣi declares:—'The learned have named a conservatory act *as kṣema,* a sacrificial one as *yoga;* both are pronounced indivisible; so are the bed and the chair.' Para. 24. "Some hold that by the compound term *yogakṣema,* those who effect sacrificial and conservatory acts, (*yoga* and *kṣema),* are intended, as the king's counsellors, the stipendiary priests, and the rest; others say, weapons, cowtails, parasols, shoes, and similar things are meant." The same term 'yogakṣema' is thus explained in the Vīramitrodaya, ch. 7, sec. 2, p. 249 of the English translation. "The term religious fund *(yoga)* means a fund for the performance of religious ceremonies; and 'charitable work' *(kṣema)* signifies a reservoir of water or the like contructed for the public benefit. The impartibility of these two, though raised or made at the charge of the paternal property, are set forth as examples; since, directly or indirectly, a partition of these is not possible, far less when they are hereditary. Accordingly Laugākṣi declares:—'The sages declare the charitable work is a reservoir of water or the like constructed for public good, and that religious fund is property set apart for the performance of religious rites; these two are pronounced impartible ; so are the bed and seat.' Some hold that the term *yogakṣenaa* intends those who perform sacrifices and charitable works, as the king's minister (of charitable works), the family priest, and the like. Others say that it signifies weapons, cowtails, shoes, and similar things."

The same term is explained in the Dāyabhāga, ch. 6, sec. 2, para. 24, where Colebrooke has rendered it 'furniture for repose or for meals,' such as beds, and vessels used for eating and drinking and similar purposes.

In the Smṛti-candrikā, the term is noticed in ch. 7, para. 40, where the same text of Laugākṣi is quoted which we find both in the Mitākṣarā and the Vīramitrodaya, and a brief explanation is suggested, in accordance therewith, which explanation would probably amount to this, that religious works and charitable works are indivisible. An alternative meaning is then suggested. " Or it may mean the wealth obtained from a king or a rich man who has been courted and followed for the purpose of obtaining one's livelihood." This leaves the expression in its original obscurity.

In the Vyvahāra-mayūkha, ch. 4, see. 7, para. 19,[1] the anchor says with reference to this term—"By the word *yogakṣema,* the Kalpataru says, is meant, the counsellors, the family priest, and the like. Laugākṣi however says:— 'The learned explain *kṣema* to mean meritorious works, and *yoga* as meaning wealth obtained by sacrifice, both of them as well as beds and seats are declared to be impartible.' Here *pūrtam* means a garden, or a tank, etc., and *iṣṭam* a sacrifice, a feast to Brāhmaṇas, and the like. The meaning is, that whatever wealth has been given up and set apart for such purposes with the consent of all when in an undivided state by a certain man, it should be used by that person alone for that same charity and not by another, nor by all together."

Yogakṣema, the Nearest approach to the modern endowed property

By piecing together what has been said in the Mitākṣarā, the Vīramitrodaya and the Mayūkha, with regard to the character of the joint property known by the name of *yogakṣema,* it seems that this is the nearest approach to anything like an endowed property, to be met with in our original texts. Babu Golap Chandra Sarkar's translation of the passage in the Vīramitrodaya relating to this matter, which translation I have adopted in full, is a little free. The original does not mention any 'public benefit,' or speak of any 'religious *fund.*' At the same time, there is no other way of attaching any sense to the original text, except by

1. P. 71, Mandlik.

supposing that here are being spoken of properties which the Mahommedans would call *wakf,* and which would in English receive the name of ' endowments.' This supposition is confirmed by the very explicit explanation given in the Mayūkha of the term *yagakṣema.* An endowment, or rather endowed property is not to be divided:—that is what Manu means. Vijñāna gives instances of a garden or a reservoir of water—the usual forms that public charity takes in India. He also mentions gifts made outside the altar, whereby I suppose we are to understand public charities consisting in daily doles of food to all chance arrivals—charities which in modern vernaculars are sometimes called *satras,* or *chatras,* or *atithiśālā,* or *dharmaśālā,* and have got different names in different Provinces of India. Our country can even now boast of numberless institutions of this kind, although our Rajahs and opulent zemindars are on the way to extinction. Manu. takes the precaution of laying it down that these charities, though endowed from the patrimonial funds, and therefore constituting a part and parcel of the general undivided property, should not be made a bone of contention between the several parceners, when they make a general partition of the patrimonial effects.

Prachāra, a kind of joint property

Pursuing our consideration of the kinds of joint property, we meet with in the very same śloka which mentions *Yogakṣema* or 'endowed property,' another article called a *prachāra,* which I have rendered as 'lands for depasturing cattle.' This would be in accordance with the Smṛticandrikā[1] and also with the Mayūkha.[2] But the Mitākṣarā (ch. 2, s. 4, para. 25) and the Vīramitrodaya (p. 250, Eng. Tran.) are unanimous in saying that this word implies the means of ingress to and egress from a house,

1. Ch. 7, para. 40.
2. Ch. 4, sec. 7, para. 19.

etc. The Dāyabhāga indeed is for making *yogakṣemaprachāra* as a single expression signifying drinking and eating vessels; but in para. 29, sec. 2, ch. 6, the author mentions '*prachāra* for water,' which can have no other meaning than that of 'drains' and 'water-channels.'

Yājya or 'pīyā dālan'

In the Mitākṣarā[1] we find mention of another kind of joint property, called a 'yājyā'; Jimūta explains it as 'the place for offering sacrifices' or as 'the divinity.'[2] 'Yajya' therefore answers to the 'poojah dālan' of modern Bengal, and also to the family idol, both which are recognized kinds of joint property, and have been dealt with in a number of decided cases. Jīmūta also mentions '*vāstu*,' 'a dwelling-house.'[3] The Mitākṣarā[4] mentions *patra* which has been elsewhere explained as 'vehicles,' including a riding horse and cars. But the Smṛti-candrikā[5] mentions a written instrument for debt or a bond as a kind of joint property not to be divided, since a division of it would destroy the very evidence for the debt. Colebrooke has translated *patra* in para. 26, sec. 4, ch. 1, Mitākṣarā, as written documents,—a rendering borne out by the observation in the Smṛti-candrikā cited above.

Joint Trade

A joint trade or a joint undertaking of any other kind has been long considered by our tribunals as a very important class of undivided family property.[6] There are indications in the original texts which leave no doubt that the carrying on of joint business by the united exertions of all the members is a practice as old as the days of Manu, who in śloka 205, ch. 9, says that if the unlearned brothers acquire wealth by a joint undertaking, the division will be

1. Ch. 1, sec. 4, para. 26.
2. Ibid.
3. Para. 30
4. Ch, 1, sec. 4 para. 26.
5. Ch. 7, para, 42.
6. *Vide ante*, p. 239.

into equal shares—save and except the portion received from the father. The comments of Kullūka are—If the brothers make money by exerting themselves in the pursuit of agriculture or trade, then with regard to that wealth, (exclusive of what is paternal,)—it being self-acquired—the division must be equal; that is to say, there will be no deductions or larger shares on account of seniority of birth. The same subject is touched upon in paras. 30 and 31, sec. 4, ch. 1, Mitākṣarā. For in Para. 29, it has been said that the acquirer of property who has made use of the joint funds in making his acquisitions shall receive a double share. Para. 30 says:—"The author propounds an exception to that maxim. 'But if the common stock be improved, an equal division is ordained.' Para. 31. "Among unseparated brethren, if the common stock be improved or augmented by any one of them through agriculture, commerce or similar means, an equal distribution nevertheless takes place; and a double share is not allotted to the acquirer." As the coparceners case a right to share the profits of a joint trading business; so, on the other hand, they are liable jointly for debts incurred in conducting the business, although the coparceners may not have directly interfered in the management of the business. If the business be ancestral, in other words, if it be a business first started by, say the father of the family, it descends like all other paternal property to his sons; who unless separated from one another, may be sued for the payment of the price of goods supplied to the business by a third party; for it is a settled principle of law that an ancestral trade is an inheritable property. The members of the undivided family become partners in such a trade ; "a partnership so created has many, but not all of the elements existing in an ordinary partnership. Nor, as a rule, can one of the partners, when severing his connection with the business, ask for an account of past profits and losses." The ordinary rule of Hindu Law in such a case makes every member of the united family liable for debts properly incurred by the manager for the benefit of the family.[1]

'Nibandha' What

A peculiar kind of joint property is mentioned in śloka 124,, ch. 2, Yājñavalkya, which śloka forms a part of para. 3, sec. 5, ch. 1, Colebrooke's Mitākṣarā. It is called *nibandha* in the original, having been translated by Colebrooke as a 'corrody.' The śloka has been rendered thus—"The ownership of father and son is the same in land, which was acquired by the grandfather, or in a corrody, or in chattels." A corrody or *'nibandha'* means, according to Vijñāna. 'so many leaves receivable from a plantation of betel pepper, or so many nuts from an orchard of areca.' This explanation is hardly sufficient to give us an idea as to what kind of property this *'nibandha'* was. Babu Golap Chand Sarkar, in his Vīramitrodaya, renders *'nibandha'* 'settled income,' and has thus translated the explanation given in the original.[2] "'Any settled income' what is given by reason of written grants by king to the following effect— 'To such and such a person so many betel-leaves or the like shall be given from such and such a plantation of betel leaves or orchard of betel nuts."' By looking at the original I find that *'nibandha' is* explained as a kind of 'vṛtti' or subsistence granted by kings, and recorded in a written instrument called a *śāsana* or royal grant. Whether a *'nibandha'* must in every case have some connection with specified land, or it is simply a periodical allowance from the royal treasury secured by a royal grant, or whether, when the allowance is made by a private individual, it is to be called a *'nibandha,'* are questions left in doubt by Vīramitrodaya. Turning to Jīmūta's work, ch. 2, pare: 13, I find a ' *nibandha* 'explained as that which is fixed by a promise in this form,— 'I will give that in every month of Kartik.' Srikrishna says;[3] "*Nibandha*' *is* anything which has been promised, deliverable annually, or monthly,

1. I. L. R. 5 Bom. 40, Samalbhai *v.* Someshwar.
2. Ch. 3, part 1, para. 13, p. 66, English Translation.
3. See footnote, Colebrooke's translation.

or at any other fixed periods:' Here we do not find that it must be by virtue of royal grant that a '*nibandha*' comes into existence, or that it must accrue from particular land. Raghunandana, however, quoted (under para. 13, ch. 2, Dāyabhāga.) by Colebrooke, says that '*nibandha*' is a fixed amount granted by a king or other authority, receivable from a mine or similar fund. It was I believe Macnaghten who first gave a restricted meaning to the word '*nibandha*.' On p. 1, Hindu Law, he says:— 'Hindu Law classes amongst things immoveable property which is of an opposite nature, such as slaves and corrodies or assignments on lands." To this opinion he was led by the circumstance that 'corrody' or its original Sanskṛt '*nibandha*' is placed in the same category with landed property in the above quoted śloka of Yājñavalkya; Vijñāna's explanation also might be taken as a periodical income accruing from a plantation of betel-leaves, or areca-nuts, the plantation no doubt being considered as a form of immoveable property. But the other commentators, Jīmūta and Srikrishna, do not so restrict the sense. Nor is it to be supposed that the śloka of Yājñavalkya is understood by Vijñāna as speaking solely of immoveable properties, or properties of the *quasi* immoveable kind ; for the śloka also mentions 'dravya' or chattels, such as gold and silver, as explained by Vijñāna. On the other hand, although Jīmūta does not connect '*nibandha*' with particular land; he yet seems to be of opinion that the śloka of Yājñavalkya intends immoveable property, or *quasi* immoveable property, for in para. 14, ch. 2, whereby he winds up his interpretation of that śloka, he says:—"The word 'dravya' denotes 'slaves,' since it has been put together with 'land.' " Now the ordinary meaning of 'dravya' is any moveable property. Jīmūta restricts its sense here to a particular kind of 'moveable property;' namely, the slaves; the reason is, he says, that the only moveable property which can be placed in the same class with land are slaves.[1] From this it would appear that according to Jīmūta '*nibandha*' also must be some property which should

1. See *ante*, p. 6.

be classified with land, though he has explained the word, in the para. which immediately precedes, as some payment promised to be made during every month of Kārtik, without reference to any landed property whatsoever. There may therefore be some reason for the supposition that *'nibandha'* probably was a kind of property having something to do with land, being for that reason classified by the writers of commentaries with immoveable property.

The nature of this property, *'nibandha'* is of importance, since according to some decided cases the right of the widow over moveable property inherited by her from her husband is absolute in all the four schools of law other than that of Bengal. In Doorga Dayee *v*, Poorun Dayee, 5 W. R. 141, the widow contended that in her position as a childless Hindu widow, and the nearest heir of her deceased husband, she had an absolute right over all the personality left by him, and might alienate it to whomsoever she chose. The judges said:—"In support of the appellant's (the widow's) case, we have a *dictum* of Hindu Law from the book most valued by the Hindus, explained by the authority of successive commentators, and the explanation supported by the concurrent opinions of the highest courts of law, both in Madras and Bombay." The purport of the Madras decisions relied upon in the above judgment is that a widow has power to dispose of moveable property left by her husband, although she cannot alienate the read estate without the consent of the next heirs, and that the widow has absolute authority over the personal or moveable property inherited by her from her husband to consume or dispose of it at her pleasure. The Bombay decisions say that a widow's right to alienate moveable property inherited from her husband, without the consent of his heirs, is absolute, and that she is absolutely entitled to moveable property left by her husband.[1] In Doorga Dayee's case, 5

1. Morley's Digest, New series, vol. I, p. 180; Becha Bagwan, 1 Bom. H. C. Rep. 56; Pranjiban Das, 1 Bom. H. C. Rep. 130.

W. R. 141, the Judges of the Calcutta High Court decided that a Government promissory note was not a corrody and was therefore at the absolute disposal of the widow.

It will be remembered[1] that according to Vīramitrodaya,[2] in a joint family the father can do what he likes with ancestral moveable property; whereas according to Vijñānā[3] the father must consult his sons even as regards the disposal of his self-acquired immoveable property. Whichever of these two contradictory opinions may be finally adopted by our courts of justice, the nature of the property called *'nibandha'* becomes of great importance. In the first place it ought to be ascertained whether *'nibandha'* has any necessary connection with land; in the second place, in case it be held that it has not, whether it should be still considered as immoveable property or not. Some approach to a solution of these two questions has been made in Collector of Thana *v.* Hari Sitaram, I. L. R. 6 Bom. 546, where the property about which the question arose was certain grants of money payment made by the Mahratta Government to a particular divinity; the written instrument of grant called 'the sanad' directed that the payments were to be made out of certain specified 'mahals and forts,' which it seems were districts of territory subject to the Mahratta Government. Upon these facts the Bombay High Court observed:—"The Hindu authorities, which we have quoted, seem to show that a pension or other periodical payment or allowance granted in permanence is *'nibandha'* whether secured on land or not. Some of them favour the supposition, that a private individual, as well as a royal personage, may create a *'nibandha'*. Whether that view is sustainable is a question on which we do not intend to give any opinion, such being unnecessary, inasmuch as the present grant is from the Peishwa's government, which it

1. See *ante*, p. 213.
2. Ch. 2, Part 1, end of para. 17.
3. Mitāk. ch,. 1, sec. 1, para. 27.

is admitted had full power to make it. We are, unanimous in holding that the grant made by the sanad here is *'nibandha,'* and that, for the reasons already we are bound to regard it as immoveable property or an interest in immoveable property within the scope of Act XIV of 1859, sec. 1, cl. 12."

Family idol a joint property

Another kind of joint property is the family idol. Family idols are not mentioned in the older treatises on Hindu Law. I believe the earliest original work in which an idol is mentioned, is Jīmūta's Dāyabhāga.[1] He here says that according to a śloka of Vyāsa which, he quotes, the joint property known as 'yājya' is not to be divided. The word 'yājya' is explained by him as either a place for offering sacrifices, or a divinity. Since this 'divinity' is named in connection with the question—what properties the parceners can divide among themselves, we naturally conclude that 'the divinity' must be a 'family idol,' and must have been viewed in the light of a kind of 'property' in the days of Jīmūta. In the Māyūkha ch. 4, sec. 7, para. 29,[2] it is said:" In the case of those who maintain the fire, the rites in connexion therewith are separate, while the worship of household deities, the *Vaiśvadeva,* and such other rites are single. Therefore says Sākala;— 'Of those whose food is cooked in one place, the worship of household deities, as also the *Vaiśvadeva,* is single; while in the case of divided members, these are performed in each house separately.'"

It is, I believe, during the last four or five centuries, that the practice of consecrating family idols has been prevalent in Bengal. A family idol is often endowed with large properties, the profits whereof are directed by the founder to be set apart for the purpose of carrying on the worship; the administration of the properties being left mostly in the

1. Ch. 6, sec. 2, para. 26.
2. Mandlik, p. 74.

hands of the members of the family, who are descended from the founder of the endowment; for this reason the possession of the idols gives rise to litigation. Both according to the rule given by Jimūta, and in consequence of the fact that an idol cannot be divided without losing its character as a consecrated object of worship, the course adopted by the coparcener is to make an arrangement for turns of worship. Thus the number of days that each parcener is entitled to worship is proportional to his fractional share in the joint property. A family idol, often becomes in course of time, a source of income ; the fame of a local divinity belonging to a particular family spreads, generally by reason of a report of some miraculous cure effected in some person who has worshipped the divinity with that object; every Hindu begins to think it a meritorious act to make offerings at its shrine. This is probably how the celebrated temple at Kalighat in the vicinity of the metropolis of India, originally the private property of the Haldar family, has become famous throughout the Hindu world, wherever resident. The shrine is now resorted to by millions of pilgrims from all parts of the Brahmanic land, and the deity represents untold wealth yearly pouring into the coffers of the above-named family of worshipping priests. The interest in the idol which the family possesses has been so minutely divided now, that some members have only a fractional share of a single day for their turn of worship.

Family idol worshipped by turns, called a 'pālā'

Cases have lone recognized these turns of worship as so many subjects of proprietary right, and have dealt with them accordingly. But although it is a kind of property, there cannot be any valid sale of it, so as to ensure to the benefit of a third party after the death of the parcener from whom he may have purchased it. The family idol is indivisible, being incapable of an out and out partition. But for the convenience of the parceners, the period of enjoyment may be so arranged for each, that he may derive the whole of his share of the benefit to be drawn from this kind of property, without coming into collision with the other members; in accordance with the principle propounded by Vṛhaspati, quoted in para. 10, ch. 1, Jīmūta's Dāyabhāga where it is said that when a single article, as a female slave, or a cow, is common to many, it is to be separately made use of in turn. Thus the female slave should serve each member for a stated number of days; and the cow should be milked for a certain period by each in turn. Vṛhaspati's text runs thus:—"A single female slave should be employed on labour in the houses of the several co-heirs successively, according to the amount of each share; and water of wells or ponds is drawn for use according to the need: such property should be distributed? by equitable adjustment; else it would be good for no purpose." I believe this principle has been extended by analogy to the case of a family idol. The whole coparcenary remains in a manner the joint owners of the idol; each during his turn of worship may employ a substitute for the purpose of carrying on the necessary duties to be performed in keeping up the seba; yet when the idol brings in an income, one member's share cannot be so transferred to a stranger as to enable the latter to receive the share of the income after the death of the transferor.[1] The principle upon which the validity of such a sale is impeachable has been thus stated by the Courts. The idol is the joint property of the members of the family of the endower ; they alone are entitled to worship it in turn, and to manage the affairs of the endowment. It is the essence of a family endowment amongst the Hindus, that no stranger shall be permitted to intrude himself into the management of the endowment. On the death of a member without heirs his right to a turn of worship and to the other attendant privileges devolves on the surviving members of

1. Ukoor Doss *v.* Chunder Sekhar Due, 3 W. R. 152.

the family. That the transfer is valid so long as the transferring member lives is owing to the reason that during his lifetime every individual member undoubtedly possesses a right to worship personally, or by a fitting proxy—the transferee being regarded as such proxy. Here, therefore, the general principle promulgated in paras. 28-31, ch. 2 of the Dāyabhāga is displaced by another that a divinity is an impartible property. In para. 31, Nārada is quoted as saying:— "When there are many persons sprung from one, who have duties apart, and transactions apart, and are separate in business and character; if they be not accordant in affairs ; should they give or sell their own shares, they may do all that, just as they please;—for they are masters of their own wealth." The purport of Nārada is that a coparcener can sell his own share of the property. This is the general rule. But the special rule with regard to a divinity is that there can be no partition of it ; the turns of worship being an arrangement agreed on for the convenience of the coparceners. A turn of worship cannot be called a 'share,' in the proper sense of the term; Nārada's rule speaks of a 'share' as alienable; but as there can be no share with regard to indivisible property, there cannot be a valid sale of an interest in such property.[1]

The language employed in some decisions may at first sight countenance the idea that partition may be predicated of an interest in an idol. Thus in Mitta Kunth Audhikarry *v.* Neerunjun Audhikarry, 14 B. L. R. 166, Couch, C. J, begins his judgment by saying that the reasons for which one of several joint owners can ask for partition of joint property apply to the case of a right to perform the worship of an idol. But a closer examination of the case and of the circumstances out of which it arose confirms the view I have stated above, that an idol is impartible property, but that a suit lies for the establishment of a reasonable arrangement,

1. See also Durga Bibi *v.* Chanchal Ram, I. L. R. 4 All. 81; Rajha Vramah Valia *v.* Ravi Varmah Mutha, L. R. 4 Ind. App. 76.

with regard to its worship, whereby the convenience of all the parties will be secured. It does not clearly appear whether in that case the parties belonged to one family. But the idol originally belonged to three persons and, was a source of income to those having an interest in it; income arising from the pecuniary offerings made by numerous devotees, whom the proprietors of the idol considered as their respective disciples. One of them brought a suit for the partition of the right to worship, Couch, C. J. said;—"The circumstance that it is a right to perform the worship of an idol is not one which deprives any of the joint owners of the right to a partition, and compels the court to say that they shall be obliged to perform the service jointly, and to undergo the many inconveniences which might arise from such a state of things." It is not necessary that there should be evidence of disputes and quarrels between the parties before the court could interfere to make a partition, or that there should be pecuniary loss or gain in order to entitle a joint owner to bring such a suit. The decree which the High Court directed to be made was that each joint owner should have a right to worship the idol in turn for a specified number of days; and that the priority of turns among the different parties, in other words, the question which party should have his turn of worship the first of all, should be determined by drawing lots in presence of the court below. The nature of the decree made in the case leaves no doubt that although it was called a suit for partition, it was virtually treated as a suit for the establishment of the several turns of worship to be enjoyed by the co-owners of the idol. Nevertheless, the principles applying to a suit for partition were generally applied to this case, inasmuch as the object in such a suit regarding a joint idol is identical with that in a suit for partition, namely, convenience in the enjoyment of a joint interest. The above view of the law relating to the impartibility of an interest in an idol is endorsed by Kemp, J., in the following observations made by him in the case of Anundo Moyee Chowdrain *v.* Bykuntha Nath Roy, 8 W. R. 193;—"These buildings are used for the purposes of worship and sacrifice; * * to divide them would be to render them utterly unsuited for the purposes and objects for which they were originally built. Such buildings when a butwarrah is made by a Collector under the provisions of Regulation XIX of 1814, are always left joint, and we see no reason why they should not be left so in this case. Under the Hindu Law places of worship and sacrifice are not divisible. The parties can enjoy their turn of worship, unless they can agree to a joint worship. Any infringement of the right to a turn of worship can be redressed by a suit." Where such a turn of worship has been already established, no coparcener can be wrongfully prevented by any other member from enjoying his turn; an infringement of this right will be a cause of action. In one case[1] the allegation on the plaintiff's part was that his turn of worship was on a specified day, and that having been prevented from performing worship on that day, he had been disgraced in the eyes of the whole family, for which he claimed damages in a sum of money. From the report of the case, it would appear that this circumstance induced Pontifex, J. to hold that there was a good cause of action ; for it had been contended on the part of the defendant that the loss, if any, suffered by the plaintiff, was a purely spiritual one, not capable of being estimated in terms of pecuniary damages. When therefore the family divinity is not the source of an income, but is worshipped in turn by the different members from spiritual motives, pure and simple, the statement of the cause of action in a case of interference of a right of worship, should include the allegation that there has been a disgrace consequent on such interference. The allegation may in every such case be truthfully made; for when there is a joint idol, it is the pious duty of every member to perform worship during his turn; in poor households, if the idol has no endowed property

1. Dobendronath Mullik *v.* Odit Churn Mullik, 1. L. R. 3 Cal. 391.

yielding an income, the duty becomes burdensome, as wages must be paid to the worshipping priest and food offerings presented daily before the god; yet the dereliction of such a duty is a cause of disgrace deeply felt by all orthodox Hindus.

Family idol to be worshipped in its shrine

Where the family idol has a house or temple set apart for it, the members must worship it in the usual shrine when their turn comes. It would also seem to be the law that where the divinity is housed in a temple, which by division has come to be the individual property of one member, that circumstance alone would furnish no reason for removing the idol to the residence of another member when this latter's turn of worship arrives. If, however, the proprietor of the temple site takes undue advantage of his proprietary right, and if he obstructs another member in making use of the same and conducting the worship, this would be a good reason for the removal of the idol to the house of the party whose worship has been obstructed, although the idol may have remained in that temple for generations, and may have been there worshipped all along. In such a case a member can claim a separation of the rights which he has previously enjoyed jointly with others, including the right of removing the idol to his own house in rotation. There is nothing illegal in such a separation or removal.[1] In one case the idol had remained in a particular temple for more than 100 years ; then it had been removed to a newly built shrine in the same village; while some of the coparceners had migrated to a different village. They wanted that they should worship the idol during their turn in their own house; the High Court held that there was no objection to their doing so; provided that the removal did not interfere with the exercise of the right by the other coparceners. With a view to that object, the High Court

1. Dwarkanath Roy *v.* Jannobee Chowdhrain, 4W. R. 79.

directed that the expenses of taking back the idol to its usual shrine must be borne by those who wanted to remove it to their own house during their own turn; and the idol must be taken back before the commencement of the turn of worship of any other member. In other words, the operation of carrying back the divinity to its ordinary residence must be so timed that another coparcener may not lose a single day of worship to which he is entitled by the mutual arrangement made. If the removal would take more than a day, the party who first removed must lose, very probably, the last two days of his turn ; since it is imperative on him to have the idol brought back at the latest in the evening previous to the day on which another member's turn of worship commences.[1]

A 'Pālā' A Periodically Recurring Right

Under Act XIV of 1859, the Law of Limitation which was in force before 1871, if a member's enjoyment of his turn of worship was interrupted by another, he was bound, to bring his suit within six years from the date of interruption. He was not entitled to the benefit of the 12 years' rule, for the suit could not be regarded as one to enforce a right to share in any property moveable or immoveable, on the ground of its being joint family property. The claim being one to exercise the right to worship an idol, cl. 16, sec. 1, of the above Act, which provided six years as the period of limitation for all suits not otherwise specially provided for, was held applicable in Gour Mohon Chowdhry *v.* Muddon Mahon Chowdhry, 6 B. L. R. 352, where it was also held that a claim of that kind was not a recurring cause of action, like a claim for rent. Under the two later enactments relating to limitation, namely, Act IX of 1871, and Act XV of 1877, Article 131 of the Second Schedule says that when a plaintiff seeks to establish a periodically recurring right, he will have 12 years as the period of limitation from the date when he

1. Ramsoondur Thacoor *v.* Tarak Chander Turkorutno 19 W.R. 28.

is first refused the enjoyment of his right. It has been decided by two cases in the Calcutta High Court that Article 131 will apply to the right to worship a family idol by turn.[1] In the later of these two decisions, the judges say that a *pala* or right to worship an idol in turn is a periodically recurring right within Article 131 of the Limitation Act and as then advised, they see no reason to differ from the decision in I. L. R. 4 Cal. 685. Apparently the case I have quoted from 8 B. L. R. was not brought to the notice of the judges.

Priestly earnings a kind of joint property

Another kind of joint property may be said to partake of the character of what is in English Law called an incorporeal hereditament. Thus the right to receive the fees due to an officiating priest may belong to a family, and is recognized as a kind of proprietary right. As between the Jajman (*i. e.*, who employs a priest in performing a rite) and the priest, the latter has no legal claim against the former for any money payment; cases have decided that it is entirely discretionary with the Jajman to employ a particular priest.[2] Nor will the law help a priest in asserting a claim to any fees by compelling the Jajman to perform particular religious ceremonies, such as the śrādh of his forefathers, the worship of the temporary clay idols periodically brought in among the Hindus at different seasons of the year, the sacraments such as the feeding with rice, the tonsure, the investiture with the sacred thread, and so forth. A priest cannot say to his Jajman:–"You must perform these ceremonies in their due times; and you must pay me the proper fees." The Jajman may wholly omit them, or may have them performed by another priest, without the law in the least interfering with his conduct. But as between the

1. Eshan Chunder Roy *v.* Monmohini Dosseo, 1. L. R. 4 Cal. 685; Gopee Kissen Gossain *v.* Thacoor Doss Gossain, 10 C. L. R. 440.
2. See Hay's Reports, July to December, pp. 365, 366.

different members of a priestly family, when the Jajmans are dutiful, and fees receivable by the officiating priest are regularly paid, the members of the priestly family have each a right to claim his proportional share; and can bring a suit if that share is withheld. Sometimes when the number of Jajmans is large, the members allot them severally among themselves. But this allotment cannot be in many cases satisfactorily made, owing to some Jajmans being wealthy and liberal in their donations, others poor and niggardly ; the usual course is to enjoy this right in common, and to divide the proceeds; or to establish *palas* or turns of ministering as officiating priests. This latter course is more suitable for the right to recite *mantras* (prayers) on the occasion of cremation ceremonies. The universal practice throughout the Hindu community is that every cremation site is held as a kind of incorporeal joint here ditament by the members of a particular Brāhman family, who have a vested right of reciting *mantras* to all persons coming to burn the dead bodies of their deceased relatives in that particular place. They receive fees for this priestly ministration, the fees constituting the profit derived from this kind of property. The class of Brāhmins who officiate on such occasions do not stand high in public estimation; they live apart, marry among themselves, are not associated with in social intercouse, and in Bengal go under the contemptuous appellation of corpse-burning Brāhmins.'

In all these priestly ministrations, the competency of the particular member to perform the requisite ceremonies, or his ability to assist his Jajman in performing the same, is hardly of any consequence. If he be himself incompetent and devoid even of the miserable'amount of Sanskrit knowledge indispensable for such ministrations, he can do his duty vicariously, in other words, by appointing a competent paid priest, whom he pays out of the fees received from the Jajman. It is therefore not open to the learned members of a priestly family to monopolize the duties and the rights, to the exclusion of the unlearned. Even the widow of a deceased coparcener can assert a right to appropriate the priestly fees, provided the Jajman has no objection to accept vicarious ministration arranged for by her. Jajmans seldom display any disinclination thereto. The terms between the priestly family and the Jajmans, when the latter are orthodox and of means, are exceedingly cordial. The Jajman would much rather like to see the widow of a deceased priest above want, rather than see all his gifts appropriated by the surviving male member of the priestly family. Thus this right to the priestly fees often becomes the means of keeping a respectable Brāhmin family secure from starvation through many generations, and is therefore looked upon as valuable property. An attempt to monopolize the profits arising from this incorporeal property, if made by the male members in exclusion of the widow of a deceased member, would give rise to a cause of action on the latter's part.[1] Where the widow of one of four brothers, who exercised a right of reciting *mantras* in turn at a particular ghaut on the occasion of the burning of Hindu bodies, sued on a claim that her husband's turn was for seven days in the month, stating that her husband had enjoyed the right during his lifetime, and she also after his decease, until she was prevented from exercising it by one of the surviving brothers; the High Court held that such a suit lay.[2] The judges say:—"The obligation of the Jujmans to employ a particular priest is a simple matter of conscience, and not an obligation that a court of law can enforce. * * But in this case it is not denied that the four brothers amongst whom was the plaintiff's husband, had a joint right in the performance of the ceremonies alluded to above, and in the profits thereby accruing to them. The parties frequenting a ghaut for the purpose of burning their dead, could not perhaps be obliged to employ a particular purohit; but that has nothing to do with the question of the

1. Khedro Ojha *v.* Muss. Deo Ranee Kumar, 5 W. R. 222.
2. Becharam Banerjea *v.* Thacoormoney Debia, 10 W. R. 114.

right to enjoy the joint profits accruing from the performance of these ceremonies."

In Madras, divinity strictly impartible

In Madras, where the principle of the Mitākṣāra law prevails, the old rule that a divinity is an indivisible property, seems to have had a development different from Bengal. In Bengal, the divinity is left undivided, but *palas* are established to be enjoyed by the several members in rotation; but in Madras, a single member of the family obtains the management of the affairs of the divinity; and the old rule of impartibility is rigidly followed.

Dhamma katta

There the person who discharges the duties of manager is called a dhammakattā, a name easily referable to its Sanskrit origin, meaning 'the performer of religious duties,' although I am not aware that the original texts anywhere have employed the expression in the sense of an 'administrator of temple property.' The office has been thus described in a decision of the Madras High Court. "An office of this kind not being in its nature partible, it is not only not unusual, but it is in accordance with general practice for some one member of a family to hold it for life. Instead of several members of the family holding the property in common, one takes it in its entirety, and the common law rights of the others who would be coparceners of partible property are reduced to the rights of survivorship to the possession of the whole."[1] The general rule seems to be that the senior surviving male member of the family holds the office of dhammakattā; therefore, if he allows any other person to hold the office, the possession of the latter becomes adverse, and in twelve years extinguishes the right of the senior member. A female descendant of the founder, being always married into some other family, is not considered as of the founder's family, but is as a stranger,

1. I. L. R. 1 Mad. 346, Chenna Kesavraya *v.* Vaidelinga.

with regard to the office of the dhammakattā. If she or her male issue takes possession of the office, such possession is adverse to the male members. This was so decided in the case cited above, where Inner, J. says :— "Whatever right to the office a female, married and estranged from the family of the founder, might have after the exhaustion of the male coparceners, it is contrary to all known principles of Hindu rights of property, that a female should take possession in preference to male survivors who are also coparceners."

In Bombay, share of earnings from a temple alienable

In Bombay, however, the law upon the subject of this kind of joint property, namely, the rights and privileges vested in an undivided family in connection with temples founded by an ancestor, is partly similar to that of Bengal, but partly also differs from the same. If a temple is founded by an ancestor with property set apart for the purposes of carrying on the worship, and if the shrine in course of time comes to yield an income from the offerings made by the public, it is in Bombay regarded exactly in the light of undivided property belonging to all the persons descended from the founder, to the extent that one member can claim a partition of his share, and can even alienate it, subject to certain restrictions. The partition is made according to the principle of enjoying the profits in rotation. The validity of such a partition is not based upon the text of Vṛhaspati cited in Jīmūta's work,[1] but upon modern usage, as has been said by Melvil, J., in Mancharam *v.* Pransankar, I. L. R,. 6 Bom. 299, whose words are :— ' No doubt hereditary offices, whether religious or secular, are treated by Hindu text writers as naturally indivisible; but modern custom, whether or not it be strictly in accordance with ancient law, has sanctioned such partition as can be had of such property, by means of a performance of the duties of the office, and the enjoyment of the emoluments, by the

1. See *ante*, p. 452.

different coparceners in rotation." With regard to the alienation of such a share, the principal objection against it is, that if the law allowed its unrestricted transfer, the purchaser might be a person altogether incompetent to perform the worship, and the religious duties might thereupon remain unattended to. Even a Christian might be a purchaser, and he might wholly omit to perform the worship. As cooked food is often presented before the deity, the purchaser may be a person of a low caste, and food cooked by him may be an abomination in the eye of a strict Hindu, far less fit to be offered in the shrine of a divinity. The law in Bombay therefore has laid down that rights in a temple cannot be transferred to a stranger. But since similar objections would not apply to an alienation made to a member of the selfsame family, the law upholds such alienations, the words of Melvil, J., in the case referred to above being:—"If the alienation of a priestly office is open to objection only on the grounds that it would be contrary to the founder's intention that the office should pass out of his family, and that it would be incompatible with the duties of the office that it should be held by a person of a different religion or caste, then (in the absence of any restriction to a particular class of heirs, imposed either by the founder or by usage) there would appear to be no reason why an alienation should not be upheld, which is made in favour of any person standing in the line of succession, and not disqualified by any personal unfitness."

Landed Estate the Usual Joint Property

In the vast majority of cases, undivided property is found in the form of landed estate, originally acquired by some ancestor, and transmitted in the family from one generation to another. Landed property, since the first introduction of the system of land tenures during the Mahommeden rule, has assumed various names, implying diverse rights and liabilities as incident to its ownership. The highest class of landed property is the lakhiraj or rent-free land; next to it is the zamindari paying revenue directly to Government; then come the putnees, the durputnees, the mokurrarees, the ijaras, and innumerable other tenures, temporary or permanent, all of which are capable of being held and owned as well by a number of individuals as by a single person. When a number of individuals owning these landed tenures are descended from a common ancestor, the land is considered as joint family property, and is subject to all its incidents. Landed property is in general, accompanied by documents of title, showing how right to it originated, whether by sale or by gift, or by inheritance, or by partition. There is an interesting passage in the Institutes of Gautama, which is quoted in most of the modern commentaries, and which shows how the ancient Ṛṣis speculated on the origin of property in land. The passage is found in the Mitākṣarā, ch. 1, sec. 1, para. 8. The purport of the passage may be thus set forth:-A person becomes owner by means of inheriting property from some one else, by purchase, by partition, by occupancy, or by finding a hidden treasure. These expedients of acquiring proprietary right are common to all creeds and castes. But a Brāhmin can acquire property by acceptance of gift; a man of the military caste by conquest ; persons of the two lowest castes by receiving wages. Those expedients are peculiar to the several castes, When the subject of propiretary right is land, and purchase or gift the means of acquisition, in the Hindu society as in other civilized societies, the practice from time immemorial has been to make out a document of title, called in Sanskrit indifferently a 'lekhya' or a 'patra,' and executed by the person in whom the proprietary right at first lay, in favour of the person to whom the right is transferred. When property is partitioned among co-sharers, then also is a document prepared, which the Sanskrit lawyers have called 'vibhāga-patra,' or instrument of partition.' In modern times, documents of title have assumed a diversified character, corresponding to the diversity of the form, of landed estates. As evidencing a transfer of right by sale, these documents are called ' kobalas;' as creating a tenure, they are 'pattas;' of which class there are various kinds, known by different names of ' sanads' putnees,' 'ijaras,' and so forth.

Precantions in purchase of joint land

Where a joint family in the aggregate owns any landed property, the instruments of title are often made out in the name of one member alone; in other words, only one member is mentioned by name in it as the party in whose favour the transfer is made. But the law will consider him *prima facie* the representative of the family corporation with regard to the property. Generally the property stands in the name of the managing member; and then not only those who are members of the same undivided family with him, but also the descendants in the male line of all such members will be considered as having an interest in such property. As a rule, the name of the manager is used in the documents relating to property; but the names of other members are not unfrequently so employed. In fact the law attaches but little importance to the character or position of the particular member in whose name the document may be; law simply recognizes the fact that it is the usual practice of Hindu families to hold joint property in the name of one. A person therefore desirous to purchase property from the member of a joint family, should look to the character of the property, whether joint or separate. He should not conclude that it is separate, simply because one member's name is mentioned in the documents of title. In other systems of law, all that the purchaser need do is to inspect the documents of title and to see whether the vendor holds the property under them or not. But among Hindus, additional circumspection and care are demanded from a purchaser. He must not only inspect the documents of title, but must also make an enquiry whether the vendor is the member of a joint family or not. In case the vendor be such a member, the next enquiry on the part of the purchaser should be whether the property to be sold was acquired by the vendor with his own separate funds or not. Should the purchaser fail to enquire, and should it be actually the case that the property was really joint, then in Bengal the purchaser gets only the vendor's share, although from ignorance of the fact that there were other sharers in it, the purchaser may have paid a price adequate for the whole property. In Shibosonndery Dossee *v.* Rakhal Das Sarkar, 1 W. R. 38, the judges say:–"The fact of the Hindu family is enough to put the purchaser upon enquiry, and if he deals with a single member, without obtaining proof that the property is separate, he does so at his own risk." This is a Bengal case ; but it will be subsequently shown that the rule is the same in all the schools. Only there is this difference that under the Mitākṣarā as administered in the North-Western Provinces, the purchaser will not get even that particular member's share, with whom he dealt. This we shall show subsequently. Under the law of the Mitākṣarā as administered by the High Court of Bengal also, the tendency of the earlier decisions was to hold that a single member could not alienate even his own share; but later decisions, especially some judgments of the Privy Council, as we shall subsequently show, have weakened the effect of the earlier rule. What we are concerned with at present is, that the fact of property standing in the name of one member does not make it the less a joint property of the entire family, the law not attaching to that fact the slightest importance whatsoever. This rule has been recognised in a number of cases, some of which alone I shall notice here.

Name of single member in title deeds of joint land

In Deela Sing *v.* Toofanee Sing, 1 W. R. 306, the question was whether a particular property belonged to one brother of a Mitākṣarā family, or to all the six brothers who jointly constituted the family. The observations of the judges of the High Court are:—" The purchase of property by a joint family in the sole name of one of the members, and the registration also being permitted in his sole name, is what we see done every day; and in a suit between the members of the family to try the question, such matters are never regarded by themselves as sufficient evidence of separate acquisition." In this case, not only the fact of the title-deed being in the name of one member is disregarded, but also the other important fact, that the property was registered in the name of that member alone; which no doubt means that the property in question was a zamindari paying revenue directly to the Collector, who according to the usual practice of the Collector's office, keeps a record of the names of the proprietors to whom a particular revenue paying estate belongs. If therefore the Collector's records alone be looked into, it would often appear that a particular zamindari was the sole and exclusive property of a single individual; when in point of fact, it was the property of an undivided family consisting, it may be, of ten or twenty individuals.

Registry in collector's books

As registration in the Collector's book of the name of one member may consist with the right of all the members; similarly if the Collector settles the zamindari with one, it will enure to the benefit of all. Where the property belonged to the father, but a settlement for its revenue was made by Government, in the name of an elder son, in other words, the elder son was recorded as the party liable for the payment of revenue, the younger brother's right in the property was not in the least affected. The elder brother, being registered in the Collector's records, was the proprietor to the outer world; but it was of no weight in the determination of the question, whether the younger brother had a right to it or not.[1] In Lalla Behari Lal *v.* Lalla Modhoo Prosad, 6 W. R. 69, the sum and substance of what the judges observe is as follows:–The correct notion of a Hindu family joint in food and estate is that its members bring their earnings of all kinds into the common stock. The mere fact of the property standing in the name of one member is no index whatever to the real owner. Even a separate possession by one member is no evidence that it is not joint property. Such a conclusion would be warranted only where the shareholder exercising separate possession is permitted by the other sharers, to open and keep a separate account of his own, and not to carry his earnings to the common stock.[2]

Sale certificates in a single member's name

Since its first establishment, the British Government in the exercise of its legislative functions have from time to time made attempts to check the inveterate practice obtaining in India of holding property by one person in the name of another.This practice, having its origin in the dishonest motive of defrauding creditors of their just and lawful dues, has had so large and widespread a prevalence here that the Legislature cannot altogether put an end to it by a drastic enactment declaring the practice absolutely illegal in all cases. Such a step would be attended with immense mischief. But as the British Government by its revenue laws has retained in its hands the supreme control over the vast majority of landed property, there have been enactments to discourage benamee purchases at a revenue sale. Under Regulation XI of 1822, the Government was empowered by secs. 19 and 20 to cancel and annul benamee purchases made at a sale for arrears of revenue. The next

---

1. Umrith Nath Chowdhry *v.* Goureenath Chowdhry, 2 Sutherland P. R. p. 381.
2. See also Huro Soondury Debya *v.* Doorgadoss Bhattacharjee, 16 W. R. 265.

enactment upon the subject is contained in Act XII of 1841, sec. 22 whereof provides that "any suit brought to oust a certified purchaser as aforesaid on the ground that the purchase was made on behalf of another person not the certified purchaser, though by agreement the name of the certified purchaser was used, shall be dismissed with costs." The object of this provision is that if benamee purchases are made at a revenue sale, the real purchaser will thereby incur a risk of losing his purchase, for the ostensible purchaser may play false to the real purchaser, may get possession of the zamindari by virtue of his sale certificate, and then although he may not have advanced a single pice of the price paid for it, the real purchaser will have no remedy. Under the ordinary principles of law and equity, the real purchaser might bring a suit upon the allegation that the purchase money belonged to him, and a court of justice, if satisfied that it was so, might give him a decree for the possession of the zamindari. But the above provision was intended to prevent the operation of these principles, in order that purchasers might be deterred from making purchases in another's name. Now, as regards a joint Hindu family, the question may naturally arise, whether when a zamindari is purchased at a revenue sale, and when the sale certificate mentions the name of one member alone, the other members will have the benefit of the purchase at all. The principle of the above provision might be contended to be that courts of justice were not to look beyond the four corners of the sale certificate, and that although the party mentioned by name as the purchaser in such a certificate might be the managing member of a joint family, yet he alone must be held as the only person interested in the purchase. But such a contention has been held to be untenable, and it has been ruled that the purchase of zamindari property at a revenue sale in the name of the managing member will enure to the benefit of all.[1] In the

1. Toondun Sing *v.* Pokhnarain Sing, 13 W.R. 347.

case in which it was so held the revenue sale was under Act I of 1845, sec. 21 whereof says the very same thing as Act XII of 1841, infact repeats the very same words. Norman, J. observed that this was a penal clause, in other words, it provided forfeiture of proprietary right on the ground of one name being used in lieu of another; therefore the clause must receive a strict construction. According to this strict construction, where the managing member is the certified purchaser, the ground of a suit brought by any other member for a declaration that he also has an interest in it will not be this, that the purchase was made on behalf of another person not the certified purchaser. What he will have to state is that the purchase was made on behalf of both the certified purchaser, and certain other persons, of whom the plaintiff is one. A suit upon such an allegation cannot be said to be one on the ground that the purchase was made on behalf of persons other than the certified purchaser. Such a suit therefore by an ordinary member to get a share in property purchased in the name of the managing member is not liable to dismissal under sec. 21, Act I of 1845. Norman, J. notices an alteration in the language of the still later enactment relating to revenue sales, namely, Act XI of 1859. In it, sec. 36 being the corresponding provision of law, runs:–"Any suit brought to oust the certified purchaser on the ground that the purchase was made on behalf of another person not the certified purchaser, *or on behalf* partly of himself *and partly of another person*, though by agreement the name of the certified purchaser was used, shall be dismissed with costs." Under this later provision, any other member seems to be precluded from alleging in his plaint that the purchased property belongs partly to himself and partly to the certified purchaser. This decision of Norman, J. was affirmed in appeal by the Privy Council, the judgment of their Lordships being reported in 22 W. R. 199, where they express their concurrence in the following proposition of law :— A purchase at a sale for arrears of revenue under Act I of 1845, made by the managing member of a joint Hindu family in his own name, but on behalf of the joint family, is not affected by the 21st section of that Act, and that notwithstanding anything contained therein, the members of such a joint family may sue to enforce rights acquired by them under such a purchase as against the managing member; though he is the sole certified purchaser. In another case the purchase was made in the name of the son of one of the members of a Mitākṣarā family, but the purchase money had come out of the joint funds. It was contended before the High Court that sec, 21 of Act I of 1845 applied, and that the sale certificate was conclusive against the rights of other members. But Conch, C. J. said :— "The purchase was made by Chundun Lall by means of the common property. The other members of the family could not be deprived of their rights by his making it in his son's name. It is as much family property as if the purchase was made in the name of Chundun Lall.

What sec. 21 of Act I of 1845 prohibits is a suit by Chundun Lall to oust his son Booniadi, and it may be, also a suit by any other son claiming a share of the property as being the separate property of Chundun Lall. It does not prevent the other members of the family claiming a share of it as joint property." Bukshee Booniadi Lal *v.* Bukshee Deokee Nundon, 19 W. R., 223. Here as the family was governed by the Mitākṣarā law, the son also was a member having an interest in the purchased property, though his father seems to have been the member who actively exerted himself in order to effect the purchase at a revenue sale in his son's name. Consequently the effect of the decision is that whether a zamindari is purchased at a revenue sale in the name of the managing member, or any other member, so long as the purchase money was furnished out of the joint funds, the rights of the members remain unaffected by the provisions of sec. 21 of Act I of 1845.

Purchase in the name of the family priest held as joint

The principle that the name stated in the documents of title is no index to the real proprietor in Hindu joint families has been carried so far, that in one case the Privy Council held a particular property to be joint, which had been purchased by the managing member in the name of the family priest. There the family consisted of two members, one being introduced into the family as a co-sharer by virtue of an adoption. He established his right as such by a suit relating to the ancestral zamindari. With regard to the acquisition made in the name of the family priest, the Privy Council observed:–"The presumption of law and the presumption of fact would be that the property acquired in that way by the managing representative member of the joint family would be joint family property."[1]

This has brought me to another rule that acquisitions made from the income of the joint property form a part and parcel of the undivided funds, every member being interested in such acquisitions in the same proportion in which he is interested in the original property. In the case of Kalee Sunkar Bhadoory *v.* Eshan Chunder Bhadoory, 17 W. R., 528, the question was, what share each member should receive, in a property purchased from the common funds. The judges observe:—"At the time when this purchase was made, the plaintiff and the defendant No. 4 were living together as members of a joint undivided Hindu family, and it is admitted that the plaintiff was the manager of the joint estate. * * *Admitting, the correctness of the defendant's allegation, namely, that the purchase of Chunder Kant's share was by the plaintiff for the benefit of the joint undivided family and with funds belonging to it, it seems to be clear that the plaintiff would be entitled to such a share of the property covered by the purchase as

1. 2 Suth. P. R. Rulings, p. 805, Chand Hari Maiti *v.* Rajah Norender Narain, Roy.

would be equal to his original share in the *corpus* of the estate. The increment must follow the same rule as the *corpus*."

Texts establishing the joint character of a acquisitions

The general proposition that acquisitions made from the joint funds are to be regarded as joint has been said to follow from certain texts in the Mitākṣarā cited below. Colebrooke's Mitākṣarā, ch. 1, sec. 4, verses 29-31:—"It is settled that whatever is acquired at the charge of the patrimony is subject to partition. But if the common stock be improved, an equal division is ordained. Among unseparated brethren, if the common stock be improved or augmented by any one of them, through agriculture, commerce, or similar means, an equal distribution nevertheless takes place; and a double share is not allotted to the acquirer." These texts occur at the end of that portion of the Mitākṣarā which deals with properties not liable to be partitioned when a general separation of the members is taking place. The intention of the passage therefore is to declare the joint character of all 'augmentations' made by making use of the patrimony, although only one coparcener may have actively exerted himself in bringing about the augmentation. This passage is an instance wherein the joint family is contemplated as composed of brothers alone, this as I have observed more than once being customary with the writers of the original texts, who generally lay down their law as applicable to a joint family in its simplest form. But we must not therefore suppose that the rule promulgated by them will not apply where the household corporation consists of persons more distantly related to one another than brothers are. The proper rule to be extracted from the above passage is, that if the common stock be augmented by one coparcener by making use of the ancestral property, each member of the family corporation will have such a share in the augmentation, or in the additions made, as is equal to the share he has in the original stock. A rule which comes to the very same thing is laid down in the Vivāda-cintāmaṇi, p. 255, where it is said that the brothers participate in that wealth which one of them gains by valour or the like, using any common property, such as a weapon or a vehicle. To him two shares shall be given, but the rest shall share alike. Here the rule of equality of shares is negatived; but I apprehend that the double share is lawful only where the acquisition owes its origin to some special qualification of the acquirer, such as uncommon learning, extraordinary exertion, and so forth. Where the acquisition is made out of the common stock with ordinary exertion, no double share will be allotted to the party who may have brought about the increase the common stock. Some such principle seems to have been in the mind of Mitter J., who in Sheo Dyal Tewaree *v.* Jadoonath Tewaree, 9 W. R. 61, says:-"As to the labour, that consisted in purchasing estates out of the funds of the joint ancestral firm, which Sheo Dyal was managing for the benefit of the joint family. This is no more than a case of augmentation at the highest. The ancestral firm was the main nucleus of this estate; and every property acquired from such a nucleus falls within the rule of equal division. The verse 29 (of the Mitākṣarā, which declares the allotment of a double share) applies to a different state of things. Where a coparcener, with comparatively small detriment to the joint estate, acquires any separate property by his own labour or capital, the property is nevertheless to be considered joint, although the acquirer gets a double share. Here, strictly speaking. there is no proof of Sheo Dyal having supplied any portion of the money required for the purchase of the properties in question from his own funds, and as to labour, his case does not stand higher than that of a manager of a joint undivided family. In our opinion it is not even a case of augmentation. The mere conversion of joint funds into lands is not an acquisition within the meaning of the Hindu Law." Where the family consists of a father and his sons governed by the Mitākṣarā law, it has sometimes been a question whether acquisitions made by the father out of the income of the ancestral property, such ancestral property under the circumstances being property joint between the father and the son, must also be joint. In Sudanand Mohapattur *v.* Bonomalee Doss Mohapattur, 6 W. R., 256, E. Jackson, J. lays down the law as follows:—All acquisitions made by the manager of a family composed of brothers, out of the profits of the joint property, belong to the joint estate. But, although a son has a joint interest with his father in the ancestral immoveable estate, he cannot, as long as that interest remains joint, call upon his father for an account of his management of the profits of the estate; he cannot sue his father for mesne profits for years during which it was under his father's management. The consequence hereof is, that the son's interest does not extend to the annual profits received from the ancestral immoveable estate while it remains joint. The father is at liberty to spend them as he pleases, and is not accountable to his son for such expenditure. Such profits do not constitute ancestral property, and immoveable property purchased with such profits is therefore not ancestral property. The difference between a joint family composed of a father and his sons, and a joint family composed of brothers, as regards their rights in the profits of the ancestral immoveable property, is this that in the former the father is the sole unaccountable owner, and in the latter all the brothers are joint owners. In the former, the son's interest extends only to the original undivided estate. In the latter, the brother's interest extends to the profits as their acquired property, as well as their patrimony. To this opinion were opposed the observations of Steer, J., the sum and substance whereof may be thus stated:—There are numerous decisions in which it has been held that, when it is presumable that property has been bought out of the assets of the ancestral property, it is itself ancestral. The law does not make any distinction between one joint family and another. A family consisting of a father and sons is as much under the rules which govern rights of property in joint families, as a family of brothers. One brother cannot by the use of joint funds acquire separate property for himself ; a father also is similarly incapable of doing so. All funds are joint till there is a separation. Although the father is the sole manager, and has the control of the expenditure of the income of the family; yet whatever he spends, he must be considered to spend for the family; and whatever he acquires, he acquires for the family. The family has a common interest with him both in the income and in the expenditure. The income is not the father's, but the family's; and though the father cannot be controlled while he is manager in the purchase of such property as he thinks fit to buy out of the income of the family estate, the estate he does buy must be considered the property of the family. Trevor, J. agreed with Steer, J. His words are:—"As the father and son or sons are co-owners in the ancestral property, so, they are co-owners in that which issues from it, namely, the profits of the joint estate; consequently any estate purchased by these joint funds follows the character of the funds, of which it is the representative."

Purhchases From ancestral Funds Joint, Even Though no Coparcener Exists

Purchases made from ancestral funds partake of the character of those funds, even though at the time the purchases are made, it may be that there is no actually existing joint family. Thus before the birth or adoption of a son, the father is the sole proprietor of the ancestral property. Both the income and the *corpus* are therefore at his entire disposal; he may dissipate either at his pleasure. But if he thinks proper to invest the income in the purchase of durable property, such as land or Government securities, the additional properties at once become a part and parcel of the ancestral property; and a son afterwards born to him, or adopted by him, acquires a vested right to the whole immediately on his birth or adoption. Previous to his birth or adoption, the fresh additions could not very well be termed joint, because there was no co-owner; but the birth or adoption immediately converts it into joint family property. There is no distinction between investment of money before the birth or adoption of a son, or after the same event.[1] This doctrine seems to be the outcome of the joint right of a father and his son under the Mitākṣarā Law. But recently some doubt has been thrown upon the soundness of the reasons for which the doctrine was carried so far. In Ganga Pershad *v.* Sheo Dyal Sing, 9 C. L. R., 422, R. Mitter, J. says:—"The result is, that a son becomes co-owner with his father only in property which was inherited from the father of the latter. But property acquired out of the income of ancestral property is not property inherited. It is true that if property be purchased out of such income after the birth of the son, the latter acquires a joint interest in it. But this is so, not under any special texts of the Mitākṣarā, but because he is jointly interested in the profits arising out of the ancestral property after his birth. But he has no such interest in the profits of such property before his birth." These observations relate only to property acquired by the father before the birth of a son; they do not therefore affect the soundness of the rule, that where there is an actually existing joint family, whether constituted by a father and his sons, or by brothers or other more distant relatives, all acquisitions made by the use of joint funds belong to the whole family. Besides the cases already cited by me as recognizing this rule, I may cite Muss. Teeknoo *v.* Muss. Mooniah, 7 W. R., 440 ; in this case, property admittedly acquired by one of two brothers from ancestral funds was held to be joint, and consequently incapable of being succeeded to by his widow, whose right under the Mitākṣarā Law is confined to only the separate estate of her deceased husband.

1. Sudanand Mohapattur *v.* Soorjo Money Daya, 11 W.R., 436.

Property distributed by Grandfather Joint as Between Father and Son

I shall conclude this Lecture by citing a case in which it has been held that property acquired by the grandfather and distributed by him among his sons does not thereby cease to be joint family property as between the recipients of such distribution and their sons.[1] In this case the contention was that the property distributed by the grandfather to his sons should be regarded as gifts made by him to his sons. Under the Hindu Law, gift being a recognized mode of acquiring property, it was urged that gifts of grandfather's property should be considered as the self-acquisitions of the father. But Norman, J. decided against the contention, upon the ground that such acquisitions by a grandfather's gift could not be said to be acquired without detriment to the ancestral estate, since it had been given not only out of that estate, but in substitution for the undivided share of that estate to which the father was entitled under the Mitākṣarā Law. It could not therefore be taken to be simply ' gifts of favour' spoken of in para. 27, sec. 1, ch. 1, Colebrooke's Mitākṣarā. 'Gifts of favour' alluded to in that para. are such as are made upon a consideration personal to the donee; as for instance, in wealthy families, the father gives rich dresses and valuable ornaments and sometimes considerable landed properties to a son on the occasion of the latter's investiture, with the sacred thread, or on the occasion of his marriage. Such gifts no doubt are in a sense acquisitions made by sons with detriment to the patrimony. Yet they are not joint property; for the Mitākṣāra in ch. 1, sec. 1, paras. 24 and 25, says that the father is competent by virtue of express texts to make 'gifts of favour' to his sons out of his self-acquired property and ancestral moveable property, although it is beyond doubt that his sons other than the recipient of the favour had before the act of gift a vested right in all these properties from the moment of their birth.

---

1. Muddon Gopal Thacoor *v.* Ram Buksh Panday, 6 W. R., 71.

Chapter 9
Alienation of Joint Family Property

Alienation in Bengal—Nārada's text taken as authorizing alienation of joint share—Stranger can purchase fractional share in family dwelling-house—Sale of whole property valid in case of legal necessity—Legal necessity, what—Alienation under Mitākshāra as administered by Calcutta High Court, when valid—Purchaser bound to enquire as to legal necessity—Śrādh a necessity—Alienation of even a single share invalid—But auction sale for debt valid—Reasons for the invalidity of a single member's share—Refund of purchase money when necessary in setting aside alienation of joint property— Law of alienation under Allahabad High Court—Gift of joint property, when valid—Alienation of joint property in Madras—Fractional share alienable in Madras—Division by metes and bounds not necessary to terminate joint character—Practical difficulties from alienation of a fractional share—Testamentary devise of a fractional share not valid—Law of alienation in Bombay—Devise valid by last survivor of a joint family-Obstructed heritage and unobstructed heritage—Unobstructed heritage extends as far 'as the great-grandson—Alienation of property by obstructed inheritance held valid.

In this Lecture the question to be dealt with is the validity of the alienation of Joint Family Property. Upon this subject the original texts have furnished us only with a few principles, which have been developed into a large number of propositions by decided cases. A general consideration of these propositions leads me to think that it will be advantageous to state the law of alienation apart in each of the schools of Hindu Law, and also as administered by each of the four High Courts. Two of these High Courts, namely, those of Madras and Bombay, man be said to correspond to two of those schools ; while the High Court of Allahabad is at present the authoritative exponent of the Benares Law. But the High Court of Calcutta has to administer three schools of Law, namely, the Benares, the Mithila and the Bengal.

Alienation in Bengal

Under the Bengal school, the question how far the alienation of joint family property is valid is not complicated. While the father lives, the sons have no ownership in the ancestral property. The father's alienation therefore of the whole or a part of it cannot be questioned by them. Its validity will depend upon principles relating to the transfer of property which are not peculiar to the Hindu Law, but which are common to it with all other bodies of Law. I allude to such rules as that an alienation is not valid unless the alienor is of sound mind, or unless his consent was properly obtained. Nor are such rules confined to the alienation of joint family property. The fundamental idea in Bengal is that when there are more than one owner of any property, the owners own it in defined shares. If there are five brothers, from the death of their father each brother is the proprietor of one-fifth share in the patrimony. So long as the father was alive, he could alienate the whole or a part; after his death each brother can alienate his one-fifth share, although the property may not have then been divided. This is unlike the Mitākṣāra Law, as I have had occasion to notice more than once. The reason of this difference between the two schools is obvious. In the Mitākṣāra school, before partition, each brother would not have a defined share; for if before partition one brother were to die, although he left a widow, the share of each of the surviving brothers would at once rise to one-fourth. In Bengal, this rise in the value of a share takes place only when the deceased died without leaving a nearer heir, a son, a wife, a daughter, a daughter's son, a father or a mother.

Narada's text taken as authorising atlienation of joint share

Now, the right of a Bengal brother to alienate his undivided share has been deduced by Jīmūta from a text of Nārada, already cited, but which I shall cite here once more for convenience' sake. It is quoted in para. 31, ch. 2, Dāyabhāga. "When there are many sprung from one man, having duties apart, transactions apart, and separate in business and character; if they be not accordant in their affairs, should they give or sell their own share, they may do all that just as they please, for they are the lords of their own property." One would think that this text refers to divided property, or at least to divided brothers, for it thrice repeats expressions implying 'separatedness,' by speaking of business apart and duties apart and transactions apart.' But such a construction would be in conflict with the fundamental idea of 'fractional ownership.' Each brother is an owner in severalty of his fractional share, although the property be undivided. Why should not each therefore be competent to sell it, or give it? This is how. Jīmūta argues, and brings forward Nārada to show that each is competent to give or sell his share. That the natural construction of Nārada's text would bear out the competency only of a divided parcener to alienate his share, not of an undivided parcener, seems to have struck Srīkṛṣṇa, the commentator of Jīmūta, for he is solicitous to explain away the first part of Nārada's text. He in his commentary says :— धर्मो ऽशौचं दश द्वादशरात्रादि। कर्म तपः शौर्य्यादि। गुणो मृदुत्व चण्डत्वादिः। क्रिया याजन पालनादिः। कार्य्येषु एकैक क्रियमाणदानादिषु। That is to say:— "By 'duties' is meant the observance of the days of impurity, such as ten days or twelve days. By 'transactions ' is meant the practice of austerities, or the performance of valorous deeds. By 'character' is meant mildness or fierceness. By 'business' is meant the performance of priestly duties and so forth. By 'affairs' is meant the making of gifts etc. by each apart from the others." Śrīkṛṣṇa then adds :—विभक्तस्येव अविभक्तस्यावरस्यापि स्वामिकृतदानादि सिध्यत्येव। अक्षपातादिना पश्चादंशे परिचयसम्भवादिति भाव:। "If the owner makes a gift or any other alienation of undivided immoveable property, it is valid, like that of the divided, since afterwards the share may be identified by the process of drawing lots and so forth. This is the purport," He in fact labours to bring the text of Nārada into an agreement with his own view of the law, and says that in an undivided family the parceners have their religions duties apart— that is to say, each must perform for himself the religious observance prescribed by the law of impurities. This law says that in a Brāhmin family, impurity extends to ten days on account of a near relation's death. During these ten days, daily prayers are prohibited, abstinence from animal food is prescribed, and so forth. Each one of the undivided brothers observes these rules separately for himself; this is what is meant by 'duties apart' in Nārada's text. Similarly each does his own transaction apart, that is, each,—if it be a family of ministering priests,—officiates as a priest separately from the others; each makes a gift apart from another, and so on. This is how it is attempted to show in the Bengal school that Nārada has sanctioned alienation of undivided property by an undivided coparcener to the extent of his share. Modern tribunals, however, have little to do with the question whether this interpretation of Nārada is forced or natural; they administer the rule as it has been propounded by Jīmūta; and he sanctions the alienation of undivided property.

Stranger can purchase fractional share in family dwelling house

The rule under the Bengal Law that a parcener can sell his joint share has been fully recognized in the case of

Koomar Bijoy Keshab Roy Bahadur *v.* Shama Soonduree Dossee, 2 W. R. Mis. Rulings, p. 30. There a stranger had purchased the share of one member of a Bengal joint family in the undivided family dwelling-house. The question was whether he could be put in possession of it, regard being had to the inconvenience and annoyance caused to the female members, were a stranger allowed to jointly occupy the dwelling-house. Four out of five judges of the Calcutta High Court ruled that the purchase was valid, while Kemp, J. dissented on the following grounds-" It would be inconvenient to give a stranger a right of tangible actual entry into a dwelling house occupied by a respectable Hindu female. * * I think with reference to Hindu customs and prejudices, it world be inequitable to permit a stranger to intrude himself upon the privacy of a joint Hindu family residence, more particularly when, as in this instance, a stranger is actuated by motives of enmity. If we permit him to do this, we shall be encouraging him in his animosity, and be driving the other members of the family to leave the ancestral house."

Sale of whole property valid in case of legal necessity

So far therefore it is clear that in a Bengal joint family, the transfer of one member's fractional share in the undivided property, whether the sale be in execution of a decree against the individual member, or be a voluntary one effected by himself, is valid to the extent of the share. Sometimes it is contended that not only the fractional share, but the whole property passes by a single member's act of alienation. In Ram Lochan Shaha *v.* Annopoorna Dossee, 7 W. R. 144, there was a decree against two major brothers out of three constituting a , joint family; in execution of the decree the interest of the two brothers in the joint property was purchased by a stranger who claimed to be entitled to the whole property on the ground that the auction sale was effectual as against the interest of the third brother also, and that the two elder brothers were to be taken as representing him in the suit which had culminated in the decree against them. But the High Court ruled that the interests of the major and the minor brothers were distinct and separate ; that the minor brother's share had not been sold under a sale advertisement, which referred solely to the rights and interests of the two elder brothers; and that the elder brothers did not necessarily represent the minor brother, simply because the latter held undivided property with them. To the same effect are the observations of Loch, J, in Sree Prosad Sarmah *v.* Soroopah Dossia, 9 W. R., 452. "The judge has very unnecessarily gone into the question whether the debt for which the property was sold was contracted for the benefit of the family, or only for the benefit of the judgment-debtor, Bhyrub Chunder. * * * It was joint family property, and as such, Bhyrub Chunder was entitled only to a moiety. The auction purchaser can obtain no more than the rights and interests of Bhyrub Chunder." Sir Barnes Peacock has held that a managing member, who simply receives the rents, is not authorized to sell the property of an adult member of the family.[1] But this rule seems to be confined to those cases where the managing member sells family property without the consent of the others, in the absence of a legal necessity for the sale. When such a necessity actually exists, the sale by a managing member is valid to the extent of the whole property. The rule is founded on the principle that where a legal necessity exists, there is an implied consent on the part of the other members authorizing the manager to make the alienation. The rule is supported by express texts showing that even a single parcener can sell or pledge or give immoveable property during distress, or for the general purposes of the family, or for the performance of religious duties. Thus para. 26, ch. 2, Jīmūta's Dāyabhāga says:—"If, however, the

1. Koylasseshwar Bose *v.* Srimati Narainee Dossee, 10 W. R., 303.

family cannot be maintained without selling the whole immoveable property then it tacitly follows that the sale of the whole immoveable property would be valid. Since the Veda prescribes that one must at all events preserve himself." This para. is but a paraphrase of the Ṛṣi text cited in para. 28, sec. 1, ch. I, Mitākṣāra. Jīmūta does not cite the text, nor expressly says that a single member can sell the whole; but the drift of the passage leads to that result.

Legal Necessity, What

Legal necessity is of various forms. All the indispensable religious ceremonies, the sacraments, such as marriage and the investiture with the sacred thread, the obsequies, the cremation, the periodical oblations to the manes, the ceremonies customary in the family, the subsistence of the family, the education of the yonger members, the payment of the ancestral debts, the giving of presents at particular seasons and on special occassions to the relatives, these and a thousand other causes of expenditure are constantly cropping up in a fairly prosperous Hindu joint family: All these are in the strict sense of the word, lawful necessities. An indigent family may evade meeting them ; but to do so lowers, the family in the eye of the caste and the kinsfolk. It is difficult to state a general rule for answering the question, whether a given expenditure is a legal necessity or not. To one acquainted with the inner life of Hindu families, it would be at once clear whether any particular instance of family expenditure is proper or not; he would know it instinetively; while no explanation can enable one not so acquainted to find out what are legal necessities, and what are not. Ancestral debts, however, or debts contracted by any one of the family for some common benefit, or to meet some common exigency, are conceded on all hands to be such legal necessities as would justify the alienation of joint property. In one case the widow of one member claimed her husband's proper share in some property which had been purchased in the name of her husband's uncle, had been all along in the said uncle's possession, and had been sold by him to a person unconnected with the family. It was found that the property belonged to the joint family, but that the consideration money for the sale, paid by the afore said purchaser, had been applied for the purposes of the joint estate. The High Court held that this fact was sufficient to protect the purchaser from the claim of the widow; that the whole property including her husband's share in it had passed by the act of alienation on the part of her husband's uncle, and that this was clearly a case of joint family property having been sold on account of legal necessity.[1]

Alienation under Mitāksharā as administered by Calcutta High Cout, when valid

I now come to the law of alienation under the Mitākṣarā system as administered by the High Court of Calcutta. On this part of the law relating to joint families, the Mithila School does not stand, out as distinct from the Mitākṣarā doctrine; many of the cases I shall here notice came from the District of Tirhoot, yet they may be safely taken as illustrative of the Mitāksharā Law. In that treatise the rules regarding alienation of joint property are found in ch. 1, all that has been said by Vijnāna on this topic being in connection with his disquisition on on the nature of ownership. The passage forms paras. 27-30 in ch. 1, sec. 1, Colebrooke's Mitākṣarā. As this is an important portion of the work of Vijñāna, containing almost all the principles applied to questions regarding the alienation of joint family property, I shall first translate it, in my own way, and then add such explanations as may be necessary.

"Therefore ownership is by birth in the paternal property, and in that of the grandfather. Nevertheless, there

---

1. Koylash Kaminee Dossee *v.* Tarinee Churn Bose, 20 W. R. 100.

is independence on the part of the father, in making use of property other than immoveable, on the occasion of indispensable religious ceremonies, making gifts of favour, maintaining the family, relieving distress, and so forth, such as are enjoined in the texts. This is settled. But as regards immoveable property, self-acquired or received from the forefathers, there is dependence upon, the sons etc. 'Immoveable property and slaves, although acquired by one's own self, cannot be given or sold, without convening all the sons. Those that are born, those that are not born, those that are lying in the womb—they expect subsistence—there can be no gift or sale.' To this there is an exception. 'Even a single person may effect a gift, or a pledge, or a sale in respect of immoveable property; in time of distress, for family purposes, and specially for religious purposes.' The meaning hereof is:—Where sons and grandson are minors, and incompetent to consent, or where brothers are so—though they be undivided—when there is distress affecting the whole family, and for maintenance thereof, and for the indispensable oblations to father and so forth, even a single competent person may make a gift or pledge or sale of immoveable property. This is the sense. But there is this text of Manu:—'Whether undivided or divided, sapiṇḍas are equal in respect of immoveable property. For a single person is in every case incompetent to make a gift or pledge or sale.' This also should be thus interpreted. Where they are undivided, since the property is common, and since a single person is not the proprietor, permission must be given by all; but where they are divided, in order that in future there may be facility of transactions (or of litigation), by removing doubts as to whether the property was divided or undivided, permission is given by all; not because a single person is not the proprietor. Therefore, even without the permission of the divided parcener, the transaction is no doubt valid."

To the above I subjoin paras. 9 and 10, sec. 5, ch. I.

"When an undivided father gives or sells grandfather's property the grandson is competent to interdict the same. But in respect of father's self acquisitions, there is no competency to interdict, because there is dependence upon him; but permission ought to be given. That is to say:— Although ownership is by birth in the paternal property, and in that of the grandfather; yet, since there is dependence on the father in respect of father's self-acquisitions, and since there is superiority in the father on account of his being the acquirer,—when a father disposes of his self-acquisitions, the sons ought to give permission. In respect, however, of grandfather's property the ownership of both is undistinguishable— thus there is a right to prohibit. This is the distinction."

The decision of the High Courts in by far the greater majority of cases involving the question of alienation may be looked upon as a running commentary upon the above passage of the Mitākṣarā; there is some conflict in them, but is has arisen because one decision gives greater prominence to one part of the above passage, and another decision opposed to it has done so to another part. In one case the father had made alienations to pay the family debts, and also for its maintenance, but there was an adult son whose consent had not been obtained. The High Court says:—"The son's power of interdiction to prevent alienations by the father ancestral estate extends to acts of dissipation or waste of the property only, and not to alienations for the payment of joint family debts and for the maintenance of the family. We fail to see why it should be legal for a father, to alienate for legal necessity, where a minor son exists, who cannot protect his interests, but illegal where there is a son who has arrived at majority; and can exercise the power of interdiction if the father commits waste, but fails to do so and stands by and allows innocent purchasers to give a good consideration for the property.[1] Somewhat opposed to

1. Bisambhur Naik *v.* Sudaseeb Mohapattur, 1 W. R., 96.

the above might seem to be the remarks of Mitter, J., in Aproop Tewaree *v.* Kandhjee Sahay, 8 C. L. R. 194. There the father had mortgaged the family property at a time when his son had arrived at majority. Mitter, J. held that if the mortgage was for the payment of an antecedent debt of the father himself, that would be a good legal necessity with in the meaning of the Mitākṣarā; but still family property could not be validly pledged without the consent of an adult son, even where there was a good legal necessity. He lays stress upon that portion of the Mitāksharā passage wherein it is said that the father can alienate for indispensable purposes independently of sons, and grandsons when the latter are not of age, and therefore unable to give their consent. From this it follows that when sons and grandsons have arrived at majority, even indispensable family necessities would not justify the father in making an alienation irrespective of their consent or permission. But Mitter, J. concludes his judgement by saying that consent is of two kinds, express and implied; law implies a consent on the part of the son, if he has stood by, and allowed the alienation to take place without protest. In such a case, a principle more general in its application than the rules of Hindu Law, comes into operation : inasmuch as conduct of the kind on the part of the son naturally creates a belief in the mind of the alience that the father was acting with his son's consent by omitting to protest or to exercise his right of interdiction, the son is prevented by the law of estoppel from contending afterwards that he did not give his content.

Purchaser bound to enquire as to legal necessity

An important rule for testing the validity of an alienation of joint family property is to see how far the conduct of the purchaser was guided by good faith. All alienations, whether in the form of a sale, or mortgage, or gift, or a permanent lease, are good if there is a legal necessity. But sometimes the actual existence of a legal necessity is not indispensable for the validity of the alienation. If the purchaser acts in good faith, if he makes enquiry as to whether the alienation was caused by family exigencies, if he satisfies himself that it is for the benefit of the family, or of the estate, and if he exercises such caution and diligence as would be exercised by a person of ordinary prudence in conducting his own affairs, then the real existence of an alleged, sufficient and reasonably credited necessity is not condition precedent to the validity of the alienation.[1] This rule was laid down with reference to the mortgage of an infant's estate effected by his guardian and manager. But courts of justice have extended it to the alienation of joint property by the head of the family.[2] Where a legal necessity really exists, as for instance where debts were at first incurred for the due performance of marriage and for funeral expenses, and then ancestral land has been sold by the undivided father for paying off the debts, the purchaser is protected in his purchase, although the father having borrowed the money ostensibly for the above purpose, may have wasted it and neglect appropriate it to the purpose for which it had been borrowed; the title of the lender is not vitiated because he does not see to the application of his money. In such cases both the lender on mortgage of joint property and the purchaser of it stand on the same footing; for the text of the Mitākṣarā places in the same category all forms of alienation, whether a sale, or a gift or a mortage.

Śrādh a Necessity

The expenses incurred for celebrating the *śrādh* of the father's grandmother has been held to be a good legal necessity, so as to justify him in burdening the family property. If the purchaser sees that family property has been

1. Honnoman Prosad Panday *v.* Muss. Babooi Munraj Kooer,6 Moore, I. A. 393.
2. Jugdel Narain Suhai *v.* Lalla Ramprakash, 2 W. R. 292.

attached under a decree against the father; if he finds that there are bonds payable by the father for such debts, or for reasonable expenses of litigation in which the father was involved, he is quite justified in advancing money and purchasing the property either at a court sale, or by private transfer.[1] But although the validity of the purchase does not require the actual existence of necessity, the purchaser is bound to prove by proper evidence that by enquiries made in good faith, he was led to believe that the sales were necessary. Neither such a belief, nor the existence of the necessity itself, will be taken for granted by a court, simply because certain old bonds and deeds of mortgage affecting the family property are forthcoming. Such documents are not a sufficient reason for a purchaser to conclude that loans or sales of family property were necessary to pay off the debts secured by those documents; nor are such documents any evidence of the existence of the debts they purport to secure.[2]

The purchaser is not bound to enquire as to the original necessity for a particular loan, for the payment of which the joint property is sold to him. In one case other joint properties had been in mortgage, and a notice of foreclosure had been issued. This was held a sufficient justification for the purchaser to purchase from the father.[3] The substance of what Macpherson, J. observed is;—"In this particular instance the lender or rather the purchaser did ascertain that there was a certain debt due, that notice of foreclosure had been issued, that the year of grace was just about to expire, and that he satisfied himself of the necessity for the debt incurred with reference to parties with whom he was dealing. The purchasers were not bound to go further, to travel back to the time when the original loan: on mortgage was contracted, or to have enquired into the original object

1. Muss. Bhoorun Kooer *v.* Shahebzadee, 6 W. R. 149.
2. Muss. Nowruttom Kooer *v.* Babu Gouree Dutt Sing, 6 W. R. 193.
3. Babu Luchmcedhar Sing *v.* Ekbal Ali, 6 W. R. 75.

for which the money was borrowed. It would be unreasonable to impose any such duty on the purchaser. It is not necessary for him to go back to enquire into the primary origin of the necessity for the mortgage he finds about to be foreclosed, and which may be of many years standing. If he must go back and enquire to the causes which led to the giving of the mortgage, the probabalities are, it would be equally necessary for him to go further back still and enquire into the causes which form the first foundation of the necessity for raising money, which ultimately resulted in the necesaity which led to the mortgage. The rights of the members of a joint family are sufficiently protected if the rule laid down in Hanooman Persad's case be strictly applied.[1]

Macpherson, J. lays down in this case another, principle with regard to the sale of joint property on account of legal necessity. He says, that only so much of the property should be sold as will meet the necessity; if a larger portion than is required is sold, it must be shown by the purchaser that the money required to pay off the claim could not be otherwise raised. But this rule does not apply to cases where the excess is comparatively small, or where the money really required could not be raised otherwise than by the course adopted.

In one case decrees had been obtained against the grandfather who had confessed judgment, and sales had taken place in execution of those decrees; the High Court held that the purchasers were not protected against the claim of the grandson; that there being no other evidence as to the existence of the grandfather's debts except judgments on confession, the case was distinguishable from the case where notice of foreclosure had been issued.[2]

But this case does not seem to give sufficient

1. See also Mahabeeer Kooer *v.* Joobha Sing, 16 W. R. 221.
2. Brojo Kishore Gojendar Mohapattur *v.* Hori Kissen Doss, 10 W. R. 57.

prominence to the rule laid down by the Judicial Committee in Honooman Prosad's case, namely, that honest conduct and enquiry on the part of the purchaser will protect him, and that the real existence of an alleged, sufficient and reasonably accredited necessity is not a condition precedent to the validity of the purchase, and that the purchaser has nothing to do with the application of the purchase money advanced by him. This rule was applied by Sir Barnes Peacock in Rajaram Tewaree *v.* Luchman Pershad, 12 W. R. 478, who says[1]:— "If the plaintiff case were sustainable in other respects; it would be necessary to direct issues as to whether the persons who advanced money to Jeetun and Oodit, upon the security of the lands, or for the purchase of them; did, after due enquiry into the necessities of the father and the uncle of the plaintiffs, act honestly in the belief that a sufficient necessity for taking up the money for the benefit of the family existed." Again:[2]—"It was for the defendants (purchasers) to prove that a legal necessity for taking up the money existed, or that after due and honest inquiry they had reason to believe that such a necessity did exist." The existence of decrees against the grandfather, if ascertained by the purchaser, should therefore be a sufficient justification for him to make the purchase, and should absolve him from the duty of making any further enquiry as to whether the decrees were founded upon actually existing debts, or were collusive ones. Rajaram Tewaree's case also lays down this other rule, that where a larger sum of money is borrowed or raised than is required for meeting the legal necessity, and a larger portion of the estate than is necessary for the purpose of raising the money legally required is sold or mortgaged, the purchasers or mortgagees are entitled to a charge upon the lands mortagaged or sold to the extent of the money required and taken up for purposes which would justify an alienation of

1. p. 480, Column 1.
2. p. 481, Column 1, last para.

joint family property. Thus if money be required for the purpose of celebrating the grandfather's *shrad,* and if according to what has been customary in the family and would be suitable to its rank and position, Rs. 5000 would be enough; but if the managing member or members borrowed or raised by sale Rs. 10,000, the rule says that in either case the property should be considered by a Court of Justice as having been validly hypothecated for Rs. 5000, on payment of which sum any member of the joint family would be entitled to recover the property from the hand of the purchaser, where there has been an out and out sale by the managing member. Or if they have mortgaged joint family property and have received Rs . 10,000, any member may pay Rs. 5,000, the sum actually required, and thereby the property would be set free from the burden. It follows therefore that the purchaser or mortgagee must not only ascertain that the necessity exists, but also the amount reasonably required : if he fails to make this latter enquiry, for all that he knows a part of the money advanced by him will be insecure.

Alientìon of even a single share invalid

The main principle laid down by Sir Barnes Peacock in the above case, however, is that when one member seeks to set aside alienations of joint property on the ground that there was no legal necessity, the suit must implead all the coparceners interested in the property. If all cannot be induced to join as plaintiffs, those unwilling must be made defendants; and the property must be treated as a whole belonging to all the coparceners jointly, and not as made up of so many shares belonging severally to the individual members. For Sir Barnes more than once emphasizes upon the doctrine, that joint coparceners have no definite fractional shares, but are unitedly entitled to the whole.

But auction sale for debt valid

This doctrine, upon which is founded the rule that the

alienation of a single member's share is not allowed by law, has been somewhat obscured by recent decisions upholding auction sales of individual shares in joint family property. Thus in the Privy Council case of Deen Dyal Lal *v.* Jugdeep Narain Sing, I. L. R. 3 Cal., 198, the father had mortgaged joint family property without the consent of his undivided son, a decree had been obtained upon the mortage bond, and in execution, the right, title and interest of the father in the property was sold by auction. One of the the questions was whether the auction purchaser had purchased anything, regard being had to the Mitākṣarā rule, according to which the father could not be said to have had a definite and distinct share in the family property, such as could be separately laid hold and taken possession of either by himself or by any one standing in his shoes as purchaser of his rights. The Judicial Committee held that the purchaser had acquired a valid title to the extent of the father's share, and that he, as occupying the father's position with regard to the latter's right in the property, was entitled to demand a partition of the father's share from the son. According to the Mitākṣarā as administered in the Province of Bengal, the Privy Council say, there is a distinction between a voluntary conveyance and the enforced auction sale by a court in execution of a decree. The distinction between the rights of a purchaser under a voluntary, conveyance and those of a purchaser under an execution sale are nice; but there are such distinctions. Thus in a trading partnership, the separate creditor of one of the partners may bring a suit and obtain a decree against his debtor, and in execution may seize and sell his debtor's share in the partnership. The effect of such a proceeding is that the purchaser of the share in the trading partnership becomes entitled to have the partnership accounts taken in order to realize and ascertain its value, for he has acquired by execution sale the interest of that member of the partnership against whom the decree had been obtained, although that member could not himself sold his share so as to introduce a stranger into the firm without the consent of his copartners.

This principle, whereby the old Mitākṣarā doctrine of aggregate ownership was trenched upon, seems to have been first introduced into our judge-made law by Phear, J. in Mohabeer Pershad v. Ramyad Sing, 12 B. L.R. 90. (S. C. 20 W. R. 192.) There the father had occasion for money in order to obtain what he considered would be a profitable lease of certain landed property; this money the father procured by mortgaging joint family property. The lease obtained did not prove profitable; the mortgagee obtained a decree upon the loan, and in execution himself became the purchaser of the joint family property. Then some of the sons sued for reversal of the sale on the ground that the sale of joint property by a single member without legal necessity and without the consent of all the members of the family was void under the law. Phear, J. in delivering judgment, observes, that the propositions of law which are clear and beyond all doubt are:—(1) that joint property may be mortgaged or sold if all the members interested in it join in the transaction, or otherwise testify their consent to it; (2) that a single member, or the manager can alienate the whole, if there is a legal necessity for such alienation; (3) that if the alienation be made by some of the members without legal necessity, and that if still benefits have been derived by all the members from the results of the act of alienation effected by some only of the members, then the money advanced by the alience would be a valid charge upon the whole joint property, and an attempt to recover it must be accompanied by a refund of that money; (4) that an alienation of joint property by some only of the members is invalid *in toto*, so as not even to pass their individual and particular shares in the property; (5) but that the alienee shall have a right to insist upon his vendors' share being called into existence by partition, in which partition all the members of the family shall get their proper fractional shares according to Law, and that even a female member who is entitled to get a share on the occasion of a voluntary family partition, shall receive her legal share on the occasion of a compulsory partition directed by an equitable decree of a court of justice. The equitable principle upon which the compulsory judicial partition, brought about not at the instance of a co-sharer, but by Court with a view to protect the interests of a third party who has advanced money upon the security of joint property, has been thus set forth in the above decision :—The father no doubt is incapable of alienating his own individual share in joint property. But he can demand partition at any time. Now when a stranger takes a deed of mortgage or a bill of sale from the father alone, the law no doubt is bound to declare such a mortgage or sale dull and void. But if the law unconditionally makes a declaration of that the result will be that the property mortgaged or conveyed will come into the hands of the joint family again, and will be again enjoyed by the very same father as manager of the family, who once pocketed an amount of money from a stranger, which was considered as equivalent for that same property. This would be palpably repugnant to all rules of equity and good conscience. What the law therefore does in such a case is that, at the same time that it declares the alienation void, it compels the father to ask for a partition, and it declares a lien upon the father's divided share for such a sum of money as was advanced or paid as price by the stranger to whom it was mortgaged or sold. This rule is not confined to the father alone; it extends also to the share of any other member who may have consented to the alienation, either by executing the deed of alienation, or by being present on the occasion, or by otherwise actively promoting the transaction.

This principle, having now received the imprimatur of the Judicial Committee, has become an elemenatary one in the joint family law, and is acted upon in cases to which it is applicable. Thus in Roy Narain Doss v. Nownit Lall, 4 C. L. R., 57, the son had contracted a debt, which was not proved to have any way benefited the family; the creditor obtained a decree against , the son and attached joint family property in execution, whereupon the father as manager sued to have the attachment removed, upon the ground, that ancestral and undivided property could not be sold for a debt contracted by a single member for purposes not amounting to a legal necessity. The High Court applied the rule established in Deen Dyal's case, and observed that the only difference between Deen Dyal's case and the case before them was that in the former the father had contracted the debt, in the latter it was the son's liability which was in question. This difference did not prevent the application of the rule, and the son's particular share in the joint family property which had been attached by the decree-holder was liable to be sold. The judges also mentioned an unreported case, Special Appeal No. 2038 of 1877, in which it had been decided by Jackson and Tottenham, JJ., that a son's interest in joint Mitākṣarā property could be sold for a decree against him on account of a debt contracted by him alone.

It seems now therefore to be settled law that the share of a member in the family property may be sold in execution of a money decree against him. The rule has now assumed a definite form which it never had before. But its germ is discernible in one or two comparatively early decisions. In Goor Surun Doss *v.* Ramsurn Bhukut 5 W. R. 54, the holder of a decree for money against some of the sons of an undivided Mitākṣarā family sought to sell their interest in the family property, and the High Court in upholding his right to do so, employed the very same arguments which were long afterwards used by Phear, J. in Moha Beer Prosad's case. This was in 1866, and it seems that at that date the rule of law declaring a Mitākṣarā son's right to be co-ordinate with that of the father in ancestral property had not established itself so firmly as it has since done ; for the judges use language calculated to lead one to suppose as if they were laying down some proposition not generally known. They say:—" The decree-holder appeals and urges that according to the Mitākṣarā system of Law, sons have from the first a vested interest in the ancestral property, and that such interest is saleable at any time. There can be no doubt that this is a correct exposition of the law as it prevails under the Mitākṣarā system, and that sons can at their pleasure force a father, however reluctant, to divide with them property obtained from a paternal grandfather. This right accrues to a son from the time of his birth, and is not, therefore, contingent on the father's death, or upon any uncertain event; it is a vested right claimable at any time during the father's life. It may be that no case of the kind is to be found in our books; but the principle is indubitable, and we have no hesitation in declaring it. * *We declare the sons to have a vested right in the ancestral property, which is liable to sale in satisfaction of any claims against them."

There is no express text in the Mitākṣarā declaring that in undivided property one member cannot alienate his own particular share. What that work expressly says is that the whole joint property cannot be alienated by one member without the consent of all, except in case of a legal necessity. But the definition of 'partition' contained in para. 4, sec. 1, ch. I, leaves no doubt that every member's right extends over the entire joint property; his right over any particular share of it does not come into existence before a partition is effected. This fractional right is a non-existent entity then; how can a non-existent entity be sold or mortgaged, or made a gift of? This is how I believe it is argued that the Mitākṣarā doctrine of aggregate ownership does not favour the alienation of fractional shares in joint property. As early as 1867, the High Court of Calcutta decided that a single member cannot make a valid alienation even to the extent of his own share.[1] One of three brothers had sold property

1. Muss. Bona Koeree *v.* Baboo Boole Sing, 8 W. R. 182.

which seems to have been acquired out of ancestral funds. The judges of the High Court quoted the observations of the Judicial Committee in Appoovier's case,[1] and held that as manager and trustee of the younger minor brothers, if he invested the proceeds of the joint ancestral estate in the purchase of other estates, he did so for the benefit of the joint family; without the consent of all, or a legal necessity, or a declaration and acts amounting to a division, he could not alienate so as to bind even his own share. In a still earlier case, Mr. Lewis Cosserat *v.* Sudaburt Pershad Sahoo, 3 W. R. 210, the judges say:–"By the Mitākṣarā, all the members of the joint family have a continuing interest in the whole of the family estate; one member cannot alienate even his own share without the consent of all; and nothing but the most urgent necessity legalizes any transfer to a third party. Each member has a life-interest and no more in the property–an interest which he can neither give away during his lifetime nor will away after his death, but which must go to the survivors of the joint family." Previous to the decision of Appoovier's case by the Judicial Committee, it had not been so distinctly laid down that a member in a joint Mitākṣarā family had no definite fractional share in the joint property, and the inalienability of a single member's share had not been founded upon this principle. It was Sir Barnes Peacock who appealed to that principle, in order to establish the rule that the share of a single member was inalienable. This was done in the Full Bench case of Sadaburt Pershad Sahoo *v.* Fool Bash Kooer, 12 W. R. F. B. 1. Sir Barnes in his judgment referred to a number of early cases, the earliest of which was decided in 1823, and which laid down on the authority of the Vyavasthas of Pandits that a, gift or other alienation of undivided property, real or personal, was not valid, even to the extent of the alienor's share. Sir Barnes also cited Appoovier's case, which rules that no individual member can predicate of the undivided

1. 11 Moore's, I. A. 75.

property that he, that particular member, has a certain definite share. He says:—"Whatever our opinions might be in the absence of the decided cases to which I have referred, I am of opinion that we should not be justified in unsettling the law by overruling that current of authorities by which or nearly half a century the law appears to have been settled, and in accordance with the principles of which it appears to have been understood and acted upon." The conclusion arrived at by the Full Bench was, that a member of a joint family governed by the Mitākṣarā cannot mortgage his undivided share in a portion of the joint family property, in order to raise money on his own account, and not for the benefit of the family.

It ought to be borne in mind that the decision of the Full Bench has not yet received the sanction of the Privy Council, although there was an appeal to England from that decision. The Judicial Committee carefully guard against expressing their assent to the proposition of law established by Sir Barnes, saying:—"They abstain from pronouncing any opinion upon the grave question of Hindu Law involved in the answer of the Full Bench to the second point referred to them, a question, which, the appeal coming on *ex parte*, could not be fully or properly argued before them. That question must continue to stand, as it now stands, upon the authorities, unaffected by the judgment in, this appeal."[1]

The rule, however, that a single member's share is not alienable was acted upon in Nuthoo Lall Chowdry *v.* Chedee Sahee, 12 W. R. 446, where some of the sons and grandsons sued to set aside sales of family property which had been effected by their father and grandfather, upon the usual ground of absence of necessity and absence of consent on the part of all. The High Court held that the sales were null, because the family had not benefited by them, and that it was not necessary to refund any part of the purchase

1. Fool Bash Kooer *v.* Lalla Jogeswar Sahay, I.L.R. 1 Cal., p. 248.

money. Here originally the sale was a private one, to a stranger; but then a second stranger had purchased in execution the right, title and interest of the first vendee, and it was the second purchaser who was forced to give back the property to the family, without receiving any portion of the purchase money. It was contended on his part that at least the father's share had passed, and also that of an adult son, who might have entered a protest against the father's act of alienation, and whose consent the law ought to imply from his having failed to object. But the High Court said that although his silence might be construed into a consent, yet that consent alone was not sufficient to render the transfer valid, since at the date of sale there were other minor members, whose consent not be inferred from silence, and since according to the Mitākṣarā, the consent of all the members was indispensable to validate the alienation of even a single share. To the argument that it was a hardship that an innocent purchaser should lose both his money and also the property for which he had parted with it, the High Court replied that he had every opportunity of making enquiry and must have known the danger of purchasing an interest which had been originally bought from a single member of a joint undivided family living under the Mitākṣarā Law. The High Court also pointed out that it was no good legal necessity if the father had stood security for a farmer of Government revenue, and had to meet in consequence thereof a demand of Government, with which the concerns of the family had nothing to do, but which was the cause of the sale by the father.

In Honooman Dutt Roy *v.* Bhagbut Kishen, 15 W. R F.B. 6, the rule was further confirmed, and it was laid down, by another Full Bench, that where alienation was made by a father of joint ancestral property in a case in which no legal necessity existed, it could not be treated as an alienation of the father's separate share; that a son suing to set it aside was entitled to a declaration that it was void, inclusive of the father's share. Here alienations were made by the father by way of private conveyance; so far therefore the decision does not conflict with the judgment of Phear, J. in Mohabeer Pershad's case, 12 B. L. R. 90. But, a later decision of Chief Justice Couch in Kalee Podo Banerjee *v.* Chaitan Pandah, 22 W. R. 214, which was a case from the District of Cuttack and therefore governed by, the Mitākṣarā, is in conflict with the principle propounded by Phear, J. Couch, C. J. says:—"There was a purchase by the plaintiffs of the right, title and interest of some of the members of a joint Hindu family in property admitted to be joint ancestial property, and there is no evidence of any transaction which would amount to a partition. The question is whether the sale in execution of a decree against some of the members of the interest of those persons in the family property can be supported where the family is governed by the Mitākṣarā Law. The grounds upon which the judgment of the Court in the Full Bench decision was rested, apply to a sale in execution." He then refers to the case of Jugdeep Narain Sing *v.*, Deen Dyal Lall, 20 W. R. 174, as an authority for holding such a sale void. But it was in appeal (I. L. R. 3 Cal. 198) from this very case that the Privy Council adopted the principle propounded by Phear, J. in Mohabeer Prosad's case. (20 W. R. 192.) They drew a distinction between a voluntary conveyance and a sale in execution of a decree, and expressed their dissent from the opinion of Phear, J., who had attempted to distinguish the two cases of Deen Dyal and Mohabeer Prosad on the following grounds. In Deen Dyal's case, the property sold in execution had not been originally mortgaged by the father to secure the debt contracted by him; whereas in, Mohabeer Prosad's case, the property given in security was ordered by the decree to be sold in execution. This distinction, according to Phear, J., was of, importance; for if the father pledges joint property, and then it is sold by order of the court to realize the creaditor's money, the father may be said to have made a false representation to the creditor; to have led the creditor to believe that the security offered was valid; therefore the creditor can insist upon the father's right of demanding a partition being exercised by him; he can urge that at least the security should be valid to the extent of the father's share. On the contrary, if property not pledged by the father be sold in execution of a decree against him, there was no false representation; therefore, the creditor has no right to insist upon the conversion of what is joint property into divided property. Such a right can be claimed by the creditor only if he can show that there is no other means of enforcing his decree against the father except by seizing family property. But the Privy Council say (I. L. R. 3 Cal., 198) that the hypothecation of the property sold in execution does not improve the position of the creditor, since the very act of hypothecation involves the violation of the rule laid down in Sadabrat Prosad's case. The judgment of the Chief Justice Couch in the case reported in 22 W. R. 214 must therefore be taken as overruled by the Privy Council, since Couch, C. J. relied upon the authority of judgment which was upset in appeal by the Judical Committee.

Reasons for the invalidity of a single member's share

The authorities which have established that the voluntary conveyance of a single member's share is invalid, ground the rule chiefly upon Appoovier'a case, (8 W. R. P. R. 1) and set forth the reason to be this, that the share of a single member not being defined, nothing can pass. It is difficult to see how the sale of a single share can be valid simply because there was legal necessity for it. At the same time I find that it has been so held in Juggarnath Khootia *v.* Doobo Mistier, 14 W. R. 80. The judges observe that the Full Bench case of Sudabart Pershad does not by any means go to the length of ruling that even legal necessity would not justify the private sale of an undivided share; that a member cannot, without the consent of his co-sharers, pledge, far less sell, his share to raise money on his own accounts; but that if the sale or pledge is executed to liquidate which are just and proper according to the principles of Hindu Law, it is valid even to the extent of a single member's share.

Refund of purchase money when necessary, in setting aside alienation of joint property

Although the rule therefore has now been established that a member can set aside a voluntary conveyance of joint property by another member, so as to leave the purchaser no benefit out of the act of alienation, some cases have added a qualification to the rule, that if the sale has benefited the joint family or joint estate, it should be set aside on the condition that a refund be made to purchaser to the extent of the benefit received. The member who seeks to set aside the sale has no right to ask that is should be set aside unconditionally. The law goes even so far, according to Norman, C. J., that the Court should presume the purchase money to have, benefited the family. This was held where a son sought to set aside his father's sale. If the son can show that he or the family or the joint estate did not receive any benefit from the transaction objected to by him, if he proves that no part of such purchase money, or the produce of it, ever reached his hands, the sale will be absolutely set aside. In the absence of such evidence, however, it must be assumed that the price received by the father became a part of the assets of the joint family; the son therefore seeking the aid of the court to set the purchase aside, must do equity, and offer to repay the purchase money.[1]

This rule, however, was dissented from by Kemp and Glover, JJ. in the Full Bench cast of Modhoo Dyal Sing *v.* Golbur Sing, 9 W. R. 511. The purport of what they say as

1. Muddon Gopal Thakoor *v.* Rambuksh Pandey, 6 W. R. 71.

follows:–A long current of decisions has settled that a father under the Mitākṣarā Law cannot alienate ancestral property without the consent of his son, unless for certain necessary purposes. In all other cases the son has an absolute veto on the sale, and must succeed in a suit to set it aside. Where there was no necessity and no acquiescence on the part of the son, there is no reason or equity which entitles the purchaser to receive his purchase money from the son. This is clear in the case of an imprudent sale, absolutely uncalled for, which no man of sense would make, and from which no member of the family derived any benefit. Even if it be not so, still the son has an absolute right to set aside his father's alienation, and is not bound to refund to the purchasers, in order to set aside imprudent or unnecessary sales. If he be compelled to make a refund, then he gets back the property, not on his joint right as son, but because he pays money for property which was already his. If the son be a man of substance, he will get it back; but a poor man will lose his undoubted right under the Mitākṣarā Law. The maxim of 'caveat emptor' should be rigidly applied in cases of this character. Every purchaser in a District governed by the Mitākṣarā Law knows or ought to know perfectly well what the father's rights are in ancestral property. If the purchaser choose to buy such property without securing the consent of all interested in it, or without assuring himself that there was a legal necessity for the sale, he has himself to blame if the son recovers the property from him, and if he loses both the money and its equivalent—The point referred to the Full Bench was whether a son can recover joint property sold by his father without necessity and without his consent or acquiescence, unconditionally, is he bound to refund the purchase money. The judgement of the Full Bench was delivered by Sir Barnes Peacock; its substance may be stated as follows:— In the absence of proof of circumstances giving the purchaser an equitable right to compel a refund from the son, the latter would recover without refunding the purchase money or any part of it. If it be proved that the money was carried to the assets of the joint estate, and that the son had the benefit of his share of it, he cannot recover his share of the estate without refunding his share of the money. If it be proved that the sale was effected for the purpose of paying off a valid incumbrance on the estate was binding upon the son, and the purchase-money was applied in freeing the estate which from the incumbrance, the purchaser would stand in the place of the incumbrancer, notwithstanding the incumbrance might be such that the incumbrancer could not have compelled its immediate discharge, as for instance where the mortgage term has still some years to run before the right to redeem is put an end to. In such a case the son shall recover the ancestral property or his share of it, subject to the right of the purchaser to stand in the place of the incumbrancer. Sir Barnes expressed his dissent from the opinion of Norman, J., who had held that in absence of evidence to the contrary, it was to be presumed that the purchase money went to the benefit of the son. According to Sir Barnes, the *onus* lies upon the purchaser to show that the son was benefited; since the father is not entitled to sell in absence of legal necessity—such absence entitles the son to set the sale aside and to recover the property back to the family. If it appears that the son consented to take the benefit of the purchase money with the knowledge of all the facts, it would be evidence of the son's acquiescence in the sale.

The rule making it obligatory upon the son to refund the purchase money or a portion of it is illustrated in the case of Mothoora Koonwaree *v.* Bootun Sing, 13 W. R. 30. There the father had to mortgage joint property for paying off debts he had previously incurred for the support of the family. The mortgage was of the zur-i-peshgee character. After the property had been for some years in the possession of the zur-i-peshgeedar, the debt was not cleared off by the proceeds of the usufruct, whereupon the father saw fit to sell half of the mortgaged property in order to pay off the mortgage debt; this, however, was done without taking the consent of his sons. One of the sons sued for setting aside the sale; the suit was decreed in his favour to the extent of his own particular share, *viz.*, onefourth out of the whole; at the same time the decree directed that the son should pay to the purchaser one-fourth share of the. purchase money, since the son's one-fourth share of the property had been benefited to that extent by being freed from the prior burdens which had been discharged by means of the said purchase money. The rule of refund is further illustrated in the case of Bhyro Prosad *v.* Bosisto Narain Panday, 16 W. R. 31, where the father's share in the family property was sold in execution of a money decree against him, but the sale proceeds went to satisfy another judgment debt which had its origin in the payment of the Government revenue of joint property, such payment having been made by the father. The High Court set aside the execution sale of even the father's share, inasmuch as under Appoovier's case the father had no definite share ; and because even a single member's share could not be sold without consent and without necessity. But the High Court directed that the sons should pay to the execution purchasers as much money as went to the liquidation of the debt for Government Revenue for which the joint property had been liable. The High Court also held that since the decree, in execution of which the father's share was sold, was not based upon the liability for the Government Revenue, the execution sale could not be supported on the ground of necessity. But the refund was equitable, inasmuch as the sons had been benefited by the sale proceeds, which for the most part went to satisfy the prior decree based upon the debt for Government Revenue. This case was decided, and in fact many of the cases I have noticed in this Lecture were decided before the decision of

Giridhari Lal's case, 22 W . R. 56, which I shall have to notice at length in my next Lecture. If some of these decisions of the Calcutta High Court had been of a later date, I doubt whether the sale by father would have been set aside at the instance of the sons.

Law of alienation under Allahabad High Court

The law relating to the alienation of joint property, as administered by the High Court of Allahabad, has followed in the footsteps of the Calcutta High Court. As early as 1860, before the establishment of the High Court, the North-Western tribunals had recognized the principle that alienation of joint property by single member without the consent of all and without legal necessity was null and void. Those courts had also settled that such an alienation was invalid even to the extent of the share of the coparcener whose act the alienation was. But where the family is of the special form in which the father is the head and his own sons are his coparceners, the High Court of Allahabad has had regard to the principle of Giridhari Lal's case, which rules that sales for father's debts are valid unless the sons can show that the debts were for an illegal or an immoral purpose. If, however, the sons do succeed in showing it, then the old rule deducible from the text of the Mitākṣarā has its force, and not only do the sons get the sale set aside as regards their own particular shares, but even as regards the share belonging to the father. If it was a private conveyance, and if the father had no occasion for the money received from the purchaser, except for she purpose of spending it in vicious pleasures, then the purchaser, although not cognizant of the fact of the having been taken for those purposes, cannot yet demand to be placed in the position of the father, and ask for a partition of his share. The answer of the Allahabad High Court to such a contention on the part of the purchaser would be that by a reasonable enquiry, he might have ascertained for what purposes the father wanted the money; that a *bona fade* purchase is not constituted by payment of the consideration money alone, but requires as an ingredient that due care and caution be exercised in dealing with one only of a number of persons interested in the property about to be sold. In the matter of a voluntary or private conveyance, the Allahabad High Court says that the rule of Deen Dyal's case will not apply; for although the Judicial Committee do not expressly confine the rule to an execution sale, yet they point out a distinction between the two kinds of alienation, one public and compulsory, and superintended by a Court of Justice, the other private and voluntary and necessarily requiring more care, caution and circumspection on the part of the purchaser.[1]

In the passages I have quoted from the Mitākṣarā it will have been seen that gift is mentioned as one form of alienation. A gift is valid if made to meet a legal necessity, or if made by all the coparceners in union, or by one with the consent of the rest, express or implied. It is invalid, if there is no legal necessity, or consent, or acquiescence, to the extent even of the donor's share. A gift becomes a legal necessity mostly on the occasion of marriage. When the daughter of a respectable Hindu family arrives at the marriageable age, it becomes the duty of the father or other managing member to find a suitable bridegroom for her. A suitable bridegroom often means one rather superior in his position in the caste to the family of the bride. Not to be able to secure such a bridegroom is derogatory to the members of the bride's family; they therefore generally try their utmost to find one. This requires expenditure of

1. See Chamaili Kuar *v.* Ramprasad, I. L. R. 2 All. 270; and also the prior North-West cases referred to in the judgment of Oldfield, J., namely, Ajodhya Pershad *v.* Lalta Pershad, S. D. A. N. W. P. 1864, vol. ii, p. 315; Baboo Ram *v.* Gajadhar Sing, N. W. P. H. C. Rep. F. B. R. 1866-67, p. 86; Byjnath Sing *v.* Rameshwar Dyal, S. D. A. N. W. P. 1864, vol. i. p. 299; Joy Naran Sing *v.* Roshan Sing, S. D. A. N. W. P. 1860, p. 162.

money. Every bridegroom, however high his position may be in the caste community—a position depending upon circustances connected with his descent from a particular line of forefathers,—has his price. Gift or large estates or large sums of money is the consideration for which a bridegroom condescends to honour a somewhat less esteemed family by giving his hand to a daughter of it. In a Mitākṣarā family, no son therefore can object to such gifts when they are made by the father on the occasion of a marriage. But in one case decided by the Allahabad High Court, the marriage had already taken place; two years after the marriage, the father redeemed a promise he had made at the time of the marriage, by giving some landed property out the joint estate, to the father of his son-in-law. At the instance of one of the sons, against whom was not proved that he had either consented or an acquiescence, the High Court set aside the expressed gift *in toto*, including even the father's share, observing that although the deed of gift was executed by the father in performance of a promise he had made to give a dowry to his daughter, yet the performance of such a promise could not be regarded as a lawful purpose justifying alienation under the Hindu Law. "Daughters must be maintained until their marriage, and the expenses of their marriage must be paid. In this case the gift was not made at the time of the marriage. It was not until two years after the marriage."[1] At first sight this decision seems to be opposed to the principle of Giridhari Lal's case; it is no doubt a pious duty on the part of the father to redeem a promise knowingly and solemnly made by himself; and it is equally a pious duty on the part of the sons to abstain raising impediments to the fulfilment of a such promise by the father. The promise also in the above case was not without a consideration. Possibly had it not been for such a promise, and had father of the bridegroom relied upon the honour of the bride's father, he might have withheld his

1. Ganga Bisheshar *v.* Pirthee Lal, I. L. R. 2 All. 636.

consent to the marriage. But I apprehend that the bridge degroom's father had made a serious omission, as he had not taken the precaution of binding the sons also by such a promise. Moreover, a marriage under the Hindu Law being an irrevocable act, the necessity had ceased after the marriage was over, and the sons therefore were under no legal obligation to make the gift. Had it been a real debt of the father in the proper sense of the terms, instead of being merely a debt of honour on his and had any money been received by the father part the principle of Giridhari Lal's case would have been applied, and the sons would have been made to the submit to the father's act of alienation.

In Ramanand *v.* Gobinda Sing, I. L. R. 5 All. 385. Allahabad High Court said:—The rule in the North Western Provinces has always been that one member of a joint and undivided Hindu family cannot mortgage or sell his own share without the consent, express or implied to be of his coparceners. Whatever may be the inference, drawn from the remarks of the Judicial Committee into two cases of Deen Dyal Lal and Suraj Bansee Kuer, we do not feel called upon to disturb a uniform and unbroken course of decisions, which have the advantage of being based on, and being in harmony with, the Mitākṣarā itself."This was a suit in which one member had mortgaged his interest in the undivided property, without the consent of the others, who sued to have a declaration that the mortgage was void. The High Court set it aside on the simple ground that joint family property could not be aliened by a single members. As in this case the mortgagor was not the father of the family, the application of the above simple rule was not complicated by any other principle, such as that the sons are bound to pay their father's debts. And as the mortgage was a private transaction, the principle of Deen Dyal's case, which upheld the execution sale of a single member's share, could not apply. Surj Bansi Kuer's case I shall have to notice at length in my next Lecture. At present it may suffice to say that there the execution sale of property which had been mortgaged by the Father four purposes not justified by law was upheld to the extent of a father's share. But being a case of execution its principle is inapplicable to a private alienation.

Alienation of joint property in Madras

In Madras the law of alienation differs widely from of the Mitākṣarā Districts of Bengal and the North-West. There although we find in the first volume of the Madras High Court Reports,[1] a case in which the Mitākṣarā doctrine that a single cannot effect a valid alienation was upheld, we are not sure whether there the conveyance to the extent of that coparcener's share would have been valid or not, if the grantee under the said conveyance had insisted upon receiving that share by partition. There,[2] one R. had conveyed all his property to his son-in-law. After his death his nephew contested the validity of the alienation upon the ground that he had been joint with his uncle and that undivided property could not be alienated by him alone. The High Courth simply held the conveyance to be invalid, inasmuch as the separation of R. from his brother had neither alleged nor proved. In 1863, the Madras High Cour held[3] the member of a joint family might alien the share of the family property, to which, if a partition took place, he would be entitled. Consequently it was ruled that a decree against a single member in an action for damages on tort, might be executed by attachment and sale of joint, family property to the extent of the judgment debtor's share. This ruling agrees principle with Deen Dyal's case; in fact, the Privy Council, in their judgment in Deen Dyal's case, reffered to this very case of the Madras High Court in order to show that the law of Madras as to the alienability of a single member's share differed from that of Bengal. In the Madras case, the joint family seemed to have consisted of

1. p. 51.
2. Tayumana Reddi *v.* Perumal Reddi, 1 Mad. H. C. Rep. 51.
3. Virāsami Gramini *v.* Ayyasami Gramini, 1 Mud. H. C. Rep. 471.

two brothers and a step-mother. Two years later, the same High Court held in nivelappa Kaundan *v.* Manuaru Naikan, 2 Mad. H.C. Rep. 416, that a sale by a father was valid, to the extent of his own particular share and that according to the Madras School there was no distinction between a father and any other coparcener. The reasons for the validity of the sale of a single share are, thus set forth:—"In argument, treating this case as an action for recovery of land, it has been contended that the sale by the father is altogether void, and that partition for the purpose of satisfying his contracts, cannot, as in other cases, be directed. The principle upon which, following the suggestion of Sir Thomas Strange and Mr. Colebrooke, this Court have of late years satisfied abontract of one individual member out of the share which would come to him on partition, is that as the coparcener has contracted, he ought to fulfil his contract; that according to the doctrine of the Madras school, if he could if disposed at any time enforce a partition; and that it is only just, that where he has incurred an obligation he shall not be allowed to escape its effects by the allegation that his own deed was *ultra vires*; that he should be compelled to give to his creditors all the remedies to which he would himself be entitled as against the subject matter of his agreement.

Fractional share alienable in Madra

"It seems therefore that it was Sir Thomas Strange who first therefore the doctrine of alienability of a single share, into the Madras School. The rule, however, has no foundation in the original texts considered as special authorities for that school. Thus we see that in Smṛticandrikā, which is by all eulogized as a very high authority of that school, and which in fact occupies in that part of India as honoured a position as the work of Jīmūta does in Bengal, there are passages which would lead to a conclusion quite contrary to the suggesion of Sir Thomas Strange and Colebrooke's. Thus in ch. 15 of that work, we find as follows: It should be borne in mind that this chapter is headed as "Acts of the divided." The meaning is that this chapter is intended to deal with such transactions as may be lawfully entered into by divided coparceners. Para. 2 says:—(I am giving here the purport, referring to Mr. Iyer's translation for a literal rendering.) If the brothers do not give their consent, then they should be disregarded, and the others should do their own duties. Further more, if those divided persons should do sell their own shares, or should give them away, they would be quite Justified in doing all that, just as they pleased; because being divided, they are the self-dependent owners of their own wealth. All this is said by way of comment upon the text of Nārada referred to as an authority by Jimūta and Śrīkṛṣṇa[1] for the proposition that undivided brothers can sell their respective individual shares in joint property. I have already hinted that the same was a very forced interpretation of the language of Nārada, wherein I am borne out by Smṛti-candrikā the author of who cites it to show individual shares are alienable after division, and not before. The is further confirmed by para. 3. "As for the text of Vṛhaspati, who says that whether undivided or divided, the co-heirs have like powers in respect of immoveable property, and that in all cases a single parcener is incompetent either to give it away, or to mortgage or sell it;—this will apply to the following case; namely where the co-heirs find that it is difficult to divide into equitable and impartially equal shares their joint undivided immoveable property, and for that reason they come to a mutual understanding that they will divide the profits from time to time, and become separate from one another by dividing property other than immoveable. For in such a case none has an independent ownership in the immoveable property." No authority could be clearer than this that sale of undivided shares in immoveable property is against the principles of Hindu Law as understood the writers of original texts.

1. See *ante*, p. 484.

Divison by metes and bound not necessary to terminate joint character

The case hypthatically put by the author of Smṛti-candrikā is one in which modern tribunals would be bound to pronounce a verdict of separation, according to Appoovier's case. There the Privy Council have laid down that division by metes and bounds is not necessary in order to convert a joint family into a separated one. The joint character ceases at once if the co-heirs arrange among themselves that they will divide the profits. And yet in a case of this kind where the division of profits is mutually agreed upon by the members, and where the same agreement is accompanied by a complete division of the moveable effects, the Smṛti-candrikā says that particular share in the landed property will not be validly sold. This is the only method that commends itself to the author of the Smṛti-candrikā to reconcile Nārada and Vṛhaspati. Nārada says that divided parceners can sell their own particular shares; Vṛhaspati says that divided or undivided, no single parcener can sell or pledge or give immoveable property. The Smṛti-candrikā brings about a harmony of the two Ṛṣis, equally authoritative equally infallible from an orthodox point of view. The rules deduced are, that undivided property can never be sold, even to the extent of a single member's share; that immoveable property, unless divided by metes and bounds, is to be considered as undivided, and incapable of being alienated by a single member, although he may be divided in suspect of the imoveables. Jīmūta and Srīkrishna and a believe the modern judicial authorities of Madras would reconcile Nārada and Vṛhaspati by supposing the latter to be declaring that a single parcener is incompetent to alienate the whole joint property, while Nārada according to them declares his competency to alienate his own individual share. But this is not what the Smṛti-candrikā says and for very good reasons; for Vṛhaspati says then even divided brothers cannot sell immoveable property. As brothers being divided means nothing else than the division of the property, it follows that according to Vṛhaspati divided immoveable property cannot be alienated by the owner of the same-a position must have struck the author of the Smṛti-candrikā as rather puzzling. He therefore construes Bṛhaspati's expression, divided co-heirs, as divided in respect of moveable property.' It should be noticed here that Vijñāna cites a couplet similar to this text of Vṛhaspati in para. 30, seo. 1, ch. I, Mitākṣarā ascribing it to Manu. The couplet quoted in the Smṛti candrikā as that of Vṛhaspati reads exactly like the one quoted in the Mitākṣarā as that of Manu, excepting only a single term. Vṛhaspati reads dāyādāh, co-heirs where Manu reads sapiṇḍāh 'of the same piṇḍa'. Vijñāna explains the declaration of the incompetion of a divided parcener to alienate, immoveable property, in a different way. He says that this is not a peremptory declaration, but simply precautionary, advising person not to buy landed property unless all the kinsfolk of the vendor consent; that such a precaution observed at the time of the sale obviates future litigation; that it estops the vendor's relatives from afterwards contending that the land is not divided; but that nevertheless the sale of divided land is valid in law, even though the kinsfolk do not give consent. The Mitākṣarā therefore' leaves it ambiguous whether according to its author the sale of a member's undivided share is lawful or not, except by way of what may be deduced from its avowed doctrine of aggregate ownership, and from its definition of partition. But that the Madras School above all should adopt the doctrine of the validity of such a sale, in the teeth of what its own special treotise says, is a matter of surprise. This seems to be one of the instances in which the law of Bengal, have been first studied by the administrators of Hindu Law, exercised an undue influence upon the development of the law of other schools, specially of the Madras School, in which Sir Thomas Strange was one of the early British promulgators of Hindu Law. That learned judge was an admirer of Jagannātha. As a European lawyer, his sympathies were naturally enlisted on the side of the only school, that had given the greatest scope to individual proprietary right, the principle of which had been established for conturies in Europe, except in the matter of entailed estates. Colebrooke moreover was a Sanskrit scholar who prosecuted his oriental studies in Bengal, was more liable to be influenced by the doctrines and principles which were topics of every day talk with the Pandits of Bengal. It is to these two authorities, Strange and Colebrooke, that the theory of the alienability of individual shares owes its origin. It was fortified by the equitable principle expounded by the High Court of Madras. If a person belonging to a joint family into a contract for selling land, he ought, to be held fast to his promise in respect of as much right and privilege as he undoubtedly has. His right of demanding partition at any time is undoubted. Why should he not therefore be made to demand partition, when he has taken money from a third person? Why should not the purchaser be at least invested with as much right as the vendor has? This equitable principle was given weight to in Madras, whereby a difference was established between the Mitākṣarā Law of that Province on the one hand, and that of Bengal, and the North-West on the other. Yet when Sir Barnes decided in an opposite way for Bengal, he had an opportunity of considering all these arguments. He seems to meet them by the following observations:—"The shares to which the members of a joint family would be entitled on partition, are constantly varying by births deaths, marriages, etc., and the principle of the Mitākṣarā Law seems to be that no sharer before partition without the assent of his co-sharers, determine the joint character of the property, by conveying away his share. If he could do so, he would have the power, by his own will, without resorting to partition, the only' means known to the law for that purpose, to exclude from participation in the portion conveyed away those who by subsequent birth become members of the joint family and titled to shares upon partition.

Practical difficulties from alienation of a fractional share

They who are and born and they who are yet

unbegotten, and they who are still in the womb, require the means of support. No gift or sale, should, therefore be made (12 W. R. F. B. 1): "This part of his judgment indicates a practical difficulty the Madras doctrine would give rise to. Thus: Suppose a member alienates joint property when the family consists of himself and two sons; suppose that when the alienee resorts to court and gets a decree for partition, another son has been born to the father. Now the practical difficulty is, what share of the property will the purchaser get? Is it a third, or is it a fourth? In favour of his getting a third share, it may be said that as the act of alienation took effect when the vendor was entitled to get a third share, the purchaser should get what the vendor had to sell at the time of executing the deed of sale. Against that condition, it may be urged that as the actual partition does not take place but at a time when the vendor, the father; was entitled to only one-fourth, the purchaser should get no more than one-fourth. What he has purchased is,–'that part of the land which should fall into the father's allowment on an actual partition. Whichever may be adopted in deciding the question, no principle furnished by the original texts will be of any help. They never contemplated such a combination of facts. Again, on the occasion of an actual partition, every wife of the father gets an equal share, equal to that of a son, some-times she gets half of what is received by a son. The Madras doctrine therefore, by offering a seeming advantage to the purchaser of joint property from a single member, places him in a tantalizing and perplexing position. Such a purchaser mush not only enquire how many sons father has, and how many wives, but he must also calculate upon the possibility of the father begetting other sons in the interval between the alienation and the decree for partition. He must ascertain whether the wives received any peculiar property from her husband or her father-in-law, in which case their shares would be one-half of that of a son. Unless he extends his enquiries to all these different directions, it must be impossible for him to estimate the real value of what he is going to purchase.

None but speculative purchasers of landed property, who thrive upon litigation, whose trade it is to spoliate the property of respectable families by fomenting quarrels and disputes, whose expedient it is to pander to the low instincts of the unworthy members of wealthy households, would enter upon purchases beset with so many risks.

There is but one justification that occurs to me for making a departure from the strict old rule of the Mitākṣarā and its most obvious and legitimate deductions. In the altered condition of our society, the necessity of property frequently changing hands has become common. The dull routine of the ancient Hindu days has been disturbed by the animation of western civilization, the principles of which have been to some extent transplated to India. On the other hand, the time honoured institution of joint family has an inherent tendency to create and perpetuate a confusion between ostensible and real ownership of property. The father is the manager, he collects rents; institutes suits in courts, pays revenue, has his name recorded in the State registers, buys articles and pays for them, is sued for family debts, even sells family properties on declared necessities, and seems to the outside world to be the only person interested in all property which really belongs not only to himself but also to a number of persons. The existence of these other persons is not prominent in the eyes of the outside world. What happens under such, circumstances is what might have been expected. People are naturally led to treat the father as sole proprietor. The greed of securing tempting bits of landed property has not a little to do with the facility with which people part with their money to the father of a joint family in exchange for deeds of sale. The practice has become so inveterate and widespread, that tribunals feel small inclination to hearken to the old Mitākṣarā rule first invented at a time when the condition of society was widely different. Whether the practice might not have been nipped in its origin if our first foreign tribunals had applied the old rule in all its rigidity from the very beginning, may be open to question. But encouraged early indulgence, the sale by single members, especially a father, has now gone too far, and our courts are under the necessity of calling in principles, which are little in unison with our original texts.

Testmentary devise of a fractional share not valid

The Madras High Court, however, does allow exceptions to the rule, that a single parcener can part with his interest in the family property. It might be supposed that the law of testamentary disposition would follow that of transfer *inter vivos.* And generally speaking, if a person can sell property during his lifetime, he can leave it by a will also. But as regards the case of a joint family, it has been held by the Madras High Courts to be otherwise. In O. Gooroova Butten. V.C. Naraina semi Butten, 8 Mad. H. C. Rep. p. 13, Holloway, J. says:—"The theory of the will of a Hindu is an anomaly and ought therefore not to be pressed. Principles of law should be followed to their logical conclusions. But where an exceptional law is introduced, such as this of wills among Hindus, it should not be carried further than the anomaly introduced requires. It is not law that a Hindu may dispose of *inter vivoa* can disposed of by him by mortuary instrument. That has never been decided by the court; but on the contrary has been distinctly found against in a late case from Mangalore." The reason why undivided property cannot be disposed of by a will is this,—that as soon as the testator dies, the right of survivorship vested in the other member of the family takes effect, and the legatee cannot take anything. The share of the deceased testator might have been alienated by him so long as he lived; but his death puts an end to all his rights, and his share lapses to the others immediately on its occurrence. But a will by its very nature is to have effect after his death; therefore it is to have effect over something which is no longer his property. Consequently the bequest of an undivided share is held in Madras to be inoperative.[1] This reasoning made use of to invalidate the bequest of undivided property by one member,̀ would, however, be equally applicable to all Hindu wills. Even in the Bengal School, the son's right to the heritable property is contemporaneous with the termination of his father's right by death, either natural or civil. Yet the Privy Council have said in the Tagore case that wills in Bengal have been established by decided cases too numerous to be now upset, although the principle underlying the testamentary disposition of property may not be quite in agreement with the original authorities of Hindu Law. But I apprehend that the tribunals on the other side of the Vindhya have stopped short in giving validity to the bequests of undivided property, because the practice of making such bequest had not rooted itself in usage before it was brought to notice that the practice was not in harmony with the older Hindu Law.

Barring this exception relating to a will of undivided property the Madras High Court has uniformly held to the doctrine of alienability of a single share, as will appear from the following cases. In Venkatachella Pillai *v.* Chinnaiya Mudaliar, 5 Mad. H. C. Rep. p. 166, the managing member of the family had sold a village which belonged to the family, besides other properties. This alienation was made not for family purposes, nor with the assent of his brother, the family it seems consisting of two brothers and a son of one. The nephew sued to recover a moiety of the village, which in its entirety would have been less in quantity and value the share the managing member would have received if a partition of the family property had been made. It seems to have been contended for the purchaser that since that was so, and since one member could part with his own share, the sale of the village should not be set aside, as the whole village was less than the managing member's share. To this

1. See Vitla Butten *v.* Yamenamma; 8, Mad. H. C. Rep, p. 6.

argument the High Court did not accede, but ruled that no more than a member's own particular share in every property could be sold by a single member. The words used by the judges were:—"The decisions of this court, as to the right of a coparcener to alienate his vested interest in the property held in coparcenary do not go beyond establishing the validity of an alienation to the extent of the coparcener's share in the particular property, which is the subject of the alienation. And they are founded upon the principle that each coparcener has a vested present undivided estate in his share which he may at any time convert into an estate in severalty by a compulsory or voluntary partition, and that such estate is transferable like any other interest in property. Further than this the title of the first defendant under the alienation in the present case cannot be carried. The estate of each coparcener gives him only a right to enjoy a fair proportion of the benefits of the whole family property in common with the other coparceners. But as respects the proprietary right to the *corpus* of the property; There is a perfect unity of title which makes the coparcenary extent of the nature of a joint tenancy, and until a partition takes place, the coparceners continue seized by one and the same title of the whole and every portion of the property alike, the law recognizing the right of one coparcener to hold possession and manage for the joint benefit of himself and the rest."

The principle adopted in this case is not sufficient to meet all the equities that demand a consideration in effecting a partition. It is seldom that co-sharers make partition by dividing every property into as many bits and parcels as there are sharers. Some sharers may take one property, some another, and so on; the principal consideration being that the shares be equal in value in every respect. Now when a part of joint property is sold by a single member, the above method of making partition is precluded ; the purchaser has his interest confined to one particular portion, and it would be a very unusual stretch of power on the part of a court to give the purchaser a part of joint property to which his purchase did not extend, as equivalent to what he purchased. This seems to be another practical difficulty and another complication created by the doctrine of the alienality of a single share. True, this difficulty is not inseparable from the law of property as it obtains in the Bengal School, where each brother may sell his share in particular property out of many properties belonging to joint family of brothers.In that case, on the occasion of a partition, that same property must be dealt with separately from the rest, and must be divided apart into as many allotments, as them are sharers, including the purchaser. But the same complication might have been averted from the schools of aggregate ownership, if a single share had from the beginning been held to be inalienable.

Law of alienation in Bombay

I now come upon the law of alienation as it obtains in Bombay. This law is based upon exactly the same principles as that of Madras. The general rule that individual shares in a joint family property are not definite is so far disregarded that every member is held competent to part with his particular share. This the High Court of Bombay has expounded as beyond all doubt. But with respect to a single member's power to deal with shares which belong to members other than himself, it is said to depend upon the existence of family necessity the power would be upheld by law if the alienation is made for the common benefit and use of the family.[1] With regard to the gift of immoveable property, in the case Gangu Bai *v.* Ramanna Bin Bhimanna, 3 Bom. H. C. Rep. A. C. J. 66, the High Court held that a gift by a single member was invalid even to the extent of his individual share. (See also 12 Bom. H. C. Rep. 229.) The

1. Gundo Mehadev *v.* Rambhat Bin Bhau Bhat, Bom. 1 H. C. Rep. 39.

High Court also says that such cannot be disposed of by will—a doctrine which agrees with the law of Madras. In Lakshman Dada Naik *v.* Ramchandra Dada Naik, I. L. R. 1 Bom., Melvil, J., says at p. 568, that it is not within the power of the father of a joint family, (whether his act be regarded in the light of a gift or of a partition), to bequeath the whole or almost the whole of the ancestral moveable property, to one son, and virtually to disinherit the other. The High Court therefore held such a will to be wholly inoperative. If however, the law in Bombay had been that a bequest was valid to the extent of the testator's share in the property, it is not difficult to see that the will in the above case, instead of being wholly set aside, would have been upheld to the extent of the father's share in the ancestral moveable property. The contention does not seem to have been raised in the High Court, and the Court probably regarded the question as one of partition, deciding it in accordance with the express texts of the Mitākṣarā which declare the unequal distribution by father of ancestral property, whether moveable or immoveable, as *ultra vires* and invalid in law. In the fifth volume of the Indian Law Reports, Bombay series, however, in the case of Rambhat *v.* Lakahman Chintaman Mayalay, we find the following observations made by Westropp, C. J. says:—"Taking this view of the adoption, we permitted Lakshman'a pleader to argue that *Bakshispatra* must be regarded as a will and not a deed of that proposition could have been maintained, we may that Lakshman should have sued for the whole; and not for a moiety only of the property, inasmuch as Chintaman being a member of an undivided family at the time of his death, could not have devised away any part of the property from his coparcener, *i.e.*, his adopted son according to the Hindu Law of this Presidency."In this proposition that an undivided member cannot bequeath his particular share, besides the case of Gangubai, the following other cases are cited in a foot-note. Vṛandavandas *v.* Yamuna Bai, 12 Bom. H. C. Rep. 229; 11 Bom. H.C. Rep. 80.

Whatever may be the decision ultimately arrived at Bombay High Court with regard to the validity of the bequest by will of an individual share, the general doctrine that such a share is alienable intervos is now settled law in that Province. In Vasudeb Bhat *v* Venkatesh Sambhao,. 10 Bom. H. C. Rep. p. 139; the question has been discussed by Westropp, CJ., the result being thus set forth in the judgement of the learned Chief Justice. "On the principle *stare decisis* which induced Sir Barnes Peacock and his colleagues strictly to adhere to the antialienation doctrine of the Mitākṣarā in the Provinces subject to their jurisdiction where the authority of that treatise prevails, we at this side of India find overselves Compelled to depart from that doctrine, so far as itdenics' the right of a Hindu parcener for valuable consideration to sell, incumber, or otherwise alien his share of the undivided family property. The foregoing authorities lead us to the conclusion that it must be regarded as the settled law of this Presidency, not only that one of several coparceners in a Hindu family may, before partition, and without the assent of his coparceners; sell, mortgage, or otherwise alien, for valuable consideration, his share in the undivided family estate, moveable or immoveable, but also that such a share may be taken execution under a judgment against him at the suit of his personal creditor. Were we to hold otherwise, we should undermine many titles which rest upon the course of decisions, that, for a long period of time, the courtsat this side of India have steadily taken. Stability of decisions is, in our estimation, of far greater importance, than a deviation from the special doctrine of the Mitākṣarā upon the right of alienation." (See p. 160.) The veiw of the law was further confirmed in Fakirapa Bin Satyapa. Chaunapa Bin Chinmalapa, 10 Bom. H. C. Rep. p. 162 by a Full Bench decision, in which Westropp, C. J. noticed in the following words a decision of the Bombay Sadr Adalat to a contrary effect:—"On examination of the opinion of the Zilla Shastri, it will be seen that there is an inconsistency in it. He says, ' Neither brother can sell his share before separation; and yet he adds, 'The part of the house containing the cookroom and the place of worship belongs to the elder brother and the other half of the house to the younger. A *dictum* at variance with the doctrine in Appoovier *v.* Ram Subha."

In Tukaram *v.* Ramchandra, 6 Bom. H. C. Rep. A. C. J. 247, a distinction is drawn between the sale of an undivided share for a valuable consideration and a gift of it without valuable consideration. The distinction is in accordance with Gangu Bai's case, 3 Bom. H. C. Rep. A. C. J. 66. A gift is said to be different from a transfer or mortgage made for valuable consideration. On this point, however, there is a difference between the Madras and the Bombay schools, as pointed out in the judgment of the Privy Council in Lakshman Dada Naik *v.* Ramchandra Dada Naik, where a contention appears to have been raised before their Lordships, that gift or devise of undivided property in Bombay to the extent of the donor's or testator's share was operative.[1] Their Lordships say:—"The argument is founded upon the comparatively modern decisions of the Courts of Madras and Bombay which have been recognized by this Committee as establishing, that one of several coparceners has, to some extent, a power of disposing of his undivided share without the consent of his co-sharers. The Madras High Court has gone further and sealed that an alienation by gift, or other voluntary conveyance *inter vivos,* will also be valid against the non assentient coparceners. Their Lordships have to apply to this case the law as it is received at Bombay. The decisions of the High Court of Bombay, notably Vasudeb Bhat *v.* Venkatesh Sambhav, 10 Bom. H. C. Rep. 139, and Udaram Shriram *v.* Ranu Panduji, 11 Bom. H. C. Rep. 76, have ruled that a coparcener cannot, without the consent of his co-sharers, either give or devise his share; that the alienation of it must be for value; and if this be law,

1. See p. 61, I. L. R. 5 Bom.

the whole argument in favour of the testamentary power over the undivided share fails."

Devise valid by last survivor of a joint family

On other hand, it has been held in Bombay that self-acquired property may be always alienated by the acquirer both *inter vivos*, and also by testamentary disposition, although he may at the same time be joint in respect of other property. Property likewise, which was originally joint, but which has become vested in a singal individual by the extinction of all the coparcener, may be willed away by the last survivor. In such a case, it may be that there is a remote kinsman who would be the heir of the last survivor by the law inheritage. But if that heir be not joint with the last survivor he cannot object to the exercise of the testamentary power by the last member in respect of property that originally belonged to the now extinct family. The property in fact as vested in the lạst survivor is considered as his separate estate, and is treated as his self-acquired property. Since there is no bar under the law to the bequest of separate or self-acquired property even in the Provinces subject to the Mitākṣarā Law, joint family property which ultimately comes to be owned by a single person in the aforesaid manner, can also be bequeathed by him to whomsoever he chooses.[1]

Obstructed heritage and unobstructed heritage

In such a state of things comes into operation a principle peculiar to the Mitākṣarā Law, which is the basis of the well-known division of heritable wealth into 'obstructed' and unobstructed; the original words respectively being 'apratibandha' and sapratibandha.' This principle has been thus explained in the Mitākṣara, ch. I, sec. 1, para. 2, *et seq*.

"Here the term heritage *(daya)* signifies that wealth, which becomes the property of another, solely by reason of relationship to the owner. It is of two sorts, unobstructed

1. Narottam Jagjiban *v.* Narsan Das, 3 Bom. H, C. Rep. p. 6.

(apratibandha) and liable to obstruction *(sapratibandha)*. The wealth of the father or of the paternal grandfather, becomes the property of his sons or grand sons, in right of their being his sons or grandsons: and this is an inheritance not liable to obstruction. But property developes on parents (or uncles), brothers, and the rest, upon the demise of the owner, if there be no male issue: and thus the actual existence of the son and survival of the owner are impediments to the succession; and on their ceasing, the property devolves on the successor in right of his being uncle or brother. That is an inheritance subject to obstruction. The same holds good in respect of their sons and other descendants." The meaning of this passage may be thus explained. We have seen that under the Mitākṣarā the sons are co-owners of the father in ancestral estate. Now let us suppose that A acquired some property and becomes the root of a family. A being separate from all his relatives. A dies leaving sons and grandsons. These sons and grandson will become joint owners of all property left by A.A's as great-grandsons also, if there be any will become joint owners with their fathers and grandfathers; for ownership is by birth, under the Mitākṣarā. If all sons and grandsons and great-grandsons were to die without being married and without adopting sons, A's widow if then living, would get his property. If there be no widow, his mother, then his father,then his brother property then his brother's son would successively inherit A's. At the same time so long as either A or any of his sons or grandsons or great-grandsons live, neither the life, nor the father or mother or brother or brother's son or any one of the successive heirs enumerated in the well-known Yājñavalkya's text[1] will have any the last right or ownership in A's property. But the sons and grandsons and great-grandsons of A not only inherit his property after his death, but also have an ownership by birth. This is the distinction between the obstructed and unobstructed

1. See *ante*, p. 184

inheritors. The son, grandson and great grandson of A are his unobstructed heritors; all other kinsmen who occupy a place in the line of succession obstructed heritors. In respect of self-acquired property. A cannot be prevented from disposing of it in any way he likes by his unobstructed heritors. At least so it has been established by modern Case Law. But as soon as the self-acquired property of A becomes by inheritance the ancestral property of B his son, A's grandsons and great grandsons will be B's co-sharers in the strict sense of term, and will be able to interdict all unustifiable alienation by B *inter vivās*, and all bequests by B to take after his death. In other words, it is the unobstructed theritors, the sons, grandsons and great-grandson of the root of the family, who have co-ownership; and power of interdiction in respect of alienations and bequests. The Mitākṣarā does not mention the great grandson as one of the unobstructed heritors. But the Virmitrodaya is clear upon the point. This appears from Para 16, ch. II, Part 1, p. 72 of Baboo Golapchandra Sarkar's English translation.

"Kātyāyana says:—"When one himself dies unseparated, his son who has not received maintenance from the grandfather, shall be made participator of the heritage; he is to get, however, the paternal share from the uncle or uncle's son ; the very same share shall equitably belong to all the brothers: or his son also shall get afterwards cessation of succession shall take place himself on signifies a brother his son—the brother son. 'Maintenance means 'share.' The question on curring sort of share is he to get?'—it is said 'The paternal share.' 'His son' intends the 'greatgrandson of the person whose estate is divided, because the case of a grandson is considered. 'Afterwards, that is after his son.' Cessation,–'that is, 'cessation of suceession takes, place. The meaning is, that the great grandson's son is not entitled to a share. According also Devala says:—'Partition of heritage among undivided parceners and second partition among divided dwelling together, extends to the fourth in descent. This is the settled law'— The meaning is that the partition of heritage extends *inclusively*,[1] to the fourth degree counting from the proprietor.[2] This rule is alike applicable if divided coparceners dwell together after reunion, by reason of the expression 'dwellling together.'"

The two texts, one of Kātyāyana, and the other of Devala, thus explained by Mitra Misra to show that descendants including the great-grandson are entitled to shares, have been cited by Vācaspati, the author of the Mithila treatise, at pp. 238 and 239 of Baboo Prosunno Hoomar's translation. The conclusion is thus set forth in the latter page. "The partition of heritage shall extend from the original owner of the estate to his descendants in the fourth degree."

The same two texts are noticed in para. 8 and para. 15 ch. 8, Smṛti-candrikā, the Madras special authority. The author concludes thus in para. 16; "If there are many persons sprung in the family of the original owner, who are sprung from different lines of his progeny, and if they have

---

1. In the original the word अभिव्याप्य, abhivyāpya, 'inclusively,' is used by the author of the Vīramitrodāya to obivate all ambiguity, in explaining Devala's text, which says,... 'extends to the fourth in descent.' It might be doubted whether the fourth in descent is kept outside or brought within the circle of those entitled to a share. The preposition आ, employed by Devala, is ambiguous, Sanskrit lexicographers explaining it as either मर्य्यादा, 'limit exclusive,' or अभिविधि, 'limit inclusive;' thus we might say 'India extends as far as Afghanistan,' or India extends unto the Punjab.' In both these cases, the Sanskrit particle आ may be justifiably used. In the first cases, it would signify मर्य्यादा, 'limit exclusive; in the second case, it would signify अभिविधि 'limit inclusive'. Mitra Misra, the author of the Vīramitrodaya, advisedly explains Devala's आ as अभिव्याप्य; that is, according to him, the word आ in the text is to be taken in the sense of 'limit inclusive'.
2. Here the word in the original is वीजिन्, 'vijin', literally, the seedsman, that is, the root of the original progenitor of the family.

all dwelt together jointly for a very long time, then the partition of heritage will take place down to the fourth, that is, to the great-grandson of the orginal owner. This is the limit of the partition of heritage where there are many lines of progeny." The application of this rule might give rise to a curious practical result. Suppose A was the original owner, he left two sons, B and C. The family remains undivided till no one is left in it, except a grandson of B and a great grandson of C. According to the interpretation given to Kātyāyana and Devala by the Smṛti-candrikā, B's grandson would be the fourth in descent from A the original owner, and C's great-grandson would be the fifth in descent. If these two persons incline to divide the family property, C's great-grandson ought not to get anything, and B's grandson should get the whole. I doubt whether modern tribunals would allow of any such result; yet I do not see what other meaning can be attached to the words of the Smṛti-candrikā, when it says that the fourth in descent from the original owner is the limit beyond which partition of heritage does not extend, where there are different lines of progeny descended from the same original owner.

The same two texts of Kātyāyana and Devala are cited in paras. 15—24, sec. 4, ch. 4, Mayūkha, (pp. 44 and 45 of Māndlik's translation). The author sets forth the result thus:— "The sons, etc., of the great-grandson do not obtain the wealth of the great-great-grandfather, if the father, grandfather and great-grandfather have predeceased such great-great-grandfather, who at his decease has left other sons and other nearer heirs alive. The meaning is that in the absence of sons, grandsons and great-grandsons and the like [of the deceased], even he [the great-grandson] takes. And this does not refer to the undivided, but the re-united." The Bombay treatise adds a qualification of its own to the rule. In order to exclude the fifth in descent, his three immedite ancestors must have pre-decease, his three immediate ancestors must have pre-deceased the fifth in ascent, that is to say, the owner of the undivided property at the root. The Bombay treatise confines the rule to the re-united coparceners.

Unobstructed heritage extends as far as the great-grandson

But whatever may the practical application of the rule intended to be laid down in the two texts of Kātyāyana and Devala, the texts at all events furnish us with an answer to the question, how far does unobstructed inheritance extend? It is clear from the Mitākṣarā that every heir does not inherit by way of unobstructed inheritance; it is also clear from that treatise that both the son and the grandson are heirs by way of unobstructed inheritance. Kātyāyana and Devala, cited by all the leading treatises, seem to say that a participation in the shares does not extend beyond the fourth in descent. From this I conclude that the line of unobstructed inheritance terminates at the fourth in descent; which is tantamount to saying that ownership by birth also terminates there.

Alienation of property by obstructed inheritance held valid

The question, what is obstructed inheritance and what is not so, becomes of importance, since the High Court of Calcutta has drawn a distinction between the two, and has deduced important results from it. In Baboo Nundo Coomar Lal *v.* Moulive Ruziooddeen Hossein, 18 W. R., 477, the Hight Court of Calcutta has thus laid down the law upon the point. A son cannot contral his father's acts in respect of property, the succession to which is liable to obstruction; and it is only in respect of property not liable to obstruction that the wealth of the father and grandfather becomes the of property his sons, or grandsons by virtue of birth. In this case, the father had inherited some property from the widows of two of his brothers and of a nephew. It was held that such property must be taken as inherited by way of obstructed inheritance, and that the father's power of disposition as, over such property was unrestricted and beyond the control of his sons. The judgment in this case also quotes approvingly the following passage from West and Bulher's Digest of Hindoo Law.

Ancestral property as among descendants comprises property transmitted in the direct male line from the common ancestor, and accretions to such property made with the aid of the inherited ancestral estate. Thus in the case of a father, the head of a family, the property inherited from his father or grandfather is ancestral property, however acquired by its previous possessors. On the other hand, property inherited by him from females, brothers, or collaterals, or directly from a great grandfather, appears to be subject to the same rules as if self-acquired ancestral property, in fact may be co-extensive with the objects of the 'apratibandhadāya or unobstructed inheritance. The view here stated agrees with that arrived at by Jagannatha, after a discussion of the contrary doctrines held by other lawyers. This discussion itself shows, however, that there is much to be said on both sides, and the question must be regarded as one still in controversy."

In the above citation, Jagannātha is referred to as authority for the doctrine of obstructed heritage propounded. I ought to mention here, however, that Jagannātha, being an authority of the Bengal School, can have title to do with that doctrine. The Bengal School does not admit ownership by birth ; under it, therefore, all hiers are alike. The son, grandson, and great-grandson do not occupy any superior position as heirs to the widow, the parents, the brothers, and so forth, except by way of priority of succession. The superiority may be attributed to the widow over the parents, to the parents the brothers, and so on. The superiority son, of grandson and great-grandson under the Mitākṣarā lies in the fact that they are not only successors after the death, but are also joint owners during the lifetime, of their father, grandfather and great grandfather. This joint ownership is only described in a different way when it is said that their inheritance is unobstructed.

In concluding this Lecture on Alienation of Joint Property. I may summarise the rules thus. In Bengal under the Dāyabhāga, joint family property may be alienated to the extent of a single share, and may also be left by will. In the same Province under the Mitākṣarā, and in the North-West, there can be no voluntary alienation of a single share; nor any bequest ; but such a share can be sold in execution of a decree. In Madras, there can be both voluntary sale of such a share for valuable consideration, also a gift without consideration; also an execution sale; but no bequest by a will. In Bombay there can be a voluntary sale, also an execution sale; but gift without a valuable consideration, nor a bequest by a will. In all the Provinces, property which was originally joint ancestral, but which is no longer so being, at the time vested in a single individual, last surviver of the family, is treated as self-acquired property, and besides being capable of alienation *inter vivos,* voluntary or compulsory, may also be left by a will, so as to disapoint the expectation of a lawful heir.

Chapter 10

Son's Liability For Father's Debts

Giridhari Lal v. Kantoo Lal; principles established by it—Sons liable for father's debts; nessesity of a princple like this—The principle of *Giridhari Lal's* case deducible from ancient texts—Texts relating to immoral debts—Decisions subsequent to *Giridhari Lal's* case—Father's powers over joint property extended—High rate of interest does not render a debt illegal or immoral—Purchaser's right confirmed to father's share, where—Suraj Buns Kooer's case P.B case of Lachman Das *v.* Giridhari Chowdry, rules established by—Creditors should sue both the father end the son—Rule where the son is adult—Loans for carrying on family trade valid—Father sued as representing the family—An instance of immoral debt.

Giridhari Lal v. Kantoo Lal; principles established by it.

In this Lecture, the matter to be dealt with is the, liability of the joint family property for father's debts.

We have seen that joint families under the Mitākṣarā are constituted either by a father and his sons, or by brothers or other remoter kinsmen living together. Now, law has established some distinctions between these two descriptions of joint families. These distinctions' have been brought into prominence and put into a definite shape by the decision of the Privy Council in the cases of Giridhari Lal *v.* Kantoo Lal, and Muddon Thakoor *v.* Kantoo Lal. The two cases were decided by a single judgement reported at p. 56 of the 22nd Volume of Sutherland's a Weekly Reporter;

to be also found 1L. R. I. A. 321 and and 14 B. L. R. 187. The propositions of law established this decision may be thus summed up:—Under the Mitākṣarā Law, the sons are bound to pay the debts of their father, unless the debts are of such a nature that it is not duty of the sons to pay them. The ancestral property inherited by the father may be sold for the payment of such debts, and by such a sale the whole property, including the son's interest in it, will pass. If there is a decree made by a court of justice, properly obtained by a creditor of the father, the ancestral property may be sold in execution of such a decree; and the exceution sale will pass even the son's interest in the peoperty. If the debt of the father has been contracted for an immoral parpose the son is not under an abligation to pay it; and he has a right to object to the ancestral property being made liable for it. If a son seeks to reverse the sale of ancestral property, which was brought about for the payment of his father's debts, he must show that the debts are bad in law; if he fails, the sales, whether private or by public auction in execution of a decree will stand. If a court of justice has decree against a father in favour of a creditor; if the court has given an order for ancestral property 'to be put up for sale under the execution; then the purchaser at such a sale is protected in his purchase against the claim of the sons. Such a purchaser stands in the same position which is occupied by the purchaser from the manager for an infant heir. The rule with regard to the purchaser from the manager for an infant heir is thus stated in Honooman Prosad's case.[1] "The power of the manager for an infant heir to charge an estate not his own under the Hindu Law a limited and qualified powre. It can only be exercised rightly in a case of need, or for the benefit of the estate. But where in the particular instance the charge is one which a prudent owner would make in order to benefit the estate, "the *bona fide* ledger is not affected by the precedent mismanagement of the estate. The actual

1. 6 Moore, I, A. 393, for the particular passage, see p. 423.

pressure on the estate, the danger to be averted, the benefit to be conferred upon it in the particular instance, is the thing to be regarded. By if that danger arises, or has arisen from any misconduct which the lender is or has been a party, he cannot advantage of his own wrong to support a charge in his own favour against the heir, grounded on a necessity which his wrong has helped to cause." This rule will apply to the case of an execution purchaser of ancestral property sold for a decree against the father of an undivided family. Such a purchaser is not bound to go back beyond the decree in order to ascertain whether the court was right in giving the decree, or having given it, in putting up the property for sale under an execution upon it. If the decree be a proper one, the interest of the sons, as well as the interest of the father, in the ancestral property, are liable for the payment of the father's debts. The purchaser is not bound to go further back than to see that there is a decree against the father; and that the property is such as would be liable to satisfy a properly given decree. Such an, enquiry made in good faith on the purchaser's part, and payment of a valuable consideration in good faith for the purchase in execution, will secure 'his purchase from the claim of the sons. If the execution purchaser, however, be privy to any transaction of bad faith, if he has knowledge of any collusive character in the decree, or of any attend on the part of the father to sell the family estate and raise for his own purposes, then the sons will have a good ground for setting aside the purchase, and for recovering the property back to the family.

The effect of this decision of the Judicial Committe has been further explained and commented upon by their Lordships themselves in the case of Ram Sahai *v.* Sheo Prosad Sing, (otherwise known as Suraj Bansi Koer's case) 4 C. L.R. 226. In this case the Judgment of the Privy Council thus sets forth the distinction between a joint family composed of a father and his sons, and one composed of brothers. "The rights of the coparceners in an undivided

Hindu family, governed by the law of the Mitākṣarā which consists of a father and his sons, do not differ from those of the coparceners in a like family consists of undivided brethren, except so far as they are affected by the peculiar obligation of paying their father's debts which the Hindu Law imposes upon sons, and the fact that the father is in all cases naturally, and in the case of infant sons necessarily, the manager of the joint estate." Then their Lordships explain the result of Kantoo Lal's case in the following words:—

"The decision of this tribunal in the before-mentioned of *Kantoo Lal** *treats the obligation of a son to pay his father's debts, unless contracted for an immoral purpose as affording, by itself, a sufficient answer to a suit brought by son either to impeach sales by a private contract for the purpose of raising money in order to satisfy pre-existing debts, or to recover property sold in execution of decrees of Courts. The judgment moreover affirms the principle laid down in the judgment of the Sudder Dewanny Adawlut, that a purchaser, under an execution is not bound to go further back than to see that there was a decree against the father; and that the property was properly liable to satisfy the decree, if the decree had been given properly against the father. In such a case one who has *bona fide* purchased the estate under the execution, and *bona fide* paid a valuable consideration for it, is protected against the suit of the sons seeking to set aside all that has bean done under joint ancestral property. This case then, which is a decision of this tribunal, is undoubtedly an authority for these propositions;—1st, that where the joint ancestral property has passed out of the joint family, either under a conveyance executed by a father in consideration of an antecedent debt, or in order to raise money to pay off an antecedent debt, or under a sale in execution of a degree for the father's debts, his sons, by reason of their duty to pay their father's debts, cannot recover that property unless they show that the debts were contracted for immoral purposes, and that the purchasers had notice that they were so contracted; and secondly, that the purchasers at an execution sale, being strangers to the suit, if they have not notice that the debts were so contracted, are not bound to make inquiry beyond what appears on the face of the proceedings." The decision of the Sudder Dewanny Adawlut, referred to in the above passage; was in some respects the foundation of the decision of the Privy Council in *Kantoo Lal's* case. The Privy Council have recapitulated the. facts and the result of this early case in the following words. The case itself was reported at p. 213, Decisions of the Sudder Dewanny Adawlut of Bengal for 1861." In it an infant sued by his guardian, in the lifetime of his father, to set aside various conveyances which had been made by the father of portions of the joint family estate, and to recover the property sold under them, and also to recover other portions of the estate which had been sold under orders of the Court in execution of decrees. The family was governed by the Mithila Law, and the first point decided was, that the restriction on a father's power of alienation over ancestral immoveable estate under that law were the same as those impossed by the law of the Mitākṣarā. This case has recognised the distinction between alienations by conveyance and those under process of execution. The Court set aside the sale by conveyance because no justifying necessit for them had been established, and it did this although the considerations for the sales were in some instances money raised in order to satisfy either judgment or bond debts. On the other hand, it dismissed the suit so far as it sought to recover property which had been sold under decrees of Court, on the ground that the son was under an obligation to pay the debts of the father if not contracted for immoral purposes, and that he had failed in this case to prove as against the purchasers under the decrees that they were so contracted. The words of the judgment on this point are:— 'Freedom on the part of the son, as far as regards ancestral property, from the obligation to discharge father's debts, under Hindu Law, can be successfully pleaed only by a consideration of the invalid nature of the debts incurred. Now we are clearly of opinion that the plaintiff has been unable to show that the expenses for which these decrees were passed were, looking to the decrees, themselves, and we cannot look beyond them, immoral, and such as the son, under the Hindu Law, would not be liable for."

The case of Giridhari Lal *v.* Kantoo Lal was decided on the 12th May, 1874. The date may be regarded as having opened a new era with regard to the Law of Property under the Mitākṣarā system. Many in the profession think that the case dealt a deatblow-institution of Hindoo joint family; that it has done away with the essential feature of that institution; that it has rendered the father independent of the control of his sons in dealing with ancestral property, which had all along been looked upon as a common fund belonging as much to the sons as to the father. Some of the judges in the High Court of Madras made an attempt to disregard the Judgment of the judicial Committee, and to uphold the rights of the sons to question sales of ancestral property on account of father's personal debts.[1] The decision has been in fact a surprise upon the world of lawyers who have had anything to do with the law of joint families governed by the Mitākṣarā.

1. See, for instance, the remarks of Innes J., in Ponnappa Pillai *v.* Pappuvayyangar, I. L. R. 4 Mad. 14. The learned judge says: (see p. 14) "The decision of the Privy Council is contrary to what is understood to be the Hindu Law in the Madras Presidency as established by a long series of decisions, which the Judicial Committee in arriving at their conclusion did not notice, I think we are not bound by the novel view taken by the Committee in this respect. The conclusion I arrive at is, that the case of Giridhari Lal v. Kantoo Lal ought not to be followed in this Presidency to the extent of laying upon the son the duty of discharging his father's debts in his lifetime, or as to the *dictum* that the son can only call in question charges created upon the property by the father, on the ground that the debts in discharge of which such charges were created were of an immoral character,"

Sons liable for father's debts; necesity of a principle like this

The promulgation of the principle, however, which was adopted by the Privy Council, had become necessity to put an end to a serious abuse, which had become rife in the Mitākṣarā districts. In those places, the fathers of families knowing well that ancestral properties were secure against the claims of their own creditors, had established almost a regular system of inveigling innocent persons of substance to lend monly to them; and when a decree was obtained and properties were attached, they used to put forward their sons to contest the creditors claims. As the text of the Mitākṣarā declares all sales of joint property by a single member invalid unless for specified legal necessity, the courts of justice in this country, bound to administer the law as it is laid down in the original texts, were powerless againts the, above named abuse, and contented themselves by stigmatizing the heedlessness of creditors, who, they said, ought to have known what the Mitākṣarā law was, and should have known better than to venture their money upon the personal security of a single member. It was to put an end to this state of things that the Privy Council invoked the old well-established rule of Hindu Law, that it is a pious duty on the part of the son to discharge his father's debts, unless the debts are of an immoral character. This rule had almost been forgotten by the tribunals in this country; its resuscitation therefore by the Judicial Committee should be regarded by all lovers of justice and equity as a timely intervention to deal blow to a revolting practice of systematic fraud.

On a first examination of the decision in Kantoo Lal's case, it does not seem to go beyond the shifting of the burden of proof from one party to another. The son sues to set aside alienation on account of his father's debts. It has been always admitted that such alienations are valid if the debts have been contracted by the father for legal necessities. If, however, they have been contracted by him for immoral purposes, to keep a concubine for instance, to meet his drinking expenses, to pay gambling debts, to meet his foolish gifts to his boon companions, his expenditure upon cock-fights, upon theatrical entertainments and so forth, it has been always held, that the son is not liable to pay his debts. But hitherto it was the purchaser who was bound to prove that there was a legal necessity. If the purchaser failed to do so, the son recovered the whole property. Now Kantoo Lal's case says that the son must show the immoral character of the father's debt for which the property was sold, and he must also show that the purchaser had notice of that circumstance, ere he can recover the property. From the purchaser showing the valid character of the nessessity which was at the root of the father's debts, the transition to the son showing the invalid character of those debts, does not at first sight seem to be so very great. Yet this shifting of the burden of proof imperceptibly introduces an important change. For between legal necessities on the one hand, and immoral expenses on the other, there is a debateable ground of expenses of an indifferent character, which are neither immoral, nor examples of a legal necessity. Take for instance a debt contracted by the father to augment the joint family property, heedless speculative enterprises ventured upon with an idea that he will thereby raise the profits of the joint property. Suppose he starts a trade, or enters upon costly schemes of draining his lands, or planting them with profitable trees, and so forth. No ethical code would pronounce such expenses to be immoral; they are the legitimate means of improving property. They often prove successful, and cause an increase of profits. On the other hand, they are some times ruinous, and bring about embarassments calculated to involve the loss of the whole property: I apprehend that under the Privy Council Judgement, the father's debts incurred for purposes like the above would bind the son; whereas formerly it had been held that debts incurred to raise the profits of the property were not legal necessities.[1] Again the shifting of the burden of proof to the son imposes upon him a difficulty which is often practically insuperable. The transactions entered into by the father may have ranged over a number of years, frequently when the son was a minor, with nobody to look after his interests except his father who is bent upon disregarding them and making the best of his own uncontrolled position, and except perhaps his mother, generally a purdanashin lady, no better acquainted with the ways of the world than the infant himself whose interests are to be protected. How can such an infant, after coming of age, show that the debt was immoral in its origin, and that the lender or the purchaser knew it? Formerly it was for the lender or the purchaser to show the character of the debt, or at least that he made *bona fide* enquiries as to its character. The shifting of the burden of proof itself to the son therefore has been of an incalculable advantage to the purchaser in relieving him from the necessity of hunting evidence connected with transactions. But the Privy Council Judgment on the face of it goes even further. Whenever there has been a decree against the father, it almost places the execution purchaser in an unassailable position. Not only must the original debts be immoral, but the auction purchaser must have had notice of the immoral character; otherwise his purchase stands. This notice is of course to to be proved by the son, to whom the auction purchaser may be, and often is, a complete stranger, never known to him in his life; yet the son is to show that this stranger had knowledge that his father was contracting debts for immoral purposes. In this part of the result of the judgment, the Mitākṣarā father has been placed nearly in the same position, which is occupied by the Dāyabhāga father. The Mitākṣarā father, if disposed to appropriate the entire benefit of the ancestral property to himself, may borrow money upon it to an amount nearly equal to its value, on

1. See 20 W. R. 38. Radha Pershad Sing *v.* Muss. Talook Raj Koer.

an understanding that it will be repaid within a short time. He fails to pay at the due date; a suit is brought and a decree obtained against him, and the execution purchaser need not be in any collusion with father for the father's purposes. The execution purchaser's knowledge that there is a, decree and an attachment, and his absence cf knowledge as to what led to the father's debts, would be quite sufficient to protect his purchase. The only means of protecting the son's interest in such a case would be to put in a claim immediately after attachment and before the auction sale, in which latter case the purchaser will get only the father's share of the property. At least such seems to be the effect of the case of Surj Bansi Koer *v.* Shev Prosad Sing 4 C. L. R. 226.

The principle of Giridhari Lal's case deduceble from ancient texts

Yet it is difficult to as that *Kantoo Lal's* case say has made a departure from the spirit of the old Hindoo Law as disclosed in the original texts, and as understood by eminent authorities like Vijñāneśvara, and Devagana Bhaṭṭa, the author of the Smṛti Candrikā. True, the Judicial Committee do not fortify their decision by citing any such original texts; but they do cite the judgment of the Sudder Dewanny Adawlut which was passed in 1861. There is little doubt that the rule, for the first time brought into light in that Sudder Adawlut Judgment, must have been suggested by some obscure Vyavasthā of some Pundit of ordinary note in an obscure case.[1] These Pundits knew where the law was to be found, so far as it and be found, when a given

1. In those days, these Pundits had a great hand in elucidating questions of Hindu Law by drawing from the store of their Sanskrit erudition. The Pundits as a class were probably liable to a just suspicion of occasionally taking bribes. In the Full Bench case of Sadaburt Pershad Sahoo, 12 W. R. F. B. I, Sir Barnes Peacock at p. 5 says, that a review was applied for in a particular case, upon a suspicion that the Pundit had delivered the Vyavasthā in the case, had taken bribe. No one would be surprised at the liability of the Pundits to such suspicions, when he reflects that the pay allowed them by Government was often no more than the fortieth part of

combination of facts was placed before them for their opinion. I therefore surmise that the doctrine of the pious duty discharge the debts of their father, first saw light in the Vyavasthā of a clever Pundit who knew well the Smṛti texts. It will be my endeavour here to point attention to some of these texts. The attention of the European Judges was, I believe, rarely drawn to these texts, since the texts are found in that part of the, Digests in the original Sanskrit, which is not directly connected with Partition or Inheritance, and which was therefore not translated by Colebrooke. And first of all, I turn to the Mitākṣarā. Śloka 51 of ch. 2 of the Institutes of Yājñavalkya, runs thus:[1]—"When the father is gone abroad in a sojourn, or is dead, or is overwhelmed in calamity, the debt should be paid by sons and grandsons, proved by witnesses in case the debt

---

what a Judge of the High Court now receives. Yet the fiat of these Pundits could decide questions of title to property, the value of which might be crores of rupees, a Darbhanga Raj or a Burdwan Raj for instance. The state of things only showed an injudicious and one-sided economy only possible under a foreign Government.

1. पितरि प्रोषिते प्रेते व्यसनाभिप्लुतेऽथवा।
पुत्रपौचे: ऋणं देयं निह्नवे साक्षिभावितं।।

पिता यदि दातव्यमृणमदत्त्वा प्रेतोऽचिकित्सनीयव्याध्याद्यभिभूतो वा। तदा तत्कृतमृणमवश्यं देयं पुत्रेण पौत्रेण वा। पितृधनाभावेऽपि पुत्रत्वेन (पौत्रत्वेन?) च। तच क्रमोऽप्यमेव। पित्रभावे पुत्र:। पुत्राभावे पौत्र:। पुत्रेण पौत्रेण वा निह्नवे कृते अर्थिना साक्ष्यादिभावितमृणं देयं पुत्रपौत्रैरित्यन्वय:।–अत: पुत्रेण जातेन स्वार्थमुतमृज्य यत्नत:। ऋणात् पिता मोचनीयो यथा नो नरकं व्रजेत्। इति। पुत्रेण व्यवहारज्ञतया जातेन निष्पनेन। इति व्याख्येयं।– पुत्रपौत्रैरिति बहुवचननिर्देशात् बहव: पुत्रा यदि विभक्ता:। स्वांशानुरूपेण ऋणं दद्यु:। अविभक्ताश्वेत। सम्भूयसमुत्थानेन गुणप्रधानभावेन वर्त्तमानानां प्रधानभूत एव दद्यादिति गम्यते। तथाह नारद:।
अत ऊर्द्धं पितु: पुत्रा ऋणं दद्युर्यथांशत:।
अविभक्ता विभक्ता वा यस्ताश्चोद्वहत्ते धुरम्। इति।
अच यद्यपि पुत्रपौत्रै: ऋणं देयं इत्यपिशेषेणोक्तं। तथापि पुत्रेण यथा पिता सवृद्धिकं ददाति तथैव देयं। पौत्रेण तु समं मूलमेव दातव्यं न वृद्धिरिति विशेषोऽवगन्तव्य:।
ऋणमात्मीयवत् पित्रयं पुत्रैर्देयं विभावितं।
पैतामहं समं देयमदेय तत्सुतस्य तु।।
इति वृहस्प्रतिस्मरणात्।
तत्सुतस्य प्रपौगृहीस्य अदेयमहयतधनस्य। एतस उत्तरश्लोके स्पष्टयिष्पयते।

is denied." On this the comments of Vijñāna are "If the father, having not paid the debt due, has died, or has gone to a distant country, or is overpowered by incurable illness etc. then the debt contracted by him must be paid by his son or grandson, even in the absence of father's property—on account of being a son, and (a grandson). Therein, this is the order, in father's default, it is the son; in son's default, it is the grandson, (who should pay). On a denial being made by the son or the grandson, when the debt has been proved by the plaintiff by witnesses etc., it should be paid by the sons and grandsons. This is the connection of the terms * * *Therefore by a son born, having given up his selfinterest-should the father be carefully released from debt—so that he may not go to hell. This should be explained,—' By a son born, that is, by a son become a major, capable of understanding transactions'. Since the plural number has been used by saying 'sons and grandsons, if there are many divided sons, they should pay the debt in accordance with their respective shares. If they are undivided—then from among those who are living together by a joint enterprise, on a footing of mutual relation of superiority and subordination, the superior alone should pay:—this is the inference to be made. So says Nārada:—' Thereafter, the sons should pay the father's debts in accordance with shares,—whether undivided or divided and he who bears the same burden, (*i. e.*, occupies the responsible post). And here, although it has been said without distinction that sons and grandsons should pay the debt, yet the son should pay with interest, in the same manner as the father, would have paid; but a grandson should pay only what is equal to the principal such not interest. This distinction should to understood;—since there is this text of Vṛhaspati. 'By the sons the paternal debt should be paid when, as if it were their own: that of the grandfather" should be paid, equal (to the original loan). By, his son 'it is not payable' Equal, *i. e.* as much was then, so much should be paid, and not interest. By his son,'—that is, 'by the great-grandson. It is note payable 'if he has not taken the wealth. And this will be made clear in the next succeeding couplet."

The next succeeding couplet, and the important parts of Vijñāna's comments are as follows:[1]

"The appropriator of the heritable wealth should be made to pay the debt; similarly, also he who appropriates the woman; a son whose wealth had not gone to another person, of one possessed of heritable wealth, who is devoid of sons:' I have in this translation purposely tried to retain the ambiguity, or rather the unintelligibility of the couplet of Yājñavalkya, in order to illustrate how our old commentators of law evolve sense out of what at first hardly appears to be sense. On this couplet, Vijñāna comments:—

"Heritable wealth is that, which being once the property of one person, becomes the property of a second person, without there being any sale, etc. The appropriator of heritable wealth is one, who by meant of partition, appropriates heritable wealth. He should be made to pay the debt. What is intended to be said is this. He who takes

---

1. ऋक्थग्राह ऋणं दाप्यो योषिदग्राह स्तथैव च।
पुत्रोऽनन्याश्रितद्रव्यः पुत्रहीनस्य रिक्थिनः।।
अन्यदीयं द्रव्यमन्यस्य क्रयादिव्यतिरेकेण यत् स्वीयं भवित तदृक्थं। विभागद्वारेण रिक्थं ग्टह्णाति इति ऋक्थग्राहः। स ऋणं दाप्यः। एतदुक्तं भवति। यो यदीयं द्रव्यं रिक्थरूपेण ग्टह्णाति स तत्कृतमृणं दाप्यः। न चौरादिरिति। योषितं भार्य्यां ग्टह्णातीति योषिद्ग्राहः। स तथैव ऋणं दाप्यः। यो यदीयां योषितं गृह्णाति। स तत्कृतमृणं दाप्यः। योषितोऽविभाज्यद्रव्यत्वेन ऋक्थयपदेशानर्हत्वात् भेदेन निर्देशः। पुत्रश्च अनन्याश्रितद्रव्य ऋणं दाप्यः। अन्यमाश्रित मन्याश्रितं मातृपितृसम्बन्धि द्रव्यं यस्य असौ अन्याश्रितद्रव्यः। न अन्याश्रितद्रव्यः अनन्याश्रितद्रव्यः। पुत्रहीनस्य ऋक्थिन ऋणं दाप्य इति सम्बन्धः। एतेषां समवाये क्रमश्च पाठक्रम एवं। ऋक्थग्राह ऋणं दाप्य स्तदभावे योषिद्ग्राहस्तदभावे पुत्र इति।–पुत्रे सत्यपि अन्य ऋक्थग्राहौ सम्भवति क्लीवान्धबधिरादीनां पुत्रत्वेऽपि ऋक्थहरत्वाभावात् । तथाच क्लीवादीननुक्रम्य भर्त्तव्यास्तु निरंशका इति वक्ष्यति। तथा सवर्णापुत्रेऽप्यन्यायवृत्तो न लभेत इति केषामिति गौतमवचनात्। अतश्च क्लीवादिषु पुत्रेषु सत्सु अन्यायवृत्ते च सवर्णापुत्रे सति ऋक्थग्राह्नौ पितृव्यतत्पुत्रादिः।– – – अनन्याश्रितद्रव्य इति वहपुत्रेषु ऋक्थाभावेऽपि अंशग्रहणयोग्यस्यैव ऋणापाकरणाधिकारी न अयोग्यस्य अन्धादेरित्येवमर्थ। पुत्रहीनस्य रिक्थिन इत्येतदपि पुत्रपौत्रहीनस्य प्रपौत्रादयो यदि रिक्थं गृह्णन्ति तक्ष ऋणं दाप्या न अन्यथा इत्येवमर्थं। पुत्रपौत्रौ तु ऋक्थग्रहणाभावेऽपि दाप्यौ इत्युक्तं।

another's property as *heritable wealth,* should be made to pay that person's debt, not a thief etc. One who appropriates the woman is, one who takes the wife. He in a similar manner should be made to pay the debt. He who takes the woman of another person, should be made to pay that person's debt. Since a woman; cannot be spoken of as heritable wealth, she has been separately mentioned. And a son, whose wealth has not gone to another person, should be made to pay the debt. 'Whose wealth has gone to another man' means 'the wealth of whose father and mother has gone to another man.' 'Should be made to pay the debt, of one possessed of heritable wealth, who is devoid of sons.' This is the connection of the terms. When these all exist together, the order of their liability is the same as the order of their mention in the text. The appropriator of heritable wealth should be made to pay the debt; in his default, the appropriator of the woman ; in default thereof the son. * * * Even though there be a son, there may be another another appropriator of wealth. Although the impotent, the blind, etc. are sons, yet they are not participators of heritable wealth Thus—(Yājñavalkya) will, (in say a future part of the work) in connection with the impotent, etc., that they are shareless, and should be maintained. So there is a saying of Gautama,—' Even a son of a wife of the same caste, which son is ill-behaved, should not get. Say some.' Therefore when there are sons who are impotent etc., or when there is a son of a wife of the same caste, which son is ill-behaved, the appropriator of heritable wealth is, the paternal uncle, his son, etc. 'A son whose wealth has gone to another.' The meaning of this is, that where there are many sons, although there may be no heritable wealth, yet it is one competent to inherit who has a right to pay the debt, not one incompetent, such as a blind man etc. 'Of one possessed of heritable wealth, who is devoid of sons'. The meaning of it is, that of one who has no son or grandson, if the great-grandson etc. take the heritable wealth, then they should be made to pay, not otherwise. But it *has* been said that a son and a grandson should be made to pay, even though they do not take the heritable wealth."

After perusing these passages, can there be any doubt that when law was administered by a Hindu king, the sons were placed in a far more unfavourable position than they have been placed in by Kantoo Lal's case. There the sons had to pay their father's debts, although it might be that they had not inherited any wealth from him. Whereas at present, only the joint property, received by them on account of their relationship the father, is liable. The definition of Riktha, which I have rendered 'heritable wealth' as given by Vijñāna at the beginning of his comments on this couplet of Yājñavalkya which I have quoted last, is significant. If some property once belonged to one person, and comes to belong to another, not by the ordinary method of acquiring property, such as purchase, etc., the same is called Riktha. Does not the interest, which a son has in the difinition ancestral property, come within the terms of that definition. Before the son was born, the whole ancestral property undoubtedly belonged to the father. Therefore, the property was then another person's. It becomes son's property, not by purchase, nor by any other ordinary method of acquiring property. Therefore it is Riktha, in the hand of the son. Consequently, the son is liable not only as a son, but also as the appropriator of Riktha or heritable wealth. Kantoo Lal's case has established the son's liability only in this latter capacity of an appropriator of Riktha. It has therefore not gone for enough in the direction, in which the old Hindu Law of the original texts went.

Texts relating to immoral debts.

I shall now cite the texts regarding the immoral, character of the debts. This topic is explained in Śloka 48 of the second chapter of Yājñavalkya, and has been discussed in Vijñāna's comments upon the same.[1] "The son should not pay such paternal debt, as is incurred on account of drink of lust, of gambling; nor the balance of a fine or of a toll; nor likewise his infructuous gifts. That debt incurred by drinking liquors; that incurred by reason of infatuation about a woman; that on account of his being a loser in a game of hazard; infructuous gifts, that is, what has been promised to a cheat, to a minstrel, to a wrestler, and so fouth. For these is a Smṛti text,—'A gift made to a cheat, a minstrel, a wrestler, a quack, a gambler, a swindler, to pimps, dancing master and thieves, bears no fruit.' Such debt, contracted by the father, the son, etc., should not pay to the liquor-seller, etc. Here, because 'the *balance* of a fine and of a toll' has been spoken of, it should not be deemed that the whole should be paid. For there is a text of Usanas, 'A fine or the balance of a fine, a toll or the balance hereof, should not be paid by the son; nor that for which no action lies.' It has been said by Gautama also,—'the intoxicating drink, the toll, the gambling money, and the fine, should not devolve on the son 'Should not devolve, that is, are not payable by the son. '(Literally, do not place themselves upon the son.) This is the meaning."

This enumeration of immoral debts is in consonance with Manu, ch. VIII, Śloka 159. "The son need not pay a

1. सुराकामद्यूतकृतं दण्डशुल्कावशिष्टकं।
वृथादानं तथैवेह पुत्रो दद्यान्न पैतृकं।।
सुरापानेन यत् कृतमृणं। कामकृतं स्त्रीव्यसनेन कृतं। द्यूते पराजयनिमित्तं।
दण्डशुल्कयोरवशिष्टं। वृथादानं धूर्त्तवन्दिमल्लादिभ्यो यत् प्रतिज्ञातं।
धूर्त्ते वन्दिनि मल्ले च कुवैद्ये कितवे शठे।
चाटचारणचौरेषुं दत्तं भवति निष्फलं। इति स्मरणात्।
एतहणं पित्रा कृतं पुत्रादिः शौण्डिकादिभ्यो न दद्यात्। अत्र दण्डशुल्कावशिष्टकमित्यवशिष्ठग्रहणात्
सर्व्वं दातव्यमिति न मन्तव्यं।
दण्डं वा दण्डशेषं वा शुल्कं तच्छेषमेव वा।
न दातव्यं तु पुत्रेण यश्च न व्यावहारिकमित्यशनःस्मरणात्।
गौतमेनाप्युक्तं। मद्यशुल्कद्यूतदण्डा न पुत्रानध्यावहेयुः। इति। न पुत्रस्योपरि भवन्ति इत्यर्थः।
अनेन अदेयमृणमुक्तं।

liability incurred by father on account of being a surety, or fruitlers gift, or gambling money, or that for liquor, or the balance of a fine or a doll."

The same subject has been very elaborately discussed to the Vivāda Cintāmaṇi, Baboo Prosunno Coomar's. Translation, pp. 22 *et seq.* I shall quote here a few lines therefrom, (p. 36.)

"Vṛhaspati says that sons are not liable for such debts of their fathers as are due for the purchase of spirituous liquors, for gaming, idly-promised gifts, love, anger surety, fines, tolls, and the balance tolls or fines. Vyāsa confirms this. Fines, tolls, balance thereof, or debts for irregular conduct, due from fathers, shall be paid by their sons. Kātyāyana speaks of debts incurred through love and anger. Debt through love means what is promised to a harlot. Debt through anger means what is promised to a man as compensation for injury done to him." The same texts are found and explained in the same manner in the Vyvahāra-mayūkha, Mandlik's Translation, pp. 112, 113.

Devagaṇa Bhatta, the author of the Smṛticandrikā, has discussed the liability of the sons for their father's debts in a disquisition, which extends over six leaves of the manuscript I have consulted.[1] The whole of his observation upon the point is of an exceedingly interesting character, and quite sufficient to dispel the idea, sons in a Hindu joint family were ever held exempt payment of their paternal debts. This author has quoted largely from Vṛhaspati, Nārada, Kātyāyana and Viṣṇu; the quotations show how minutely these Ṛṣis have dealt with the liability of the sons, and how little reason there is for supposing that the doctrine promulgated in Kantoo Lal's case is novel, or repugnant to the old law of joint families. As space will not allow of my citing the whole discussion from the Smṛti-candrikā, I must

1. See *ante*, p.146

content myself by quoting the following passage from leaf 140, p. 2 of the manuscript.[1]

"Kātyāyana says:—'Even though the father be living, if he is afflicted with disease, of gone to sojourn away from his own country,—the debt contracted by the father should be paid by sons after the twentieth year.' After the twentieth year,' that is, commencing from the date of going abroad. The sons should pay, if it is not known to what place the father is gone. For otherwise, the father himself can pay, by sending the money. If he is afflicted with a disease, if there be disagreement as to kind and amount, it should be paid only after ascertainment. So says Vṛhaspati. 'Even when the father is alive, if he be afflicted with disease, such as consumption, leprosy, etc., or if he be a born blind person then the sons should pay the debt when it has been—proved.' When there is no disagreement, it should be paid immediately after a demand, as the text says,—'To one

1. कात्यायनः। विद्यमानेऽपि रोगार्त्ते स्वदेशात् प्रोपितेऽथवा।
विंशात् संवत्सराद् देयं ऋणं पित्रकृतं सुतैः।
विंशात् संवत्मरात् प्रवासमारभ्येति शेषः। कुत्र गत इत्यज्ञातविषये सुतैर्देय। अन्यत्र प्रस्थापनादिना पित्रैव दातुं शक्यत्वात्। रोगार्तें तु स्वरूपसंख्यादिविप्रतिपत्तौ निर्णयात् पश्चादेव देर्य। तथाच वृहस्पतिः।
सान्निध्येऽपि पितुः पुत्रैः ऋणं देयं विभावितं।
जात्यन्ध पतितोन्मत्त क्षयश्वित्रादिरोगिणः।।
अविप्रतिपत्तौ तु याचमानाय दातव्यमित्यादिनोक्त याचनानन्तरादि कालएव दातव्यं कालांतरास्मृतेः। क्षयश्वित्रादीत्यत्र आदिशब्देन क्षयश्वित्रादिसदृशा दुश्चिकित्स्या एवं रोगा गृह्यन्ते न पुनर्ज्वरादयः। जात्यन्धादिभिः पुत्रैः पितर्य्युपरते प्रोषिते जात्यन्धत्वादिना प्रतिदानासमर्थेऽपि न देयं। जात्यन्धदीनां पितृद्रव्यभागानर्हत्वात्। क्षयादिरोगिणामत्यन्तो पद्रुतत्वात्।
तथाच कात्यायनः। ऋणं तु दापयेत् पुत्रं यदि स्यान्निरुपद्रवः।
द्रविणार्हश्च धुर्य्यश्च नान्यथा दापयेत् सुतं।।
द्रविणार्हः पितृद्रव्यभागार्हः। धुर्य्यो वोढ़ा। अर्ह इति वदन् पितृद्रव्याग्रहणेऽपि अर्हत्वे सति पुत्री दाप्य इति दर्शयति।– –धुर्य्यश्च इत्येतत् असमानभावेन वर्त्तमाननानापुत्रविषयं। तथात्र नारदः।
पितर्य्युपरते पुत्रा ऋणं दद्युर्यथांशतः।
विभक्ता: अविभक्ता वा यस्तामुद्धरते धुरं।।
यथांशत इति विषमांशविधायकशास्त्रानुसारेण विभक्तपुत्रविषयं। समभागविभक्त स्तु समानमेव धनं दद्युः। अविभक्ताश्च समप्रधानतया वर्त्तमानाः सम्भूयसमुत्थानेन दद्युः। गुणप्रधानतया वर्त्तमानेषु अविभक्तेषु प्रधानभूत एव सर्वं दद्यात्। गुणभूतस्यानधिकारात्।

demanding, should be paid etc.' For there is no text inculcating any other time for payment. By the term etc. (in consumption, leprosy; etc.') are included only the diseases difficult to cure, like the consumption, and the leprosy—but not fever etc. If the sons themselves are born blind etc., then even if the father dies, goes abroad, or becomes unable to repay on account of being born blind etc., the sons should not pay; for, sons who are born blind etc. are incompetent to receive a share of father's property; and since sons who are afflicted with consumption etc. are themselves in very great trouble. So says Kātyāyana. 'The son should be made to pay the debt, if he be free from trouble, and competent to inherit, and a bearer of burden otherwise he should not be made to pay.' Competent to get a share of father's wealth. By saying the Ṛṣi shows that even though the son does not actually get his father's wealth, still he should pay, if he be a person free from a defect that disqualifies. 'Bearer of burden'—this applies to a case where there are many sons living together is an unequal manner. That is, some are superior, some subordinate. So says Nārada. 'When the father is dead the sons should pay the debt according to their shares, if divided or if undivided, then he who bears the same burden.' 'According to their shares.' This has reference to those texts of the law that inculcate unequal allotment. Those who have divided with equal allotments, shoal pay an equal share each. Those who are undivided are living together, all being invested with an euqal authority; should pay by combined exertions. Where the undivided live under an arrangement of 'unequalauthority, some being superior, some subordinate—then he having the superior authority alone should pay the whole. For one inferior in authority is not competent to pay."

I have thus cited passages from each one of the special treatises 'accepted in the four schools of 'aggregate ownership,' to show that the principle adopted in Kantoo Lal's case is repugnant to none of these schools. The principle had been virtually inoperative for a long period of time, from the date when the post of law-officers attached to the tribunals of this country, whose duty it was to inform the Judges in questions relating to Hindu Law, was abolished on the ground that the Pundits could not be relied upon. Happily there was that Sudder Dewanny case in which the true law had been once enunciated, and happy the Appellote Court in England, by the eminent training of its members in the various systems of jurisprudence, with which they have to deal in discharging their august functions, could by their very instincts catch hold of the hidden rule of equity and good conscience, that lay buried in obscure and rarely explored regions of our original texts. Had it not been for these two circumstances, it is difficult to see how otherwise the perpetuation of systematic iniquity in connection with the administration of the Mitākṣarā Law could have been obviated.

Decisions subsequent to Giridhari Lal's case.

A large number of cases has now been decided by the four High Courts of India, in which regard has been had to Kantoo Lal's case. He would be bold who should say that all these decisions can be reconciled with one another. At least a most eminent Judge of the Calcutta High Court, who has been more than ordinarily outspoken on other occasions, begins one of his judgments by the following observation:—"This appears to be one of those fraudulent cases on the part of a Mitākṣarā Father and son's which have led to the late *fluctuating* developments of the Mitākṣarā Law.[1]" The duty which is cast upon me is to notice a number of these decisions *seriatim* and to point out the principles upo which they rest.

---

1. See *per* Pontifex, in Laljee Sahoy *v.* Fakir Chand, 7 R. C. L. Ft. 99. As to the outspokenness, see the remarks of the same learned Judge on what he calls the 'spasmodic character of Indian legislation,' in Kally Nag *v.* Chander Nath Nag, 10 C. L. R. 216.

When ancestral property is purchased at an auction sale in, execution of a decree against the father, the sons, will not be entitled to recover the property on the ground that the debts contracted by the father were of an immoral character, merely because it appears that the father used occasionally to attend nautch parties, and also to give such parties at his own expense in his own house". In the case in which the above rule was laid down one of the learned Judges says[1]:—"If that is to be considered an immorality, and an estate is not to be made liable for a father's debts because the father attends nautches and gives nautches at his own expense, all I can say is that there is not an estate in the country that could decree-holder in execution if sales are to be set aside on such a ground." In this case, the decision rested also upon the circumstance, that the sons who wanted to set aside the sales could not satisfactorily prove that they had been born previous to the mortgages, which led to the sales in execution of decrees. It was moreover found; that a considerable portion of the monies had been borrowed for legitimate purposes, such as would have been a valid incumbrance on the estate. If the sons have not been born at the time when the father makes the alienation, the father being the sole owner, his act of alienation must necessarily be valid. At least the case-law has so established it, although the general rule against alienation of ancestral property, which is found in para. 27, sec. I, ch. I, Mitakṣarā, if strictly applied, would not allow of an alienation of even this kind, since the rule says that these that are yet unbegotten are in expectation of the means of subsistence, for which reason there can be neither a gift nor a sale of ancestral property. In practice, so large a scope was never given by Courts to the above saying of the of Vyāsa.

Where the debts are incurred for the performance of a family ceremony, such as an obsequial rite, or a nuptial rite;

1. Budree Lal *v.* Kantee Lal, 23 W. R. 260.

or where the reality of the debts is guaranteed by the existence of a decree against the father; if a creditor lends money on the security of the ancestral property, whereby the judgment-debt is paid, he has a charge upon the whole ancestral property including the sons' interest. Such loans of the father, to save the property from sale in execution of a decree against him, can never be said to be of an immoral character. And a loan for the performance of an obsequial or nuptial ceremony has been always held to be a valid legal necessity.[1] The father can also contract valid loans, so as to be a charge upon the whole ancestral property, in order to pay off debts left by his own father, the grandfather of his sons who contest the validity of such loans. Any disposition of property which is reasonably made by the father for the purpose of discharging his own father's debts, must necessarily be an unavoidable cause of expenditure, within the meaning of Paras 28 and 29 sec. 1, ch. I, Mitākṣarā. Such a debt is one, for which the ancestral property would be ultimately liable; and the act of alienation, whether it be a mortgage or a sale by the father upon reasonable terms, for the purpose of discharging the debt, must be substantially an unavoidable, transaction.[2] The case from which I draw the above rule thus describes the result of Kantoo Lal's case. "The interest which under the Mitākṣarā Law a son acquires in ancestral property of his father, by, and in the event of being born, is of the nature of an inheritance, and remains liable to the payment of the personal debts of the father even though subsequently contracted, in the same way as the entire property would have been liable had the son not been born, except only in the case where these debts are illegal or were contracted for an immoral purpose. The interest of the sons as well as the interest of the father in the property, although it is ancestral, is liable for the payment of the father's debts." These are the words of Phear, J., according

1. Muddon Gopal Lal *v.* Muss. Gowrun Butty. 23 W. R. 365.
2. Ibid.

to whom, if there is but once a money decree against the father, he authorised to enter into any reasonable transaction relating to the ancestral property, provided the transaction is for the purpose of settling the judgment debt.

I have already said that one apparent result of Kantoo Lal's case is, that it has shifted the burden of proof to the son, when he seeks to set-aside sales of ancestral property of his father's debts. According it has been held, on account that where a zur-i-peshgee lease was given by the father in order to pay off certain judgment debts against himself, and where it was found that excepting a small portion of the money borrowed on the security of that lease, the whole went to the payment of the decrees against the father, it was for the son to show that the debts contracted by the father were for an immoral purpose. After citing from the Privy Council Judgement, the learned Judges of the High Court say:—"Clearly by this their Lordships mean to throw the *onus* both in this case and in the case of a decree on the plaintiff to show, that the debts which were incurred by his father were debts contracted for an immoral purpose, and that therefore he is not under any pious obligation to pay those debts.[1] As nothing but absolute immorality of the purpose which a debt is contracted by the father will invalidate an alienation in consequence of that debt, it has been held that where the father executed a bond to raise money or the purpose of paying the zur-i-peshgee of a farming lease taken by himself, and the lease ultimately proved a loss, the sons were nevertheless bound, by the decree on the basis of that bond and the consequent execution sale of the ancestral property.[2] It should be borne in mind that within the jurisdiction of the Calcutta High Court, in those parts of the Province where the Mitākṣarā Law prevails, one of the commonest methods adopted by men of substance for investing their money is to take zuri-

1. Muss. Kooldeep Kooer *v.* Runjeet Sing, 24 W. R., 231.
2. Ram Sahoy Sing *v.* Mohaheer Pershad, 25 W. R., 185.

peshgee leases. This is a transaction which belongs to the category of speculation in landed property. The zamindar class of the Behar and the Mithila Districts, like their prototypes all over the world, are mostly an idle class. On the other hand, the upstart mahajans, fresh from the pursuit of the exciting business, which consists in trading and money-lending operations, lay out their earnings in securing leases of land, which run for a pretty considerable number of years. They advance a large ready sum to the zamindar, bind themselves also to pay a rent, sometimes nominal, sometimes substantial, and are put in possession of extensive tracts of land, mostly tenanted, in order that by rack-renting and other harassing measures, they may make good to themselves not only the advance of ready money, and rent and legitimate interest, but also in large profits. This is the reason of the existence of these transactions, known in the world of business and of law as zur-i-peshgee, which literally means 'money advanced.' Law regards it as a kind of mortgage; but from an economical point of view, it cannot but be looked upon as additional engine of harassment, over and above the many that operate upon the Indian agriculturist.

Father's powers over joint property extended

However that be, in the case quoted above, it has been held that the father of a joint family can legitimately contract loans for the purpose of speculating in leases of land of the above-named kind; and that such loans are not immoral, so as to authorize the son to claim exemption from paying the same. This is an illustration of what I have already said, that whereas formerly the doctrine of legal necessity could not protect such loans, now the theory of the son's liability to pay all but immoral debts, has given a new sanctity to them. In other words, the sons and their interest in the ancestral property are liable for such loans of the father. The equitable principle that may be lurking within this rule of law appears to be this. If the father borrows money on the security of ancestral property, thereby speculates in leases of land, and makes large profits by the transactions, the sons' right to lay a claim to the share of such profits as made by the assistance of ancestral funds, has been always admitted, and is in fact an established proposition of law. That being so, where the father's speculations in that direction do not prove a success, it would lie ill in the mouth of the sons to say, that their share of the ancestral property would not be liable. As the profits, so the eventual losses, should be borne by all the member of a group of individuals which is not unoften likened to a corporation.

The above case illustrates a large extension of the father's powers in dealing with ancestral property. The following case proves, if possible, a still larger extension of the same powers. The father acted as an agent for a third person unconnected with the family. He under a mistaken notion that he was authorized to grant a lease in the name of his principal, exercised the supposed authority in leasing his principal's lands to a fourth person. The principal, far from ratifying the act of his agent, repudiated the grant of lease; whereupon the lease being annulled, the aforesaid agent incurred heavy liabilites. The father borrowed money on mortgage of family lands; the mortgagee sued, obtained a decree, and sold the mortgaged lands in execution; the High Court held that the lands had been rightly sold, and that the entire interest of the family, including both the father's and the son's interest, had passed; Garth, C. J., observing." It is a mistake to suppose that father and son had several undivided shares in the family estate. The father was in fact in possession of the whole; and although he might not have had power to dispose of it for immoral purposes, so as to defeat his son's inchoate rights, he had still such an entire proprietary interest, that when his rights and title were sold under a decree *bona fide* obtained upon a debt properly contracted, and which the son in the event of his father's death would have been bound to pay, the whole interest passed to the purchaser under that sale.' The

Chief Justice also said that it was impossible to declare under the circumstances that the debts had been improperly or unreasonably contracted by the father.[1]

The chain of argument by which the above result would be arrived at may be thus set forth in a different manner. It is not an immoral act on the part of the father to be employed as agent for another person; nor is it immoral, if he makes a mistake as to the extent of his authority as such agent, whatever obtuseness of intelligence it may indicate. If the father therefore by an erroneous exercise of his agent's authority, renders himself liable for damages; a decree may be obtained against him; he may be put in jail; and I apprehend that this would be a distress or calamity expressly provided for by Vyāsa's text quoted in para. 27, sec. 1, ch. I, Mitākṣarā Vyāsa says that in *āpatkāla*, or time of distress; a single member can alienate the whole family property. The incarceration of the father of the family is certainly a calamity. Any measure, even including the sale of the whole property, would be legitimate, not only to remove the calamity when it has actually happened, but also to avert it when it is impending. What more certain than that when the father is liable to pay damages for wrongful conduct, he will be put in jail unless he pays them by some means in his power? He therefore rightly sells or pledges ancestral property, to avert such an impending danger.

High rate of interest does not render a debt illegal or immoral

Similarly, it seems, he may purchase property by contrading loans on payment of exorbitant interest, say 50 per cent; and when the loan is converted into a judgement-debt against him, the whole ancestral property will be liable for it. The auction-purchaser of such property in the execution sale need not make any other enquiry, except that there has been a decree and an attachment. When the Privy Council

1. Shah Wajed Hossein *v.* Baboo Nankoo sing, 26 W. R., 311.

say in Kantoo Lal's case that, such a purchaser is bound to see that the decree has been properly obtained; according to Markhy, J.,[1] all that the Privy Council mean is, that the purchaser will see that the decree is in proper form; not that the transactions which were the basis of the decree were proper. That would be imposing an amount of trouble upon the purchaser, which is unreasonable in itself, an obligation that it would be impracticable for the purchaser to perform. Nor would the exorbitant rate of interest, (according to the same learned Judge), which may have been decreed, and which may be patent on the face of the decree, derogate from the propriety of the decree. Hindu law may have laid down express prohibitions against high rates of interest. But those rules have been disregarded by modern tribunals, which, since the repeal of the Indian Usury law by Act XXVII of 1855, have guided themselves upon this point by the most advanced European notions relating to the law of interest. The award of a high rate of interest can be scarcely said to taint a judgment-debt with such an immoral character, as would exempt the son's interest in the ancestral property. Nor would the decree, and the attachment of property based upon it, be bad in form, simply because the mortgaged property has not been first ordered to be sold. In general, where there is a mortgage, the Courts, in awarding a decree for money, direct, that the mortgaged property shall be sold first; and that if the sale proceeds be insufficient to discharge the whole judgment-debt, then other property shall be liable. But supposing that no such direction were contained in the decree, it would not be bad in law; nor should the auction-purchaser be deterred, by absence of such a direction in the decree, from purchasing joint family property in execution of a decree against the father.

Purchaser's Right Confined to Father's Share, Where

On the other hand, the Privy Council case of Suraj Bunsi

1. Muss. Luchmee Dai *v.* Asman Sing, 25 W. R., 421.

Kooer, 4 C. L. R. 226, is an authority for saying, that if before the sale, the son's intervene and plead that the father's debts were originally immoral, that if the auction-purchaser makes his purchase in spite of such objection on the sons' part, that if subsequently in a suit between the sons and the auction-purchaser, the sons substantiate their plea of the immorality of the debts–in such a case the auction-purchaser will at best get only the father's share of the property, and the sons' interest in the ancestral property will be protected. For, in every case, even though there be a decree against the father, the immoral character of the debts in their inception, if known to the auction-purchaser, will be a ground for, the invalidity of his purchase. If that fact be not positively known, still if it be brought to his notice, if the sons give notice that they object to the valid nature of their father's debts, then it becomes the duty of every person who desires to bid for joint property, to make a searching enquiry as to the truth of the sons' objection. After such a notice has been once given to the purchaser before the purchase, his purchase as regards other persons share, over and above that of the father, will stand or fall, according as the sons fail or succeed in making good the objection that the debts were immoral. The father's share, however, will always remain to the purchaser, whatever the character of the debts may be, provided the purchase, be made in execution in the lifetime of the father. If the father, however, be dead at the time when the execution sale takes place, a fresh complication is added to the circumstances by the strict rule of survivorship. By that rule, as soon as the father dies, his share, or rather; his interest, lapses to his sons. Although therefore the law says, that a single member's share passes under an execution sale, (Deen Dyal'a case, p. 499, *ante*), yet where the member himself no longer exists, his share must be at an end, and nothing can pass. In Suraj Bunsi's case (4 C. L. R. 226) the Judicial Committee upheld the claim of the purchaser to the extent of the father's share, although at the time of the auction sale the father was no longer living, resting their conclusion upon the exceptional circumstances of the case; and saying[1] that at the time of the father's death, the execution proceedings, under which the joint family property had been attached and ordered to be sold, had gone so far as to constitute, in favour of the judgment-creditor, a valid charge upon the land, to the extent of the father's undivided share and interest therein, which could not be defeated by his death before the actual sale.

Suraj Bansi Kooer's Case

This case of Suraj Bunsi Kooer has also settled, that if there be some debts owing by the father, that if in order to pay off such antecedent debts, the father contracts fresh loans by pledging family property, then such pledge will be binding upon the sons, unless they can show that the loan was immoral. Accordingly, it has been held that a zur-i-peshgee lease, granted by the father, will entitle the creditor who has advanced money to him, in order to pay off antecedent debts, to take possession of the family lands by virtue of his zur-i-peshgee deed, unless the sons succeed in showing the loans to be of an immoral character.[2] In deciding this case, the learned "Judges of the Calcutta High Court had occasion to refer to a previous decision by White, J., in the case of Bheknarain Sing *v.* Janak Sing, I. L. R. 2 Cal., 438. The judgment of Mr. Justice White illustrates how the ruling in Kantoo Lal's case was at first attempted by the tribunals in this country to be confined to as narrow limits as liable. In that case of Becknarain Sing, the father had mortgaged the whole joint property belonging to himself and his two minor sons; he failed to repay at the due date, whereupon the mortgagee brought a suit for realizing his money by the estate that had been pledged. In this suit the

1. P. 241, 4 C. L. R.
2. Gunga Pershad *v.* Sheo Dyal Sing, 5 C. L. R. 225.

sons also were made parties. The District Judge gave a decree for the sale of the whole property, inasmuch as the sons failed to show that the father's loans were immoral. White, J. in the High Court, however, distinguished the case from that of Kantoo Lal, on the ground that it was a suit by the mortgagee of the father for a declaration, that the whole interest of the three members, namely the father and two sons, was liable for the mortgage debt. In such a suit by the creditor, it was, according to White, J., for the creditor to show that there was legal necessity at the bottom of the father's loans, not for the sons to prove the immoral character of the loans. Were, it otherwise, says that learned Judge, then "the interests the ancestral immoveable property, which, under the Mitākṣarā Law, are vested in sons by their birth are entirely unprotected from the selfish or wasteful or capricious acts of the father, except in the single instance of money borrowed by him upon the estate for immoral purposes." The learned Judge therefore held that only the father's share in the ancestral property was liable for the mortgage debt. But this case is considered by Miner, J. as overruled by the Privy Council in Suraj Bunsi Kooer's case.[1] These differences of opinion justify what Pontifex, J, says as to the fluctuating decisions under the ruling in Kantoo Lal's case.[2]

These differences of opinion led to a reference of the following questions to a Full Bench of the Calcutta High Court, the decision in which has been reported in Luchman Das *v.* Girdhari Chowdry, 6 C. L. R., 476. The propositons of law established by the Full Bench judgement may be thus summed up:—

---

1. See 5 C. L. R, p. 226;—I should have mentioned that Suraj Bunsi Kooer'e case is the same as Ram Sahai *v.* Sheo Prosad Sing, 4. C. L. R. 226, Suraj Bunsi being, I believe, the guardian of the minor Ram Sahai. I have referred to the case in these Lectures under both the titles.
2. See *ante*, p. 566.

Full bench case of Luchman Das v. Giridhari Chowdry, rules established by

1. If the family consists of a father and one minor son, the father being necessarily the manager, if then the father hypothecates family property, if there be no legal necessity, nor on the other hand any suggestion or evidence that the loan was made for an illegal or an immoral purpose, nor does it appear that the lender made any enquiry as to purpose for which the money was required by the father; in such a case, the money advanced by the creditor may be sued for in a suit against the father and the son, and the lender can get a decree directing the debt to be paid out of the whole ancestral estate, inclusive of the mortgaged property; but the mortgage itself could not be enforced by him. This latter part of the rule seems to say, that supposing the mortgage were usufructuary, the mortgagee cannot take possession of the family property by virtue of the mortgage deed; his remedy is limited to realizing his money, from whatever family property may be in the possession of the father and the son.

2. If under the circumstances named above, the father dies before a suit is brought for the money, the lender will be competent to sue the minor son alone, and to enforce the very same remedy against him.

3. If, however, under the above circumstances, the mortga-gee sues the father alone, gets a decree for payment and for sale of the property, and at the sale buys the property himself, he cannot be considered as a *bona fide* purchaser for value, nor will he be entitled to the property, except to the extent of the father's interest, as against the infant son.

4. If the son be adult at the date of the father's executing the mortgage deed, then the son may be, made a party to the suit for money against the father, and the mortgagee will be entitled to a decree directing the debt to be paid out of the whole ancestral estate.

5. As to what would constitute an antecedent debt, within the meaning of the expression as used by the Privy Council in Suraj Bunsi Kooer'a case, (4 C. L. R., 226), the Full Bench seems to hold that whatever money is borrowed by the father, except for an illegal or immoral purpose, would be an antecedent debt, and would be a good foundation for an action jointly against the father and the sons.

6. If the family consists of two brothers and their sons, and if the brothers have recourse to a circuitous process for raising money, first by giving a zur-i-peshgee lease to the lender on taking an advance from him, and then by taking a sub-lease of their own property as undertenants, whereby they actually retain possession of the property in their own hands; in such a case the Full Bench held that a decree for rent of the sub-lease obtained by the lender against the two brothers alone would bind only their own shares of the property; and that the sons not having been made parties to the rent suit, will not be affected by the decree made in it; even after an execution sale under such a decree, they would be entitled to recover their shares from the purchaser, if the holder of the rent decree be himself the purchaser.

Creditors should sue both the father and the son

The effect of this Full Bench Decision, when closely examined amounts to this, that unless the debt be immoral or illegal, the lender of money to the father of a Mitākṣarā family, in which his sons alone are his cosharers, would do well to sue both the father and the sons in an notion for the money; that the hypothecation of the family property effected by the father hardly places him in any advantageous position; that the father's share is in every case liable to make good his claim; that a decree obtained only against the father will bind only his share; that in case of such a decree made solely against the father, the decree-holder can not improve his position by purchasing the family property at the execution sale; although a third party by so purchasing might get the whole interest of the family; and that, however, circuitous the transactions may be, where the money borrowed by the father be not required for meeting any necessity of the whole family and where the transactions are in their essence, nothing more than a loan of money taken by the father,—nothing less than an actual decree against the sons will affect their interest, save and except where the purchase is made at an execution by a stranger, entirely unacquainted with the previous history of the transactions.

Within a short period after the appearance of the above Full Bench decision, it became necessary to make a still further advance towards the protection of the purchaser's interests, under the following special circumstances.[1] The father borrowed money by pledging the whole family property, in which he and an adult son were jointly interested. The money was required for paying off two decrees which had been obtained by the creditor against the father alone, also another decree which had been obtained against both the father and the son. A small part of the money borrowed was spent in some religious ceremony on account of the deceased grandfather. The creditor sued the father alone on the mortgage deed of the latest date, without making his adult son a party to it, obtained a decree, and in execution sale, himself became the purchaser and took possession of the whole family property belonging to both the father and the son. after he had been thus in possession for 11 years, the son sued recover his share. But Pontifex, J. disallowed the son's claim, although such a claim might be sustainable on the rules laid down by the Full Bench, since the son had not been a party to the last suit which culminated in the execution sale. The special circumstances relied upon by Pontifex, J. to distinguish the case from those

1. Lalji Sahay *v.* Fakir Chand, 7 C. L. R., 100.

to which the Full Bench Decision would apply, were these: (1) A great part of the money borrowed on the last occasion by the father went to satisfy a judgment-debt enforceable as well against the son as the father; (2) The son had acquiesced in the possession of the creditor purchaser for 11 years, and also had allowed him to discharge other incumbrances in the estate; (3) The son had been present when the father executed the mortgage bond, and after the decree, had asked the mortgagee to postpone the execution. For these reasons, the Full Bench Decision was not followed in this case, although it came within it on the following two grounds expressly declared by the Full Bench as sufficient to exempt the son's share in the family property, namely, that the son had not been made a party, and that the creditor himself was the auction-purchaser. In the course of his judgment in the above case, the learned Judge incidentally made the following declarations of the law upon the subject. It is a pious duty on the part of a son to pay an antecedent debt of the father, even during the father's lifetime. The father can make a valid sale or mortgage to discharge such antecedent debts, although the debts may have been contracted for a purpose which does not strictly come within the definition of a legal necessity, given in the Mitākṣarā, ch. I, sec. 1, paras. 27-29. The expression 'antecedent debt' means 'a debt antecedent to the transaction,' *vis.*, the sale or mortgage purporting to deal with the property. As regards ancestral property, the son is as much liable to pay out of it his father's debts not contracted for an immoral purpose, as he would be liable to pay his own debts out of it. But the interests of an adult son are not affected unless he be made a party to the suit. I apprehend that this latter ruling by the learned Judge requires to be qualified by saying, that the son's interest will be affected by a decree against the father alone, where in execution of that decree, a third party, other than the creditor, purchases the property without knowledge that the debts of the father were of an immoral character.

Rule where the son is adult

In the case of Aparoop Tewaree *v.* Kandhjee Sohoy, 8 C. L. R., 192, a distinction is drawn, between a minor son and an adult son, and Mitter, J. has held that in the case of an adult son an express or implied consent on his part is necessory to authorize the father in mortgaging family property in order to pay off his own antecedent debt. If there be no such consent on the part of the son, his share will not be bound by such mortgage transaction. The learned Judge further says, that if the son stands by, and allows the creditor to believe that he is a consenting party, he will be bound by the transaction. He here assimilates the father's mortgage for paying his own actecedent debt, to the case of a legal necessity as provided for in the Mitākṣarā. But as those provisions (ch. I, Sec. 1, para. 27) limit a single member's power to alienate the family property to a case in which the other members are minors, the learned Judge has laid down that when the son is adult, his consent is necessary.

Loans for carying on family trade valid

If the father purports to mortgage the whole interest of the family for an antecedent debt, then a decree obtained upon that mortgage and the consequent auction sale of the property will bind the son's share, although from the execution proceedings, it might appear that only the father's right, title and interest in the property was advertised for sale. In such a case, since the antecedent debt would be a valid consideration for pledging the whole interest of the family including that of the sons, the auction sale of the father's right and title will be construed by the law as having passed the right of the whole family.[1] Sometimes the debt incurred by the father, obviously savours of a legal necessity, as for instance, where the father of a family

1. E. J. C. Studd *v.* Birjnundon Pershad Sing, 9 C. L. R., 351.

'consisting of himself, his sons and grandsons, is carrying on a trading business, and in the course of his dealings connected with that business, contracts debts; such debts partake very much of the character of a legal necessity, if the trading business be one in which the whole family is interested. This may appear, by other members taking part in its management. In one case,[1] one of the sons was the cash-keeper of the business, which consisted in aratdaree operation. The debts were incurred in course of the business; a decree was obtained solely against the father, in execution of which the whole family property was sold, and purchased in good faith by a third party. The High Court upheld the sale of the entire family property, holding that the father was sued in his representative capacity as the manager of the joint family. In the course of his judgment, Mitter, J. pointed out the erroneousness of the supposition, that when joint family property is sold in execution, no more than the interest of the judgment-debtor can pass. The learned Judge has laid down the rule in such cases to be, that the entire property belonging to all the members of the family will pass, if it appears that the judgment-debtor represented the whole family in the suit. Whether he did so or not, will depend upon the particular circumstances of each case. The first thing to be considered was, whether the debts had any concern with a matter, in which all the members may be supposed to have an interest; secondly, it must also be seen what was sold, whether the interest of one member, or of all the members ; in order to ascertain this last point, the sale proceedings must be carefully scrutinized. Thus, in the particular instance, the family property consisted of 4 anas' share in a certain mouzah, and the family was composed of the father, his two sons and one grandson. In such a family, the father on partition would be entitled to one-third of the four-anna

1. Ambika Prosad Tewari *v.* Ram Sahai Lal, 10 C. L. R., 506.

share in the mouzah. If, however, it appeared from the sale proceedings, that all the 4 annas were advertised for sale, and were sold by auction, the execution purchaser, being actuated by good faith in making a purchase in execution of a decree against the father, would get the whole 4 annas, according to the ruling of the Privy Council in Mudden Thacoor *v.* Kantoo Lal, 22 W. R., 56. Mitter, J. also observed that the real principle established by Deen Dyal's case (I. L. R. 3 Cal. 198) was, , that under the Mitākṣarā Law, a single member's share was seizable in execution, howsoever inalienable it may be by voluntary conveyance. That case never intended to lay down, that in execution, only that member's share ' would pass by auction sale, who had been made a party to the suit.

Father sued As representing the family

This principle, that on many occasions the father of the family will be regarded as having been sued in his representative capacity as the manager of the joint family, has been extended in some cases to members other than the father. In fact, law seems to invest the Courts of Justice with a certain discretion in deciding, whether a particular suit brought nominally against a single member, is to be regarded as having really been so intended; or the single member is to be considered as having stood for the whole family corporation. The determination of this question becomes important, whenever family property has been sold by execution of a decree against a single member. Such a sale is sure to raise a contention between the other members and the auction purchaser, as to how much of the joint property the latter is entitled to get, by virtue of the auction sale, whether only the judgment-debtor's share or the entire property. The Privy Council in Bissessur Lal Sahoo *v.* Luchmissur Sing, 5 C. L. R., 477 held that one brother represented, as defendant in a suit, his co-sharer the other member of the family. The reason for so holding in that case seems to be, that the suits were for rent in respect of property, which, although held in the name of a single deceased member of the family, was yet family property. This principle of representation has been recognized in a judgment of the Allahabad High Court, where the learned Judge who delivered it, observed,[1] in a case where the son wanted to protect his share of the family property from being sold in execution of a decree solely against the father, that the whole ancestral property was liable for a debt contracted by the father of an undivided family, the property being in the father's possession and management, and the debt having been incurred for the support of the family. " No weight is to be attached in the present case to the contention, that the decree being against the father only, it is his interest that can be sold. * * * In a recent case before the Judicial Committee of the Privy Council, Bisseasur Lal Sahoo *v*. Luchmessur Sing, L. R., 6 Ind. All. 233 ; (s. c. 5. C. L. R:, 477, * their Lordships appear to consider that where the family is joint, there may be a presumption that the party sued is sued as a representative of the family, and that when the decrees are substantially decress in respect of a joint family and against the representatives of the family, they may be properly executed against the joint family property." Here the High Court seems to lay down that a decree against a single member of a joint family will be *prima facie* taken to be a decree against him as representing the family; for the learned Judge speaks of a presumption. But I apprehend that even in case of a father, it might be hard upon the sons to hold them tied to such a presumption of law, rebuttable though it be. In case of any other relative, the proposition, that any decree against him, simply because he happens to belong to an undivided family, or even because he happens to be the managing member, will *prima facie* bind the other members, would not be in unison with those authorities, which lay down, that, as a general rule,

1. Deva Sing *v*. Ram Manohar, I. L. R., 2 All. 751.

the decree will bind the judgment-debtor alone. In fact, the safest statement of the principle, whereby one member is taken as having represented all, seems to be, that the facts of each particular case will be the best guide as to whether the principle is applicable or not. When the decree is against a father, every auction purchaser in execution, other than the judgment-creditor, who has paid consideration in good faith, will get the whole family property provided the sale proceedings show that the whole interest of the family was sold. In such a case, it does not become necessary to decide, whether the father represented the whole family or not. That question arises where the sale has not yet been had, and the sons have come forward to object and to protect their share from being available for the decree holder. If the decree was on a debt which constituted a legal necessity, the father will of course be taken as having been sued in his representative character. Sometimes the debt may partake of the character of a *quasi* legal necessity, the father, for instance, having incurred debts to improve the family property. Such debts are not immoral, and the sons must pay them. It is idle for the son to contend, that he was not made a party to the suit against the father. Even if such a contention be given effect to, nothing will prevent the creditor from suing the sons for a declaration that their shares are liable to pay the debts. Such a suit must be decreed unless the debts are immoral. It is only when the family is managed by a member, who bears some other relationship than that of a father, that the question, how far he represented the others in that particular suit, assumes a difficulty. For there, the rule that sons are under a pious obligation to pay their father's debts, does not come into operation. I apprehend, that the nature of the claim, which was the foundation of the suit against a single member, will be the only criterion. The question will be whether the claim was connected with the general concerns of the family. A tradesman who has supplied goods for the use and consumption of the family, may sue the managing member alone for their value. The decree will no doubt bind the whole family property; in other words, it may be enforced by attachment and sale of the joint property. It may be that the other members can give the decree-holder some trouble by contesting their liability. But the trouble will consist in this, that the tradesman will have to prove the facts of his case a second time against these other members, in a properly framed suit; will have to show that the articles supplied by him were consumed by the family. Similarly, I apprehend, money borrowed by the managing member, which benefited the whole family, will be a good charge upon the family property. It may even be said that the principle of Honooman Prosad's case will apply; that all that is necessary on the part of the person who gives credit to the managing member is, that he made enquiries in good faith and satisfied himself that the money was for family purposes.

In Bika Sing *v.* Lachman Sing, I. L. R., 2 All., 804, Pearson, J. held, that where no more than the father's interest has been actually sold in execution of a decree solely against him, it is not necessary to inquire whether the father's debts were of an immoral character or not. The sale being limited in its character, the execution purchaser will get no more than the father's share, and the sons will recover from him if he has taken possession of anything more than the father's share.

An instance of immoral debt

When the father misappropriated certain jewels belonging to a third party, who obtained a decree for damages against him, and in execution sold the father's right, title and interest in the family property, the Allahabad High Court held that the sons were entitled to recover their shares; that they were not bound in duty to pay the debt.[1]

1. Chundra Sen *v.* Gangaram, I. L. R 2 All., 901.

In this case the action-purchaser was other than the judgment-creditor. The learned Judges said, that if the property had passed out of the family by the execution sale, the sons could not have recovered it from a stranger to the original suit, as pointed out in the case of Suraj Bunsi Kooer; but as no more than the right, title and interest of the father had been sold in execution, and as the claim was not for a family debt, but was a personal claim against the father, who was alone represented in the original suit, and the decree was against him personally for a money claim, the sons' share had not passed by the auction sale.

Where money had been borrowed by the grandfather, before his grandson was born, in order to protect ancestral property from sale, the debt is one which the grandson would be liable to pay, and for which the ancestral property would also be liable. If the grandson is a minor at the time when the lender brings his suit, and therefore is necessarily under the guardianship of his father, the head of the joint family, it is not necessary to make the grandson a party to the suit of the lender. In such a case it is presumable that the father and the uncle, being the grandfather's heirs, have been sued in their representative capacity, representing the joint family in respect of a family debt. This is in accordance with Bissessur Lal *v.* Luchmessur Sing, L. R. 6 I. A., 233, (S. C. 5 C. L. R. 477) where the Judicial Committee held, that the entire joint property was liable for two decrees against a member, who had been sued as heir of his grandfather to recover a debt for which the joint family was liable, and the family being joint, it was to be presumed that the suit had been brought against the member in his representative capacity.[1]

A certain firm was first established by the grandfather, its business was carried on by the father, who having entered into some time-bargains connected with produce business, which seemed to have formed a part of the ordi-

1. Ram Sevak *v.* Raghubar, I. L. R. 3 All. 72.

nary dealings of the firm, incurred heavy liabilities, and was alone sued, although he had a minor son joint with him. In execution, the family property was sold, the sale certificates describing a portion of the property sold as belonging to the judgment-debtor, and not describing the remaining portion as belonging to anybody. The Allahabad High Court upheld the purchaser's claim to the extent of even the minor son's share, who had not been made a party to the suit which had culminated in the execution sale. The sum and substance of the judgment of Straight, J. may be thus set forth. The firm was a joint family concern, the father was the manager, the debts were incurred in the course of the business of the firm, and they were not immoral or improper; on the contrary, if profit had accrued from the transactions out of which they arose, the minor son would have participated in it. The only contention on the part of the son is the technical one, that as he was not a party to the suit against his father, his share is not liable. But this contention is not favoured by the course of recent decisions, and the opinion of the Privy Council, expressed in one case, thus—"In execution proceedings the Courts will look to the substance of the transaction, and will not be disposed to set aside an execution sale upon mere technical grounds, when they find that it is substantially right." The minor son in this case by birth became entitled to share in the business established by his grandfather and carried on by his father; he was one of the joint proprietors; he therefore must contribute his proportion towards the discharge of any debts that might be incurred, or losses made by the managing member. Looking to the nature of the debts, it must be assumed that the father was sued as the head of the family. In the majority of suits for setting aside sales on account of father's debts, the suit is really instigated by the father for the purpose of depriving his creditors of a considerable portion of the fruits of their execution against him. Litigation of this kind involves a direct breach of the first duties of allegiance and respect due from Hindu sons towards their fathers, and is rarely instituted without collusion on the part of the latter. Consequently a claim by a son, alleging the immorality of his father as the ground for setting aside a transaction entered into by the latter, must always be viewed with great suspicion, especially where the, interests of a *bona fide* purchaser for value at sale in execution of a decree have to be considered.[1]–

In the Madras case of Chockalinga *v.* Subba Raya, I. L, R., 5 Mad., 134, the family consisted of two brothers, and two minor sons of one of the brothers. The father of the minor sons hypothecated family property in order to raise money for the purpose of rebuilding the family house, and partly also for the marriage of one of his sons. When the mortgagee brought his suit, his remedy against the person of the mortgagor had become barred, he therefore obtained a decree against the hypothecated house. The decree was solely against one of the brothers, namely, against him alone who had executed the mortgage deed. In execution, only his right was sold. But the representative of the mortgagee brought a fresh suit to have it declared that the shares of the other members were liable for the mortgage decree. The High Court disallowed the claim. The reasons upon which the judgment of the High Court proceeded may be thus set forth. Although the debt was no doubt a family debt, it could be recovered solely from the hypothecated family property, the personal remedy having become barred. But in order to bind all the coparceners by a decree upon the hyphothecation, it was necessary to make all of them parties to the suit, so as to give them an opportunity of redeeming the ancestral estate. If a suit is brought against one coparcener on an obligation entered into by him, and a decree obtained against him, and it is afterwards sought to extend the scope of the decree by making other coparceners liable upon the obligation, according to the authorities this course is not permissible, because the cause of action on the

1. Phul Chand *v.* Lachmi Chand, I. L. R., 4 All., 490.

obligation is one and indivisible, and a second suit cannot be entertained upon the same cause of action.-It should be remembered that in this Madras case, there was another brother interested in the hypothecated property, and therefore the principle of the sons' pious liability could not be applied. The remedy again upon the basis of the hypothecation had been exhausted in the first suit; therefore the second suit which sought to extend the liability over other parts of the same property, was open to the well-known objection of law, that a cause of action cannot be split into parts. That where the sons alone are their father's cosharers, their shares also would be bound by a mortgage executed by their father, appears from Srinivasa *v.* Yelaya, I. L. R., 5 Mad., 251, where it was not shown that the debt contracted by the father was an immoral one, and the High Court held that the share of the sons was also liable for it.

Although, however, the interests of the sons are liable to satisfy the father's debts, yet if the holder of a money decree against the father does not attach the joint family property, except after the death of the father, he cannot execute that decree, after such death, by attachment and sale of ancestral property in the hands of the sons. Whatever share the father had in such property during his lifetime, lapsed by survivorship to his sons immediately on his death; it is not therefore property of the deceased judgment-debtor come into the hands of his representative.[1] Turner, C. J. observed, that the decree-holder should have recourse to a separate suit, if he sought to enforce his decree against the ancestral property after the death of the father. This was a converse case of what was decided by the Privy Council in Suraj Bunsi Kooer's case, for there the property had been attached during the father's lifetime, therefore his share was held as having passed to the purchaser.

1. Hanumantha *v.* anumayya, I. L. R., 5 Mad., 233.

That the father's share in the ancestral property is not his assets after his death in the hands of his sons as his legal representatives, was further corroborated in Karpakambal Ammal *v.* Ganapathi Subbayyan, I. L. R. 5 Mad., 234, where the decree had been obtained by, it seems, some female member of the family, directing the father to make an annual payment to her by way of maintenance, and it was held that ancestral property could not be attached in execution of the decree.

In the Bombay case of Sadasiv Dinkar Joshi *v.* Dinkar Narayan Joshi, 1. L. R., 6 Bow. 522, Westropp, C. J. made the following observations:—"Subject to certain limited exceptions (as, for instance debts contracted for immoral or illegal purposes), the whole of the estate of a Hindu undivided family would be, when in the hands of sons or grandsons, liable to the debts of the father or grandfather." The burden of proof, he continues, that the debt was for an illegal or immoral purpose, lies upon the son or the grandson who seeks to contest such liability. Simply because the father kept a mistress would not prove the debt to be immoral, unless it be established that the debt had some connection with that fact.

Chapter 11

Partition

Practical importance of the question, Is a family joint or separate—partition how made evident—According to Mitākṣarā—According to Vīrāmitrodaya—According to Smṛti candrikā—To declare, 'I am separate' tantamount to partition—Division by metes and bounds not essential— Written instrument tantamount to partition- Separation in mess takes place first—Separate appropriation of profits may amount to partition—A suit for partition and proceedings of Courts—How to effect partition-Partition effected by father-Preferential share to an eldest son—Deductions or 'uddhara'—Partition of father's acquisitions'—Time for partition during father's life—Father's wives receive a share—Wife's deductions—Deductions obsolete-Partition after father's death—Father's wife's share in Bengal—Whether mother's share on partition her absolute property—Right of representation in dividing grandfather's property—Law of partition in Bengal—In ancestral property, Bengal father takes a double share—Also in sons' acquisitions-Deduction in Bengal-Division by brothers in Bengal.

Partition is that act of the members of a joint family by which they terminate the unity of the family group. As soon as partition has been effected, there is no longer a joint family; its members lose that particular legal character, which they previously had as belonging to a union of relations. Henceforward the acts of one can have no effect upon the rights and liabilities of the others. They are now separate individuals, having no other claims against one another, and in all respects are like strangers, except that under particular contingencies, they may succeed as heirs to the property of each other. This right of heirship being dependent upon relationship, either by blood, marriage or adoption, cannot of course be put an end to by the termination of the joint character.

Practical importance of the question—Is a family joint or separate, practical how made evident

In the schools of aggregate ownership, that is to say, under the Benares, the Mithila, the Madras and the Bombay law, the effects of a partition are of a more momentous character, than under the Bengal school. For in those schools it is after a partition that the female members of the family, a wife, a daughter, a mother, a grandmother, begin to obtain an independent right in the property. During the pendency of the joint character, their rights are confined to receiving maintenance; their rights of succession come into existence when the family is separate. For this reason, in the practical administration of law, a frequent question of the utmost importance is, whether the family is joint or separate. It is the interest of the female members to contend that it is separate, while the male members, who profit by the doctrine of survivorship, try as strenuously to maintain that the family is joint. The best proof that the family is separate would be to show, that the property belonging to the family has been demarcated by metes and bounds, and that the members of the family are enjoying the several portions of the property separately and independently of one another. Thus, if it be a house, and if it be shown that the two brothers have raised a party-wall between the two portions of it, one brother, being in exclusive possession of the portion on one side of the wall, the other brother of the other portion, then it would be indisputable that the brothers are separate; if one of them dies leaving no male issue, his widow, would certainly get his part of the house, and it would be preposterous for the other brother, supposing always that it is a family governed by the Mitākṣarā Law, to contest the widow's claim on the ground of non-separation and consequent survivorship. So again, if it be a field, and if the two brothers have marked off their several shares of it by constructing the customary boundary line in the middle, namely, the line of narrow earthwork about half a foot or a foot in height, (specimens of which may be seen running along mile after mile in the vast cultivated tracts of this country,) the partition of the field would be of ocular demonstration, specially if it be shown that the brothers till each his own portion apart from the other; in such a case the widow's right to succeed would be secure against any claim of her brother-in-law. These are obvious instances of a separation. In practice, however; facts assume a more complex combination; it is then that the question of partition or no partition tasks to the utmost the judicial acumen of our administrators of justice. If the law as laid down by our original texts had not allowed any, other evidence of partition, except a division by metes and bounds, practical questions would have been less difficult to solve. But the original texts are far from capable of bearing so simple an interpretation. In the oldest of the special treatises, the Mitākṣarā, the topic is touched upon in the last part of the Inheritance Portion, and has been thus treated in sec. 12, ch. II.

According to Mitākṣarā

If partition is denied, that is to say, if one brother says that there has been a partition, and another says that there has been no partition, and thus a question arises as to which statement is true, then the dispute will have to be settled by calling in the evidence of the paternal relatives, or maternal relatives, or of other unrelated witnesses. Sometimes the dispute will be settled by some written deed of partition, where such a deed exists. Sometimes the question will be determined by referring to the fact that the houses are separate or the fields are separate. There are other marks also of a separation. If the brothers carry on their transactions separately, if they perform religious rites apart from one another, if one brother becomes a witness for another, or a surety for another, or if one brother makes a gift of property to another, and the other accepts, these are marks which would establish the fact of partition. According to the old Hindu Law, undivided coparceners were not accepted as witnesses for one another, nor as sureties for one another.

According to Vīramitrodaya

The subject is thus Further elucidated by Mitra Misra in his Vīramitrodaya, Ch. X. He here says that the paternal relatives and the maternal relatives have been specially mentioned as proper and preferable witnesses in a question of partition or no partition, because such relatives are more likely to know the truth of the matter than a stranger. When a partition is effected by coparceners, generally, their relatives act as arbitrators; they have access to the female apartments ; they see how the household economy is carried on; whether they mess together, or perform their father's śrādh or mother's śrādh together, or worship their family divinities in combination, and so forth. That these paternal relations are separately mentioned argues, that the evidence of the relatives is of greater weight than that of strangers. Mitra Misra then quotes the opinion expressed in some other treatise which he names as the Paribhāṣā, that a written instrument of partition is the best evidence of the fact of separation among coparceners. Then follows a passage from Nārada who says, besides what has been referred to in the Mitākṣarā, that the separate coheirs have their cattle apart, and food apart; they have their income and expenditure apart; that although there may be no written instrument, yet the separateness of the above concerns and transactions, of religious rites, and so forth, would be suificient to show that the brothers are no longer joint. To the above, Vṛshaspati adds that the fact of partition is a matter of inference, where there is neither instrument, nor a witness. If trade and money-lending operations be separate, if one brother lends and another borrows from him, if one sells and another purchases from him, then it is to be inferred that they are separate, for transactions of the above character would not be probable in the joint state. Nor is it to be supposed, adds Mitra Misra, that all these marks must combine to show the fact of separation; but that evidentiary character attaches to them, whether all these marks are found together or not. If all are not found together, even some of these marks will be sufficient evidence, sometimes even a single mark. For, these declarations of law have reason and experience for their basis. If however, there is no means of making an inference, no witness, no written instrument, then Manu says that a sound partition will be indispensable.

Accroding to Smṛti-Candrikā

In connection with this topic, the Smṛticandrikā quotes[1] a couplet of Kātyāyana, which may be of service in some cases of disputed partition. Kātyāyana says, that if for ten continuous years, the brothers have lived separate in religious rites and in business, then they should be taken as having separated themselves in respect of the paternal wealth. Thus, it frequently happens in actual life that brothers live in different localities, having separately gone away from their home in infancy ; one of them subsequently amasses a fortune; probably their father left hardly anything likely to be the subject of a conspicuous act of partition. The brothers have not met one another for a lengthened period; in such a case the above text of Kātyāyana would probably be a good answer to the claim of the poorer brother to a joint ownership with the other. *

1. Ch. 16, para. 14.

To Declare 'I am Separate,' Tantamount to Partition

Nīlakaṇṭha, the author of the Bombay special treatise, has made a pregnant remark at the beginning of his Chapter on Partition.[1] "Even where there is a total absence of all property, a partition is effected by the mere declaration, 'I am separate from thee; for partition is but a particular condition of the mind; and this declaration is an indication of the same[2]"

I wish to draw attention to this observation of Nīlakaṇṭha as very important, because the notion implied thereby has been the parent of the modern doctrine of partition, that division by metes and bounds is not an essential feature of separation among coheirs.

Divison by metes and bounds not essential

This doctrine has been of gradual growth. No doubt the passage of the Mayūkha seems to have early come to the notice of our tribunals. In 1865, in a judgment bearing the name of Trever and Norman, JJ.,[3] the Calcutta High Court said, that in a joint Hindu family, a separation may take place at any time at the will of and member of the joint family, that any act or declaration showing unequivocally

1. p. 38, Mandlik.
2. I have here made a slight departure from Mr. Mandlik's translation. The original is, द्रव्यसामान्याभावेऽपि. Mr. Mandlik makes it, 'even where there is a total absence of *common* property.' This would have been unexceptionable, if the original had been सामान्यद्रव्याभावेऽपि. The word सामान्य has been used here as a substantive, and has that sense which was first attached to the word by the Vaiśeṣika philosophy, and means 'a class,' 'a genus.' Therefore Nīlakaṇṭha's expression means, 'even in the absence of every *class* of property, even in the absence of all property whatsoever.' The word सामान्य, when used in the sense of 'common' in a compound word, precedes the substantive which it qualities. As I entertain a very high respect for Mr. Mandlik' ability and scholarship, I could not pass over the slight alteration with which I have adopted his rendering, without showing why I have thought the alteration necessary.
3. Bulakee Lal *v.* Muss. Indurputty Kooer, 3 W. R., 41.

an intention on the part of any shareholder to hold or enjoy his own share separately and to renounce all rights upon the shares of his coparceners, constitues a complete severance or partition. Then they quote from the Mayūkha the passage I have quoted above. But in Badamo Kooer *v.* Wazeer Sing, 5 W. R., 78, L. S. Jackson, J, in concurrence with SetonKarr, J., says—"Unless there has been a definitive separation in estate; indicated by separate enjoyment and istinct liabilities, the family must be held joint, and it will not establish a separation in estate to show that the different members of the family dealt separately with their shares of the proceeds, or even that they collected rents and, profits from different parts of the estate, for that might simply result from some arrangement made for the general convenience of the family, and would not indicate any cessation of the joint rights or responsibilities."

In Muss. Jussoda Koonwar *v.* Gouri Byjnath Sahai Sing, 6 W. R., 139, Macpherson, J., after going through a, large number of authorities, came to the conclusion that nothing in the text books of Hindu Law, or in the decisions of the Sudder Court, would justify the supposition, that no partition can be effected save by the actual division of lands into parcels, and the allotment of those parcels to the different shares, to be held by them in severalty. In Shunker Lall *v.* Muss. Rohmer Koonwur, N. W. P. Rep. for 1865, p. 373, four'judges of the North West tribunal held, that in order to constitute a partition in law, particular portions of the aggregate area of land must have been divided off and assigned separately to the sharers. In this judgment, two other previous decisions of the same Court to the same effect are referred to and relied upon. In the Madras case of Nagappa Nynour *v.* Midundi Swara Nynour, Madras Sadder Court Reports for 1853, p. 125, the decision is, that the mere execution of a deed to effect a division of family property, does not suffice to constitute a division, which can only be held to have taken place, when the members of the family have actually divided their property, each taking possession of his allotted share.

The matter, however, was set at rest by the Privy Council in Appovier *v.* Ram Subha Aiyan, 8 W. R. P. R p. 1. In that case, a deed of division had been executed between the members of the family. The salient features of this deed seem to be contained in the following words inserted therein. " But inasmuch as it is not convenient now to divide one moiety of the villages, we shall divide every year in six shares the produce of them and enjoy it, after deducting the Sarkar sist and the charges on the villages. * * * We have henceforward no interest in each other's effects and debts, except friendship between us." Besides the above deed, there had not been anything like a partition, nor had the lands been divided by metes and bounds. On these facts the Judicial Committee held that the deed of division had converted the joint family into separate ownership, that it was sufficient to make a divided family, and to make a divided possession of what was previously undivided, without the necessity of its being carried out, into an actual partition of the subject matter. The reasons upon which their Lordships based this conclusion may be thus set-forth. When the members of an undivided family agree among themselves with regard to particular property, that it shall thenceforth be the subject of ownership in certain defined shares, then the character of undivided property and joint enjoyment is taken away from the subject matter agreed to be so dealt with; and in the estate each member henceforth has a definite and certain share which he may claim a right to receive and enjoy in severalty, although the property itself has not been actually severed and divided.

Written Instrument Tantamount to Partition

It is an error to suppose that an instrument of partition is ineffectual to convert undivided property into divided property, until it has been completed by an actual partition by metes and bounds. The error lies in confounding the division of the title with the division of the subject to which the title is applied. In a true joint family, no member has a defined share; every member has his right extended over the whole; therefore to define shares is to divide the title. This doctrine is further confirmed in another decision of the Judicial Committee[1] in which their Lordships interpret the passage in the Mitākṣarā, which I have already referred to,[2] that as separated fields and houses are good indications of a division, so is an instrument of partition, or an agreement to divide, though the agreement has not yet been carried out by an actual division of the property by metes and bounds. If the rents accruing from the property be divided among the members in accordance with the agreement, that would be quite sufficient to constitute a division in the eye of law.

An instrument of partition is sometimes called an ikrarnaṃah, or agreement. If such an ikrarnamah defines the shares, if it declares, after enumerating the different descriptions of property in the possession of the members of the family, that the said properties shall be the properties of the parties executing the ikrarnamah in equal shares, that they shall enjoy the profits and losses of the business of the family in equal shares, the ikrarnamah will be quite sufficient to constitute a division. In one case,[3] the very same ikrarnamah recited that the business of the kotee, or a banking business which the family had, was in future to be conducted and carried on as heretofore ; that the affairs of the kotee were to be managed is the best possible manner in consultation with, and with the consent of all the sharers; and that the profits were to be shared, each party to the ikrarnamah receiving one-fourth share. This naming of the

1. Rajah Suraneni Venkata Gopal Narasinha Row Bahadur *v.* Rajah Suraneni Latchmi Venkama Row, 12 W. R. P. R., p. 40.
2. See *ante*, p. 595.
3. Lalla Mohabeer Pershad *v.* Muss. Kundun Kooer, 8 W. R., 116.

share that each should receive, was enough to convert the joint into a separate condition. That the banking business was to be jointly conducted, did not derogate from the fact of separation; this joint management was necessitated by the nature of the business itself; which would have been, destroyed, if the arrangement for conducting it separately had been adopted by the sharers. In this case it also appeared, that the sharers had certain other properties, which exclusively belonged to the several sharers. Yet what remained joint; subject to the above definition of shares, was held to be separate property mingled together. The consequence thereof was, that the widow of one of the sharers who had died childless, *died* succeed her husband to his particular share, in spite of the opposition of the other sharers who contended that they were entitled by the rule of survivorship.

Separation in mess takes place first, Separate, appropriation of profits may amount to partition

Generally speaking, the members of the family first separate in mess; even after separation in mess, the property may remain joint. But sometimes, it so happens that the members agree to take the rents and profits of the property in several shares, and yet commensality is not broken up. As on the one hand, the breaking up of commensality would not be a legitimate indication that the property has been divided;[1] so on the other hand, simply because the members mess together, it would not be a valid conclusion that the members constitute an undivided family. Common mess or separate mess may consist with both a divided and an undivided condition. True, our old texts lay down, that separate mess should lead to the inference of a general

1. See Rewun Pershad *v.* Radha Bibee, 7 W. R. P. R. p. 37, Col. 1, where the Judicial Committee say, "Separation from commensality does not as a necessary consequence effect a division of property, or at least of the whole undivided property."

separation in estate. But this, I apprehend, will be only in the absence of all evidence to the contrary. Similarly, common mess, if coupled with evidence that the collections of rents are made in distinct shares, would not baran inference that the family is divided in estate.[1] This was so held in a Bengal case, but the principle seems to be applicable to the case of a Mitākṣarā family. For I find a dictum by Romes-chunder Mitten, J., to the effect that separate appropriation of profits by the members, would in certain cases be very good evidence of a tacit agreement amongst the members, to hold their property according to their separate shares.[2] This would lead to the supposition, that even written instruments are not indispensable to cause a separation of the family, but a verbal understanding, carried into effect by taking the profits of the property separately, or dividing the same after they have been collected, is tantamount to that state of mind, which, according to the author of the Vyavahāra Mayūkha, renders a person separate from his coheirs. For the principle propounded in Appovier's case is, that the members must not contemplate the joint property as belonging to themselves by so much for each individual, or by fractional shares. Such an idea would be inconsistent with the constitution of a true joint family. An instrument in writing, by which an agreement to divide is put into a durable form, is but one of the many means whereby the agreement can be proved. A course of conduct therefore may be an equally unexceptionable proof of the agreement.

On the other hand, it has been held, that vague expressions, contained in petitions presented to a Court, cannot have the effect of solemn deeds and agreements between parties, whether reduced to writing or not, but

1. Shibuarain Bose *v.* Ram Nidhi Bose, 9 W. R., 87.
2. See 23 W. R., p. 397, Col. 2, in the case of Cheytnarain Sing *v.* Bunwaree Sing.

contemplating the 'very subject of separation.'[1] The Allahabad High Court says, that mere definement of shares, not followed by separate enjoyment of profits, will not amount to a separation. The fact that there is a definement of shares followed by entries of separate interests in the revenue records, is an important piece of evidence towards proving separation of title and interests, but it will not necessarily amount to a separation; it must be shown that there was unmistakable intention on the part of the shareholders to separate their interests, and that the intention was carried into effect. The best evidence is, separate enjoyment of profits and separate dealings with the property. If it appears, that during a long course of years, the definement of shares was not in any way acted on, that the parties continued to enjoy the property on the same footing as before, it is but reasonable to suppose, that although the co-sharers may have taken some steps towards a separation—from some cause or other, for instance, a reconciliation, the co-sharers may have abandoned the intention that may have been formed, in the excitement of a rupture or family quarrel. Whether the separation was carried out or not may also appear from the manner of managing of the property, whether the properties are managed by a single sharer, or by different sharers. In the former case, the inference that subsequent reconciliation may have made up the breach in the family circle which is evidenced by a definement of shares, would be strengthened.[2] In one case a suit was brought on behalf of a minor, to set aside the execution sale of the joint property on account of his father's debt, and recover the minor's share of it. In the course of this litigation the minor died, and his mother claimed to be his heir, inasmuch as, she contended, that the suit by the minor to obtain his share of

---

1. *Per* L. S. Jackson, J., Mooktakasee Debee *v.*Omabutty, 14, W. R. 31.
2. Ambika Dat *v.* Sukhmani Kuer, I. L. R., 1 All., 438.

the joint property, was tantamount to the definement of a separate right, and therefore equivalent to a division. But the Allahabad High Court held that the mere fact that the minor asserted his right to a certain portion of the ancestral estate, and brought a suit to set aside an alienation thereof effected by the father, did not create a separate title in him, so as to be exempt from the operation of survivorship, and inheritable by his particular heir.[1] In another case the same High Court has said,[2] if there has been ascertainment and definition of the extent of right and interest of the several co-sharers in the whole, and of the proportion of participation each of them is to have in the income derived from the property, this is enough to effect a severance and destruction of the joint tenancy, and to convert it into a tenancy in common. In such a case, if a female member, such as a widow, or a daughter, seeks to succeed to the property of a deceased shareholder, as her right depends upon the fact of separation, it is for her to prove that fact; so also it is for any one who claims through a female member, such as a daughter's son. In the above decision Straight, J. says that there is a prejudice among many Hindus against succession following in the female line, and that since separation favours such successions, evidence of separation is less easily forthcoming than the evidence of a contrary tendency.

A suit for partition and proceedings of courts

Besides an agreement to decide, and separate enjoyment of the family income in shares, there is another indication that the family is no longer joint, which consists in proceedings had in a Court of Justice to effect a partition. In a family consisting of two cousins, one of the cousins separated himself in food from the other, left his paternal home on account of the ill-usage he received from his

1. Padarath Sing *v.* Raja Ram, I. L. R., 4 All. 236.
2. Adi Deo Narain Sing *v.* Dukaharam Sing, I.L.R., 5 All. 532.

cousin, and also because his rights were denied him. He brought a suit to establish his rights, obtained a decree, which was contested by the other cousin up to the Privy Council. He applied to execute the decree, was resisted, and while the appeal to England was pending, died. The Calcutta High Court held that this was a case in which the principle established by Appoovier's case was applicable, that the proceedings in Court between the two cousins had effected a separation, that the deceased cousin had not only declared his intention to separate, but had done everything in his power to carry it out, and that his failure to have the joint property divided off had been entirely the result of his cosharer's determined opposition.[1] In a Madras case, the younger brother brought a suit for his half share of a certain zamindari which the elder brother claimed to be impartible property, exclusively vested in himself, and not liable to be shared between the two. In the course of determining this question, the Court of first instance recorded a judgment to the following effect, that the property was partible, and that the younger brother was entitled to a moiety of the property left by his father, whatever that moiety might be.[2] The Privy, Council upon this have held, that by this judgment there was a clear adjudication that the property was partible, and that the rights of the two brothers were that each should have a moiety, that this adjudication was equivalent to a declaratory decree, which determined that there was a partition of the estate into moieties, and made the brothers separate in estate from the date when the above judgment was recorded. When the younger brother died, the actual division of the property had not been completed, but as the case fell within the principle of Appoovier's case, the interest of the younger brother passed, not to his elder brother by survivorship, but to such representatives of himself as were entitled to succeed to his separate estate.

---

1. Joy Narain Giri *v.* Goloke Chunder Mytee, 25 W. R. 355; s.c. I. L. R., 5 Cal. 434.
2. Chintambaram Chettiar *v.* Gouri Natchier, 5 C. L. R., 6,.

In Babaji Parshram v. Kashi Bai, I. L. R., 4 Bom. 158, the words in the decree in a partition suit between two members of a joint family, an uncle and a nephew, were that the estate should be divided, and that a mortgage debt secured on the joint property should be paid by halves, each co-sharer paying one-half of the same. Before, however, the execution of the decree, the uncle died. Her daughter sued to have one-half share of the property, claiming it on the ground that the aforesaid decree had effected a separation between the uncle and the nephew, and that the rule of survivorship did not apply in favour of the nephew. The Bombay High Court, however, rejected her claim, holding that such a decree as above had *not* effected a separation between the uncle and the nephew. The judgment says:— "We know of no authority for the broader proposition of law, that where there is no indication of an intention presently to appropriate and enjoy in a manner inconsistent with the ordinary state of enjoyment of an undivided family, an agreement to divide without more is of itself sufficient to effect a separation.* * *' The direction that 'the estate be divided' was at best but an inchoate partition, which remained to become legal by an appropriation in execution of the respective shares." In this case it seems to me that the dictum of the Vyavahāra-mayūkha has not been considered. That treatise says that the mere declaration of an intention to divide[1] is sufficient to effect a partition. In this case the nephew had first brought a suit for a partition; he must therefore have filed a plaint; he must have stated in that plaint his desire to divide the property. I apprehend that this would be quite sufficient, according to the opinion of Nīlakaṇṭha, to fasten the divided character upon the family property. It does not matter whether the particular shares were named or not in the decree. The distinction between this case and the case of Chithambaram Chettiar[2]

1. See *ante*, p. 598.
2. See *ante*, p. 606.

seems to consist solely in the circumstance, that the judgment of the First Court in the latter case mentions what fractional share each brother should obtain on partition ; whereas in the case before the Bombay High Court, the decree simply directed a division to the made, without naming what fractional share each was to get. But this distinction is nearly effaced by the next following direction contained in the decree, that each should pay only one-half of the mortgage debt secured on the family property, which implies and involves the proposition, that the interest of each co-sharer was one-half out of the whole family property. It is difficult therefore to see, why a decree for partition in a suit for that purpose should not have the result of terminating the joint character of the family.

In another case decided by the same High Court, one of the party to a partition suit died after a decree for partition had been passed by the Court of First Instance, but before the decision of an appeal from that decree which was pending in the High Court. A question therefore was raised before the High Court, whether the decree of the Lower Court was to be considered as having effected a separation of the family or not. If after that decree, the family was separate, then the widow of the deceased member got his share; if, however, the family continued joint, notwithstanding the said decree, then the shares of the remaining shareholders were enlarged , since the share of the deceased member lapsed to the general funds of the family. It devolved upon the High Court therefore to determine the question, whether the family at the time of the appeal before it was joint or separate. The High Court decided that the family was still joint, that the decree of the Lower Court, so long as the appeal was pending, was not sufficient to terminate the joint character of the family.[1] This decision also seems to ignore the opinion of Nīlakaṇṭha.

1. Sakharam Mahadeo Dange *v.* Hari Krishna Dange, I. L. R., 6 Bom. 115.

How to effect a partition

With regard to the manner in which a partition ought to be effected, the writers of the original texts have contemplated it under dfferent lights. They speak of what they call a Jīvadvibhāga, 'the living partition' and ajīvadvibhāga, 'the non-living partition.' By 'living partition is meant a partition carried out during the lifetime of the father, while that by the sons after his death is spoken of as non-living partition. All the commentators treat the subject of partition under the above two separate heads.

Partition efected by father

According to the Mitākṣarā, the father as the head of the family can always effect a division of the family property between himself and his several sons. The family property is in such a case considered as of two kinds, that acquired by the father himself, and the property which has come down from the grandfather or any remoter ancestor. With regard to the self-acquired property of the father, the Mitākṣarā allowed him some latitude in making a partition, in respect of the value of the different allotments given to his sons. Were we to confine our attention solely to the Ṛṣi texts, we might be led to suppose, that the father had unlimited power in giving unequal shares, both of his self-acquired and of the ancestral property, for in the śloka 116 of the 2nd chapter of Yājñavalkya, cited in para. 1, sec. 2, chap. I of the English translation of the Mitākṣarā, the Ṛṣi says, that when the father is desirous of making a partition, he should divide the sons in accordance with his will. He may either allot a superior share to the eldest born son; or all the sons may get allotments equal in value. But this śloka the Mitākṣarā declares in para. 7, sec. 5, chap. I, to be confined to the self-acquired property of the father. Vijnāneśvara also says in para. 6, sec. 2, chap. 1, that the allotment of shares unequal in value can be made by the father only with regard to his self-acquired property. Again, the Mitākṣarā says that we are not to understand by the expression 'superior share,' directed to be given to the eldest born, that it is competent to the father to give any share he pleases to the eldest born, making the shares of the other sons as small as the father likes. Such unlimited power in making the shares small or large is not vested in him. The superior share to be obtained by the eldest born has been expressly defined by a text of Manu, cited in the Mitākṣarā, para. 4, sec. 2, chap. I. In that text it is said, that the eldest born is entitled, to what the English translators have called 'a deduction,' to the value of one-twentieth part; he also has a right to some particular article, select and choice, out of the whole property. The word for deduction in the original Sanskrit is uddhāra.This word literally means a 'lifting up,' ' something picked up.' Imagination might dwell upon the idea called up by this Sanskrit term, and might picture a simple state of society, all the paternal effects being, on the occasion of a partition about to be made, gathered at a single spot, and the eldest born coming up and taking one twentieth part out of the whole, as something allowed to him by way of a token of honour and superiority.

Preferential share to an eldest son

He also selects what appears best to him out of the whole property, a fine horse or a fine car or a fine sword, supposing it to be a family belonging to the military caste. This is the uddhāra or the deduction. Nor is Manu partial to the eldest born in giving the deduction; for he allots a fortieth part as the deduction proper for the son who stands next to the eldest in the order of birth; and each one of all the other younger sons is given an eightieth part. When therefore Yājñavalkya says that the father may give a superior share to the eldest born, all that the Ṛṣi means to lay down is, that the father must mind what has been indicated by Manu, in making up the shares for each one of his sons. And this inequality of shares is limited to his self-acquired property. For, the ancestral property is owned in equal right by both the father and his sons; in respect of ancestral property, the inequality of shares would be repugnant to law.[1] Not that the sons have no ownership by virtue of their birth in the self-acquired property of their father. No proposition can be more free from doubts than this, that as well in the self-acquired property of the father, as in the ancestral, the sons have an equal right by virtue of their birth.[2] But there are certain texts of some of the ancient Ṛṣis, the application whereof must be somehow defined.

Thus there is a Ṛṣi text— "The father dividing, shall take two shares, of himself.' There is another— "while those two are alive, he must not be independent, although he be arrived at a decrepit ago." There is a third— "for that they are not lords, while those two are living."[3] Now all these texts being the authoritative sayings of the Ṛṣis, must be applicable to some case. Therefore, it becomes proper to apply them to the case of the self-acquired property of the father, says the Mitākṣarā. According to this limited application, the meaning of the first text is, that in dividing his own self-acquired property, the father may appropriate to himself two shares to one that he gives to each one of his sons. The meaning of the second text is, that with regard to the father's selfacquired property, the son cannot be independent, he cannot restrict the paternal power in making unequal distribution, he cannot even demand a partition of it, if the father be not willing, he cannot prevent any alienation of it which is made by the father. The meaning of the third text is the same as that of the second, the word 'lord' being employed in the sense of 'independent owner.' This view of the law, says the Mitākṣarā, is confirmed by another text of Manu, cited in para. 11, sec. 5, ch. I. The purport of this couplet is— 'If the father obtains any property belonging to his own father, which had not

1. Mitāk, chap. I, sec. 2, para. 6.
2. Mitāk Chap. I, sec. 5, para. 10.
3. Mitāk. chap, I, sec. 5, para. 7.

been obtained before, he, if unwilling, need not share it with his sons, being acquired by himself.' Here the last expression in the couplet, ' being acquired by himself,' has evidently been added as the reason for the father's appropriating it wholly to himself. The meaning of the whole couplet is this : Sometimes ancestral property is lost to the family; a stranger may have stolen it, or forcibly seized it; sometimes a stranger may have dispossessed the family from some family land; sometimes the family land may have been mortgaged by some deceased ancestor, and has not since been redeemed. The father may have recovered it by having recourse to litigation; he may have spent his time and money upon the recovery of it. This recovered property, the law says, although originally ancestral, is to be regarded as the acquisition of the father. Now, when Manu says that the father need not give a share of it to his sons, he there by implies that all other ancestral property must be shared with the sons; he also implies that the father's own acquisitions are free from the control of his sons. For Manu says, that the father need not share the recovered ancestral property, it being his self-acquired property. Consequently the proposition implied is, that what is self-acquired need not be shared. But this proposition must be taken in a limited sense. The father may altogether withhold his self-acquired property from the sons; but if he makes a partition of it, he cannot transgress the rules of law. He must not take more than a double share; he must not give more than a twentieth part to the eldest born. If he does so, such a partition will be bad in law, and may, I believe, be set aside in a court of justice. This I gather from paras. 13 and 14, sec: 2, ch. 1, Mitākṣarā. The purport of those paras. may be thus set forth.

Deductions or Uddhāra

It should be observed, that the authority for the proposition of law laid down here is a half-couplet of Yājñavalkya being the latter half of śloka 118 of the 2nd chapter; the meaning of it is, that when sons are divided with larger and smaller shares, then the division shall be considered as one made by the father, provided the division be in every respect conformable to law. Vijñāna says, that the object of this half couplet is to declare the illegality of a division, which does not follow the law of deductions,' as laid down in the Smṛtis. The father in every case has a legal right to institute a division of his self-acquired property among his sons. Neither the mother nor the eldest brother nor an uncle can exercise any such right of making a division among a number of brothers, when the father is living. Therefore, there is a character of legality attaching to a division made by the father. The sons cannot repudiate it. But this division must follow the strict rules of law relating to unequal shares; otherwise it will be illegal, and liable to be set aside. It is not then a 'division made by the father.' A division made by the father, to be valid, must be properly so made. This is the interpretation put by Vijnāna on this text. Therefore according to him, the father can either give equal shares to all his sons, out of his self-acquired property, reserving a double share to himself, or he may give deductions of a twentieth part and so forth, and then divide the residue equally ; his own double share, it seems, being always proper to be taken by himself.

Partition of father's acquisitions

A question may be raised here, whether the father, when dividing his self-acquired property among his sons, can appropriate to himself more than a double share. Modern cases have decided, that even in a Mitākṣarā family, the father can dispose of his self-acquired property in any way he pleases. These cases rest on the authority of para. 10, sec. 5, ch. I of the Mitākṣarā. The translation of Mr. Colebrooke is— "The son must' acquiesce in the father's disposal of his own acquired property (in the original,स्वार्जितद्रव्ये)." But in para. 27, sec. 1, ch. I, are the following words:—" But he is subject to the control of his sons, in regard to the immoveable estate, whether acquired by himself or inherited from his father or other predecessor." Here is a direct contradiction between the two passages. I am afraid that the contradiction owes its origin to an inaccuracy in the translation of the first passage. There, the word in the original for property is द्रव्य dravya, 'a thing,' 'an article.' 'Property' is a general name, and includes both moveables and immoveables. 'Dravya' is more special, I have grave doubts whether land may be called 'dravya.' At least the text of Yājñavalkya, which stands at the head of that long string of comments made by Vijñāna, out of which the first passage has been extracted, evidently makes a distinction between 'land' and 'dravya'. The text of Yājñavalkya is— "Whether it be land, or nibandha, or 'dravya', etc.— Can there be a doubt that here 'dravya' is something other than land? The same word 'dravya' is made use of by Vijñana, when he says, that the son must acquiesce in the disposal by father of his own acquired'dravya.' It was an unfortunate and misleading method of translation, which was adopted by Mr. Colebrooke in regard to his English Mitākṣarā. By reading his translation, can anybody even guess, that the work is nothing but a perpetual commentary on a metrical treatise on law? What prevented Mr. Celebrooke from giving the text, separately from the commentary, however discursive the commentary may be, it is impossible now to say. In the original; the separation between the text and the commentary is palpable to the most inattentive reader. Possibly, the absence of properly printed copies of the work had much to do with the arrangement adopted by Mr. Colebrooke. Be that as it may, it is clear that when Vijñāna is commenting upon a text of his author, in which dravya' is mentioned as different from land, he cannot have made a heedless use of the word 'dravya.' I have little doubt that he by 'dravya' means moveable property.' His proposition is, that sons must acquiesce in the disposal by father of his self-acquire *moveable* property. This is corroborated by what

Vijñāna says in para. 27, sec. 1, ch. I, cited above. The father is subject to the control of his sons in disposing of immoveable property, though acquired by himself. Such an explanation would remove all contradiction. Vijñāna was one of the most lucid, careful and conscientious of commentators of Hindu Law. His language is the beau-ideal of clearness, simplicity, and straightforwardness of statement. He seems to be above the vulgar solicitude for graces of style. Yet his work is one of the most graceful specimens of Sanskrit composition. He is an almost unknown author, so far as his birth and dwelling-place are concerned,. Yet that his work has commanded so durable and wide spead a circulation as an authority of Hindu law, must be partly owing to the magic of his language. We should therefore hesitate before ascribing contradiction or heedless statement to such an author. To my mind, therefore, the modern cases that have decided the father's uncontrolled power over all kinds of self-acquired property, have gone on an inaccurate translation of the Mitākṣarā, and have supposed a non-existent contradiction between para. 27 of the first section, and para. 10 of the fifth section, of the first chapter of the Mitākṣarā.

There is also another matter to be considered. The father may alienate or dispose of his self-acquired property. But from this it need not follow, that he can make any unequal partition he likes of his self-acquired property. A partition infringing the rules of law is an illegal act liable to be set aside. The rules of partition say, that the father is to take a double share out of his self-acquired property. Vijñāna says that this double share is limited to only the self-acquired property. If we therefore be disposed to give full effect to all these different declarations of law, which are equally authoritative, what other conclusion can we come to but this, that the father can alienate his self-acquired moveable property uncontrolled by his sons ; that he cannot alienate his self-acquired immoveable property; that he cannot take more than a double share out of that property, when he makes a division of it among his sons ; that if he likes, he may give to the sons their legal deductions. These are the propositions deducible from the Mitākṣarā.

Time for partition during father's life

With regard to the time for making a partition, Vijñāna has laid down the following rules. The father can make a partition whenever he chooses. His desire therefore determines one time for it. Another is, when his sexual powers are extinct, the mother is past the child-bearing age, and when the father has no longer any inclination for worldly pursuits. In such a case, the sons can divide, although the father be unwilling. Another time is, when the father is vicious, or afflicted with a chronic and protracted illness. Under such circumstances, the sons can divide, even though the father be unwilling, and even though the mother has not passed the child-bearing age.[1]

Father's wives receive a share

On all occasions of a partition made by the father, his wives must each receive a share equal to that of a son. This rule has an exception, where the wives of the father have any property given to them by their husband or by their father-in-law. If any such property has been obtained by father's wives, then they each shall receive a share equal to a half of what each son receives. The word in the original is 'strīdhana,' or the peculiar property of a woman. Vijñāna does not attach a technical sense to that expression, for in paras. 3 and 4, sec. 11, ch. II, he says that the expression must be taken in its plain literal sense; it has no technical meaning. The rule of interpretation is that when a word is capable of a double meaning, one technical, and another plain and literal, and where there is no objection to its being taken in its literal sense, then the literal sense is preferable.

1. Para. 7, sec. 2, ch. I, Mitāk.

So that any property which belongs to a woman is strīdhana; unlike what the law is under the Bengal school; for in that school, although property may belong to a woman, yet it may not be her strīdhana. For instance, wealth inherited by a woman from her husband does no doubt belong to her; yet it is not her strīdhana. * Vijñāna would no doubt have said that it is strīdhana. He would also have said, that property inherited by a daughter from her father is her strīdhana. But modern tribunals, influenced always to an undue extent by the doctrines of the Bengal school, have long ago decided[1] that even under the Mitākṣarā, the word 'strīdhana' bears a technical sense, and that property inherited from a husband or a father does not come within the term. With regard to the question with which we are just now concerned, it does not matter whether 'strīdhana' is to be understood in its technical sense or not. If neither the husband nor the father-in-law has given a woman any property, her share is equal to that of a son. If property has been given, it is half a son's share. Therefore, whatever other property a woman may have, her share is not reduced. A husband or a father-in-law generally gives ornaments to his wife or daughter-in-law. In wealthy families, valuable landed properties are given by the father-in-law by way of jautuka or marriage gift. In all these cases, those belongings of the mothers and stepmothers must be taken into account, when the father is dividing his own property among his sons. In commenting upon the text here, Vijñāna adds that his author, that is, Yājñavalkya, will on a future occasion say, that a, half-share should be given if the father's wife has had property. I apprehend that he here alludes to śloka 151 of the second chapter, which is found in para. 35, sec. 11, ch. II of the English translation. In that part of the work is declared, the claim of a superseded wife to compensation; this compensation is equal to the sum spent by the husband in marrying his second wife. If, however, the superseded

1. See Chotayal *v.* Chunnoo Lal, I. L. R. 4 Cal. 744.

wife has obtained any strīdhana property beforehand, she will receive half the marriage expenses. In interpreting the word 'half' here, Vijñāna says that it does not mean an equal moiety; but it means such a fractional part as will make up the whole property of the superseded wife equal to the sum spent on the second marriage. In the case of partition, he applies the rule of a half-share, by analogy with the superseded wife. If the analogy is to be carried to its whole extent, then the rule of partition would stand thus. Every wife of the father gets a share equal to that of a son. If the father's wife has received anything before from her husband or her father-in-law, she will get as much at the time of partition as will make up what she formerly received from her husband or her father-in-law equal to a son's share. It should be carefully borne in mind here, that the father's wife may have received very large properties from her own father; yet that will not reduce her share. It is what she has received in the husband's family, that will form a part of the whole which will be equal to a son's share.

Wife's deduction

When the partition, however, is unequal, and deductions have been given to sons,—then the balance is to be divided among the wives and the sons equally or unequally, according to the rule laid down above. The wife again is said to have a right to certain special 'deductions.' These consist in the furniture of the house and ornaments. As an authority for this proposition, Āpastamba is quoted. His text seems to be one of those puzzles, that frequently arise in the study of the Ṛṣi texts. If literally translated, the text would stand thus:—"The whole of the utensils and the ornaments in the house, are the wife's." The commentator Bālambhaṭṭa, cited in a footnote by Colebrooke,[1] explains without a thought, that the chairs, and the stone and the earthen utensils and the ornaments worn by the wife belong

1. Mitāk. ch. I, sec. 2, para. 10.

to her. It should be recollected, that Vijñāna has cited this text of Āpastamba to show what the special perquisites of a wife are. He is talking of the wife's uddhāra to be given her at a general partition. By what has been already said, it must now be clear that uddhāra is something given at a partition to a particular person, as a recognition of the special character which that person bears. Thus, the eldest born, on account of being so, gets, a twentieth; the second born, a fortieth; and so on. Therefore what already belongs to a person cannot be said to be that person's, uddhara. Yet Bālambhaṭṭa says, that ornaments worn by a wife are her uddhāra. If these ornaments already belong to her, they cannot be her uddhāra. The fact of her wearing them is some proof, that they do' already belong to her. No doubt, there is a custom in many middle-class Hindu joint families, of keeping a set of ornaments as belonging to the family in general, to be worn by any female member as she may have occasion for doing so, in paying visits to other families as a guest, in going to relatives' houses on festive occasions, and so forth. This custom owes its origin to motives of economy, since, unless the family is very wealthy, it cannot afford to appropriate a complete set of ornaments to every one of the female members. But this practice furnishes no solution of the difficulty met with in construing Āpastamba's text. For then the ornaments cannot be said to be worn by one female member. The solution which I would propose is, that by the expression 'ornaments in the house ' were probably meant 'the decorations of the house,' consisting it may be in pictures, and whatever other specimens of decorative art were fashionable in the days of Āpastamba. A canopy, for instance, is frequently mentioned in Sanskrit works of general literature. These canopies, often decked with strings of pearls in wealthy families, would not be at all insignificant articles of property. Āpastamba therefore, not only bestows on the wife, the pestle and the mortar, the slab and the muller, the baskets and the plate, but also canopies, screens, pictures, and so forth.

Deductions Obsolete

It ought to be mentioned here, that the law of giving deductions or of making an unequal partition is not approved by the generality of commentators. Thus Vijñāna himself has said, that this unequal partition, although prescribed in the ancient authorities, is yet repugnant to the popular feeling. It should not therefore be practised in actual life.[1] Mitra Miśra has developed this point in the following manner.[2] He says, that the ancient law authorizes unequal partition, both when the father is alive, and when after his death the division is made by the sons themselves. "But there are certain other texts which prohibit the practice of unequal partition in this age of Kali; there is a text of Yogīśvara, which says that what is detrimental to the future life, and hateful in the world, should not be practised, though 'it be in accordance with the law.' Here by the expression 'hateful in the world' is to be understood that which is prohibited for the special age. A practice may be lawful in one cyclical age; yet interdicted in another age; such a practice should not be adopted during that age for which it is prohibited. For otherwise, nothing lawful can be detrimental to the future life; nor will people learned in the law hate that which is laid down by the law. Nor can a practice be detrimental to the future life, simply because it is not to the taste of illiterate and ignorant people. Now in the Ādipurāṇa, it is prohibited that in the Kali age there is no second marriage of a woman who had been once married, no superior share for the eldest born, no cohabitation with the widow of the elder brother, no slaughter of kine on sacrificial occasions, no adoption of a mendicant life. These five practices are unlawful in the Kali."

According to Jīmūta,[3] unequal partition may take place

1. Ch. I, sec. 3, para. 7.
2. Ch. II, part I, sec. II, (p. 61).
3. Ch. III, sec. 2, para. 26.

if the co-sharers agree to do so; but in the present age, an eldest son is rarely found who deserves to be so distinguished from the rest; nor are the younger sons of this degenerate period loyal and dutiful, as they used to be in the past ages of the world. Unequal partition therefore has gone out of use. If, however, the brothers among themselves do agree to conform to the ancient rules, an unequal partition made by them would not be repugnant to law, nor liable to be set aside: This also is the opinion expressed in the Smṛticandrikā.

Partition after father's death

We have seen how partition is effected during the lifetime of the father. A partition after the death of the father follows on the same lines. The property is divided equally among the sons, and also their mothers. Here however, there seems to be a difference in the opinion of the different commentators. The question is, whether at a partition after the death of the father, only such widows of the father as have a son receive a share, or all the widows indifferently. This question has been discussed by Mitra Miśra in see. 19, Part 1, ch. II. Upon this point, there are two Ṛṣi texts to be disposed of. One is that of Yājñavalkya, Mitāk. Ch. I, sec. 7, para. 1. The other is that of Vyāsa, cited by Mitra Miśra. The two texts may be thus placed side by side.

Yājñavalkya.—"The mother also of those, dividing after the father's death, should take an equal share."

Vyāsa.—" The sonless wives of the father are declared as having an equal share; and also the grandmothers. They all are declared equal to the mothers." The substance of the discussion in the Vīramitradaya[1] may be thus stated. "As in the case of partition during the lifetime of the father, the father is to make his wives equal sharers with his sons, so after his death the sons are to make them partakers of shares

1. P. 79, English Translation.

equal to that of themselves. If, however, they have received strīdhana, so much should be given to each of them as will make her, the strīdhana being included, an equal sharer with a son. The text of Vyāsa, however, relates to a partition during the lifetime of the father. For in that text the term used is,—'the wives'—its correlative being 'the husband'. Therefore it follows that it is the husband who is making the partition; the husband then will give to each of his wives a share equal to that of a son. But in Yājñavalkya's text, which expressly, relates to division after the father's death, the word 'mother' has been used. This word cannot be meant for a stepmother as well. The word 'mother' in its primary sense is applied to the female parent; in a secondary sense, it may mean a stepmother. But in the same sentence, a single word cannot properly be taken both in its primary and also in its secondary sense. Therefore the correct opinion is, that after the father's death, the stepmother does not take a share at a partition by the sons. She is entitled only to food and raiment. But Vijñāneśvara introduces the above text of Yājñavalkya, by saying, that as in the lifetime of the father, so after his death also, his widows get a share equal to that of a son.[1] This also is the opinion of Madanaratnākara." But the majority of the authorities, says Mitra Misra, are in favour of the contrary doctrine.

The above is the opinion of Mitra Miśra. But I apprehead that the authority of Vijñāneśvara being the highest in the schools of aggregate ownership, it may be safely laid down that at all partitions, the wives or the widows of the father each gets an equal share, whether she has a son or not.

Father's wife's share in bengal

Under the Bengal school, the opinion of Jīmūta, propounded by him in paras. 30-32, sec. 2, ch. III, Dāyabhāga, is different. These paras. run thus:—

1. Mitāk. ch. I, sec. 7, para. 1.

"Since the term 'mother' intends the natural parent, it cannot also mean a stepmother. For a word employed once cannot bear the literal and the metaphorical senses at the same time. The equal participation of the mother with the brethren' takes effect, if no separate property has been given to the woman. But if any has been given, she has half. And if the father makes an equal partition among his sons, all the wives must have equal shares with the sons *' * Wives of the father who have no male issue, not those who are mothers of sons, are equal sharers." These words of Jīmūta have been thus cleared up by Śrīkṛṣṇa in his commentary on the Dāyabhāga.[1]

"Therefore, at a partition made by the husband, the sonless wives alone are sharers, not those who have a son. But at a partition made by the sons, only the mothers are sharers, not stepmothers."

With regard to the ancestral property, all the above rules will apply, except that under the Mitākṣarā, the father cannot take a double share for himself. Ancestral property must be divided equally among all the sons, an equal share being reserved by the father for himself, and equal shares being given to all his wives, or such shares as will raise their already received strīdhan to the value of a share received by each of the sons. After the death of the father also, ancestral property will be shared by his widows with his sons; and I apprehend that if there be a paternal grandmother living at the time, she should get a share, according to the text of Vyāsa quoted in the Vīramitrodaya.[2] That the father's widows receive a share of the ancestral property may not have been declared in so many words by the Mitākṣarā; but it has been so decided in the case of Lall Jeet Sing *v.* Rajcumar Sing, 20 W. R. 336, where Phear, J. lays down the law in the following words:—" The father, during

1. तस्मात् पतिकृतविभागे पुत्रहीनपत्नीनामेवांशित्वं न पुत्रवतीनां। पुत्रकृतविभागेतु मातृणामेवांशित्वं न विमातृणाम्। इति व्यवस्था।
2. See *ante*, p. 623.

his life, may at his pleasure, partition the whole of the property in his hands, or any of it; and if he does so, he must allot a share to his wife for her maintenance, in addition to the share which he takes himself, also the sons can at any time, during the father's life, at their pleasure, (even when any of the contingencies which entitle them to divide have not happened), call upon him to partition the ancestral property, and in that event also the mother must have her share as before. After the father's death again, the sons may divide the property among themselves, but then, too, they must give a share to their father's widow, and to an unmarried sister if there is one. In all the cases alike, the mother's share in the ancestral property must be equal to that of a son."

Two observations must be made with regard to the above declaration of law. The first is that the mother's share is equal to that of a son, only when she has not received any separate property given to her by her husband or father-in-law. The second is, that although the Mitākṣarā nowhere says that the share which the mother receives is intended for her maintenance, it is possible that the law will preclude her claim for any further maintenance after she has once received a share of the joint property. The sons also would be similarly debarred from making a claim of that kind after a partition. The reason for this seems to be, that the maintenance is a claim that usually attaches upon joint property; and when the joint character has terminated, and every member has appropriated as much out of the joint property as could be legally claimed by him or her, there is nothing upon which the claim for maintenance can attach. The share, received by a wife or a widow therefore, is considered her maintenance. As an authority I may mention, that not only Phear, J. in the above judgment, couples that share with the name of maintenance; but Dwarkanath Mitter, J., in the case of Sheodyal Tewaree *v.* Jadunath Towaree, 9 W. I3,. 61, said:—"There can be no doubt that the share which is given to a Hindu mother at the time of partition, is given to her for no other purpose than as a provision for her maintenance. She has no right to ask for maintenance after she has got such a share."The only textual authority for a distinction between a mother's share and a son's share received at the time of a partition, that I have been able to light upon, is found in Smṛti-candrikā ch. IV, paras. 7, 8 and 9. There the author raises an objection grounded on the well-known text of Baudhāyana that a woman has no right to any inheritance, If, says the author, a woman has no heritable right, how then is she declared by Yājñavalkya as entitled to an equal share with her son? How then does Vyāsa say, that the sonless wives of the father, and also the paternal grandmothers, are equal sharers? How then does Viṣṇu say, that mothers participate, by getting a share equivalent to a son's share. Surely, says the author, persons having no heritable rights, cannot be properly declared entitled to shares. To answer these objections, the author draws a distinction between 'a share' and' dāya or 'heritable property.' The distinction seems to be rather finely drawn. If the author had said, that the wife or the mother had no independent ownership, irrespective of the act of partition, then there might be some substance in the distinction. But that does not seem to be the author's meaning; for immediately after he says, that the mother has ownership in the 'heap of wealth about to be divided', that this right is founded upon her *status* as the wife of the father; that when she takes her share, her ownership is simply made definite and tangible.

Whether mother's share on partition her absolute property

Now, this is language which places the wife or the widow at a partition almost on a par with the sons; for these latter also, in the schools of aggregate ownership have a prior ownership in the divisible property, which ownership is made definite and tangible by the act of partition. The Smṛticandrikā therefore may be cited to support the proposition that the widow's share at a partition is her maintenance. On the other hand, inconvenience may sometimes arise if we regard it in that light. There is authority for saying that maintenance is resumable, if the woman proves unchaste. Thus, p. 153 Vīramitrodaya, Nārada is cited who says—"If she behave otherwise, they may resume the allowance." Again there is authority for saying that maintenance property belonging to a woman is her strīdhana. Thus Dāyabhāga, ch. IV, sec. 1, paras. 15. "Her subsistence, her ornaments, her perquisites, her gains, are the separate property of a woman. She herself exclusively enjoys it; and her husband has no right to use it, unless in distress." By calling a wife's or a widow's share received by her at a partition her maintenance, we place it in the category of her strīdhana, whereby it becomes subject to all the legal incidents that attach to that kind of property.

Phear, J., in the above case, says that the father can divide as mach of his self-acquired property as he likes among his sons, and that on such a partition his wife gets an equal share for her maintenance. Now supposing that the share received is insufficient for her maintenance, she can demand adequate maintenance from the managers of the joint family, if there be ancestral property in their hands. By her prior receipt of a share, she had partially received her maintenance—which proving inadequate, may be increased, on a demand being made by her.

Right of representation in dividing grandfather's is property

Here I must enunciate another important rule relating to partition. This rule is laid town in paras. 1 and 2 in sec. 5, ch. I of the Mitākṣarā. It relates to the division of the grandfather's property by the grandsons, and is therefore applicable to the partition of all kinds of ancestral property. The rule has been thus propounded by Vijñāna—Although the grandsons are owners of the grandfather's property from the moment of their birth, yet when they divide the grandfather's property, they must make their respective shares, by reference to their fathers. Thus where all the brothers have did before a partition; one brother has left two sons, another three, another four; there the two sons together take their father's share; the three sons also take the one share belonging to their father; similarly the four sons. Likewise, if some sons of the grandfather are alive, and others are dead, this very rule will apply. The living sons take their own respective shares; the sons of the deceased take their respective fathers' shares. This is a limitation of the general rule that sons and grandsons are co-ordinate owners of the grandfather's property. The above rule, whereby the grandsons' shares are made up by reference to their father is otherwise called the right of representation. The grandsons are taken to represent their respective fathers at a partition, and the number of shares at first made is equal to the number of fathers who have left sons.[1]

Law of partition in bengal

I shall now point out certain peculiarities in the law of partition as by Jimūtavāhana. According to him, there are two times for dividing the father's property, as distinguished from ancestral property. One is when the right of the father terminates, and the other when the father desires a division. The cesser of the father's right is caused by his becoming a fallen man,[2] by his giving up worldly concerns, or by death. It may be briefly put thus: Father's right ceases by death, natural or civil. Civil death takes place either when the father becomes a fallen man, by committing a sin, or when he relinquishes the world. With regard to the division of the ancestral property, one time is when both the parents die; for although ancestral property is claimed through the father, and not through the mother, yet brothers

1. Ch. I. para. 44.
2. See *ante*, p. 424.

of the whole blood ought not to divide the ancestral property so long as their mother is alive.[1] Another time is when the mother is past her child-bearing age, and at the same time the father desires to make a division of the ancestral property. The reason for the necessity of the mother being incapable of bearing any more children is, that the subsequently born sons may not be deprived of their just rights in ancestral property. The necessity for the father's willingness is peculiar to the Bengal Law. Under the Mitākṣarā, whether the father be willing or not, the division of ancestral property may be always demanded by the son. The Mitākṣarā Law supplements this rule by further enacting, that if a son is subsequently born to the father, he takes the whole of what had been taken by the father at the partition.[2] According to the Bengal school, as there can be no division of ancestral property unless the mother is past her child-bearing age, the objection that future sons will lose their birthright does not arise. Yet the Bengal school recognises the right of the subsequently born son to the father's share of his own self-acquired property. It is only the self-acquired property of the father, which can be divided when there is a possibility of a son being again born. Such a subsequently born son will appropriate the whole of the property which fell to the father's share at the time of dividing the self-acquisitions of the father. This is made clear by the comments of Śrīkṛṣṇa on paras. 1-6 of the second chapter of the Dāyabhāga. There the commentator says[3]:—"As regards grandfather's property, the father is

1. Ch. II, para. 5.
2. Mitāk. ch. I, sec. 6, para. 1, *et seq.*
3. पितामहधने पितुः पुत्रेभ्यः स्वेच्छाकृतन्यूनाधिकदानस्यापि निषेधेन उत्पत्स्यमानपुत्रनिरं शतायाः सर्व्वथैव निषिद्धत्वात् तत्रैव मातृरजोनिवृत्तेः सहकारित्वौचित्यात्। न च पित्रा स्वयं गृहीते द्व्यंशे तदनन्तरं तस्यैवाधिकारात् न निरंशता इति वाच्यं। तस्य पित्रुपभोगोपक्षीणत्वे निरंशताया दुर्वारत्वा। पैतृके तु तस्य स्वेच्छा स्वयमुपात्ते ऽर्थे इति विष्णुवचनेन इच्छाया नियामकत्वाभिधानात् इच्छया डत्पत्स्यमाननिरंशतायाप्यविरोधात् न तत्र अस्य सहकारिता इति। अतएव वृत्तिलोपो विगर्हित इति प्रागुक्तवचने वृत्तिपदं पितामहधनपरमिति सुधीभिर्भाव्यं।

strictly prohibited from following the dictates of his own will in giving larger or smaller shares to his sons; he ought not therefore to deprive his subsequentlv born son; therefore the divison of the grandfather's property must be subject to the condition that the mother's monthly courses have ceased. True, in dividing grandfather's property, the father takes a double share; and the subsequently born son may take the same; and so, may not be deprived of his birthright absolutely. But if that double share be entirely consumed by the father before he dies, what will the subsequently born son take? In such a case the deprivation of his brithright becomes inevitable. But as regards the father's self-acquired property, Viṣṇu syas that the father can do just as he likes. It is the father's will which is the sole determining cause in such a case. There is no objection against the father's willingness absolutely to deprive the subseqently born son of all share in his self-acquired property. The cessation of the mother's monthly courses need not, therefore, be a condition to the divison of the father's self-acquired property."

The text of Yājñavalkya, declaring the equality of the father and the son as regards ancestral property, is not ignored by the Bengal school; but it is explained in the following manner.[1] Since the right of the grandson is equal to the right of a son as regards grandfather's property, if A dies leaving a son B, and a grandson D by a deceased son C, B and D both inherit A's property, and divide it equally between themselves. Here D the grandson has the same right to A the grandfather's property, as C the deceased son would have had, if he had been living at the time of the partition. This is the meaning of the equality of the father and the son with regard to the grandfather's property. There, is also another kind of equality between the two. When the father divides his self-acquired property, he may give any share he likes to any son. But he cannot give

1. Dayābhaga, ch. II, para. 9.

unequal shares at his pleasure of the property received by him from his father or any other ancestor in the paternal line.[1] This is the law as laid down by Jīmūtavāhana himself. How far, however, the modern tribunals will act according to this doctrine may well be questioned. Modern tribunals have long settled, that in Bengal the father can sell, give, or otherwise alienate the ancestral property in any manner he likes, from doing which he cannot be prevented by his sons. There may still be a distinction between alienation and partition. Although the Bengal father may alienate at his pleasure, it does not follow that he should be allowed to partition ancestral property in a manner, that runs counter to the express declarations of law as contained in the work, which is universally accepted as the highest authority in the Bengal school. It seems also to be settled law, that the Bengal father can make a will regarding the ancestral property, whereby he may even absolutely disinherit his sons. This is very near allowing him an unlimited power of partitioning the same property entirely at his pleasure. Still, inasmuch as the theory regarding wills ascribes its origin to customary law, which has had little to do with written authorities, the validity of a disinheriting testamentary instrument may depend upon a separate set of considerations. The conformity of a will to the principles inculcated in the written authorities may have nothing to do with its validity; for there are no provisions in those authorities that bear upon a will. Its existence dates from a period long subsequent to the time when the Dāyabhāga was written, But partition is expressly provided for in that work. If therefore a Bengal father affects to make a partition of ancestral property among his sons, and at the same time transgresses the plain rules of partition, it may be fairly argued that his acts are without the sanction of law. If, for instance, he has divided ancestral property before the mother has past her child-bearing age, the subsequently

1. Ch. II, para. 17.

born son can well challenge such a partition as null and void. If, again, he takes more than a double share out of the ancestral property, the sons may well oppose his proceedings. But I am afraid, that it is now too late to turn back the current of decisions upon these points. Somehow or other, the legal world is deeply imbued with the notion, that the Bengal father's power over ancestral property is absolute, unlimited and uncontrollable. It does not matter that you can cite scores of passages from the Dāyabhāga to controvert the same. The notion is deep and ineradicable; every doubtful point of law is decided in accordance with that notion. It has had a permanent and wide-spread influence on the body of our case-law. Possibly an attempt now made to restore the Bengal law to a strict conformity with the Dāyabhalga would be of too unsettling a character to be seriously contemplated. But the matter is nevertheless worthy of note, that though we are accustomed to profess a deep respect for the authority of the Dāyabhāga, we have already learnt to disregard it in practice, in many an essential point of law having an intimate connection with the administration of justice.

In ancestral property, bengal father takes a double share

That the father cannot take more than a double share out of the ancestral property appears from para. 20, ch. II. It also appears therefrom that the sons, unlike under the Mitākṣarā school, cannot demand a partition of ancestral property. The father is the sole arbiter as to when the division will be made, subject, however, to the cessation of mother's monthly courses. From para. 23 it appears that ancestral moveable property can be sold or given away by the father at his pleasure, not the ancestral immoveable property. He can dispose of everything ancestral, however, if the maintenance of the family makes it imperative.[1]

1. Para. 26.

With regard to the law of Uddhāra or deductions, the Bengal school lays down the following peculiar rule.[1] If all the brothers be of the whole blood, and if the eldest born be superior in learning and merit, he takes a double share. If the brothers be sons of different mothers the eldest born will get one-twentieth part as his special additional share.

Also in son's acquisitions

The father takes a double share not only in partitioning the ancestral property, but also out of any property which may have been acquired by a son of his.[2] When a general partition takes place, the acquisitions made by the sons during the joint state must of course be separated. Upon this part of the subject, the Bengal school lays down this peculiar rule, that whether their acquisitions be made by the help of the joint property or not, the father always takes a double share. If the son's acquisitions have been made by making use of the joint funds, then the father takes two shares, the acquirer takes two shares, and the rest of the brothers one share each. If the acquisitions were made without using the joint funds, then the acquisitions are divided half and half between the father and son.[3] As an illustration of how acquisitions are made by a single brother by using or by not using joint funds, the following cases may be supposed. One brother tills an ancestral field by his own money and labour; the crops will be acquitisions made with the help of the joint property. Or he trades with the money taken from the family coffers, then the profits will be acquisitions made with the help of the joint funds. But suppose he is employed as a servant, rises by his merit to high posts, and earns money. These acquisitions will not be shared by the other brothers. But the father will always take a half share of such earnings. Other examples of earning money without the help of joint

1. Paras. 42, et seq.
2. Para. 73.
3. Paras. 71.

funds may be thus imagined. A coolie goes to Demerara and after a few years' sojourn there, returns with a sum of money. The money made by a boatman, a day-labourer, a carrier who carries burdens on his shoulders, in general, money made in an occupation which does not require any previous training or any out lay of capital, are instances of acquisitions made without the help of the joint funds.

It is of course settled law that out of his own acquisitions, the father can give as much or as little as he likes to his sons, he may give a large share to one son, a very small share to another son. The reasons for which the father is ordinarily induced to make an inequality of shares are thus set forth.[1] One son may be possessed of special and extraordinary merit; the father surely has a right to reward him by giving a preferential allotment. Another son may be burdened with a large family; unless his means are made adequate to maintain his family, it would be in distress. In such a case the father is not bound to observe the rule of equality. A third son may be incapable, would not be able to support himself unless special kindness were shown to him. The father is not precluded from showing such special kindness by giving him a larger allotment. A fourth son has been all along exceedingly and uncommonly dutiful obedient, and diligent to please his parents. Surely the father can mark his appreciation of that son's filial affection by giving him a distinguished share. Of course, remembering always that all these distinctions are to be made solely out of the father's self-acquired property. In making these distinctions, not only is the father within the law; but any attempt on the part of the sons to raise objections to or to repudiate or to set aside the unequal distribution would render them liable to be punished by the king.[2] On this point, Śrīkṛṣṇa adds a note[3]—"In the absence of any of the above-named causes, an unequal

1. Para. 74.
2. Para. 75.
3. उक्तान्यतमकारणं विना स्वार्जितधने पुत्राणां विषमभागो न धर्म्य इति भावः।

distribution among his sons of his self-acquired property would not be lawful. This is the purport."

Deduction in Bengal

Jīmūtavāhana takes special care to point out, that the unequal partition made by the father of his self-acquired property must not be confounded with the uddhāra or deductions, or with the unequal partition expressly enjoined by the ancient Ṛṣis. Uddhāra may be given of ancestral property also. In para. 80, *et seq.*, he says that although the father may be out of the question, there maybe two kinds of partition. In one the shares are equal; in the other, there is an inequality of shares on account of seniority of age. Now the unequal distribution of his self-acquired property made by the father does not follow seniority of age as its basis. The reasons for it are as stated above. Whereas inequality following the seniority of age must be in accordance with certain rules expressly laid down by the ancient Ṛṣis. That is to say, if the brothers of the whole blood are dividing, the eldest born takes two shares, the son next to him in point of birth takes one share and a half ; all the other sons each takes one share and a fourth. If the brothers be sons of different mothers, the eldest born takes one twentieth out of the whole; the next senior takes one-fortieth and all the others one-eightieth each.[1] If it be ancestral property, the father always takes a double share.[2] If it be the father's acquisitions, the above rule must strictly be observed if the division be made by the brothers after the father's death; that is to say, if they at all incline to make an unequal partition. If the division be made by the father himself of his self-acquired property, he need not observe any rules whatsoever. In all these rules, it should be carefully remembered that the eldest born is that male child, who was born the first of all other sons; if he dies, the senior survivor of the living sons would not be entitled to

1. See Dāyabhāga, ch. II, para. 36; and para. 44.
2. Para. 36.

the appellation of the 'eldest born,' nor to the rights and privileges attached to that status.[1] It should also be borne in mind, that unlike the Mitākṣarā, the Dāyabhāga does not absolutely discountenance unequal partition made either by the father or by the brothers after his death. For in para. 26, see. 2, ch. III, it says:—"It must not be argued, that the practice of equal partition is indispensable, as the only mode authorised by law. For the brethren may consent to the deductions by reason of great veneration for the eldest. An option exists, like that of making or omitting partition. Accordingly, since persons of the present day who are younger brothers, entertain no great veneration for their elders, equal distribution is alone seen in the world ; as also because elder brothers deserving of deducted allotments are now rare." There the author does not take any notice of the text of Ādipurāṇa cited in the Vīramitrodaya,[2] which withdraws the sanction of law from the practice of unequal partition in the Kali age. He nevertheless arrives at nearly the same conclusion, and testifies that even in his time the practice had gone out of use. At this day therefore even in the Bengal school, the hope of an eldest born son to revive the practice by an appeal to the ancient Ṛṣi texts, must necessarily be slender; since no Court would give a moment's hearing to a contention based upon law, that has been obsolete from before the date of Jīmūtavāhana. At the same time, under the Dāyabhāga, there is nothing to prevent a father from dividing ancestral property among his sons, by giving them such unequal shares as are conformable to the rules stated above. If he, however, be of unsound mind on account of illness, or be influenced by unreasonable antipathy against one son, or by undue partiality for the son of a favourite wife, then he is not competent to make a partition.[3] In other words, the division made by him under those circumstances will be liable to be

1. Ch. I, para. 36.
2. See *ante*, p. 622.
3. Ch. II, para. 83.

set aside. If again the sons themselves persuade him by importunities to make a division of his self-acquired property, he should not make an unequal distribution at his pleasure; although he may give the legal deductions as laid down in the law.[1] In connection with this topic of deductions, as under the Mitākṣarā, the household furniture and decorations form the perquisites of the wife; so under the Dāyabhāga, there are certain special articles to be exclusively appropriated to the different sharers at the time of a general partition.[2] Thus it is said that a car drawn by a horse is the special deduction for the eldest born.

Division by brothers in Bengal

When the division is made by the brothers after the death of the father, the brothers, if of the whole blood, should wait till the death of their mother, or should divide if she dives permission. It is also said, that if there are different mothers, and all the mothers have an equal number of sons, then after the death of the father, the property should be divided into as many shares as there are mothers; and the sons of each mother should live together under the superintendence of their mother, until her death; when they may divide among themselves. It is not said how it will be, if the number of sons sprung from each mother be not the same. I apprehend that then the sons of each mother will together take their share of the property, and live unitedly under the superintendence of their respective mothers.[3] But this law is more directory, than imperative. The death of the mother is not a condition precedent to a division by brothers of the whole blood; otherwise there would have been no provision for a mother's share in a division made by her sons.[4] Or if such division requires as an indispensable condition the permission of the mother,

1. Ch. II, para. 86.
2. See ch. II, pats. 37.
3. Ch. III, sec. 1, paras. 12-14.
4. Para. 29, sec, 2, ch. III.

then such permission will not be difficult to obtain, when the mother sees that by giving permission she entitles herself to a share of the property. The existence of a minor brother will be no impediment to a partition. All that need be done is, that the minor's share is to be placed in trust with some relative or friend of the family.[1] This division after the death of the father is not confined to the sons alone, but extends equally to sons and grandsons and great-grandsons. If there be only grandsons, they will divide among themselves ; always remembering that their shares are to be made up by reference to their fathers; if there be only great-grandsons, a division on the very same principles will take place. If there be sons, grandsons and great-grandsons, all together, then only such grandsons and great-grandson will, receive shares, whose fathers and grand-fathers are dead at the time of the partition. The general rule may be thus stated. Supposing A were the person whose property is to be divided; supposing also that it is to be divided among his sons, grandsons and great-grandsons. First divide the property into as many shares as there are sons of A., either living at the time of the partition, or deceased and represented by a living grandson or by a great-grandson. Then let each of these shares be set apart for each son, either living, or represented as above. If there are more than one grandson by a deceased son, then that son's share must be divided according to a similar principle among those grandsons. Similar allotments on similar principles must be made in respect of great-grandsons whose father and grandfather are both dead. This rule has been briefly indicated in paras. 21-23, sec. 1, ch. 3; where it is said that if there be one son, and many grandsons by another son; then one son takes half, and the many grandsons together take the other half ; and that if there be two grandsons by one deceased son, and three grandsons by another deceased son; the two grandsons together take

1. Para. 17, sec. 1, Ch. III.

one half ; and the three grandsons together take the other half. I also think that in every case the widow of the person whose property is being divided, if living at the time of the partition, should receive a share, the value of which will depend upon her having previously received or not received strīdhana from her husband's family. This appears from paras. 31-32 sec. 2, ch. 3. I have already said in a previous part of these Lectures; that under the Bengal school, the unmarried daughters take nothing, but that their interest in the family property is limited to receiving a sufficient marriage portion; while the Mitākṣarā gives such daughters a right to one-fourth part of what each brother receives.

The above are the principles of the law of partition properly so called, as propounded by the two rival schools of aggregate ownership and partial ownership. But the writers of the original texts understood partition in a far more comprehensive sense, as comprising in fact all the questions of succession, reunion, inheritance, woman's peculiar property, disqualification, and a number of other chapters of the law of property. Since many of these questions have been handled in these Lectures under other heads, I need not lengthen my present Lecture on Partition, on the lines adopted by the writers of the original texts.

Chapter 12
Property Not Liable to Partiton

Separate property in a joint family—Separate property exempt from partition or survivorship—Ancient text as to rise of proprietary right—Eight modes of acquiring property—Riktha means unobstructed heritage, Sanvibhāga obstrocted heritage—Separate property acquired by obstructed inheritance— 'Seizure' as a means of acquiring property—Hidden treasure—Hindu law averse to separate property—Modes of acquisition according to Manu—Where acquisitions joint, where separate Nuptial gifts—Reocovered ancestral property—Gains of science—Gifts obtained where separate—Property impartible by its nature—Gains of science in the Mithilā law—The same in the Madras law—Exclusive property in Bengal—Learning money in Bengal-Case law upon separate property.

Separate property in a joint family

It has been said that although a Hindu be the member of a joint family possessed of property in which all the members are commonly interested, yet he is not debarred from holding property belonging exclusively to himself. This capacity of an undivided member was recognised in the Sivaganga case, in which the Judicial Committee ruled, that the separate property of an undivided member went by descent to his widow, if he left neither a son, nor a grandson, nor a great-grandson. To such separate property the rule of survivorship does not apply. This decision necessarily implies the possibility of the existence of such separate property within a joint undivided Hindu family.

Separate property exempt from partition or survivorship

Such property is not only exempt from the operation of the rule of surviroship, but is also free from a liability to be partitioned with the other members. This is one reason for there being property within a joint family which is not liable to partition,—the property is separate, and exclusively belongs to a single member. There are certain other kinds of property, which by their very nature and character are not liable to partition. For instance, a family idol ; every member owns it in part; but it cannot be divided into pieces and taken separate possession of. In this Lecture I shall briefly dwell upon both these kinds of property, not liable to partition when a general division of the family estate takes place.

Ancient Texts as to Rise of Proprietary

The separate properties of an undivided member have been enumerated and discussed in sec. 4, ch. I, of the Mitākṣarā. The general rule with regard to separate property, as stated in the Mitākṣarā, is this, that whatever has been acquired by a single coparcener without consuming the wealth either of the father or of the mother will belong exclusively to him. He is not bound to share it with his co-heirs when a general partition takes place. In order to understand adequately the drift of this rule, we must have recourse to those texts of the ancient Ṛṣis, which speak of 'the nature of an acquisition; in other words, which deal with the question, when is a person said to acquire property? Upon this point, the text of Gautama, ch. X, verses 39-42, and cited in the Mitākṣarā, ch. I, sec. 1, para. 8, is accepted as the principal authority.

Right, Eight Modes Acquiring Property

The passage is as follows:—'An owner is by inberitence, purchase, partition, seizure, or finding. Acceptance is for a Brāhman an additional mode; conquest for a Kṣatriya; gain for a Vaiśya or for a Sūdra." The meaning of this passage is, that there are five methods of acquiring proprietary right which are general to all mankind. These are,–first, inheritance; a person who was not the owner of some property before, may be the owner of it, if he becomes the heir of the previous owner. The second method is purchase. A person acquires a right to something for which he has given a price. The distinction between the first and the second method is this, that to be an heir of another person requires no exertions; but to purchase requires that the purchaser should be the owner of some other equivalent property, which must have been acquired by his exertions, or by becoming an heir, or by some other method which is independent of previous possession of some other property. This distinction is not unimportant in connection with the subject with which we are just now concerned. That subject is the separate property of a single member. The rule is, that property acquired without consuming paternal property is separate. But as purchase is a method of acquiring property, which implies that something is given in exchange, unless that something given in exchange be wholly unconnected with the paternal property, purchase will not be the means of acquiring separate property. The third method of acquiring property is partition. The Mitākṣarā distin-guishes inheritance and partition thus.

Rikhta Means Obstructed Heritage, Sanvibhāga Obstructed Heritage

The word in the original which has been rendered as 'inheritance' is रिक्थ, Rikhta; while that for 'partition' is संविभाग, 'Saṁvibhāga.' The Mitākṣarā says that by Riktha is meant unobstructed heritage; by Saṁvibhāga is meant obstructed heritage.[1] Thus if a son a grandson, or a great-grandson comes to the property of his father, grandfather, or great-grandfather, his acquisition is Riktha. If, however, a daughter's son comes to the property of the

1. Pars. 13, sec. 1, ch. 1, Mitāk; see also *ante* p. 538.

maternal grandfather, he acquires it by that method of acquisition which is styled as 'Saṁvibhaga' by Gautama. Both these kinds of acquiring property would be comprised in the word inheritance. Were it allowed to suggest some interpretation of the above text of Gautama, different from that of Vijñāneśvara, I would say that Riktha comprises all kinds of inheritance, obstructed and unobstructed; and Saṁvibhāga, which ordinarily means 'partition,' imports that method of acquiring property, whereby a mother gets a share at a general partition. This interpretation is suggested to me by the following words of Mr. Justice Dwarkanath in his judgement in the case of Shib Dyal Tewaee *v.* Jadunath Tewaree, 9 W. R. 61. "The mother or the grandmother is entitled to a share, when the sons or the grandsons divide the family estate between themselves. But the mother or the grandmother can never be recognized as the owner of such a share, until the division has been actually made. She has no pre-existing vested right in the estate except a right of maintenance. She may acquire property by partition, for partition is one of the recognized modes of acquiring property under the Hindu Law. But partition in her case is the sole cause of her right to the property." According to the Mitākṣarā interpre-tation, Gautama intends to say, by naming Riktha as a mode of acquiring property, that a son, a grandson or a great-grandson acquires property by birth; and that birth is one of the modes of acquiring property. This view is somewhat confirmed by what appears from para. 13, ch. I of the Dāyabhāga. We all know that the Bengal school has emphatically discarded the idea, that birth on the part of a son is the means of acquiring property. But in doing so, the author of the Dāyabhāga recites the doctrine opposed to his own, and puts into the mouth of his opponent an anonymous text in para. 13 ch. I. There the propounder of the opposed doctrine is made to say:—"Is not birth therefore, as the act of the son, rightly deemed his mode of acquisition? And have not sons consequently a proprietary right, during their father's life, even without his being degraded or otherwise disqualified? And not by reason of his death? And therefore it is declared, 'In some cases birth alone is a mode of acquisition, as in the instance of paternal estate.' This anonymous text therefore, cited by Jīmutavāhana to be explained away, being in the way of his favourite theory that sons have no right during the lifetime of their father, is an authority for saying, that in the schools of 'aggregate ownership,' birth is viewed as a mode of acquiring property; and that this notion is indicated in the text of Gautama, where he says that Riktha is a mode of acquiring proprietary right, Vijñāneśvara having explained Riktha as unobstructed heritage. For, it will be remembered, that unobstructed heritage as explained by Vijñāna in para. 3, sec. 1, ch. I, is nothing else than that property, to which the son or the grandson acquires a right by virtue of his birth.

For our present purposes, however, we must remember, that in a joint family, unobstructed inheritance can seldom be a mode of acquiring separate property. Such a family is necessarily composed of persons descended from a common ancestor. All therefore must have an interest in property which originally belonged to that common ancestor. In a peculiar sense, however, unobstructed inheritance may be the means of acquiring separate property, even within a joint family. Thus, suppose the family were composed of many brothers, and their sons and grandsons. One of the brothers A acquires some separate property for himself. When he dies leaving a son B ; B inherits exclusively the separate property of A; it also becomes the separate property of B. This inheritance must be of the unobstructed kind; because the property is inherited by a son from his father. The son had a right to it by birth, if the property had been acquired by his father before his birth. I also believe that the son would acquire a right to it immediately on its acquisition by A, if A acquires it after B's birth. The brothers of A can have nothing to do with such property, because it is A's self-acquisition. Here therefore A's self-acquisition may be said to descend or to survive to B, separately and quite apart from the general family property. This was in fact very nearly the state of things in the Sivaganga case. The only difference is, that there the member of the undivided family, Gauriballabha Tevar, acquired separate property; he, however, had no son when he died. But the Judicial Committee expressly declare, that the separate property follows its own special course of descent. They therefore declared in that case the widow's right to succeed to Gauriballabha in respect of the zamindari which had belonged exclusively to Gauriballabha. If this gentleman had left a son, instead of a widow, the said son would have got the zamindari in exclusion of the other members of the undivided family to which Gauriballabha belonged. But though under a state of things imagined above, the son, an unobstructed inheritor, would acquire property exclusively belonging to himself, yet the same property could not be properly called separate, to all intents and purposes. It could not properly be called separate, because so long as the father A lived, the son B had a joint right with A in it; although the brothers of A had no such joint right. Nor can B be said to *acquire* it after the death of A. To *acquire* is to become the owner of something to which one had no right before. But B had a joint right before the death of A; he only becomes the sole owner after the death of A. To become a sole owner from a joint owner is not to acquire property. Therefore, unobstructed inheritance, which necessarily implies previous joint ownership, cannot properly be said to be a mode of acquiring separate property.

Separate property acquired by obstructed in heritance

On the other hand, the member of a joint family may frequently acquire separate property by the mode of obstructed inheritance. Thus if the family consists of a father and a son, the son may inherit the property of his maternal grandfather; this is an instance of obstructed inheritance; for so long as the maternal grandfather lived, the daughter's son had no joint right with him. Again if the daughter be alive, her son has nothing but a reversionary interest. If there be a son to the maternal grandfather, neither the daughter nor her son has any right whatsoever. These are the obstructions to the inheritance of the maternal grandfather's property. But as the daughter's son may inherit in the absence of the aforesaid obstructions, when he does so, while he is at the same time the member of a joint family with his father, his inheritance becomes a separate property exclusively belonging to himself. Thus it becomes an instance of acquiring property by way of what Gautama calls ' Saṁāvibhaga,' which according to the Mitākṣarā interpretation, as shown above, is obstructed inheritance. It is obvious that if there be two or more sons and a father who constitute a joint family, the two or more sons will jointly inherit their maternal grandfather's property, which will be common separate property of all the sons, with which the father will have no concern. This will be an example of a joint family within a joint family. For, while all the brothers will possess a joint right with their father in the paternal property, and will so constitute the larger joint family; they at the same time will form a smaller joint family composed solely of themselves, with which the father has no connection. The joint right of this smaller joint family will be limited to the property inherited from the maternal grandfather. Yet we must remember that the two joint families do not bear the same character in all respects. According to the decision of the Calcutta High Court cited before,[1] obstructed heritage cannot be claimed by sons as subject to their ownership by virtue of birth. Therefore, supposing in the above-mentioned case that there are grandsons in the family, these grandsons will have no

1. See *ante*, p. 541.

interest in the property inherited by their fathers from the maternal grandfather; but the grandsons will be members of the larger joint family in which their grandfather is comprised.

We may multiply instances of separate property acquired by the mode of obstructed inheritance to any extent we please. According to the Mitākṣarā school and all the schools subordinate to it, wherever the property of a separated and unreunited Hindu is inherited by his legal heir, it is done by way of obstructed inheritance. Thus, in the Vyavahāra-Mayūkha, this point is clearly discerned by the author; when he sets out to speak of the heritable rights of the widow, the daughter, the daughter's son, and so forth, he introduces that part of his work as 'order of succession to obstructed heritage.[1] He says:—" Yājñavalkya thus states the order of succession to the wealth of one dying separated and not reunited. The wife, daughters, both parents, brothers, and likewise their sons, Gotrajas, bandhus, a pupil, and a fellow-student. Of these, on failure of the preceding, the next following is the heir to the estate of one who has departed for heaven leaving no male issue." It has now been decided by the Judicial Committee in the Sivaganga case, that a widow will succeed to the separate and self-acquired property of her deceased husband, though the latter at the time of his death may have been the member of an undivided family. The result of this decision is, that such a widow, although she herself remains a member of the joint family, may have separate property acquired by way of obstructed heritage from her deceased husband. For, there is no authority for saying, that she ceases to be a member of the joint family by the death of her husband, who himself up to the moment of his death was a member of that family. There is no authority for saying, that the widow's succession to the separate property of her husband terminates her rights, privileges and liabilities as a female

1. Mandlik, p. 76.

member of that same joint family to which her husband belonged. If a male member can acquire exclusive property, and yet remain connected with the family, there is no reason why a female member should not be able to do so. It is now beyond question, (see *ante*, p. 141), that the wives of the male members are to be considered as themselves members of the household corporation. Once a member, always a member, unless a separation in form has intervened. The rights of the female members are limited, in the schools governed by the Mitākṣarā, to the receipt of maintenance from the joint funds. The widow of a member has still her right to the maintenance from those funds. The widow of a member who inherits separate property of her deceased husband cannot forfeit that right simply by reason of so inheriting. It therefore logically, follows, that the widow of a male member is an example of 'how an individual member of a joint family may be in possession of separate and exclusive property not liable to partition with the rest. That this view of the position of the female members is not unsupported by original texts will appear from para. 19, sec, 4, ch. 1 of the Mitākṣarā, where the author is speaking generally, of properties not to be divided by coheirs at the time of a general partition. The para. cites a couplet of Manu, which runs thus:—"Such ornaments, as are worn by women during the life of their husbands, the heirs of the husband shall not divide among themselves; they who do no are degraded from their tribes." In lieu of ornaments worn during the life of their husband, we are to suppose moveable or immoveable separate property of the husband, which at his death is succeeded to by his widow. Suc inheritance is beyond the reach of the co-parceners of her husband, and is not liable to be divided by them.

The very same remarks may be made with regard to the daughter who acquires property by way of obstructed in heritance from her deceased father while she remains a member of the family of her father. This can only be while she remains unmarried. Marriage would at once cut off her connection with the family of her father; after that event, she can no more be said to be a member of her father's family; though there is nothing to prevent her succeeding to her father's separate property. But when unmarried, she remains a member of the paternal household, succeeds to her father's separate property, and holds it free from the partition rights of her father's coparceners. An unmarried daughter therefore, succeeding to her father's separate property, is another example of how Saṁvibhāga or obstructed inheritance enables a member of a joint family to hold property not liable to partition. In her case, as well as in the case of a son succeeding to the separate property of the father, the rule of Yājñavalkya seems to be trenched upon. That rule is, that whatever is acquired by an individual member of a joint family without consuming the father's or the mother's wealth, is not to be partitioned with the other coheirs. When a son or an unmarried daughter, who is the member of a joint family, succeeds to the separate property of his or her deceased father, he or she cannot be said to acquire property without consuming the father's wealth. In fact it is the very wealth of the father which is obtained by a son or daughter in succession to the father. Yet there can be no doubt that it is not to be shared by the other members. How is this to be reconciled with Yājñavalkya's rule. This reconciliation is to be made by a proper explanation of the rule. As in so many other instances, the ancient Ṛṣis are found to contemplate a joint family consisting solely of brothers; so here also, the rule has been propounded under the supposition that the family is composed of a father and his sons. In such a case the rule is quite accurate. In order to frame a rule applicable to families composed of more distant relatives, cousins, uncles, nephews, grand-uncles, cousins to the second or the third remove, we must say, that whatever is acquired by an individual member without making use of the joint property is not liable to partition. By 'joint property' will have to be understood the property left by the common ancestor of the male members of the family, be it a grandfather, or great-grandfather or even a remoter ancestor. The expression will also include all increments to ancestral property, which have gradually accrued to the original nucleus in course of time. Thus put into a general form, the rule I believe will cover all cases, whenever the separate property of an individual member is inherited by another member, by Saṁvibhāga or obstructed inheritance.

But Saṁvibhāga, as a means of acquiring separate property within a joint family, presupposes the existence of separate property belonging to another individual member. It cannot therefore be said to be a primary method of acquiring separate property. These primary methods are, as enumerated in Gautama, what have been called 'seizure' and 'finding,' and acceptance of a gift, and conquest, and wages received for work done.

Seizure as a Means of Acquiring Property

'Seizure' is explained in the Mitākṣarā as consisting in the act of appropriating something which never belonged to anybody else before. Thus the water of a flowing , river, it would seem, was supposed in Hindu times to belong to nobody; it is put into his jars by the water-carrier ; the water becomes his property by seizure; convertible into money, which belongs exclusively to him. How far this theory will accord with the state of things under the British Government may be doubted. For that Government has appropriated the rivers and forests to itself ; and a jar of water drawn even from a navigable river may be said to be a trespass upon Government property, and would not probably be an example of what Gautama calls acquisition of property by seizure. The Mitākṣarā also instances grass and wood as capable of being appropriated by seizure; and evidently in the Hindu times, the extensive tracts overgrown with grass, or reeds, or fragrant shrubs, and the vast forest lands, were considered as belonging to nobody, and any person so inclined might appropriate the spontaneous produce of those tracts, and thereby acquire wealth.

Hidden Treasure

Again the finding of hidden treasure was another recognized mode of acquiring property in the former times. This mode could not well be included, in the previous one of 'seizure,' for ' seizure' presupposes unappropriated articles fit for the use of man; whereas it cannot be said in respect of hidden treasure that it never belonged to anybody. On the contrary, the very care and caution, and attempt at concealment, which are betrayed by the fact of the treasure having been stowed away, would show that the treasure had an owner, although he may not be traced when the treasure is discovered. Hidden treasure is in the original called 'nidhi;' it implies a quantity of coined money or precious stones, which has lain buried in the earth, probably during more than one generation, and is discovered by chance. The mention, of finding a hidden treasure as an ordinary mode of acquiring property by so early a writer as Gautama, shows that discoveries of hidden treasure were rather frequent in ancient times. We may come to the same conclusion by remembering, that India has been always noted as a wealthy country, that under the generally peaceful government of the Hindu kings, vast riches used to be produced and accumulated by its inhabitants, and that a good deal of the wealth so acquired used to be stowed away in concealment, whether bricked up in the walls of the house, or buried in a neighbouring forest, or thrown into a tank. The modern methods of investing money had not then been invented; and although a rudimentary banking system had been introduced by the Śreṣṭhis, the ancient prototypes of the Chetties of Madras, the system was not sufficiently attractive, or secure, or trusted, so as to draw in the whole disposable capital of the country. The inborn thrift of the nation found its scope in the practice of burying treasures. When therefore Gautama and Vijñāna speak of the discovery of a hidden treasure as a means of acquiring property, they have simply recorded a fact ordinarily seen by them in actual life.

Hindu Law Averse to Separate Property

In connection with the subject of separate property which may be acquired by the member of a joint family, I am drawing attention to these old texts, because these texts show how an individual member may in a manner create wealth for himself, without the least imaginable assistance from the common estate of the family. Hindu law, we shall see ere long, seems to have been rather jealous, and reluctant in the matter of allowing exclusive property to the individual member of an undivided family. The spirit of the old law, as disclosed in the original texts, is such, that the faintest shadow of a connection with the joint effects would destroy the separate character of the acquisition. I have therefore tried to show how, under the old ideas, a man was able to earn property which would be exclusively his beyond all dispute, by pointing out what the old ideas about acquiring property were. If an individual member went to a forest, and collected a load of dry twigs solely by the use of his hands, and sold it in the market, he might thereby acquire some capital. He might employ that capital in trade; such small capitals not unfrequently lead to the making of vast fortunes; instances of a very poor man rising to large fortunes, by diligence and luck combined, are not rare. Now it is wealth made in this manner by an individual member, which is indisputably his separate property; it is the crucial example of property acquired without using the joint funds. Similarly, the discovery of a hidden treasure is a crucial example. But inheritance, whether obstructed, or unobstructed, would not be an example of that kind. Inherited property belongs exclusively to an individual member, when it was already the separate property of the previous owner, as we have seen above. We are therefore naturally led to enquire how the previous owner acquired it. In order to be the separate property of the previous owner, it must have been earned by him without using the common funds. Our enquiry therefore places us again face to face with the question, how is it possible for an individual member to earn property, without the assistance of the common funds? Similarly, as I have already hinted, it would not do to say, that a given property belongs exclusively to one, because he has purchased it. The question would immediately follow, whence did he derive the purchase money ? If from the common funds, then it cannot purchase exclusive property. But if we can say that he discovered a treasure, and made the purchase therewith, all doubts, and all further enquiry, would at once cease.

Modes of acquisition according to Manu

In śloka 115, ch. R, Manu has given an enumeration of the different modes of acquiring proprietary right. "There are seven unexceptionable means," he says, "of coming by property; inheritance, finding, purchase, conquest, investment, occupation, and acceptance of a gift from an approved donor." Kullūka explains this śloka as follows:—"The seven means, beginning with inheritance, of coming by property, are unexceptionable, respectively for those for whom they are enjoined. Out of these, inheritance is that wealth which has come down from the ancestral line; finding, that is, the discovery of hidden treasure, etc., also the receiving of that which is obtained on account of friendship; purchase is what everybody knows; these three are unexceptionable for all the four castes; the wealth acquired by conquest is unexceptionable for the military caste alone, since that caste alone can have recourse to conquest for earning wealth. Investment is the means of coming by such money as the interest on loans, etc; occupation means agriculture and trade. These two means, investment and occupation, are unexceptionable for the Vaiśya caste. Acceptance of gift from an approvers party is unexceptionable for the sacerdotal caste." Gautama has put the last two castes, the Vaiśyas and the Śūdras together, and has declared the wages of labour as the means by which they acquire property. The Mitākṣarā (ch. I, sec. 1, para 13) explains the wages of labour sanctioned for the Vaiśyas, to be what a Vaiśya gets by agriculture, or by tending cattle, or by similar other occupations; the same is to be considered as his wages or 'bhṛti,' as the original word is, which signifies 'the means of subsistence." The wages of the servile caste consists in what they receive as subsistence from the service the three superior castes. According to Vijñāna, the word 'bhṛti' includes also, the profits which are made by all the mixed castes from the pursuit of the trades, professions and occupations, appointed for them respectively in the Institutes of Manu. Besides the well-known occupations of the four principal pure castes, the following occupations have been enumerated by Manu in ślokas 47-56, of the 10th chapter. Driving a car, or the occupation of a coachman; the profession of a physician; the occupation of guarding the female apartments; the inland trade; the fisherman's employment; that of a carpenter, that of a hunter of wild animals; that of catching snakes; the business of working in leather; the business of a drummer; and the occupation of the lowest of all the castes, the Cāṇḍālas, who were public executioners, and had to dispose of unclaimed corpses. This enumeration was not evidently meant as exhaustive, but simply as illustrative.

Where acquisitions joint, where separate

I have given above a brief outline of the different modes of acquiring property, as they were understood by our Ṛṣis and our commentators of law. The acquisitions made by these different means by an individual member of a joint family were either joint or exclusive, according as the acquirers were supposed to have had any help from the common funds or not. The opinion of Vijñāna is, that although Yājñavalkya specifially mentions (Mitāk., ch. I, sec. 4, para. 1) certain kinds of acquisition as exempt from partition, still they are not exempt if assistance has been taken from the common funds. Acquisitons specifically mentioned by Yājñavalkya as 'impartible[1] are, the gifts from a friend, the nuptial gifts, the recovered ancestral property, and the gains of science. Yājñavalkya specifies the above kinds, after having said in general terms, that whatever is acquired without consuming the parental wealth is exempt from partition with the coheirs. From this way of speaking of the different kinds of acquisitions, it might have been inferred, that gifts of friendship and the following three are exempt from partition, though acquired with the assistance of the common funds. But Vijñāna (Mitāk., ch. I, sec. 4; para. 6) guards against such a supposition. The condition implied by the general rule attaches to all descriptions of separate acquisions. Thus, gifts from a friend may be received by way of reciprocation; presents have been made to a friend out of the common funds; if the friend repays the obligation by sending equivalent presents to an individual member, that member cannot claim them as his exclusive property. In our days, the practice of sending presents to a friend, and receiving presents from a friend, by an individual member of a joint family, is not so common; we cannot imagine the state of things, in which this practice was of so general a prevalence, as to have necessitated the enactment of a special provision of law. The exchange of periodical presents between families connected by marriage are frequent enough in these days; but such presents would not fall under the category of 'friendly gifts,' within the meaning

1. Mitāk., ch. I, sec. 4, para.

of the original taste. For the word is 'maitra,' that is, 'gifts from a mitra.' There is a distinction between a 'mitra' and a 'bandhu.' The former implies some one who, without being related to us, is the object of an affectionate feeling, and reciprocates the same. But 'banhu' in Sanakrit generally, implies relationship. I apprehend that in times gone by, the relation of a patron and a protege was more common; that the protege used to repay his obligations by sending large presents to his patron; this he often did with the, consent of his family, who had an interest in keeping up the good name of the family; the patron, if generous-minded, rarely failed to reciprocate the presents, which were considered as friendly gifts obtained by the assistance of the common funds, and therefore liable to be partitioned by all.

Nuptial Gifts

Nuptial gifts also may be of two kinds—some are received without the consumption of joint funds; others for which joint property has had to suffer. Vijñāna instances the 'āsura' form of marriage, to show how joint property may suffer, on account of nuptial gifts received by an individnal member. In the 'āsura' form of marriage, the bridegroom has to pay money to the father of the bride. If this money is advanced by the joint family, the marriage gifts received by the individual member who has had to marry in the ' āsura' form, cannot be his exclusive property. They have been at the charge of the common estate; and they consequently must form a part of the same. In our times, the Calcutta High Court has decided that all modern marriages are of the Brāhma form. (16 W. R. 105, Jadunath Sarkar). But the practice of taking money from the bridegroom, specially among the Bansaja Brāhmans of Bengal, is not obsolete. As among the more respectable classes of Brāhmans, the bride's father often ruins himself by celebrating the marriage of a daughter; so, among the Bansaja Brāhmans, the bridegroom pretty frequently sells all that he has, simply for the purpose of getting a wife. Practically, therefore, the 'āsura' form of marriage is not gone out of use. Again, in almost every case, the nuptial gifts of the present day involve a reciprocation of gifts of nearly the same value from the recipient family. They are therefore at the charge of the family property. A young man belonging to a joint family of good circumstances in life, marries into a wealthy family, and receives very valuable presents in the shape of ornaments, clothes, furniture, jewellery, and a variety of other articles. If he is joint with his father and uncle, he can hardly congratulate himself on having secured a large amount of property. These gifts may have been ostensibly made to him; but general opinion regards them as gifts to his family. This opinion is, I believe, in strict accordance with the law of the original texts. As there is a reciprocal exchange of gifts between the two families which have formed a connubial relationship, these gifts must be regarded as obtained by consuming the family estate. It is only in the case of the Kulin Brāhmans and the Kulin Kāyasthas of Bengal, that nuptial gifts of an opposite character can be said to occur. In their case the bride's party considers the honour of having a high-born son-in-law to be a sufficient repayment for the profuse donations they make to the bridegroom, who is often poor, and whose parents are not expected to make return presents. These gifts made to a Kulin bridegroom are nuptial gifts answering the description of a nuptial gift not at the charge of the common property. It should also be noted here, that wherever there are any return gifts made by the bridegroom's family, the character of exclusiveness must drop from the nuptial gifts received by the bride groom ; and I apprehend that comparative largeness or smallness of the presents on either side will have nothing to do with the question. The bride's family may have made very large gifts; the bridegroom's family may have made very small returns; yet the rule is, that there must not be any detriment to the common property, if the bridegroom seeks to appropriate thorn wholly.

Recovered Ancestral Property

The third kind of separate acquisition specifically mentioned by Yājñavalkya is the recovered ancestral property. Upon this point Vijñāna says, that if any property, come down in the family by descent, was forcibly seized by strangers, and the father and the previous ancestors had not been able to bring it back to the family—then one of the sons may recover it by the permission of the other brothers; if he does so, he is not bound to divide it with his coheirs. There is a special rule attached to the general proposition. If the recovered property be a field, he who recovers gets only one-fourth part as his special share and his reward; the remainder must be equally shared by all. As an authority for this special rule, Vijñāna cites a couplet of Śaṅkha; in this couplet[1] the word ' bhūmi,' or ' land' is used; while Vijñāna speaks of a 'khetra' or a 'field.' The word 'khetra' implies a cultivated area of land; while 'bhūmi' is more general, and may include houses and orchards. I apprehend that Vijñāna's explanation will be accepted; It is likely that in an agricultural community, the special rule with regard to arable land was framed in accordance with a general sentiment, which regarded it as inequitable to deprive the other members from all share in a kind of recovered, property, which was the principal means of carrying on agricultural operations.

Gains of Science

The fourth kind of special acquisition mentioned by Yājñavalkya is what is acquired by means of learning. It has been in other treatises briefly called ' Vidyādhana,' literally 'learning-money.' Colebrooke has called it' gains of science:

1. Ch. I sec. 4 para. 3.

Vijñāna explains it as follows:[1]—learning here means the study of the Veda, the teaching of the Veda, and the expounding of the sense of the Veda; any money acquired by doing so, 'the acquirer is not bound to give to his co-heirs; he shall take it all. Here a difference is made between the teaching of the Veda, and the expounding of the sense of the Veda. It need not puzzle no, since the practice in former times was, (and still is, wherever anything like a systematic study of the Veda prevails among the Brāhmans in India, as for instance in the Mahratta and the Dravida countries), that the student of the Veda was first made to recite with proper intonation and melody, the texts of the Veda under the tuition of his preceptor; the tuition was commenced immediately after the investiture with the sacred thread. This ceremony used to take place when the Brāhman was only nine years old; at that age it was not likely that he could have mastered the rules of grammar; this explanation of the meaning of the Veda was therefore postponed to a date when the boy had far advanced in learning the texts by heart, and in reciting them with proper melody. The gains made by a learned Brāhman by this professorial employment were received by him at the termination of his pupil's studies. To teach on the understanding of receiving fixed wages was denounced as a sin, expiable by a penance.[2] When the pupil went home after finishing his studies, it was then for him to offer what was called his 'gurudakṣiṇā,' or presents to a preceptor.' The amount of these presents made by a student depended upon the extent of his means. It could not have been small; the son of a royal minister, or a king's appointed judicial functionary, probably used to make enormous gifts to his preceptor, with whom, under the normal condition of a Hindu society, the student used to live for ten or twelve

1. Ch. I, sec. 4, para 5.
2. See *ante* p. 424, Sin No. 16.

years. On the other hand, a poor Brāhman's son was often discharged by his preceptor with a blessing, and an assurance that the dutiful conduct of the pupil during his sojourn in the preceptor's family was considered by the latter as sufficient compensation for the trouble and care he had taken in teaching the pupil. Everyone who has read Raghuvaṁśa will call to mind the touching story of Kautsa, the pupil of Varatantu, who was first directed to go home without having to pay anything, but who foolishly insisted upon making a money payment; whereupon the preceptor got annoyed, and by way of punishment, laid upon him the fearful obligation of paying a crore of gold coins for each branch of learning that he had learnt; the branches of learning being fourteen in number, the young Brahman unwittingly took upon himself the duty of procuring fourteen crores of gold coins, in order to pay his preceptor. How he went a begging from king to king, how he came to Raghu, the renowned universal monarch of the day, who had just then exhausted his whole treasury in the celebration of a religious ceremony, how yet Raghu helped Kautsa in obtaining his wish, are topics immortalised in the verse of Kālidāsa. The story furnishes a graphic picture of the state of society. It gives us an insight into the amount of money which the learned Brahmans of past times used to make by means of learning. We can thus solve the mystery of the strange provisions of law with regard to this Vidyādhana, (gains of scince), which I am going to set forth. It is in this part of the law relating to separate acquisitions, that our ancient Ṛṣis have evinced a very illiberal and jealous spirit, in cutting down the separate acquisitions of the member of an undivided family. What earnings can be imagined as more unconnected with the common funds of the family, than the income made by a learned and diligent teacher in carrying on his calling? But the keen eye of our old law-givers could even here perceive a connection between such earnings and the family funds. Vijñāna says,[1] that if the learning has been acquired by the expenditure of the paternal wealth, any money made by means of that learning must be shared with the father and the brothers. The 'learning-money' which is not partible has been characterized by Kātyāyana thus:[2]—"That money is to be regarded the real gains of science, where the learning was acquired, while eating the' rice of a stranger, and where the knowledge was acquired under the tuition of a stranger." Not only the, teacher must be a stranger, but the pupil's daily sustenance must come from a source other than the family funds, so long as he is engaged in his pursuit of knowledge, in order that future profits to be made by him by means of that knowledge might become his exclusive property. It might be supposed that such unreasonable conditions could never be satisfied in actual life. But such a supposition would be besides the truth. Even now in Bengal, scores of students resort to Nuddea and other celebrated seats of learning, which have become famous as the residence of highly considered professors of Sanskrit learning; there they are fed and clothed by their preceptors so long as they study. The income of the preceptors mainly consists in presents received at the religious ceremonies celebrated by the opulent Hindus. It is on occasions of śrādhs that large presents are bestowed. Some renowned professors have to travel not only all over Bengal at the invitation of wealthy people, but their, fame has spread beyond Bengal, and brings in presents to them from even the up-country districts. Again, even now in Calcutta, scores of students, chiefly from Eastern Bengal, educate themselves, and have their food supplied to them by some rich citizen who has established an eating-house, specially intended for the student class. It costs the students nothing;

1. Ch. I, sec. 4, para. 6.
2. Para. 8.

the rich citizen's motives are purely philanthropic. Whatever little additional expense the students require is supplied by their own earnings made in the line of private tuition. Thus, almost without costing a pice to their families, these students acquire high attainments, obtain posts endowed with very large salaries, and amass sums of money. Acquisitions like these answer to the letter the description of the 'learning-money given by Kātyāyana. It is money acquired by means of a learning, which itself was acquired while eating the rice of a stranger, and from a teacher totally unconnected with the family. Similarly, when students like those of Nuddea finish their course of study, and themselves set up as professors of Sanskrit knowledge, in those indigenous school-houses of Bengal which are known by the name of Chatushpāthīs, they begin to earn money in the same way as their preceptors, from presents at the religious ceremonies of pious and wealthy Hindus. This learning-money they need not divide with any of their co-heirs.

Besides that of Kātyāyana, Vijñāna has quoted two social texts relating to the subject of the 'learning money.'[1] One runs thus:— "If any money is obtained by the eldest born after the death of the father, his younger brothers have a share therein, provided they have cultivated science." Vijñāna explains this as embodying an exception to the general rule, which says that whether before or after the death of the father, whatever is earned by an individual member without detriment to the paternal property, is impartible. The above text is the same as śloka' 204th of the 9th chapter of Manu. Kullūka explains it thus :—"After the death of the father, "whatever wealth the eldest born son, who is undivided with his brothers, earns by his own individual exertions, is to be shared by him with all his learned younger brothers, but not with the unlearned ones:" Here the provision does not appear to be confined to the

1. Para. 13, sec. 4, chap. I.

'learning money' of the eldest brother, but extends to all sorts of acquisitions made by him. The word in the orginal is, Jyeṣṭha,' and I have understood by it the 'eldest born,' not simply 'the eldest surviving son;' for in the chapter on Inheritance, that word 'Jyeshṭha,' which elsewhere may, indifferently mean either the eldest surviving son or the eldest born son, is limited to the latter sense; as appears from an opinion expressed by Jimūta.[1] I apprehend that, the modern tribunals will hardly be disposed to give effect to this rule, which gives a right to the learned younger brothers in all the earnings of their undivided eldest brother subsequent to the father's death. The chief reason for refusing countenance to this rule will probably be, that learning or literary attainments are a kind of qualification, the existence of which is not susceptible of a sufficiently certain determination. An indispensable attribute of a provision of law must be the certainty of application. To say that one possessed of learning shall get a, share, and one not possessed of learning shall not get a share, would not be enough; we must have a criterion, whereby we may ascertain who is possessed of learning and who is not. This is a specimen of the reasoning, with which modern tribunals often testify a disposition to give a go-by to the provisions of the Hindu law involving uncertainties of the above character. But in the matter of learning or literary attainments, I believe Courts of Justice under a Hindu king had large discretionary power to decide, whether a particular individual was to be taken as a learned man or not. We cannot imagine that these provisions of law were a dead letter; they are found in treatises which must have been constantly consulted ; they could not be overlooked or explained away.

The other provision relating to the gains of science which has been quoted by Vijñāna is found in para. 8. This text seems to be an exception to the one from Manu. It says

1. See *ante* p. 637.

that if while one brother is prosecuting his studies, another maintains the family of the first, the gains of Science acquired by the first must be participated in by the second, although the latter be himself an unlearned man. From this text it would seem, that all the learned members of a family had a sort of indefeasible right in the gains of science acquired by any one of them; this privilege is given to an unlearned co-heir only when he has been of a special service to the acquirer, by taking care of his family in his absence. But a further consideration will make it evident that the text must refer to divided brothers. During the undivided condition, the family of every brother who is absent from home must be cared for either by the head of the family, or by the other members if there is no recognized head. There is no possibility therefore in a joint family of one brother taking special care of the family of an absent member. But if we understand the text as applicable to two divided brothers, one of whom goes abroad to prosecute his studies, leaving his family under the supervision of his brother, the latter will be a sharer in all the gains of science, subsequently earned by the learned brother. To share them it will not be necessary that the other brother should be a learned man. Learned or illiterate, he has benefited his brother, and partakes, in the name of equity, of the good fortune of his learned brother.

Gifts obtained, where separate

As Vijñāna would allow no property to be exclusive, if the common property has had to suffer in acquiring the same, he distinctly says that even gifts made to a Brāhman on account of his caste irrespective of his learning are partible, if these gifts have been obtained by detriment to the common property.[1] So he says that if ancestral property be recovered by spending father's money, that would not be impartible. How donations made to a Brāhman on

1. Para. 7, chap. I, sec. 4.

account of his caste can ever cause any detriment to the common funds is not explained, by Vijñāna. The only circumstances under which I can imagine that it could be so are, when a number of cows is made a gift of to a Brāhman who is the member of an undivided family; he brings the cattle home, but feeds them out of the common funds, or constructs a cow-house for them from the same source; here the cattle will belong to the family in general. Or suppose the Brāhman, the member of a joint family, receives a donation of a large quantity of rice, or paddy, or sesamum seed, but has no wherewithal to pay out of his own exclusive pocket the charges for conveying the gift to his house; he has recourse to the family funds for that purpose. I believe by doing so he loses his exclusive right. In para. 29, Vijñāna says that the acquirer gets a double share when his acquisitions fail to be his exclusive property by reason of his having had the assistance of the family property in acquiring the property. It should be never lost sight of, that it is while the undivided condition lasts that individual acquisitions made by the help of the joint funds merge into the joint estate, the acquirer having a lien to an additional share. After a division, one brother may receive any help he likes from another in making acquisitions, without risking his exclusive right. He may be liable to give such compensation as may be agreed on; but the law will attach no joint character to such acquisitions, even though made with very material assistance from another, who was formerly a joint coparcener, but is no longer so.

Property impartible by its nature

With regard to property which is impartible on account of some special character it bears, Vijñāna has enumerated clothes, vehicles ornaments prepared food, and women. All the articles of clothing, which during the undivided condition, are part of the special wardrobe of an individual member, are not to be partitioned, however valuable they may be. The father has an authority of presenting valuable shawls, laced clothing, and jewellery, to one son, out of the common means, if these means are large enough to admit of such presents being made. These pieces of clothing or jewellery or vehicles specially appropriated to an individual member, should be allowed to that very member at the time of the general partition. They in fact are exclusively his. But I am afraid that modern practice is not always in accordance with this salutary provision of law. With regard to the articles of a very small value, such as clothing of ordinary daily wear, the coparceners do not grudge them to the particular individual who has used them previously. But this generosity or indifference is not extended to valuable property, such as shawls, and laced clothing, and jewellery and so forth. Although previous to partition, every coparcener knew that a certain set of these articles had been intended for a particular member, had in fact been constantly and exclusively used by him, yet there is a reluctance and a strain exhibited by the others in allowing them to be appropriated by that individual, unless indeed every parcener possesses specimens of similar articles of a corresponding value. In very wealthy families that is generally the case; few have reason to complain that they have not had a sufficiency of these necessary articles, or that the managing member had been partial to any one member in his allowance of these articles. But in the middle class families, the means common to all may be insufficient to furnish every member with necessary articles for constant use of exactly the same value. If the disproportion in value be appreciable, then an attempt is made to bring everything into the hotchpot. For this proceeding, the reason set up is that the articles had not been intended for the exclusive use of the particular members, but that they were the common property of the family, and had been used by particular members for the sake of convenience or by a temporary mutual arrangement. Then of course the question resolves itself into one of fact; but the law is clear, that if cloth has been worn by a particular member, or a carriage has been driven, or a horse has been ridden by a particular member, before partition, it should be given to him at the partition without diminishing his share in other property. Pieces of new clothing, however, are to be shared by all. Again, clothing which had been used by the deceased father are to be made a gift of to the Brāhman who eats the śrādha food; for it must be remembered, that formerly the śrāddha was performed by inviting a Brāhman to represent the manes of the deceased; choice food of diverse kinds was served up to him with the recitation of proper texts from the Veda. The Brāhman partook of the food, and the hunger of the manes was supposed to have been appeased thereby. This Brāhman was called the eater of the śrāddha, and he had a right to all clothing and ornaments, and beds, carriages and horses, etc. which had been in the use of the father. As the practice now is obsolete, and as a make-believe Brāhman figure of kusa grass now occupies the place of the living Brāhman of former times, there is no one now to claim these articles of the father's special use. It has been said, that a horse which has been ridden by a particular member before division, shall belong to him. But if it be a family of horse-dealers, owning a large number of horses, the beasts must be shared by all; only if there be a residual number, not capable of an equal division, it becomes the exclusive property of the eldest born. This rule applies not only to horses, but to goats, sheep, asses, and all animals of an uncloven hoof. The rule is based on the śloka 119, ch. IX, Manu. Kullūka's comments upon the same are:—"Goats and sheep, etc., together with animals of an uncloven hoof, which cannot be equally divided at the time of the partition, should belong to the first-born; these should not be divided by exchange of other articles of equal value; nor should they be sold, and the price divided." It is not clear whether cows, buffaloes and camels are included in the rule. Kullūka says, 'goats and sheep,' etc. Sanskrit writers are often in the habit of adding this word 'etc.,' 'adi,' without attaching a definite meaning to it. Manu speaks of particular animals only; the rule derogates from the equal rights of all; it should therefore be strictly construed. Cows and buffaloes and camels should not come within it, but although unequal in number, must be equally divided in either of the two ways indicated by Kullūka,— of other articles of equal value, or division of the price received by selling them.

To illustrate the application of the rule, suppose there are five brothers, and eleven, or twelve or thirteen or fourteen horses; the brothers get two horses each; but the eldest gets three or four or five or six. If the number of brothers be large, and if the number of animals be one less than a multiple of the number of brothers, the eldest gets a disproportionately large number of the animals. But I do not see how such a result can be prevented. The residual number of particular animals, which becomes the exclusive property of the eldest, cannot be said to be uddhāra or deduction, and therefore the rule does not come within the prohibition, whereby partition accompanied by deduction has been interdicted in the Kali age. Vijñāna, who elsewhere, sets his countenance against all unequal partition, expressly, introduces this rule with approval in para. 18, sec. 4, ch. I. He then says—"In case of the horses, etc. being numerous—they must indeed be divided by persons making their subsistence by selling them. But in case of indivisibility on account of inequality, they belong to the eldest." Then he cites the text of Manu. I apprehend therefore that even now the eldest can assert his claim thus declared by Manu's text.

Gains of science in the Mithilā law

According to the Vivādacintāmaṇi, gains of science are of two kinds; earnings made by one proficient in letters, and those made by skill in the military art. In the translation of this treatise, the subject of separate acquisitions will be found discussed in pp. 249-266. I shall here point out the peculiarities in its doctrine relating to this topic. The author says, that if skill in literature or in the military art has been acquired from the instructions of the father or of any coparcener, all acquisitions made by means of that science must be shared with the rest. To illustrate acquisitions made by scholarship, he says, that where a prize has been offered for the solution of a difficulty, the prize earned by the scholar, who solves the difficulty is his 'learning-money.' So are presents obtained from a pupil, from a jajamana or a person celebrating a religious ceremony, on account of officiating as a priest; or for answering a question, or for determining a doubtful point, or through display of knowledge, or by victory in a disputation, or for superior skill in reading. An officiating priest receives a fee or gratuity as compensation for his labours. The author says that there may be earning made by setting questions.[1] This is exemplified by the fees, which an examiner in our time receives for setting papers. Again, where there is a doubt with reference to a particular passage in some literary work, a scholar gives expression to his own views; if they appear satisfactory to those, able to judge, he receives a reward. The author also says that what is earned by skill in a mechanical art is subject to the law of the ' learning-money.' Similarly, if some valuable article has been sold at a small price by an ignorant seller, the profit belongs exclusively to the purchaser, the co-heirs having no right to it. Again, a scholar says, ' I alone know this particular branch of learning;' he substantiates his assertion and gets a reward; that is an instance of ' learning-money. ' As regards the liability of the learning-money to be shared with the rest, the author

1. Here, as on other occasions, I have mostly referred to the original of the Vivādacintāmaṇi; and therefore my summary of the text may not be altogether in unison with the English Translation, which, I am afraid, is too free in many places.

summarizes thus:—'That learning-money is not to be shared, which is earned even with the assistance of the common property, by one who has acquired his learning or his military skill from a strange; and fed himself with food received from a stranger; provided that while he was learning the science, his co-heirs were not supporting his family: The author does not say; how gains of science are to be acquired with the assistance of the common property. But since he includes skill in arms as well as skill in a mechanical art, in the name of 'science,' we may suppose, that if the weapons belong to the family wherewith a soldier exercises his calling and acquires money, such acquisitions will be common or exclusive, according as the soldier received his professional instruction from some member of the family or not. So if the mechanical art has been learnt from a stranger, then the artizan may employ the tools belonging to the family in plying his trade, and yet he will not lose his exclusive right to acquisitions so made. This follows directly from the rule laid down in the Mithila Treatise. The separate acquisitions made by means of the military art are thus illustrated: "If a soldier risks his life, and performs a gallant deed, and receives a reward from his lord well-pleased at the deed, that would be money obtained by valour. The acquisition which is made with a standard is not to be shared. That is said to be won with a standard, which is gained by one who risks his life in the cause of his employer, gains a victory over the hostile force, and brings home a prize from the field of battle." Besides the above, the author mentions two other kinds of exclusive property, one is called madhuparkika, which word means 'hospitable offerings made to a guest or a visitor.' The practice of making these offerings remotely owes its origin to the institution of castes. As it is only the several limited sections of the Hindu community that can partake of each other's cooked food; there is a custom prevailing all over India, that when an honoured guest or a visitor arrives at the place of another person of a different caste, the latter offers him raw articles of food, which the guest will either cook himself or have cooked by his own men. These offerings are known by the name of madhuparka, which in Bengal goes by the vernacular name of 'sidha.' We may easily imagine how when a learned and famous Brāhman pays a visit to a Rajah or an opulent zamindar, the madhuparka assumes the shape of an assortment of costly presents, including not only rice and butter and similar articles of daily consumption, but even a carriage, a horse, ornaments, and gold and silver. This is the madhuparka which seems to be alluded to by our original texts, when they provide that mādhuparkika becomes the separate property of the recipient. The other kind of separate property mentioned by Vivādacintāmaṇi is the gift of favour received from a relative. Vyāsa quoted as declaring, that what has been bestowed by the paternal grandfather, or by the father, or by the mother, to one parcener as a mark of favour, it should not be taken away from him. This is known as a gift of favour; such a gift can be made by the father, according to the Mitākṣarā, from moveable property, whether acquired by himself, or ancestral.[1]

The same in the Madras Law

In the Smṛticandrikā, ch. VII, the following special light is thrown upon the subject, over and above what is common to it with the Mithilā treatise. One kind of learning-money is said to be, what a learned Brāhman receives by declaring, what expiatory penance a man must undergo, when he has committed a sin. It is his fee for propounding a proposition of sacred. law. He also receives a similar fee for giving his opinion upon a question of temporal law, as where the two opposite parties in a suit refer a question to him. Where the learning money is not exclusive, because the learning was acquired from the instruction of a member of the family, the

1. Mitāk, ch. I, sec, I, para, 25.

acquirer nevertheless receives a double share. Vyāsa is quoted as declaring that if a soldier acquires money, by making use of weapons, or of horses and cars, which belong to the family, then the acquirer receives a double share, and the rest receive a single share each. The author explains that this rule will apply to every joint family, whether it is composed of brothers, or of more distant relatives. Another text of Vyāsa is quoted, wherein it is said, that when partible property which went out of the family, being seized by a stranger, is recovered by an individual sharer, whether that recovery takes place before or after partition, the recoverer takes a double share, the rest receiving a single share each. This rule, the author says, extends to the recovered landed property. It therefore, conflicts with Śaṅkha, quoted (see *ante* p. 661) in the Mitākṣarā, who says that the additional share to be received by the recoverer is only one-fourth. With regard'to the gifts of favour, the author is of the same opinion with Vijñāna, and lays down that immoveable property can never be given as a mark of favour to an individual member; even if given, it will be partitioned.[1]

Exclusive Property in Bengal

In the Dāyabhāga of Jīmūtavāhana, the subject of separate property has been discussed more at length than in any other treatise.[2] He adopts the general rule, that what an individual member acquires by making use of his paternal property is to be shared by others; what is not so acquired belongs exclusively to him. The root of this distinction is, that in the case of common property not having been so used, the others have made no contribution to the acquisition, either by their wealth, or by their personal exertions; therefore they cannot claim a share. Besides the kinds of exclusive property enumerated in the Mitākṣarā,

1. Ch. VII, para, 48.
2. Ch. VI.

Jīmūta mentions a new kind called Saudāyika,[1] which he explains as what has been received. as a mark of favour from the father or the paternal uncle, or other relatives likely to entertain an affectionate feeling for the recipient. According to thus author, there is a peculiar rule applicable to 'gains of science,' which he says must be shared with coparceners of equal or superior learning, although the learning may have been acquired under the instructions of a stranger.[2] In para. 24, he says that whatever kind of acquisitions it may be, the acquirer will always get a double share, wherever the acquisitions are for any reason to be shared with the rest. The reasons for sharing one's acquisitions with the other members of the family are, either that the common property was used in making the acquisition, or that the science was acquired under the instructions of a member of the family, or that a share is claimable on account of equal or superior learning. The general rule with regard to the acquisitions made by an individual member under the Bengal school has been explained in paras. 38-40, ch. VI. Whatever has been acquired by consuming, or by the help or assistance of, the joint property, is to be shared with the rest. That the ancient Ṛṣis particularly mention 'learning-money,' or 'valour-money,' or other descriptions of separate earnings, ought not to lead us to suppose, that these earnings are exempt from division, even though acquired by the help of the joint property. Nor are we to suppose, that whatever is acquired by an undivided member is joint property. That the liability or non-liability to division depends upon the fact of common property having been or having not been used, extends even to donations a Brāhman receives. Acceptance of gifts may seem never to require any outlay of joint money; but the author says, that instances often do occur of presents being made in order to induce a donation.

1. Para. 11
2. Para. 21

Again, if joint property be spent expressly for the purpose of making the acquisitions, it is then that the acquisitions become joint. It is no reason for partibility, that the acquirer has received his subsistence from the common funds while he was earning his separate property.[1] This is an important rule, and ought to be carefully borne in mind. Had it not been for this rule, no separate acquisition could possibly have been made, which would not have involved the use of joint funds. For every member must have been fed and clothed from the common funds during the years of his infancy, that is, until he arrives at an age when he can earn for himself. The preservation of life, therefore, is attended with some consumption of joint property; and as no earning is possible unless life has been preserved, all acquisition depends indirectly upon the assistance received from joint property. It might therefore have been supposed, that separate acquisition, absolutely independent of any help from the general family estate, would be a non-existent entity. Accordingly Jīmūtavāhana takes special care to point out, that the rule is not to be understood in so rigorous a sense. If that had been the real meaning, argues Jīmūta, how could Manu, Yājñavalkya, Viṣṇu, Vyāsa and other Ṛṣis say in the same strain, that whatever is acquired by one's self-exertions without consuming the common property must belong exclusively to him. Surely these provisions of law must have been intended to be operative. We must therefore attach a reasonable meaning to the phrase, 'without consuming the common wealth.' Such consumption, as is inevitable in the preservation of life, by receiving food and clothing and the other necessaries of life, is not within its meaning. But it is consumption which has for its express purpose the acquisition of wealth, that will take away the exclusive character of the wealth acquired. Thus trade or agriculture requires capital; if this capital is supplied by the family, of course income derived from the

1. Paras. 48-50.

trade or the agricultural operations carried on with that capital must be shared by all. The acquirer, however, had a share in the capital equally with the others ; over and above the same, he bestowed his time, labour and exertions in conducting the operations; his claim therefore is double; and he receives a double share. If on the contrary, he has borrowed the money which he uses as capital, if he has not pledged the family credit in order to borrow it, then the profits will be his; though during all the time his maintenance has been obtained from the joint funds.

Jīmūtavāhana lays down a special rule, that[1] if the brothers live under the presidency of the eldest after the death of the father, then all the subsequent acquisitions made by the eldest must be shared with his learned brothers, the illiterate brothers being entirely excluded. This is a distinction between the father and the eldest brother; for the father's acquisitions are shared by all, learned or illiterate. I have already pointed out (see *ante*, p. 666) the difficulty in the practical application of this rule, because the Courts of the present day will most probably consider learning ' to be an indeterminate qualification for a claimant to property.

Learning Money in Bengal

Jīmūta has illustrated (ch. VI, See. 2) 'learning-money' by the following explanations. A person says, 'If you can give a satisfactory solution of this difficulty of mine, I shall pay you so much.' The learned man does solve it, and gets the reward, which is not to be shared. So is a gift made by a pupil who has received instruction. So are the fees of an officiating priest; nor are these fees to be taken as gift-money (pratigraha dhana); for gift-money is something paid without a consideration; whereas the fees of a priest are his wages for labour done. Similarly, a learned man may get a reward by explaining a difficulty, although no reward had

1. Para. 54. Sec. 1, ch. VI.

been promised beforehand. A man learned in law gets a sixth part of the disputed property, if he arbitrates between two contending claimants. Sometimes a disputation takes place between two learned men, upon the understanding that the defeated disputant will lose a sum of money to the winner. Likewise a prize is offered to be competed for by many learned men, one of whom establishes his superior ability and gains the prize. So, since science includes skill in art, the earnings of a goldsmith or of a painter are subject to the rules applicable to the earnings made by a man of literary attainments. Even a gambler's skill may be the source of profits, which are not to be shared with the rest. So that the real drift of the textual law upon the subject is, that earnings made by any kind of knowledge belong exclusively to the acquirer, and are not liable to be partitioned by the others. What is called the gift-money, that is to say, property acquired by acceptance of a gift, is a particular class of learning money. Acceptance of gift is a mode of acquiring proprietary right, which is proper only for a Brāhman. Now, it is only a learned Brāhman who can be properly made the object of a donation; the illiterate are utterly unworthy to receive gifts. The object of making gifts to a Brāhman is, that it will do good to the donor in the next world. None but a learned and righteous Brāhman can do that good; it is as impossible for an illiterate Brāhman to be of any service to the donor in the next world, as it is impossible to cross a river by embarking in a boat made of stone. Nor is it to be supposed that the vidyādhana (learning-money) is confined solely to the gains made by giving literary instruction; for the term 'vidyā' comes from the root, *vid*–to know; any knowledge therefore comes within the word ' vidyā.' With regard to the gains of valour and the nuptial gifts, the Dāyabhāga has not adopted any peculiar doctrine, but has cited the same Ṛṣi texts, which are found in the Vivāda-cintāmaṇi, and have been noticed by me. In para. 28, sec. 2, ch. VI, it is said, that books forming a part of the joint property should not be shared by illiterate members and that tools of art are not to be got but by those proficient in the art. Similarly, if one coparcener has constructed a dwelling house or laid out a garden, on a piece of joint land, it should be given to him, provided the father gave him permission. Permission may be inferred if the father, while alive, did not expressly laid his interdiction.

Similarly, ancestral property recovered by an individual member, by his sole exertions and the expenditure of his exclusive money, must belong to him, excepting land, which, according to Śaṅkha, must be shared with the rest, the recoverer receiving a fourth part of the recovered property as his additional share. Thus, if the land recovered, measures four bigahs, and there are three brothers; one bigah is first set apart for him who recovered it; then the three brothers divide the three bigahs equally among themselves; the result being that he who recovered gets two bigahs, and each of the two other brothers one bigah of land. It is to be remembered, that this rule of an additional fourth share obtains only when the land has been recovered without any use of the joint funds, and by the exclusive exertions of a single member.

Case-Law Upon Separate Property

I have thus given above a summary of the law relating to the separate property of an individual member in an undivided family. The case-law upon the subject is not extensive. In Dhunookdharee Lal *v.* Ganpat Lal, 10 W. R. 122, Dwarkanath Mitter, J. said, that because an individual member received his education from the joint estate, it would be no reason that acquisitions made by him should be joint property. In Bolakee Sahoo *v.* Court of Wards, 14 W. R. 34, Markby, J. says:— "According to a passage of the Mitākṣarā, if the father recovers property, which had been acquired by an ancestor, and taken away by a stranger, and not redeemed by the grandfather, he need not himself share it, against his inclinations, with his sons, any more than he need give up his own acquisitions. If this be the case where are property is recovered by a single member of the family upon the strength of the ancestor's title, the same principle will seem to apply with still greater force where the property would have been irrevocably lost to the family, but was repurchased by a person, who was solely entitled to it at the time, and who advances the money out of his own self-acquired property." In Behary Lal Roy *v.* Lalchand Roy, 25 W. R. 307, Macpherson, J. held, that the shop and business having been acquired by one brother from his father-in-law, having been in fact given to him on account of his having married his daughter, was the separate property of that brother, to which the other brother had no right to share.

In Durvasala Gangadhar Udu *v.* Durvasala, 7 Mad. H. C. Rep. p. 47, the question was whether the professional earnings of a vakeel were generally his self-acquired and impartible property. The judgment of Kindersley, J. may be thus summarised. It is easy to find isolated texts of Hindu Law which will support either of the two views, that they are partible and that they are not partible. On the one side, there is a text of Nārada, laying down the broad principle, that wealth gained by valour, property received with a wife, and the gains of science, these three are indivisible. On the other side, there are texts which lay down that any property acquired by an unseparated brother by means of science, which science he was unable to learn but by assistance from his father's funds, will be participated by his brothers. It may be that a member of an undivided family, specially trained by the head of the family in some special manner, started in a scientific profession by the same means, and for a time at all events, trusting for support to the family means, and leaving his wife and children to be maintained in the family house while he was pursuing his at first unremunerative profession, might be called upon to place in the general stock, any income he might eventually derive from that profession. There is a natural inclination in favour of such an interpretation of the law as would secure the fruits of a man's professional earnings for his own branch of the family. But it is impossible to read the authorities without concluding, that the question must be upon the facts in each case, how far the common family means were instrumental in enabling the professional man to earn the property which is claimed as subject to partition. When the professional man received from his father, nothing more than a general education, and it does not appear that he was distinguished by his professional learning, the fair presumption would be that such attainments as the vakeel possessed, had been acquired with the assistance of the family means. According to the opinion of Holloway, J. in this very case, the ordinary gains of science by one who has received a family maintenance are certainly partible; moreover, within the meaning of the authorities, a vakeel's business is not matter of science at all.

The above opinion will hardly be endorsed in this part of India. In the present day, it requires a course of at least ten years' severe study to attain the privilege of a vakeel of the Calcutta High Court. No one therefore can entertain the idea that it is not a learned profession. Jīmūta says, that if common property has been spent in giving a member a particular course of instruction, in order that he may in future be able to earn money, then the acquisitions made are joint. At present, goodly sums of money have to be spent to attain the status of a vakeel of the High Court. If the father of the family has advanced these sums, I do not see how we can fail to arrive at the conclusion, that the vakeel's earnings will be shared by the rest. Under the Bengal doctrine, a similar observation will apply to the earnings of those, who go to England with a view to enter the covenanted civil service, or the higher branch of the legal profession. If their expenses have been paid by the father, a reasonable interpretation of what Jīmūta has said will support the proposition, that a share will belong to all the other brothers in the future earnings of the civil servant or the barrister-at-law, besides a share claimable by the father of the family.[1]

The Privy Council have not yet had occasion to express their view of the law upon the question, namely, how far the future earnings of a member who has received his education from the common funds are to be shared with the rest. But the inclination of their opinion is discernible from the following extract out of their judgment in Pauliem Valoo Chetti *v.* Pauliem Suryah Chetty, I. L. R. 1 Mad. p. 261.

"This being their Lordships' view, it does not become necessary to consider whether the somewhat startling proposition of law, 'put forward by the appellant,—which, stated in plain terms, amounts to this: that if a member of a joint Hindu family receives any education whatever from the joint funds, he becomes for ever after incapable of acquiring by his own skill and industry any separate property—is or is not maintainable. Very strong and clear authority would be required to support such a proposition. For the reasons that they have given, it does not appear to them necessary to review the textbooks or the authorities which have been cited on this subject on this may be enough to say, that according to their Lordships' view, no texts which have been cited go to the full extent of the proposition which has been contended for. It appears to them further, that the case reported in the 10th volume of Sutherland's Weekly Reporter,[2] in which a judgment was given by Mr. Justice Jackson and Mr. Justice Mitter, both very high authorities, lays down the law upon this subject by no means so broadly as is laid down in two cases which have been quoted as decided in Madras; the first being to

1. For details of law on this point, see *ante*, p. 678.
2. P. 122, Dhnnnookdharee Lot, Appellant, already noticed.

the effect, that a woman adopting a dancing-girl, and supplying her with some means of carrying on her profession, was entitled to share in her gains;[1] and the second to the effect that the gains of a vakeel who has received no special education for his profession are to be shared in by the joint family of which he was a member,[2] decisions which to a certain extent have been also acted upon in Bombay.[3] It may hereafter possibly become necessary for this Board to consider whether or not the more limited and guarded expression of the law upon this subject of the Courts of Bengal is not more correct than what appears to be the doctrine of the Courts of Madras."

Now, in the Dāyabhāga at least, in para. 50, sec. 1, ch. VI, it is distinctly laid down, that where the common property is spent expressly for the purpose of earning money, the earnings made thereby must be common property. Therefore, if education be given to a member to enable him to become a vakeel, and such education costs money, this must be an instance of spending property for the express purpose of earning money. Therefore, if the money spent for that education come out of the common funds, the conclusion is irresistible that the earnings of the vakeel so educated must be shared by all.

---

1. Chalakonda Alasani *v.* Chalakonda Ratnachalam, 2 Mad. H. C. Rep. 56.
2. Durvasula Gangadharudu *v.* Durvasula Narasamma, 7 Mad. H. C. Rep. 47, already noticed by me.
3. Bai Manchha *v.* Norotam Doe Kasi Das, 6 Dom. II. C. Rep. (A. C.) 1.

Chapter 13

Presumptions In Relation To Joint Hindu Family

Three kinds of presumptions—No text authority for them—Property joint though purchased in one name—Family presumed joint in food, worship and estate—Property presumed joint after reunion—Self-acquisition proved by the party pleading it—Nucleus theory—Cases sanctioning nucleus theory—Cases recognising the ordinary, presumptions—Separation in estate presumed from separate mess and residence—Facts rebutting the presumption—rebutted by a will in a Mitākṣarā family—Mere separation in mess does not rebut presumption—Nucleus theory still more extended—Presumption weak where the common ancestor is remote—Presumption rebutted by conduct—Separate food and residence not conclusive as to separate estate—Party alleging separation cannot rely upon presumption—Best mode of rebutting the presumption—Views of Chief Justice Couch—Result of his decision—Presumption rebutted by disruption of family union—weakened by separate mess.

Three Kinds of presumption

This part of the subject of the present course has had its origin from the application of the principle of English Law of Evidence to the trial of suits involving questions of Hindu Law. Under the English Law of Evidence, the effect of legal presumptions is to shift the burden of proof, to answer the question, namely, who ought to give evidence, when a particular combination of facts arises in a suit. As regards a joint Hindu family, since the earliest days of Hindu Law being administered by British Judges, certain legal presumptions have been recognized as legitimately applicable to the case of a Hindu family. These presumptions may be classified under three heads, namely, I, a presumption of law that every Hindu family is to be taken as joint, unless the contrary is proved; I that the property in the possession of any member of such a family is to be taken as joint, unless the contrary is proved; III., that the fact of commensality is a legitimate basis for the inference that the family is joint. It will appear that the above are the propositions to be deduced from the observations made by Judges in deciding cases relating to joint family. It will also appear, that some of the judges of the High Court of Bengal, chief among whom were Sir John Budd Phear and the late Mr. Justice Elphinstone Jackson, made attempts to minimise the effect of these presumptions of law. But such attempts have ultimately failed; subsequent decisions by other judges having distinctly held, that the above presumptions are applicable in all cases.

No text authority for presumptions

The original texts furnish us with hardly any principle, which might be taken as the foundation of these presumptions. I have only been able to lay my finger upon the following text of the Mitāksharā, upon this subject.

समवेतैस्तु यत् प्राप्तं तत्र सर्व्वे समांशिनः।

Chap. I, sec. 4, para. 15.

"In what has been acquired, however, by all united, all have equal shares." As the decisions of the tribunals therefore are the sole authority, and in fact, the source, from which our knowledge of this part of the law is derived, I shall here give a number of cases upon the point. It will be borne in mind, that the five schools of Hindu Law do not differ among each other upon this question.

Property Joint, Though Purchased in One Name

The Judicial Committee have held, that where a family lives in commensality, eats together, and possesses joint property, it is to be presumed that all property in their possession is joint, and that purchase of some property in the name of one member, and receipts standing in his name, is consistent with the notion of its being joint property.[1] A family once joint retains the joint condition unless a division is proved; and the family property is to be taken as joint, unless it is shown that the property has become separate.[2] The normal state of every Hindu family is joint.

Family Presumed Joint in Food, Worship and Estate

Presumably, every such family is joint in food, worship, and estate. In the absence of proof of division, such is the legal presumption. But the members may sever in all or any of these three things.[3] Here the Judicial Committee have expressly laid down the law to be, that the presupmtion to be made with reference to a Hindu family is of a threefold character. We must presume, that the property is common, likewise that the members of the family live in commensality ; and thirdly that they worship in common. I have noticed in a previous part of these lectures what is understood by the word 'worship' in cases, like these. It ought to be said here, however, that unless it be shown that there was once a family to which the parties in a suit belong, no presumptions of law can possibly arise with reference to the family being joint.[4]

Property Presumed Joint in Re-union

Where two brothers, members, of a joint family, having once separated, and having remained in separation for

1. Dhurmodas Panday *v.* Shama Sundari Devi, 3 Moore's 1. A. 229, S. C., 6 W. R. P. R. 43.
2. Cheethah *v.* Meheen Lal, 11 Moore's I. A. 369.
3. Neel Kristo Deb Burmono *v.* Beer Chunder Thacoor, 12 Moore's 1, A, 523, S. C. 12 W. R. P. R. 21.
4. See per Garth, C. J. in a case quoted *ante* p. 268.

eleven months, again united, forming what is in the phraseology of Hindu Law called a re-union, it was held that this re-union relegated the brothers to their former joint condition; and that the legal presumption relating to a joint Hindu family would again apply in their case; consequently, where the eldest brother was long in the management of the joint estate, had received the collections from it, and had purchased talooks with moneys which formed part of those drawn from the joint estate, the younger brother on re-union was entitled to share in them, as acquisitions made with the joint funds.[1]

Self-Acquisition to be Proved by the Party Pleading it

In one early case, the judgment in which was delivered by the Judicial Committee in 1831, the *onus* of proving a certain property to be separate was thrown upon the party who had set up the plea that it was his self-acquisition.[2] Their Lordships say:—" There was some family property in which the Bhow had a share, although not large, and that property was never abandoned, * * by the Bhow." It seems to me that these remarks gave origin to an opinion, adopted by Phear, J., and Elphinstone Jackson, J., who held that the presumption of all property being joint in a Hindu family does not arise, unless it be in the first place shown that there was some nucleus of family property from which acquisitions could be made.

Cases Sanctioning the Uncleus Theory

The earliest case, so far as it appears, wherein doubts were thrown as to the soundness of the doctrine that all property in the hands of any one of the members of a joint family is to be presumed joint, is to be found in p. 3, S. D. A. D. for 1852, where the Judges say:— "The *onus probandi* in this case appears to us to be clearly on the plaintiff. By his own admission the properties in dispute were not

1. Prankishen Paul Chowdry *v.* Mothoora Mohun Paul Chowdry, Suth, P. C. Judgments, vol. 1, p. 609, S. C. 5 W. P. R. 11.
2. Luximon Sada-Sew *v.* Mullar Row Baju, Suth. P. C. J. vol. 1, p. 1.

acquired by the use of the patrimonial funds, nor have the defendants even acknowledged that they were acquired by joint exertions and aid of the plaintiff and his father. It was therefore for the plaintiff to prove, his own allegations as to the original joint interest in the purchase of the properties. The mere circumstance of the parties having been united in food raises no such sufficient presumption of a joint interest as to relieve the plaintiff from the onus of proof." This decision was referred to with approval by Peacock, C. J., in Muss. Subheddur v. Boloram Dewan, Sp. No. W. R. p. 57, where, no part of the property was ancestral, one brother being a Dewan of the Maharajah of Tipperah, and so in a position to acquire more than the other brother, who was a mere peon. No evidence having been given that the brothers ever treated their acquisitions as joint, it was held that the Dewan was not bound to give a half-share to his brother's widow. This principle was followed by Phear, J., in Sheo Golam Sing *v.* Burra Sing, 10 W R. 198, where he said:—"The plaintiff says that he is entitled by purchase to the property of one of three brothers, alleging that the land in suit is the joint property of the three brothers, and he seeks to recover the undivided share of his vendor. The defendants deny that the land belonged to the three brothers jointly, but aver that it was the self-acquired property of the elder brother, who was not the vendor of the plaintiff." Under these circumstances, the judgment goes on to say in substance, no presumption arises that the brothers lived jointly until the contrary is proved, or that all property acquired by one member of a joint family must have been acquired for the benefit of the whole family until it is shown to be otherwise. The normal condition of a Hindu family is no doubt joint, and it is to be presumed to remain joint unless a separation is proved. Again, property shown to have been once joint, is to be presumed to remain joint, until the contrary is proved. But the single fact of a family living joint or in commensality is not enough to raise a presumption that property acquired by an individual member is joint. To render it so, consideration for its purchase must have proceeded either out of ancestral funds, or have been produced out of joint property, or by joint labour. Neither of these alternatives is matter of legal presumption. The plaintiff claiming a share in property as joint must show that the defendants constitute a joint family, and that the acquisition was joint at the time it was made, or became so by being jointly enjoyed at a subsequent period. He must at least show that the family lived joint in estate at some antecedent period, not unreasonably great, and that the property was either a portion of the patrimonial estate, or was acquired by joint funds.

In Kisto Chunder Kurmokar *v.* Rughoonath Kurmokar, 10 W. R. 328, Phear,' J., expressed his views in these words:—"There is no presumption as to the sources of the funds which constituted the purchase money, arising merely from the circumstance that the person in whose name the property was acquired was living jointly or in commensality with others. * * I do not understand that any presumption arises by law against the plaintiff's title merely on the ground of his having been at the time of the purchase a member of a joint family." This contradicts directly the presumption that all property in the hand of a member of a joint family is to be taken as joint. As to the necessity for there being a nucleus of joint funds, in Dhunnookdhari Lal *v.* Ganpat Lal, 10 W. R. 122, p. Mitter, J., says:—"It is a mistake to say that in every case in which a Hindu pleads separate acquisition, it is incumbent on him to show the source from which the money came. No doubt, as remarked by their Lordships of the Privy Council in the case of Dhurm Das Panday, (6 W. R. P. R. 43), the source from which the money comes is the 'chief criterion' for determining as to whether a particular property is joint or separate ; but their Lordships never said that it is the only criterion, so as to render it obligatory on the party who pleads self-acquisition, to give evidence of the particular source from which the money was derived." Again:—'The defendant having shown that in acquiring the property in suit, he did not use any property which belonged to the joint family, the presumption of joint ownership is at once rebutted, and it is for the plaintiff to show that the property was acquired in the manner alleged by him." In this case the findings of facts were, that the joint property was not sufficiently large, after supporting the members of the family, to leave any surplus funds from which the property in suit could have been acquired; and that two brothers were at the time of purchase pursuing lucrative employments, the plaintiff himself being a minor. The effect of this decision seems to be, that acquisitions will not be presumed to be joint, unless, some nucleus of family property is shown to have existed, from the profits of which the acquisitions could be made. The indispensableness of a nucleus of family property in order to raise the presumption, seems to have been tacitly admitted in the following words of E. Jackson, J., in Shib Prosad Chuckerbutty *v.* Gungamoney Deby, 16 W. R. 291;— "The acquisitions seem to have been made from time to time with very small sums of money.

Considering that there was a certain nucleus of ancestral property from which a beginning might have been made, and that on the other hand, there is no evidence to show that the defendants acquired any special profits by any exertions of their own, the inference that can follow is that this property was acquired from ancestral funds."[1] A very similar principle was adopted in Khelat Chunder Ghose *v.* Kunjo Lal Mar" 10 'W. R. 333, as will appear from the following extract of the judgment.—" It appears to have been admitted that the three brothers lived in commensality; and the Lower Appellate Court has considered this fact sufficient to warrant the presumption that a property purchased by one member of the family was purchased for the benefit of all, without ascertaining whether there was

1. See p. 293, Col. 1, bottom.

any ancestral property from which funds were derived for the purchase of this property, and he has required the defendant, who is the representative of the auction purchaser of one brother's share, to prove that the said brother purchased from his separate funds. * *

But the plaintiff should have shown that there was some joint source from which funds were available for the purchase of this property for the family:' In Goalm Mustapha Khan *v.* Sheo Sundury Burmonee, 15 W. R. 304, it is said:— "The second objection is that the mere finding that the plaintiff's husband lived with his brothers in commensality is not sufficient to raise the presumption that they were members of a joint undivided family. But on this point the Sub-judge found not only that the parties lived together, but also the fact of the property being joint. Taking the two facts, he raised a very warrantable presumption that the family was joint. It was for the defendant to rebut this presumption." In Gangadhur Chatterji *v.* Soorjonath Chatterji, 15 W. R. 446, Loch, J., said:—"In this case there appears to be no family property from which the funds could have been procured for the building of the house. Therefore the presumption of Hindu law does not arise. ** The judge throws the *onus* on the defendant, because the parties being members of a joint Hindu family, when the defendant claimed an exclusive right, he was bound to prove. Looking to the fact that there was no ancestral source of wealth, that plaintiff was absent for many years, and has failed to prove that he made remittances to be used for the purpose of building the house, I think that this was not a correct course." Paul, J., said:—"The presumption of Hindu law arises only when the family is joint, having possession of joint property."

Cases Recognising the Ordinary Presumption

On the other hand, the following cases may be cited as recognising in an unqualified manner the validity of the ordinary presumptions of Hindu law, that the family is joint, that all property is joint, and that the members live in commensality. I shall here extract the propositions laid down in the different cases which involved questions of the validity or otherwise of these presumptions.

The rule of law is that a presumption arises from the status of Hindu society that a family of two or more Hindu brothers live in commensality and with joint funds, and that all property is ordinarily acquired from such funds. But it is a rebuttable presumption. It may be shown that the nucleus of the purchase money did not come from the joint funds, that the property is held separately, though the family lived in the same mess; and that the member claiming exclusive right purchased the property for himself out of his own funds, with title deeds written out in his own name, and not as manager or trustee. If these facts be proved, then the burden shifts on the party who pleads joint acquisition. He must then show that the single name was used in the title deeds for convenience for joint names, or that it is only as the name of the manager or trustee that it appears in the title deeds.[1]

Separation in estate presumed from separate mess and residence

It has been said, however, in one case, that when a family is separate in residence and food, it is to be presumed to be separate in estate.[2] The burden of proof in case of an alleged separate acquisition by the member of an undivided family possessing joint estate is upon the party advancing such a claim. But it is not necessary, in order to discharge it, that he should trace the very funds with which such purchase was made. The source from which the purchase money comes is a good criterion. But the following facts also may rebut the presumption. The party relying on his

1. Lokenath Surmah *v.* Oomamoyee Debi, 1 W. R. 107.
2. Badamoo Kooer *v.* Wazeer Sing, 5 W. R. 78.

self-acquisition had a separate employment yielding him an income; the amount of the purchase money was not disproportionate to what might be supposed to be the possible savings out of such income; the title deed ran in his name; he held the property openly in his exclusive possession; the proceeds were applied to his own use without the interference of the family.[1]

Facts rebutting the presumption

It is not singly, but a combination of facts like these, has the effect of rebutting the presumption; as, for instance, the single name in the title deed has hardly any effect of that kind; while the exclusive appropriation of the proceeds would be almost conclusive. In Mon-Mohinee Debee *v.* Soodamoney Debee, 3 W. R. 31, it is said that the presumption is that all Hindu families are joint and undivided, and that the *onus* of proving that a family is separate in mess and business is on the party making such assertion. The mere fact of property standing in the name of one brother does not prove that it is that one brother's separate and self-acquired property. These observations were thus noticed and explained in a subsequent case, Dhurm Chand Shatea *v.* Rajmohishi Debee, 5 W. R. 145;—"We do not read the precedents to rule that brothers must always be living together, but that if they are found to be living together as a family, they must be presumed to be joint in property, until the contrary is proved. * * Clear admission or clear proof of the non-existence of ancestral property is to be taken as rebutting to a certain extent the presumption of joint property." In Hurihur Mukerji *v.* Nobin Kishore Banerji, 5. W. R. 251, the Judges remark:—"A case is quoted in which it seems to be laid down that when the party are separate in mess, it lies on plaintiff to show some sort of joint or other enjoyment of the estate; but that remark is at most *obiter*, since in fact in that case the

1. Bipro Prosad Mytee *v.* Kena Dayee, 5 W.R. 82.

party was not thrown out on this ground; and it seems probable, that if the case be examined, it will turn out that though the words 'separate in mess' are somewhat broadly used, the case is like another case also quoted, in which there was not only, as in this case, a separate messing by parties living in the same enclosure and with no apparent separate incomes, but in fact an apparent separation in mess, purse, and means of maintenance, the parties having adopted separate professions, the one being a Dewan and the other a Jemadar of the Rajah of Tipperah. We are by no means prepared to say that in this case, as a mere presumption of law, we must not assume the estate to be joint till it is proved to be separate." The case referred to in the latter part of this extract is the one already cited by me, and to be found in p. 57, Sp. No. W. R. In Guru Prasad Roy *v.* Devi Prasad Tiwari, 6 W. R. 58, the facts were that joint property had been sold under a decree against some members, and another member of the family had repurchased it from the auction purchaser; upon these facts it was said:— " The family were originally joint in food, residence and business; the property in question was ancestral; it was sold for the debts of some of the members of the family and re-purchased by the plaintiff, but whether from his own private funds or from other resources belonging to the family has not been found.* * As the family have all along been joint, and they are still living in commensality, the presumption of Hindu law that the property is joint does arise." In Muss. Pitum Kunwur *v.* Joy Kishen Doss, 6 W. R. 101 two brothers governed by the Mitākṣarā law were originally joint; subsequently, after the death of one brother, his son lived jointly with his uncle, the surviving brother. Then this brother executed a will with the concurrence and attestation of his nephew, whereby he bequeathed some property to his daughter, which will had effect given to it by the daughter coming into possession of the property bequeathed to her. A dispute then arose as to certain *churs,* the nephew claiming it on the ground that it was joint family property. Presumption rebutted by a will in a Mitakṣarā family.

Under these circumstances the High Court held that here the presumption of Hindu law did not arise that the *onus* lay upon the nephew that the *churs* were joint, that the fact of a will by his uncle with his concurrence showed that the uncle dealt with his estate as separate; that where a member unquestionably had separate property, as well as a share in joint property, no presumption arose that a particular property was joint; that because originally the two brothers had been joint, it did not follow that the surviving brother at the time of his death was joint with his nephew. In Hurrihur Mukerji *v.* Tincowrie Dossee, 6 W. R. 170, the auction-purchaser of the rights and interests of one of two brothers sued for the half share of a property which stood in the name of the other brother, who claimed it as his separate acquisition. Upon these facts, the High Court said :— "The defendant pleads that for twelve years before the plaintiff's purchase, neither plaintiff nor plaintiff's vendor ever were in possession, either by receipt of rent, or otherwise, of any portion of the putni taluk. Evidence on this point should be required from both parties, and if defendant's allegation be substantiated, plaintiff is out of Court under the Statute of Limitations. Should, however, plaintiff prove that his vendor is within time, it will then be necessary for the judge first to demand from the plaintiff evidence of the source whence the money came for the purchase. If plaintiff proves his allegation, this fact together with the fact of commensality, will *not* raise a presumption under Hindu law in a case like the present, that the family was joint, but it will be a strong evidence in favour of plaintiff's contention, and when considered together with the will of which probate has been taken out, and the evidence of the signature of Kisto Chunder on that document, and with the failure of the defendant, to file the best evidence procurable as to the source whence the purchase money for the putnee came, will be sufficient to prove the plaintiff's case."

Case Not in harmony

Here it is difficult to understand upon what principle the learned judges held that in a case like the present the presumption of Hindu law did not arise; but we shall see a little further on, that Chief Justice Couch expressly said in one case, that the decisions on the subject of this presumption, are not reconcilable with each other. In Ram Gobindo Koondoo *v.* Maulavi Syud Hossein Ali, 7 W. R. 90, Norman, J. held that after a general separation in food, and a partition of estate, and after the brothers have commenced to live separately, if any one of them name into Court alleging that a particular portion of property originally, joint continued to remain so, the onus properly lay on him. But in Sriram Ghosh v. Srinath Dutt, 7 W. R,. 451, Macphereon J. said:—" So long as no partition is proved the presumption is that the property is joint. * *

Mere separation in mess does not rebut presumption

The fact that certain parcels are admittedly held in severalty does not do away with the presumption as regards the rest of what originally constituted the joint estate. In Beney, Madhab Mukerji *v.* Bhuggobutty Churn Banerji, 8 W.R. 270; Dwarkanath Mitten J. said:—"Mere separation in mess is not sufficient to rebut the presumption of joint ownership, which arises when there is a nucleus of joint property either admitted by the party pleading sole acquisition or proved against him by his opponents. In Taracharan Mukerji *v.* Joynaran Mukerji, 8 W. 8 226, the question arose, whether the presumption that purchases made in a joint family are joint would be applicable to a case, where the original joint property was so small, that there could have been no surplus after providing for the wants of those members of the family who were living on the joint funds. Those who maintain, that in such a case the ordinary presumption would not arise, ground their opinion upon the reason, that the foundation of the presumption is that there should be a surplus capable of being made a nucleus for further acquisition. It is in fact the nucleus theory in a more extended form. That theory says that unless it is proved that there was some joint property, the presumption does not arise that acquisitions are joint.

Nucleus theory still more extended

In its more extended form it says, that not only must the existence of joint property be proved in order to raise the presumption, but it must also be shown that the said property could yield an income sufficient to leave a surplus whereby the acquisitions could be made. But Markby, J. sitting with L. S. Jackson and Kemp, JJ., said:—"Whether or no this view of the law is in all respects correct, it does not appear to me to be necessary to consider, because I understand it to be conceded by Mr. Doyne, that the existence of family property being admitted the *onus* of showing that it was all absorbed in the family expenditure rested with the party setting up self- acquisition."

Presumption weak where the common ancestor is remote

In Rung Lall Misser *v.* Rughubur Sing, 9 W. R. 169, Dwarkanath Mitter, J. held that where the parties belonged to two different branches of a Hindu family sprung from a very remote common ancestor, and the disputed properties stood in the sole name of the ancestor of only one of the parties; where the two branches of the family had been separate from one another since a long time; where exclusive title had been previously asserted by one of the parties, and title-deeds and documents relating to possession were all is their favour; there was no basis for the presumption of a joint undivided Hindu family.

In Badul Sing *v.* Chutterdharee Sing, 9 W. R. 558, the facts were, that the family estates had been partitioned long before certain property in possession of some of the members were claimed as joint; that ever since that time, down to the making of the claim, more than eleven years had elapsed, during which time properties had been held by those members in their exclusive possession. No explanations were given as to why and under what circumstances those properties had not been included in the general partition. Dwarkanath Mitter, J., upon these facts said:—"These are not cases in which the plaintiffs can and ought to be permitted to take their stand upon the naked presumption of Hindu law, according to which every property acquired during a state of union is to be considered as joint unless the contrary is shown."

Presumption rebutted by conduct

Again:—"There can be no stereotyped mode of rebutting the presumption of Hindu law above alluded to, and I do not see any reason why in the .present instance it should be held that that presumption has not been amply rebutted by the conduct of the parties themselves." *Per* L. S. Jackson, J.—"The separation between the parties having taken place so long ago as eleven years before the commencement of suit, and there being nothing to show that anything was reserved at that separation, it certainly lay on the plaintiffs to show why they remained silent so long; and the presumption in favour of the members of a joint family, at all times capable of being easily rebutted, had no force at all in a case like the present."

Separate food and residence not conclusive as to Separate estate

Jagan Kooer *v.* Raghoonundon Lall, 10 W. R. 148, it was observed that separation in food and dwelling could raise a presumption that there was separation in estate also, though it might not be conclusive evidence of separation in estate. In Nund Coomar Mukerji *v.* Juggessur Mukerji, 11 W. R. 167, the plaintiff sued upon the allegations that there had been a partition between himself and the defendant, that a certain debt secured by a bond in the name of the defendant had been reserved as an asset recoverable by both the parties, that the defendant had recovered a portion of the debt: and the plaintiff sued for his half-share. Upon these facts L. S. Jackson, J., in concurrence with Markby, J., ruled that this was not a case in which the question of presumption or *onus* of proof should be considered."

Party alleging separatio cannot rely upon presumption

The plaintiff did not rely upon his right as member of a joint family. He relied and sued expressly upon the allegation that this was a debt which under the butwarrah papers he was entitled to recover jointly with the defendant. Those butwarrah papers the Court of first instance found to be fabrications ; and** with that finding unaltered and undisplaced, it was idle to talk of presumptions in favour of the plaintiff." In Chundro Tara Debea *v.* Buksh Ali, 11 W. R. 305, the Court observed that where the two brothers lived in commensality and carried on business together and there was some ancestral property, it was for the widow of one brother who relied upon separate acquisition on the part of her deceased husband to rebut the presumption of the acquisition being joint. "In regard to the Privy Council Decision, reported at page 207, Moore's Indian Appeals, Vol. III, it is true that there is some reference to patrimonial property; but the substance of the ruling is that in a Hindu family living in commensality, and possessing some joint property, the presumption of law is that all the property they are in possession of is joint, until it is shown that some member of the family acquired separately." In Dharoo Sooklain *v.* Court of Wards, 11 W. R. 336, the words of the Court are:—"Although under a recent ruling of the Privy Council, direct evidence of a butwarrah in the shape of a deed and a partition by metes and bounds is very properly no longer required, still *prima facie* presumption is not lost sight of, namely, that every Hindu family is presumed to be joint unless circumstances point clearly to a contrary conclusion."

Best mode of rebutting the presumption

The Court also holds that the best method of rebutting this presumption is to prove partition by the testimony of kinsmen, it being laid down in the Vivāda-cintāmaṇi[1] that where there is a doubt about the fact of partition among co-heirs, it should be removed by the evidence of kinsmen

1. p. 310.

and the like. In Radhika Prosad Dey *v.* Dhurm Dossee Debea, 11 W. R. 499, L. S. Jackson, J., ruled that the mere fact of commensality is not sufficient to raise the presumption of property being joint, but that it must be shown in addition that joint funds existed out of which acquisition could be made. Where there had been once a partial separation, by one brother going out, and again another separation on a subsequent occasion, and where separation had been alleged by the parties in proceedings before a Court of Justice, the High Court held that no presumption of the property being joint arose from the fact of the parties being members of a Hindu family; and that it lay upon the party pleading joint property to prove what portion of the property, remained joint after the separation.[1]

I have cited all these cases to show that the opinion expressed by judges upon the question of the presumptions to be made in connection with a joint Hindu family has not been uniform. This absence of uniformity was, pointedly noticed by Sir Richard Couch in Tarok Chunder Totadar *v.*, Judhistheer Chunder Koondoo, 19 W. R. 178.

Views of chief Justice Couch

The following extract will show the views of the learned Chief Justice upon this point.—"The Judicial Committee of the Privy Council, in the case in 12 Moore's Indian Appeals, p. 523, Neelkisto Deb *v.* Beer Chunder have laid down* * * that every Hindu family is presumably join in food, worship, and estate; and the same law had been laid down in a previous case in 9 Moore's Indian Appeals, p. 92, where it is said that the presumption with regard to a Hindu family is that it remains undivided." Then the Chief Justice quoted from the judgment in the case of Dhurm Das Pandey, 3 Moors, p. 229,[2] and says:—"With regard to what their Lordships say as to the family being possessed of

1. Premchand Dan *v.* Darimba Debea, 15 W. R. 238.
2. See *ante*, p. 688.

property, and that the presumption of law is that all the property the family is in possession of is joint property, the rule that the possession of one is the possession of all would apply to this extent, that if one of them was found to be in possession of any property, the family being presumed to be joint in estate, the presumption would be not that he was in possession of it as separate property acquired by him, but as member of a joint family. *** There is no doubt a conflict of decisions in this Court upon this subject. I can see no way of reconciling them." Then the Chief Justice, notices some of the cases already cited by me, and says that they are opposed to the principle laid down by the Judicial Committee.

Result of the decision by Couch, C. J.

The result of this decision must necessarily be, that whenever the parties in a case are Hindus not very remotely related to one another, the Court is bound, at the instance of any of the parties, to presume that the form a joint family, and that their property is joint. If it be the interest of any other party to traverse either of the above two suppositions, it is for him to give evidence of some fact that may lead to a contrary conclusion. I apprehend that a strict and logical application of the principles involved in the decision of Sir Richard Couch demands that we should take the law to be as I have here set forth. These principles received a further confirmation from the Judicial Committee in the case of Chand Huree Maitee *v.* Rajah Norindur Narain Roy, 19 W. R. 231, where a property had been purchased in the name of the family priest, and one brother attempted to set up a plea of self-acquisition with regard to it, upon which their Lordships said that with regard to what was purchased in the name of the priest, the presumption of law and the presumption of fact would be that the property acquired in that way by the managing representative member of the joint family, would be joint family property. The burden of proof, therefore, lay upon those who insisted that these two lots did not form part of that joint family estate.

Presumption rebutted by disruption of family unity

In Radhacharan Das *v.* Kripa Sindhu Das, I. L. R., 5 Cal. 474, Chief Justice Garth laid down that the presumption of the continued unity of the joint family did not apply where a disruption of the unity had already taken place, by one of the members having separated from the rest. In such a case no inference should be made that after the separation of one, the rest remained joint. The reason is said to be that even one member cannot separate from the rest, unless the shares of all are ascertained at the time, and such an ascertainment of shares would be tantamount to a partition, under the Mitākṣarā law, as explained in Appoovier's case.

Presumption weakened by seperated in mess

In the case of Shunkur Ram *v.* Dabee Ram, reported in p. 77 of Shome's Reports, Vol. 3, Mr. Justice Rameschander Mitter says —"The ordinary presumption in the case of a purchase by a member of a joint Hindu family in favour of the purchase being joint is considerably weakened if the purchase is found to have been made after separation in mess. This has been held by their Lordships of the Judicial Committee in the well known case of Khudu Lall."

APPENDIX

Original Sanskrit Text

No. 1

Manu, chap. 8, Śloka 415.

ध्वजाहृतो भक्तदासो गृहजः क्रीतदत्रिमौ।
पैतृको दण्डदासश्च सप्रैते दासयोनयः।।

(In English, word for word.)

By banner procured, rice-slave, in the house born, bought and given, paternal, fine-slave, and, seven, these, (are) slaves' sources.

Purport.

Slavery has its source in seven causes;—a man fights under a banner, and makes a captive; or gives rice to one, and the latter becomes his slave; or one is a slave, being the son of a slave of the house; or bought or given; or inherited, or has become a slave, having been unable to pay a fine imposed upon him.

Śloka 416.

भार्य्या पुत्रश्च दासश्च त्रय एवाधनाः स्मृताः।
यत्ते समधिगच्छन्ति यस्यैते तस्य तद्धनं।।

(Word for word.)

Wife, son, and, slave, and, three, even, wealthless, remembered (declared in the law). What they earn, whose, they (are), his, that wealth.

Śloka 299, chap. 8.

भार्य्या पुत्रश्च दासश्च शिष्यो भ्राता च सोदरः।
प्राप्तापराधास्ताड्याः सूरज्ज्वा वेणुदलेन वा।।

(Word for word.)

Wife, son, and, slave, and, pupil, brother, and, uterine, received-offence, strikeable, should be, by a rope, by a bamboo-splitting, or.

'Received-offence' means having incurred a liability to punishment for an offence committed..'

Manu, chap. 8, Śloka 167.

कुटुम्बार्थेऽध्यधीनोऽपि व्यवहारं यमाचरेत्।
स्वदेशे वा विदेशे वा ज्यायांस्तन्न विचालयेत्।।

"For family need, even a dependent's dependent, what transaction, may enter into; in own country, or in a foreign land; the elder should not disturb that."

There are two peculiar words in this Śloka, Adhyadhīna and Jyāyan. The former may be analyzed into adhi, adhi, and ina ; these three words may be literally rendered into 'under, under, a master or a lord.' The preposition adhi preceding ina, would mean 'under a master,' 'having a master or a lord to obey;' this gives the compound adhīna. The same preposition adhi, again placed before the compound adhīna, gives a doubly compound word adhyadhīna, 'under a dependent,' 'one who has a dependent to obey; ' a dependent's dependent.' I think therefore that Kullūka, the commentator of Manu, may be safely trusted when he explains the word 'adhyadhina' as' a slave.'

The other word jyāyan is explained by Sanskrit Grammarians as jyatīyas. The form 'jya' again is, according to them, inter changeable with ' vṛddha,' ' big,' 'senior;' while the 'īyas' is the suffix implying a comparative degree.

Therefore ' Jyāyān literally means ' the bigger,' ' the senior', 'the elder; hence 'the head of the family;' because headship of the family went by seniority in years.

Original Text, No. II.

Dāyabhāga, chap. II, para. 14.

द्रव्यं भूसाहचर्य्यात् द्विपदमभिहितं ।।

"The word 'property,' on account its being placed side by side with land, intends the 'biped' (species of property)."

Original Text, No. III.

Mitākṣarā, chap. I, sec. 1, para. 27.

स्थावरं द्विपदञ्चैव यद्यपि स्वयमर्जितं।
असम्भूय सुतान्सर्व्वान् न दानं न च विक्रयः ।।

"Immoveable, and also biped, (species of property), although acquired by one's own self; without convening all the sons, there is neither a gift nor a sale."

As the purport is quite clear, I have not changed the broken and elliptical form of the original, deeming that the above rendering will give a more vivid idea of the manner in which the Ṛṣis expressed views on law.

Original Text, No. IV.

Manu, chap. IX, Śloka 219.

वस्त्रं पत्रमलङ्कार कृतान्नमुदकं स्त्रियः।
योगक्षेमं प्रचारं च न विभाज्यं प्रचक्षते।।

"Clothing, vehicle, ornament, prepared food, water, women, sacrificial acts, and common path;—not partible;—(they) say."

The original for 'sacrificial acts' is 'Yogakṣema.' In another Lecture, I have treated at length of this kind of indivisible joint property. (See p. 438).

Original Text, No. V.

Mitākṣarā, chap. I, sec. 4, para. 26.

अविभाज्यं सगोत्राणामासहस्रकुलादपि।
याज्यं क्षेत्रं च पत्रं च कृतान्नमुदकं स्त्रियः।।

" Impartible is, among those of the same gotra, even as far as one thousand families (generations), the sacrificial place (or gains), and arable field, and vehicles, prepared food, water, women."

I have elsewhere noticed the peculiarity of the expressions,' as far as one thousand families.' (See p. 72). As regards yājya and pattra, the original respectively for 'sacrificial place and vehicles,' see p. 443.

Original Text, No. VI.

Dāyabhāga, chap. I, sec. 10.

एकां स्त्रीं कारयेत् कर्म्म यथांशेन गृहे गृहे।

" One should cause a single woman to perform duty, according to share, in each house."

Original Text, No. VII.

Manu, chap. VIII, Śloka 342.

असन्धितानां सन्धाता सन्धितानां च मोक्षकः।
दासाश्वरथहर्त्ता य प्राप्तः स्याच्चौर किल्विषं।।

"One who ties (animals) untied—one who sets free (those) that are tied—and the stealer of a slave, a horse, and a car; should be (deemed to have) committed the offence of a thief."

Original Text, No. VIII.

Nārada quoted in the Mitākṣarā on Śloka 183, chap. II, Yājñavalkya, p. 268 of the Edition of the Vyavahāradhyāya, issued by the Committee of Public Instruction in 1829.

गृहजातस्तथा क्रीतो लब्धो दायादुपागतः।
अनाकामभृतस्तद्वदाहितः स्वामिना च यः।।

मोक्षितो महत्तश्चर्णाद्युद्धप्राप्तः पणे जितः।
तवाहमित्युपगतः प्रव्रज्यावसिनः कृतः।।
भक्त दासश्च विज्ञेय स्तथैव वड़वाहृतः।
विक्रेता चात्मनः शास्त्रेदासाः पञ्चदश स्मृताः।।

The substance of the above text of Nārada has been given in the body of the Lectures, p. 10.

Original Text, No. IX.

Mitākṣarā, Vyavahārdhyāya, pp. 56-57; comments on Yājñavalkya chap. II, śloka, 32.

यत्तु स्मरणं। गुरोःशिष्ये पितुः पुत्रे दम्पत्योः स्वामिभृत्ययोः। विरोधे तु मिथस्तेषां व्यवहारो न सिध्यतीति। तदपि गुरुशिष्यादीनामात्यन्तिक व्यवहार प्रतिषेधपरं न भवति। तेषामपि कथञ्चिद् व्यवहारस्येष्टत्वात्। तथाहि। शिष्यशिष्टिरबधेन। अशक्तौ रज्जु वेणु विदलाभ्यां तनुभ्यां। अन्येन घ्नन् राज्ञा शास्यः। इति गौतमस्मरणात्। नोत्तमाङ्गे कथश्चन। इति मनुस्मरणाच्च। यदि गुरुः कोपावेशेन महता दण्डेन उत्तमाङ्गे ताड़यति। तदा स्मृतिव्यपेतेन मार्गेण आधर्षितः शिष्यो यदि राज्ञे निवेदयति। तदा भवत्येव व्यवहारपदं। भूर्य्या पितामहोपात्ता इत्यादि वचनात् पितामहोपात्ते भूम्यादौ पितापुत्रयोः स्वाम्ये समाने यदि पिता विक्रयादिना पितामहोपात्तं भूम्यादि नाशयति। तदा पुत्रो यदि धर्म्माधिकरणं प्रविशति। तदा पितापुत्रयोरपि भवत्येव व्यवहारः। तथा दुर्भिक्षे धर्म्मकार्य्ये च व्याधौ सम्प्रतिरोधके। गृहीतं स्त्रीधनं भर्त्ता नाकामो दातु मर्हति। इति स्मरणात्। दुर्भिक्षादिव्यतिरेकेण यदि स्त्रीधनं भर्त्ता व्ययीकृत्य विद्यमानधनोऽपि याच्यमानो न ददाति। तदा दम्पत्योरपि इष्यत एव व्यवहारः।

"As to the declaration,—'A judicial proceeding between preceptor and pupil, father and son, husband and wife, master and servants, is not valid,'—that, however, cannot intend to declare an absolute prohibition of a judicial proceeding, between preceptor and pupil, etc. Thus :— Gautama declares;— 'A pupil is to be corrected without killing. In case of inability, (the correction should be) by thin rope or thin split bamboo. (A preceptor) beating by any other (instrument of correction) is punishable by the king.' And Manu has declared.— 'Never on the head."—Therefore if the preceptor, being subject to wrath, strikes on the head with a big stick ; then if the pupil, being subject to an illegal assault, complains to the king—it would undoubtedly be a subject of judicial proceeding.

Similarly, by a text of Yājñavalkya, it having been declared that in grandfather's land, etc., the father and the son have equal right,–if the father by sale, etc., makes away with the grandfather's land, etc.; then if the son enters a court of justice; in that case, a judicial proceeding undoubtedly takes place between the father and the son.

Similarly, there is a declaration,—' In famine, in religious ceremony, in disease, in (being made a captive by) a robber, what peculiar property of a woman has been taken by the husband, he need not give (back), if unwilling.' Without there being famine, etc., if the husband having spent (his wife's) peculiar property, does not on demand pay it, although he has got money; then even between a husband and a wife, a proceeding in Court is allowable."

Original Text, No. X.
Institutes of Vaśiṣtha, chap. 15.
Jivānanda's edition, p. 484.

शोणित शुक्रसम्भवः पुत्रो मातापितृनिमित्तकः। तस्य प्रदानविक्रयत्यागेषु माता पितरौ प्रभवतः। नत्वेकं पुत्रं दद्यात्। स हि सन्तानाय पूर्व्वेषां। न स्त्री दद्यात् प्रतिगृहणीयाद् वा। अन्यत्र अनुज्ञानाद् भर्त्तुः।

"A son born from blood and seed, has his (efficient) cause in the father and the mother. The father and the mother possess an absolute power, as regards making a gift of him, selling him, and abandoning him. But (one) should not give a single son. For he is to continue the line of *his* forefathers. A woman should not give, or take. Unless it be on account of the permission of the husband."

No. XI.

Manu, chap. IX, Śloka 168.

माता पिता वा दद्यातां यमद्भिः पुत्रमापदि।
सदृशं प्रीतिसंयुक्तं स ज्ञेयो दत्रिमः सुतः।।

Literal.

"The mother, or the father, what son should give, with water, in distress, equal, with affection, he should be known the given son."

Purport.

That son, whom either the father or the mother, should both give, in distress— the son being of the same caste, the ceremony being attended with the sprinkling of water, and the gift of the son being made from motives of friendship, is to be deemed as the given son.

No. XII.

Kullūka's Comments.

तस्मैव पुत्राभावनिमित्तायामापदि।

"When that very person [the adoptive party] is in distress, on account of his having no son."

Original Text, No. XIII.

मन्वर्थविपरीता या सा स्मृतिर्न प्रशस्यते।
वेदार्थोपनिबन्धृत्वात् प्राधान्यं हि मनोः स्मृतम्।।

No. XIV

Mitākṣarā, chap. I, sec. 11, para. 10.

आपद् ग्रहणादनापदि न देयो दातुरयं प्रतिषेधः।

" Since distress is spoken of, a son should not be given, when there is no distress. This prohibition is directed to the giver."

No. XV.

Nanda Pandita's Dattaka Mimanśa, sec. 1,para. 7.

व्याख्यातञ्चापरार्केणापि तथा। आपदि प्रतिग्रहीतुरपुत्रत्वे इति। यद्वा। आपदि दुर्भिक्षादौ।

"Aparārka also has explained it in that way. Thus :— In distress,' that is, in case of the adopter being sonless.' Or; In distress' means in a time of scarcity etc.'

No. XVI.

Kātyāyana quoted in Nanda Pundita's Dattaka Mīmāṁsa, sec. 1, para. 7.

आपत्काले तु कर्तव्यं दानं विक्रय एव वा।
अन्यथा न प्रकर्त्तव्यमिति शास्त्रविनिश्चयः।।

"In a time of distress should be made a gift or a sale. Otherwise it should not be made. This is the settled law of the Śāstras."

Original Tests, Nos. XVI—2, and XVII, Manu, chap. 8, Sloka 169.

त्रयः परार्थे क्लिश्यन्ति साक्षिणः प्रतिभूः कुलम्।।

"The three suffer for another's sake ;—the' witnesses, the surety, (and) and the family."

Kullūka's Comments.

साक्षिणः प्रतिभूः कुलञ्च धर्म्मार्थव्यवहारेषु त्रय एते परार्थं क्लेशमनुभवन्ति। तस्मादनेन साक्ष्य प्रातिभाव्यं व्यवहारेक्षणञ्च नामी कारयितव्याः।

"The witnesses, a surety, and the family, in righteous litigation these three suffer trouble on another's account. Therefore he (the king) should not force these to do the duty of a witness, or a surety, or try cases (respectively)."

No. XVIII.

Yājnavalkaya, Ch. II, Sloka 30.

नृपेणाधिकृताः पूगाः श्रेणयोऽथ कुलानि च।
पूर्व्वं पूर्व्वं गुरु ज्ञेयं व्यवहारविधौ नृणाम्।।

"The king's functionaries, the village communities, the guilds, the families; of these, the each one that precedes is superior, in administering justice among men."

Vijñāneśvara's Comments.

पूगाः समूहा भिन्नजातीनां भिन्नवृत्तीनामेकस्याननिवासिनाम्। यथा ग्रामनगरादयः। श्रेण्यो नानाजातीनामेकजातीनामपि एकजातीयकर्म्मोपजीविनां सङ्घाताः। यथा हेड़ावुकानां ताम्बूलिक कुविन्दचर्म्मकारादीनां च। कुलनि ज्ञातिसम्बन्धिबन्धूनां समूहाः। **। एतदुक्तं भवति। नृपाधिकृतैर्निर्णीते व्यवहारे पराजितस्य यद्यप्यसन्तोषः कुदृष्टिबुद्धयापि भवति। तथापि पूगादिषु पुनर्व्यवहारो न भवत्येव। एवं पूगनिर्णीतेऽपि न श्रेण्यादिगमनं। तथा श्रेणीनिर्णीते कुलगमनं न भवति। कुलनिर्णीते तु श्रेण्यागमनं भवति। श्रेणीनिर्णीते पूगादिगमनं। पूगनिर्णीते नृपाधिकृतगमनं भवति।

For its purport, see Lectures, p. 23.

Original Text, No. XIX.

Smṛti-candrikā, leaf 15, page 2, line 8, (MS. belonging to the Calcutta Government Sanskrit College, No. 2898.)

कुलानि अर्थिप्रत्यर्थिनोः सगोत्रानि।
कुलिकाः केचन अर्थिप्रत्यर्थिगोत्रजा वृद्धाः।।

"Families are those of the same gotra with the plaintiff and the defendant. Family men are some seniors born in the family of the plaintiff and the defendant."

In this passage the author of the Smṛti-candrikā cites a text of Brigu, which mentions 'kulas' or families, and kulikas' or family-men as assisting in the administration of justice.

Original Text, No.XX

Manu, Ch: VIII, Śloka 158.

यो यस्य प्रतिभूस्तिष्ठेत् दर्शनायेह मानवः।
अदर्शयन स तं तस्य प्रयच्छेत् स्वधनादृणम्।।

"If one man stands surety to a second for the appearance

of a third; then he being unable to produce the third to the second, should pay the debt from his own wealth.

Yājñavalkya, Ch. II, Śloka 54.

दर्शने प्रत्यये दाने प्रातिभाव्यं विधीयते।
आद्यौ तु वितथे दाप्यौ इतरस्य सुता अपि।।

" Suretyship is constituted in the matter of appearance, trustworthiness, or guarantee. The first two classes of sureties should be made to pay in case of failure of what they undertook. Even the sons of the last class should be made to pay."

The Mitākṣarā explains the above thus :—

The first class of surety undertakes to produce a particular person; the second class asserts the trustworthiness of the debtor, by saying that he will not deceive the creditor, since he is the son of so and so; he has got a quantity of fertile lands or he owns a fine village. The third class of surety undertakes to pay the debt if the debtor fails.

Original Text, No. XXI.

Manu, Ch. VIII, Śloka 166.

ग्रहीता यदि नष्टः स्यात् कुटुम्बार्थे कृतो व्ययः।
दातव्यं बान्धवैस्तत् स्यात् प्रविभक्तैरपि स्वतः।।

Kullūka's Comments.

ऋणग्रहीता यदि मृतः स्यात्। तेन च पूर्व्वविभक्ताविभक्तसर्व्वभ्रातृकुटुम्बसवर्धनार्थं तदृणव्ययः कृतः। तदा तदृणं विभक्तैरविभक्तैश्च स्वधनाद्दातव्ययं।

Kullūka on Sloka 167.

तद्देशस्थे देशान्तरस्थे वा स्वामिनि स्वामिसम्बन्धिकुटुम्बव्ययनिमित्तं दासोऽपि यत् ऋणादानादि कुर्यात्। स्वामी तत् तथा अनुमन्येत।

Original Text, No. XXII.

Vijñāneśvara's Comments on Śloka 46, Ch. II, Yājñanalkya.

अविभक्तैर्बहुभिः कुटुम्बार्थं एकैकेन वा यदृणं कृतं। तत् ऋणं कुटुम्बी दद्यात्। अस्मिन् प्रेते प्रोषिते वा तदृक्थिनः सर्व्वे दद्युः।

Original Text, No. XXIII.

Yājñavalkya, Ch. II, Śloka 47.

न योषित् पतिपुत्राभ्यां न पुत्रेण कृतं पिता।
दद्यात् ऋते कुटुम्बार्थात् न पतिः स्त्रीकृतं तथा।।

Comments of Vijñāneśvara.

पत्या कृतमृणं योषिद् भार्य्या नैव दद्यात् पुत्रेण कृतं योषित् माता न दद्यात्। तदा पुत्रेण कृतं पिता न दद्यात्। तथा भार्य्याकृतं पतिर्न दद्यात्। कुटुम्बार्थादृते इति सर्व्वशेषं। अतः कुटुम्बार्थं येन केनापि कृतं। तत् कुटुम्बिना देयं।

No. XXIV.

Mitākṣarā, Ch. I, s. 1, para. 27, *et seq.*

तस्मात् पैतृके पैतामहे च द्रव्ये जन्मनैव स्वत्वं। तथापि पितुः आवश्यकेषु धर्म्मकृत्येषु वाचनिकेषु प्रसाददानकुटुम्बभरणापद्विमोक्षादिषु च। स्थावरव्यतिरिक्तद्रव्यत्रिनियोगे स्वातन्त्र्यम्। इति स्थितम्। स्थावरे तु स्वार्जिते पित्रादिप्राप्ते च पुत्रादिपारतन्त्र्यमेव।

स्थावरं द्विपदञ्चैव यद्यपि स्वयमर्जितम्।
असम्भूय सुतान् सर्व्वान् न दानं न च विक्रयः।।

ये जाता येऽप्यजाताश्च ये च गर्भे व्यवस्थिताः।
वृतिञ्च तेऽभिकाङ्क्षन्ति न दानं न च विक्रयः।।

इत्यादि स्मरणात्। अस्यापवादः।
एकोऽपि स्थावरे कुर्य्यात् दानाधमनविक्रयम्।
आपत्काले कुटुम्बार्थे धर्म्मार्थे च विशेषतः।।

अस्यार्थः। अप्राप्तव्यवहारेषु पुत्रेषु पौत्रेषु च। अनुज्ञानादावसमर्थेषु। भ्रातृषु वा तथाविधेषु। अविभक्तेपि। सर्व्वकुटुम्बव्यापिन्यामापदि। तत्पोषणे च। अवश्यकर्तव्येषु च पितृश्राद्धादिषु। स्थावरस्य दानाधमनविक्रयामेकोऽपि समर्थः कुर्य्यात्। इति।

Original Text, No. XXV.

Nārada cited in Vivādacintāmaṇi, p. .8, Sanskrit,

पितृव्येणाविभक्तेन भ्रात्रा वा यद्दृशं कृतम्।
मात्रा वा यत् कुटुम्बार्थे दद्यु स्तत् सर्व्वरिक्थिनः।।

Vṛhaspati.

पितृव्यभ्रातृपुत्रस्त्रीदासशिष्यानुजीविभिः ।
यद् गृहीतं कुटुम्बार्थे तद् गृही दातुमर्हति।।

Nārada, (p. 19).

न च भार्य्याकृतमृणं कथञ्चित् पत्युरातरेत्।
आपत्कृताहते पुंसः कुटुम्बार्थो हि दुस्तरः।।
अन्यत्र रजकव्याधगोपशौण्डिकयोषिताम्।
तेषाञ्च तत्परा वृत्तिः कुटुम्बञ्च तदाश्रयम्।।

Vācaspati's Comments.

एवमन्यत्रापि यत्र स्त्रीप्राधान्यं। तत्र तथैव। न तु जात्यादरः कार्य्यः। इदं तु प्रपञ्चनमात्रम्। कुटुम्बार्थं ब्राह्मणादिस्त्रीकृतस्यापि कुटम्बिदेयत्वात्।

Jīmūtavāhana's Dāyabhāga, Ch. 1, para. 42, Śaṅkha quoted.

पितरि अशक्ते व्यवहारान् ज्येष्ठः प्रतिकुर्य्यात्। अनन्तरो वा कार्य्यज्ञः तदनुमतः। न तु अकामे पितरि रिक्थविभागः। वृद्धे विपरीतचेतसि दीर्घरोगिणि वा ज्येष्ठ एव पितृवत् अर्थान् पालयेत् इतरेषां। ऋक्थमूलं हि कुटुम्बम्। अस्वतन्त्राः पितृमन्तः। मातुरप्येवमवस्थितायाः।

Original Text, No. XXVI.

Mitākṣarā, Ch. T, s. 4, para .8

कुटुम्बं बिभृयाद् भ्रातुर्यो विद्यामधिगच्छतः।
भागं विद्याधनात् तस्मात् स लभेताश्रुतोऽपि सन्।।

Original Text, No. XXVII.

Dāyabhāga, Ch. XI, s. 1, para. 37.

प्रपितामहः। पितामहः। पिता। स्वयं। सोदर्य्या भ्रातरः। सवर्णायाः पुत्रः। पौत्रः।

प्रपौत्रः। एतान् अविभक्तदायादान् सपिण्डान् आचक्षते। विभक्तदायादान् सकुल्यान् आचक्षते। सत्सु अङ्गजेषु तङ्गामी हि अर्थो भवति। सपिण्डाभावे सकुल्यः। तदभावे च आचार्य्यः अन्तेवासी ऋत्विग् वा। हरेत्। तदभावे राजा।

Original Text, No. XXVIII

Devala cited in Vivādacintāmaṇi, (Sanskrit, p. 154).

ततो दायमुपुत्रस्य विभजेरन् सहोदराः।
तुल्या दुहितरो वापि ध्रियमाणः पितापि वा।।
सवर्णा भ्रातरो माता भार्य्या चेति यथाक्रमम्।
एषामभावे गृहणीयुः सकुल्याः सहवासिनः।।

Vṛhaspati cited in Smṛticandrikā MS., Sanskrit College, leaf, 253, p. 2, line 2, also p. 77, Sanskrit, Edition by the late Professor .Bharatachandra Śiromaṇi, this Edition being confined to that portion of the work which deals with Inheritance.

बहवो ज्ञातयो यत्र सकुल्या बान्धवा स्तथा।
यश्चासन्नतर स्तेषां सोऽनपत्यधनं हरेत्।।
ज्ञातयः सपिण्डाः। सकुल्याः समानोदकाः।

Original Text, No. XXIX.

Mārkaṇḍeya Purāṇa, cited in the Dāyabhāga, Ch para. 41.

पिण्डलेपभुजश्चान्ये पितामहपितामहात्।।
प्रभृत्युक्तास्त्रयस्तेषां यजमानश्च सप्तमः।
इत्येवं मुनिभिः प्रोक्तः सम्बन्दः साप्तपौरुषः।।

अशौचकरः। इत्यर्थः।

Original Text, No. XXX.

Yājñavalkya, Ch. I, Śloka.

श्रुतिः स्मृतिः सदाचारः स्वस्य च प्रियमात्मनः।
सम्यक् संकल्पजः कामो धर्म्ममूलमिदं स्मृतम्।।

Manu, Ch. VIII, Śloka 41.

जातिजानपदान् धर्म्मान श्रेणीधर्म्मांश्च धर्म्मवित्।
समीक्ष्य कुलधर्म्मांश्च स्वधर्म्मं प्रतिपादयेत्।।

Śloka 46.

सद्भिराचरितं यत् स्याद् धार्म्मिकैश्च द्विजातिभिः।
तद् देशकुलजातीनान् अविरुद्धं प्रकल्पयेत्।।

Kullūka's Comments.

विद्वद्भिः धर्म्मप्रधानैः द्विजातिभिः यत् दृश्यमानशास्त्रम् अनुष्ठितम्। तत् देशकुलजात्यविरुद्धमादाय व्यवहारनिर्णयं प्रकल्पयेत्।

The rendering of the last two words in the Comments should strictly be—

"Should carry on the adjudication of lawsuits."

My rendering in the body of the Lectures gives only the purport.

Yājñavalkya, Ch. II, Śloka 188.

निजधर्म्माविरोधेन यस्तु सामयिको भवेत्।
सोऽपि यत्नेन संरक्ष्यो धर्म्मो राजकृतश्च यः।।

Vijnāneswara's Comments.

श्रौतस्मार्त्तधर्म्मानुपमर्द्देन समयात् निष्पन्नो यो धर्म्मो गोप्रचारोदकरक्षणदेवगृह पालादिरूपः। सोऽपि यत्नेन पालनीयः। तथा। राज्ञा च निजधर्म्माविरोधेनैव यः सामयिको धर्म्मः। यावत्पथिकं भोजनं देयम्। अस्मदरातिमण्डलं तुरगादयो न प्रस्थापनीयाः। इत्येवरूपः कृतः। सोऽपि रक्षणीयः।

Yājñavalkya, Ch. II, Śloka 194.

अणिनैगमपाषण्डिगणानामप्ययं विधिः।
भेदञ्चैषां नृपो। रक्षेत् पूर्व्ववृत्तिञ्च पालयेत्।।

Vijñāneśvara's Comments.

एकपण्यशिल्पोपजीविनः श्रेणयः। नैगमा ये वेदस्य आप्तप्रणीतत्वेन प्रामाण्यमिच्छन्ति पाशुपतादयः। पाषण्डिनः ये देवस्य प्रामाण्यमेव नेच्छन्ति नग्नाः सौगत्तादयः। गणो व्रातः आयुधीयादीनामेकर्म्मोपजीविनाम्। एषां चतुर्विधानामपि

अयमेव विधि र्या निजधर्म्माविरोधेन इत्येवमादिना प्रतिपादितः। एतेषाञ्च श्रेण्यादीनां भेदं धर्म्मव्यवस्थां नृपो रक्षेत्। पूर्व्वोपात्तां वृतिञ्च पालयेत्।

Original Text, No. XXXI.

Manu,.Ch. IX, Śloka 215.

भ्रातृणामविभक्तानां यद्युत्थानं भवेत्सह।
न पुत्रभागं विषमं पिता दद्यात् कथञ्चन।।

Original Text, No. XXXII.

Mitākṣarā, Ch. I, sec. 4, para. 6.

अत्र च पितृद्रव्याविरोधेन यत्किञ्चित् स्वयमर्जितमिति सर्व्वशेषः। अतश्च। पितृद्रव्याविरोधेन यन्मैत्रमर्जितं। पितृद्रव्याविरोधेन यदौद्वाहिकं। पितृद्रव्याविरोधेन यत् क्रमायातं। पितृद्रव्याविरोधेन विद्यया यल्लब्धम्। इति प्रत्येकमभिसम्बध्यते। तथा च। पितृद्रव्यविरोधेन प्रत्युपकारेण यन्मैत्रं। आसुरादिविवाहेण यल्लब्धं। तथा पितृद्रव्यव्ययेन यत् क्रमायातमुद्धृतं। तथा पितृद्रव्यव्ययेन लब्धया विद्यया यल्लब्धं तद् सर्वं सर्व्वैर्भ्रातृभिः पित्रा च विभजनीयम्।

Original Text, No. XXXIII.

Mitākṣarā, Ch. I, sec. 1, para. 4.

विभागो नाम द्रव्यसमुदायविषयाणामनेकस्वाम्यानां तदेकदेशेषु व्यवस्थापनम्।

Para. 23.

विभागशब्दश्च बहुस्वामिकधनविषयो लोकप्रसिद्धः।

Literally.

"The word Vibhāga' is current among people as having its application in case of wealth of which the owners are many."

Original Text, No. XXXIV.

Mitākṣarā, Ch. II, sec. 1, para. 30.

तस्मात् विभक्तासंसृष्टिनि अपुत्रे स्वर्य्याते पत्नी धनं प्रथमं गृहणाति। इत्ययमर्थः सिद्धो भवति।

Para. 35.

शङ्खवचनमपि संसृष्टभ्रातृविषयम्।

The text of Śaṅkha cited in the first part of para. 35.

स्वर्य्यातस्य हि अपुत्रस्य भ्रातृगामि द्रव्यं। तदभावे पितरौ हरेयातां। ज्येष्ठा वा पत्नी।

Original Text, No. XXXV.

Mitākṣarā, Ch. I, sec. 1, para. 30 ; Manu cited.

अविभक्ता विभक्ता वा सपिण्डाः स्थावरे समाः।

Yājñavalkya, Ch. II, Śloka 46.

अविभक्तैः कुटुम्बार्थे यदृणं तु कृतं भवेत्।

Manu, Ch. VIII, Sloka 166.

ग्रहीता यदि नष्टः स्यात् कुटुम्बार्थे कृतो व्ययः।
दातव्यं बान्धवैस्तत् स्यात् प्रविभक्तैरपि स्वतः।।

Original Text, No. XXXVI

Yājñavalkya, Ch. II, Śloka, 127.

भगिन्यश्च निजादंशात् दत्वांशन्तु तुरीयकम्।

Original Text, No. XXXVII.

मटचीहतेष कुरुषु

Chāndogya Upaniṣad, Ch. III, Part 10.

Original Text, No. XXXVIII.

Mitākṣarā, Ch I, sec. 4, para. 26.

अविभाज्ये सगोत्राणामा सहस्त्रकुलादपि।
याज्यं क्षेत्रं च पत्रं च कृतान्नमुदकं स्त्रियः।।

Original Text, No. XXXIX.

Mitākṣarā, Ch. I, sec. 4, para. 18.

पत्रं वाहनमश्वशिविकादि।

'Pattra' is the means of conveyance, horses, palanqueens, etc."

Original Text, No. XL.

Mitākṣarā, Ch. I, sec. 4, para. 26, last part.

यत्तूशनसा क्षेत्रस्य अविभाज्यत्वमुक्तं। **। तत् ब्राह्मणोत्पन्न क्षत्रियादिपुत्रविषयम्।

"The impartibility of a field which has been declared by Uśanas has its application in the case of the son of a Kṣatriya mother begotten by a Brāhmaṇa father."

Original Text, No. XLI.

Manu, Ch. IX, Śloka 111.

एवं सह वसेयुर्वा पृथग् वा धर्म्मकाम्यया।
पृथग् विवर्धते धर्म्मस्तस्माद् धर्म्या पृथक्क्रिया।।

"Thus they should dwell either together or separately, from a desire for religious merit. Religious merit increases by separation. Therefore, separation is a pious act."

Original Text, No. XLII.

Mitākṣarā, Ch. I, sec. 1, para. 81.

स्वग्रामज्ञातिसामन्तदायादानुमतेन च।
हिरण्योदकदानेन षड्भिगच्छति मेदिनी।

Original Text, No. XLIII.

Manu, Ch. VIII, Śloka 245.

सीमां प्रति समुत्पन्ने विवादे ग्रामयोर्द्वयोः।
ज्यैष्ठे मासि नयेत् सीमां सुप्रकाशेषु सेतुषु।।

Śloka 248.

तड़ागान्युदपानानि वाप्यः प्रस्रवणानि च।
सीमासन्धिषु कार्य्याणि देवतायतनानि च।।

Śloka 258

साक्ष्यभावे तु चत्वारो ग्रामाः सामन्तवासिनः।
सीमाविनिर्णयं कुर्य्युः प्रयता राजसन्निधौ।।

Śloka 259.

सामन्तानासभावे तु मौलानां सौम्नि साक्षिणाम्।
इमानप्यनुयुक्तीत पुरुषान् वनगोचरान्।।

Śloka 260

व्याधान् शाकुनिकान् गोपान् कैवर्त्तान् मूलखानकान्।
व्यालग्राहान् उच्छवृतीन् अन्यांश्च वनचारिणः।।

Śloka 261.

ते पृष्ठासु यथा ब्रूयुः सीमासन्धिषु लक्षणम्।
तत् तथा स्थापयेद् राजा धर्म्मेण ग्रामयोर्द्वयोः।।

Original Text, No. XLIV.

Manu, Ch. VIII, Śloka 237.

धनुः शतं परीणाहो ग्रामस्य स्यात् समन्ततः।
शम्यापातास्त्रयो वापि त्रिगुणो नगरस्य तु।।

Kullūka's Comments.

चतुर्हस्तो धनुः। शम्या यष्टिः। तस्याः पातः प्रक्षेपः। ग्रामसमीपे सर्व्वासु दिक्ष चत्वारि हस्तशतानि त्रीन् वा यष्टिप्रक्षेपान् यावत्पशुप्रचारार्थं शस्यवपनादिसरोधपरिहारः कार्य्यः। नगरसमीपे पुनः अयं त्रिगुणः कार्य्यः।।

Yājñavalkya, Ch. 11, Śloka 169.

ग्राम्येच्छया गोप्रचारो भूमिराजवशेन वा।

Vijñāneśvara's Comments.

ग्राम्येच्छया ग्राम्यजनेच्छया। भूम्यल्पत्वमहत्वापेक्षया। राजेच्छया वा। गोप्रचारः कर्त्तव्य। गवादीनां चरणार्थं कियान् अपि भूभागः अकृष्टः परिकल्पनीयः। इत्यर्थः।

Original Text, No. XLV.

अविभक्ता विभक्ता वा सपिण्डाः स्थावरे समाः।
एकोह्यनीशः सर्व्वत्र दानाधमनविक्रये।।

इति। तदपि अविभक्तेषु द्रव्यस्य मध्यस्थत्वात् एकस्य अनीश्वरत्वात् सर्व्वाभ्यनुज्ञा अवश्यं कार्य्या। विभक्तेषु तु उत्तरकालं विभक्ताविभक्तसंशयव्युदासेन व्यवहारसौकर्य्याय सर्व्वाभ्यनुज्ञा। न पुरेकस्यानीश्वरत्वेन। अतो विभक्तानुमतिव्यतिरेकेणापि व्यवहारः सिध्यत्येव। इति व्याख्येयं। यदपि

स्वग्राम ज्ञातिसामन्त दायादानुमतेन च।
हिरण्योदकदानेन षड्भिर्गच्छति मेदिनी।।

इति। तत्रापि। ग्रामानुमतिः।

प्रतिग्रहः प्रकाशः स्यात् स्थावरस्य विशेषतः।

इति स्मरणात्। व्यवहार प्रकाशनार्थमेव अपेक्ष्यते। न पुनर्ग्रामानुमत्या विना व्यवहारासिद्धिः। सामन्तामतिस्तु सीमाविप्रतिपत्ति निरासाय। ज्ञातिदायादानुमतेस्तु प्रयोजनमुक्तमेव। हिरण्योदकदाननेति।

स्थावरे विक्रयानास्ति कुर्य्यादाधिमनुज्ञया।

इति स्थावरस्य विक्रयप्रतिमेधात्

भूमिं यः प्रतिगृह्णादि यश्च भूमिं प्रयच्छति।
उभौ तौ पुण्यकर्म्माणौ नियतौ स्वर्गगामिनौ।

इति दानप्रशंसादर्शनाच्च। विक्रयेऽपि कर्तव्ये सहिरण्यमुदकं दत्वा स्थावरविक्रयं कुर्य्यात्। इत्यर्थः।

For the Text, No. XLVI.

See the preceding extract.

Text No. XLVII.

Tāranāth's explanation of the word jñāti.

सपिण्ड सकुल्य समानोदक सगोत्रज रूपे एकगोत्रोत्पन्ने पितृव्यादौ।

Literally.

"The word jñāti [is applied] to paternal uncle and others, born in the same gotra, such as the sapiṇḍas, the sākulyas, the samānodakas, and the sagotras."

Original Text, No. XLVIII.

Mitākṣarā, Ch. II, sec. 5, para. 6.

तेषाम् अभावे समानोदकानां धनसम्बन्धः। ते च सपिण्डानामुपरि सप्त वेदितव्याः। जन्मनामज्ञानावधिका वा। यथाह वृहन्मनुः।

सपिण्डता तु पुरुषे सप्तमे विनिवर्तते।
समानोदकभावस्तु निवर्त्तेताचतुर्द्दशात्।।
जन्मनाम्नोः स्मृतेरेके तत्परं गोत्र मुच्यते।।

For Text, No. XLIX.
See Text, No. XLV.

Text, No. L.

Dattaka Mīmāṁsā, see. 2, para, 76.

क्षत्रियाणां प्रातिस्विकगोत्राभावात् गुरुनिर्देशः।

Original Text, No. LI.

विश्वामित्रो जमदग्निर्भरद्वाजो गौतमः अत्रिर्वशिष्ठः काश्यप इत्येते सप्तर्षयः। सप्तर्षीणामगस्त्याष्टमानां यदपत्यं तद्गोत्रमित्याचक्षते।

No. LII

एतेषाश्च गोत्राणामवान्तरभेदाः सहस्त्रसंख्यकाः।

No. LIII.

Manu, CL. IX, Śloka 105.

ज्येष्ठ एव तु गृहणीयात् पित्र्यन्धनमशेषतः।
शेषास्तमुपजीवेयुर्यथैव पितरं तथा।।

Śloka 106.

ज्येष्ठेन जातमात्रेण पुत्री भवति मानवः।
पितृणामनृणश्चैव स तस्मात् सर्व्वमर्हति।।

Śloka 107.

यस्मिन् ऋण संनयति येन चानन्त्यमश्नुते।
स एव धर्म्मजः पुत्रंः कामजान् इतरान् विदुः।।

Śloka 108.

पितेव पालयेत् पुत्रान् ज्येष्ठो भ्रातृन् यवीयसः।
पुत्रवच्चापि वर्तेरन् ज्येष्ठे भ्रातरि धर्म्मतः।।

Śloka 109.

ज्येष्ठः कुलं वर्धयति विनाशयति वा पुनः।
ज्येष्ठः पूज्यतमोलोके ज्येष्ठः सद्भिरगर्हितः।।

Original Text, No. LIV.

Āpastamba quoted in Mītākṣarā, Ch. I, sec. 3, para. 6.

ज्येष्ठो दायाद इत्येके। देशविशेषे सुवर्णं कृष्णा गावः कृष्णं भौमं ज्येष्ठस्य। तच्छास्त्रविप्रतिषिद्धम्।

No. LV.

Sāyaṇa's Comments on the Ṛg-veda hymn inculcating female exclusion.

तान्च स्तनूज औरसः पुत्रो जामये भगिन्यै ऋक्थं पित्र्यं धनं न अरैक् न प्ररेचयति न प्रददाति। किं तर्हि। सवितुः एनां संभजमानस्य भर्त्तुः। गर्भं षष्ठायर्थे द्वितीया। गर्भस्य निधानं रेतः सेकनिधानीमेनां। करोति। न तु तस्यै रिक्थं ददाति। इत्यभिप्रायः। असंस्कृतास्तु संस्कार्य्या भ्रातृभिः पूर्व्वसंस्कृतैः। भगिन्यश्च निजादंशाङ्कदत्वाशन्तु तुरीयकम् इति याज्ञवल्क्यस्मरणत्। 2। 124। स्त्रीपुंसलक्षणस्य अपत्यस्य एकोत्पाद्यत्कविशेषात् पुमपत्यस्य को विशेष इत्याशङ्का विशेषं दर्शयति। यदि यद्यपि मातरो मातापितरौ। वह्नि। अवह्निः स्त्री। वह्निः पुमान्। स्वभार्य्याया वोढृत्वात् अवह्निश्च वहिः। तादृशं स्त्रीपुंसलक्षणमपत्यं जनयन्तः तथापि तयोर्मध्ये। अन्यः। पुंलक्षणः। सुकृतोः शोभनस्य पिण्डदानादेः कर्म्मणः कर्त्ता भवति। अन्यः स्त्रीलक्षणः। ऋन्धन् वस्त्रालङ्कारादिना ऋध्यमान एव भवति। पिण्डदानादिकर्तृत्वात् पुत्रो दायार्हः। दुहिता तु तथा न इति न दायार्हा। सा तु केवलं परस्यै दीयते।

Original Text, No. LVI.

अर्हति स्त्री। इति अनुवृतौ। बौधायनः। न दायम्। निरिन्द्रिया अदायाश्च स्त्रिया मता इति श्रुतेः।

Dāyabhāga, Ch. XI, sec. 6, para. 11.

Original Text, No. LVII.

Manu, Ch. IX, Śloka 130.

यथैवात्मा तथा पुत्रः पुत्रेण दुहिता समा।
तस्यामात्मनि जीवन्त्यां कथमन्यो धनं हरेत्।।

No. LVIII.

Mitākṣarā, folio edition, leaf 7, p. 1.

तथा च पुत्रादयः षट् सपिण्डाः। पुत्रादयश्च षट्। आत्मा च सप्तमः। सन्ताना भेदेऽपि यतः सन्तानभेदः। तमादाय गणयेत्। यावत् सप्तमः। इति सर्व्वज योजनीयम्।

Leaf 6, p. 1.

सपिण्डता च एकशरीरावयवान्वयेन भवति। तथाहि। पुत्रस्य पितृशरीरावयनन्वयेन

पित्रा सह एकपिण्डता। एवं पितामहादिभिरपि पितृद्वारेण तच्छरीरावयवान्वयात्। एवं मातृशरीरावयवान्वयेन मात्रा। तथा मातामहादिभिरपिमातृद्वारेण। तथा मातृष्वस्ट मातुलादिभिरपि एकशरीरावयवान्वयात्। तथा पितृव्यपितृष्वस्रादिभिरपि। तथा पत्या सह पत्पा एकशरीरारम्भकतया। एवं भ्रातृभार्य्याणामपि परम्परमेकशरीरारम्भैः सह एकशरीरारम्भकत्वेन। एवं यत्र यत्र सपिण्डशब्दः। तत्र तत्र साक्षात् परम्परया एकशरीरावयवान्वयो वेदितव्यः।

Original Text, No. LIX.

Mitākṣarā, folio edition, leaf 33, p. 1.

श्राद्धं नाम अदनीयस्य तत्स्थानीयस्य वा द्रव्यस्य प्रेतोद्देशेन श्रद्धया त्यागः तच्च द्विविधं पार्व्वणमेकोदिष्टञ्चेति। तत्र त्रिपुरुषोद्देशेन यत् क्रियते तत् पार्व्वणम्। एकपुरुषोद्देशेन क्रियमाणमेकोद्दिष्टम्। पुनश्च त्रिविधं नित्यं नैमित्तिकं काम्यञ्चेति। तत्र नित्यं। नियतनिमित्तोपाधौ चोदितं नित्यम्। अहरहरमावस्याष्टकादिषु। अनियत-निमित्तोपाधौ चोदितं नैमित्तिकम्। यथा पुत्रजन्मादिषु। फलकामनापाधौ विहितं काम्यम्। यथा स्वर्गादिकामानां कृत्तिकादिषु नक्षत्रेषु। पुनश्च पञ्चविधम्। अहरहः श्राद्धं पार्व्वणं वृद्धिश्राद्धं एकोद्दिष्टं सपिण्डीकरणं चेति। तत्र अहरहः। श्राद्धमन्नं पितृमनुष्येभ्य इत्यादिनोक्तम्। तथा च मनुः। दद्यादहरहः श्राद्ध मन्नाद्येनोदकेन वा। पयोमूलफलैर्वापि पितृभ्यः प्रीतिमक्षयम्। अधुना पार्व्वणं वृद्धिश्राद्धश्च दर्शयिष्यंस्तयोः कालानाह। अमावस्याष्टका वृद्धि कृष्णपक्षोऽयनद्वयं। द्रव्यं ब्राह्मणसम्पत्तिर्विषुवत् सूर्य्यसंक्रमः। व्यतीपातो गजच्छाया ग्रहणं चन्द्रसूर्य्ययोः। श्राद्धं प्रति रुचिश्चैव श्राद्धकालाः प्रकीर्त्तिताः।।

Index

C

N